W9-ADR-503

JAMES L. HESKETT, Ph.D., Stanford University, is
1907 Foundation Professor of Business Logistics at
the Graduate School of Business Administration,
Harvard University. Previously he was on the
faculty of the College of Commerce and Administration, The Ohio State University, and was
President of Logistics Systems, Inc. Dr. Heskett
has written many professional articles, is a co-
author of a book on highway transportation management, and serves as Director of Distribution
Centers, Inc., and several other organizations.

NICHOLAS A. GLASKOWSKY, JR., Ph.D., Stanford
University, is President of National Distribution
Services, Inc., in Atlanta. Dr. Glaskowsky was
formerly Professor of Management and Logistics
at the School of Business Administration, University
of Minnesota. He is the author of many articles in
the professional journals and is also a co-author of
a book on highway transportation management.

ROBERT M. IVIE, M.B.A., Stanford University, is
President of Guild Wineries and Distilleries, San
Francisco. Prior to his present position, he was
Traffic Manager and then Vice President—Distri-
bution at United Vintners in San Francisco.

BUSINESS LOGISTICS

Physical Distribution and Materials Management

JAMES L. HESKETT

HARVARD UNIVERSITY

NICHOLAS A. GLASKOWSKY, JR.

NATIONAL DISTRIBUTION SERVICES, INC.

ROBERT M. IVIE

GUILD WINERIES AND DISTILLERIES

SECOND EDITION

THE RONALD PRESS COMPANY • NEW YORK

Copyright © 1973 by
THE RONALD PRESS COMPANY

Copyright © 1964 by
THE RONALD PRESS COMPANY

All Rights Reserved

No part of this book may be reproduced
in any form without permission in writing
from the publisher.

Library of Congress Catalog Card Number: 73–78570
PRINTED IN THE UNITED STATES OF AMERICA

Once again,
To three patient wives

Preface

The purpose of this book is to provide a comprehensive and up-to-date study of logistics systems design and management. It has been planned to help develop the ability to organize and analyze logistics information, to foresee and coordinate the interrelated aspects of a problem, and to make recommendations or take action that will effectively resolve a problem situation.

Our treatment of the field of business logistics deals with the management of physical supply and physical distribution activities. It involves the total effort required to make particular kinds and specific quantities of goods available in an acceptable condition, at a certain place, at the time they are desired by the customer or ultimate consumer. It has evolved from concepts developed by marketing and transportation economists, geographers, electrical and industrial engineers, systems analysts, and students of production and marketing management.

McLuhan has pointed out that it is difficult to describe and discuss a system, any system, in the linear format of a book. Our approach in this Second Edition has been to proceed from the descriptive to the analytical, from early general presentation to a specific discussion of elements, constraints, and activities. It then becomes possible to consider the broader interpersonal and functional problems of a logistics manager. Throughout, we have attempted to assemble the related pieces of a logistics system and to present them as early in the discussion as possible.

As strategic aids to this integral approach, we have embedded in the text itself a series of questions for each chapter. They are intended as learning devices, for their answers will confirm understanding of the material under discussion and stimulate awareness to other fields and other influences upon the specific topic of the section. This multifield view is intended to provide a more natural basis for class discussion of case material appearing in a companion volume, *Case Problems in Business Logistics*.

Part I of the text introduces the subject by offering background information, concepts, and definitions intended to establish a basic foundation for the understanding of ideas presented later. This is extremely important in light of the constant confusion of physical distribution activities in the macroeconomic sense and business logistics activities in the individual firm, or microeconomic setting. The relationship of logistics to systems management is established at this point.

Part II is devoted to a brief presentation of the elements of a logistics system, including the costing and pricing of their services. Inventory processing elements, with emphasis on warehousing, data processing, and communication, are considered first. Succeeding chapters concentrate on transportation services, costs, and rates.

The focus of the book shifts in Part III to topics with which logistics system design and management are closely related—procurement, pricing, and customer service standards. These might be called constraints on the logistics system, since they are decision areas outside the full control of the logistician which nevertheless serve as some of the determinants of the system. Basic changes in a firm's logistics cost structure are caused by changes in procurement policies. The nature of a firm's physical distribution cost pattern will in turn influence its price level, its quantity discount schedule, and the geographical area to be served. Finally, planning of physical distribution depends in part upon an analysis of the various possible levels of customer service and the cost of providing each of these levels. Instead of viewing these matters as constraints, we prefer to regard them as negotiable by the manager of logistics activities.

Part IV describes the operation of the Warren G. Wonka Manufacturing Company, our vehicle for discussing the complexities of logistics system design. Progressing again from theory to practical application, the system design process at the Wonka Company is described from audit to implementation. This approach of building on data, and interrelating case facts, is used to study several major segments of the design effort—inventory control, location, and scheduling strategies.

The chapters of Part V discuss the managerial aspects of packaging and material handling, warehousing, and traffic and transportation, as well as the managerial machinery necessary for the integration of these logistics activities in the individual firm. The organization and controls necessary for their successful management are included in this discussion. The final chapter speculates on the nature of the future of logistics.

There have been varied sources of support and encouragement for our work on this revision. In particular, the 1907 Foundation gave important indirect support by freeing up time for research and writing activities.

We also wish to thank those people who contributed their time and effort to helping us during the various phases from manuscript to publication, especially John Nystuen, Graham W. Rider, Robert N. Rice, Thomas L. Keltner, Michael J. Evers, Richard B. Taylor, Georgia G.

Albritten, Carmen M. Gay, Carolyn Ann Taylor, Susan Bradshaw, Linda Brown, Karen Peters, and Denise Erwood.

Over half the material in this Second Edition is completely new. Literally hundreds of students, teachers, and business executives have contributed to the formulation of the ideas in this book and the adaptation of the principles set forth in the First Edition to the dynamic changes that have taken place in the field since then. The comments and suggestions of the users of the earlier book, both in the classroom and in practice, have been most helpful in the planning and structuring of this edition. For any errors, misconceptions, or fuzzy thinking that appears between these covers, however, the buck stops with us.

James L. Heskett
Nicholas A. Glaskowsky, Jr.
Robert M. Ivie

Cambridge, Massachusetts
Atlanta, Georgia
San Francisco, California
August, 1973

Contents

PART ONE

THE SCOPE AND IMPORTANCE OF LOGISTICS

Labels often convey a confusing array of ideas. On consumer products they are backed by large amounts of advertising. In the academic world, vested interests represent the backing for various labels. The resulting semantic confusion can be colossal. Thus, a well-known professor of marketing management has criticized our ideas because they portray "physical distribution as falling outside the field of marketing management." Those coining the word "rhochrematics" to describe the field will be disappointed by our choice of words. Others would prefer to use uniform references made to the field which conform to their terminology and definitions. In this portion of the book, one of our objectives is to state a frame of reference which makes sense in the field and, perhaps more important, is the one we will use throughout the book.

In 1964 we said that a certain amount of confusion could be expected in the definitions of terms, the scope of various subject areas, executive responsibilities and titles, and other structural devices in a newly organized field of management. The state of business logistics is not very different today.

Many firms continue to consolidate various responsibilities for incoming materials supply under a function called materials management. At the same time, another group of firms (including

1

some corporate members common to the first group) is busily realigning responsibilities for the control of finished product distribution under a single function called physical distribution. Their objectives are the same and the results are likely to be similar. The names are different.

The confusion has worked certain specific, identifiable hardships on various individuals and groups in the field. At an American Management Association Special Conference on Distribution Management, a recognized authority in his field addressed the assembled executives about costs of distribution, including such costs as sales salaries, travel expenses, clerical services, accounts receivable, credit authorization and collections, bad debts, and others. The group of business logisticians assembled for the presentation had expected to hear about the control of costs of transportation, warehousing, inventory carrying, and order processing. What appeared to be the scope of distribution to the audience was not that envisioned by the speaker. Such presentations are still being made, although their number is slowly diminishing.

The use of clearly defined terms can provide a ready frame of reference to elements of a field in which time saving is important in these early phases of growth. It has taken marketing and production scholars and executives six decades to organize their terminology in a usable, time-saving, and almost universally understandable form. The field of business logistics has benefited from this experience.

A second purpose of this section is to offer an explanation of how the field of business logistics got where it is. It did not just happen. In the process, perhaps we can dispel an old wives' tale or two.

The word "systems" in the business world is becoming comparable in its attractiveness to "sex" for the general public. No book about business is complete without it. The systems approach is the underlying philosophy for this book. Therefore, these opening chapters describe general systems concepts, explain their appropriateness for logistics, and indicate the nature of the influence which these concepts have on the organization and content of the rest of the book.

Perhaps the least intelligible and most often made statement about logistics activities is that they represent "the third largest cost of doing business, right behind labor and materials." This approach to measurement ignores both the fact that logistics is not at all an economic resource comparable to labor and materials and that, in itself, it is made up largely of the very same labor and materials costs with which it is being compared. Although available cost information, in its present state, yields only general (and sometimes misleading) orders of magnitude, a fourth objective of this portion of the book is to set forth what information exists, and give warning accordingly.

Because these early chapters provide a frame of reference for material following, we suggest review of their charts and diagrams from time to time throughout the reading of the book, in order to reestablish the structure within which the discussion is presented.

1

Logistics in the Economy

Logistics is an "in" term, guaranteed to stir a chorus of "What is it?" in a conversation. Without bothering to define it, we speak of the logistics of solid waste disposal, fighting a battle, operating a hospital, or getting people from home to work.

The word hints darkly of automation and the computer-oriented control of geographically far-flung, complex transportation and supply networks. It is brought into focus as we sit bumper-to-bumper in a traffic jam, pick up a leaky carton of milk in the supermarket, or unexpectedly run out of grinding wheels as a $200,000 machine which requires them has to be shut down.

Logistics is a word that sounds scientific. It implies that we know the answers and have the techniques. It may hint at a field of activity relatively devoid of human content until we remember that, even in this golden age of technology, there are still more people in this world *and in this country* lifting and transporting things than are engaged in any other principal job assignment. Logistics, in a figurative as well as a somewhat literal sense, deals with man's burden in this world. At one and the same time, it signifies scientific and somewhat romantic planning activities as well as back-breaking, day-to-day work.

ORIGINS OF LOGISTICS

Origins of the field of logistics can be traced to early man. And it is perhaps appropriate that they antedate the invention of the wheel. The individuals or families stockpiling food in their caves at certain times of

5

the year in order to survive the rigors of winter practiced a basic approach to inventory control. Later, as families produced more of certain foods or clothing than they could consume, the distribution of such goods from place to place began. Possibly as a response to the growing needs for more efficient transportation, the wheel was discovered.

Mass manufacture resulting from the Industrial Revolution in the United States in the last century provided the potential for expanding production capacities far beyond the ability of customers to use consequent output. The forces which made the Industrial Revolution possible included a rapidly growing labor force, a new railroad system for the transportation of larger quantities of products faster than had previously been possible, and new and rapidly growing markets inland as well as along the eastern seaboard. These same forces were to provide markets to match the productive capacities for many years. Fifty years later, in the 1920's, Henry Ford could still presume to offer customers any color of automobile "as long as it is black."

As the nation began to flex its industrial muscle, financiers occupied the spotlight along with production and efficiency engineers. Although historians label them frequently as the "robber barons" of industry, railroading, and finance, they were needed to provide the fuel to stoke the industrial fires and make the rapid growth possible. The revolution propelling the country into a position of world industrial leadership continued apace until the 1930's, when the Great Depression convinced some people that we could not concentrate forever on productive capacity and its attendant financing without comparable attention to the desires of the market and to the ability and inclinations of individuals to consume the output of the industrial machine.

It was at this point that attention was turned to the inefficiencies of the distribution system, with its great universal villains, the "middlemen." A pioneering voice of concern was that of Ralph Borsodi, who in 1927 concluded that:

. . . in 50 years between 1870 and 1920 the cost of distributing necessities and luxuries has nearly trebled, while production costs have gone down by one-fifth . . . what we are saving in production we are losing in distribution. . . .
. . . manufacturers engaged in mass production and mass selling have been the active factors in the development of extravagant marketing and unnecessary transportation. . . .[1]

It seems ironic that at precisely this point in time retailers and wholesalers were developing concepts of chain-store marketing and cooperative wholesaling organizations, to make their operations more efficient through economies of scale, mechanization, and better organization and control of effort.

[1] Ralph Borsodi, *The Distribution Age* (New York: D. Appleton & Co., 1929), p. 3.

As the pent-up demand for durables and other goods subsided in the aftermath of World War II, the nation was left with an abnormally expanded production capability. Attention shifted to the consumer and his wants as a means of encouraging consumption and providing opportunities for diversification of output to take up some of our production slack. The "age of marketing," which probably began in the 1930's, was confirmed.

It would have been natural for the logistical capabilities for moving products more efficiently from production to consumption points to have come under review as a part of the growing emphasis on the distribution system. Surprisingly, this development did not occur until the mid-1950's. By then, logistics offered perhaps the most fruitful area for potential improvement of industrial and commercial activity, in terms of both the quality and the cost of its output. This is the stage of development in which we find ourselves today, and it suggests that the subject of our discussion requires, and in many cases is receiving, disproportionately heavy attention in relation to other functional aspects of economic activity.

THE PLACE OF LOGISTICS IN ECONOMIC ACTIVITY

Once products or services in excess of need are created at any one location, they must be made available elsewhere unless they are to remain unused. This process of exchanging and making available the fruits of production has long been labeled distribution. Economists have lectured themselves voiceless on the need to capitalize on comparative cost advantages in the production of goods and services. The ability to utilize low labor costs, favorable locations with regard to raw material sources, and low costs for construction and land depends upon the degree to which barriers to exchange and the physical transfer of goods from one place to another can be lowered.

The Flow Concept

One way of viewing the economic process, encompassing both commercial and governmental activity, is as a variety of flows involving material, money (transactions), information, and people. Through the process, existing combinations of the basic "factors of production" (using a traditional term from economics)—land, labor, materials, and money—are merged into new combinations to start the cycle again. What some have claimed is the fifth "factor of production," management, is the vehicle by which the necessary flows are achieved. This concept is diagrammed in Fig. 1–1.

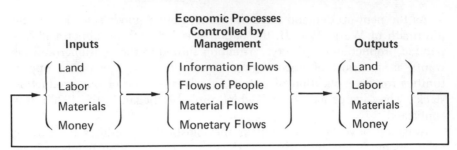

Fig. 1–1. The flow concept of economic activity.

Viewing the economic process in this manner, we would say that logistics in the broad sense is concerned with flows of material, people, money, and associated information. In this sense, it encompasses both production and physical transfer.

The Functional Concept

More traditionally, economic activity can be viewed as being comprised of so-called basic or core activities of production, finance, and distribution. Production may involve the manufacture of goods from raw materials, the extraction of minerals from the earth, agricultural activity, or the creation of skills and services (for example, through education as a production process). Finance involves the procurement and allocation of funds. Distribution involves both the creation of demand (transactions) through promotional effort and the logistics of making goods and services, once "sold," available.

The functional concept of economic activity is represented in Fig. 1–2. It differs in an important respect, at least to us, from the flow concept. (1) **What is the difference?** (Check this out by comparing Figs. 1–1 and 1–2.)

In the functional sense, then, our interest centers on the term "distribution."

Distribution. Converse articulated the distinctly different areas of activity in distribution this way:

Marketing [distribution] has been defined as matter in motion. There are two kinds of motion in moving goods from the farm, the mine, and the factory into the hands of the ultimate consumers. Goods must be moved through the

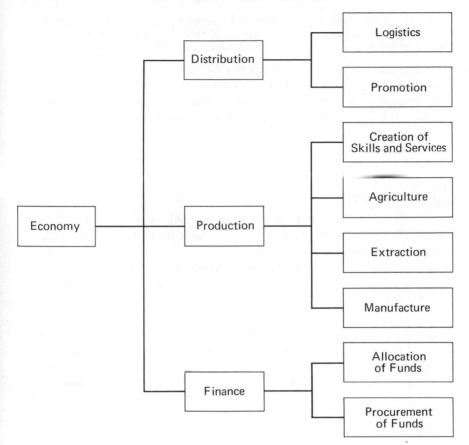

Fig. 1–2. Functional activities in the economy.

trade channel and gotten into the possession of customers—that is they must be bought and sold. . . . [Second,] goods must be moved physically.[2]

In doing so, he revived a long dormant discussion begun by Arch Shaw who wrote in 1916:

The problem of distribution today is . . . complex. Broadly speaking, it divides into two sub-problems closely related and interdependent but each having to do with a different set of factors and reactions. The first takes shape in the question: Given a particular article, how can a demand for it be created of sufficient volume to make its production and distribution profitable? The second is: Through what channels can the article itself be conveyed from the

[2] Paul D. Converse, "The Other Half of Marketing," in *Twenty-Sixth Boston Conference on Distribution* (Boston: Boston Trade Board, 1954), pp. 22–25; reprinted in Alfred L. Seelye (ed.), *Marketing in Transition* (New York: Harper & Row, 1958), pp. 114–21.

factory warehouse where it is of least value, into the hands of those consumers who will pay the most profitable price for it, though this price may not be the highest at which a more limited volume could be sold? [3]

In answering his two questions, Shaw concluded that distribution was composed of two types of effort, demand creation and physical supply.

For purposes of discussion the areas of demand creation and physical supply will be referred to in this chapter as promotion and logistics.

Promotion.   Promotion includes all ways in which organizations and individuals create awareness of real or perceived attributes of a product or service on the part of a potential customer. It concerns itself as well with the completion of sales transactions, and the maintenance of customer loyalty and post-purchase satisfaction. The end objective of these efforts, of course, is to increase the consumption of their firms' output, hopefully at a profit.

Promotional endeavors include direct selling, advertising, merchandising, and marketing research, ways in which potential customers are persuaded either directly or indirectly.

Logistics.   It was not until 1948 that the American Marketing Association (AMA), a leading organization in the field of marketing, formulated a set of definitions which included one for physical distribution: "The movement and handling of goods from the point of production to the point of consumption or use." [4] Besides formulating the definition, the AMA's Definitions Committee made a special effort to differentiate the terms "physical distribution" and "distribution" by cautioning:

> The word "distribution" is sometimes used to describe this activity. In view of the technical meaning of the word "distribution" in economic theory and of the fact that it is used by the Bureau of the Census and increasingly by marketing students and businessmen as synonymous with "marketing," the Committee recommends that its use as a synonym of, or substitute for, "physical distribution" be discouraged.[5]

Thus, a standard, generally accepted definition which distinguished "demand creation" from "physical distribution" activities were formed. **(2) How would you translate the AMA's definition for physical distribution into an acceptable one for logistics, as we have pictured it in Figs. 1–1 and 1–2?**

---

[3] A. W. Shaw, *An Approach to Business Problems* (Cambridge: Harvard University Press, 1916), pp. 99–100.
[4] Definitions Committee of the American Marketing Association, "1948 Report," *The Journal of Marketing,* October, 1948, p. 202.
[5] *Ibid.*

Distinctions Between Promotion and Logistics. Promotion and logistics have, for years, been thrown together under the category of marketing or distribution. For several reasons it appears desirable to treat them now as related but separate fields of study and activity.

Utility Creation. Promotion and logistics efforts are undertaken to create different types of utilities in goods.

Through direct and indirect contact with the market, promotional efforts increase the desire, or call latent desire to mind, on the part of the customer to possess a good or benefit from a service. This effort presumably leads to sales transactions or some type of exchange. We say then that promotion is primarily concerned with creating possession utility.

Logistics creates place and time utility in goods and services. Place utility is created primarily by transportation, time utility primarily by inventory maintenance and the strategic location of goods and services. In these terms, logistics activities are means by which customer demands for time and place utility in goods and services are translated into a supply of these same types of utility.

Channel Composition. Promotional channels and logistics channels for the same item may involve different institutions. The study of marketing has long concentrated on some consideration of the institutions through which a good or service passes on its way from initial manufacturers to ultimate consumers. A series of such institutions is said to make up a channel of distribution.

Logistics and promotional channels for a family of products are illustrated in Fig. 1–3. The logistics channel includes those firms that are involved in the physical transfer of product, those that actually take possession of the wheat seed, wheat, and flour. The promotional channel includes firms that buy and sell the family of products, often taking title (financial responsibility) for a product in the process.

Note that the firms included in these two types of channels are not the same. Only in recent years have we begun to differentiate between the basic functions of the so-called channel of distribution, and between the logistical and promotional needs within channels of distribution. Such differentiation has opened the door for the improved design of both logistics and promotional efforts, as we shall see later.

In Fig. 1–3, each transfer of goods from one business entity to the next requires the coordination of demand and supply among many different institutions in the channel, from the original grower of wheat seed to the ultimate consumer of flour. The length of time from the original

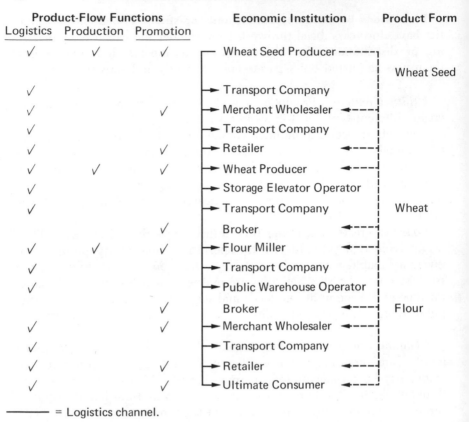

Product-Flow Functions			Economic Institution	Product Form
Logistics	Production	Promotion		
✓	✓	✓	Wheat Seed Producer	
				Wheat Seed
✓			Transport Company	
✓		✓	Merchant Wholesaler	
✓			Transport Company	
✓		✓	Retailer	
✓	✓	✓	Wheat Producer	
✓			Storage Elevator Operator	
✓			Transport Company	Wheat
		✓	Broker	
✓	✓	✓	Flour Miller	
✓			Transport Company	
✓			Public Warehouse Operator	
		✓	Broker	Flour
✓		✓	Merchant Wholesaler	
✓			Transport Company	
✓		✓	Retailer	
✓		✓	Ultimate Consumer	

——— = Logistics channel.

– – – – = Promotion channel.

Fig. 1–3. The logistics and promotional channels for a product family.

planting of wheat for seed to the ultimate consumption of flour may be as much as three years or more. Allowing for two growing seasons, storage time of nearly two years may be required, with attendant costs of storage and investment in inventory. Transportation and material-handling activities are also repeated six or more times. Is it any wonder that a large proportion of the price paid for flour at the local grocery store defrays the expenses of logistics throughout the channel?

Figure 1–3 is a vastly oversimplified representation of what goes on in a channel of distribution, or in its component logistics and promotional channels. Management in the logistics channel has as its basic objectives: (1) providing the desired level of physical product availability, in terms of quantities and the physical or temporal distance between the product and its customer, (2) providing products in the assortments in which they are desired by the potential customer, and (3) offering the desired physical service levels at an attractive cost level, often through the consolidation of products for physical movement wherever it can be accomplished.

The importance of product assortment for "merchandising" and consolidation for storage and transportation means that related products and product families are assembled together and dispersed from each of several institutions in both logistics and promotional channels. This allows producing organizations to specialize in the goods they produce and various types of retailing institutions, for example, to specialize in selling different assortments of products from a variety of sources.

Further, each institution in a logistics channel encompasses one or more facilities or terminals to and from which goods flow in a physical sense. The terminal for a trucker may be just that; for a retailer it is his warehouse and his retail stores. Even though the resulting assortment of goods may change at each level and each terminal in the channel, the total volume of economic activity may be sufficiently large to allow for the efficient movement of a given product to and from channel "terminals" by means of its consolidation with changing assortments comprising other products as well.

Overall, the resulting accomplishment of a logistics channel may be the dispersal of goods from a relatively few sources to many eventual users, as would be the case with flour. Or it might be the reverse, as is typical of the company offering solid waste disposal services.

The Application of Quantitative Techniques. To date, logistics has offered great opportunity for the application of quantitative techniques in problem solving by managers. Although theoretical research regarding promotional problems, particularly those concerning consumer behavior, has utilized such techniques, relatively little of it has been put into actual use by marketing managers. Some possible explanations are:

1. The human factor is great, but not as important in carrying out logistics as opposed to promotional activities.
2. Logistics goals often can be more clearly defined than those for promotional efforts.
3. Alternative methods to achieve goals are becoming better known.
4. Logistics system alternatives lend themselves to quantification and mathematical analysis.
5. Mathematical tools to attack more complicated logistics system problems are becoming available.

(3) Do these factors suggest a continuing differentiation in the application of quantitative techniques to logistical and promotional problems?

Because of basic differences in the fields of promotion and logistics, it is well to consider them separately while at the same time keeping in mind that, together, promotion and logistics make up a powerful combination which accomplishes a vital task: distribution in our economy.

THE IMPORTANCE OF LOGISTICS

What is a valid measure of the importance of logistics in the economy? What is the current magnitude of logistics costs? What is the estimated trend of these costs based on the recent past? Different measuring sticks can be applied to suggest answers to these questions. Among them are: (1) people employed, (2) investment in facilities, and (3) logistics as a cost of doing business in the economy.

People Employed

Statistics compiled by the Transportation Association of America from Bureau of Labor Statistics reports indicate that the average number of people employed in freight and passenger transportation activities in 1969 was 2,561,000, or 3.3% of the total number of employed persons in the United States.[6] This was down from 4.5% of employed persons in 1950, due solely to the fact that during the nineteen-year span of time, railroad companies reduced their labor force by 747,000 persons, or more than half of their 1950 total, while increasing their ton-miles of freight carried by nearly 30%.

Employment in transportation-related industries has increased with sufficient rapidity to make up for the lag in employment in transportation services, and produced a total employment in transportation services and related industries of 13.2% of the persons employed in the United States in 1970. The large groups of employees counted among those in transportation-related industries included those employed in the manufacture and distribution of transportation equipment, parts, and service, the manufacture and distribution of petroleum for transportation purposes, and state and local highway department employees.

If there is any doubt about the orientation of the United States transportation system, it should be dispelled by the fact that over 72% of the employment in transportation and transportation-related industries is devoted to highway transportation, as contrasted with less than 28% for rail, water, pipeline, air, and the U. S. Postal Service combined.

[6] *Transportation Facts and Trends*, 9th Ed. (Washington, D. C.: Transportation Association of America, 1972), p. 22, based on statistics reported by the U. S. Department of Labor, Bureau of Labor Statistics.

Investment in Support of Logistics Activities [7]

The net investment in support of freight and passenger logistics and logistics-related activities is shown in Table 1–1. In 1965, we estimate that it amounted to about $417 billion, or about 18.5% of the national wealth. Gross assumptions were required to arrive at these figures, but they at least suggest that it requires a lot of capital to support our logistics system.

Who supplied these vast amounts of money? Over 80%, or about $338 billion, resulted from investment by private enterprise or individuals This was 17.7% of the total of net private tangible assets in the United States. The $79 billion in net assets financed from public funds represented about 23.4% of the estimated total of net tangible assets held in public title by national, state, or local governments.

What is the money invested in? Information in Table 1–1 allows us to identify investment by both the private and public sectors for freight and passenger logistics activities, for transportation and non-transportation activities, and for single important segments of logistics activity.

Nearly 65% of the investment by the private sector was identified with freight logistics activities. Of this, slightly more than one-fourth supported transportation as opposed to non-transportation logistics activities. In particular, major investments of more than $144 billion in inventory, nearly $16 billion in warehousing facilities, and more than $28 billion in railroad facilities contributed significantly to the total of nearly $218 billion which the private sector invested in freight logistics activities.

The dominant item of investment by the private sector in passenger logistics reflected the individual's "love affair" with the automobile. In 1965, individuals and private organizations had a net investment of more than $89 billion in automobiles, nearly three-fourths of the total investment for passenger logistics by the private sector.

In contrast to patterns of private investment, the federal, state, and local governments of this country have invested primarily on behalf of passenger logistics activities, devoting more than three-fourths of their net investment to these purposes.[8] Most of the nearly $60 billion invested in support of passenger logistics activities has been devoted to highway construction, the rest to the construction of airports and installation of equipment necessary to maintain effective airways. These figures, be-

[7] Much of this and the following section is based on J. L. Heskett and D. Daryl Wyckoff, "Macroeconomic Logistics Cost Trends," to be published.

[8] This particular figure may be the most arguable in Table 1–1, in that it is based largely on the courageous assumption that investments in airports, airways, and highways are allocated in the same proportions as private investment in air and highway freight and passenger vehicles, respectively.

TABLE 1-1. Net Investment for Logistics Activities, 1965
(Millions of Dollars)

	Primarily Freight	Primarily Passenger
Private		
Transportation:		
Air carrier:		
Commercial	$ 198[a]	$ 3,730
General		1,005
Equipment manufacturers:		
Motor vehicles and equipment		13,791
Other than motor vehicles	9,064	
Highway:		
Automobile		89,070
Truck and trailer	12,642	
Bus		389
Dealers, service stations	1,018[b]	7,200[b]
Repair, garages, etc.	378[b]	2,668[b]
Oil pipe line	2,988	
Railroad	28,400[c]	1,567[c]
Transit:[d]		
Rail and trolley		2,282
Bus		466
Water carrier:		
Inland	730	
Ocean	2,091	
Great Lakes	309	
Subtotals, private transportation	$ 57,818	$122,168
Inventory:		
Farm	$ 23,300	
Manufacturers	68,000	
Wholesalers	18,300	
Retailers	34,600	
Warehousing:[e]		
Public	512	—
Private	15,360	—
Order Processing:	n.a.	—
Subtotal, private non-transportation	$160,072	—
Government (Federal, State, and Local)		
Transportation:		
Airports and airways[f]	$ 670	$ 16,180
Highways[g]	6,140	43,750
Waterways[h]	8,340	—
Subtotals, government transportation	$ 15,150	$ 59,930

TABLE 1-1 (Continued). Net Investment for Logistics Activities, 1965
(Millions of Dollars)

	Primarily Freight	Primarily Passenger
Inventory:		
Farm	$ 4,400	–
Other	n.a.	–
Warehousing	n.a.	–
Order Processing	n.a.	–
Subtotal, government non-transportation	$ 4,400	–
Total, private logistics	$217,890	$122,168
Percentage of total net private tangible assets of U. S. invested in private logistics activities[i]	11.4%	6.3%
Total, government logistics	$ 19,550	$ 59,930
Percentage of total net government tangible assets of U. S. invested in government logistics activities[j]	5.8%	17.6%
Total, private and government logistics	$237,440	$181,920
Percentage of national wealth invested in private and government logistics activities	10.5%	8.0%

n.a. = not available.

[a]Allocated on the basis of the relative proportions of revenue derived from passengers on the one hand and freight and mail on the other.

[b]Allocated on the basis of net capital investment in automobiles and buses (passenger) and trucks and trailers (freight) above.

[c]Allocated on the basis of 1965 revenues derived from freight and passenger revenues.

[d]Includes municipally owned operations.

[e]Based on an average valuation of $2 per square foot for warehouse space and $.25 per cubic foot for refrigeration space in the 1963 *Census of Business* for public warehousemen and wholesalers, and using an estimate of private space owned by retailers and manufacturers based on inventory value/space occupied ratio for wholesalers.

[f]Based on an estimate of the depreciated value (20-year, straight-line) of expenditures for projects on which some federal funds are used (probably understating the total), currently reported in the *FAA Statistical Handbook of Aviation*, and allocated on the basis of previously calculated investments for commercial and general aviation.

[g]Based on an estimate of the depreciated value (20-year, straight-line) of capital outlays for interstate, state, county, and local roads, currently reported in *Highway Statistics*, Annual Report, Federal Highway Administration, Department of Transportation, and allocated on the basis of previously calculated investments for freight and passenger vehicles.

[h]Based on an estimate of the depreciated value (20-year, straight-line) of federal funds allocated to the Army Corps of Engineers (including funds spent for maintenance, but including no state or local investments), currently reported in the *Annual Report*, Corps of Engineers, Department of the Army.

[i]Based on an estimate of $1,909,000 million for total net private tangible assets in 1965, appearing in *Transportation Facts and Trends*, published annually by the Transportation Association of America, Washington, D. C.

[j]Based on an estimate of $339,000 million for total net public tangible assets in 1965, prepared from the national wealth estimates presented in the *Statistical Abstract of the United States*, published annually by the Government Printing Office, Washington, D. C.

cause of the relatively rapid rates of depreciation on which they are based, offer a conservative view of the current worth of government investments in support of freight and passenger logistics.

To the extent that 18.5% of national wealth was invested in activities employing 13.4% of persons employed in 1965, we might conclude that logistics and logistics-related activities are capital- as opposed to labor-intensive, even though tens of thousands of those employed are still moving freight with a combination of a $50 hand truck and their hands and backs.

Logistics as a Cost of Doing Business

Dollar logistics costs are rising. But when compared to a measurement of cost increases in, or incomes derived from, all types of economic activity, logistics costs can be shown to be rising more slowly than the nation's tangible gross national product which they facilitate. For this purpose we divided all logistics costs into three major categories: movement (transportation), inventory holding, and logistics management costs. In total, these costs were nearly $148 billion in 1970. As shown in Fig. 1–4, the ratio of such costs to tangible gross national product in 1970 was 26.0%, the highest in recent years. However, significant increases in inventory carrying costs in 1969 and transportation rates in 1970 appeared to precede a large increase in tangible gross national product in subsequent years which will bring total logistics cost levels back nearer their recent lows in 1968.

Movement.[9]   Movement costs exceeded $84 billion in 1970. Most of them were incurred for highway transportation not subject to economic regulation, such as local pickup and delivery, private transport operations of firms engaged largely in other businesses, and the hauling of agricultural commodities. Movement costs made up roughly 58% of all estimated logistics costs in 1970.

Although constant in relation to tangible gross national product (at about 15%) for many years, such costs dropped significantly in 1968 and 1969 as the tangible GNP rose at a faster rate than returns to transportation activities. However, because of several rounds of rate increases by regulated carriers during 1970, the previous relationship has been restored. This typifies at least the regulated portions of the transportation industries, in that they usually receive rate increases months after an upturn

---

[9] The most complete and accurate estimates of transportation costs prepared on a year-to-year basis are those published in the form of a booklet entitled *Transportation Facts and Trends* by the Transportation Association of America, Washington, D. C.

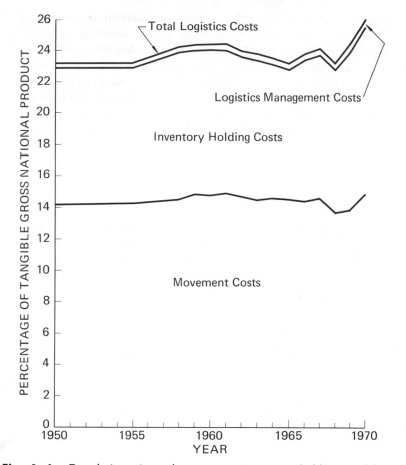

Fig. 1–4. Trends in estimated movement, inventory holding, and logistics management costs, as a percentage of tangible gross national product, 1950 through 1970.

in general economic activity and following increases of prices for labor and goods in general.

Inventory Carrying Costs. Matters of inventory control vary in complexity from those of a service establishment with very little inventory to those of a large variety store which may have a complicated inventory of 10,000 items or more. Collectively, inventories made up about 7.5% of the net tangible assets of the United States in 1965, a year in which American business had an average investment of about $144 billion in inventories. Until 1969, the ratio of inventory carrying costs to tangible GNP, shown in Fig. 1–4, remained relatively constant at about 9%. Rapidly escalating interest rates drove carrying costs to nearly 11% of the tangible gross national product in 1970. They have since returned to near their former levels, but promise to fluctuate more in the future than they have in the past. Inventory carrying costs make up about 41% of all logistics costs.

Our estimates of inventory carrying costs are based on the commonly accepted ratio of such costs to the average value of inventory on hand over the period of a year, 25%.[10] There is some argument over how this figure should be constructed. Alford and Bangs made their well-known allocation as follows: storage facilities, 0.25%; insurance, 0.25%; taxes, 0.50%; transportation, 0.50%; handling and distribution, 2.50%; depreciation, 5.00%; interest, 6.00%; obsolescence, 10.00%; for a total of 25.00%.[11] While few dispute the total magnitude of these costs, there is good cause to believe that storage facility costs are underestimated, and costs of depreciation and obsolescence are overestimated by this particular allocation. Nevertheless, it provides one of the few published guides available.

In order to avoid double counting of expenses between movement and inventory holding costs, transportation costs (assumed to be expended for transfer movements between storage points) and handling and distribution costs (to avoid inclusion of local transportation and warehouse shipping and receiving) were excluded from the inventory carrying cost factor which we used. Instead of 6% interest on money invested in inventory, we employed an annual figure representing 1.5 times the average prime rate of interest charged by banks to their most valued customers. This produced a carrying cost factor ranging from 19.5% of average inventories in 1950 to 28.7% of average inventories in 1970.

In spite of a generally rising cost of money over the twenty-year period considered in Fig. 1–4, inventory holding costs remained relatively constant in relation to tangible GNP until 1969, actually dropping at times on a year-to-year basis. One such drop in 1964 and 1965 gave rise at the time to the following interesting speculation:

. . . A number of economists and businessmen have begun to argue that inventories may not be, at this point, the reliable economic indicator they have traditionally been. The economists say that "secular" influences (mechanical processes unrelated to traditional economic events) have tended to keep inventories at lower levels.

[10] For the results of one informal study which indicates values in use ranging from 12% to 35%, see John B. Holbrook, "A Simple Tabular Method for Determining Economic Order Quantities," in *Managing the Materials Function* (New York: American Management Association, 1959), AMA Management Report No. 35, p. 66.

[11] See L. P. Alford and John R. Bangs (eds.), *Production Handbook* (New York: The Ronald Press Company, 1955), pp. 396–97. See also Gordon B. Carson, Harold A. Bolz, and Hewitt H. Young (eds.), *Production Handbook*, 3rd ed. (New York: The Ronald Press Co., 1972), p. 5.10, for several alternative types of allocations.

These secular influences include the use of computers for inventory control, more rapid communications and transportation, and a growing business concern with inventory.[12]

(4) **Do the statistics for years following 1965 bear out this opinion?**
(5) **What explanations can we offer for inventory carrying cost trends?**

It is somewhat misleading to measure the importance of logistics activities in the economy in terms of employment, investment in facilities, or the relationship of logistics costs to tangible gross national product. These measures describe only the inputs to our national logistics system.

What have we gotten for our money? Are more goods more readily available in better condition to a greater extent than ever before? As we will see, high productivity and low costs in logistical activities often are easiest to achieve in a company with a few products, each of which may be selling in large volume to concentrated markets. There is evidence to suggest that just the reverse has been happening in the United States. More and more product variations are being produced and sold in many industries, compounding logistics problems, impairing productivity, and adversely affecting logistics costs. Under these circumstances, the achievement represented by cost trends and relationships discussed earlier is all the more remarkable.

THE SYSTEMS APPROACH TO LOGISTICS

Systems, systems analysis, systems design, and systems management became bywords in technology-oriented companies in the 1950's. This emphasis grew out of the demand for products of greater and greater complexity whose production could not be completed by a single firm. For a nation confronted with growing complexity in its problems, products, and way of life, the term "system" somehow vaguely conveyed the idea of increasing complexity. It is now the darling in the language of the world of the corporate state. Little wonder, then, that a paint manufacturer announced not too long ago that its products would no longer be known as paints, but rather as "protective coating systems," or that an airline has become not a company but an "air system," or that the word "systems" appears in a growing number of corporate names, particularly those preparing to sell stock to the public.

What is a system? One leading textbook on the subject of systems management tells us that it is "a complex whole." That is an indication either of the difficulty of defining the term or of what currently is wrong with higher education in this country. As it has been used in practice,

---

[12] Philip Shabecoff, "Inventory Ratio Shows a Decline," *New York Times,* June 7, 1964, p. F–3.

however, the word seems to signify a mechanism or process composed of many interrelated parts. If the word is overused, then, perhaps it is because it seems to be a pretty good substitute for the process of life itself.

If we cannot define a system very satisfactorily, perhaps we can enumerate some of its common characteristics. We have already described it as having many interrelated parts. Further, the performance of one part influences, and is influenced by, the performance of other parts. To examine the parts of a system individually may lead to undesirable results.

Typically, a system's performance is more sensitive to changes in certain of its components than in others. The exploration of these sensitivities is referred to as sensitivity analysis. A well-conceived analysis of sensitivities can be a great aid in establishing priorities for changes to be made in system design.

System performance depends on the "balance" which is achieved between system components, measured in terms of capacity, timing, economics, or other measures. Often, performance reflects the effectiveness of the weakest or least efficient element in the system, regardless of the degree of technical sophistication or capability associated with other elements in such a system.

Optimum system performance does not depend necessarily on: (1) the optimum performance of each individual system component, (2) the ability to cut the single most important cost item in the system budget, or (3) the use of the most advanced technology for system components.

The management of systems involves cost trade-offs, the trading of one type of cost for another. This approach relies on the belief that all activities and results can be translated into costs, whether they might be costs resulting from activities such as transportation or those resulting from foregone opportunities, such as service failures resulting in "costs" of lost sales.

Finally, systems management often is not compatible with existing organizational arrangements.

This is all rather profound. What does it mean for us? To the extent possible, we will attempt to take a systems-oriented approach to the exploration of logistics in this book. In looking at logistics system elements, constraints, activities, design, and management, we will move from the examination of specific elements to interrelationships between elements; from the somewhat descriptive (designed to provide necessary background) to the analytical; from the technical aspects of design to the real pay-off, systems management; from the management of logistics systems in individual firms to those encompassing several firms doing business with one another. This essential scheme of the book is laid out in Fig. 1–5.

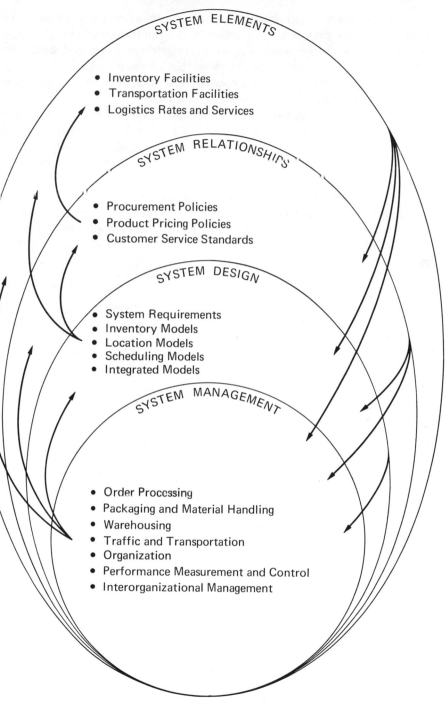

Fig. 1–5. Plan of the book.

A system-oriented approach to study means more than a fancy diagram. It means that wherever possible in examining individual system elements and activities we will make every attempt to suggest important interactions to be expected between related elements. As we go along, numerical examples drawn from experience will help us measure and visualize interactions between system elements.

There is on the market a plastic toy designed for small children. It consists of several gears mounted on spindles in such a way that the teeth of the various gears mesh. As the handle on one gear is turned, it draws all the rest into action. In many ways, this toy typifies our logistics system. Starting with the basic elements of nodes and network, and given system relationships (constraints), a logistics system is designed within which a variety of logistics activities are managed. We are poised with our version of the toy, getting ready to turn the handle and find out more about how the mechanism works.

2

Logistics
in the Enterprise

The military provides, as with so many other management concepts, a likely origin of the term "logistics." Together with tactics and strategies, logistics is one of the three major functions of the military mission. In adopting logistics management concepts from the military, business has also adapted such concepts to meet somewhat different needs.

Military logistics has been defined as "The process by which human effort and facilitating resources are directed toward the objective of *creating and supporting* combat forces and weapons." [1] Logistics, as a function of the business enterprise, devotes primary attention to the movement and storage of products and supplies and is concerned only incidentally, if at all, with the movement of people. The military logistician can set up priorities for filling demand that constantly exceeds supply, making possible a degree of "customer control" that is virtually impossible in business except under extraordinary circumstances. In many businesses, all orders are considered "top priority" due to the pressures of a competitive economy. In recent years, the excess of supply (i.e., capacity) over demand in many industries has encouraged this philosophy.

With this in mind, business logistics will, for our discussion, refer to the management of *all activities which facilitate product movement and the coordination of supply and demand in the creation of time and place utility in goods.*

[1] James L. Quinn, *Logistics Management Concepts and Cases* (Wright–Patterson Air Force Base, Ohio: School of Systems and Logistics, Air Force Institute of Technology, 1971), p. 8. Emphasis supplied.

25

THE SCOPE OF BUSINESS LOGISTICS

The direct relationship between product-flow activities of production and distribution in the economy and functions of production, marketing, and logistics in the business firm is illustrated by Fig. 2–1. Although these product-flow activities are basic to the economy as a whole, they have varied levels of importance in individual firms. For example, few marketing institutions also engage in production, especially if the narrower term, manufacturing, is meant. On the other hand, brokers buy and sell goods, but assume little responsibility for logistics activities. Some firms may utilize the marketing or supply organizations of others, confining themselves basically to the management of production and logistics activities.

Figure 2–1 illustrates also how the various managerial and operational functions of business logistics in the firm are grouped and aligned. Familiarity with the diagram will facilitate understanding of the use of terminology throughout the text.

Physical Supply (Materials Management) and Physical Distribution

In Fig. 2–1, logistics is made up of two related subsets of activity, physical supply and physical distribution. Each of these, in turn, involves movement control and demand–supply coordination.

Physical supply, or as it is more popularly known, materials management, involves the accumulation of materials from various supply points and the coordination of such activity with the demand for the firm's products or services. Ammer, while acknowledging different views about the functions that comprise materials management, concludes:

. . . in a typical company they would embrace all activities concerned with materials *except* those directly concerned with designing or manufacturing the product or maintaining the facilities, equipment and tooling. These would include most, if not all, of the activities performed by the following departments in the typical company: purchasing, control, shipping, traffic, receiving, and stores.[2]

Once materials are procured, assembled, blended, and refinished, they must be moved on either to another production facility in a vertically integrated firm or to a customer, again with the attendant coordination of demand and supply. This movement and demand–supply

[2] Dean S. Ammer, *Material Management*, Rev. Ed. (Homewood. Ill.: Richard D. Irwin, Inc., 1968), p. 12.

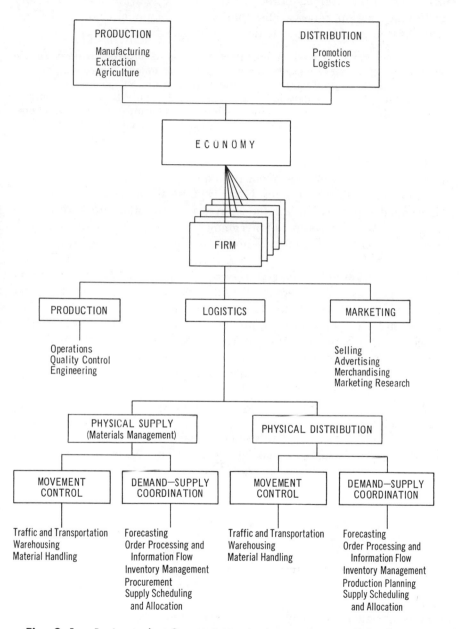

Fig. 2–1. Basic product-flow activities in the economy and the firm.

coordination for products outbound is, from the viewpoint of the facility or firm in question, physical distribution. The National Council of Physical Distribution Management defines physical distribution as:

. . . the term employed in manufacturing and commerce to describe the broad range of activities concerned with efficient movement of finished products from the end of the production line to the consumer, and in some cases includes the movement of raw materials from the source of supply to the beginning of the production line. These activities include freight transportation, warehousing, material handling, protective packaging, inventory control, plant and warehouse site selection, order processing, market forecasting and customer service.[3]

In a logistics channel comprising those firms engaged in the physical exchange of goods, the movement from a supplier to its customer is physical distribution to the supplier, but it is physical supply to the customer. Conceptually, physical supply and physical distribution are both accomplished by the supervision of a common set of activities dealing with movement control and demand–supply coordination.

Movement Control.   Every business firm using, making, or dealing in tangible goods must concern itself with problems of moving goods from one point to another, obviously involving transportation in some form. This includes not only the various forms of long-distance transportation which normally come to mind, but also a second aspect of movement control: the handling of materials over very short distances.

Storage is often necessary to hold goods until the time when they are needed. Thus, storage is the third aspect of movement control. It is important to remember that the apparent contradiction between "storage" (which implies the absence of physical motion) and "movement" can be resolved when one reasons that storage actually *moves goods closer* to sale or consumption, *in time*, by making goods available when and where they are needed.

Demand–Supply Coordination.   To coordinate demand and supply effectively, it is important to be able to estimate what the demand might be. This is the goal of forecasting activities, and it allows a firm to anticipate the demands of its customers or its production facilities, thereby providing more time to respond to such needs. Once demand develops, it can be identified through order processing and information flow. The information must be acted upon, and this is the primary function of inventory management, involving the updating of inventories for shipments and receipts; the identification of replenishment needs in terms of quantities, times, and locations; and the preparation of replenishment orders.

[3] Quoted from various pieces of literature circulated from the executive offices of the National Council of Physical Distribution Management, Chicago, Ill.

This, in turn, may trigger the procurement of raw materials or release of goods purchased previously for physical supply, or the planning of the time and place at which production is to take place for physical distribution. Whether for physical supply or distribution, the timing and placement of product to be made available must be determined before such plans are turned over to those in charge of movement control activities for follow-through.

Logistics Management in the Channel of Distribution

Unlike manufacturing and marketing responsibilities, logistics management in the channel of distribution often is beset by problems of varying or overlapping responsibilities for timing, methods, and other considerations in the shipping and storage of goods. Such responsibilities will vary with the terms used in the purchase and sale of goods.

With the large numbers of institutions involved, an overlap of authority regarding matters of logistics is inevitable in the channel, as indicated in Fig. 2–2. What is physical distribution to a producer, whether he is a wheat seed grower or a flour miller, must by its very nature be physical supply to a consumer, whether he is a wheat grower or wholesaler. Such overlap poses problems in the determination of responsibility for logistics activities and in the measurement of their costs and performance.

DEVELOPMENT OF THE LOGISTICS FUNCTION—
PRACTICE AND THEORY

The development of the current logistics function in the business firm has its origin in traffic and inventory management. There are many views as to just how these functional areas of management have developed. However, before we become too smug about the recent development of a system-oriented view of the field, consider the following example of such thought:

The fact is that carriage by road being quicker, more reliable and less subject to loss or damage, it possesses advantage to which businessmen often attach a considerable value. However, it may well be that the saving of 0 fr. 87 induces the merchant to use the canal; he can buy warehouses and increase his floating capital in order to have a sufficient supply of goods on hand to protect himself against the slowness and irregularity of the canal, and if all told the saving of 0 fr. 87 in transport gives him an advantage of a few centimes, he will decide in favor of the new route. . . .[4]

[4] Jules Dupuit, "On the Measurement of the Utility of Public Works," reprinted in *International Economic Papers*, No. 2, translated from the French by R. H. Barback (London: Macmillan and Co., Ltd., 1952), p. 100.

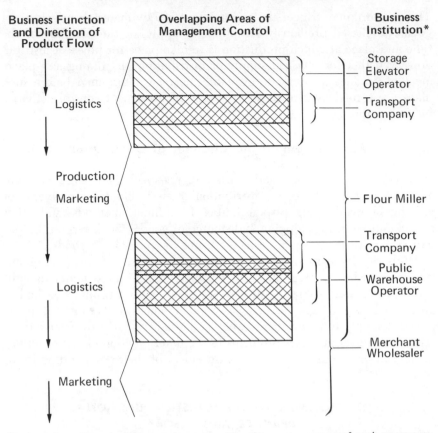

| Business Function and Direction of Product Flow | Overlapping Areas of Management Control | Business Institution* |

*Braces show functional control exercised by the management of each company in the logistics channel.

Fig. 2–2. Overlap of control in adjacent firms in a portion of a logistical channel.

The author? Jules Dupuit, a French engineer. The date of his publication? 1844. A countryman of Dupuit already had formulated the commonly accepted military definition of logistics in 1838:

Logistics comprises the means and arrangements which work out the plans of strategy and tactics. Strategy decides where to act; logistics brings the troops to this point.[5]

[5] Antoine Henri Jomini, *Précis de l'Art de la Guerre*, 1838, quoted in Robert Debs Heinl, Jr. (ed.), *Dictionary of Military and Naval Quotations* (Annapolis, Md.: United States Naval Institute, 1966), p. 315.

Early Development

Traffic management perhaps gained initial identification and recognition in this country when the first alternative to water transportation, the railroad, was developed and the distribution of manufacturing outputs over wide geographic areas began to take place.[6]

As railroad capacity far in excess of need was built, intensive competition was experienced in many geographic areas. In an era of unregulated rates, the traffic manager able to "wheel and deal" in such a manner as to produce a competitive advantage through rate differentials or rebates from the railroads gained an important position in many industrial and commercial organizations.

With the passage of the Interstate Commerce Act in 1887, the role of the traffic manager changed dramatically from that of an entrepreneur to one of a technician charged with the responsibility for translating an increasingly complex set of rate tariffs into management action. The prohibition of rebates and the publication of all regulated rates greatly restricted the latitude of the traffic manager to negotiate preferential rates. Later, the introduction of in-transit rates (allowing commodities to be stored or processed en route to their ultimate destination upon proof or identification of the commodity) required the traffic manager in some industries using bulk transport to immerse himself in a commodity accounting system. Because of the typically great significance of transportation costs in these industries, traffic managers employed in them were able to maintain a high status in the organizational ranks of their respective companies. However, the technical nature of the task, necessitating the use of a largely "private" language and producing somewhat narrow managerial interests, did nothing to enhance the traffic manager's candidacy for top management positions.

Concurrent with the development of industrial capacity, featuring large plants capable of taking greater advantage of production economies of scale, and accompanying large capital investment, the need to use such productive capacity efficiently became apparent. Efficiency experts, the forerunners of industrial engineers, came forward to meet the need at the outset of the twentieth century. Among them were such men as Frederick Taylor, the "father of scientific management," whose experiments in the more efficient handling of pig iron culminated in a famous demonstration at Bethlehem Steel in 1898 of his methods of personnel selection, motivation, and training as well as improved procedures for han-

[6] For an interesting discussion of the evolution of the traffic management function, see Roy J. Sampson, "Evolution of the Traffic Management Function," *Northwest Business Management*, Spring, 1966, pp. 13–17.

dling. Contemporary with Taylor's work was that of Frank and Lillian Gilbreth and their "therbligs" (measured units of work), and Camp and others and their "economic lot size" formulas for determining the most efficient production runs on the expensive and newly developed machinery.

Camp's work and that of his contemporaries provided the basis for modern inventory control theory. It is natural that the work of these men and women was almost totally oriented to production. The "economic lot size" or EOQ (economic order quantity) formulas had as their objective the balancing of machine set-up costs against inventory holding costs resulting from production in excess of immediate shipment requirements. Unfortunately this production orientation was to pervade and dominate the field for another half-century, greatly restricting the potential benefits of scientific inventory control, the organizational aspirations and breadth of view of most inventory managers, and the ability of top management to deal with questions regarding the effectiveness of company-wide inventory management.

This "two-headed monster" of uncoordinated traffic and inventory management was to continue until after World War II, with isolated exceptions. One such exception occurred at Goodyear when the President, Paul Litchfield,

. . . assumed a personal role in the creation in 1939 of an organization to coordinate demand and supply and take full responsibility for all investment in goods, including supporting activities of sales forecasting and the balancing of production schedules against anticipated sales needs. With the later addition of transportation and warehousing management responsibilities, this organization, under a General Merchandise and Materials Control Manager, has been a pace-setter in modern logistics management.[7]

Other forerunners of today's materials (physical supply) managers began to emerge during World War II, especially in defense-oriented companies with significant supply problems. Pioneer physical distribution managers began to provide the moving force for reorganization in consumer-goods companies with sizable physical distribution problems. Although top management interest in logistics had long been a fact, a remark attributed to Admiral Ernest J. King of World War II fame would be heard a generation later in many business organizations:

I don't know what the hell this logistics is that [General] Marshall is always talking about but I want some of it.[8]

Studies designed to document the early organizational growth of materials (physical supply) and physical distribution management offer a

[7] "Invention To Satisfy a Manifest Management Need," *Handling & Shipping,* July, 1966, pp. 43–47.
[8] Quoted in Heinl, *op. cit.,* p. 175.

more detailed review of developments since World War II. A study conducted by one of the authors provides the basis for much of the following discussion.[9]

The study markedly pointed out the preponderance of interest in the management of problems of physical distribution as opposed to physical supply. In fact, measurable trends of development were found to exist only in the former management area. For this reason, the discussion of business logistics development in the following sections will be confined largely to physical distribution management.

Historical Growth, 1945–1956

Three characteristics of the early growth of the physical distribution function are noteworthy. First, physical distribution management in manufacturing firms was recognized as a separate organizational function or field and developed almost entirely after World War II. It may have stemmed from certain physical merchandising techniques used by large retail mail-order houses at that time. Second, its early growth was based on the assignment of additional responsibilities to reorganized traffic departments. Third, the most commonly mentioned initial objective of the newly established departments was to cut physical distribution costs.

By the end of World War II several industrial firms contained strong departments, essentially in charge of all elements of movement control.[10] Expansion of the responsibilities of some of these groups led to the establishment of what are now recognized as the first physical distribution departments.

Early growth of the function occurred in manufacturing firms marketing a wide line of products through retail grocery and drug outlets. Thus, in 1945, such firms as Lever Brothers Company, H. J. Heinz Company, and General Foods Corporation contained departments which supervised both transportation and warehousing activities, particularly on outbound movements. These were followed by the establishment of similar departments by Gerber Products Company several years later, by American Home

[9] Firms included in this study were selected from eight industry groupings: electronics, ladies' ready-to-wear, machine tool, chemical manufacturers, dairy food processors, grain millers, steel millers and fabricators, and brewers. In addition, a sample of "progressive" firms chosen from among those known to have engaged in organizational development for logistics management was surveyed. All firms surveyed were industrial firms reporting gross sales over $1 million in 1958. In all, 206 firms supplied information by mail, and 60 executives in 43 of the companies were questioned further in personal interviews. For further discussion of methods employed in the study, see J. L. Heskett, "Ferment in Marketing's Oldest Area," *Journal of Marketing*, October, 1962, pp. 40–45.

[10] Traffic and transportation, warehousing, and material handling. See Fig. 2–1.

Foods in 1948, by Sunshine Biscuit Company in 1949, and by Armour & Company and the International Latex Corporation in 1952.

In 1948, Whirlpool Corporation, a major firm in the consumer durable goods field, was one of the first firms producing goods of this type to place transportation and finished product warehousing activities under a single administrator. In 1950, Lever Brothers' "movement control department" was expanded in scope to include the management of inventory, but not control of the actual determinants of inventory levels.

In 1954, a pioneer physical distribution department, under the previously stated definition of the term, was created at H. J. Heinz.[11] Here an existing traffic and warehouse division with control over traffic, material handling, privately owned transportation equipment, and warehouse real estate was combined with the planning and distribution division. This action added responsibilities for customer order processing, finished goods inventory control, internal order processing, and manufacturing planning, to create a physical distribution department under the former Manager of Traffic and Warehousing reporting to the Executive Vice President of the firm.

Several physical distribution divisions grew out of cost-cutting investigations initiated during periods of austerity within their respective firms. The timing of early departmental reorganizations coincided closely with periods of recession in the economy. In each of these cases, the initial mission of the new departments was to reduce costs of transportation, storage, and inventory, with only secondary regard for customer service.

Historical Growth Since 1956

The publication of a study by Lewis, Culliton, and Steele in 1956 was a milestone, in that it crystallized and communicated an idea which a few firms had begun to implement and which has since dominated thinking in the field: the total cost concept of logistics.[12] In identifying the role which air freight could play in physical distribution, Lewis, Culliton, and Steele concluded, among other things, that: (1) a cost identification system breaking out fixed and variable logistics costs and (2) a breadth of system evaluation which included both transportation and inventory-related costs would be necessary to encourage firms to trade higher out-of-pocket costs for air freight against potential cost savings from inventory

[11] For a full description of the organization of H. J. Heinz' physical distribution division, see John H. Frederick, *Traffic Department Organization* (Philadelphia: Chilton Co., 1956), pp. 27–32.

[12] Howard T. Lewis, James W. Culliton, and Jack D. Steele, *The Role of Air Freight in Physical Distribution* (Boston: Division of Research, Graduate School of Business Administration, Harvard University, 1956).

reductions. In many respects, this was a restatement of the concept advanced by Dupuit 112 years earlier. But in the context of a developing air freight industry, the concept took on more drama and glamour.

The total cost concept, in a simplified form, is shown in Fig. 2–3. The logistics system alternatives at the right of the cost graph are typified by high inventory costs (perhaps resulting from the use of many market-oriented warehouses and inventories), low transportation costs (possibly as a result of using low-cost forms of transportation such as water or rail), and low-cost, mail-speed order processing. Those at the left feature relatively low inventory costs (as in systems with one or a few somewhat centralized inventories from which large geographic areas are served), high transportation costs (for relatively small shipments by air or truck),

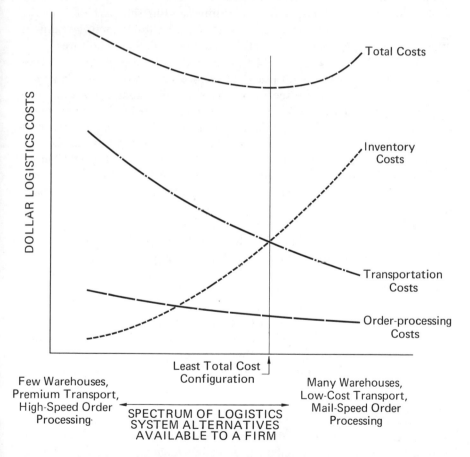

Fig. 2–3. A simplified illustration of the total cost concept, showing hypothetical trade-offs among transportation, inventory, and order-processing costs.

and high-speed order processing (for which costs may be relatively high). However, the lowest total cost system configuration is typified by the use of an intermediate number of inventory locations and a mixture of low- and high-priced transportation services. For many firms operating logistics systems at the right side of the spectrum, the idea that a firm could spend more dollars for transportation services in order to reduce its total costs of logistics was pinpointed for the first time.

Identifying the concept was one thing. But, as Lewis, Culliton, and Steele pointed out, implementing it was another. In fact, implementation could only be accomplished through such means as (1) revised costing methods to identify relevant costs, (2) coordination of related management functions through improved communication, a revised system of management incentives, and a centralized control in one department of all related logistics functions, and (3) willingness on the part of firms to revise their distribution systems, in some cases closing facilities and in others relocating employees as well as making capital expenditures.

What has happened since 1956? The total cost concept, great in theory, remains an elusive one in practice. However, several trends have become apparent in the more recent development of management for physical distribution activities: (1) development has been far more rapid in certain types of industries than in others, (2) physical distribution management organizational concepts are being employed by firms producing a growing range of products, (3) an upsurge in the number of new physical distribution departments arriving on the business scene has occurred recently, and (4) once costs of physical distribution are initially reduced, customer service typically has been given primary emphasis over costs of service in physical distribution planning.

It is not surprising to find that attention to physical distribution management has been greater in certain types of industries than in others. Among the factors favoring the establishment of separate departments to supervise physical distribution activities are: (1) multiple sources of raw materials, or stocks, (2) a number of manufacturing or storage locations, (3) many consumption points, (4) seasonal or cyclical demand for finished products, (5) problems—primarily inventory holding costs—arising from production to stock rather than to order, (6) multi-item product lines, and (7) perhaps most important, the need to establish a balance between onerous customer service requirements on the one hand and sizable logistics costs on the other.

There is an inevitable exchange of ideas and procedures among firms belonging to industry associations, such as the Grocery Manufacturers of America, Inc. As a result, changes in management techniques frequently occur on an industry-by-industry basis. Executives of firms in industries where initial growth of physical distribution management has been rapid often have felt compelled to reorganize logistics activities in order to remain competitive in terms of customer service, price, and profit.

A significant medium for the exchange of such ideas was created in the spring of 1962 with the founding of the National Council of Physical Distribution Management (NCPDM) by seven representatives from industry and academia sitting around a table in St. Louis. This organization has grown rapidly, offering channels of communication across industry categories through its annual meetings, regional meetings, university seminars, and publications.

Firms thought to possess fully developed physical distribution departments deal in an increasing range of products. Although development gained early impetus in firms manufacturing grocery products, it soon spread to manufacturers of electrical appliances, business machines, pharmaceuticals, biological preparations, and chemicals. Some idea of the types of industries in which organizational development for physical distribution management was greatest up to 1960 can be obtained from the data in Table 2–1.

TABLE 2-1. Primary and Secondary Product Categories of Industrial Firms Which Were Leaders in Physical Distribution Management, 1960

Number of Firms	Category of Product
15	Food products
5	Paper products for home and industrial use
4	Biologicals, pharmaceuticals
4	Office machines
4	Home appliances and heating equipment
3	Industrial organic and inorganic chemicals
2	Cleaning agents, for home and industrial use
2	Toilet preparations
4	Others

Compare this with an analysis of the primary Standard Industrial Classification (SIC) codes which identify the firms employing current members of the National Council of Physical Distribution Management, presented in Table 2–2.

The development of the physical distribution function as an organized department in the American firm occurred at an increasing rate during the 1960's. Confirmation of the early acceleration of this trend was provided by studies conducted by *Transportation & Distribution Management* magazine. For example, in 41 of the 50 firms included in one survey in 1962, the average age of the physical distribution department was about

TABLE 2-2. Standard Industrial Classifications for Companies Employing
Members of the National Council of Physical Distribution Management, 1971

SIC Category	Number of NCPDM Members Employed*
Manufacturing Companies:	
Pharmaceutical preparations	32
Industrial inorganic chemicals (n.e.c.)	30
Industrial organic chemicals (n.e.c.)	18
Canned fruits, vegetables, preserves, jams and jellies	16
Medicinal chemicals and botanical products	15
Paper mills (operation)	15
Plastic materials, synthetic resins, and non-vulcanized elastomers	14
Perfumes, cosmetics, and other toilet preparations	13
Photographic equipment and supplies	12
Motor truck vehicle parts and accessories	11
Meat-packing plants	9
Metal cans	9
Radio and television transmitting, signaling, and detection equipment and apparatus	8
Crude petroleum and natural gas	8
Soybean oil mills	8
Pulp mills	8
Alkalies and chlorine	8
Other (161 other categories)	347
Non-manufacturing Organizations:	
Business consulting	55
Public warehousing	47
Universities	22
Trucking, except local	19
Air transportation, certified carriers	15
Railroads, line-haul operating	12
Other (42 other categories)	106
Total, all categories	849

n.e.c. = not elsewhere classified.

*Where a company was included in two or more SIC categories, the first two such categories were tabulated. Therefore, the total exceeds the membership of the NCPDM.

Source: Authors' tabulation of the 1971 roster of the National Council of Physical Distribution Management.

three years.[13] The remaining nine firms included in the study contained departments which had existed for significantly longer periods of time.

As a physical distribution department matures, its major mission appears to undergo change to reflect greater emphasis on customer service

[13] Warren Blanding, "Profile of P.D.M.," *Transportation & Distribution Management,* June, 1962, p. 14.

than on the cost of providing that service. This was found to be the case in the firms surveyed.[14]

There is little doubt that techniques and organization for effective physical distribution management will continue to spread to an even wider variety of industries. Further, the field of materials (physical supply) management, through more widespread application of logistics system concepts, will likely come in for a greater share of management's attention in the future. The decade of the 1970's also will witness a similar development of interest in the coordinated management of logistics activities in European as well as American firms. Finally, increasing emphasis will be placed on the coordinated management of logistics activities by two or more interdependent organizations.

WHY THE REBIRTH OF INTEREST IN LOGISTICS?

A number of explanations have been advanced for the upsurge of interest in, and development of, logistics management. Among them are: (1) rapidly escalating costs, particularly for transportation and warehousing services, (2) the development of mathematical techniques and computer equipment capable of handling efficiently the mass of data typically required for the analysis of a logistics problem, (3) growing complexities of materials management and physical distribution as the *Fortune* 500 firms and their smaller competitors grow even larger, requiring more complex systems, (4) the availability of a wider range of logistics services than ever before, offering both variety and more competition for the shipper's dollar, (5) changing markets and channels of distribution, especially for consumer goods, (6) tendencies for retailers and wholesalers to shift responsibilities for inventory management back to manufacturers, and (7) the evolution of the "marketing concept" in many firms.

Rising Costs

Our previous analysis of logistics costs in the economy, at least up to 1970, suggests that the oft-quoted manager denouncing "the outrageous increases in transportation" might have been using a myth to support his cause. This is not to say that particular industries may not have been hard hit by logistics cost increases. But in the aggregate, American industry has fared rather well in this regard.

Information in Fig. 2–4 indicates that rates per ton-mile paid for most regulated transportation services rose less rapidly than the price index

[14] *Ibid.*, p. 15.

for wholesale products between 1947 and 1971. For example, using 1947 as a base, rail rates per ton-mile rose 47%, air freight rates declined 6%, and oil pipeline rates actually dropped 5% compared with a 49% increase in wholesale prices during this period. Only truck rates increased a larger amount, 65%, during this period. (1) **What explanations would you offer for the trends shown in Fig. 2–4?**

Development of Techniques and Equipment

The development of operations research techniques such as linear programming, queuing theory, and simulation, as well as the further development of computer technology, was an important byproduct of World War II. It was a short step and an easy transition from the application of techniques for allocating equipment to provide optimum military firepower to the solution of problems of vehicle assignment for the local delivery of consumer products. The availability of techniques and equip-

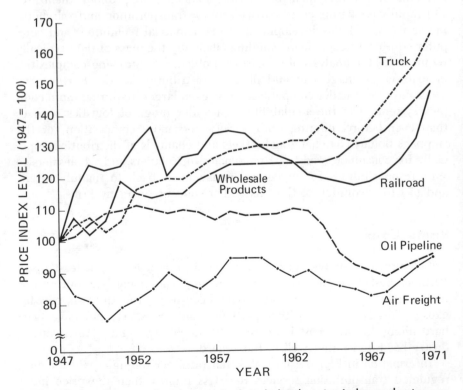

Fig. 2–4. Comparative changes in the wholesale price index and rates per ton-mile for regulated transportation services, 1950 through 1969.

ment provided an opportunity for more sophisticated management. It was not until leading firms in various industries began making use of techniques such as linear programming in the planning of their distribution systems that pressure was created for their competitors to apply such techniques similarly.

Increasing Complexity of Business

It is true that as a business grows, the logistical alternatives open to that business increase as well. There is a strong tendency toward the use of managers with more and more specialized knowledge to deal with each now-important facet of logistics. At the same time, the need for overall coordination and direction increases if logistics activities are to be managed as a system.

However, in some respects growth relieves logistics problems. Through growth, for example, a company may achieve the "critical mass" necessary to allow frequent shipments in carload and truckload quantities, a happy situation that often provides better inventory coverage and system response as well as faster and more dependable transportation service. A growing company certainly acquires power which can be applied in bargaining for logistics services.

Expanding Range of Logistical Alternatives

Since World War II, air freight service and coordinated forms of transportation such as trailer on flat car (TOFC) have become viable alternatives for the transportation of freight. The capabilities of bulk handling methods and bulk transport vehicles have greatly increased in speed and capacity. Containerized methods of shipment have become available. A wide variety of mechanized approaches to warehousing and material handling have been developed.

While introducing complexities to the task of logistics system design and management, the development of alternative methods has produced a healthier competitive situation based not as much on price competition as on new, more creative ways of accomplishing various tasks, alternatives which result in reduced costs to their users. It cannot be denied, however, that in many situations the questions of "what service or combination of services to use when" have become much more complex.

The development of new logistical alternatives has, in some instances, had a profound impact on ways of doing business in certain industries. New rates and technology, in the form of the "Big John" hopper car, forced significant changes in the location of facilities used in the distribution of grain in the early 1960's, for example. The increasingly rapid development of such alternatives may make existing logistics systems obsolete faster. It also introduces an air of impermanence to the field that suggests the need for more frequent and comprehensive appraisals of available systems.

Changing Markets and Channels of Distribution

More than half of all Americans now live in suburban areas, according to the 1970 Census of Population. This diffusion of people away from metropolitan centers has greatly increased the problem of product distribution, particularly for those types of products for which the consumer is unwilling to travel great distances. Although more a problem for retailing organizations than for manufacturers, the diffusion of population has fragmented distribution efforts which depend on mass transport and storage for efficient operation.

Consumers purchase items in supermarkets today that were formerly sold through drug stores, hardware stores, appliance retail outlets, and dry goods stores. So-called "scrambled merchandising" techniques have greatly increased the breadth of product lines which many retailers elect to stock today. As food stores expand into non-food items, discount department stores respond by opening discount food departments. This trend has reduced the quantities of product moving from manufacturers to a single wholesale or retail customer, requiring the establishment of new working relationships for purposes of supply and distribution, and has made a distribution system designed on the assumption of relative stability in markets and business relationships a somewhat risky undertaking.

Shifting of Inventory Maintenance Task

In the past two decades, retailers and wholesalers, particularly of consumer products, have attempted to improve or at least maintain their profit performance by reducing storage space, maintaining lower inventories, and ordering replacement stocks more frequently in small quantities. The introduction of the computer into retail and wholesale inventory planning and control has had the same effect, with frequent computer review producing "grocery list" orders comprised of one or two units of many items, often on a daily basis. These developments have not only reduced the average sizes of shipments moving from processing and manufacturing facilities, but have shifted some of the costs of warehousing and inventory maintenance back to primary suppliers who must provide higher levels of logistics services to remain competitive. The inevitable result has been that logistics, especially physical distribution, has been elevated in importance as an element in a manufacturer's marketing strategy, thereby drawing attention to its management.

The Marketing Concept

We noted earlier that the nation's economy shifted from a seller's to a buyer's market in the late 1940's. As a result, many companies moved their primary emphasis from production to marketing. It took several years to place a label on what had been transpiring. The new emphasis was the "marketing concept," the process of detecting and satisfying consumer needs or desires *at a profit*. Among other things, a conscious adoption of the marketing concept as a way of doing business usually led to the grouping of sales and advertising under common "marketing" management; it encouraged the creation of more marketing research groups; and it brought about in some companies the establishment of product manager positions encompassing responsibility for bringing the focus of corporate functional departments to bear on the product, its markets, and appropriate marketing strategies for them. It is possible that the adoption of the marketing concept has had a greater impact on logistics, especially physical distribution management, than any of the other factors previously discussed in this chapter.

Consider a typical sequence of actions in a company adopting a marketing-oriented corporate strategy. First, a marketing research department is formed and charged with the task of detecting customers' wants and needs. Second, the marketing research department recommends a higher level of customer logistics service, leading to the establishment of a greater number of warehouse locations to make the company's product more readily accessible to a greater number of customers. Third, desires for new or slightly altered products are discovered, leading to the introduction of new products to stand alongside existing products in the line.

Problems and costs of inventory control vary inversely with the sales per stock-keeping unit location. Both product-line items (stock-keeping units, or SKU's) and locations for their distribution have been increasing in many industries. One example of this trend is provided by information in Fig. 2–5, which shows the marked increase in the number of items carried in an average supermarket, the number of supermarkets, the resulting number of supermarket stock-keeping unit locations and the average annual sales per stock-keeping unit location in supermarkets for the period of 1950 through 1969.[15] The number of supermarkets in the United States more than tripled between 1950 and 1969, reaching a total of 37,180 in 1969. During this same period of time, the number of line items (stock-keeping units, or SKU's) carried in an average supermarket more than doubled, reaching a figure of 7,700 per store in 1969. The combined effect of these increases produced more than a sixfold growth in the number of stock-keeping unit locations (SKUL's), or basic inventory control units. Thus, even though real dollar sales through supermarket outlets increased about four times between 1950 and 1969, reaching a figure of more than $42 billion in 1969 (deflated to 1950 dollars), the average annual dollar sales per stock-keeping unit location declined from about $238 in 1950 to about $143 in 1969. Little wonder that inventory turnover rates in supermarkets (measured by dividing annual sales by average inventories), dependent in part on sales volume per SKUL, declined about 9% between 1958 and 1968, even during a period when more systematic attention was being given to the problem of inventory control.

These trends highlight the need for a more effective appraisal of alternative systems of inventory control in the context of systems also encompassing transportation, warehousing, and order-processing activities.

LOGISTICS COSTS IN THE FIRM

Estimating logistics costs in an individual firm is an imprecise art, given the current state of accounting for such costs. Inbound transportation costs may be buried in a "Cost of Materials for Manufacturing" account in a manufacturing organization or a "Cost of Goods Sold" account in a retail enterprise. Outbound transportation costs may not be known if a firm sells on an "f.o.b. plant" basis, requiring customers to arrange for their own transportation away from the plant. Material-handling labor at a plant or warehouse may be charged to "Manufacturing Labor." Order-processing costs may be a part of "Sales Service." A portion of inventory carrying costs is contained in the "Interest Expense" category. Currently, no functional area of the organization is more poorly served by accounting practice than logistics.

We saw earlier that logistics costs are of major importance from a macroeconomic point of view. Naturally, their degree of importance will vary greatly from firm to firm. The following sections explore several basic factors accounting for such variations: product characteristics, se-

15 For an example from the motor truck and farm equipment parts industry, see the International Harvester Company case in James L. Heskett, Lewis M. Schneider, Robert M. Ivie, and Nicholas A. Glaskowsky, Jr., *Case Problems in Business Logistics* (New York: The Ronald Press Co., 1973).

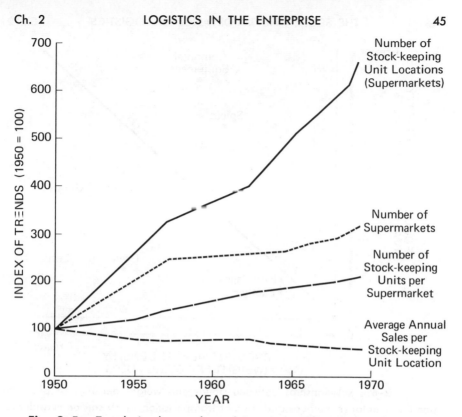

Fig. 2–5. Trends in the number of items carried in an average super-market, the number of supermarkets, the number of supermarket stock-keeping unit locations, and the average annual sales (in real dollars) per stock-keeping unit location in supermarkets, selected years between 1950 and 1969. *Source: Progressive Grocer* magazine.

lected top management policies which influence logistics costs, geographic location, and the role played by a firm in its channel or channels of distribution.

Product Characteristics

Two product characteristics can be used to illustrate roughly the comparative differences in products which affect the major logistics costs of transportation and inventory maintenance: (1) dollar density (value per cubic measure) and (2) weight density (weight per cubic measure). This assumes, for the moment, that we hold constant the level of customer logistics service needed to sell the product.

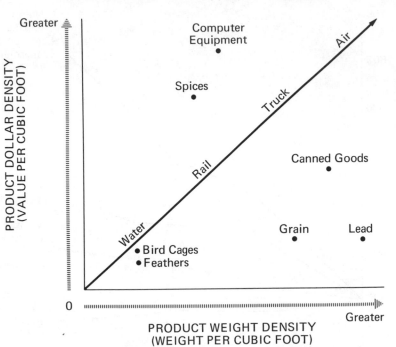

Fig. 2–6. Relationships between dollar and weight densities of products and the alternative methods and costs of transportation which can be considered in distributing them. (The graph shows the general nature, not the magnitude, of the relationships.)

Figure 2–6 illustrates the relationship between dollar and weight density and the alternative methods and costs of transportation which can be considered in distributing various products. A variety of products are plotted on this graph. Clearly, as we move to products with higher dollar and weight densities (from the lower left-hand corner toward the middle of the graph), the cost of transportation as a proportion of the total sales value of the product will decline and the number of viable logistics alternatives available to us increases. (2) **Try your hand at positioning on this graph additional product categories with which you are familiar. (3) What happens as we then move up toward the upper right-hand corner of the graph? (4) For what category of products are our** *viable* **alternatives the greatest?**

The manner in which we distribute our goods will depend on the way in which transportation and inventory management (including warehousing) costs are likely to be altered under different alternatives. For this consideration, look at Fig. 2–7(a), showing the cost of various transportation–inventory alternatives for computing equipment. Assume we start with configuration X in graph (a). Clearly, the high value of our product suggests that we can spend much more money for faster, more dependable forms of transportation to enable us to reduce the number of our inventories, our overall inventory level, and our inventory carrying costs. The converse is true for crude oil, as shown in Fig. 2–7(b). **(5) Check out Fig. 2–7(b) to assure yourself that you can explain it.**

Notice that although our total costs are perhaps 3% of sales for computing equipment and 37% of sales for crude oil, in both cases a redesign of the respective systems resulted in a higher proportion of expense for transportation than for inventory maintenance.

In the case of computing equipment we decided to spend more for transportation in order to reduce inventory carrying costs substantially. From a configuration in which we were actually spending more to carry our inventory than to transport goods, we shifted to an alternative requiring about twice the amount of transportation costs as inventory carrying costs. Just the reverse was decided for crude oil.

Snyder, in analyzing logistics costs incurred by manufacturing firms in eight industries, compiled information presented in Table 2–3.[16] Although a number of questions may be raised about this survey and the high cost estimates which it produced, if the numbers have internal consistency, they indicate that the sum of transportation, warehousing, material handling, and administrative costs as a proportion of sales varied in 1961 from 29.6% for food products manufacturers to 8.8% for machinery manufacturers. Interestingly, the relative proportions of transportation-related and inventory-related costs do not appear to vary in direct relationship to the probable dollar density or weight density of the broad product categories for which information was collected. **(6) Can you explain the ratios in the bottom line of Table 2–3?**

From industry to industry, regardless of the nature of the product involved, economic relationships suggest that the most effective logistics systems do not involve extremely large expenditures for one major category of logistics expense (transportation or inventory maintenance) vis-à-vis the other. Rather, a total cost solution is suggested which, for most commodities under most circumstances, suggests a moderately greater expenditure for transportation than for inventory maintenance. This, of course, assumes that all relevant costs associated with inbound or outbound goods are assessed, regardless of the terms of purchase and sale and their impact on cost accounts.

Neuschel offers further confirmation of the general cost relationships cited above in his composite report of logistics costs incurred by 26 large

---

[16] Richard E. Snyder, "Physical Distribution Costs—A Two-Year Analysis," *Distribution Age* (now *Distribution Worldwide*), January, 1963, pp. 45–56.

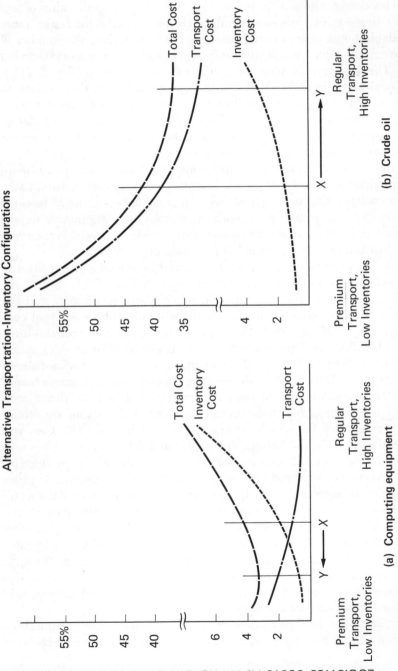

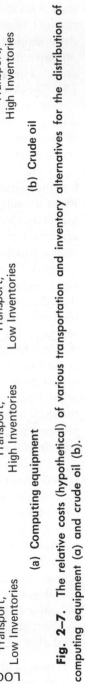

Fig. 2-7. The relative costs (hypothetical) of various transportation and inventory alternatives for the distribution of computing equipment (a) and crude oil (b).

TABLE 2-3. Selected Physical Distribution Expenses as Proportion of Sales in Manufacturing Industries, 1961

Selected Expense Items[a]	Industries[b]							
	Food and Food Products	Primary and Fabricated Metals	Chemicals, Petroleum, Rubber Products	Paper and Paper Products	Wood Products	Transport Equipment	Machinery (Elec. and Non-Elec.)	Average of Seven Industries
1. Common carrier	9.6%	5.1%	9.3%	5.6%	8.8%	5.3%	5.3%	7.9%
2. Private trucking	6.0	3.5	3.5	2.5	2.5	1.8	.8	3.8
3. Public warehousing	1.9	.6	1.1	1.4	.1	—	.4	1.1
4. Private warehousing	4.0	9.5	2.9	2.0	1.0	.7	.5	3.9
5. Material handling	2.3	1.5	1.4	1.3	1.1	.8	.4	1.5
6. Shipping room	3.9	2.5	2.4	3.0	1.4	1.1	1.0	2.6
7. Over, short, damage	.3	.0	.2	.2	.1	.0	.0	.2
8. Selected administrative	1.6	3.6	1.0	.6	.8	.5	.5	1.6
Totals[c]	29.6%	26.4%	21.7%	16.6%	15.8%	13.2%	8.8%	22.6%
Rate of transport-related expense (items 1 and 2) to inventory-related expense (items 3, 4, 5, and 6)	1.3	.6	1.6	1.1	3.1	2.7	2.7	1.3

[a]Costs omitted from the survey included all inbound costs, investment in inventory, and order processing.
[b]Based on median figures obtained from an unstated number of returns from a sample of indeterminate size.
[c]Totals may not add exactly because of rounding.

Source: Richard E. Snyder, "Physical Distribution Costs—A Two-Year Analysis," *Distribution Age* (now *Distribution Worldwide*), January, 1963, pp. 45–56.

firms from the food processing, chemicals, petroleum, building materials, and metal fabricating industries: [17]

Cost Item	Percentage of Total Distribution Costs *
Carrier charges	44%
Warehousing and handling	20
Inventory carrying cost	18
Shipping room	11
Administrative	7
Total	100%

* Based on available company data and/or author's estimates. Percentages assigned to various items themselves vary as much as ± 20% among the 26 individual companies in the sample.

Top Management Policies

The conscious adoption of something other than a lowest total logistics cost strategy can influence the relative importance of cost categories. Such strategies include support for speculative purchasing (in advance of price increases, for example), a high level of customer service, or a continually expanding product line.

Geographic Location

The relative importance of the costs of physical supply and distribution in an individual firm is affected by the distances by which the firm is separated from its sources of supply and its markets. The firm with lower production costs may be willing to incur heavier proportions of transportation or inventory costs in realizing roughly the same profit margins as its competitor. Also, an increase in logistics expenditures can help reduce production costs in a firm by enabling it to expand its geographical marketing territory and share of the market; the resultant increase in sales volume may allow lower costs of production if economies of scale are present.

Firm's Role in the Channel of Distribution

The role which a firm plays in a channel of logistics, including the terms of sale under which it does business, determines not only the relative importance of physical supply and physical distribution costs in its cost structure, but also influences the degree of knowledge which the firm's

[17] Robert P. Neuschel, "Physical Distribution—Forgotten Frontier," *Harvard Business Review*, March–April, 1967, pp. 125–34.

management may have concerning the actual costs of logistics activities in its operation. Consider Fig. 2–8, which shows four firms in a channel of distribution, all contributing to the ultimate distribution of the same product.

Firm A is a supplier of raw materials to processors in the channel who subsequently distribute finished products. Several things can be said about its logistics costs. First, it is likely that Firm A is located closer to its sources of supply than to its customers. Thus, physical distribution costs probably are much greater than physical supply costs in this firm. Second, its product may have relatively low value, producing logistics cost levels in relation to sales similar to those for crude oil in Fig. 2–7. Finally, there are few costs of physical supply obscured in the value of the product stored in Firm A's warehouses at the supply source. Firm A probably has extensive knowledge of the costs of business logistics as a proportion of its sales.

Firm B is a processor and distributor of the product under consideration. Because of its location in the channel, costs of both physical supply and distribution will be important to the firm. The degree to which these costs are recorded and controlled will depend on: (1) whether the firm purchases its raw materials for a price which includes delivery to its processing plant or arranges its own transportation for such raw materials, and (2) whether it sells its products on a basis which does not include outbound transportation, in which case it will have little information about physical distribution costs or methods, or on a delivered basis, with outbound logistics arranged and paid for by Firm B.

Firm C, a retailer, largely experiences costs associated with the inbound movement of product to its stores. In this firm, the individual consumer typically assumes responsibility for, and the costs of, the least efficient link in a channel of distribution, that of transportation from the store to the home. The costs of logistics as a proportion of the total cost of products which a retailer stocks will be made up of those costs incurred by the supplier at the supply source, by the processor at both his plant and warehouse, and by the wholesaler serving as the retailer's immediate source of supply. In this situation, costs of logistics to the retailer are almost totally submerged in an account labeled "Cost of Goods Sold," often causing misleading assumptions about the importance of logistics costs to the firm and the desirability of retailer participation in logistics problem solving in a channel of distribution.

Firm D in Fig. 2–8 owns its own supply sources, processing plant, warehouses at the processing location, and market-oriented distribution warehouses. Both physical supply and physical distribution activities will constitute important elements of the total cost of doing business in Firm D. Greater control over the channel also provides more complete in-

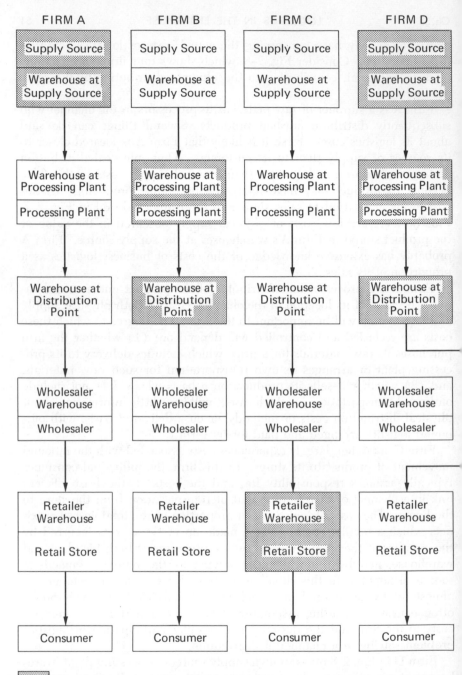

	FIRM A	FIRM B	FIRM C	FIRM D
	Supply Source	Supply Source	Supply Source	Supply Source
	Warehouse at Supply Source	Warehouse at Supply Source	Warehouse at Supply Source	Warehouse at Supply Source
	Warehouse at Processing Plant	Warehouse at Processing Plant	Warehouse at Processing Plant	Warehouse at Processing Plant
	Processing Plant	Processing Plant	Processing Plant	Processing Plant
	Warehouse at Distribution Point	Warehouse at Distribution Point	Warehouse at Distribution Point	Warehouse at Distribution Point
	Wholesaler Warehouse	Wholesaler Warehouse	Wholesaler Warehouse	Wholesaler Warehouse
	Wholesaler	Wholesaler	Wholesaler	Wholesaler
	Retailer Warehouse	Retailer Warehouse	Retailer Warehouse	Retailer Warehouse
	Retail Store	Retail Store	Retail Store	Retail Store
	Consumer	Consumer	Consumer	Consumer

Ownership or control by firm in question.

Fig. 2–8. A channel of distribution for a single product, indicating the relative logistical role of Firms A, B, C, and D.

formation in regard to logistics costs incurred at various points in the channel.

SUMMARY

Logistics in an organization encompasses activities associated with both materials management (for inbound raw materials, supplies, components, and products purchased for resale) and physical distribution (for outbound components and finished products, for example). The President of the Norge Division of Borg–Warner Corporation once gave an excellent rationale for this coordinated approach to the planning and management of physical flows:

> We have a production lead time of 90 days or better and if we stop the line abruptly, material continues to arrive for weeks afterward or we incur very substantial cancellation charges. In our business, and I suspect in many others, an effective system of physical distribution cannot begin at the end of the production line. . . . It must also apply at the very beginning of the production process—at the planning, the forecasting and the scheduling stages and not simply from the end of the production line.[18]

Further, coordination must extend beyond corporate boundaries to deal with the inevitable overlap in responsibility and conflicts of logistical goals which arise in a channel of distribution.

The field of logistics management has evolved from specific ideas which can be traced back in the literature at least as far as the nineteenth century, and in a more general sense back to the earliest recordings of man. However, forces emerging since World War II have greatly accelerated the emphasis on logistics as the last major neglected area of management. Among such forces are rising costs, the development of new analytical techniques and computing equipment, the increasing physical complexity of business operations and organizations, the expanding range of methods for transporting and handling materials, changes in the marketplace and in channels of distribution through which goods move, the shifting of responsibilities within such channels, and the pressures created by the widespread adoption of the marketing concept, or a marketing-oriented approach to business.

As it has evolved, emphasis has spread from the early development of logistics management approaches in the grocery and chemical products manufacturing industries to a much wider spectrum of commercial organizations.

Costs form an important part of the decision process for logistics management. As we have seen, they vary widely in importance from industry

18 "From Red to Black," *Handling & Shipping*, September, 1966, pp. 69–72, at 72.

to industry as firms attempt to balance basic costs of transportation and inventory maintenance in such a way that a relatively low total cost results. The relative importance of these costs will depend on such factors as the physical characteristics of the product, management policies which consider logistics in relation to other major cost categories or service objectives, the geographic location of a company's facilities in relation to its supply sources and markets, and the role that the firm in question may play in a channel of distribution.

The effective management of costs and service levels is a central theme of this book. We will get to these matters after we have had an opportunity to consider the basic framework of physical resources available to a logistics manager to help him carry out his responsibility for storing and moving his company's materials and products. We call this basic framework the elements of a logistics system.

PART TWO

ELEMENTS OF A LOGISTICS SYSTEM

There are several basic elements in the logistics system of a business firm. The first of these is a set of fixed points (inventory processing facilities) which may vary in number from two to several thousand. The second is the hardware, computerized or manually operated, for the processing of orders and management of inventory. These points are connected by the other elements of a logistics system, transportation and communication networks.

The complexity of a logistics system is largely a function of the variety of time and distance relationships between its fixed points and the degree of regularity and predictability of the flow of goods entering, within, and leaving the system. Chapters 3 and 4 set forth these elements in a form designed to provide both a clear picture of the elements and some appreciation of the alternatives encountered in the job of designing logistics systems.

A discussion of logistics rates and services in Chapter 5 completes the discussion of basic transportation concepts. There is no intent to present a complete description of what one needs to know about transportation. We suspect that the necessity for this has been overemphasized in the past. The presentation has, however, been heavily referenced to suggest sources of additional information where they are believed necessary. Its major value to the student or manager of logistics is perhaps that it emphasizes the role of transportation in the logistics system of the firm.

Chapters 3, 4, and 5 are descriptive in nature. If you are already familiar with their subjects, they provide a review; if you are not, they are intended to serve as an introduction. The analysis of inventory location, fixed facility operation, and transportation operations and services is stressed in later chapters.

For now we turn our attention to trucks and trains, ships and planes. But first, a look at hardware for the storage and management of inventory.

3

Inventory Processing Elements

The inventory processing elements in a logistics system are the fixed facilities required to perform logistics activities. A logistics system comprises two components for analysis: *product* and *information*. The definition of product is dependent upon the particular segment of the logistics cycle, i.e., it may be a raw material or a finished product. Information is defined as data utilized in the planning, design, implementation, and operation of a logistics system. Figure 3–1 shows how the basic components for analysis are related to logistics functions and the types of fixed facilities required to perform them.

Consistent with the components of analysis just discussed, a logistics system utilizes two general types of fixed facilities, those for the *storage and handling of product* and those for the *transmission, processing, and storage of logistics information*. The product support category includes two types of facilities: warehousing facilities and transfer facilities. These facilities are utilized to accomplish the movement control function. The logistics information support category includes two types of facilities: communication facilities and data processing facilities. These facilities are primarily utilized in support of the demand–supply coordination function. To a limited degree, they are also utilized to satisfy information requirements in the performance of movement control.

PRODUCT SUPPORT FACILITIES

A product support facility in the logistics system of a business firm can be defined as a regularly established facility at which there is planned

57

Logistics Functions	Basic Components for Analysis in a Logistics System	
	Product	Information
Movement Control: Transportation Warehousing Material Handling	*Product Support Facilities:* Warehousing Facilities Transfer Facilities	*Logistics Information Support Facilities:* Communication Facilities Data Processing Facilities
Demand–Supply Coordination: Supply Scheduling and Allocation Inventory Management Order Processing		*Logistics Information Support Facilities:* Communication Facilities Data Processing Facilities

Fig. 3–1. Interrelationships of basic components for analysis, logistics functions, and fixed facilities required to perform them in a logistics system.

storage and/or material-handling delay in the movement of inventory (raw materials or finished goods) from point of origin to ultimate delivery to the customer of the firm. A delay in movement of a particular material or product at a product support facility might range from less than a day to more than a year.

There are two basic classes of product support facilities in commercial, extractive, agricultural, and industrial logistics systems. These are warehousing facilities and transfer facilities. Warehousing facilities are defined as gathering/dispersing points where products are added to or deleted from an inventory of similar products on a regular basis. Transfer facilities are defined as points associated with transportation or warehousing facilities wherein a product shipment encounters material-handling delay in the process of being transferred from one vehicle to another vehicle. Thus, in terms of the definition for product support facilities, transfer facilities involve material-handling delay while warehousing facilities involve both product storage and material-handling delay. Another distinction between warehousing facilities and transfer facilities is that the former are closely associated with the existence of an accountable inventory while the latter are closely associated with the continuation of a specific and identifiable shipment.

Unlike manufacturing facilities, which are devoted primarily to the creation of form utility, warehousing and transfer facilities exist to create time and place utilities.

Warehousing Facilities

Warehousing is a functional activity which involves the storage and transshipment of goods without any change in the form of the goods. It takes place in buildings which are separated from, attached to, or an integral part of a manufacturing plant. It is carried out in the back room of a sales office located in a metropolitan area, where goods are stored for delivery to customers who place "rush" orders. It is accomplished in the receiving and marking area of a department store. It occurs at the point of production of a manufacturing or processing facility. It may be performed by company employees in a company-owned or leased facility; or it may be performed by a warehouseman in public warehousing facilities.

Structure of Warehousing Operations.   There are at least five bases for the classification of types of warehouse operations. All of these are valid, and in fact all must be included in a description of a warehouse in order to describe it completely. These five bases of classification are: physical function, commodities handled, ownership, legal status, and place in the logistics system of the firm.

Physical Function.   Some warehouses are used primarily as storage facilities for raw materials or finished goods. It is necessary for firms to hold goods in storage for a variety of reasons. For example, producers of products as diverse as cheese, liquors, and baseball bats find it necessary to hold raw materials or semifinished products in storage warehouses for varying periods of time while these products undergo aging.

The primary use of storage warehouses occurs in relation to, and usually in advance of, various production processes. It is unusual for finished goods in condition to be delivered to customers of the firm to be stored for any length of time. This may occur, however, in situations where the firm has, for one reason or another, produced or purchased an extremely large amount of a particular product at one time, and must store some portion of this amount for later sale or use. Example cases are industries in which production is seasonal but sales are not, where sales are seasonal but production is not, where both production and sales are seasonal at times which do not coincide, or where large quantities of product are purchased on a speculative basis to take advantage of favorable prices. **(1) Can you think of specific industries which meet each of these characteristics? (2) What form do storage facilities take in each?**

Storage warehouses may be located at any point in a logistics system, but usually have a strong locational relationship to production facilities of one type or another. (3) **Why is this often the case?**

Distribution warehouses are used to maintain and adjust product inventories and assortments utilized in the day-to-day coordination of demand requirements and supply availability in the movement of materials from raw material sources to production facilities, trade outlets, and ultimate customers. Functionally the distribution warehouse is very different from the storage warehouse, and it must be designed somewhat differently to meet different operational requirements.

The distribution warehouse, often called a distribution center, is characterized by the rapidity with which goods flow through it. Many goods are actually "stored" less than a day within its walls. For example, this is often the case in the operation of receiving and marking departments in retail stores. A distribution warehouse therefore will require more in the way of flexible and high-speed material-handling equipment and facilities than will a storage warehouse. It follows that unless the facility is highly mechanized there will ordinarily be more persons employed in a distribution warehouse operation than in a storage warehouse operation for a given level of average inventory on hand.

(4) **Given the nature of their functions, would you expect most distribution warehouses to be located near facilities producing or processing goods which they handle? (5) Why?**

A warehouse may serve as both a storage and a distribution facility. For example, a dairy food distributor may utilize a portion of a warehouse for the aging of cheese (storage) and utilize the remainder of the warehouse for maintaining an inventory of products ready for shipment to customers (distribution). In this case, the portion of the warehouse used for distribution will be characterized by easily accessible inventory locations to allow rapid picking and packing in the filling of customer orders, and specialized material-handling equipment for rapid movement and accumulation of customer orders in preparation for shipment.

(6) **Would you expect a multistory building to be more suitable as a storage or distribution facility? (7) How about a building with a 35-foot as opposed to a 15-foot ceiling? (8) Why? (9) In what other respects would you expect storage and distribution warehouse facilities to differ?**

Commodities Handled. A warehouse may be designed to handle chilled or frozen products which must be kept at temperatures ranging from 40° above zero to 20° below zero. There are also many types of specialized bulk storage facilities for such commodities as grain (elevators), oil (tank farms), aging wine (steel lined or redwood tanks), and many others. Coal is frequently stored in the open in very large piles; this is, in effect, "outside warehousing." Some warehouse facilities are specially designed and operated for the storage of household goods. The variety of possible examples is nearly limitless.

Ownership. Warehouse facilities may also be classified as to whether they are owned by the user or leased by him, or are public warehouses used by him for the storage or handling of his goods.

There is an interesting set of relationships among these three classifications. Warehouse facilities which are owned or leased by a particular company can be classified as private warehouse facilities. These contrast with public warehousing, operated to provide storage facilities to the public for hire on an as-needed basis. On the other hand, leased facilities and public warehouse facilities together form a classification which is characterized as rented by the using firm, in contrast to owned warehouse facilities. The latter is an important distinction, because a using company's capital is not invested in the case of leased or public warehouse facilities, whereas a substantial amount of capital may be required for owned warehouse facilities.

Leased private warehousing may be differentiated from public warehousing in the following manner: When a company leases warehousing facilities, it literally rents all or a portion of a *structure* for periods of a month up to several years. A company utilizing public warehousing pays only for space utilized on a day-to-day basis (typically estimated on the basis of a monthly measurement of product in storage).

These considerations and relationships are summarized in Fig. 3–2.

Table 3–1 provides a breakdown of owned versus leased buildings in one segment of the business community, that performing wholesale trade. Approximately one-third of the number of wholesale establishments reporting ownership information indicated use of company-owned buildings; about two-thirds indicated use of leased buildings. (10) **Looking again at Table 3–1, what is the relative size of wholesaling companies using each combination of owned and leased warehousing space? (11) How would you explain this? (12) Do you think the same relationship would hold true for manufacturing and retailing firms as well? (13) Why?**

Legal Status. Examples of warehouses possessing special legal status are bonded warehouses in which goods are kept under government bond, and warehouses which are being used for storage of materials on which field warehouse receipts have been issued. Of course, a warehouse may have no particular legal status other than as an integral part of a business operation.

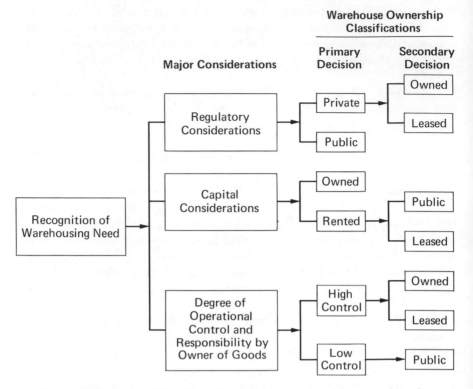

Fig. 3–2. Major considerations in evaluating warehouse ownership alternatives.

The term "field warehouse" refers to the legal status of a warehouse rather than to any physical aspect or location of such a facility. It describes a situation in which the goods or materials stored are under the actual supervision of a designated public warehouseman, who is legally responsible for their custody. When a company's goods are stored in its own or a leased facility all or part of which has been designated as a "field warehouse," the public warehouseman, in accordance with the provisions of the Uniform Commercial Code (superseding The Uniform Warehouse Receipts Act), may issue a "warehouse receipt" for the goods. This receipt, which may be either negotiable or non-negotiable, can be used by the owner of the goods as an instrument of credit for the purpose of obtaining loans on the goods so stored.[1]

The term "bonded warehouse" is applied to both public and private warehouse facilities in which goods are stored under bonding arrange-

---

[1] A comprehensive presentation of this subject is given in Albert G. Sweetser, *Financing Goods* (Newton Highlands, Mass.: The author, 1957), chap. 17.

TABLE 3-1. Breakdown of Warehouse Ownership
in the Wholesale Trade Industry, 1967

	Establishments		Sales		Total Floor Space	
	Number	Percentage	Thousands of Dollars	Percentage	Thousands of Sq. Ft.	Percentage
Company-owned buildings	49,385	31.7%	$77,723,738	37.0%	667,362	39.9%
Leased buildings	101,394	65.1	121,185,621	57.7	901,966	53.9
Space partly owned, partly leased	5,041	3.2	11,168,159	5.3	104,408	6.2
Total	155,820	100.0%	$210,077,518	100.0%	1,673,736	100.0%

Note: Limited to establishments reporting 1,000 square feet or more of floor space and ownership vs. leasing. Includes merchant wholesalers, manufacturers' sales branches (with stock), merchandise agents and brokers, and assemblers of farm products.

Source: 1967 Census of Business, Wholesale Trade (Washington, D. C.: Department of Commerce, Bureau of the Census, 1971), Table 8, p. 5–85.

ments made with the government. Goods cannot be removed from such warehouses until the required taxes or duties have been paid on them, except for movement to another bonded warehouse by a bonded common carrier. Basically, there are two variations of this arrangement, and they have a common purpose. Goods imported and stored in a bonded warehouse need not have import duties paid on them until they are removed from the bonded warehouse. Taxes on goods subject to certain internal revenue taxes, such as liquor and tobacco, are not required to be paid until the goods are removed from the bonded warehouse for movement to other than bonded facilities. In each case, the result is that the owner of the goods need not tie up his funds in paid duties or taxes until such time as he wishes to remove the goods from the bonded warehouse for sale or other disposition.

Place in the Logistics System. Finally, a warehouse may be classified according to its place in a logistics system. That is, it may be used as a storage or distribution facility for incoming or outgoing goods by retailers, wholesalers, manufacturing companies, extractive enterprises, or other types of businesses. Within the operation of an individual manufacturing company, for example, it could be a facility for handling raw materials which are stored temporarily outside the immediate manufacturing area until needed for processing. It could be a storage facility located at a company's plant to receive and transship finished goods coming off an assembly line. Or it could be a warehouse, located at some point between the company's plant and its customers, which is used for inventory storage and transshipment of finished goods. Thus, a warehouse may be described in terms of its position in the logistics system of a particular firm.

Performance Capabilities. Public warehousing offers space and services on a "for hire, as needed" basis for industrial and commercial firms in need of storage, collection, and distribution services and facilities. In addition to performing the basic functions of storage and handling, public warehouses offer many services, as indicated in Table 3–2.[2]

TABLE 3-2. Public Warehousing Services Offered
by 120 Larger Public Warehousing Companies

Service	Proportion of Firms Surveyed Offering Service
Inventory records	100%
Warehouse receipts	100
Storage	100
Break bulk handling	100
Marking and tagging	100
Over, short, damage reports	93
Prepaying freight (on behalf of warehouse users)	88
Local pickup and delivery	72
Accredited customer lists (for credit and other purposes)	72
Recoopering and repairing (for broken and damaged packages)	68
Packaging	52
Field warehousing	32
Make bulk handling	28
Loans on goods in storage	23

Source: McKinsey & Co., Inc. survey of public warehousing industry conducted in 1970. Authors' comments are in parentheses.

The most important feature of public warehousing is that it requires no investment of capital for its user. Instead, costs vary somewhat directly with the volume of business done by the user, and presumably with his ability to incur the expense. Other important advantages are that public warehousing: (1) may be used to accommodate peak, as opposed to more constant base, warehousing, and handling needs; (2) can be obtained in hundreds of locations, perhaps on a basis which reflects changing costs, transportation rate patterns, and other factors plac-

[2] For a comprehensive treatment of the subject of public warehousing, see Kenneth B. Ackerman, H. W. Gardner, and Lee P. Thomas, *Understanding Today's Distribution Center* (Washington, D. C.: Traffic Service Corp., 1972); John H. Frederick, *Using Public Warehouses* (Philadelphia: Chilton Co., 1957).

ing a premium on the flexibility of a user's operations; (3) can provide specialized storage and handling facilities on a short-term basis; (4) offers in some states preferential property tax treatment in comparison with goods stored in privately owned warehouse space; and (5) provides a more definitive documentation of warehousing costs than the operation of owned space. As a result, public warehousing occupies a particularly important position in the logistics systems of many companies.

The services of the public warehouseman in the warehousing industry are somewhat comparable to those of the common carrier in the transportation industry. Although he is not required by law to serve all comers, the public warehouseman does provide space and services to a great variety of customers to meet a wide range of user needs.

The functions performed by firms using private warehouses are essentially the same functions discussed above. Particular advantages to the user of private warehousing include: (1) lower per-unit costs in situations where there is a large, constant flow of product or need for space; (2) cash flow advantages achieved from the depreciation of owned facilities; (3) greater direct control of warehousing operations and response time in filling customer orders; and (4) specialized or unique operations not generally available from public warehouses.

Industry Size.   *Public Warehousing.*   The public warehousing industry is composed of small companies, with no dominant firm. The largest firm in the industry in 1970 operated perhaps 9 million square feet of space in about 50 cities, or about 5% of general warehouse space, and no more than 2% of all types of public warehousing space in the United States. According to the *Census of Business* for 1967, there were 9,433 public warehouse establishments (separate facilities, regardless of whether a firm might own two or more such facilities) in the United States. They comprised about 390 million square feet of non-specialized warehouse space, 534 million cubic feet of refrigerated space, 520 million gallons of bulk liquid storage space, and 2.7 million cubic feet of space for frozen food. They produced revenue of about $1.6 billion and paid an annual payroll of $634 million.

Public warehousing businesses are categorized by the *Census of Business* in six ways: household goods, general goods, refrigerated goods, farm products, food lockers, and special warehousing. In terms of total revenues reported by the *Census of Business* for 1967, household goods warehousemen and general goods warehousemen dominated the industry with 39.6% and 23.4% of industry revenues respectively. These types of warehousing operations, along with special warehousing, have enjoyed growth rates considerably above those for all industries, as shown in Table 3–3. (14) **To what would you attribute these relatively high**

TABLE 3–3. Public Warehousing Revenues and Growth Rates,
by Category of Operation

Category of Operation	Proportion of Total Revenue in 1967[a]	1963–1970 Annual Revenue Growth Rate[b]
Household goods	39.6%	12.8%
General goods	23.4%	11.9
Refrigerated goods	14.1	7.6
Farm products	12.3	4.4
Food lockers	5.9	3.9
Special warehousing	4.7	14.4
	100.0%	10.2%

[a]Data from *1967 Census of Business, Public Warehousing* (Washington, D. C.: Department of Commerce, Bureau of the Census, 1970).
[b]McKinsey & Co., Inc. survey of public warehousing industry conducted in 1970.

growth rates? Table 3–4 provides additional data by category of warehousing business.

Most public warehouse businesses serve a limited geographic area. According to the McKinsey and Company survey of 120 larger firms in the industry, over 80% of general-goods public warehouse companies do business in only one city.

Private Warehousing. The Bureau of the Census has published information about non-public warehousing only in conjunction with wholesale trade data. Table 3–5 presents information about warehouse floor space utilized in 1967 by the four major kinds of wholesale businesses: merchant wholesalers, manufacturers' sales branches and offices, merchandise agents and brokers, and assemblers of farm products. In total, wholesalers reported the use of over 1.7 billion square feet of space, of which about two-thirds was in single-story buildings. Merchant wholesalers who provided a full range of services, including the holding of inventory, were by far the largest users of warehouse space. Each square foot of warehousing space they reported was supporting about $90 of annual sales and a year-end inventory valued at about $10.

Other information collected by the 1967 *Census of Business* indicates that, of the total warehouse floor space used by wholesalers in 1967, 41% was built prior to 1940 and 75% was built prior to 1960.

(15) **Compare the relative square footages represented by public warehousing and wholesalers' warehousing space in 1967. What do you conclude? (16) Would you expect the growth rate for public or for private warehousing space to be greater? (17) Why?**

Public Warehousing. *Costs.* Roughly two-thirds of all costs of public warehouse operations are thought to be fixed, at least over the short term.

TABLE 3–4. Public Warehousing, by Type of Warehousing Facility, 1967

	U. S. Total	Category of Warehousing Facility					
		Household Goods Warehousing and Storage	General Warehousing and Storage	Refrigerated Warehousing, Except Food Lockers	Food Lockers, With or Without Food Preparation Facilities	Farm Products Warehousing and Storage	Other Special Warehousing and Storage
Establishments (number)	9,433	3,701	1,677	749	1,772	1,131	403
Revenue ($000)	$1,624,632	$643,361	$379,910	$228,902	$96,085	$199,780	$76,594
Payroll, entire year ($000)	$ 634,429	$282,405	$163,816	$ 83,123	$16,451	$ 60,585	$28,049
Occupiable public storage space, December 31:							
Floor space (000 sq. ft.)	392,865	100,502	163,168	8,666	438	103,628	16,463
Refrigerated space (000 sq. ft.)	533,960	1,059	3,543	525,938	3,293	127	–
Bulk liquid storage space (000 gal.)	519,601	15	258	515	95	131	518,587
Frozen food lockers, December 31:							
Individual lockers installed (number)	742,316	40	5	9,108	733,163	–	–
Bulk freezer storage space (000 cu. ft.)	2,674	11	44	59	2,560	–	–

Source: 1967 Census of Business, Public Warehousing (Washington, D. C.: Department of Commerce, Bureau of the Census, 1970), Table 1, p. 9–1.

TABLE 3-5. Wholesale Trade Industry Warehouse Floor Space, by Kind of Business, 1967*

	U. S. Total	Kind of Wholesale Business			
		Merchant Wholesalers	Manufacturers' Sales Branches, Offices	Merchandise Agents, Brokers	Assemblers of Farm Products
All establishments:					
Number	267,265	212,993	16,709	26,462	11,101
Sales ($000)	$344,732,247	$206,055,065	$67,174,649	$61,347,022	$10,155,511
Inventories at end of year, at cost	$ 26,843,645	$ 21,463,112	$ 4,259,852	$ 559,355	$ 561,326
Establishments reporting 1,000 sq. ft. or more of floor space:					
Number	129,937	108,428	10,844	6,479	4,186
Sales ($000)	$187,875,759	$126,039,265	$44,995,856	$12,954,130	$ 3,886,508
Inventories at end of year, at cost	$ 18,381,724	$ 14,652,071	$ 3,244,373	$ 206,002	$ 279,278
Occupiable warehouse floor space, end of year (000 sq. ft.):					
Total	1,746,147	1,395,198	205,118	50,182	95,649
In single-story buildings	844,988	672,506	137,338	24,073	11,072
In multistory buildings	426,295	348,490	51,512	11,066	15,227
Type of building not reporting	501,184	387,762	17,086	16,038	80,298

*Excludes manufacturers' sales offices (without stocks) and petroleum bulk stations and terminals.

Source: 1967 Census of Business, Wholesale Trade, Warehouse Space (Washington, D. C.: Department of Commerce, Bureau of the Census, 1971), Table 1, p. 5–1.

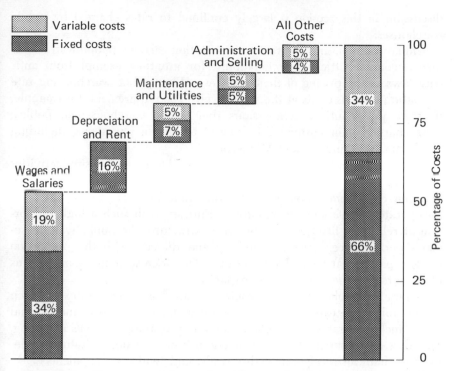

Fig. 3–3. The cost structure of public warehousing operations. *Source:* McKinsey & Co., Inc.; survey of public warehousing industry conducted in 1970.

Important elements of these fixed costs, as shown in Fig. 3–3, include a significant proportion of wages and salaries, all depreciation and rent, and lesser amounts of maintenance and utilities as well as administration and selling.

Differences in the fixed versus variable cost structure for major types of services such as storage, handling, and office services are great. For example, nearly all costs of storage are fixed, while significant elements of handling and office services are variable in nature.

(18) How would you expect the difference in cost makeup to affect the pricing policies for each of the major categories of public warehouse service? (19) In general, would you expect prices for public warehousing services to be somewhat uniform among competitors, as they are among for-hire transportation companies? (20) Why?

Rates and Services. Rates are prices charged by public warehouses for the performance of specified functions or services. In contrast, private warehouse expenses are treated as internal costs to the user. The discussion in this section is largely confined to rates charged by public warehouses.

Unlike common and contract transportation carriers, public warehouse-men encounter little rate regulation. Nor are they exempt from anti-trust laws in the pricing of their services. What public warehousing rate regulation there is exists at the state level. The requirement, for example, by state public utility commissions that public warehousemen publish rates charged their customers is limited to only a few states, including California, Washington, and Minnesota.

Costs can be allocated in various ways to basic warehousing activities of storage and handling, with contrasting prices resulting for each, even between close competitors handling the same product. Costs may vary for operators in various communities. Further, with such a high propor-tion of relatively fixed costs in his price structure, the public warehouse-man's performance varies significantly and directly with the proportion of his capacity that he is able to utilize. The price structure is one means of encouraging the use of excess capacity.

Generally, public warehousing charges are based upon rates for each of the following categories: storage rates, handling rates, and special rates (including rates for functions such as preparation of bills of lading, repairing or recoopering, cash collections from customers, returned de-liveries, small lot receipts or withdrawals, and "will call" shipments).

Factors of greatest importance in the pricing of basic public ware-housing services for a specific commodity and customer are:

1. The cubic dimensions per case, pallet, or other unit of the product
2. Whether the product will be palletized (allowing a number of cases or packages to be handled as a unit)
3. The height to which the product can be stacked
4. The square footage under the stack which the product will require
5. The rate at which the product will move through the warehouse during each season or period of time
6. Special handling, packaging, or other requirements associated with the product

On the basis of this and other information which the shipper often is asked to provide, the square footage, cubic footage, and handling rate and labor which a given type of product will require can be estimated.

Storage rates typically are assessed on the basis of square feet, cubic feet, weight, or units. The rate assessed may also vary with the value, fragility, or degree of hazard represented by the product in question. Time storage charges are assessed in many different ways, but most of the differences are matters of detail inasmuch as nearly all methods of assessment are based on periods of a month and/or half-month. The following provisions, quoted from a Minnesota public warehousing tariff, are reasonably typical of industry practice:

Storage Period and Charges

(a) All charges for storage are per package or other agreed unit per month.

(b) Storage charges become applicable upon the date that warehouseman accepts care, custody and control of the goods, regardless of unloading date or date of issue of warehouse receipt.

(c) Except as provided in paragraph (d) of this section, a full month's storage charge will apply on all goods received between the first and the 15th, inclusive, of a calendar month; one-half month's storage charge will apply on all goods received between the 10th and last day of a calendar month, and a full month's storage charge will apply to all goods in storage the first day of storage for the initial month and thereafter on the first day of the calendar month.

(d) When mutually agreed by the warehouseman and the depositor, a storage month shall extend from a date in one calendar month to, but not including, the same date of the next and all succeeding months. All storage charges are due and payable on the first day of the storage month.

"Space rental" rates provide for a specified amount of space to be set aside for the exclusive storage of the renter's goods. These rates are assessed on a square footage basis and are charged even if the space is not fully utilized.

The application of standard costs (including an allowance for profit) to estimated storage and handling volumes will produce a price per case or price per pallet for such services. Such standards will, of course, vary with time and location. Standards for storage might range, for example, from 20¢ to 30¢ per square foot under the pile per month. Standard handling costs might range from $10 to $15 per hour for labor and equipment employed in handling activities.

Handling rates too are usually based upon the volume, weight, or number of units (often cases) of goods handled. Specialized handling may be quoted as a special rate or on the basis of a man-hour charge.

What do these factors suggest about the range of prices which you, as a logistics manager for your firm, might expect to encounter in purchasing public warehousing services? As you might expect, it can be large. The experience of one manufacturer of low-density paper products is summarized in Table 3–6. Here we see that storage costs, in cents per case per month, were five times as high in the Pittsburgh public warehouse as in the Minneapolis warehouse used by this manufacturer. Handling costs, on the other hand, were higher in Minneapolis. The overall bill for a standard set of services under these pricing arrangements was about 50% higher in Pittsburgh. (21) **What other interesting contrasts do you see in Table 3–6?**

TABLE 3–6. Public Warehousing Charges Paid Recently by a Paper
Products Manufacturer at Various Locations

Warehouse Location	Case Per Month[a]	Handling In, in Cents Per Case[b]	Handling Out, in Cents Per Case[b]	Preparation of Bill of Lading[c]	Annual Charge for a Standard Set of Services[d]
Pittsburgh, Pa.	$.15[a]	$.12	$.12	$.50	$3,340
New Orleans, La.	.10[a]	.12	.17	.35	3,010
Kansas City, Kan.	.094[a]	.145	.15	.50	3,000
Dallas, Tex.	.09	.135	.135	.50	2,800
Chicago, Ill.	.10[a]	.12	.12	.70	2,780
Charlotte, N. C.	.066[a]	.08	.22	.45	2,680
Atlanta, Ga.	.101[a]	.108	.108	.45	2,590
Worcester, Mass.	.09	.14	.09	.50	2,560
Bayonne, N. J.	.10[a]	.10	.10	.50	2,500
Milwaukee, Wis.	.085	.11	.11	.35	2,410
Denver, Colo.	.06[a]	.07	.19	.40	2,360
Des Moines, Iowa	.08[a]	.11	.10	.50	2,320
Syracuse, N. Y.	.09	.09	.09	.40	2,240
Minneapolis, Minn.	.03	.15	.15	.35	2,230
Pennsauken, N. J.	.06[a]	.095	.095	.75	2,010

[a]Designates warehouses that assess one-half month vs. full month charges on cases in inventory 15 days or less.

[b]Rates assume that shipments in and out exceed minimum quantities established by some warehouses.

[c]For shipments outbound from the warehouse.

[d]Charges shown are based on the assumption of a 6,000-case throughput with an average inventory of 1,000 cases and an average shipment size out of 30 cases (1,000 pounds).

In addition to handling and storage charges, a wide variety of accessorial charges for special services may make up a smaller proportion of the total public warehousing bill. Figure 3–4 consists of excerpts from a Minnesota public warehousing tariff. It contains rates for a wide variety of special services performed in addition to routine storage and handling rates. It also illustrates, in terms of differing charges depending on cube, weight, and other factors, how the logistics characteristics of goods are taken into consideration when rates and charges are set. Since rates are, to a fair degree, based on costs, this illustrative information is also indicative of the cost variances which might be expected in private warehousing operations by firms dealing in various types of goods.

(22) Look over Fig. 3–4. What cost/value relationships are assumed by the Space Rental Schedule of charges? (23) Refer to the Base Rate Storage Table. Do these rates seem to be based on cost of service, or value of service, or a combination of the two? (24) Check out column no. 3 in the Handling Charge Table of Fig. 3–4. You might graph it. Are the handling charges linear or not? (25) Why? (26) What is the

SPACE RENTAL SCHEDULE

SPACE RENTAL—The term as used in this Tariff means space specified for the exclusive use of a customer on which the storage Company assumes responsibility as a public warehouseman such as the keeping of stock records, making of reports, etc. When using this schedule, the customer shall pay for the gross space, i.e., lost space in piling, aisles, etc., and a just proportion of the main aisle serving the area used.

The following rates will apply up to 10 foot ceiling height:

Up to 500 square feet......................14¢ per square foot per month
501 to 1000 square feet....................12¢ per square foot per month
1001 square feet and over..................10¢ per square foot per month

The following rates will apply up to 16 foot ceiling height:

Up to 500 square feet......................16¢ per square foot per month
501 to 1000 square feet....................14¢ per square foot per month
1001 square feet and over..................12¢ per square foot per month

The following rates will apply over 16 foot ceiling height:

Up to 500 square feet......................18¢ per square foot per month
501 to 1000 square feet....................16¢ per square foot per month
1001 square feet and over..................14¢ per square foot per month

SPACE TABLE SCHEDULE

Merchandise listed in this Tariff as "SPACE TABLE" and other merchandise which may be offered and which does not lend itself to the application of the unit package or per cwt. basis will be stored at a monthly rate of 14¢ per square foot; except on merchandise or customers requiring additional space due to excessive marks, brands, or varieties apply the "SPACE RENTAL SCHEDULE."

If merchandise can be stored in reduced space through reduced access space, reduced aisle space, increased pile height, or reduced service space, warehouseman may compute a storage rate per piece or per hundredweight based on space rental table above.

If for any of the reasons listed in the Standard Modification Table, Page 3, merchandise requires an unusual amount of space, the warehouseman may con.pute storage rate per piece or hundredweight on this table also.

DEFINITIONS

AVERAGE CUBE—Means to determine average cubic measurement per package in each consignment and charge by the package.

AVERAGE WEIGHT—Means to determine average gross weight per package in each consignment and charge by the package weight.

CUBE—Means to store according to the cubical dimensions of the package.

CWT.—Means to store by gross weight only.

Fig. 3–4. Excerpts from Minnesota–Northwest Warehousemen's Association Merchandise Tariff 23M.

BASE RATE STORAGE TABLE

CLASS	RATE PER CWT.	RATE PER CU. INCH	PER CU. FOOT
"A"	.07	.0000133	.025
"B"	.08	.0000161	.029
"C"	.09	.0000177	.030
"D"	.10	.0000190	.034
"E"	.12	.0000202	.036
"F"	.13	.0000221	.044

EXPLANATION

A normal package is one weighing 25 pounds per cubic foot. If, therefore, a package weighs 25 pounds or less per cubic foot, the storage rate should be based on the "bulk" or cubic inches; if it weighs more than 25 pounds per cubic foot, the storage rate should be based on "weight".

In classifying commodities listed in this Tariff, the following exceptions have been used, and the same exceptions will be followed on commodities not listed. Class "C" shall be the starting classification for such commodities.

STANDARD MODIFICATIONS

1. Value
2. Fragility
3. Liability to claims — double
4. Small volume-double
5. Possible damage to other goods because of leakage
6. Protection against freezing
7. Isolation-double
8. Attractive to vermin

9. Hazardous
10. Malodorous
11. Dusty
12. Mussy
13. Require access for examination or treatment-double
14. Lost space in piling-double
15. Fermentation, causing explosion
16. Large variety-double

After the classification of a commodity is found, other factors in addition to space consumption must be taken into consideration as modifying the rate.

When using the above schedule of listed modifications advance one or more classes as modifications are applicable to commodities offered for storage.

Fig. 3–4. Continued.

HANDLING CHARGE TABLE

TO BE USED ONLY ON ITEMS NOT LISTED SPECIFICALLY IN THIS TARIFF.

COLUMN NO. 1	COLUMN NO. 2	COLUMN NO. 3
Pounds per Cubic Foot	Pounds per Cubic Inch	Handling Rate per Cwt.
Pounds to 3 pounds	.00000 to .00173	1.24
ver 3 pounds and not exceeding 6 pounds	.00174 to .00347	.98
ver 6 pounds and not exceeding 9 pounds	.00348 to .00520	.82
ver 9 pounds and not exceeding 11 pounds	.00521 to .00636	.68
ver 11 pounds and not exceeding 14 pounds	.00637 to .00810	.57
ver 14 pounds and not exceeding 17 pounds	.00811 to .00983	.47
ver 17 pounds and not exceeding 20 pounds	.00984 to .01157	.44
ver 20 pounds and not exceeding 23 pounds	.01158 to .01331	.40
ver 23 pounds and not exceeding 26 pounds	.01332 to .01504	.35
ver 26 pounds and not exceeding 29 pounds	.01505 to .01678	.31
ver 29 pounds and not exceeding 32 pounds	.01679 to .01851	.28
ver 32 pounds and not exceeding 35 pounds	.01852 to .02025	.27
ver 35 pounds and not exceeding 38 pounds	.02026 to .02199	.26
ver 38 pounds and not exceeding 43 pounds	.02200 to .02488	.25
3 pounds and up	.02489 and up	.24

No. 1 The above Handling Charge Table will be used according to relative bulk and weight for computing handling charges on commodities not listed herein.

Exceptions All merchandise packed in glass, bulk liquid merchandise in wood containers, and other merchandise having objectionable handling features, will be charged for at the rate of 1 cent per cwt. in excess of the rates indicated in the above table. When merchandise is tendered for storage, and/or shipped from storage by a mechanized handling system, the warehouseman may compute a rate for handling such merchandise by using the hourly labor rates shown below.

TO USE THE ABOVE TABLE, THE WEIGHT SHOULD BE DIVIDED BY THE NUMBER OF CUBIC INCHES IN THE PACKAGE.

This will give the weight per cubic inch in decimals similar to those shown in Column No. 2 of the table. If the resulting decimal is less than .00173, the handling charge will be at the rate of $1.24 per hundredweight. If the decimal is between .00521 and .00636, the handling charge will be at the rate of 68¢ per hundredweight; and so on as shown in the above table. When the decimal is over .02489 the handling charge will be at the rate of 24¢ per hundredweight.

EXPLANATION OF HANDLING CHARGE

The word "handling" as used in this Tariff, includes not only the actual cost of manual labor taking the merchandise into and out of the warehouse, but also such items of expense as salaries of foreman and checkers, nonproductive labor, lost time, liability insurance, repairs, depreciation, taxes and insurance on equipment; power, light and heat; loss and damage; Social Security Taxes, compensation insurance and other expenses incidental to labor, together with a proper proportion of office salaries and general office expense chargeable to the handling of the merchandise. CLERICAL SERVICES performed by the warehouseman will be services listed in Note 12; and one inventory report per month, one physical inventory per year, and one warehouse receipt. Additional clerical services including transmission of extra reports or documents will be assessed at the rates listed in Note 4.

Storage, and/or handling, and/or accessorial charges, computed per the several provisions of this tariff may be calculated on a composite basis, either per hundredweight, or per unit, if requested by storer and agreed to by warehouseman.

In addition to the above Handling Charge Table, apply the Small Lot Receipt Charge and/or Withdrawal Charge when applicable. (See Note 11 and Note 12.)

HOURLY RATES FOR "PER HOUR" COMMODITIES

Warehouse labor will be furnished at $6.80 per hour, standard fork lift equipment at $8.80 per hour, clerical labor at $5.80 per hour; and the total of these charges will be the handling rate for commodities listed in this tariff as assessable on the "per hour" basis, or as handling rate for any commodity if agreed to between warehouseman and storer.

Fig. 3—4. Continued.

SPECIAL NOTES

HANDLING CHARGES

Note 1. The handling charges scheduled herein cover the receiving of merchandise in good condition from freight cars or tail gate of trucks at the warehouse, handling into the warehouse and making delivery to shipping platform and shall be billed with the first month's storage charge. Per hour rates listed herein may be converted to hundredweight or unit rates by agreement between storer and warehouseman using hourly rates per Note 4.

DISTRIBUTION

Note 2. Consignments received by cars, truck or trailer for immediate distribution will be assessed the full handling rate as specified in the tariff; unless the car is not loaded order by order, in which case the warehouseman will charge based on the hourly rate set forth in Note 4. A charge of two cents per package, minimum charge of 60¢ per shipment, will be made for outgoing shipments via railway, common carrier truck, express, parcel post, or air transport from distribution or pool cars. Free time of 48 hours will be allowed after goods are ready for delivery. Monthly storage charge as contained in this tariff to apply thereafter.

MINIMUM CHARGES

Note 3. Except as otherwise provided herein the following minimums will apply:
a) Minimum handling charge per lot (includes small lot charge): $3.40
b) Minimum storage charge per lot, mark, brand or variety: $1.00
c) Minimum monthly storage charge: $15.00
d) Minimum handling charge for any car placed on siding for storage or distribution: $25.00
These charges will apply also to each account where one customer has several accounts each requiring separate record keeping and billing.

EXTRA LABOR CHARGES

Note 4. Extra service during normal working hours will be furnished to regular storers for sampling, inspections, weighing, breaking original packages, repiling, leveling, bracing, sorting or special physical warehouse checking and any other extra service at $6.80 per man hour; minimum charge one hour's time. For these services, a man and a standard 2000 lb. fork lift will be furnished for $8.80 per man hour; minimum charge one hour's time. These extra labor charges do not include the use of special tools, attachments, or equipment; nor do they include supervision.

Extra clerical service for special statements of stock on hand, or shipped, or other extra services will be furnished to regular stores for $5.80 per hour; minimum charge one hour's time. Damage free rail cars—When merchandise is loaded or unloaded from this type rail car, a charge of $10.00 will be made. This fee covers the cost of removing the special DF equipment from the rail car, placing same into point of storage within our warehouse, and then, the necessary labor to reset the equipment into the car after your portion of the merchandise has been removed. Similar charges will apply to reefer cars requiring other than normal handling.

REPAIRING AND RECOOPERING

Note 5. A charge of 70¢ per bag, box or carton, minimum charge of $3.00 will be made for recoopering, inspection, extra handling, repacking or repairing ordinary damage to original packages received in bad order condition major appliances $1.50. After warehouseman has notified carrier or his agent, rejected goods must be picked up within 48 hours. After 48 hours, regular charges including storage minimums, shall apply. For repairing extraordinary damages, a time and material charge will be made as per Note 4 and Note 14.

WEIGHTS

Note 6. When rates are quoted by weight, they will be computed on the gross weight, and the term "cwt." when used means one hundred (100) pounds.

COLLECTIONS AND ADVANCES

Note 7. When the warehouseman is requested to make collections in cash for account of the storer, the charge therefor will be one fourth of one per cent of the amount involved, minimum $1.00. An additional charge of $1.00 will be made when advance charges are to be collected.

EXPENSE BILLS

Note 8. A charge of one-half of one per cent, minimum 60¢ per expense bill, will be made to cover the cost of clerical work necessary in paying and handling transportation companies' expense bills.

DELIVERIES RETURNED

Note 9. When a delivery is authorized to be made and delivery cannot be affected, the regular handling charge will be made when goods are returned to storage.

PERISHABLE GOODS

Note 10. Perishable goods or others susceptible to damage through changes in temperature or other causes incidental to ordinary storage, will be accepted only at owner's risk. Warehouseman may assess special charges for product protection. Such charges will not alter storer's risk under this article.

SMALL LOT RECEIPT CHARGE

Note 11. When merchandise is received for storage in L.C.L. or L.T.L. quantities of less than 20,000 pound lots, an additional charge will be made as follows:
Receipts of less than 5,000 lbs.—8¢ cwt. minimum 60¢ per mark, brand or variety
Receipts of 5,000 lbs. to 10,000 lbs.—6¢ cwt., minimum 60¢ per mark, brand or variety
Receipts of 10,000 lbs. to 20,000 lbs.—4¢ cwt., minimum 60¢ per mark, brand or variety

WITHDRAWAL CHARGE

Note 12. When merchandise is released from the warehouse in less than 20,000 lb. quantities, an additional charge will be made of 5¢ cwt., minimum 60¢ per withdrawal, but not less than 1¢ per package. This charge includes the following: selecting and preparing the order, marking, providing and preparing delivery ticket and/or bill of lading on outbound L.C.L. or L.T.L. shipment, telephoning the trucking company or consignee to pick up shipment at the warehouse delivery platform, and sending signed delivery ticket to storer. All outbound orders are subject to a line item charge of 10¢ per line, minimum charge 35¢ per order.

WILL CALL SHIPMENTS

Note 13. All will call shipments will be subject to an extra charge of $1.50.

SUPPLIES

Note 14. Materials furnished to be charged for at current market prices plus 10 per cent.

Fig. 3–4. Continued.

COMMODITY	STORAGE	MODIFICATION	PER CWT. HANDLING
MISCELLANEOUS			
Anti-Freeze . . . . { Drums	Weight C		22¢
Batteries, Storage { Cartons	Weight C		25¢
Dry	Weight D		28¢
Wet	Weight E		31¢
Beet Pulp, Dehydrated	Weight A		21¢
Bottles, Empty			
Cases and Crates	Cube C	2-14	31¢
Cans, Empty			
Cartons, Crates, Bundles	Cube C		80¢
Loose	Cube C		Per Hour
Cosmetics, Drugs, Medicines and related			
articles	Weight E	16	41¢
Feed, Animal			
Millfeed in bags	Weight A		22¢
Feed, Animal: Vitamin Mixtures, Mineral			
Supplements or other enriching compounds. . . .	Weight D	1-10	30¢
Fertilizer			
Bags 80# and over	Weight A		22¢
Furniture, New	Space Rental		Per Hour
Metals: Bars, Pigs, Ingots Unitized.	Weight A		18¢
Nails, Kegs & Boxes	Av. Wt. A		20¢
Paints and Varnishes			
Cases, Assortment	Space Rental		Per Hour
Soap and Soap Products			
Dry and Liquid, Cases	Weight E	5-6-10-16	28¢
Tires	Space Rental		Per Hour
Twine, Baler & Binder	Weight C		22¢
Wax, Polish - Cases.	Weight C	16	31¢
PAPER PRODUCTS			
Paper Bags in bundles	Cube E	4-14-16	Handling Table
Paper Boxes, Chipboard			
Strawboard or Pulpboard			
Bundles and Cartons	Cube D	14	Handling Table
Paper Boxes, Corrugated			
In Bundles	Cube E	14	Handling Table
Paper, Book & Print			
Cardboard on			
skids not exceeding	$1.50 per skid stacked		
4 x 4	$3.00 per skid not stacked		$3.00 per skid
Paper Cups.	Cube D		Handling Table
Paper Envelopes	Cube D		Handling Table
Paper, Newsprint	Weight B		15¢
Paper, Building and Roofing			
Rolls and Bundles	Weight B	14-16	27¢
Paper, Napkins, Toilet, Towels or Tissue and			
Sanitary Napkins			
Cases.	Cube E	14	Handling Table
Paper, Waxed, Cartons	Weight D		27¢
Paper, Wrapping			
Bundles and Rolls	Weight D	14	31¢

Fig. 3—4. Continued.

reasoning underlying each of the special charges listed on the Special Notes page? (27) Why, for example, should there be a "small lot receipt charge"? (28) On the sample commodity listing page, look at the Storage, Modification, and Handling columns. Review the classification of each commodity in each column. Can you reason out why each commodity should be so classified and charged for storage and handling?

Regulation. The public warehousing industry is regulated primarily by the Uniform Commercial Code, which prescribes legal conditions of contractual procedures to be followed by public warehousemen in dealing with their customers. There is little economic regulation of the industry comparable to that which exists for common carrier transportation firms. However, rates and charges of public warehouses are regulated in three states: California, Minnesota, and Washington.

In California uniform rates are established in each of five distribution areas. Rates are based upon negotiation between the public warehousing firms in the area and the California Public Utilities Commission. An individual firm can file separately for special rates, but they cannot be lower than the rates negotiated for the distribution area in which the warehouse is located. Minnesota and Washington require filing of rates with the Utilities Commission, and a determination by the Commission that such rates are fair and reasonable.

Private warehousing is subject to state and local municipality laws concerning such matters as zoning, safety, and pollution. Laws administered by federal agencies may be applied to the storage of food and drugs, and when duties or taxes are due on the goods stored, bonding may be required.

Transfer Facilities

The second major class of product support facilities is transfer facilities. The various major types of transfer facilities can be characterized best by the nature of the freight or item they are designed to accommodate. They include: terminals for assembling, sorting, transferring, or distributing packaged freight; terminals for handling and transferring containers used in coordinated transportation service; specialized bulk commodity terminals dedicated to particular commodities ranging from grain to oil; and carrier yards, terminals, and ports for combining and/or separating carrier equipment.

Packaged Freight. Carriers engaging in small shipment transportation (anything less than a vehicle load) may utilize terminals for the consolidation, mixing, or deconsolidation of packaged freight shipments. This is especially typical of highway and air carrier operations.

Shipping and receiving docks operated by individual shippers to serve as staging points for the shipment or receipt of packaged freight shipments also fall into this category.

Container Terminals. With the growth of coordinated transport, characterized by the use of two or more modes in the transportation of a single shipment, large containers compatible with two or more modes have come into common use. The transfer of a standard $20' \times 8' \times 8'$ container from one mode to another typically requires the use of a crane capable of lifting 85 tons at one time. Perhaps the world's largest container terminal is located at Port Elizabeth, New Jersey, for the transfer of containers from truck to ship and vice versa.

Typical packaged freight transfer facilities often involve transfer between vehicles of the same mode of transportation.

The design and operation of packaged freight terminals has proven to be one of the most difficult of all logistics tasks. Given the non-standard nature of packaged freight, most packaged freight operations have not been able to make use of automation, or even mechanical equipment to any great extent. The tedious nature of the work performed in these facilities has made their operation particularly susceptible to labor difficulties.

Bulk Commodity Terminals. The transportation of commodities in unpackaged form has a great economic attraction. It requires the construction of facilities for assembling, transferring, and breaking bulk commodity shipments. Such facilities typically are designed to handle one or a limited number of bulk commodities in great quantities and at speeds ranging up to 20,000 tons or 2 million gallons per hour, and often offer the capability of transferring such commodities between vehicles of two cooperative transportation modes.

Bulk commodity terminals may be owned and operated by carriers, shippers, or public organizations such as port authorities.

Carrier Equipment Transfer Facilities. Rail, highway, and water carriers operate terminals for the transfer of cars, trailers, and barges, respectively. The sorting of railroad cars at "yard" terminal facilities has long been a feature of railroad freight transportation. With the advent of the Interstate Highway System and other superhighways, motor carriers have been permitted to haul heavier loads and more trailers per powered vehicle between terminals at which such trailer combinations are assembled and disassembled for handling over more closely restricted highways. The LASH system of water transportation, involving the use of a "motor ship" capable of carrying a number of barges, may or may not require terminals for the handling of such barges.

In general, productivity increases at product support facilities have lagged behind those for the transportation of these same products. (29) **What factors do you think contribute to this problem?**

LOGISTICS INFORMATION SUPPORT FACILITIES

Information support facilities include both communication facilities and data processing facilities. While these facilities are used primarily to aid in demand–supply coordination, they are also used to a limited degree in the support of movement control. Communication facilities are used to transmit data from an origin point to data processing facilities, and then to transmit the processed data to a required destination. Operating efficiency is usually enhanced to the degree that the data processing facility becomes accessible to more people for wider use in an expanded operation. Therefore, the relationship of the communication facility to the data processing facility is an important one, and if properly understood and implemented, will allow maximum support of the logistics system.

In the discussion that follows, our interest will be confined to communication facilities as data transmitters. For example, our interest in the telephone is restricted to data, not voice, transmission. The discussion of data processing facilities will be limited for the most part to computers since they represent a large portion of the data processing facilities used in the support of logistics systems today.

Communication Facilities

Data communication is a rapidly expanding field that has emerged because of rapid advances in data processing technologies. In order to utilize effectively the data processing facilities that are available, it is necessary to have high-speed communication links to transmit data to these processing facilities. Figure 3–5 demonstrates the role of data communication facilities in the transmission and processing of data. They are so vital to an effective data system that business corporations have imposed strong pressures upon both communication common carriers and computer manufacturers to develop the necessary techniques and equipment for efficient and economical data transmission.

A data communication system is a combination of people and machines whose primary purpose is to transfer digital data between two or more terminals in a reliable manner.

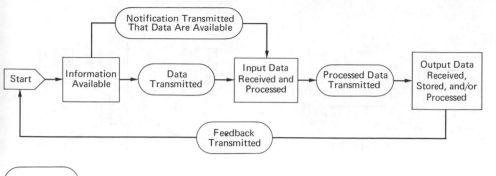

Fig. 3–5. The role of data communication facilities in the transmission and processing of data.

The functions, structure, and complexity of data communication systems vary widely. For example, some systems transfer messages between remote terminals; other systems may transmit from remote terminals to a central processing facility. Figure 3–6 illustrates several patterns of data transmission that may occur in communication systems.

(30) **Which of the patterns shown in Fig. 3–6 do you think would be most expensive, given the same volume of information flowing between the points shown in the diagrams? (31) Why? (32) What factors would influence the configuration for data transmission in a communication system?**

Electrical data communication systems first became possible when Samuel Morse invented the telegraph in 1844. However, only recently have data communication systems been able to meet industry requirements effectively; this has in part been due to the development of reliable medium- and high-speed terminal equipment and communication processing equipment, in conjunction with the availability of reasonably priced standard communication facilities and flexible common-carrier service. Computer users in the United States are beginning to recognize the advantages of company-wide data communication networks and of the closely related concepts of real-time data processing and integrated management information systems.

Although only about 1 percent of the computers sold in 1965 were linked in a data communications system, Western Union has predicted that 60 per cent of the computers likely to be sold in 1975 will be so linked. A.T.&T. expects that the volume of information transmitted in the form of digital data will eventually equal the volume transmitted by voice.[3]

[3] *Auerbach Guide to Data Communications* (Philadelphia: Auerbach Info, Inc., 1970), p. iii.

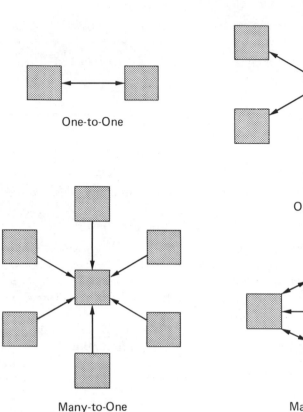

One-to-One

One-to-Many

Many-to-One

Many-to-Many*

⟶ = Direction of data flow.

*There are many variations of this pattern. Only the direct line connection is shown here.

Fig. 3–6. Several basic data transmission patterns in communication systems.

Structure of the Communication Industry. Communication common carriers are companies in America which furnish communication services to the public. Reference to the communication companies by this name dates back to the days when messages were carried by stagecoach or the Pony Express. These common carriers offer facilities for the transmission of voice, data, television, and telephoto pictures. Some are now beginning to offer on-line computer services also, and it appears that in the future their business will branch out widely in this direction. This may pose a problem for the computer manufacturers who also provide on-line computer services in that the communication common carriers as an industry are public utilities and are regulated by state and federal governments. As they begin to offer on-line computer services, many feel that companies providing these business services, whether communication common carriers or computer manufacturers, may become regulated.

It is surprising to note that there are more than two thousand telecommunication common carriers in the United States. Many other countries have only one such organization, which is run by the government. Most of these common carriers are very small. Only about 250 of them have more than 5,000 subscribers.[4]

Nevertheless, there are three major domestic telecommunication common carriers: The Bell System, General Telephone and Electronics Corporation, and Western Union

The Bell System.   The American Telephone and Telegraph Company, commonly referred to as the Bell System, is a vast network of telephone and data circuits with many switching offices as well as television and other links which are operated across the United States. It is by far the largest communication common carrier and operates more than 80% of the telephones installed in the United States.

The data communication facilities and services that the Bell System offers include the telephone, the teletypewriter, *Data-phone,*[5] and Telpak. The performance capabilities of these technologies are discussed in a subsequent section.

General Telephone and Electronics Corporation.   The General System is the second largest telephone company, but is a distant second, accounting for only 7% of the telephones in the United States. The General System is totally compatible with the Bell System, allowing for direct interconnection. Unlike the Bell System, the General System offers only the teletypewriter for data communication.

Western Union.   The Western Union Telegraph Company operates a national telegraph message service to all parts of the United States and overseas via suboceanic cables. It also operates and leases private communication links, as well as the American Telex System, a direct dial-up teleprinter service very similar to the Bell System's teletypewriter service. Telex is Western Union's primary service for transmitting data in a logistics system.

The United States Independent Telephone Association (USITA).   The remainder of the two thousand or so telephone companies are very small

[4] James Martin, *Telecommunications and the Computer* (Englewood Cliffs, N. J.: Prentice-Hall, Inc., 1969), p. 81.

[5] *Data-phone* is a trademark and service mark of the Bell System.

and belong to the United States Independent Telephone Association, which coordinates their practices. Their tariffs are established by committees, and literature is distributed to the various member companies. USITA members are interconnected with the Bell and General Telephone systems.

Performance Capabilities of Communication Facilities. Performance capabilities of a communication system are best assessed in the context of the objectives of a company's particular logistics system. Some of these may include: (1) improvement of customer service, (2) shortening of the time required to determine stock availability in order to quote delivery dates more rapidly to customers, (3) reduction of inventories without delaying order shipments, and (4) reduction of costs of order processing, inventory management, and related data processing tasks.

Once objectives have been developed, the performance capabilities of the different data communication facilities can be evaluated in terms of distribution, volume, speed, language, and accuracy of information to be transmitted. For example, *Data-phone* has more capability in terms of speed and volume than the Telex or the teletypewriter, but the Telex (offering a hard or typed copy of information as it is entered into the system) has more capability in terms of transmitting information accurately than does *Data-phone*. Further, Telpak service has greater capabilities in all areas than any other type of communication facilities.

Perhaps the most critical characteristic in determining the capabilities of communication facilities is the speed at which information can be transmitted. Current services provide basically three different ranges of speeds. The first of these is the narrow-band line designed for telegraph and similar machines transmitting at speeds ranging from 45 to 150 bits [6] per second. Communication facilities which have this speed capability include the Telex and the teletypewriter. The second range of speeds is provided by telephone channels transmitting at speeds ranging generally from 600 to 2,400 bits per second. Communication facilities with these capabilities are the Wide Area Telephone Service (WATS) system and *Data-phone*. Wide-band services are high-speed data transmission facilities with speeds up to 500,000 bits per second. An example of this third type of facility is Telpak.

To summarize, the steps for planning a data communication system are shown in Fig. 3–7. Note that the selection of terminal equipment (communication facilities) is only one step in the design of a communication system and must be evaluated in terms of other aspects of the system.

[6] A bit is a unit of information content. A contraction of "binary digit," a bit is the smallest unit of information in the binary system of notation. It is the choice between two possible states, usually designated one and zero.

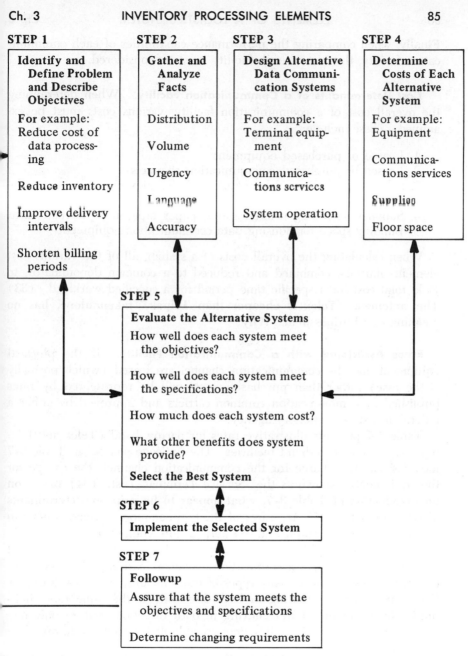

Fig. 3–7. A summary of the steps involved in planning a data communication system. *Source:* Edgar C. Gentle, Jr., *Data Communications in Business —An Introduction* (New York: American Telephone and Telegraph Co., 1966), p. 79. Copyright © 1965 by American Telephone and Telegraph Co. All rights reserved.

Finally, when comparing the performance capabilities of each communication facility, the cost of each facility must be considered.

Cost Determinants of a Communication Facility. When determining the overall cost of a communication facility, various costs must be examined. These include:

1. Leased or purchased equipment
2. Leased or purchased communication channels
3. Salaries (including all benefits) of the employees who operate the facility
4. Supplies, including printed forms, paper tape, and punched cards
5. Building space for housing data communication equipment

When calculating the overall costs of a system, all of the various cost elements must be combined and reduced to a common denominator, to yield total cost for a specific time period for a specified workload. (33) **The statement, "Telex is cheaper than Telpak," taken alone, has no meaning to a businessman. Why?**

Rates Associated with a Communication Facility. If the physical equipment and the communication channel are leased (which normally is the case) rather than purchased, costs will be represented by rates published by communication common carriers and approved by either a federal or a state regulatory agency.

Table 3–7 presents illustrative rates for narrow-band (Telex and teletypewriter) and voice-band facilities. The "mileage charge" in Table 3–7 includes only the charge for the communication channel; the charge for the equipment is shown as the "Service Terminal" cost. (34) **Based on an examination of Table 3–7, what appear to be primary determinants of rates quoted? (35) Are rates of the two common carriers, American Telephone and Telegraph and Western Union, competitive?**

Lest you be misled by the simplicity of Table 3–7, it should be noted that rates offered by communications common carriers are very complicated. They comprise many types of transmissions, such as full-duplex lines capable of transmitting in both directions at the same time, half-duplex lines capable of transmitting in both directions but in only one direction at a time, and simplex lines capable of transmitting in only one direction.

Regulation of the Communications Industry. Rates for interstate communication services are regulated by the Federal Communications Commission. Rates for intrastate services are regulated by state public utility commissions. Different states frequently have different rates for the same

TABLE 3-7. Data Communication Rates

Illustrative Rates[a] for Narrow-Band and Voice-Band Facilities

	Narrow Band (Teletypewriter and Telex)	Voice Band[b]
Approximate bits/second	150	2,400
Available from	A.T.&T. and Western Union	A.T.&T. and Western Union
Mileage charge ($/mile/month)	Base rate + 37.5%	Base rate A + 10%
Service terminal ($/month)	$34.38	$13.75

Base Rate Schedule for Narrow Band

	Cost per Mile
Base rate per month:	
1-100 miles	$1.40
Next 150 miles	0.98
Next 250 miles	0.56
Next 500 miles	0.42
Additional miles	0.28

Base Rate Schedule for Voice Band

	Cost per Mile
Base rate per month:	
1-25 miles	$3.00
Next 75 miles	2.10
Next 150 miles	1.50
Next 250 miles	1.05
Next 500 miles	0.75
Next 500 miles	0.75
Additional miles	0.75

[a]These rates were in effect on August 1, 1967, and reflect full-duplex transmission.

[b]These rates do not include charges for conditioning. A voice line can be conditioned so that it has better properties for data transmission.

Source: Adapted from *Auerbach Guide to Data Communications* (Philadelphia: Auerbach Info, Inc., 1970), pp. 105-14.

services, and there are also wide differences in the prices of facilities among the different states. Interstate rates, however, are uniform across the country.

The Federal Communications Commission (FCC) is an independent federal agency which regulates radio, television, telephone, telegraph, and other transmissions by wire or radio. The powers of the FCC are defined in the Communications Act of 1934. The FCC's overall goal is ". . . to make available, so far as possible, to all the people of the United States a rapid, efficient, nation-wide, and world-wide wire and radio communications service with adequate facilities at reasonable charges. . . ." [7] The provisions of the Act require that regulated communications common carriers furnish services at reasonable charges upon reasonable request. Every common carrier subject to FCC regulation must have its plans for facilities offered to the public approved by the FCC before they become effective. To do this, carriers must file tariffs (or concur with existing tariffs) showing all services and charges offered to the public. A tariff, unless suspended or explicitly disapproved by the FCC, automatically becomes effective.

Data Processing Facilities

Structure of the Industry. The computer industry is composed of computer manufacturers, peripheral equipment manufacturers, and software suppliers. The total sales value of equipment shipped world-wide in 1969 was $7,170 million, and by 1970 there were about 77,000 computers in use in the United States.[8] Today, there are nearly 2,000 computer equipment manufacturers of which 20 are manufacturers of large digital computers. The remainder are manufacturers of smaller digital computers and peripheral equipment.[9]

Performance Capabilities. Computer and peripheral equipment performance may be expressed in terms of central processing speed, storage capacity, printing speed, cost, and software capabilities among others.[10] Information about selected computers, compared on these dimensions, is presented in Table 3–8.

Cost of Data Processing Systems. The basic elements in a data processing system, whether computerized or not, are input, data storage, data processing, and output. They are related in the manner shown in Fig. 3–8.

There are essentially two tasks which a data processing system must perform: the *facilitating* tasks, which include input preparation and file maintenance, and the *result* tasks, which include transaction processing,

[7] *The Communications Act of 1934, With Amendments and Index Thereto* (Washington, D. C.: Government Printing Office, 1961), Title I, Sec. I.

[8] *Computer Industry Profile* (Newton, Mass.: International Data Corp., 1970).

[9] These numbers are estimates, and are based on entries in the directory of manufacturers and suppliers in *Infosystems* (formerly *Business Automation*), December, 1971, pp. 234–61.

[10] For an excellent technical discussion of the computer and associated equipment, see Gordon B. Davis, *Computer Data Processing* (New York: McGraw-Hill Book Co., 1969).

TABLE 3–8. Selected Computers and Peripheral Equipment and Their Associated Characteristics

Manufacturer and Model Number	Purchase Price ($000)	CPU Cycle Time (μsec)	Minimum Core Capacity (in Characters)	Printer (Lines per Minute)	Time Share Capability	Software Languages Accommodated	
						COBOL	Fortran II, IV, or VI
Control Data:							
3300	$ 700	1.2	652,000	1,200	Yes	Yes	Yes
6200	1,525	.125	1,310,000	1,200	Yes	Yes	Yes
7500	9,500	.0275	650,000	1,200	Yes	Yes	Yes
International Business Machines:							
Sys. 360, Mod. 20	$ 99	3.6	16,000	300–1,100	No	No	No
Sys. 360, Mod. 30	420	1.5	65,000	240–1,400	Yes	Yes	Yes
Sys. 370, Mod. 195	3,505–6,719	2 milliseconds	n.a.	2,000	Yes	Yes	Yes
Univac Div.:							
492	$ 800	4.8	327,000	1,500	Yes	Yes	Yes
1106	1,500	1.5	262,000	1,500	Yes	Yes	Yes
1110	2,000	.75	131,000	1,600	Yes	Yes	Yes

μsec = microseconds (millionths of a second).
n.a. = not available.
Source: Infosystems (formerly *Business Automation*), December, 1971, pp. 168–77.

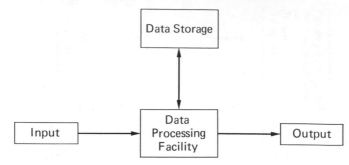

Fig. 3–8. The elements of a data processing system.

inquiry processing, and report preparation. Data processing systems differ in the degree of mechanization utilized. A system may be:

1. Manual, in which case all processing is performed by hand
2. Electromechanical, utilizing a manually operated bookkeeping or posting machine
3. Punched card, in which all input and data files are keypunched
4. Computerized, in which all processing tasks are performed by the computer

Figures 3–9 and 3–10 show representations of the relationships between the total and average costs for the different data processing methods discussed above. As you might expect, the more mechanized the process, the lower the total cost beyond a certain volume. Therefore, if

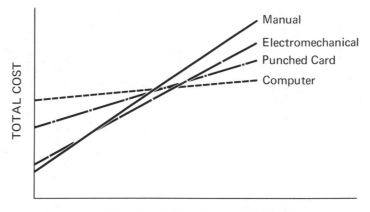

Fig. 3–9. Total costs for different data processing methods. *Source:* Gordon B. Davis, *Computer Data Processing* (New York: McGraw-Hill Book Co., 1969), p. 15.

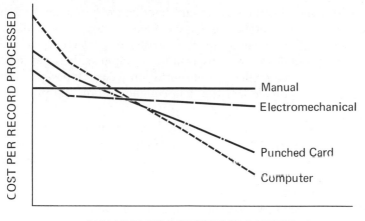

Fig. 3–10. Average cost for different data processing methods. *Source:* Same as for Fig. 3–9.

a logistics system involves a large amount of data processing, it is desirable to consider computerizing the system.

Two types of costs make up the total costs of a data processing system. Direct costs include those incurred in operating the equipment, particularly salaries, power, and certain types of equipment maintenance. Indirect costs are those associated with system design (designing data contents, establishing output formats, designing the reporting system, designing required computer systems, selecting equipment), selecting and training personnel, equipment depreciation or rental, clerical and management personnel, and other general overhead items.

Finally, as a rule of thumb, the "total cost of any information system is approximately 5½ times the hardware cost,"[11] with indirect costs accounting for approximately 36% of the total cost. **(36) If these statements are true, why is it we hear most often about the "cost of a computer?" (37) In a company with before-tax profits of about 5% of its annual sales volume of $50 million, would this knowledge lead you to be somewhat cautious about the installation of computer equipment (hardware) renting for $30,000 per month? (38) Why?**

SUMMARY

Product support and information support facilities are two major categories of fixed facilities in support of logistics activities. Product support

[11] R. L. Martino, *Management Information Systems* (Wayne, Pa.: MDI Publications, 1969), p. 51.

facilities, designed for the storage and handling of products, basically can be regarded as (1) warehouses for the receipt, storage, and distribution of products or as (2) facilities for the transfer of packaged products, bulk commodities, containers, or transportation equipment between carriers of different or the same modes of transportation. Basic types of information support facilities provide logistics data communication and processing services.

These types of fixed facilities, located and coordinated for use in conjunction with transportation services, comprise a large portion of any logistics system. They are arrayed to serve and provide the logistical link for products and information for over 2,000,000 farms, over 310,000 manufacturing and extractive (mining and related) facilities, nearly 270,000 wholesaling establishments, about 1,190,000 service establishments, and more than 1,760,000 retail establishments in the United States.[12] The number of relationships which exist among these establishments, and the quantities of goods and information moved among them, suggests the number and complexity of identifiable logistics systems in this country.

Clearly, no firm or facility can be "an island unto itself" in the general scheme of business logistics. Coordination and cooperation are more than desirable, they are essential.

SUGGESTED READINGS

ACKERMAN, KENNETH B., R. W. GARDNER, and LEE P. THOMAS. *Understanding Today's Distribution Center*. Washington, D. C.: The Traffic Service Corp., 1972.
A practical guide to the use and operation of distribution centers. Of particular interest at this point in our discussion are sections on the origins, history, and role of merchandising warehousing, establishing the distribution center, communications, and cost of warehousing.
Auerbach Guide to Data Communications. Philadelphia: Auerbach Info, Inc., 1970.
DAVIS, GORDON B. *Computer Data Processing*. New York: McGraw-Hill Book Co., 1969.
GENTLE, EDGAR C. *Data Communications in Business*. New York: Publishers Service Co., 1966.
JENKINS, CREED H. *Modern Warehouse Management*. New York: McGraw-Hill Book Co., 1968.
A good general reference on the subject.
MARTIN, JAMES. *Telecommunications and the Computer*. Englewood Cliffs, N. J.: Prentice-Hall, Inc., 1969.
MARTINO, R. L. *Management Information Systems*. Wayne, Pa.: MDI Publications, 1969.
MATHISON, STUART L., and PHILIP M. WALKER. *Computers and Telecommunications: Issues in Public Policy*. Englewood Cliffs, N. J.: Prentice-Hall, Inc., 1970.

[12] As reported by the 1967 Censuses of Manufacturers, Business, and Agriculture.

4

Transport Facilities

Transport facilities are by far the most glamorous elements of a logistics system. If you are in doubt on this point all you need do is conduct a poll of children to determine the number of young aspirants to careers as airline pilots and locomotive engineers. Compare this with the number hoping to become warehousemen or inventory controllers. To the logistician this is nonsense, of course. Performance, not appearance, is the thing.

This chapter is organized under four principal headings: (1) the structure of the transportation industry, (2) the relative magnitude of various types of transportation service, (3) cost characteristics of the various modes and methods of transportation, and (4) operating characteristics of the various modes and methods of transportation. The discussion is designed as a concise presentation of existing transport modes, legal forms of transportation, auxiliary users of transportation systems, and coordinated systems of transportation.

STRUCTURE OF THE TRANSPORTATION INDUSTRY

The five basic modes of transportation are rail, highway, water, pipeline, and air.[1] The structure of the transportation industry is based on these five modes plus a number of variations and subgroups derived from (1) their several legal forms (2) a number of auxiliary users of transportation, and (3) various modal combinations (coordinated systems). The relationships among these groups are shown in Fig. 4–1. You may wish to refer several times to this graphic presentation during the discussion which follows.

[1] Two others are conveyor and wire. As a mode of transportation, conveyors have experienced very limited growth, except within fixed facilities. Wire is not generally included in this type of discussion because of its specialized application.

93

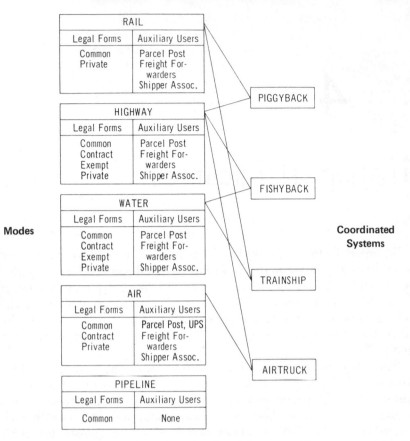

Fig. 4–1. The relationship of modes, legal forms, auxiliary users, and principal coordinated systems of transportation.

Legal Forms

The term "legal form" refers to the manner in which a transportation operation is regarded for regulatory purposes. There are four basic legal forms of transportation: common, contract, exempt, and private.[2] The

---

[2] Subtleties of legal status between, among, and within the various legal forms of transportation, if not already understood by the reader, are discussed in many of the suggested readings. You are strongly advised to familiarize yourself with them, as there are many circumstances in which an apparently "trivial legal difference" in the status of alternative transportation operations may have profound consequences for the planning and operation of a logistics system. This consideration will be touched upon at many points throughout this book.

first two are subject to economic and safety regulation by national or state regulatory bodies, ordinarily depending on whether operations cross state borders. The latter two are subject only to the safety regulations of the states through which they operate, and the cities which they serve. Common, contract, and exempt carriers are generally grouped into a category termed "for-hire" carriage.

Common carriers are the backbone of the transportation industry. They accept responsibility for carrying goods (as permitted by their operating authority) any time, any place. They are required to publish and make available to the public all rates charged for their services, which must be the same to all for a given service. The public nature of these carriers is further typified by the fact that the Interstate Commerce Commission and the Civil Aeronautics Board must first approve all rights to operate on the basis of proven "public convenience and necessity."

Contract carriers, on the other hand, make themselves available for business on a selective basis. They may charge different rates to different customers for the same service, although they are required to publish the actual rates which they charge shippers. Permits to operate in contract transportation service are issued by regulatory bodies on a basis less restrictive than that for common carriers. A permit will be specific as to commodity, routes to be used, and other characteristics of the operation.

Exempt carriage is a legal form which embraces a wide variety of transportation activities. Carriage of "unprocessed" products of agriculture and fishing is largely exempt from economic regulation, although any common carrier transporting such freight must publish its rates. Originally established to allow farmers to haul their products over public roads, the agricultural exemption has since been extended to a wider range of products.

Another class of exempt movement involves water carriers, whose cargoes are exempt from economic regulation if, among other things: (1) their cargoes are liquids being transported in tank vessels and (2) in a single ship or barge tow, not more than three commodities (in bulk) are carried. A third class of exempt carriers are those engaged in local cartage in municipalities or "commercial zones" contiguous to municipalities. Such carriers are generally exempt from federal economic regulation, and in all but a few states are exempt from economic regulation by the various state regulatory bodies. One of the principal reasons for this is the administrative near-impossibility of keeping track of the operations of so many small, local cartage operators. There are a number of other "exempt" examples including newspaper delivery trucks and hotel limousines, none of which conduct operations having any significant effect on interstate or intrastate commercial transportation.

Private transportation refers to the common ownership of goods transported and the lease or ownership of the equipment in which they are moved. This not-for-hire category allows firms to transport their own goods without facing economic regulation at the state or national level. Private transportation must be carried on as an activity incidental to the primary purpose of the business.

Freight brokers are sometimes cited as an additional legal form of transportation although the broker merely "matches" freight with carriers. He neither possesses nor operates equipment of his own. The Interstate Commerce Commission has not exercised its power to regulate brokers, leaving this to states which rely heavily on exempt carriers for agricultural commodities, the group of carriers for which freight brokers are most important.

Auxiliary Users

Auxiliary users are defined as transport agencies which purchase a major portion of their transportation from other carriers via one or more of the basic modes. They concentrate their operations on the handling of shipments of several pounds to LTL,[3] LCL, or container[4] quantities. They generally own limited amounts of long-distance transportation equipment of their own, concentrating their operations on the collecting of freight at origin and dispersion of freight at destination. While they utilize the services of other carriers for long-distance transportation, they provide a somewhat different service for shippers than carriers grouped under basic modes. Auxiliary users include the U. S. Postal Service (parcel post), United Parcel Service, freight forwarders, and shipper associations.

Parcel post service is one means of transportation commonly used by nearly everyone, yet it is frequently ignored in discussions of methods of

[3] The abbreviations LTL and LCL stand for "less than truckload" and "less than carload," respectively. These terms cannot be strictly defined. The reason is that there are no definitions of the terms "truckload" and "carload" which are meaningful to those concerned with transportation and logistics. A carload of one commodity (for tariff purposes) may be as little as 10,000 pounds; for another commodity, the minimum quantity considered a carload might be 30,000 pounds or more. In each case, any amount less than these carload (or truckload) quantities would be considered LCL or LTL freight.

[4] Containers are "boxes" of varying dimensions, constructed from a variety of materials (wood, metal, fiberglass, etc.) for the purpose of holding many small shipments or commodities in bulk. Some are designed for transfer from one carrier to another, and from one mode to another.

transporting goods. The small-quantity, low-weight nature of parcel post shipments [5] makes them eligible for shipment by any of the basic modes except pipeline (although pneumatic tubes should not be discounted as a possible method of the future). In areas of the country having limited transportation service, parcel post is even carried by water. The volume of packages handled by United Parcel Service, the nation's largest trucking company, now exceeds that of parcel post.

Freight forwarders are considered by some to be a separate legal form of transportation. This attitude derives from the fact that they are subjected to regulation similar to that for common carriers. However, freight forwarders utilize the services of other common carriers for all their long-distance shipments, accepting responsibility for shipments tendered to them by shippers. Their major function is the consolidation of small shipments into large ones. While obtaining lower line-haul rates and faster service for shippers, freight forwarders rely upon a portion of the differential between LTL and TL rates and LCL and CL rates, respectively, for revenue to defray expenses of their operation.

One well-known organization has been separately identified but in fact operates in much the same manner as a freight forwarder. This is REA Express, which has working agreements with railroads to pull its equipment, and agreements with highway, air, and water carriers for the movement of freight for which it is responsible.

Shipper associations perform much the same function as freight forwarders, but are voluntary organizations composed of several members, each of whom uses the service to take advantage of consolidation economies. These associations are the private counterparts of the "for-hire" freight forwarders.

Coordinated Systems [6]

For the purpose of this discussion, coordinated systems are defined as those offering point-to-point through-movements by means of two or more modes of transportation, on the basis of regularly scheduled operations. Modal combinations, commonly referred to as coordinated transportation services, are shown in Fig. 4–2, where each of the five modes

[5] The average weight of parcel post shipments has declined steadily from 6.3 pounds in 1950 to 4.9 pounds in 1970. See Annual Reports of the Postmaster General.

[6] Much of the material in this chapter relating to coordinated systems of transportation is adapted from Nicholas A. Glaskowsky, Jr., *An Analysis and Evaluation of the Development of Coordinated Air-Truck Transportation with Special Reference to Northwest Airlines, Inc.* (Minneapolis: School of Business Administration, University of Minnesota, 1962, Business Report No. 2), and is used with permission.

Modes of Transportation	Highway	Rail	Water	Air	Pipeline
Highway	· X	Piggyback	Fishyback	Air-truck	n.d.
Rail	Piggyback	X	Train-ship	(Sky-rail)[a]	n.d.
Water	Fishyback	Train-ship	Ship-barge[b]	(Air-barge)[a]	n.d.
Air	Air-truck	(Sky-rail)[a]	(Air-barge)[a]	X	n.d.
Pipeline	n.d.	n.d.	n.d.	n.d.	X

n.d. = Does not ordinarily meet the requirements of the definition of Coordinated Transportation Service.

[a] These combinations do not exist at the present time, and it is unlikely that they could be developed as regular commercial services.

[b] Defined as ship-to-barge or barge-to-ship, not barge-to-barge or ship-to-ship.

Fig. 4–2. Transportation coordination possibilities.

of transportation is matched against the other modes to illustrate the maximum number of types of coordinated transportation service which theoretically might be established. Each "box" contains a term which is used, or might be used, to denote that particular combination of modes.

Truck–Rail. The best known type of this combination is piggyback or trailer-on-flat-car (TOFC) service, shown in Fig. 4–2 as "piggyback." In 1960, the number of cars loaded with highway trailers and containers handled by Class I railroads in freight service was 554,115; this number increased to 1,034,377 in 1965 and 1,264,501 in 1970. (The 1970 figure represents a 6% decrease from 1969.) [7] Several types of piggyback service are made available by various rail carriers. Not all types or plans are provided by all railroads.

Plan I piggyback service allows common carrier truckers to place their highway trailers on railroad-owned flat cars. It is "substituted" service for the trucker, because trailers can be hauled only in territories where both highway and rail carriers involved have operating rights. The trucker sells the service, charges the shipper his rates, and pays the railroad a fee (based on distance) for hauling his trailers.

Plan II is an all-rail service, consisting of rail-owned trailers on rail-owned flat cars. For this service, railroads have quoted rates comparable to those of highway common carriers.

Plan II½ service is one in which the railroad supplies the equipment but the shipper performs the pickup and delivery of trailers.

[7] *Yearbook of Railroad Facts* (Washington, D. C.: Association of American Railroads, April, 1971), p. 25.

Plan III enables shippers to place their trailers or containers on rail-owned flat cars, paying a flat rate (based on distance) to have them hauled either loaded or empty.

Plan IV requires shippers to provide not only highway vehicles or containers, but also the rail cars on which the equipment is placed. In effect, the shipper pays the railroad a distance fee for pulling his equipment loaded or empty.

Plan V is a system built around the quotation of joint rates (rates quoted by two or more carriers) for truck–rail–truck service. Both the highway and rail carriers participating in such a joint agreement haul the vehicle through the territory for which each has rights, even though one or more of the participating carriers may not have rights in a particular area. In effect, it allows each carrier to extend his operating rights into the area served by the other. Each may originate shipments for the other, and typically both sell the coordinated service. The participating carriers then divide the revenue paid for the through service.

In total, Plans II and II½ comprise over 70% of all TOFC volume. The latter plan has been by far the fastest growing in recent years.

Truck–Water. Coordinated truck and water service, referred to in Fig. 4–2 as "fishyback," includes coordination of truck movements with water movement on coastal and intercoastal routes, as well as on inland waterways, the Great Lakes, and between West Coast ports and ports in Hawaii and Alaska. One type of system makes use of roll-on, roll-off ships, while another uses large container cargo boxes and specially constructed container-carrying ships.

Truck–Air. This service is the newest combination to be offered to shippers. It was first established in 1957 by a single air carrier in cooperation with a number of trucking firms. It is now widely available throughout the United States.

Rail–Water. Rail–water coordination is shown in Fig. 4–2 as "train-ship." It has been offered to shippers for many years. East Coast and Gulf Coast rail–water service involves the use of specially constructed ships on which strings of loaded freight cars are placed and then moved over water to the port nearest their ultimate inland destination.

Ship–Barge. This type of system is found most frequently in the shipment of bulk commodity cargoes such as coal, grain, wine, petroleum, and lumber. With the increasing use of cargo containers in maritime transportation, it is probable that future developments of this type of service will include increased numbers of containerized shipments of mixed dry cargo.

Pipeline Combinations.   Because combinations of two modes of transportation, one of which is pipeline, almost always involve bulk storage in transit at a terminal and transfer from one type of vehicle to another, this series of combinations does not come within the meaning of the definition of coordinated transportation service given earlier.

Containerization.   Containerization is the packing of goods of like or unlike characteristics in an enclosed box to eliminate rehandling of materials in their transportation from point to point. Containers are commonly fitted with fixtures which allow them to be transferred easily from vehicles of one mode of transportation to those of another. As such, containerization is necessary to the full development of the potential of most coordinated transportation services.

Containers have generally provided their users with: (1) lower handling costs (resulting in lower freight rates), (2) lower in-transit insurance costs, (3) reduction of product damage in transit, and (4) the reduction or elimination of pilferage during shipment. To date, these advantages have been offset somewhat by the cost of containers, the general lack of adequate facilities for handling them, and the problem of the return of empty containers to a point of reuse. Containerization, in common with other labor-saving methods of transportation, has been delayed in some sections of the country by labor union reluctance to change working rules which would allow their use.

Containers are currently used in all modes of transportation except pipeline. They range in size from a small box (airline type-E container) to the largest standard container, which is 8′ × 8′ × 40′ (commonly used in rail, ocean, and truck movements). By agreement among shippers and carriers, large intermodal containers have been standardized with external dimensions of eight feet in width and height, and lengths of ten, twenty, thirty, and forty feet.

A listing of products containerized indicates the ability of containers to serve in the handling and transportation of a wide range of products. Some of these are household goods, machinery, soap, paint, wheels and axles, pre-cut houses, citrus concentrates, ice creams, wearing apparel, plastics, chemicals, letter mail, dry ice, baggage, and CARE materials. One aircraft manufacturer has even reported the early use of containers in the transportation and handling of huge vertical tail stabilizers for its jet transport aircraft.[8]

Containers are replacing other types of equipment, particularly the highway trailer, in coordinated transportation. It is likely that many of

[8] Norton Wood, "Meeting the Problems of Warehousing, Inventory Control, and Production Planning," *Transportation & Distribution Management*, April, 1962, pp. 22–27.

the trailer-on-flat-car movements made today will eventually be converted to container-on-flat-car movements. The development of detachable axles and other features have made this possible. Further economic reasons for this substitution include: (1) elimination of multistate highway licensing, (2) special routing requirements caused by limited clearances for piggyback trailers, (3) off-balance load characteristics and high center of gravity of trailers on flat cars, (4) lower train speeds required by unbalanced trailer loads, and (5) equipment purchase savings. Some of these same economic savings dictate the current and future use of containers in other forms of coordinated transportation as well.

Summary

Only combinations of two modes have been considered in this discussion. In some cases, three or more modes may be involved in a coordinated transportation movement. For example, a popular combination now in existence involves ocean–truck–rail; this has become possible with the development of ocean vessels and material-handling equipment capable of loading and unloading containers from ocean vessels to motor vehicles. However, lack of communication and organization among carriers has restricted the availability of coordinated systems utilizing more than two modes.

RELATIVE SIZE OF INDUSTRY COMPONENTS

Only several of the many measures of the relative importance of transportation services are considered in this section. Where revenue or weight–distance statistics are not available, other measures are presented.

Modes

Statistics related to trends in revenues received by all regulated and non-regulated transportation activities are presented in Table 4–1. Trends in the relative importance of regulated transport are shown by mode in Table 4–2. In the discussion which follows, repeated reference will be made to figures drawn from these tables.

Rail. Historically, rail carriers have accounted for the largest percentage of the freight tonnage moved within the United States. The ability of the railroads to transport large quantities of freight efficiently over long distances is the primary factor which has provided them their current share of transport business. Even this has not prevented the

TABLE 4-1. Estimated Revenue Generated in All Domestic Freight
Transportation, by Methods, 1960, 1965, and 1971

	1960		1965		1971	
	Millions of Dollars	Percentage of Total	Millions of Dollars	Percentage of Total	Millions of Dollars	Percentage of Total[a]
Highway:						
Truck–intercity:						
ICC-regulated	$ 7,214	16.2%	$10,068	16.7%	$16,800	17.6%
Non-ICC-regulated	10,744	24.2	13,560	22.5	21,690	22.6
Truck–local	14,289	32.2	23,041	38.2	41.103	43.0
Bus	42	.1	70	.1	125	.1
Subtotal	32,289	72.7	46,739	77.5	79,718	83.0
Railroads	9,028	20.3	9,923	16.5	11,650	12.2
Water:						
Coastal, intercoastal	747	1.7	692	1.2	752	.8
Inland waterways	312	.7	381	.6	525	.5
Great Lakes	227	.5	213	.4	210	.2
Locks, channels, etc.	287	.7	391	.6	385	.4
Subtotal	1,573	3.6	1,677	2.8	1,872	2.0
Oil Pipeline:						
ICC-regulated	770	1.7	904	1.5	1,247	1.3
Non-ICC-regulated	125	.3	147	.2	238	.2
Subtotal	895	2.0	1,051	1.7	1,485	1.5
Air (Domestic)	220	.5	428	.7	758	.8
Other Carriers:						
Forwarders and						
REA Express	393	.9	470	.8	428	.4
Total	$44,398	100.0%[b]	$60,288	100.0%[b]	$95,911	100.0%[b]

[a]Preliminary TAA estimate.
[b]Totals of percentages may not add exactly due to rounding.
Source: Transportation Facts and Trends (Washington, D. C.: Transportation Association of America). Various annual editions, and the October, 1972, Quarterly Supplement.

railroads' share of total for-hire and private intercity freight tonnage from falling from 56.2% in 1950 to 44.1% in 1960 and to 38.7% in 1971. The railroads' share of freight revenues registered an even greater decline during the same period, indicating a loss of high-revenue freight movements to other modes.

TABLE 4-2. Distribution of Domestic For-Hire and Private Freight
Transportation, By Mode, 1960 and 1971

	Ton-Mile Distribution Among For-Hire and Private Freight Carriers				
	1960		1971		Percentage Change in Volume, 1971 vs. 1960
Mode	Billions of Ton-Miles	Percentage of Total	Billions of Ton-Miles	Percentage of Total	
Railroad	579.0	44.1%	744.0	38.7%	+ 28.8%
Highway	285.0	21.8	422.0	21.9	+ 67.7
Great Lakes	99.0	7.5	104.0	5.4	+ 4.3
Rivers and canals	121.0	9.2	205.0	10.7	+ 70.0
Oil pipelines	229.0	17.4	444.0	23.1	+ 93.8
Air	.9	.1	3.5	.2	+288.0
Totals*	1,314.0	100.0%	1,923.0	100.0%	+ 43.5%

	Revenue Distribution Among For-Hire and Private Freight Carriers				
	1960		1971		Percentage Change in Revenue, 1971 vs. 1960
Mode	Gross Operative Revenue (Billions)	Percentage of Total	Gross Operative Revenue (Billions)	Percentage of Total	
Railroad	$ 9,028	20.5%	$11,650	12.2%	+ 29.2%
Highway	32,289	73.3	79,718	83.4	+146.5
Great Lakes	227	.5	210	.2	− 7.2
Rivers and canals	1,346	3.1	1,662	1.7	+ 23.5
Oil pipelines	895	2.0	1,485	1.5	+ 65.5
Air	220	.6	1,758	.8	+244.0
Totals*	$44,129	100.0%	$95,473	100.0%	+116.0%

*Totals may not add exactly due to rounding.

Source: Same as for Table 4-1. These figures exclude ton-miles and revenues realized by
other (auxiliary) carriers such as freight forwarders and REA Express.

Highway. During the past thirty years, highway carriers have developed from one-truck operations serving limited requirements into
large carriers, several with revenues in excess of $200 million annually.
During the last decade the route structures of individual motor carrier firms, once limited to regional coverage, have expanded to become
transcontinental in coverage. The flexibility of highway transportation,

ranging from coast-to-coast operations to city delivery movements, has given motor carriers an inherent advantage in many spheres of competition with railroads. The regulated motor carriers have increased their share of the total revenues from regulated transportation from 29.4% in 1950 to 53.1% in 1971 (representing more than a fourfold increase in revenue). When both regulated and non-regulated transportation are taken into consideration, as in Table 4–1, the overwhelming importance of highway transportation is clear. In 1971, local and intercity highway transportation accounted for about 83% of all revenue generated in freight transportation activities in the United States. This compares with 72.7% in 1960.

Water.   Water carriers have been faced with the problems of restrictions on automation on the waterfront, wage increases in excess of those granted to other transportation industries, and selective rate cutting by competing modes of transportation. Great Lakes traffic (excluding international shipping) has fallen in importance while inland-waterways, coastwise, and intercoastal (Atlantic-to-Gulf-to-Pacific) carriers have increased their share.

Pipelines.   Pipeline carriers significantly increased their share of total transportation ton-miles during the period from 1960 to 1971. The number of pipelines has increased basically because of the need for economical volume movement systems for fluids and solids in hydraulic suspension. This demand has justified the expansion of existing facilities, and extensions to new areas where pipelines were not considered feasible as recently as 1950.

Air.   Air freight has shown the most significant increase in the percentage of tonnage during the same period. This might be expected for a previously undeveloped service with important inherent advantages of service.

You can draw further comparisons from Table 4–2, which shows the changes in volume and revenues realized by each of the modes from 1960 to 1971.

Legal Forms

Common and contract carriage, those forms falling under the economic regulation of national and state agencies, have declined in shares of revenue generated, according to the information in Table 4–1. The shares of private and exempt carriage have increased accordingly. It is estimated that in 1950, 49.8% of transportation revenue was generated by common and contract carriers. This had fallen to 40.1% by 1960 and 34.1% in 1971.[9] A major portion of this drop can be attributed to the growth of highway transportation, largely private and exempt in nature. This growth has taken place largely at the expense of rail transportation.

Auxiliary Users

Parcel post shipments approximated 2.1 million tons in 1969. The revenue derived from this activity totalled nearly $704 million in fiscal 1969, or about 2.4% of the total paid to regulated carriers in calendar 1969. The general trend in the importance of parcel post in relation to total revenues has been downward, reflecting competition from private small-shipment services.

Freight forwarders reporting to the Interstate Commerce Commission in 1969 recorded a continued increase in their relative importance with revenues of over $591 million, or 2.1% of total regulated carrier freight revenues in 1969; over half of this amount was realized by just three forwarders. In addition, REA Express handled shipments which returned it $341 million in 1969, or nearly 1.3% of total revenues received by regulated carriers.

Freight assembled and distributed by shippers' associations has been increasing rapidly in volume in recent years, although no statistics have been collected on the nature and volume of this traffic.

It should be kept in mind that the revenue figures reported above for auxiliary users are gross revenues. Much of this money was subsequently paid to common carriers for services hired from them. Of freight forwarder revenue, for example, typically more than 70% is paid for long-haul transportation service. And, of course, local pickup and delivery charges must be paid to carriers by the forwarder (if he does not furnish such services himself) to the extent that they are not included in the rates for a long-haul transportation company's services.

Coordinated Systems

Statistics for most coordinated transportation operations are obscured in currently collected data. They are "divided" among participating modes because of the systems of reporting required by the Interstate

---

[9] Based on the assumptions that all of ICC-regulated highway, bus, railroad, and pipeline; domestic air; other carrier; and about 10% of water carrier revenues are earned in regulated transport.

Commerce Commission and Civil Aeronautics Board. However, all indications are that the use of these services is growing steadily. More and more are being instituted each year, with the greatest growth in volume in the past decade being experienced by piggyback service.

COST CHARACTERISTICS

Similar to any industrial or service activity, total transportation cost is a combination of fixed and variable costs. Fixed costs in transportation can be defined as expenses which do not vary with the amount of service that is offered. It can generally be assumed that expenses such as equipment and facility depreciation and taxes are fixed. Variable costs can be defined as those expenses which vary directly with the amount of service offered by a carrier. Transportation expenses that can be considered variable include, but are not limited to, fuel and labor.

The fixed and variable costs of the modes of transportation vary considerably. Within each mode there are borderline situations where a "cost element" is partly fixed and partly variable. The relationship between fixed and variable cost also may vary as the volume of activity changes. Also, whether a cost is fixed or variable depends upon the time period involved, because in the long run all costs are variable.

The analyses which follow are based on cost estimates in the short run. The short run is defined as a period of time which does not permit large-scale additions or deletions of facilities, which might change the nature of a cost element from fixed to variable.

Modes

The relationship between fixed and variable costs in each of the five modes of transportation is shown graphically in Fig. 4–3. The break-even point graphs in Fig. 4–3 are not intended to portray particular firms, or even composites or averages. They are generalizations which indicate the degree of sensitivity of each of the modes to variations in traffic volume. For example, variations in traffic volume resulting in the operation of the firm above or below the break-even point have a much greater effect on the profits (or losses) of a railroad than would be the case with a trucking firm. Risk, in this sense of the term, varies directly with the proportion of fixed costs encountered in providing the transportation service. This is why the performance of railroads is particularly vulnerable to economic recession.

Pipeline. The fixed costs of pipeline operations include interest on land acquired or rights purchased for construction of the pipeline, de-

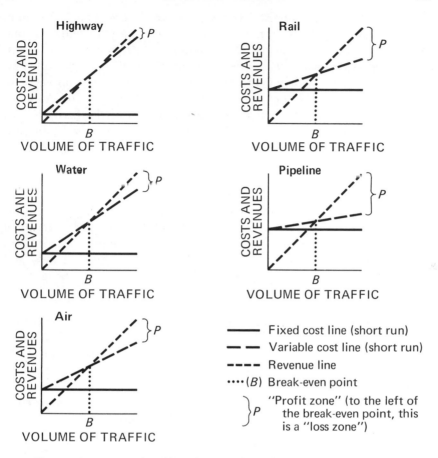

Fig. 4–3. Generalized break-even charts for five modes of carriers.

preciation of the cost of construction of the line itself, and depreciation charges against costs of constructing necessary terminals and pumping stations. Because of these large fixed cost elements, and others such as property taxes, pipelines have the greatest percentage of fixed costs of operation of any of the modes of transportation.

Rail. In the railroad industry, the requirements for extensive fixed facilities, including land for rights-of-way, yards, and terminals, make fixed costs a relatively high percentage of total cost. This extensive resource of fixed facilities permits the rail carrier to operate long trains with a minimum of motive power and manpower in relation to the volume of tonnage moved, but it also results in rail fixed costs being higher as a proportion of total costs than those of any other mode except pipeline.

Air. Although the largest jet transports cost more than $20 million apiece, airline fixed costs do not represent as large a percentage of total cost as in the railroad industry. An important contributing factor in this relationship is the fact that almost all terminal facilities are provided by local communities (with federal government support), and airways are established, maintained, and operated by the Federal Aviation Administration. This relieves air carriers of a good portion of the fixed costs of their operations. Further, a portion of fixed costs is converted into variable costs due to the fact that airplanes must pay user taxes and landing fees to help maintain the terminal facilities.

Water. The fixed costs of water transportation as a percentage of total cost are in most cases less than those of the airlines, although greater than those of highway carriers. Large bulk and dry cargo terminal facilities essential to water movement are most commonly leased from port authorities or other administrative bodies. Navigational aids and waterway improvement and maintenance are provided by the government.

Highway. Contrasted with railroads and pipelines, the truck operator has a relatively small investment in terminal facilities and operates truck and trailer units over publicly owned highways instead of privately owned rights-of way. Contrasted with rail, air, and water carriers, equipment investment depreciation is not as large an element in trucking costs. These two factors combine to give trucking the lowest fixed costs as a percentage of total costs of any mode of transportation.

The total costs of transportation by the various modes are reflected by the average rates charged for services, shown in Table 4–3. In 1971, these ranged from .20¢ per ton-mile for transportation on the Great Lakes to 22.61¢ per ton-mile for air freight service. Notice too the relative trends in the rates charged by the various modes. (1) **Does this help explain any of the trends you observed in Table 4–2? How?**

Legal Forms

Cost comparisons between legal forms of transportation vary with consideration of the various modes which may make up each form. A comparison of costs for the legal forms of highway transportation, however, should serve to provide representative relationships which apply to other modes as well.

Common carrier costs serve as the standard against which those of other legal forms are compared. In comparison, costs of contract and exempt carriage are significantly lower because of the inherent differ-

TABLE 4–3. Estimated Revenue per Ton-Mile on For-Hire and
Private Intercity Transportation, By Mode,
1960 and 1971

Mode	1960	1971
Railroad (Class I)	1.40¢	1.59¢
Highway (Class I)	6.31	8.00
Great Lakes	.23	.20
Rivers and canals	.26	.22
Oil pipelines	.32	.28
Air	22.80	22.61

Sources: Same as for Table 4–1; data in Table 4–2.

ence in their operations. By the latter two forms, most freight moves in truckload quantities, thus requiring no terminal facilities for its handling. On the other hand, common carriers incurred $7.19 terminal cost per ton of freight handled over terminal docks in 1970, compared to an average cost of $18.11 per ton for over-the-road, local transportation, and equipment maintenance.[10] Based on partial reports to the Interstate Commerce Commission, it is likely that common carriers obtain about one-half of their revenue from LTL shipments (defined in this case as shipments of less than 10,000 pounds).

Costs of private transportation are subject to considerable differences of interpretation. In comparison with common carrier transportation, private costs can be significantly lower if the equipment can be utilized in a balanced, or two-directional, haul, if it moves in truckload quantities, and under certain other conditions discussed later. Not all private transportation operations meet these low-cost requirements.

Auxiliary Users

The major operating cost of auxiliary users, the amount of money spent for transportation services bought from intercity carriers, largely is variable with volume. The amount spent per unit of freight shipped will, of course, vary with the type of service utilized. It is difficult to generalize on the nature of costs of auxiliary users, but two characteristics of the freight handled by parcel post and REA Express tend to make this a relatively high-cost method of transportation. These services deal in freight moving in particularly small quantities. In addition, REA Express freight moves on an expedited basis via the various modes which it utilizes.

[10] *American Trucking Trends* (Washington, D. C.: American Trucking Associations, Inc., 1972), pp. 24 and 26.

Coordinated Systems

The costs of operation of a coordinated transportation system ordinarily will be less than if the movement were made entirely by the more costly component mode, and more than if the movement were made entirely by the less costly component mode. Thus the pattern of costs of each of the several types of coordinated systems is, in effect, a compromise.

This "difference splitting" cost relationship holds true in regard to piggyback, fishyback, rail–water, and air–truck services almost without exception and it has been a key reason for the success of these services.

OPERATING CHARACTERISTICS OF
TRANSPORTATION SERVICES

Operating characteristics include the dependability, speed, frequency, and availability of service, and the operational capabilities of various transportation services. These, in combination with cost, are the considerations which are relevant to most users of each method.

Dependability of service is measured in terms of performance according to published or promised schedules. It may be subjected to influences over which carriers have no control such as storms, winter ice, floods, or snow. Speed refers to the total door-to-door time required to move goods from point of origin to point of destination. Frequency of service designates the number of schedules or units (trains, trucks, airplanes) moving between city pairs during a given period of time. It concerns local pickup and delivery only insofar as this affects the ability of the shipper to take advantage of intercity schedules.

The ability to handle out-size, fragile, frozen, liquid, explosive, perishable, or easily contaminated goods is an indication of the operational capabilities of a particular transportation service. This ability, resulting from the inherent nature of a shipper to offer special services, is also included here. Availability refers to the number of geographical points to and from which a shipper can obtain a given service. The term can be applied in reference to both a town or city in the broader sense, or to a specific facility site within a community.

Throughout the discussion to follow, it should be remembered that the characteristics are presented in a general manner which is intended to provide an acquaintance with the various services, some of which are rarely considered for particular freight movements. These characteristics will not apply to every situation; services may compare differently in specific situations. However, through the comparative analysis which follows, it is possible to present general relationships among the various modes.

Modes

In any particular situation, the characteristics of the points involved, volume of movement, terrain, or other factors may materially change comparisons of the operating characteristics of modes of transportation. While each service characteristic will be considered singly for simplicity, an actual selection process would involve the comparison of two or more modes by taking all characteristics into account simultaneously.

Dependability of Service. Shippers typically rate dependability of service higher than all other factors, except possibly cost, in selecting modes of transportation. Dependability is thought of most often as the percentage deviation from the normal or promised performance which occurs often enough to inconvenience a shipper to a significant degree. Thus, a steamship company whose vessels are often one day late on scheduled 33-day voyages would be considered "more dependable" by a shipper than an airline which is frequently one day late with a shipment schedule for 24-hour movement. The absolute deviation in each example is one day, but the percentage deviations are 3% and 100% respectively.

A 1957 survey of shippers indicated that "reasonable reliability" on a given movement did not necessarily mean performance exactly as scheduled. These men were asked the question, "How much leeway, in general, should be allowed before a carrier should be considered as not having performed reliably?" Their answers are shown in Table 4-4.

Pipeline. Pipelines are in a class of their own with regard to service dependability. In relation to the amount of tonnage transported, there is no equal to the efficiency and dependability of the pipeline facility.

Highway. Dependability, for the purposes of this discussion, depends on both controllable and non-controllable factors. The motor carrier is vulnerable to non-controllable factors which may inhibit performance and dependability. The primary non-controllable factor which affects motor carrier dependability is weather. Few motor carriers have the authority to select or change routes depending upon weather conditions as can ocean vessels and aircraft.

One of the elements which makes motor carriers more dependable than the modes discussed below is that they depend upon relatively few people (principally drivers) in order to accomplish effective performance. On a truckload movement from Cleveland, Ohio, to Houston, Texas, where a sleeper cab operation is used, the dependability of the motor carrier service will depend upon the two drivers and their ability to

**TABLE 4–4. Acceptable Levels of Transport Dependability,
as Expressed by Shippers**

Difference in Promised and Actual Performance	Percentage of Respondents*
10% leeway (percentage deviation)	46%
10–15% leeway	9
15–20% leeway	11
20–30% leeway	9
Over 30% leeway	9
Variable, depending on time of advertised schedule	12
Delivery during hours of promised day	5
	100%

*Percentages do not add to 100 because of rounding.

Source: "What Is Transport Reliability?," *Railway Freight Traffic*, November, 1957, pp. 21–22.

perform over a period of time. By comparison, a rail carload shipment between these points must depend upon adequate performance by literally hundreds of people in the organizations of several rail carriers in order to accomplish the same movement.

Air. Air transportation has shown the most marked improvements in service dependability of all modes in recent years, due primarily to: (1) the introduction of jet-powered aircraft with lower maintenance requirements and more dependable operating characteristics, and (2) the installation of terminal electronic systems which permit aircraft operations in all but the very worst weather. It now remains for air freight organizations to improve ground handling operations to match improvements in "line-haul" activities if the dependability of air freight service is to be increased even further.

Rail. The basic reason for the past lack of dependability among rail carriers is that there has been too much volume for the "bottleneck" points of the railroad system. This important fact has, in the minds of most of the public, been obscured by frequent references to "our excess rail capacity" and "unnecessary duplication of rail facilities." These references are true only in regard to main-line trackage; they are misleading if applied to factors of capacity and efficiency of terminals and classification yards. However, as new "electronic" classification yards are built, and as some traffic such as piggyback bypasses classification yards entirely, the bottleneck points of the rail system of the country are steadily being reduced in number and effect.

In recent years, many major railroads have established extensive car reporting systems with the objective of providing shippers with fast, accurate information on the location and movement of individual freight cars. These systems are known by various names—"Tops," "Coin," "Clic," "Carfax," and others.

Water. The dependability of inland-waterway, intercoastal, and coastwise water carriers is restricted primarily by uncertainties connected with the loading and unloading of the vessels and the non-controllable element of weather. Their dependability can also be adversely affected by tides and currents.

Speed. *Air.* No other mode of transportation even approaches the "block to block" speed of aircraft.[11] An air freight shipment picked up in midtown New York in the afternoon can easily be delivered in Los Angeles the following morning. In contrast, an LTL shipment could take 10 to 12 days to move from New York to Los Angeles.

The "speed" of air movements does not exceed that of all other modes of transportation in all cases, however. Consider a shipment from Berkeley, California, to Los Angeles, picked up in the afternoon. Allowing for pickup and delivery requirements and airport terminal handling at each end of the move, an air carrier would make delivery of this shipment the next morning in Los Angeles. However, a reasonably well managed highway common carrier or piggyback service can match this schedule, and many do. The two situations discussed in this section serve to illustrate that speed is relative to the points to be served.

Truck. Many modern tractor-trailer units can travel at a speed of 60 mph on a dual-lane, controlled-access interstate highway. Allowing for fuel stops, meals, mountain driving, etc., a block speed of 35 mph can be achieved. The twenty-four-hour operation of trucks is a functional reality and is achieved either through the use of sleeper cabs, where one driver is driving the truck while the other driver is sleeping in a special compartment above and behind the driver's seat, or by "relays" of drivers domiciled at spaced intervals along a trucking company's routes.

The transit time for truck movement depends in part on whether the movement is a less than truckload or truckload shipment. A truckload shipment can be scheduled to move from the loading to unloading points without the necessity of terminal delays.

---

[11] The term "block to block" (sometimes expressed as "block time") refers to the time interval between the time the aircraft leaves its loading gate at one airport until it arrives at its unloading gate at another airport. "Block speed" is therefore block distance divided by block time. These concepts are critical to transportation operations scheduling, as is well known by anyone who has ever personally experienced frustrating delays in airport holding patterns, buses in city traffic, and ships maneuvering in a harbor.

Less than truckload shipments usually involve pickups by a local service truck, unloading and dock handling at the origin terminal facility, loading into the line-haul vehicle and line-haul movement to the destination terminal, line-haul vehicle unloading, dock handling, and reloading to a local delivery truck for final delivery to the ultimate destination of the shipment. Some truck movements involve several line-haul changes of equipment which result in handling of shipments at several terminals. Such a shipment would be characterized by distances in excess of 1,000 miles.

Relative speeds of TL and LTL service are governed by distances involved and the competitiveness of the market as well. Measured in relation to the transit time for a truckload shipment, it would not be unusual for a transcontinental LTL shipment passing through several terminals to take as much as four or five days longer than a TL shipment between the same points. In contrast, for example, it is typical for LTL shipments to be picked up in San Francisco at four o'clock Tuesday afternoon, transported 450 miles, and delivered in the Los Angeles area by ten o'clock Wednesday morning, equal to either air or TL service between these points.

Rail. The average speed of freight trains, including stops for switching, pickup, and "setting out" of cars was 20.1 mph in 1970.[12] However, this figure does not take into account delays of cars in railroad classification yards and terminals. Thus, the overall "speed" of rail movement is something less than the figure given above. A "normal" or "average" time for movement of a carload of freight from San Francisco to New York City is about ten days, whereas the figure of 20.1 mph, divided into the rail distance of 3,200 miles between these two cities, would yield a transit time estimate of just a little less than seven days. The latter figure is obtainable only in the case of special merchandise express movements, particularly the movement of perishables in "fruit express" trains.

Water. When moving goods or materials by water, speed cannot be an important factor. There are exceptions to this general statement which arise when the commodities moved by water are necessary for timely continuation of production activities. Usually, however, where water transportation is used, the replenishment cycle is such that the commodity is stored for some time and in some quantity before its use. The speed of water vessels ranges from a low of 2 miles per hour for barges moving "upstream" against strong currents to 20 knots for the modern ocean freighters in coastwise service. The speed of the vessel while "underway" is not the only determinant of transit time. It is necessary to determine

---

[12] *Yearbook of Railroad Facts, op. cit.,* p. 43.

and allow for the number of stops or delays required to remove barges from a tow or to stop at intermediate ports-of-call to discharge cargo.

Pipeline. Pipeline tonnage moves at slow rates of speed varying from 1 to 5 mph. However, during a 24-hour period, a large pipeline can transport a stream of as much as a million barrels of product past a given point. Though the slowest "moving" form of transportation, pipelines are not subject to many of the delays which affect movements of other modes.

Frequency of Service

Pipelines. Pipelines run quietly, day and night, with the only interruption being infrequent repair on a part of the line. A pipeline is thus almost always operating and available for use. It therefore ranks as the transportation mode which offers the greatest amount of frequency, although an individual shipper may have to wait his turn until his "tender" can be accepted.

Highway. As a generalization, it can be stated that between most points trucks are dispatched more frequently than aircraft. This relationship varies between city pairs; it would be more likely to be true for origin and destination pairs of smaller size.

Air. Relatively frequent air freight service is available from most major cities through the use of passenger planes to carry "belly cargo," although such methods may seriously restrict shipment or container sizes. The use of all-cargo aircraft, operated in so-called "freighter service," with a much greater range of shipment-carrying capability, is restricted to relatively few major cities. The replacement of smaller with larger passenger aircraft such as the 747, DC 10, and L 1011 has, in some cases, reduced the frequency of service for air freight operations.

Rail. Although rail service is generally considered to be available on a once-a-day basis, it is also frequently available twice a day (morning and afternoon "switches"). Even if the rail carrier provides daily service to a shipper's siding, this by itself is of little significance unless, when the car reaches its first classification or marshalling yard, there are frequent departures from that point. The same applies to other points of rail classification and interchange which are included in the movement. It is not unusual for a car to arrive at a classification yard and then remain there for a period of 24 hours until a train leaves for the car's next destination point.

Water. Because of the large capacity of water-borne vessels and their limited number (in relation to the number of units or vehicles used by other modes of transportation), the frequency of movement by water is less than that available from the other modes of transportation. Another factor which impedes the frequency of water movement is the speed of the vessel itself. Because it is slower than the other modes of transportation, it is restricted to fewer "turn-arounds," or round trips, in the service it renders. Inland waterway frequency is greater than intercoastal and coastwise transportation because there are more units or vessels per ton of freight to be moved.

Commodity Movement Capability

Water. The inland waterway barge is the most "capable" unit of transportation available. Any type or size of shipment which is transportable in any sense can be moved on a barge. Barge movement is generally considered economically feasible only in those situations where multiples of barges can be moved at the same time. Nevertheless, as a vehicle the barge is the most capable unit for transport. Because of design features, Great Lakes and coastwise vessels are less capable than the barge.

Rail. Rail carriers are less capable than water and ocean carriers because of the necessity of unitizing shipments into the standard length, height, and width limitations of rail car equipment.

Highway. Motor carriers are considered to be less capable than rail carriers because of equipment limitations and the limitations of highway regulations governing the loaded weight and movement of trucks.

Air. Aircraft capabilities are determined (and limited) by the lift capacity of the aircraft and the tight space and design limitations of the fuselage of the aircraft, which are quite limited even when compared to highway trailers. However, with the advent of the new wide-body jets, the capability of aircraft appears to be increasing. For example, a Boeing 747F has cargo capacity of 23,890 cubic feet and 218,500 pounds.[13]

Pipelines. Pipelines are restricted to the movement of liquid commodities, or commodities which can be placed in hydraulic suspension.

---

[13] D. H. Reeher, *The Domestic Air Freight Industry and Introduction of Large Subsonic Transports* (Falls Church, Va.: Independent Research Program, Analytic Services, Inc., August, 1967), p. 100.

As indicated previously, the pipeline has the ability to transport enormous volumes of tonnage in a given day, and in that sense, it is an extremely capable system of transport. However, in terms of the ability to transport any commodity, it lacks capability.

Availability of Service

In the discussion which follows each mode is evaluated as to the availability of its service without considering the possibilities of coordinating it with other modes of transportation. For example, air freight "service" is "available" to and from many very small towns, but only as a result of its being coordinated with truck service. This type of "availability" will be discussed in detail in a later section of the chapter.

Highway. It has been suggested that the primary attribute of the motor carrier, and the chief reason for the spectacular growth of this mode, is its ability to render door-to-door service. With the exception of remote locations, inaccessible by any means other than light aircraft or boats, highway service is available to practically every shipper. There is a wide gap between the extent of the availability of motor carrier service and the availability of any other mode of transportation.

Rail. Rail service is available at any city, town, or other place served by a rail route. However, unless the shipper has a rail siding at his plant or place of business, it will be necessary for him to use public team tracks at the railroad freight station to load or unload his freight. Less-than-carload shipments by rail must be picked up and delivered by truck between the shipper's place of business and the railroad freight house.

Air. The areas encompassed by the local freight pickup and delivery services of the airlines at air terminal cities cover only a small fraction of the land area of the United States. However, within these areas are concentrated many present and potential users of air freight service; thus the availability of this service is not quite so limited as it might first appear.

Water. The availability of water transportation is highly deceptive. One glance at a map of the United States will show that most cities are not served by water transportation. However, there is a concentration along inland waterways, on the Great Lakes, and at coastal locations of shippers whose products or raw materials are particularly suited to water transportation. Thus the availability of water transportation to shippers particularly desirous of using it is greater than might at first seem likely.

The development of the inland waterway system has been remarkable. A recent achievement of this effort was the opening of the port connecting Tulsa, Oklahoma, to the great ports of the world via a navigable inland waterway. It has been estimated that fully 90% of the markets of the United States, measured in terms of population, now lie within 50 miles of a navigable waterway.

Unlike any other mode of transportation, there is one special situation which affects only water carriers operating on certain northern inland waterways and the Great Lakes in the wintertime. These routes are frozen during a part of the year and therefore are not usable during that period.

Pipeline. Because of the nature of pipeline facilities, they are generally available to move large shipments of bulk liquid or gas between major terminal points only. Further distribution and delivery of these products often must be made by other carriers. For these reasons, pipelines must be considered to be the least "available" of any of the modes of transportation. They require the greatest relative amount of fixed capital investment and therefore are not constructed to serve points unless there is literally a long-term guarantee that large quantities of liquid or gas products will be moved between such points.

Legal Forms

No attempt will be made to rank legal forms within each of the characteristics discussed above. Instead, considerations necessary to evaluate each form will be presented.

Operating characteristics have no relevance for a discussion of legal forms unless the discussion is limited to a single mode, understanding that the relative nature of the various legal forms within all modes is somewhat the same. Because highway transportation provides the best example of a mode operated under all legal forms, it will be used again for discussion purposes.

Dependability of Service. Dependability is a function of control and responsibility. In this respect, private transportation methods must once again be considered the most dependable, assuming proper maintenance of equipment and normal operator capability.

Among other forms, common carrier transportation is most competitive (on a day-to-day basis, at least) and most likely to offer dependable service on a short-run basis. This is not necessarily true for a contract carrier operating on a long-run arrangement. Dependability of service is subject to negotiation only periodically for these carriers. On the other hand, many contract carriers serve fewer than five shippers, thus placing great emphasis on the need to continue dependable service for every one of their customers. Exempt carriers, especially those hauling exempt commodities by highway, have gained a reputation for unreliable service. This has been attributed to poor maintenance of equipment, limited facilities for communication, and underfinancing of operations. These faults obviously do not apply to all exempt carriers.

Speed.   Private transportation offers the potential for the greatest speed in service of all forms. Whether the potential is realized for a given shipment is up to the shipper–owner. The potential in this case results not only from the tendency to haul truckload (or vehicle load) quantities and to have available a completely tailored service, but also from the direct control which the shipper has over the shipment in transit.

Contract, exempt, and vehicle-load common-carrier transportation all offer roughly comparable potential for service speed. Less-than-vehicle-load common-carrier transportation, involving the consolidation of as many as 150 shipments into one vehicle, one or more long-distance hauls, one or more "sorting" operations at terminals en route, and end-of-haul distribution, requires a greater amount of time to accomplish a movement.

Frequency of Service.   Theoretically, there is no limit on frequency of service provided by private transportation. Financial limitations may restrict the number of vehicles a firm can afford to own. Once dispatched, the physical limitations of time required for an out-haul plus a return would place restrictions on the availability of a piece of equipment for subsequent movement. Depending on financial limits, therefore, private transportation frequency can range from very high to very low.

In general, common carriage offers the most frequent schedules in that more intercity hauls, in number, are made by common than contract carriers. However, to a particular firm served by a contract carrier with a large fleet, frequency of service may be greater between two points by contract than by common carriers.

It is difficult to obtain any measure of frequency for exempt carriers. They do not report volume of movement, nor do they publish or maintain operating schedules (even though many may adhere to schedules in serving their customers).

Commodity Movement Capability.   The effect of legal forms on the commodity movement capability of a group of carriers is slight, except in several outstanding circumstances. Theoretically, common carriers can be found who can carry any commodity produced. Because of their larger size, they are usually financially more capable of meeting the needs of a shipper for special equipment. A shipper might have to finance personally such equipment for contract or exempt, and of course private carriage.

Exempt carriers, by definition, are prohibited from hauling non-exempt commodities, which include all those goods which have undergone a significant change from their natural state. They are unable to provide additional services such as diversion and reconsignment of shipments in transit, vital to the movement of agricultural products which make up the bulk of exempt commodities. This latter service is adequately provided only by common carrier railroads.

Availability of Service. This characteristic must be discussed with an important point in mind. If a shipper owns private transportation equipment, it is likely to rate as the most readily available form for that shipper. If he does not, financial barriers may make it the least available of the legal forms.

Common-carrier service is the most universally available. Contract carriage, especially in the situation where a shipper is willing to finance a new carrier in order to obtain service, could also be considered universally available. However, as pointed out above, exempt service may be completely unavailable for certain types of commodities.

Auxiliary Users

On several of the important characteristics, service characteristics of auxiliary users must, of necessity, take on the character of the mode of transportation used by each type of auxiliary user. As shown in Fig. 4–1, all auxiliary users may, at one time or another, use rail, highway, water, or air transportation modes. Only shipments by air mail and air express designate a specific mode to be used; these affect primarily the speed and frequency of service, which will not be included in the following discussion.

Dependability of Service. Shippers' cooperatives, because of the direct control they exercise over freight moving in their name, probably demonstrate the most dependable service of all small-shipment, auxiliary-user methods.

Shippers repeatedly have rated privately owned small-shipment operations, such as United Parcel Service, as much more dependable than parcel post service. Perhaps as a result, the new management of the

U. S. Postal Service has as one of its major objectives the improvement of service.

Commodity Movement Capabilities.   Any quantity of any commodity can move by freight forwarder, shippers' cooperatives, and REA Express. But the basic business purpose of these auxiliary users is to provide the shipper economies or speed in the movement of smaller quantities of goods.   For this reason, the practical capability of each is limited to less-than-vehicle-load quantities.

There is a definite limitation on the service provided by the U. S. Postal Service.   Parcel post service will accept packages of no more than twenty pounds in weight moving between Class I post offices, generally those serving all but rural settlements.   Post offices of other Classes are allowed to accept and handle shipments of up to 70 lb. in weight.

Availability of Service.   The U. S. Postal Service provides the most readily available service for small-package shipments.   In 1970, there were 32,029 post offices in the United States, serving all but the most remote locations.   Privately owned organizations such as United Parcel Service and REA Express provide service which is available, by means of pickup and delivery, at many points in the United States.   Finally, shippers' cooperatives are the least available of auxiliary users.   Relatively few of these associations have been formed, and these have been limited to shipments between the larger cities in the nation, i.e., movements which offer some savings from the consolidation of heavy movements of small packages in vehicle-quantity loads.

Coordinated Systems

The cost and service characteristics of a successful coordinated transportation service derive from the cost and service characteristics of its component modes, and as such do not warrant specific comparison here. In each successful coordinated service some of the desirable characteristics of each component mode are retained or emphasized, while some undesirable characteristics are reduced or eliminated.

For example, TOFC or piggyback methods typically offer a shipper faster and more dependable service than all-rail service, but at a comparable rate (and a lower total cost to the carrier organizations than all-truck shipment).   The LASH ship system, composed of vessels operating in coastal and intercoastal waters and capable of taking on, carrying, and discharging smaller barges, offers the economy and speed of deep-water transportation and the availability of "pickup and delivery" service by barge on the inland waterways.

The limitations of coordinated transportation services similarly arise from the "compromise" nature of the services themselves. For example, such combinations as air–water and air–rail probably cannot be established successfully because these combinations tend to retain the less desirable characteristics of each mode while minimizing the more desirable characteristics. They would offer slower service at higher cost than alternative services available to a shipper.

CONCLUSION

On the basis of this brief review, perhaps you have formulated some opinions about the relative types of freight hauled, the size of shipments, and the distances shipments typically are transported by the various modes. (2) **What methods of transport do you think are predominant in the transportation of canned fruits and vegetables as opposed to wearing apparel? (3) Over what range of shipment sizes? (4) Over what range of distances? (5) Why?** Before proceeding, you might wish to jot down some opinions.

For the first time in 1963, the Census of Transportation, through a national sample of documents describing shipments of manufactured goods, provided a wealth of information regarding the questions posed above. Although the Census has provided us with information for only two years (1963 and 1967), is limited to data about the transportation of manufactured goods, and is collected in a manner which may understate the use of non-regulated forms of transportation (for which documentation may be less complete), it represents the definitive source of data regarding commodity-by-commodity transportation patterns.

Information from the 1967 Census regarding the transportation of canned fruits and vegetables, certain types of wearing apparel, and several other categories of manufactured products is presented in Tables 4–5 and 4–6. (6) **Does it bear out your opinions? (7) Why is private truck the predominant mode of transportation for relatively short hauls of canned fruits and vegetables? (8) Why is rail the predominant mode for longer hauls? (9) Why are "other" forms of transportation so important for women's, misses', girls', and infants' clothing? (10) At what ranges of distance does rail or water become the predominant form of transportation for each of the shipper classes shown in Table 4–5? (11) Why? (12) Looking at the four shipper classes again, for which do you think the selection of transportation methods would be most difficult? (13) Why? (14) Can you support your opinion with information from Tables 4–5 and 4–6?**

TABLE 4–5. Relationships Between Distance Shipped and Modal Choice,
for Selected Shipper Classes, 1967

Shipper Class and Method of Transportation	Proportion of Total Tons, By Distance Shipped					Percentage of Total Tons
	Under 200 Miles	200–399 Miles	400–599 Miles	600–999 Miles	1,000 Miles and Over	
Shipper Class 021—Canned Fruits and Vegetables:						
Rail	11.6%	39.8%	55.9%	60.2%	85.2%	51.8%
Motor carrier	36.3	32.0	25.5	29.4	6.4	23.7
Private truck	49.4	28.2	18.5	7.8	3.7	21.8
Water	2.5	–	–	2.6	4.4	2.5
Other	.2	–	.1	–	.3	.2
Total	100.0%	100.0%	100.0%	100.0%	100.0%	
Percentage of total tons	25.3%	19.6%	8.0%	13.8%	33.3%	100.0%
Shipper Class 052—Women's, Misses', Girls', and Infants' Clothing:						
Rail	–	.1%	24.3%	19.1%	6.0%	10.0%
Motor carrier	53.5%	70.3	60.0	49.6	69.3	59.0
Private truck	36.4	9.0	.3	12.2	–	14.1
Other	10.1	20.6	15.4	19.1	24.7	16.9[a]
Total	100.0%	100.0%	100.0%	100.0%	100.0%	
Percentage of total tons	29.1%	10.3%	20.0%	21.0%	19.6%	100.0%
Shipper Class 091—Products of Petroleum Refining:						
Rail	8.4%	8.1%	19.6%	3.3%	1.4%	5.7%
Motor carrier	27.9	8.2	5.8	.5	.2	9.9
Private truck	12.4	2.3	.4	.1	–	4.0
Water	51.1	81.1	74.2	96.1	98.4	80.3
Other	.2	.3	–	–	–	.1
Total	100.0%	100.0%	100.0%	100.0%	100.0%	
Percentage of total tons	29.7%	14.0%	4.8%	22.4%	29.1%	100.0%
Shipper Class 242—Measuring, Controlling, and Indicating Instruments:						
Rail	.2%	2.1%	.6%	5.9%	11.6%	3.9%
Motor carrier	90.1	85.9	71.1	78.5	71.8	81.3
Private truck	4.2	3.8	7.5	6.7	2.1	4.6
Other	5.5	8.2	20.8	8.9	14.5	10.2[b]
Total	100.0%	100.0%	100.0%	100.0%	100.0%	
Percentage of total tons	28.2%	22.6%	11.6%	18.9%	18.7%	100.0%

[a]Includes 1.4 percentage points for air and the remainder for parcel post and privately owned small-package transportation services.

[b]Includes 2.2 percentage points for air, 1.1 for water, and much of the remainder for parcel post and privately owned small-package transportation services.

Source: Census of Transportation (Washington, D. C.: Department of Commerce, 1967).

TABLE 4-6. Relationships Between Size of Shipment and Modal Choice, for Selected Shipper Classes, 1967

Shipper Class and Method of Transportation	Proportion of Total Tons, By Mode, By Size of Shipment						Percentage of Total Tons
	Under 1,000 Pounds	1,000–9,999 Pounds	10,000–29,999 Pounds	30,000–59,999 Pounds	60,000–89,999 Pounds	90,000 Pounds and Over	
Shipper Class 021—Canned Fruits and Vegetables:							
Rail	2.2%	3.9%	11.0%	17.2%	84.0%	87.6%	51.8%
Motor carrier	48.9	31.0	31.2	46.2	10.4	6.8	23.7
Private truck	46.7	63.1	55.8	32.5	4.9	2.8	21.8
Water	1.2	1.9	2.0	4.0	.4	2.5	2.5
Other	1.0	.1	–	.1	.3	.3	.2
Total	100.0%	100.0%	100.0%	100.0%	100.0%	100.0%	100.0%
Percentage of total tons	.4%	5.9%	11.3%	30.2%	17.5%	34.7%	
Shipper Class 052—Women's, Misses', Girls', and Infants' Clothing:							
Rail	2.5%	–	58.4%	94.2%	–	–	10.0%
Motor carrier	68.8	43.9	31.4	5.8	100.0%	85.2%	59.0
Private truck	2.1	48.4	10.2	–	–	14.8	14.1
Other	26.6	7.7	–	–	–	–	16.9[a]
Total	100.0%	100.0%	100.0%	100.0%	100.0%	100.0%	100.0%
Percentage of total tons	56.8%	25.0%	6.8%	5.0%	5.5%	.9%	

Shipper Class 091 – Products of Petroleum Refining:

Rail	1.2%	1.5%	3.1%	5.1%	55.8%	4.6%	5.7%
Motor carrier	78.5	49.9	60.9	65.6	31.0	1.8	9.9
Private truck	17.0	46.5	35.6	29.0	12.9	.3	4.0
Water	1.7	2.1	.4	.2	–	93.2	80.3
Other	1.6	–	–	.1	.3	.1	.1
Total	100.0%	100.0%	100.0%	100.0%	100.0%	100.0%	100.0%
Percentage of total tons	–	.1%	.7%	11.0%	2.2%	86.0%	100.0%

Shipper Class 242 – Measuring, Controlling, and Indicating Instruments:

Rail	3.8%	3.8%	2.9%	8.1%	–	–	3.9%
Motor carrier	72.8	86.3	94.7	85.0	–	–	81.3
Private truck	4.6	6.0	2.4	–	–	–	4.6
Other	18.8	3.9	–	6.9	–	100.0%	10.2b
Total	100.0%	100.0%	100.0%	100.0%	–	100.0%	100.0%
Percentage of total tons	37.6%	42.0%	13.8%	5.4%	.0%	1.2%	100.0%

aIncludes 1.4 percentage points for air and the remainder for parcel post and privately owned small-package transportation services.
bIncludes 2.2 percentage points for air, 1.1 for water, and much of the remainder for parcel post and privately owned small-package transportation services.

Source: Census of Transportation (Washington, D. C.: Department of Commerce, 1967).

TABLE 4-7. Share of Ton-Miles of Transportation Service Provided, By Mode,
All Types of Manufactured Goods, 1963 and 1967

Shipper Group	Mode of Transport and Year							
	Rail		Motor Carrier		Private Truck		Other	
	1963	1967	1963	1967	1963	1967	1963	1967
01 Meat and dairy products	46.5%	46.0%	36.2%	37.7%	16.2%	15.1%	1.1%	1.2%
02 Canned and frozen foods and other food products, except meat and dairy products	74.9	73.7	16.8	15.9	6.6	7.2	1.7	3.2
03 Candy, beverages, and tobacco products	53.5	56.6	27.5	25.6	15.6	15.0	3.4	2.8
04 Basic textiles and leather products	25.3	16.6	58.8	63.2	11.5	16.1	4.4	4.1
05 Apparel and related products	10.0	15.0	62.1	66.1	6.7	7.8	21.2[a]	11.1[a]
06 Paper and allied products	70.9	77.3	20.7	15.7	4.6	4.2	3.8	2.8
07 Basic chemicals, plastics materials, synthetic resins, rubber, and fibers	61.8	64.2	13.8	16.7	3.7	3.0	20.7[b]	16.1[b]
08 Drugs, paints, and other chemical products	61.5	52.6	24.3	30.4	7.3	7.9	6.9	9.1
09 Petroleum and coal products	4.3	3.2	1.7	1.8	1.1	.7	92.9[c]	94.3[c]
10 Rubber and plastic products	37.0	34.5	52.4	57.0	5.9	5.5	4.7	3.0
11 Lumber and wood products, except furniture	83.8	77.8	6.7	5.5	6.9	6.6	2.6[d]	10.1[d]
12 Furniture, fixtures, and miscellaneous manufactured products	41.4	32.6	35.9	49.2	18.1	12.3	4.6	5.9
13 Stone, clay, and glass products	45.5	52.1	31.2	30.9	14.9	9.7	8.4	7.3
14 Primary iron and steel products	61.7	58.8	24.3	24.6	2.3	3.5	11.7[e]	13.1[e]
15 Primary non-ferrous metal products	73.2	67.7	21.0	26.1	3.8	4.5	2.0	1.7

16 Fabricated metal products, except metal cans and miscellaneous	40.6	34.9	36.6	49.0	17.7	13.1	5.1	3.0
17 Metal cans and miscellaneous fabricated metal products	41.6	34.7	46.9	50.2	7.0	11.3	4.5	3.8
18 Industrial machinery, except electrical	25.4	26.8	62.2	57.1	4.0	8.4	8.4	7.7
19 Machinery, except electrical and industrial	51.5	44.4	40.0	45.0	4.5	7.6	4.0	3.0
20 Communications products and parts	28.1	30.8	49.5	55.6	3.9	3.6	18.5f	10.0f
21 Electrical products and supplies	48.4	46.7	39.5	42.7	7.4	7.1	4.7	3.5
22 Motor vehicles and equipment	69.8	75.8	26.2	21.0	2.9	1.7	1.1	1.5
23 Transportation equipment, except motor vehicles	33.0	47.4	44.0	33.4	16.0	16.8	7.0	2.4
24 Instruments, photographic equipment, watches, and clocks	28.2	25.6	57.8	62.7	3.4	2.9	10.6g	8.8g

aIncluding 1.5 percentage points of share by air in 1963 and 1.9 percentage points of share by air in 1967, with much of the remainder accounted for by parcel post and small-parcel shipments by privately owned organizations.

bIncluding 20.3 percentage points of share by water in 1963 and 15.8 percentage points of share by water in 1967.

cIncluding 92.8 percentage points of share by water in 1963 and 94.3 percentage points of share by water in 1967.

dIncluding 2.5 percentage points of share by water in 1963 and 10.0 percentage points of share by water in 1967.

eIncluding 11.2 percentage points of share by water in 1963 and 13.0 percentage points of share by water in 1967.

fIncluding 4.3 percentage points of share by air in 1963 and 4.8 percentage points of share by air in 1967, with much of the remainder accounted for by parcel post and small-parcel shipments by privately owned organizations.

gIncluding 2.1 percentage points of share by air in 1963 and 3.4 percentage points of share by air in 1967, with much of the remainder accounted for by parcel post and small shipments by privately owned organizations.

Source: Census of Transportation (Washington, D. C.: Department of Commerce, 1963 and 1967).

A number of interesting and rather marked shifts between modes for particular commodity groupings, shown in Table 4–7, are obscured by the relatively small changes in the proportions of manufactured goods carried

TABLE 4–8. Tons and Ton-Miles of Manufactured Goods Carried in Domestic Transportation, 1963 and 1967, by Mode of Carriage

Mode of Transport	Proportion of Total Tons Carried		Proportion of Total Ton-Miles Carried	
	1963	1967	1963	1967
Rail	32.8%	32.9%	36.4%	36.8%
Regulated motor carrier	25.9	26.7	14.2	14.7
Private truck	16.2	13.8	4.6	4.3
Air	–	–	.1	.1
Water	24.5	26.3	44.0	43.7
Other	.5	.2	.6	.3
Unknown	.1	.1	.1	.1
	100.0%	100.0%	100.0%	100.0%

Source: Census of Transportation (Washington, D. C.: Department of Commerce, 1963 and 1967).

by the various modes in 1963 and 1967, shown in Table 4–8. **(15) How would you explain the shift in the share of traffic for motor vehicles from truck to rail between 1963 and 1967? (16) Or the significant shift in volume from rail to truck for the shipment of furniture and fixtures?**

Transportation facilities, and services provided, have undergone remarkable changes in recent years. This emphasizes the dynamic nature of logistics and the need for the successful logistics manager to maintain an awareness of such changes and their possible impact on his area of responsibility.

SUGGESTED READINGS

GARFIELD, PAUL J., and WALLACE F. LOVEJOY. *Public Utility Economics.* Englewood Cliffs, N. J.: Prentice-Hall, Inc., 1964.
Part IV of this book provides an excellent source of information about pipelines.
LEWIS, HOWARD T., JAMES W. CULLITON, and JACK D. STEELE. *The Role of Air Freight in Physical Distribution.* Boston: Division of Research, Graduate School of Business Administration, Harvard University, 1956.
Generally considered to be the most authoritative study yet made of air freight cost and service characteristics.
LOCKLIN, D. PHILIP. *Economics of Transportation,* 7th Ed. Homewood, Ill.: Richard D. Irwin, Inc., 1972.
A long-time standard work on the subject.

NORTON, HUGH S. *Modern Transportation Economics,* 2nd Ed. Columbus: Charles E. Merrill Publishing Co., 1971.
Provides a concise discussion of modal characteristics.
SAMSON, ROY J., and MARTIN T. FARRIS. *Domestic Transportation,* 2nd Ed. Boston: Houghton Mifflin Co., 1971.
Offers a good profile of various types of transportation services.
TAFF, CHARLES A. *Commercial Motor Transportation,* 4th Ed. Homewood, Ill.: Richard D. Irwin, Inc., 1969.
Discusses operating characteristics for motor carriers.
————. *Management of Physical Distribution and Transportation,* 5th Ed. Homewood, Ill.: Richard D. Irwin, Inc., 1972.
Presents an excellent discussion of carrier service availability of all types.

5

Logistics Rates
and Services

TRANSPORTATION RATE MAKING UNDER REGULATION

The Interstate Commerce Act of 1887 was the first federal regulation of interstate transportation in the United States.[1] Prior to this Act, several states in the East and Midwest had granted "charters" to railroads. The charters retained for these states the authority to prescribe a maximum level of rates. A second type of regulatory authority developed as a result of the Granger movement. The Granger movement gained impetus because of seriously declining agricultural prices received by farmers. Many farmers believed that the combination of high prices to consumers for agricultural commodities and low farm earnings was the result of discriminatory practices of the rail carriers. The Granger laws led to Supreme Court cases which established the right of the individual states to regulate intrastate transportation.

Once it was established that individual states could regulate transportation within their borders, the next question was whether the states could also continue to regulate interstate transportation (particularly in regard to rates) in the absence of federal regulation. The Supreme Court, in a reversal of its earlier view, decided in 1886 they could not do so.

This decision left a void in transportation regulation which was filled when the Interstate Commerce Commission (ICC) was created by the

---

[1] Actually, the original act in 1887 was titled "Act to Regulate Commerce." The change in the name to the "Interstate Commerce Act" was made by the Transportation Act of 1920. The later and current name will be used throughout this discussion.

Interstate Commerce Act of 1887.[2] The Interstate Commerce Act is a lengthy and complex piece of regulatory legislation dealing with nearly all aspects of rail, water, pipeline, and highway transportation, and the regulation of surface freight forwarders. In this chapter we will be concerned primarily with those portions of the Act which affect transportation rates.

1887–1905

After enactment of the Interstate Commerce Act the rail carriers formed associations through which rate levels were determined. These associations were adjudged illegal in 1897. The necessity of freight interchange and joint rates, however, required some degree of cooperation among railroads. Less formal traffic associations and rate bureaus continued to exist. They served as channels through which rate change proposals could be funneled. The Elkins Act of 1903 was intended to restrict some of the discriminatory practices which had developed under independent rate making by the carriers. The Elkins Act, which was supported by the carriers, outlawed rebates and special concessions and strengthened penalties for discriminatory practice and the quotation of rates other than those in published tariffs. However, it did not solve the carriers' revenue problems which continued to mount because of intense rate competition resulting from independent rate making.

1906–1919

The Hepburn Act of 1906 clarified the position of the ICC with respect to its authority over maximum rates. Prior to 1906 the Interstate Commerce Act had given the Commission authority to determine whether a rate or group of rates was "just and reasonable." The Hepburn Act gave to the ICC the authority to establish maximum rates, on the ground that it would be illogical to require the Commission to determine that a rate was unjust and unreasonable without permitting it to prescribe maximum rates. Pipeline regulation was also placed under the juridiction of the ICC in 1906.

The Hepburn Act established the ICC's authority over rates which were already in effect but did not give it the power to rule upon the reasonableness of proposed rates. Although reparations were available to shippers who had paid unreasonable rates, there was no machinery

[2] For a detailed discussion of the events leading up to the enactment of the Interstate Commerce Act in 1887, see D. Philip Locklin, *Economics of Transportation*, 7th Ed. (Homewood, Ill.: Richard D. Irwin, Inc., 1972), pp. 211–24.

through which the reasonableness of proposed rates could be challenged.[3] Provisions which permitted the ICC to rule on the reasonableness of *proposed rates* were established by passage of the Mann–Elkins Act in 1910. This law provided that the Commission could suspend, for a period of 120 days, a rate increase which had been challenged by an interested party as unreasonable or unjustly discriminatory.[4]

1920–1932

The prohibition of joint carrier action in the apportionment of freight and revenue among cooperating railroads (pooling) was based on the concept that competition between carriers would cause rates to seek a "natural level" as a result of individual carrier action. However, experience between 1898 and 1920 indicated that rate competition between the carriers had in some respects been detrimental to the carriers and the economy. In many instances rates resulted in revenues which did not cover out-of-pocket costs. To remedy this situation, the Transportation Act of 1920 permitted pooling agreements when approved by the Commission. For many of the same reasons, the Act empowered the Commission to prescribe *minimum* as well as maximum rates.

The Transportation Act of 1920 added a new section to the Interstate Commerce Act: Section 15a. Section 15a, indexed in the Act as the "rule of rate making," stressed that the Commission should *initiate* rates, *modify* established rates, or *adjust* rates in such a manner as to provide a "fair return" on the carrier's investment in property.

The Emergency Transportation Act of 1933

By 1933 the situation of many railroads had become desperate. The effects of the Great Depression on a derived demand industry having high fixed costs were severe. The 1920 "fair return" concept was further extended to the point where the Commission was assigned responsibility for assuring adequate carrier revenues. Section 15a was restated as follows:

In the exercise of its power to prescribe just and reasonable rates the Commission shall give due consideration, among other factors, to the effect of rates

---

[3] Reparation is the procedure by which the shipper or injured party could recover from the carrier the difference between the "unreasonable" charge and the rate that was determined to be reasonable by a regulatory body.

[4] An additional period of 120 days was provided when the original 120 days was not adequate to evaluate the reasonableness of a proposed rate. The period which presently governs the ICC's suspension powers is seven months.

on the movement of traffic; to the need, in the public interest, of adequate and efficient railway transportation service at the lowest cost consistent with the furnishing of such service; and to the needs of revenues sufficient to enable the carriers, under honest, economical, and efficient management, to provide such service.

Gone was the optimistic "fair-weather" provision for a fair return, and in its place was what amounted to an urgent Congressional plea for the ICC to find some way to keep the depression-plagued railroads solvent and protect the public interest.

The Motor Carrier Act of 1935

In 1935 the regulation of motor carriers involved in interstate commerce was placed under the jurisdiction of the ICC. With respect to rates the 1935 Act (enacted as Part II of the Interstate Commerce Act) prescribed for motor carriers the same general rules of rate making which were applicable to rail carriers. Two exceptions to this, which were to have profound effects on the development of for-hire motor carrier transportation, were: (1) contract carriers [5] were subject to only minimum rate regulation by the ICC and were not required to publish the actual rates they charged, being required instead to publish the minimum rates that they might charge, and (2) exemption from economic regulation (i.e., rates) was granted to certain commodities (primarily agricultural). The latter action had the effect of creating "exempt carriers"—transportation firms which specialized in the carriage of exempt, largely agricultural commodities free from rate regulation.

Civil Aeronautics Act of 1938

Many administrative, technical, and safety aspects of civilian aviation had been brought under federal regulation by the Air Commerce Act of 1926, which dealt primarily with such matters as aircraft registration, establishment of air traffic rules, designation of civil airways, and installation of air navigation aids. Economic regulation of the airline industry did not, however, become a matter of much concern until the late 1930's when the industry had developed to the point where the need for com-

[5] A contract carrier can be defined as any person that, under individual contract or agreement, engages in transportation for compensation by motor vehicle over any route of interstate or foreign commerce. In 1957, the basic definition of contract carriers was amended to restrict contract carriers to the movement of commodities for ". . . one person or a limited number of persons . . ." and contract carriers were required to publish actual rates.

prehensive federal regulation, including economic regulation, was pressing.

The Civil Aeronautics Act of 1938 established the Civil Aeronautics Authority with general powers and duties similar to those of the ICC, plus a very significant difference. The Civil Aeronautics Authority was given a Congressional mandate to *develop and promote* actively the growth of the airline industry, a duty and responsibility which had no parallel for rail, water, pipeline, and highway transportation in the Interstate Commerce Act.

In 1940 the functions of the Authority were reorganized by executive order, and the result was the establishment of the Civil Aeronautics Board, having essentially the duty of economic regulation of the industry, and the Civil Aeronautics Administration (placed in the Department of Commerce), having responsibility for administrative and technical aspects of civil aviation. In 1958, in response to the many pressing problems of the jet age, all functions of the Civil Aeronautics Administration were transferred to a newly created independent executive agency, the Federal Aviation Agency.

Transportation Act of 1940

Full regulatory control over the systems of interstate surface transportation (with the exception of transportation specifically exempt from regulation) was completed by the Transportation Act of 1940 when regulation of water transportation was made Part III of the Act.

Through its interpretation of the 1933 legislation, the ICC had generally permitted particular rates for one mode of transportation to stand only to the extent that such rates did not adversely affect the traffic of another mode. Congress did not consider this "umbrella" concept to be a reasonable policy for the Commission to follow and therefore once again changed Section 15a. Section 15a was amended by the 1940 Act to read:

. . . no carrier should be required to maintain rates which would be unreasonable, judged by other standards, for the purpose of protecting the traffic of a competitor.

Reed–Bulwinkle Act of 1948

This act legalized carrier rate associations formed for rate-fixing purposes, allowing them exemption from antitrust laws, and created a specific system by which the ICC could control the operating procedures of such associations.

Transportation Act of 1958

The Commission, in its interpretation of Section 15a of the 1940 Act, did not eliminate umbrella rate making. Congress believed this to be essential to a sound national transportation policy, and to clarify uncertainty and reaffirm its position, Congress once again changed Section 15a by adding the following subsection in the Transportation Act of 1958:

(3) In a proceeding involving competition between carriers of different modes of transportation subject to this act, the commission, in determining whether a rate is lower than a reasonable minimum rate, shall consider the facts and circumstances attending the movement of the traffic by the carrier or carriers to which the rate is applicable. Rates of a carrier shall not be held up to a particular level to protect the traffic of any other mode of transportation, giving due consideration to the objective of the National Transportation Policy declared in this Act.[6]

(1) As a shipper, would you favor this action? (2) Why?

In interpreting the Transportation Act of 1958, both the Commission and the courts have attempted to resolve two major questions posed by the Section 15a amendment:

1. Under intermodal competition, what level of cost constitutes a "reasonable minimum rate" for the inherent low-cost carrier:
   a. In the case where competition is another regulated carrier?
   b. In the case where competition is a non-regulated operator?
2. How does the competitive situation impinge on the "objective of the National Transportation Policy?"

Considerations attendant to the above questions are not mutually exclusive or independent. The Commission still tends to judge the reasonableness of a rate in terms of its possible injurious effect on a competing mode, considered as needing protection in keeping with the objective of the National Transportation Policy. However, as indicated in the wording of Section 15a, the Commission shall determine the reasonableness of the low-cost rate upon "the facts and circumstances attending the movement of the traffic by the carrier or carriers to which the rate is applicable" and not upon the protection of traffic of any other mode, giving *due consideration* to the objective of the National Transportation Policy.

An important "test case" on the rate-making provisions of the Transportation Act of 1958 is the *Pan-Atlantic Commodities* case.[7] The rail carriers had established piggyback rates which were competitive with "roll-on, roll-off" truck–water–truck rates between Eastern and Gulf points.

---

[6] Interstate Commerce Act, Section 15a (3) as amended by the Transportation Act of 1958.

[7] *New York, New Haven & Hartford R.R. Co. v. United States of America and Interstate Commerce Commission*, C.A. 8679 (D.C. Conn., 1961).

In disapproving these piggyback rates, the Commission (1) ruled that the rates were a destructive competitive practice, and (2) established a differential of 6% for piggyback rates over sea–land rates. The Commission was again deciding upon the reasonableness of a rate in relation to the effect of the proposed rate on competing modes of transportation. In supporting a Federal District Court ruling on the case, the Supreme Court unanimously decided that competitive rates could not be condemned by the ICC as inconsistent with the National Transportation Policy unless such rates reflect a patent disregard for costs or "genuinely threaten the continued existence of a transportation service that is uniquely capable of filling a transcendent national defense or other need." [8]

The ICC has utilized fully allocated cost as the basis for computing the "reasonable minimum rate" for the low-cost carrier. This position has been documented through ICC rulings in *Grain from Idaho, Oregon, and Washington to Ports in Oregon and Washington* (1963) [9] and *Ingot Molds, Va. to Steelton, Ky.* (1965).[10] The Supreme Court, in the latter case, upheld the position of the ICC. In cases where the competition has been between a non-regulated operator and a regulated carrier, the ICC has utilized variable costs, plus a contribution to fixed costs, as the basis for computing the "reasonable minimum rate" for the regulated carrier. This position has been documented through the ICC ruling in *Grain in Multiple-Car Shipments—River Crossings to the South* (1965),[11] also known as the Big John case.

Department of Transportation Act of 1966

The Department of Transportation (DOT) was established by the Department of Transportation Act of 1966. Although the DOT is primarily concerned with research, promotional, safety, and administrative functions of transportation rather than economic regulation, there easily could be a long-range impact in the area of economic regulation. The DOT has the authority and the mechanisms to develop plans and recommendations that concern national transportation objectives, policies, and programs. For example, the DOT might encourage the type of philosophy

[8] For a complete discussion of this important case and the relationship of Section 15a to the National Transportation Policy, rate discrimination, and national defense, see the full review of the case in "I.C.C. Rate Order 'Protecting' Water Lines Violates Sec. 15a (3), U.S. Court Says," *Traffic World*, Part III (November 25, 1961), pp. 97–100; and "Court Says I.C.C. 'Held Umbrella' Over Water Carriers," *Traffic World*, Part III (April 27, 1963), pp. 131 ff.
[9] 319 ICC 534 (1963).
[10] 323 ICC 758 (1965), and 326 ICC 77 (1965).
[11] 325 ICC 752 (1965).

noted in the Ash Report,[12] which recommends a single regulatory agency for all modes of transportation. Clearly, such a move could have considerable future impact on rates and rate-making policies.

RATE SYSTEMS

There are basically two types of rate systems which govern most of the transportation in the United States. These are distance and blanket rate systems.

Distance Rate Systems

This type of transportation rate system is based on the tapering rate principle in which rates increase with distance, but do not increase as fast as the increase in distance. Frequently, distance rates are established for "key points." Although the distances to several points may be different, they are grouped together for rate purposes. When rail key-point rates are established, the key-point rates are maximums for points which are intermediate to them to avoid conflict with the long- and short-haul clause. Terminal expenses have an important effect on distance rates. Terminal expenses for short-haul movements represent a greater portion of total movement cost and therefore of the total rate.

Blanket Rate Systems

Blanket rate systems involve the grouping of points, either at origin or destination or both, into the same rate group. Blanket rate groupings are more extensive; i.e., a larger area is included in a group, than is the case with key-point groupings discussed above.

Figure 5–1 illustrates the Transcontinental Freight Bureau rate groups for shipments originating in the Western Territory (as defined for this purpose) and terminating east of the line shown running through North and South Dakota, Wyoming, Colorado, and New Mexico. (Shipments from the North Pacific Coast and South Pacific Coast territories to points in the "no man's land" between the Western Territory and the border of Eastern Territory are not governed by the transcontinental freight rate tariffs.)

[12] Roy Ash, *et al.*, *A New Regulatory Framework*, Report on Selected Regulatory Agencies, The President's Advisory Council on Executive Organization (Washington, D. C.: Government Printing Office, January, 1971).

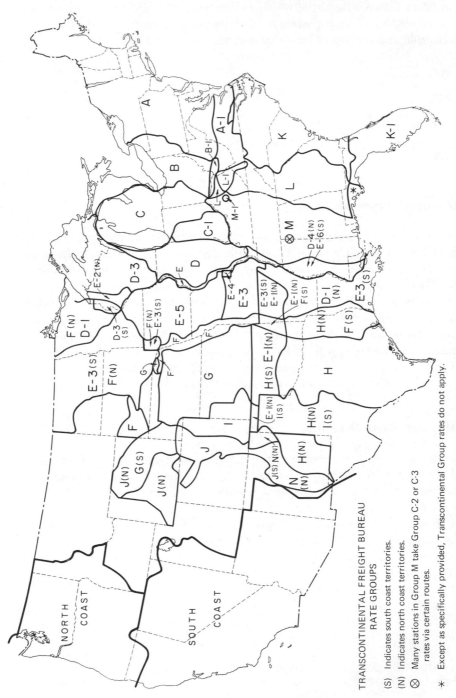

TRANSCONTINENTAL FREIGHT BUREAU
RATE GROUPS

(S)   Indicates south coast territories.

(N)   Indicates north coast territories.

⊗   Many stations in Group M take Group C-2 or C-3
      rates via certain routes.

✻   Except as specifically provided, Transcontinental Group rates do not apply.

Fig. 5–1. Transcontinental Freight Bureau rate groups.

TYPES OF RATES

For many years there have been complaints about the complexity of the transportation rate system, and it is undeniably true that much could be done to simplify freight classifications and tariffs. It is equally true, however, that the rate structure is inherently complex to an extent that precludes any gross simplification of the system.

There are a number of reasons for this complexity. First, there are thousands of possible origins and destinations for shipments in the United States, and thus there are millions of possible origin–destination pairs of places. Second, there are literally thousands of commodities, ranging from iron ore to ironing boards, which are sufficiently different to require that varying rates be charged for transporting them. Third, the volume and regularity of movement of commodities vary between different origins and different destinations, to a great enough extent in some cases to warrant a lower rate per pound, because carriers transport sufficient quantities of the commodity to realize significant economies of scale in handling it. Fourth, there are many additional "modifying factors" which affect particular situations (and therefore rates), such as competition between or within modes, differing cost characteristics of the various modes of transportation, special routings, and special carrier services.

It has been estimated that the ICC has on file something on the order of 43 *trillion* rates, and this does not, of course, include air rates on file with the CAB.[13] Even a substantial reduction in numbers would still leave a very complex situation.

Of course the logistician is not concerned with all rates on all commodities between all points under all circumstances by all modes. He is concerned primarily with the rates that he (and his competitors) must pay for the movement of the types of commodities bought or sold by his firm.[14]

Charges assessed by carriers can be divided into two classes: line-haul rates and accessorial charges. A line-haul rate is a payment made by a shipper for the movement of his goods between two points which are not in the same local pickup and delivery area (or switching district). All other types of payments made by shippers to carriers in connection with the movement, handling, or servicing of their shipments are defined here as accessorial charges.

[13] William B. Saunders, "Why All the Paperwork in Transportation?" *Handling and Shipping,* January, 1962, p. 29.
[14] Methods by which this particular problem of "information management" is approached are discussed in Part V.

Line-Haul Rates

Class Rates or Commodity Rates. Transportation rates are either class rates, exception rates, or commodity rates. Some of the more common of these will be discussed in following sections of this chapter. Commodity rates are more commonly established when there is a significant volume of a commodity moving with some degree of regularity between particular points or areas; the less this is the case the more likely it is that class rates or exception rates will prevail. There is nothing *inherent* in most goods or materials which would cause them to be transported under class rates, exception rates, or commodity rates. However, some commodities "naturally" move regularly in large volume and therefore will typically move under commodity rates rather than under class or exception rates.

Classification and Class Rates. A classification is essentially a method of relating products to one another for transportation movement pricing purposes. A classification gives weighted consideration to basic movement costs, susceptibility of the product to loss or damage, waste or theft in transit, injury to other freight with which the material comes in contact, risks due to hazards of carriage, expense of and care in handling, weight per cubic foot as packaged, adaptability to movement in carload quantity, and ratings on analogous articles. The classification does *not* establish the rate to be charged for the movement of a product between two points.

Products are classified by percentage relationships.[15] Table 5–1 is an illustration of the classification relationship in the National Motor Freight Classification, Uniform Freight Classification, and Western Classification for alcoholic liquors and related products. (3) **In Table 5–1, why do you think that classification numbers (directly reflecting rate relationships) are higher for LTL than for TL shipments? (4) For wine than vinegar? (5) For wine "in glass, in wicker baskets, covers sealed" than for wine "in bulk"? (6) For wine in bulk under the National Motor Freight Classification than under the Western Classification?**

Any product that moves by for-hire common carrier can be governed by a class rate. If there is not a specific category into which a product "fits," then it can be classified within the group of items with which it is most closely associated. To determine a class rate, the applicable classi-

---

[15] Products can be classified in one of two ways: (1) by percentage variations from 100% (Class I), and (2) by classes where Class I equals 100% and as the class numeral increases (i.e., from I to V), the relationship to 100% decreases. In this type of classification, percentages below 50% are sometimes indicated by letters (i.e., A, B, C, D, E).

(In Percentage of First Class)

Product	National Motor Freight Classification		Uniform Freight Classification		Western Classification[a]	
	LTL	TL	LCL	CL	LCL	CL
Alcohols, other than alcoholic liquors and alcohols (noibn):						
In carboys	125	70	125	70	125	70
In glass, in boxes or barrels	100	55	100	55	100	55
In metal cans, in barrels, boxes, or pails	100	55	100	55	100	55
In bulk, in barrels, steel cylinders, or tanks	100	50	100	50[b]	85	55
Juice, grape, other than frozen, in barrels, boxes or packages; also CL in glass, in crates with solid tops or in tank cars	60	35	60	35[c]	55	37.5
Vinegar (applies to wine vinegar):						
In glass, in crates	60	35	60	35	70	37.5
In barrels or boxes; also CL in tank car	60	35	60	35	55	37.5
Liquors, alcoholic (noibn) (applies to brandy):						
In glass or in metal cans, in barrels or boxes, or in packages; also in containers named in mixed CL in bulk, in barrels	100	50	100	50	100	55
In bulk, in barrels; also CL in tank cars	100	50	100	50	100	55
Vermouth:						
In containers, in barrels or boxes	100	50	100	50	100	55
In bulk, in barrels	100	50	100	50	85	55
Wine (noibn):						
In glass, in wicker baskets, covers sealed	150	50	150	50	150	55
In containers, in barrels or boxes	100	50	100	50	85	55
In bulk	100	50	100	50	85	55
Wine, sherry concentrated fortified with brandy, in bulk, in barrels	100	50	100	50	85	55
Wine, lees:						
In bags	70	37.5	70	37.5	85	37.5
In barrels	70	37.5	70	37.5	55	37.5
Champagne:						
In glass, in wicker baskets	n.c.	n.c.	150	50	150	55
In containers	n.c.	n.c.	100	50	100	55

noibn = not otherwise identified by name.

n.c. = not classified.

[a] In the Western Classification, commodities are classified by the "class system" (Class I, II, etc.) and are converted here to a percentage system of classification for comparability.

[b] UFC includes shipments in tank cars.

[c] UFC includes "with sugar or other sweetening and water added."

fication within the appropriate classification tables [16] is determined and reference is then made to the applicable rate tariff [17] which indicates the applicable rate per hundredweight for any conceivable distance the product will be transported.

Exception Rates. Under certain circumstances (which may include the volume of movement of a particular product or the specialized nature of it) exceptions to the classification (deviations from the standard classification grouping of the product) are established. Exceptions to the classification are generally lower than the standard classification. The deviation from the standard classification may be with respect to the rules of the classification or the specific classification assigned to the product. The objective is to provide a special privilege, generally in terms of a lower transportation cost, for a specific commodity or movement.

The trend has been to restrict the number of exceptions to the classification. Recent efforts have been made to establish commodity rates, instead of exceptions to the classification, when the volume of individual movements is in excess of 10,000 pounds.

Commodity Rates. Commodity rates are usually established in cases where a sufficient volume of a commodity is transported between two points or areas with enough regularity to result in some economies of scale to the carrier(s) handling such shipments. Commodity rates supersede and are frequently much lower than class rates and exception rates on the same item.

Commodity rates are established as the result of shipper requests for rates which will be lower than class rates, or by carrier efforts to offer rate concessions to particular commodities or geographical areas to develop movement from, to, or within specified points or areas.

Studies by the ICC have indicated that of the carload traffic originated on specific days, 2% was shipped on regular class rates, 7% on exception rates, and 91% on commodity rates. It is impossible to determine the volume of motor carrier tonnage that moves under commodity rates, but an "educated guess" would place the estimate at less than 20% of common-carrier truck movements. Of course, this does not mean than 80% of

[16] The "appropriate" classification table is that classification which the carrier(s) designate(s) for movement between certain areas or points. For example, the Western Classification governs truck movements within the state of California, but the National Motor Freight Classification governs movements between California and Nevada.

[17] A tariff is basically a volume–distance price list and may contain a specification of charges for any special services a carrier may offer, and rules under which the carrier transports goods.

all truck traffic is freight moving under class rates, because exempt and private trucking operations haul approximately twice as many ton-miles of freight as common and contract carriers combined.

Most airline and water carrier shipments are made on specific commodity rates. The airlines, particularly, have done a great deal of rate experimenting during the last few years as part of their general effort to increase the use of air freight transportation by shippers.

In addition to "regular" commodity rates there are special types of commodity rates which are examples of rates and rate-making techniques brought about by: (1) intermodal competition, (2) the desire to realize economies resulting from better equipment utilization by carriers, (3) the special position of government agencies as shippers, (4) the carrier–shipper "middleman" position of the freight forwarder, (5) the value of certain commodities, and (6) situations in which a shipper is willing to accept a slower movement time for his shipment in return for a lower rate. Although most of them apply to commodity rates only, some of these rate-making techniques are also applied to modify class rates. It should be emphasized that there are many other types of rates which, because of space limitations, will not be discussed here, but which might be of importance to a particular shipper.

All-Commodity Rates. Known also as "freight-all-kinds," or FAK rates, the number of such rates in effect has increased in recent years. Under all-commodity rate provisions the carrier specifies the rate per shipment whether in dollars per hundredweight or in total dollars for a specified minimum weight, irrespective of the commodity or commodities which may be included in the shipment. The all-commodity rate tends to establish rates based on transportation costs rather than on "value of service." Such rates are frequently quoted by freight forwarders, and are used primarily by shippers who send mixed commodity shipments to single destinations.

Minimum Rates. Carrier rates are based on specified minimum quantities ranging from "any quantity," on which the minimum is 100 lb. (or at least based on a 100-lb. quantity) to the carload or truckload capacity of a transport vehicle. In some tariffs, rates are provided only for the "any quantity" and "vehicle capacity quantity," e.g., "any quantity and a 30,000-lb. minimum." In other tariffs, multiple minimums may be established for various sized shipments, e.g., "any quantity 2,000-lb., 4,000-lb., 10,000-lb., 20,000-lb., and 30,000-lb. minimums." The shipper is billed on the basis of the rate which results in the lowest charges.

Rules governing shipments in excess of vehicle capacity are made a part of carrier tariffs. There are two principles which govern such "overflow" shipments. In some cases, the overflow is moved at the same rate as the quantity loaded in the vehicle. In other situations, carrier tariffs provide that segments of shipments which exceed the capacity of the vehicle will be considered separate shipments and billed at their appropriate rate.

In Excess Rates. These are a type of incentive rate, the purpose of which is to bring about heavier loading of individual carrier vehicles so as to improve carrier equipment utilization. The name "in excess rate" derives from the fact that one rate is charged up to a certain minimum weight for a vehicle load, and a lower rate is charged for any amount in excess of the established minimum. For example, the rate on a particular commodity might be 75¢/cwt. for a minimum of 30,000 lb. and 65¢/cwt. for the weight of the shipment in excess of 30,000 lb. The calculations shown in Table 5–2 for a 34,600-lb. shipment illustrate the application of an in excess rate.

TABLE 5–2. Comparison of Minimum Rate and In Excess Rate

Type of Rate	Rate (per Cwt.)	Minimum (Pounds)	Total Weight of Shipment (Pounds)	Total Freight Charges
Minimum	$.75	30,000	34,600	$259.50
In excess	.75	30,000	34,600	254.90*
	.65	Weight in excess of 30,000 lb.		

*The rate of $.75/cwt. is assessed on the first 30,000 lb. of the shipment, and the rate of $.65/cwt. is charged for the weight in excess of 30,000 lb., i.e., 4,600 lb. The effective rate per cwt. is $.737/cwt., $254.90 ÷ 34,600 lb.

Multiple Vehicle Rates. These are another type of incentive rate offered to shippers who ship more than a single vehicle load of a commodity at one time to a particular destination. There are several reasons for the existence of such rates. A rail car generally has greater capacity than a truck trailer. To overcome this type of competitive disadvantage, motor carriers can establish multiple vehicle (multiple truckload) rates. For example, where rail carriers might establish carload rates for 80,000-lb. shipments, a motor carrier might match this by quoting a competitive 80,000-lb. rate and transporting the shipment in two 40,000-lb. truckloads. It should not be assumed, however, that motor carrier economics necessarily justify this type of rate.

A second reason for quoting multiple vehicle rates has been to reduce transportation costs for commodities and thus permit them to move to markets from which a higher transportation cost formerly excluded them.

It is asserted that saving in transportation costs is achieved by economies of handling many vehicle loads at one time from one origin. Such rates are exemplified by a few trainload rates for such commodities as coal, ore, molasses, and petroleum products. These trains are specified as special trains, sometimes referred to as unit trains (although "unit" may have the wrong connotation, implying that the train is composed of a single unit rather than of a variable number of individual cars). The rail carrier(s) assume complete responsibility for the operation of a special train. Reduced unit rates are possible through greater efficiency as a result of bypassing intermediate freight classification yards and high utilization of equipment.

Another example of multiple vehicle rates involves the rent-a-train concept. The rail carrier is paid a yearly rental for specified equipment and crews plus a charge per ton-mile or train-mile. Train utilization is the responsibility of the *shipper* rather than the carrier. The difference in responsibility for train utilization is the fundamental difference between a special train and a rent-a-train. The rent-a-train concept has the effect of private carriage in the rail mode. In order to utilize rent-a-train effectively, a shipper must move a large volume of shipments on a regular basis between specific origin and destination points. An example of rent-a-train involves the shipment of grain from Eastern Illinois to Baton Rouge, La., for export.[18] The reduced transportation cost permits Eastern Illinois grain to move to export markets from which a higher transportation cost formerly excluded them. This is entirely consistent with the second reason stated above for quoting multiple vehicle rates.

Value Rates. The general rule of carrier liability for shipments handled is that the carrier is liable for the value of any goods lost or damaged while in its custody. This fact is the principal reason for the existence of various types of value rates, of which two of the more important types are "released value rates" and "actual value rates." Released value rates are, as the term suggests, rates which are based on carriers assuming a certain fixed liability, usually stated in dollars and cents per pound, for goods transported by them. This liability is ordinarily substantially less than the actual value of the goods, and the shipper is granted a lower rate in return for this "concession" on his part.

A second type of value rate is the "actual value" rate. This type of carrier pricing is employed when there is a great variation in the values of goods considered to be the *same commodity*. In such cases it would not be desirable to have a single rate because some shipments would have a high liability potential for a carrier handling them, while others

[18] "Rent Your Own Freight Train," *Business Week*, October 26, 1968, pp. 104 ff.

would have a very low liability potential, and yet both would have to be charged the same rate unless actual value rates were established.

Value rates are quoted on goods moving under commodity, class, and exception rates.

Guaranteed Schedule Rates. Guaranteed schedule rates are utilized when the carrier and the shipper agree on a guaranteed schedule for the movement of a shipment. Livestock and perishables are examples of commodities for which a guaranteed schedule would be functional. If the carrier fails to meet the schedule and an actual loss is incurred, the carrier may be held liable for the resulting loss. Under normal rates, i.e., other than guaranteed rates, the carrier is responsible for exercising "reasonable dispatch," which provides greater latitude than a guaranteed schedule.

Deferred rates are a second type of guaranteed schedule rate. Deferred rates, found most frequently in air transportation, take the following general form: the carrier has the option of deferring the arrival time of a shipment, and in return for accepting the possibility of delay the shipper is charged a rate which is lower than that assessed for standard (non-deferred) service. The reason for such rates is that they allow the carrier to move shipments at the carrier's "convenience" so long as they arrive within a reasonable time or by the scheduled deferred delivery date. This enables the carrier to use such shipments as "filler freight" to achieve fuller loading of vehicles. In terms of economic theory this practice amounts to carrying marginal cost freight for a marginal revenue return. This is an area of historical and continued experimentation. The underlying problem is that the theory conflicts with operational consideration, e.g., the use of deferred rates may result in heavily congested air terminals. The nature of claims arising out of the use of guaranteed schedule rates will be discussed in Chapter 19.

Seasonal Averaging Rates. In October, 1970, the Interstate Commerce Commission ruled that rates between Saskatchewan, Canada, and points in the United States were not in compliance with Section 6(4) of the Interstate Commerce Act.[19] The rates, which were suspended by the Commission, are an example of a more innovative approach to rate making. The proposed rates governed the movement of potash and would have provided for a $1.90 per ton discount if the shipper agreed to move no less than 6% and no more than 10% in any month; in actual practice, the movement requirement ranged between 2% and 18% in the various months. (7) **As a shipper, would you favor the introduction of seasonal**

---

[19] Interstate Commerce Commission, I. & S. Docket No. 8528, *Allowances on Controlled Shipments of Potash, Canada to U. S.,* April 1, 1970.

averaging rates in the United States? (8) Would they make sense to you as a carrier? (9) Is the action of the Interstate Commerce Commission consistent with your responses?

Section 22 Rates. The Interstate Commerce Act provides that the general rules of rate making need not apply to shipments made by government agencies. Section 22 of the Act provides that carriers may furnish transportation for certain parties, including government agencies, "free or at reduced rates." A thorough understanding of Section 22 rate-making procedure is essential for logistics managers for firms supplying military and governmental installations.

Joint or Local Rates. In addition to being a class rate or a commodity rate, every rate is also either a "joint rate" or a "local rate." When only one carrier participates in the line-haul movement of a shipment, the rate is a local rate. Thus, in this connection, the word "local" does *not* mean movements only within local areas or for short distances. For example, a movement from San Francisco to Chicago via the Santa Fe Lines is a local rate movement because only the Santa Fe Lines would participate in the line-haul movement. The same movement, accomplished by routing the shipment by The Western Pacific Railroad Company from San Francisco to Salt Lake City, Utah, thence by The Denver and Rio Grande Western Railroad Company from Salt Lake City to Denver, and finally by the Burlington Northern from Denver to Chicago would be made under a joint rate because more than one carrier participated in the line-haul movement.

It may be a matter of some concern to a logistics manager whether a movement between two points can be made under a local rate, a joint rate, or both. Figure 5–2 illustrates such situations. In case 1, only carrier Z serves the two points, and rates quoted will be local rates. In this situation the carrier has no intramodal competition, and this may tend to keep rates at a higher level than they might otherwise be.

In case 2 there are three variations shown: in (a) each carrier gets about half of the line-haul movement; in (b) carrier X gets very little of the line-haul movement; and in (c) carrier Y gets very little of the line-haul movement. In each variant of case 2, both of the carriers have terminal expense. Once again there is no intramodal competition—(a), (b), and (c) are alternatives. There is an additional factor which may tend to make rates higher in situations (b) and (c): one carrier has half of the terminal expense but only a very small portion of the line haul, and is likely to demand, perhaps justifiably, a larger than proportional (distance) share of the revenue to compensate it for having to carry out costly terminal operation with little line-haul mileage to make up for it.

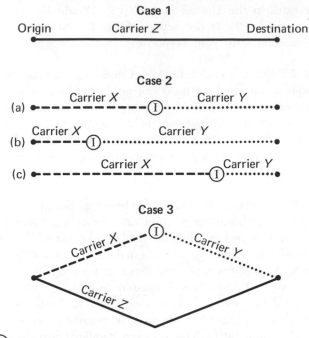

$\textcircled{I}$ = interchange point

Fig. 5–2. Illustrations of local and joint rate situations.

The result is likely to be some pressure for higher rates in situations (b) and (c) than would occur in (a).

In case 3 a third carrier enters the scene, and the first reaction of the observer may be that the rate via carriers X and Y will be determined by the costs of "local" carrier Z. But in practice this is simply not likely to be so. There is some tendency to reciprocate, and there are likely to be other traffic situations in which the roles of carriers X, Y, and Z are reversed. The result is that in case 3 the rate is likely to relate to the joint costs of carriers X and Y rather than the local costs of carrier Z.

By this time you may wonder whether there are any situations in which, in the absence of intermodal competition, rates would tend to be lower rather than higher. The answer is that there are very few, and the moral would seem to be that intermodal competition is a good thing for shippers. Only the existence of intermodal competition or the alternative of a private transportation system for a shipper serves to keep rate levels truly "competitive." There are, to be sure, some spectacular historical exceptions to this conclusion. There have been intramodal "rate wars" at times in the past as, on occasion, carriers have cut rates to survive, or to grow at the expense of other carriers. These are usually temporary aberrations and once the "crisis" is resolved the rates tend to restabilize at their former levels.

Through or Combination Rates.   In addition to being a class or commodity rate, and a joint or local rate, every rate is either a through or combination rate. The words "through" and "combination" mean just what they imply. A through rate is a rate from one point to another which is stated specifically in a tariff as applying between the points involved, and it can be either a "joint through rate" or a "local through rate." A combination rate is a rate which is made up of two or more existing rates to cover a shipment between two points. The rates involved in a combination rate may be either class or commodity rates, or both.

There are two basic types of combination rates: "aggregate of intermediates" and "proportional" rates. Both a limitation of and a reason for combination rates is the necessity of complying with Section 4 of the Interstate Commerce Act, the "Long and Short Haul Clause." This clause and problems of rate making connected with it are discussed later in this chapter.

Aggregate of Intermediates.   An aggregate of intermediates rate occurs when two or more rates are added (combined) to apply from origin to destination. If an aggregate of intermediates rate results in lower charges than a through rate, the former may sometimes be used as a substitute for the through rate. A combination rate which is lower than the through rate will only apply if the applicable tariff has a rule which protects such combinations. Such rules are common but tariffs should always be checked for the rule. The complexity of the rate structure is the cause of situations where the aggregate of intermediates rate results in lower charges than a through rate. This complexity frequently makes it necessary to determine both a through rate and an aggregate of intermediates rate. When there is a sufficient volume of movement to justify altering the rate structure, carriers usually are willing to adjust the through rate down to the aggregate of intermediates rate level.

Proportional Rates.   A proportional rate is "a separately established local or joint rate applicable to through transportation." [20] It is most frequently found in joint rate situations and is always *part* of a combination rate; i.e., it is never used alone. It is used primarily for two purposes. Assume Fig. 5–3 illustrates a carload movement from *A* to *C* through *B*. If a proportional rate were not available, charges per hundredweight

[20] Kenneth U. Flood, *Traffic Management,* 2d Ed. (Dubuque, Iowa: W. C. Brown Co., 1963), p. 157.

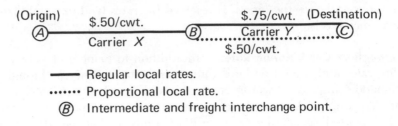

- Regular local rates.
...... Proportional local rate.
Ⓑ Intermediate and freight interchange point.

Fig. 5–3. Illustration of proportional rate application (1).

from A to C would be \$1.25 (\$.50 + \$.75). If a \$1.00/cwt. rate is necessary to develop traffic from A to C, carrier Y can accomplish this (without upsetting the regular local rate from B to C of \$.75/cwt.) by publishing a proportional rate of \$.50/cwt. from B to C *which requires a prior movement* from A to B. Carrier X could also have accomplished this purpose by quoting a proportional rate of \$.25 from A to B, or both carriers could have quoted proportional rates low enough to reduce the total charges for an A-to-C movement to \$1.00/cwt.

Figure 5–4 illustrates another use of proportional rates. Carrier Y operates routes AC and AB, while carrier X operates route BC. It would be possible for carrier Y to establish AC and AB rates which would pre-

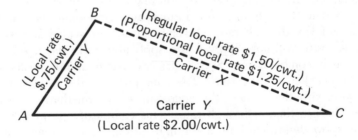

Fig. 5–4. Illustration of proportional rate application (2).

vent traffic from moving from A to C on an ABC routing. Carrier Y might attempt to do this by establishing a rate from A to B which, when combined with carrier X's local rate from B to C, would be in excess of carrier Y's local AC rate.

To answer this competitive threat, carrier X might establish a proportional rate from B to C which would equal carrier Y's AC rate without affecting carrier X's regular local rate from B to C.[21]

---

[21] For a more extensive and detailed discussion of the subject of proportional rates, see Flood, *ibid.,* pp. 157–59.

Accessorial Service and Terminal Charges

In addition to line-haul rates, carriers also assess charges for special-ized services. These charges will be discussed in the following sections under the headings of services and terminal charges.

Services. *Diversion and Reconsignment.* Technically, diversion means a change in the routing of a shipment, and reconsignment means a change of consignee for a particular shipment, but in practice the words are used interchangeably. Diversion is used most frequently in connection with the movement of perishables, grain, and lumber. The purpose is to per-mit the delivery of shipments to one of many possible alternate points, depending upon changes in market conditions or in the terms of sale sometime after the shipment has been originated but before it has reached its originally designated destination. A charge, usually $20 or less per shipment, is assessed by carriers for diversion and reassignment services.

Diversion is also a method of using the carrier as a warehouse. Through diversion, a shipper can route a shipment circuitously so that transit time will be in excess of normal. When a market for the cir-cuitously routed shipment develops, the shipper can change the routing to direct movement to destination or a point of reconsignment. This practice has been engaged in extensively by lumber brokers. Extreme abuses of it have recently come under close scrutiny by the rail carriers because of the costs involved in circuitous movement, and by the ICC because of the discriminatory aspects of this practice.

Protective Service. Carriers provide protective service for goods which are affected by temperature. The services include ventilation, re-frigeration, and heater service. In some situations, the carriers render these types of services without charge as a necessary element in the trans-portation of a commodity. In other instances, where the shipper specifies the type of service to be given to a particular shipment, charges are as-sessed for the additional service.

Transit Privileges. Generally transit privileges are established to facil-itate the flow of goods requiring some handling or processing at an inter-mediate point between origin and ultimate destination. Below are listed several of the types of transit privileges and the commodities for which they are designed:

Milling	(grain)
Compressing	(cotton)
Planing	(lumber)

Fabrication   (steel)
Blending   (wine)
Storage   (commodities produced seasonally and
                     consumed non-seasonally)

Figure 5–5 provides an illustration of the transit privilege. Assuming an inbound movement of raw materials from A to B at a rate of $.90/cwt., the transit operator would pay the inbound $.90 rate, record the tonnage

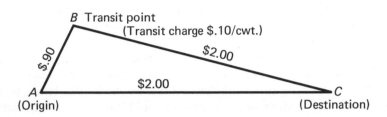

Fig. 5–5. Illustration of the processing-in-transit privilege (points A and B in the same origin-rate group for destination C).

for transit with the carrier, perform the transit operation, and then file with the carrier for the refund ($.80/cwt.) of the difference between the $.90 inbound rate and the transit charge ($.10/cwt.). Therefore, the cost of movement from A to C via transit point B would be $2.10/cwt., as compared with that of a direct movement from A to C or from B to C without a transit stop, which would be $2.00/cwt. If the transit point were not in a direct line to the destination, out-of-line charges would be assessed for the movement from the "main line" to the transit point and back to the "main line."[22]

Another type of transit privilege is that which permits the shipper to stop a shipment at a point intermediate to destination to partially unload. This is diagrammed in Fig. 5–6. If a transit privilege is provided, a shipment which originates at A can stop at B, a point intermediate to C, to partially unload. Even though the rate to B is, as illustrated in Fig.

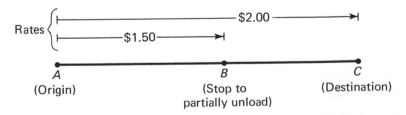

Fig. 5–6. Illustration of unloading-in-transit privilege.

[22] Out-of-line charges are usually not assessed if the movement is less than 150 miles (round trip) from the main line.

5–6, $1.50/cwt., the rate from *A* to *C* ($2.00/cwt.) may be assessed for the movement to *B*.

A receiver who elects to purchase from two suppliers can (where tariff provisions permit) have a rail car or truck partially loaded at one point and moved to a second point for completion of loading. The rate from the original loading point to destination will apply unless the rate from the point where loading was completed is higher than the rate from the origin, in which case the rate from the stop-off point will apply to the entire shipment.

Assume that the same receiver has warehouses located at three points and wants to make partial delivery of segments of a carload shipment to each of them. Tariff provisions are frequently established for stopping carload or truckload shipments to partially unload. The rate from origin to destination would apply to the through shipment plus two stop-off charges, there being no charge for the final destination delivery of a shipment which involves stop-offs. Current stop-off charges to complete loading are generally about $40, and stops to partially unload are usually about $30. Stop-off charges can and do vary significantly by mode, commodity, and geographic points. Logistics system planning involving stop-offs will require that specific charges are known in order to develop accurate transportation cost data for logistics system planning and analysis. Figure 5–7 presents an illustration of a shipment which, as in the discussion above, includes one stop to complete loading and two stops to partially unload. By using the stop-off tariff provision to complete loading and to partially unload, the charges for the movement from *A* and *B* to the three delivery points would be $932.50, as shown in Table 5–3.

If there were no stop-off privileges in the case just discussed, charges would be calculated as shown in Table 5–4.

Charges for shipments which are to be stopped for partial unloading must be prepaid at the origin point, as carrier rules require that charges for specific shipments will be collected from only one source. Normally, the shipper is limited to one stop to complete loading and three stops to partially unload. Some recent piggyback tariffs, however, have provided as many as five stops to partially unload.

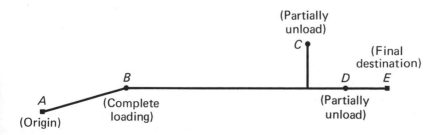

Fig. 5–7. Illustration of a movement involving stop-off charges.

TABLE 5–3. Example of Volume, Rates, and Charges for a Movement
Involving Stop-Offs with Stop-Off Privileges

Volume (Pounds)			Rates (per Cwt.)			
			From	To	Rate	Minimum[a]
Loaded at A	21,600		A	B	$ .75	20M
Loaded at B	33,900		A and B	C	1.30	50M
Unloaded at C from A	8,500	10,300	A and B	D	1.40	50M
Unloaded at C from B	1,800		A and B	E	1.50	50M
Unloaded at D from A	7,100	19,200	A	C	2.65	10M
Unloaded at D from B	12,100		B	C	4.16	AQ[b]
Unloaded at E from A	6,000	26,000	A	D	2.85	10M
Unloaded at E from B	20,000		B	D	2.95	10M
			A	E	3.25	10M
			B	E	1.90	20M

Calculation of Charges				
From	To	Weight	Rate	Charges
A and B	$C, D,$ and E	55,500 lb.	$1.50/cwt.	$832.50
One stop to complete loading		–	40.00/stop	40.00
Two stops to partially unload		–	30.00/stop	60.00
		55,500		$932.50

[a]Amount of weight (in thousands of pounds on which charges are based, unless the lading
exceeds this minimum, in which case charges will be for actual weight).
[b]Any quantity.

TABLE 5–4. Example of Volume, Rates, and Charges for a Movement
Involving Stop-Offs Without Stop-Off Privileges

From	To	Weight (Pounds)	Rate (per Cwt.)	Charges
A	C	8,500	$2.65	$ 265.00
B	C	1,800	4.16	75.88
A	D	7,100	2.85	285.00
B	D	12,100	2.95	356.95
A	E	6,000	3.25	325.00
B	E	20,000	1.90	380.00
	Total	55,500		$1,687.83

A problem connected with stop-off shipments are the delays incurred
as a result of moving cars to several points, which in many cases are not
in a direct line with each other. To help solve this problem and to
accomplish better car utilization, several rail carriers have established
transloading stations. Where a transloading station is available, a car
containing goods for three points can be moved to the station where the
contents of the car will be unloaded and reloaded into separate cars for

direct movement to each destination. An illustration of a transloading operation is shown in Fig. 5–8. The charges for transloading are the same as stop-off charges in specific tariffs.

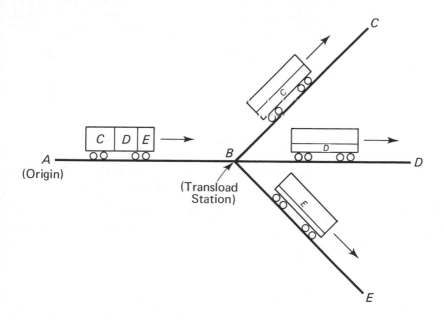

Fig. 5–8.   Transloading.

Split Delivery. Both rail and highway carriers offer stop-off service. Split delivery service is an additional service provided by highway carriers. It permits an unlimited number of segments of a larger shipment to be delivered within the limits of a specific split delivery area. Special split delivery charges are made for each segment delivered to a different point. Split delivery charges are the same regardless of the total weight of the shipment. Table 5–5 shows examples of split delivery charges.

Similar services are offered by air carriers and freight forwarders. Air carriers have developed a service which provides for movement of a consolidated shipment by air to a break-bulk point where the parcels (segments of the shipment) which have been addressed by the shipper are delivered to the Postal Service for parcel post delivery to destination. This service has the advantage of speed and reduced cost similar to that of the rail transloading station described previously.

One of the services of freight forwarders is the consolidation of shipments at an origin point for delivery to numerous destinations. If rate advantages will accrue to the shipper, the forwarder will arrange for transportation of the consolidated shipment (for example, 20,000 lb. made

TABLE 5–5. Split Delivery Charges

Weight of Individual Split Deliveries (in Pounds)		Split Delivery Charge for Each Individual Delivery
Over	But Not Over	
0	100	$ 3.05
100	250	3.70
250	500	3.95
500	1,000	5.50
1,000	2,000	8.50
2,000	4,000	9.90
4,000	10,000	11.55
10,000		13.45

up of twenty 1,000-lb. segments) to a break-bulk point and then arrange for movement of the twenty segments to their ultimate destinations.

Minimum Charge. Due to the relatively high cost to the carriers of handling small shipments, many tariffs include provisions for minimum charges for shipments in specified weight categories, usually below 1,000 pounds.

Single Shipment Charge. Some motor carrier tariffs provide for an additional service charge if the carrier is required to pick up a single shipment weighing less than 500 pounds. The extra charge helps to offset the costs of providing pickup service and, perhaps more importantly, it discourages shippers from initiating single shipments of small size.

Terminal Charges. *Demurrage and Detention.* The words "demurrage" and "detention" both refer to the same thing: charges assessed by the carrier against the shipper or consignee for delay of a car, vessel, or vehicle beyond a specified time allowed for loading or unloading and releasing the equipment to the carrier. The term demurrage is used in rail, pipeline, and water transportation. Rail demurrage is charged after a detention of rail cars for unloading beyond the "free time" period, which is usually 48 hours from the time a car is placed for loading or unloading. The demurrage charge in 1971 was $10/day for the first four days after the 48-hour "free time," $20/day for the next two days, and $30/day for each subsequent day. There are numerous rules exempting certain types of cars from demurrage, and there are special charges and rates for specific types of freight.

Demurrage control is supervised by bureaus established by the carriers. Most rail users enter into "average demurrage agreements" with the various demurrage bureaus. Under an average demurrage agreement, during a one-month period demurrage credits (credits for unloading or loading cars in less than the "free time" periods) are offset by demurrage debits (charges for detaining cars beyond the free time period). A restriction is that demurrage credits may not offset more than four days' demurrage charges for detention of an individual car.

Pipeline demurrage is charged when the receiver is not capable (usually because of insufficient storage space) of receiving the quantity delivered to it by a pipeline. The charge for pipeline demurrage is a maximum of $.01/barrel/day beginning with the time that the consignee was unable to receive the shipment.

For water movement, demurrage charges for vessel detention are based on the size of the vessel and are usually specified in the applicable tariffs or contracts. Free time is based on the volume and characteristics of the cargo to be unloaded.

Detention is the term applied to the delay of highway vehicles. Uniform practices have not been established by the highway carriers for detention charges but some tariffs specify charges for unreasonable delay of highway equipment. For example, there is a tariff provision whereby loading or unloading time in excess of three hours is charged at the rate of $2.50/15 min. for tank trucks moving liquefied propane gas (LPG) shipments.

Switching Charges. Line-haul rail rates usually include switching service to the consignee's point of unloading. Carriers frequently establish reciprocal switching arrangements. Reciprocal switching means that the switching carrier will deliver to destination (within certain switching limits) a car which it did not handle in line-haul movement, and settlement of switching charges is made directly between the line-haul and the switching carrier. When the line-haul carrier does not have access to the destination point (i.e., siding) and the destination is "closed" to reciprocal switching, the shipper or consignee must pay for the switching, which is charged on a per-car basis. Most frequently the cost is less than $30/car but it can be as high as $200/car.

In individual industrial plant complexes, where there are extensive track facilities, the carrier is required only to switch to the "first spot" designated by the consignee or shipper. If additional switching is required or there are any unreasonable delays in switching, the carrier is required to charge for diesel engine time according to the prescribed tariff.

Interstate and Intrastate Rates

An *interstate* shipment is defined as the movement of goods "between any place in a state and any place in another state, or between places in the same state through another state."[23] Conversely, an *intrastate* shipment is the movement of goods wholly within a particular state. Based upon a number of Supreme Court decisions, an *interstate* shipment is defined by the intent of the shipper[24] and the nature of the service rendered (i.e., actual movement); it is *not* defined by the billing for the shipment,[25] or the plurality of carriers that may have participated in the shipment.[26]

The specific blend or mixture between interstate and intrastate shipments (and the rates and charges applicable to each) will vary from company to company depending upon the pattern of logistics movements. Generally, *intrastate* shipments will involve (1) raw materials which possess greater weight-reduction tendencies (that is, they lose much of their weight in the manufacturing process), and (2) finished goods moving from a distribution center to customers in the local market (physical distribution). Generally, *interstate* shipments will involve (1) raw materials which possess lesser weight-reduction tendencies (physical supply), and (2) movement of finished goods from the plant to distribution centers (primary movement) and from the distribution center to customers in surrounding states (secondary movement). The proportion of intrastate shipments is increased with an increase in the number of distribution centers (either company-owned or managed, or public warehouses).

Intrastate shipments and rates tend to be underemphasized, or even forgotten. Yet they are important.

The regulation of rates for intrastate shipments is the responsibility of state regulatory agencies, sometimes identified as "public utilities commissions." The degree of regulation varies significantly among the states.[27] For example, the California Public Utilities Commission (PUC) operates a relatively strict and complex system of economic regulation for intrastate transportation movements. The California PUC publishes several tariffs which specify minimum rates applicable to California intrastate shipments. In addition to intercity rates, special intrastate rate systems are applied to shipments moving within, into, or out of the metropolitan areas (geographically defined by the California PUC) of San Francisco, Los Angeles, and San Diego.

---

[23] Part II, Section 203 of the Interstate Commerce Act. Although the Part II definition deals primarily with motor carriers, Part I provides a similar but more detailed definition applicable to rail carriers.

[24] *Baltimore and O.S.W.R. Co. v. Settle,* 260 U. S. 166 (1922).

[25] *U. S. v. Union Stock Yards and Transit Co. of Chicago,* 226 U. S. 286 (1912).

[26] *South Covington Ry. v. Covington,* 235 U. S. 537 (1915).

[27] Donald V. Harper, *Economic Regulation of the Motor Carrier Industry by the States* (Urbana: University of Illinois Press, 1959).

RATE LEVEL DETERMINANTS

There are two basic elements which are evaluated in the rate-making process. These are "cost" and "value." With regard to a specific rate, it can be said that the value of service element most often establishes the upper level that a rate might tend to seek. Carrier out-of-pocket cost tends to set the lower level of a specific rate. The factors which are outlined below are those which substantiate rate levels either at the bottom or top of this range. In addition to various characteristics of the product shipped, other factors which influence rate levels are distance and direction of movement, quantity shipped, restrictions on discrimination, and competition.

Cost of Service

Carrier costs to provide a service consist of four types, each of which has several names: (1) fixed, overhead, irreducible, constant, or indirect costs, (2) variable, out-of-pocket, reducible, inconstant, or direct costs, (3) joint and common costs, and (4) fully allocated, full or total costs. The first are those which are essentially constant over a period of time, generally considered to be short-run in nature (all costs are variable given a long enough period of time for consideration). The second category are those extra costs incurred to provide services without which the costs would not exist. The third type are: (a) joint costs incurred simultaneously by different shipments moving by the same mode, the same carrier, over the same route, and even in the same vehicle at the same time, i.e., from any process by which capacity is made available for the use of a machine or vehicle for two different "tasks" or purposes simultaneously at one cost, and (b) common costs which must be apportioned to various services, such as the allocation of railroad right-of-way maintenance costs to both freight and passenger service. Together, fixed and variable costs of a given service make up its fully allocated cost, the fourth type listed above.

The line drawn between joint and common costs is fine indeed, and often subject to debate. Both joint and common costs may be present at the same time and either fixed or variable in nature, further complicating theoretical cost identification.

Value of Service

The value of service concept in rate making is characterized by the assessment of the ability of a product to bear a given transportation rate burden. For example, high-value items can probably bear higher per-unit, per-hundredweight, or per-cubic-foot rates than items of lower value.

Items of very low value, on the other hand, may be given very low rates, based on the value of service concept. It has been suggested by Locklin that preferential (low) rates based on the "value of service" concept are not a burden on other traffic if the rates cover carrier direct, or out-of-pocket, cost and if the traffic will not command higher rates.[28] If these two conditions were actually met in low "value of service" rate making, there would be little objection to this method of determining rates. It is likely, however, that low value of service rates do not always cover out-of-pocket carrier costs, nor are carriers precise in their determination of whether the same volume of traffic would move at higher rates.

Direction of Movement

Whether a shipment moves in the light-haul or heavy-haul direction will also have an important effect on the rate level. When a shipment is moving in a heavy-haul direction, the rate tends to be higher than a comparable movement in the light-haul direction.

In many situations, changes in the direction of movement have presented serious problems to both carriers and shippers. If, for example, the light-haul direction were to become the heavy-haul direction, and previously mentioned light-haul rates were based on filling unused capacity, the carrier's revenue structure would become upset. Such situations often lead to inadequate service by the carrier as it attempts to adjust operations to the changed movement pattern.

Quantity and Regularity of Shipments

Two elements of quantity affect the level of rates: the volume shipped in the individual movement (minimum), and the quantity and regularity of shipments over a period in time. The significance of the quantity per shipment has already been discussed. The elements of time and regularity are significant because of the carriers' desire to obtain regular utilization of equipment, and thus avoid "peaks and valleys" of operations.

Restrictions on Discrimination

Between Commodities. Many differences in rate levels cannot be justified or explained by differences in carriers' costs of transporting the

[28] Locklin, *op. cit.*, p. 163.

commodities. The earlier discussion pertaining to the development of
regulation of transportation dealt exclusively with regulation governing
rates and the rate-making process. Equally important in the development
of regulation were the provisions against unjust and unreasonable discrimination. These provisions prescribed the general rules for control of
transportation and established the limits of the rate-making process.

The following excerpts from Part I of the Interstate Commerce Act
indicate the limitations placed by the Act on unjust and unreasonable
discrimination. Note that the Act prohibits only unjust and unreasonable
discrimination. Discrimination, in the sense the term is used in economics, is actually widespread in the rate structure and is not necessarily
unlawful:

Section 2. That if any common carrier subject to the provisions of this
part . . . receive from any person or persons a greater, or less compensation
for any service rendered, or to be rendered, than it receives from any other
person for doing him or them a like and contemporaneous service . . . under
substantially similar circumstances and conditions, such carrier shall be deemed
guilty of unjust discrimination and is hereby prohibited and declared to be
unlawful.
Section 3. (1) It shall be unlawful for any common carrier subject to the
provisions of this part to . . . give . . . any undue or unreasonable preference
or advantage to any particular person, company, firm, corporation, association,
locality, port, port district, gateway, transit point, region, district, territory, or
any particular description of traffic, in any respect whatsoever: *Provided, however,* that this paragraph shall not be construed to apply to discrimination,
prejudice, or disadvantage to the traffic of any other carrier of whatever
description.[29]

With respect to discrimination between commodities, the Commission
is primarily concerned with the relationship between the rates on various
commodities rather than any specific rate. Discrimination does not exist,
however, merely because rates are different. To prove unlawful discrimination it must be demonstrated by a complainant that the alleged
discrimination has truly placed it at a disadvantage in marketing its
products; further, it must be demonstrated that the commodities alleged
to have been given unduly preferential rates are actually "substitutable"
for the products against which discrimination is alleged.

Local and Regional Discrimination. Local and regional discrimination
occur when rates offer some economic advantage to one area as compared
with another. The discrimination is unlawful when the localities are in a
direct competitive relationship and the discrimination cannot be justified
by cost or operational considerations which make discrimination between

[29] A similar provision is provided in Part II of the Act for motor carriers in Section
216 (d), and for water carriers in Section 305 of Part III.

points reasonable. For example, several years ago, rail carriers established rates from the Gulf Coast area to the West Coast which were considerably less than rates for movements from Midwestern points to the West Coast. The Gulf Coast–West Coast rates were $.95/cwt. as compared with $1.47/cwt. from the Midwest to the West Coast. The basis for the justifiable "discrimination" against the Midwest in this case was the necessity to meet water competition which was available to Gulf Coast shippers but not available to Midwestern shippers.

Personal Discrimination. Personal discrimination is manifested either by special rate concessions to individuals or by special service made available to one shipper and not to another. The granting of special rate concessions outright is no longer a serious problem. Personal discrimination does develop, however, in situations where shippers are permitted to use inadequate or incorrect commodity descriptions to obtain lower rates. This occurs when the carrier either knowingly permits the incorrect description or when the carrier fails to "police" adequately the description of items by shippers.

Individual service discrimination presents a more difficult problem of control. Service discrimination is found in the supply of premium and specialized equipment to individual shippers in excess of the reasonable proportion of this premium equipment that should be assigned to them. Other forms of personal discrimination are found in the number of pickups, deliveries, or switches that are made available to various shippers and receivers. Special concessions with regard to the installation of spur-track facilities or loading docks, and more recently the provision of warehouse facilities by carriers for shippers, are other areas where discrimination exists.

Long and Short Haul Discrimination. This type of discrimination applies to the charging of a higher rate for movement of goods a shorter distance as opposed to a longer distance *over the same route by the same mode.* Such discrimination, resulting in early complaints of suffering shippers, has been ruled largely illegal under Section 4 of the Interstate Commerce Act, the "long and short haul clause." Section 4 applies only to rail and water carriers. Motor carriers have such a high proportion of variable costs that long and short haul discrimination by them would only rarely make economic sense. The Federal Aviation Act contains no provision against long and short haul discrimination in the airline industry.

Railroads, for which long and short haul discrimination has been most troublesome, have attempted to justify it on the basis of their high percentage of fixed costs which are partially defrayed by revenue created by low rates to a further point in order to secure the business. In other words, rates to the shorter point would be much higher in the absence of revenues produced by long and short haul discrimination.

Long and short haul clause "relief" has been granted railroads carrying on intense intermodal competition at some points while encountering almost no competition at other points. In addition, relief has been granted to more circuitous rail routes in competition with more direct rail routes between two points. Carriers in poor financial condition may receive "Section 4" relief to enable them to compete with healthier operations at competitive points.[30]

Competition

Intermode. On the present transportation scene, intermodal competition is the most important factor in the determination of rate levels. The struggle by the various modes of transportation for increases in volume (and in some cases survival) is intense. If a shipper has no competitive alternative for the movement of its products, the rate levels at which his products will move will tend toward the higher limits of the range and will be based to a large extent on the value of service concept of rate making.

Intramode. Intramodal competition does not have the same effect on the level of rates as does intermodal competition. In fact, in many instances, it has been suggested that intramodal competition actually has an adverse effect on rate levels and causes them to increase. The basic reason for this is the duplication of routes and facilities that results from intramodal competition. Common carriers within the same mode of transportation must charge the same rate between two points. The only factor which differentiates one from the other is the service that they can render. Competitive service, which frequently has only intangible value, is frequently reflected in a higher cost of transportation. For example, there are many situations where the volume of movement between two points or within a regional area would justify the existence of only three carriers. However, the regulatory body has authorized more than three carriers to operate within the area. If the volume of traffic is allocated evenly among the available carriers, it might be said that all of them are operating at less than capacity and therefore are operating inefficiently. The results of inefficiency are always higher transportation costs and often higher rates. In addition, when the supply of transportation services

---

[30] A very detailed and lucid description and discussion of long and short haul discrimination is given in Locklin, *op. cit.*, pp. 488–510.

exceeds the demand for it, intense traffic solicitation and special concessions in connection with traffic solicitation tend to increase the cost of transportation without any economic benefit to the shipper.

Private Transportation. Private transportation has developed for two basic reasons. First, private transportation is an attractive alternative to for-hire service when a shipper's traffic has volume and movement characteristics which permit it to operate at lower cost than possible under the rates charged by regulated carriers, or when the service rendered by available carriers is inadequate to the customer service demands of the shipper.

Second, private transportation is also used as a lever to obtain rate concessions from carriers. When a shipper is unable to obtain a rate concession which he believes reasonable (or unreasonable) and private transportation is a feasible alternative, the shipper can install a private transportation system in order to bring about the rate adjustment. In addition, the threat of private transportation is used in the same manner as a "bluff" in a poker game; the shipper develops a private transportation system plan and "bluffs" that if rate concessions are not granted, the system will be installed.

TRANSPORTATION RATE LEVEL EXAMPLES

Instead of discussing generally the rate level relationships between the various modes of transportation (plus auxiliary users) we will use several rate comparisons to illustrate actual rates for movements of various quantities of a particular commodity between various points. These are shown in Tables 5–6 (opposite) and 5–7 (page 166).

(10) Referring to Tables 5–6 and 5–7, plot the relationship between distance and truck rates for both small and large shipments. What do you find? (11) How do you explain it? (12) In Table 5–6, how can freight forwarder rates be lower than truck rates between Minneapolis and certain destinations when the freight forwarder has to pay published truck rates to have his shipments transported by truck?

SUMMARY

Our objectives in this chapter have been to: (1) convey a feeling for the complexities of the rate structure for regulated transportation carriers, and (2) indicate the opportunities for differentiated rate "treatment" among competitors that exist in a system often assumed to provide uniform rates for all competitors under similar circumstances. This

TABLE 5-6. Analysis of Alternate[a] Transportation Rates and
Cost of Shipment from Minneapolis to Points Indicated

Weight of Shipment: 160 lb.
Commodity: Recordings, sound, disc type, plastic, non-breakable, in boxes

	Truck			Freight Forwarder		
Minneapolis to	Rate/100 Lb. (Cwt.)[b]	Minimum Charge	Cost	Rate/100 Lb. (Cwt.)[b]	Minimum Charge	Cost
Boston, Mass.	$ 8.07	$12.72	$12.91	$ 8.07	$15.39	$15.39
Atlanta, Ga.	6.63	11.81	11.84	6.63	12.71	12.71
Chicago, Ill.	5.45	9.33	9.33	4.31	7.95	7.95
Houston, Tex.	8.35	14.81	14.81	8.35	15.65	15.65
Denver, Colo.	7.99	12.41	12.78	X	X	X
Los Angeles, Calif.	10.36	16.75	16.75	10.36	15.82	16.58

X = no rates or services.

[a]Rail service for this size shipment is not available.

[b]A shipment which weighs less than 100 lb. is charged for as if it were 100 lb. Shipments which weigh in excess of 100 lb. are charged for based on the actual weight of the shipment. The calculated charge is then compared to the minimum charge, and the *higher* charge becomes the cost of transportation service.

material, together with our coverage in Chapter 3 of parallel topics relating to warehousing and communications, contrasts the degree of regulation in the three most important segments of for-hire logistics activity—transportation, warehousing, and communications. This should provide at least some perspective for use in considering related matters on which carrier, warehousing, and communication rates and services will have an important bearing.

SUGGESTED READINGS

Cookenboo, Jr., Leslie. *Crude Oil Pipelines and Competition in the Oil Industry.* Cambridge: Harvard University Press, 1955.
Of particular interest for a history of the development of pipeline companies, and for a thorough analysis of pipeline costs.
Daggett, Stuart. *Principles of Inland Transportation.* New York: Harper & Row, 1955.
Presents a historical and complete discussion of long- and short-haul discrimination, modern regulation by the states, and the most complete and thorough discussion of transportation regulation.
Flood, Kenneth U. *Traffic Management,* 2nd Ed. Dubuque, Iowa: W. C. Brown Co., 1963.
Presents an especially valuable discussion of tariffs, tariff publishing agencies, and tariff interpretation, a detailed discussion of freight rates footnoted with key Interstate Commerce Commission cases, discussion of the determination of applicable rates, stop-off rules, reconsignment and diversion, switching, and demurrage.

TABLE 5–7. Analysis of Alternate Transportation Rates and Cost of Shipment from Minneapolis to Points Indicated

Weight of Shipment: Maximum quantity examples[a]

Commodity: Recordings, sound, disc type, plastic, non-breakable, in boxes

Minneapolis to	Truck Rate	Truck Cost	TOFC[b] Rate	TOFC[b] Cost	Freight Forwarder Rate	Freight Forwarder Cost	Rail Rate	Rail Cost
Boston, Mass.	$3.19[e]	$ 765.60	$2.83[g]	$1,132.00	$3.19[e]	$ 765.60	$3.49[f]	$1,047.00
Atlanta, Ga.	3.05[e]	732.00	3.40[e]	816.00	3.05[e]	732.00	3.17[f]	951.00
Chicago, Ill.	1.67[e]	400.80	1.46[g]	584.00	2.35[c]	376.00	1.80[f]	540.00
Houston, Tex.	3.61[e]	866.40	3.77[d]	754.00	3.50[e]	840.00	3.53[f]	1,059.00
Denver, Colo.	2.85[e]	684.00	3.19[e]	765.60	X	X	2.74[f]	822.00
Los Angeles, Calif.	5.06[e]	1,214.40	X	X	5.06[e]	1,214.40	5.03[f]	1,509.00

X = no rates or services.

[a]Based on the highest minimum weights for which rates are provided.
[b]Trailer-on-flat-car or "piggyback" service.
[c]Minimum weight 16,000 lb.
[d]Minimum weight 20,000 lb.
[e]Minimum weight 24,000 lb.
[f]Minimum weight 30,000 lb.
[g]Minimum weight 40,000 lb.

FREDERICK, JOHN H. *Commercial Air Transportation,* 5th Ed. Homewood, Ill.: Richard D. Irwin, Inc., 1961.
Offers a complete discussion of air freight rates from the inception of the use of air freight by the airlines in 1944.

HARPER, DONALD V. *Economic Regulation of the Motor Trucking Industry by the States.* Urbana, Ill.: University of Illinois Press, 1959.
Presents the most definitive work on motor carrier regulation at the state level.

LOCKLIN, D. PHILIP. *Economics of Transportation,* 7th Ed. Homewood, Ill.: Richard D. Irwin, Inc., 1972.
An excellent general reference for the material covered in this chapter with especially good coverage of regulation, discrimination, and rate making.

PEGRUM, DUDLEY F. *Transportation: Economics and Public Policy,* 0ld Ed. Homewood, Ill.: Richard D. Irwin, Inc., 1973.
Discusses the principles and practices of carrier rate making.

SAMPSON, ROY J., and MARTIN T. FARRIS. *Domestic Transportation,* 2nd Ed. Boston: Houghton Mifflin Co., 1971.
Offers a useful discussion of the preparation and use of freight classifications and tariffs, a description of types of freight rates, and a consideration of freight rate structures.

TAFF, CHARLES A. *Commercial Motor Transportation,* 4th Ed. Homewood, Ill.: Richard D. Irwin, Inc., 1969.
Discusses the rate-making procedure for motor carriers.

————. *Management of Physical Distribution and Transportation,* 5th Ed. Homewood, Ill.: Richard D. Irwin, Inc., 1972.
Presents a discussion of carrier service availability.

PART THREE

SYSTEM RELATIONSHIPS

Just as no man is an island unto himself, certainly no logistics system exists without significant and constraining relationships with other activities, both within and outside the firm. The field of logistics thus provides no exception to the rule that activities of a business are subject to externally and internally imposed constraints.

Part Three is confined to our consideration of logistics system relationships in the form of internally imposed constraints on logistics systems. For our purposes, we choose to define an internal constraint as a limitation set by executive action of persons other than individuals directly in charge of specific or overall matters of logistics. Three of the most important sets of logistics system relationships and constraints, in terms of their impact on the logistics system, are procurement policies, product pricing policies, and customer service standards.

Of course, many factors external to the firm must be taken into account in establishing these limits or constraints. For example, the actions of competitors in the marketplace, the service capabilities of the transportation system, and government regulatory restrictions all may influence internal decisions of the firm. External relationships such as these are discussed, where appropriate, throughout the book. They have not been singled out or grouped for discussion because they are largely constraints on all firms, outside the influence of any one business organization. They cannot be significantly altered by the action of any single firm.

It may be pointed out that we have omitted a constraint of overwhelming importance in the firm, money for financing. In our discussion we have assumed that money for a potentially *profitable* action on the part of the logistician can be found (and will be found) somewhere. The discussion is heavily cost-oriented, of course, and money stands as a silent factor in many problems discussed in this section.

A logistics manager may exercise some control over the establishment or alteration of constraints on operations under his authority. It is more likely, however, that he will only participate in, or supply information for, decisions regarding intra-corporate relationships and resultant constraints which affect the operations he directs. In order to participate intelligently he must know what information is likely to be required of him to assess the impact of alternative actions on the logistics system, and to support any proposal or report he might make. This requires a good working knowledge of analytic approaches to the establishment of procurement of policies, product pricing policies, and customer service standards.

The limits imposed by the types of internal constraints discussed in this section of the text exert a powerful influence on the day-to-day operation of the logistics system and are changed infrequently in most firms. For these reasons, decisions affecting logistics system relationships and constraints are the most important in which the logistician participates.

One of our colleagues has argued that a better word than "relationship" or "constraint" would be the current buzz word "interface." We have deliberately minimized use of this word in Part Three because we are not talking about interfaces here; we are talking about relationships and constraints. Our view is that an interface is something you worry about operationally after you understand the existence and nature of a relationship in the first place.

In Part Five (System Management) we will get around to interfaces. Here in Part Three we explore some important logistics system relationships, and we will try to give you a healthy respect for the meaning of the fact that the logistician is not a lone wolf in the corporate forest.

6

Procurement Policies

Whether it is called buying, purchasing, or procurement, no other function in a typical firm involves as great a dollar responsibility per unit of manpower. Routine decisions involving millions of dollars in the purchase of raw materials, component parts, equipment, supplies, or products for resale are the day-to-day rule for personnel engaged in procurement activities.

But the act of buying is merely the tip of the iceberg representing procurement activities. It may be preceded and followed by many less visible and spectacular activities falling under the responsibility of a progressive, aggressive procurement group.

Our major concern here is with the procurement policies and procedures which make up an integral part of the logistics planning and implementation process. Our focus will be on items purchased repeatedly and in some volume, such as raw materials and component parts used in manufacturing, consumables (supplies consumed in the manufacturing process), and goods purchased for resale. After considering procurement, and more particularly purchasing department functions and operations, we will explore in greater detail those specific policies with importance for logistics efforts. Finally, we look into the relationship among purchasing, procurement, and materials management, and the way in which all of these relate to the logistics of the firm.

THE MISSION AND IMPORTANCE OF THE
INDUSTRIAL PURCHASING DEPARTMENT

Most procurement actions are executed by the purchasing department in the industrial firm. Figure 6–1 indicates the influences exerted upon

171

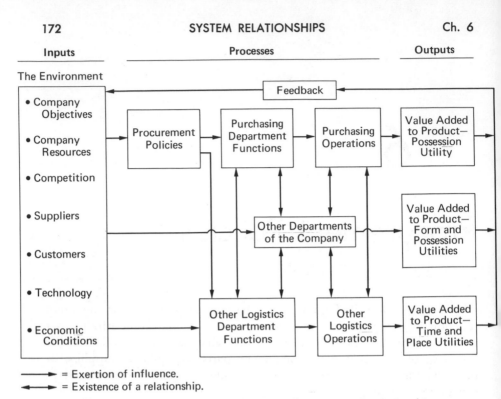

Fig. 6–1. Purchasing Department influences and relationships.

and from the purchasing department, and the relationships between purchasing and other logistics functions.

Environmental inputs serve as constraints to purchasing as well as other departments. These constraints include company objectives and committed levels of resources, outside influences from competitors, suppliers, and customers, industry and/or company levels of technology, and general economic conditions. Top management establishes procurement policies based upon environmental constraints and departmental inputs in terms of feedback information. Procurement policies define purchasing department functions. In turn, these functions define purchasing operations. The output of the purchasing department, as well as other departments, is the value added to the product, through the creation of possession utility, which in turn supplies feedback to the environment, both internal and external to the company.

Purchasing Department Functions

Within the guidelines established by company procurement policies, the purchasing department is responsible for conducting procurement functions. The purchasing department has been defined as:

. . . corporate management's group of professional and expert specialists for the procurement of materials, supplies, tools and services required by all other groups in the enterprise in the over-all process of adding value.[1]

Among the general functions of a purchasing department are those of providing purchasing services, obtaining the most effective value in items purchased, controlling financial commitments, conducting negotiations, and providing input to associated management information systems.

Providing Purchasing Services. The purchasing department is an organization of specialists performing company procurement functions on a centralized basis. Other departments which have procurement needs submit purchase requests to the purchasing department. Purchasing must be able to coordinate all of the factors affecting procurement, including those emanating from within the company as well as those external to the company, such as actual and potential suppliers. This suggests the continuing importance of relationships between purchasing and other departments of the firm.

Obtaining Effective Item Value. Value, as opposed to costs, is a measure of the worth of items to an individual or a firm. Typically, when value exceeds cost by some amount, a purchase takes place. A basic function of purchasing is to coordinate the inputs necessary to create the most effective, favorable relationship between value and cost for the firm. As such, the purchasing department can be regarded as an organization's defense against the man once described by John Ruskin: "There is hardly anything in this world that some man cannot make a little worse and sell a little cheaper, and the people who consider price only are this man's lawful prey."

Any savings that can be accomplished in the procurement process have a direct effect upon profits. In fact, in most firms, each dollar saved in purchasing is equivalent to the profit earned on many sales dollars. However, cost savings should not be overemphasized, because sometimes it is necessary to spend additional purchasing dollars in order to provide proper product availability in terms of timing, quality, or quantity. For example, in producing the best overall product value, it would not be wise to haggle over a few purchasing dollars at the risk of closing down the production line. Thus, the economic functions of purchasing must be properly balanced against the needs of the firm.

Controlling Financial Commitments. Purchased materials represent a significant portion of sales dollars in most manufacturing firms, as

[1] George Aljian (ed.), *Purchasing Handbook*, 2nd Ed. (New York: McGraw-Hill Book Co., 1966), pp. 1–3.

TABLE 6-1. Purchased Materials as a Proportion of Sales Dollars in Selected Industries

Industry	Materials Costs as a Percentage of Sales	Industry	Materials Costs as a Percentage of Sales
Aircraft	53%	Gray iron foundries	44%
Aluminum	53	Machine tools	35
Business forms	39	Metal stampings	50
Cans, metal	66	Motors and generators	41
Chemicals, organic	46	Paper mills	50
Cigarettes	52	Paperboard mills	49
Computers	51	Plastic materials	53
Construction machinery	57	Screw machine products	41
Containers, corrugated	55	Steel (fabricated	
Cotton finishing	62	structural)	59
Cotton weaving	57	TV and radio sets	60
Electronic components	36	Tires and tubes	57
Furniture, wood	49		

Source: Reprinted by special permission from the April 16, 1962, issue of *Purchasing Week* (now *Purchasing World*; Technical Publishing Co.). Copyright © 1962 by McGraw-Hill, Inc.

shown in Table 6–1. This significant financial obligation is a strong reason for identifying and centralizing procurement functions. It requires the management of procurement activities within limits suggested by a firm's ability to pay, defined by its cash flows. It requires a close control over personnel authorized to make procurement commitments on behalf of the firm. Above all, it suggests the need for close coordination between finance and purchasing in most firms.

(1) **What factors influence the importance of purchased materials for an individual firm?** (2) **Do you see any relationships between the nature of the product produced and the relative importance of purchased materials in Table 6–1?**

Conducting Negotiations. One of the major functions of the purchasing department is to conduct contract negotiations between the firm and suppliers. In order to effectively bargain over proposal and contract issues, a firm must maintain tight control over the negotiating process and the various personnel involved in the process. Such control generally is exercised by appointing a purchasing department representative in charge of negotiations. All communication with the supplier is performed through, or with the knowledge of, this purchasing representative. In this manner, conflicting or otherwise harmful statements can be monitored and adjusted to match overall company strategies prior to actual communication with a supplier.

Providing Information Input. As previously indicated, the procurement process involves large amounts of information flowing among a number of departments. It is a function of the purchasing department to obtain the information required to process specific purchases and to provide appropriate information feedback to the departments for whom procurement actions are being accomplished. The nature of information exchanged between purchasing and other departments within a firm is illustrated in Fig. 6–2.

The Role of the Purchasing Department in the Procurement Process

As a framework for exploring relationships between purchasing and other functions party to the procurement process in the industrial firm, the following discussion is focused around basic questions about procured materials. Figure 6–3 identifies this framework in terms of basic procurement questions, significant criteria that help further to define the questions, the primary functions often having responsibility for action, and the other functions with which coordination is required.

What To Procure? The prerequisite to any procurement action is to define what will be procured. Three different but related criteria are helpful in specifying the "what." These criteria include the purpose, design, and quality of the material to be procured.

Purpose concerns the overall manner in which material (or services) will fit into, or be utilized in support of, the end product. Because production is responsible for manufacturing the end product, it often has the greatest single voice in determining how the elements of production will be united. Further, production personnel typically are in the best position to determine what is to be purchased from suppliers. However, additional, specialized inputs may be required from engineering, purchasing, accounting, inventory control, and sales. (3) **What types of desirable inputs from each of these groups can you think of?**

Design also defines the material or product to be procured. In an industrial firm, engineering typically develops drawings and specifications, from which a bill of materials is obtained. These documents provide input information to production (for the planning of production processes), purchasing (for design requirements), and logistics (for inventory definition). Quality assurance assists engineering, production, and purchasing in the specialized areas of determining the desired level of quality assurance and quality conformance (inspection and related techniques). Generally, purchasing prefers design documentation that allows flexibility and competition in the procurement process, perhaps

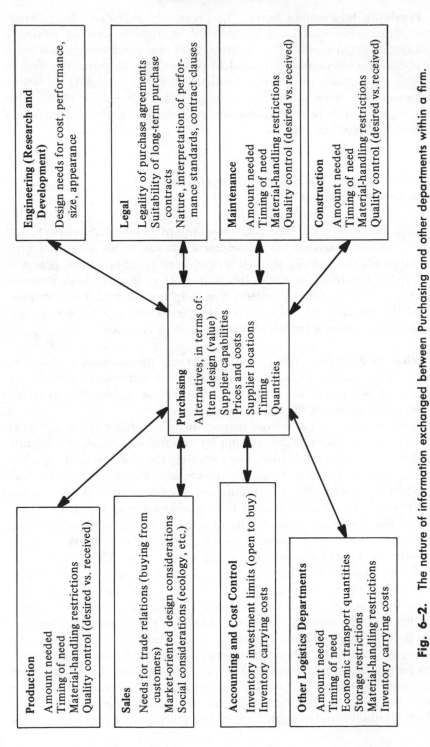

Fig. 6–2. The nature of information exchanged between Purchasing and other departments within a firm.

using standardized nomenclature or specifications. Sales inputs to engineering may include information about market conditions, competitive products, and customer preferences in design considerations.

Basic quality characteristics may be planned to conform to the desired image of company products. Within these bounds, many cost and performance combinations need to be evaluated and decided. In their deliberations regarding product design and quality, engineering and production personnel will receive inputs from sales and purchasing as well. Final quality determinations are incorporated into material and product design. They may have an effect on inventory management, particularly if relatively low-quality materials are procured and subsequently found to be inadequate, thus creating a supply of unusable material simultaneous with a shortage of proper material.

Whom To Procure From? Within the guidelines established by procurement policies concerning "alternative sources of supply" and "reciprocity" (buying from customers on a preferential basis), purchasing has the primary responsibility for identifying, evaluating, and establishing contact with potential suppliers for materials and services required by the firm. Purchasing may establish a "shopping list" of potential suppliers and maintain up-to-date records regarding supplier products, prices, services, and general policies. Purchasing has a responsibility for keeping other departments informed about suppliers and their products. Such information is useful, both in procurement negotiations and as an input to the "what to procure" decisions discussed above.

Where To Procure? The location of the procurement source is defined by the designation of a specific supplier. However, in some cases, suppliers may offer alternative origins from which an order may be filled and a shipment initiated. Those concerned with traffic and transportation will then identify the "best" origin point in terms of transportation charges, transit time, and the pattern of other shipments to or from the firm offering a potential for shipment coordination. Based upon an existing pattern of shipments, a more distant point might provide faster and more economical supply than a less distant point. This may be especially true when a firm operates privately owned equipment to meet a portion of its shipment pattern. Coordination is required between traffic and purchasing in the selection of transportation mode and routing, the performance of receiving and storage functions upon receipt of the material, and matters regarding the effect of transportation methods on the condition in which purchased goods are received.

Which Item To Procure? Once product materials and components have been identified and the product has been placed into production, inventory replenishment decisions must be made. Here, the output from the inventory management program for materials and components will provide the necessary inputs to the purchasing action.

How Much To Procure?   For inventoried purchases, the question of "how much" to order is subject to continual review. Two aspects are the magnitude of desired investment (in terms of dollars) in inventory and the determination of specific reorder quantities (usually in terms of economic order quantities). Proper reorder quantity size is influenced by such factors as customer demand rates for the end product, production requirement rates, purchase quantity discounts on supply materials, ordering costs, inventory carrying costs, and the available lead time for acquiring and receiving materials. The relationship among these influences will be discussed in detail in later chapters. In many firms, inventory control is the primary function concerned with "how much." Coordination, as indicated in Fig. 6–3, is required among production, sales, accounting, and purchasing.

When To Procure?   "When to procure" is keyed to delivery requirements and the schedule lead time (or order cycle), defined as the total time period between the notification to replenish stock in inventory and the actual placement of materials in inventory. The length of lead time will be influenced by order cycle times at both the firm initiating the order and its supplier, and transportation considerations between the supplier and the ordering firm. "When" is a primary function of inventory control, as coordinated with production (in terms of production needs) and purchasing (in terms of procurement time requirements).

In What Form To Procure?   Purchasing responsibilities include those for determining: (1) alternative methods or forms in which items may be procured, (2) assessing constraints which may dictate the form in which such items must be received, and (3) matching the two. The following example illustrates the nature of the opportunity:

A Philadelphia chemical producer's purchasing department discovered how material handling costs climb when vendors are unfamiliar with a customer's facilities for handling inbound products.

Not long ago the company ordered several chemical processing coils. No instructions were given on how the coils were to be packed and shipped, however.

What happened? The coils arrived, packed in containers so bulky that: (1) fork lifts couldn't handle them; (2) packaged coils wouldn't fit through doors leading from receiving dock to warehouses; (3) the coils couldn't be stored anywhere but on the floor (where they blocked off a large section of storage space) because the racks designed to hold them were not large enough.

Basic Procurement Question	Significant Criteria	Primary Functions	Other Functions With Which Coordination Is Required
What to procure?	Purpose: Materials	Production	Engineering, Purchasing, Accounting, Inventory Control, Sales
	Consumables	Using Function	Accounting
	Services	Using Function	Accounting
	Design	Engineering	Production, Purchasing, Quality Control
	Quality	Production	Engineering, Inventory Control, Quality Control, Sales, Purchasing
Whom to procure from?	Alternative suppliers	Purchasing	Production, Traffic, Engineering, Accounting
	Price negotiation	Purchasing	Production, Traffic, Accounting
	Procurement schedule	Purchasing	Production, Traffic
Where to procure?	Alternative supply points	Traffic	Purchasing
	Alternative modes	Traffic	
	Alternative routes	Traffic	
	Receiving & storage	Warehousing	Production, Purchasing, Quality Control
Which item to procure?	Replenishment order	Inventory Control	Production, Sales, Purchasing, Accounting
How much to procure?	Total dollar investment	Inventory Control	Production, Purchasing, Accounting
	Reorder quantity (EOQ):	Inventory Control	Production, Sales, Purchasing, Accounting
	Customer demand rate	Inventory Control	Sales
	Production requirements rate	Inventory Control	Production
	Quantity discount	Purchasing	Production, Inventory Control, Warehousing
	Ordering costs	Inventory Control	Purchasing, Sales
	Inventory carrying costs	Inventory Control	Purchasing, Production, Sales
	Lead time	Inventory Control	Purchasing, Production, Sales
When to procure?	Schedule: Delivery requirements	Inventory Control	Production, Purchasing
	Lead time	Inventory Control	Production, Purchasing
In what form to procure?	Characteristics of use	Purchasing	Production, Traffic, Warehousing
	Receiving, handling, and storage capability		

Fig. 6–3. Basic procurement questions and functional relationships in an industrial firm which procures to inventory.

Purchasing learned its lesson. Now it tells vendors what types and sizes of packaging it can handle, and cautions suppliers that their shipments must conform to this pattern. It is made clear that shipments that do not conform will be rejected.[2]

In some cases, the proper form in which to order goods may be suggested by material-handling requirements and the nature of patterns (quantities and frequency) with which an item is used in the production processes. In other cases, receiving and storage capabilities may be the major constraints. In any event, prior coordination with production, traffic, and warehousing can save the purchasing function a great deal of grief.

LOGISTICS OF THE PROCUREMENT PROCESS

Our concern here is for the set of factors that determine the importance of various logistics activities in the procurement process as well as the types of specific procurement policies that have the greatest importance for other logistics activities.

Factors Defining the Importance of Logistics Activities in the Procurement Process

Factors determining the importance of various logistics activities in the procurement process include: (1) the nature of a company's operation, (2) the nature of the product or service being procured, (3) the function supported by the procurement action, (4) whether the item procured is inventoried, and (5) whether the end product for which an item is procured is inventoried. Figure 6–4 (pages 182 and 183) presents the relationship of these factors in diagram form.

The Nature of a Company's Operation. As we have seen, the value of purchased products in relation to sales dollars approximates 50% in many firms involved in converting raw materials, components, and other purchased products and services into different products for resale. In contrast, the cost of procured items in relation to sales, often called the "cost of goods sold" in a firm engaged in reselling purchased products may range from 50% to 80% for retailers and even higher for wholesalers. (4) How would you expect this to influence the importance of purchasing (buying in a resale business) in such firms? (5) How would

2 Harvey Berman, "Turn Transport Problems Into Savings," *Purchasing*, July 14, 1966, pp. 78–80, at p. 79.

you expect the degree of importance of logistics considerations to vary between these basic types of firms? (6) Which category of firm would you expect to exert greater control over transportation and other logistics matters on inbound shipments?

The Nature of Products or Services Procured. Firms engaged in both converting and resale activities procure a number of different types of goods (including assemblies, equipment, components, raw materials, and consumables) and services. Materials, in varying mixtures dependent upon the particular requirements of each firm, are procured to support the production function. Certain consumables (fuel and tooling such as jigs and fixtures) are procured to support production or other departments (such as supplies for the office). Services, such as subcontracted labor or specialized functions such as photography, are procured to support the utilizing department. An important category of service, transportation, often is treated as a separate and specialized type of procurement performed by the traffic department. In a resale firm, buying will concentrate on finished goods in support of the sales or merchandising function, with the procurement of consumables and services occupying a lesser role and one often carried out in a less well-organized fashion.

(7) In general, how would you expect the importance of various logistics activities in the procurement process to vary with product and service categories discussed above? (8) More specifically, how would you rank the following items in terms of the role of such activities in their purchase: machine tools used in the manufacture of automobile parts, paper cups for an industrial firm, paper cups for a fast-food franchise organization, part-time secretarial service, or grain in a cereal-manufacturing company? (9) Why?

The Function Supported by the Procurement Action. The most important functions supported by procurement often are production in a converting firm and sales in a resale organization. To a lesser degree, all functions require such support. (10) In most cases, would you assume the logistics of procurement would play a greater role in support of production or sales? (11) Why? (12) What types of exceptions to this generalization could you envision?

The Degree to Which the Procured Item Is Inventoried. Functions served may require procurement to order or to inventory. In the former, the procurement process is linked closely to and initiated by the receipt of customer orders. This may eliminate the need for most inventories.

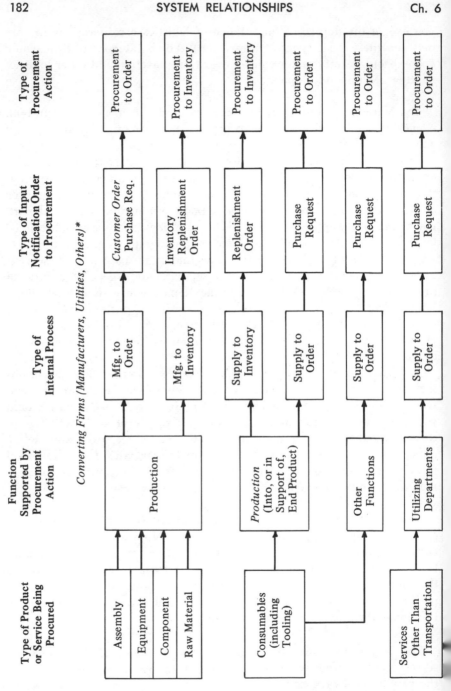

Fig. 6-4. Factors influencing the importance of logistics in procurement.

*Converting is used here to denote any firm engaged in transforming product or service inputs into basically different products or services.

Resale Firms (Wholesalers, Retailers)

Transportation Services → Traffic → Special Processes → Performed by Traffic Dept. → Procurement to Order

Finished Goods → Sales → Sell via Special Order → *Customer Order* Purchase Req. → Procurement to Inventory

→ Sell from Inventory → Replenishment Order → Procurement to Inventory

Consumables (Largely Supplies) → Utilizing Departments → Supply to Order → Purchase Request → Procurement to Order

Services Other Than Transportation → Utilizing Departments → Supply to Order → Purchase Request → Procurement to Order

Transportation Services → Logistics → Special Processes → Performed by Traffic Dept. → Procurement to Order

However, procurement to order often involves "one-of-a-kind" planning and coordination efforts, and can consume a great deal of time and effort.

Procurement to inventory, the purchase of goods for stock, requires an inventory replenishment order, often handled on a routine basis. Based upon this order, the purchasing department procures the needed materials or products to be supplied to inventory for later withdrawal by production, the using department, or sales, as appropriate.

Procurement to inventory has the greatest significance for logistics. Usually inventories are required for standardized products (where individual units are interchangeable), and competitive pressures require rapid response to customer needs. In such cases, finished goods and supporting material requirements may be estimated in advance and inventories established as buffers to assure support of customer needs (finished goods inventory) and production needs (materials inventory).

Many firms engage in both types of procurement. Here, the significance of logistics functions will depend upon the degree to which procurement to inventory is utilized.

The Degree to Which the Procured Item Is Used in Inventoried Finished Product. This consideration is relevant only to converting firms (engaged in form-converting production activities). Here, two opportunities to uncouple the demand for finished product from the need to procure raw materials or components exist in the form of finished product and raw material inventory buffers. Where they can be utilized, they may provide greater flexibility in planning the timing, quantities, and increments of goods purchased, thereby providing a greater opportunity for the exploration of logistics alternatives. On the other hand, the absence of finished product inventories may require logistics to expedite incoming goods and to insure the highest possible degree of carrier and supplier dependability and product availability to the production functions.

Procurement Policies Influencing Other Logistics Activities

Here we are interested primarily in specific procurement policies which have the greatest importance for other logistics activities. These are policies often formulated by top management rather than by purchasing or any other single department. In many companies, a formal management committee may be formed to evaluate and recommend such policies to top management. In any company, it is necessary to obtain inputs from the various functional areas (such as procurement, production, engineering, traffic, quality control, and marketing) in order to develop effective procurement policies which take into account cost/benefit trade-offs.

Procurement policies having the greatest impact on other logistics activities include make or buy decisions, the inbound material pricing method, the maintenance of alternate sources of supply, contract or "blanket" ordering, reciprocal agreements, value analysis, standardization, systems contracting, purchase order draft (POD) systems, customer–vendor coordination programs, and the use of computerized buying methods.

Make or Buy Decisions. "Make or buy" refers to a company's decision of the level(s) at which materials (assembly, equipment, component, or raw materials) will be either manufactured or purchased in support of the finished product. The comparative cost to make or buy an item is a primary criterion in the evaluation of such alternatives. Therefore it is necessary for the purchasing department to obtain supplier prices and for manufacturing, accounting, and other internal company departments to estimate the cost of internal manufacture.

However, cost comparisons are not the only criteria for make or buy decisions. The manufacture of an item not only requires investment in equipment, personnel, raw materials, space, and supervision, but also involves various overhead or indirect expenses. In some cases, a company may benefit from such investment in terms of additional control that it can achieve over its own operations, including control over design, schedule, quality, personnel and equipment utilization, and continuity of supply. On the other hand, procuring an item permits lower investment in company resources, thereby permitting investment in the manufacture of those items on which a company enjoys the greatest comparative return on investment. Thus, procurement of specified items from outside sources may permit cost savings resulting from greater specialization on the part of a supplier, lower in-plant inventories, application of competitive bidding, and greater flexibility to change design and quantity requirements.

Make or buy decisions affect the inventories that must be moved, stored, and coordinated. The specific impact on other logistics activities may depend upon the level of item under consideration for manufacture or purchase.

Assembly (or Subassembly) Level. Procurement at this level may require fewer items of greater value. Under these circumstances, the logistics system will deal with fewer origin points (suppliers) for incoming materials. The inventory carrying cost per unit will tend to be higher because of the value added to the product by the supplier.

Logistics scheduling and coordination (including the management information system) may require rapid response times in order to minimize inventory investments while maintaining an adequate supply for the production line. In some cases, such as assembly line production, the latter factor may be extremely critical to avoid a plant shutdown due to the non-availability of incoming materials.

Higher valued items generally incur higher transportation rates per hundred pounds. However, the higher rates might be offset by significant weight reductions achieved in the supplier's manufacturing process. Greater value and susceptibility to damage of assembled goods could result in increased damage during transportation and subsequent damage claim activity.

Equipment Level. Here we assume that equipment signifies a self-contained product which performs a specialized function in the conversion process but does not become a part of the end product.

Similar to other materials, equipment involves logistical movement, storage, and coordination of requirements. Unless a firm procures equipment from the same supplier over a long period of time, changing shipment patterns may require special logistics planning for each purchase. Perhaps most important of all, equipment spare parts and/or repair requirements tend to further complicate the logistics task. Spare or repair parts involve small shipments, often to scattered locations, and a relatively high degree of accompanying paperwork. Unless purchased equipment and supporting parts are highly standardized, complex inventory management needs can be created.

Component Level. Procurement at this level will tend to result in greater quantities of purchased parts and a greater number of suppliers than the other configuration levels. Unless component purchases are consolidated, the logistics system will have to comprise many origins, some initiating relatively small-sized shipments.

Raw Material Level. Procurement at the raw material level presumes a policy of manufacturing the item. This may create the need for special transportation and handling equipment and special warehouse facilities to accommodate raw materials. Although inventory carrying costs are likely to reflect the generally lower value of raw materials per unit of measure, transportation costs will have a tendency to play a greater part in a determination of the landed costs of such items. Thus, the geographic locations of sources become increasingly important. Raw material buying may involve speculation (buying in advance of need) to take advantage of price fluctuations or trends. Where this is the case, the major logistics mission may shift from inventory control to the handling and storage of unusually large stocks.

In most industrial companies, conditions are such that some combination of all four design levels is represented in make or buy decisions. Thus, in reality, the logistics system must be able to achieve multiple objectives and functions.

Inbound Material Pricing Method. Up to now we have assumed that purchases are made on an origin basis (exclusive of freight charges) on inbound materials (or items). If, in contrast, the purchase price includes transportation (and consequently seller control over carrier selection and routing on inbound shipments), logistics responsibilities in the purchasing firm may be confined only to purchasing, receiving, storing, handling, and inventorying of materials at destination. There are several other pricing policies that fall in between the complete inclusion or exclusion of transportation costs and control, and include varying logistics responsibilities.

Alternate Sources of Supply. Top management sets the policy regarding the degree to which alternative sources of supply will be developed, established, and maintained. There are a number of ingredients in this decision. For example, what degree of competition (between alternative suppliers) is desired? What is the risk associated with a *single* source of supply? Are satisfactory substitute materials available? What is the cost implication of spreading a procurement to more than one supplier, thereby reducing economies of scale for any one supplier?

Alternate sources of supply may be maintained at a somewhat higher cost to the purchaser in order to prevent significant material shortages in case of a single supplier strike, adverse weather, or other unplanned event such as supplier discontinuance of the product line or bankruptcy. They will increase the number of origin points in the inbound logistics system. Because purchases are more widely dispersed, individual shipments may be smaller and relatively more expensive to transport, store, handle, and coordinate. Also, if sources are continually added or deleted, the pattern of shipments will be continuously changing, resulting in a premium on flexibility in the planning and management of transportation, warehousing, and inventory requirements.

Contract or "Blanket" Ordering. This concept is illustrated by the following example:

. . . Braniff uses 7 million envelopes a year and the company used to buy them all at once each year to get the best volume price. Now Braniff seeks bids on the 7 million envelopes but doesn't take delivery right away. "The supplier sends them as he can as long as he keeps a 30-day supply in our hands," Mr. Bolding (vice president for purchasing and stores for Braniff) explains. "We not only get a lower unit cost but save the cost of possession." [3]

The savings in purchase order processing costs as a result of this procedure can be significant. Estimates of the costs of each purchase order in individual companies range from $7.50 to as high as $40 to $60.[4] Several years ago, for example, purchase order costs at the Ford Motor Company were estimated to be $58 for each of 85,000 purchase orders issued each year.[5] Note the impact of a blanket order program on one company's procurement program:

A North American Aviation purchasing executive, A. G. Pearson, says the Downey division has 275 blanket orders out. As a result, the department issued only 8,750 purchase orders in one recent month; 19,000 would have been required had it not been for blanket ordering. "Once a year we go out and get bids and that's it," says Mr. Pearson.[6]

In addition to eliminating repetitive order processing, contract purchasing programs may enable logistics to pre-plan movement and storage schedules and requirements, and should drastically reduce the storage capacity required for incoming goods.

Reciprocal Agreements. Purchase and sales reciprocity, or "trade relations" as some prefer to call it, refers to the purchase of product from customers in a manner designed to support sales effort. Whether reciprocity is profitable or unprofitable is arguable.[7] Our purpose here is to indicate the reality of reciprocity, and assess constraints which it represents for both the procurement process and logistics efforts.

Reciprocal agreements are generally viewed independently of logistics considerations. However, all other things being equal, the practice of reciprocity often increases the number of suppliers and supply points served by logistics in cases where it is practiced with a large number of customer-suppliers. Also, the average size of shipments may be decreased where procurements are dispersed.

Value Analysis. Value analysis has been defined as:

. . . the study of the relationship of design, function, and cost of any product, material or service with the object of reducing its cost through modification of design or material specifications, manufacture by more efficient pro-

---

[3] James C. Tanner, "Canny Buyers," *The Wall Street Journal,* June 23, 1964, p. 1.
[4] *Ibid.*
[5] Dean Ammer, "Ford's Cost Control Center," *Purchasing,* May 23, 1960, pp. 53–63. See pp. 54–55.
[6] Tanner, *op. cit.*
[7] Dean S. Ammer, "Realistic Reciprocity," *Harvard Business Review,* January–February, 1962, pp. 116–24.

cesses, change in source of supply (external or internal), or possible elimination or incorporation into a related item.[8]

The way value analysis (or value engineering) is carried out is suggested by the following procedure:

The trained VE practitioner, alone or in a team, selects a target—either a high-price-tag item, or perhaps some small part which is used in large quantities. He asks three basic questions:

1. *What does it do?* The discipline requires that the answer be reduced to two words, a verb and a noun. A pencil, for example, "makes marks." This breaks habitual patterns, pulls the thinking back to fundamentals, puts the emphasis on function rather than on "the way we've always done it."
2. *What does it cost?* The answer should already be known, but frequently it is not. It is often an eye-opener.
3. *What else would do the job, at what cost?* This calls for a brain-storming session in which alternatives may be suggested. . . . Value engineering starts from scratch and approaches each product as if it had never existed. . . . "On the average," says Miles [Larry Miles, a General Electric design engineer generally credited with organizing existing techniques into the concept of value analysis in 1949], "one fourth of all manufacturing cost proves unnecessary—or half, if it's a new rush product." [9]

To date, value analysis largely has been applied to the examination of component parts. (13) **Why do you think this is so?**

Value analysis, in the short run, may tend to increase the number of inbound and inventoried items as designs are revised and new part numbers issued. As a result, inventories may have to be more closely monitored to reduce the risk of obsolescence of various inventoried items. However, in the long run, value analysis may contribute to the standardization of parts and other items.

Standardization.   There is a natural tendency on the part of engineers, product designers, and marketing personnel to introduce nonstandard product features. Over time, this can result in an uneconomically large product line, component inventory, or logistics bill per dollar of sales.

Executives asking themselves the following set of questions have, in many cases, eliminated over half of the raw materials, components, and supplies purchased and inventoried by their companies:

1. Can this item be eliminated from stock?
2. Can an existing item be used in more than one application?

---

[8] "What Value Analysis Is All About," *Purchasing*, May, 1957, pp. 38–53, at p. 38.

[9] Lloyd Stouffer, "Biggest Thing Since Mass Production," *Reader's Digest*, January, 1964, pp. 107–10, at p. 108.

3. Can one item, with capabilities sufficiently high to meet several needs, replace several items with lesser capabilities?
4. Until item usage becomes extensive, can we avoid ordering a specially designed component?

Potential logistics savings from standardization include those resulting from a reduction in the number of inventoried items and the shipment of larger quantities. In many cases, companies standardizing around more extensive, more versatile items have found that higher per-unit purchase prices have been more than offset by such logistics cost savings. In other cases, greater quantity discounts have offset potentially higher prices for the more versatile item.

An example of this occurred at the Bogen Division of Lear Siegler, Inc., a manufacturer of public address systems and high-fidelity home entertainment products:

. . . the purchase of both transistors and carbon resistors was standardized for greater savings. Transistors were being bought in two grades, but by standardizing on the better grade, better than needed for one particular use, a quantity saving was achieved. Also, by buying 5% ½-watt resistors, instead of cheaper 10% resistors, purchasing was able to negotiate a blanket order from one, instead of several, suppliers at a lower unit price for a superior product. In addition, special packaging, which formerly cost 80¢ per thousand, is now supplied free.[10]

Systems Contracting.[11] Developed in 1962 by the Carborundum Company, systems contracting involves: (1) the identification of families of low-value, frequently ordered items (absorbing 80% of the time of purchasing department personnel but comprising only 20% of the value of goods purchased), (2) the selection of a supplier for one or more families of related items, (3) the selection of, and standardization on, selected brands offered by the supplier, (4) the preparation of in-company catalogues of such items for all individuals involved in requisitioning (requesting) such supplies, (5) the passing of requisitions from the originating department through purchasing directly to the vendor, without the preparation of purchase orders, (6) the numbering of each customer's requisitions *by the vendor* for control purposes, and (7) the prompt filling of requisitions by the vendor *from its inventory* rather than by the using company from its storeroom.

Systems contracting typically has been used for so-called maintenance, repair, and operating supply (MRO) items which, within a large company, may be ordered from company storerooms several times per day.

---

[10] Peter Wulff, "It Doesn't Have to Be Official . . . ," *Purchasing*, February 8, 1972, pp. 49 ff. See p. 53.
[11] This section is based on Ralph A. Bolton, "Systems Contracting: A New Way to Reduce Purchasing Costs," *Management Review*, May, 1967, pp. 25–32.

(14) Based on the description above, what effects would systems contracting have on logistics activities and costs (either for purchasing or, more broadly, for the management of inbound materials)? (15) What controls does it provide for managing the procurement process?

POD Systems.　Purchase order draft (POD) systems involve: (1) the preparation of a purchase order and an accompanying blank check by the customer, (2) the completion and deposit (at his bank) of the blank check by the vendor at the time he ships the ordered goods, and (3) auditing by the customer (often by computer) of receiving reports for vendor error.

A POD system, for example, was initiated at Kaiser Aluminum & Chemical Corporation after it was found that of about 18,000 checks written each month to vendors, those under $200 accounted for about 75% of the number of checks but only 4.5% of the total cash amount disbursed. A subsequent check indicated that Kaiser had made payments on its first 175,000 POD's without suffering a single loss.[12]

More recently, Kaiser announced the success of the latest application of POD in logistics, a method of paying freight carriers with blank checks. Under this program, known as "cash-in-fist" (CIF), the check is part of the bill of lading; the carrier simply computes the shipping charges, fills in the correct amount on the check, and deposits it in his bank account.

Other Customer–Vendor Coordination Programs.　There are many approaches to the problems of coordinating the logistics of procurement, particularly for the frequent, low-value, often routine, repetitive type of requisition or order. Some of the more imaginative and potentially significant are the following.

Dundee Cement Company passes much of the responsibility for buying to its vendors' salesmen under its "honor system." On his visit to Dundee's storeroom, a salesman will take stock, write up a requisition, leave it with purchasing for approval, and send a copy to his company for immediate order picking and assembly. When the approved requisition (or purchase order) is received from Dundee, shipment is made immediately. This is not unlike the way in which many items delivered directly to supermarkets by vendors' salesmen are purchased on a store-by-store basis, typically by the store manager or a department manager.

Several years, ago, one major vendor established its storeroom on the premises of the Kearfott Division of General Precision's Aerospace Group. Under this arrangement, goods were issued from requisition by Kearfott

---

[12] Lassor Blumenthal, "How to Cut Purchasing Costs," *Dun's Review,* March, 1964, pp. 53–54 and 66–69. Descriptive data on Dundee Cement Co., Kearfott Division of General Precision, and Beals, McCarthy & Rogers in subsequent sections are also from this source.

personnel, the vendor staffed the storeroom and owned the stock in it until it was issued, and the vendor billed Kearfott monthly on the basis of the value of requisitions issued.

(16) What are the advantages of each of these systems to the buyer? (17) To the vendor? (18) What are the operating characteristics which would tend to contribute to the success of each?

Computerized Buying. Buying that utilizes punched cards, tapes, or machines to reproduce handwriting, for order initiation; high-speed telephone (*Data-phone*) or telegraph transmission; and computer inquiry and immediate confirmation by the vendor are becoming increasingly popular.

For example, Beals, McCarthy & Rogers of Buffalo, a large mill supply house selling about 30,000 steel and industrial items, several years ago installed a *Data-phone* transmitter at the Towanda, Pennsylvania, plant of one of its customers, Sylvania Electric Products. This system, utilizing punched cards read by the transmitter, offered immediate inquiry of Beals, McCarthy's inventory, eliminated purchases, and provided for next-day delivery of shipments. Based on the transmission, Beals, McCarthy prepared all the paperwork ("hard copy" print-out from its computer).

As a result of this system, Sylvania has been able to reduce the number of its order clerks by 25%. Within a year after the installation of the program, Beals, McCarthy's sales to Sylvania increased by more than 50 times to about 25% of the total purchases of the Pennsylvania plant.

(19) What effects do this and similar systems have on the stability of customer–vendor relations? (20) On the jobs carried out by purchasing department personnel? (21) On the tasks assumed by vendors as opposed to buyers? (22) On other activities in a logistics system?

A buyer-oriented computerized system may take on a different set of tasks. For example, a scientific research and development laboratory has an operating EDP purchasing system which: (1) is triggered automatically when the reorder points for several thousand stocked items have been reached, (2) automatically and immediately prints out a purchase-order release to be sent to a preselected supplier for a quantity which is determined by the computer, and (3) signals the buyer if the material is not received on time or if other discrepancies occur. Others now are developing systems that will, in addition: (1) store price quotations and other departmental records, (2) calculate economic order quantity and price breaks to determine whether a quantity should be increased over the amount requisitioned, (3) evaluate stored information on price and delivery, then place the order with the supplier offering the best combination for that quantity, (4) print the purchase order to the chosen supplier, (5) check the supplier for order acknowledgment and acceptability, (6) note the receipt of material delivered against the order, and (7) compare invoices with receiving reports and with the order, printing the check to the supplier if they agree.[13]

(23) **How do the functions performed and economies realized by the vendor-oriented and buyer-oriented systems described above vary from the standpoint of the buyer?**

BUYING FOR RESALE

Thus far, we have concentrated on purchasing in an industrial firm. If anything, purchasing and other logistics activities play even more important roles in a wholesale or retail firm which buys products for resale.

As indicated in Fig. 6–1, the creation of form utility in a resale firm is limited to that produced through repackaging, sometimes including minor assembly operations. Thus, more emphasis is placed on possession utility (buying of merchandise) and on time and place utilities (logistics, such as giving rapid customer response from a local inventory maintained for a number of customers, none of whom could singly afford to hold such inventory).

Role of Buying

Within the wholesale or retail firm, the function of buying (sometimes referred to as merchandising) is to purchase goods to be resold without significant change in their physical properties. This definition is contrasted with the function of purchasing in an industrial firm, where the emphasis is on the procurement of materials and/or services which are required for the production process. Both buying and industrial purchasing functions are performed by personnel commonly referred to as buyers.

In a retailing organization, a buyer often is responsible for merchandising a department or an entire store. The buyer's decisions, and the way in which individual purchases relate to one another, may well be the major determinant in establishing the "character" of the store in the customer's mind. Thus, buying and merchandising represent major functions within the organization.

A number of contrasts can be drawn between the purchasing function in a resale organization as opposed to an industrial firm. In the former, the buyer is more likely to establish product specifications; in purchasing

---

[13] J. William Widing, Jr., and C. Gerald Diamond, "Buy by Computer," *Harvard Business Review*, March–April, 1964, pp. 109–20.

for an industrial firm, production or engineering departments may play a much greater role in establishing such specifications. In many purchases for resale, there is a much greater need for personal judgment, or feel, on the part of the buyer, particularly for "style" merchandise. This judgment may have to be exercised several months in advance of the actual receipt of goods for resale, because many manufacturers of style merchandise base their production runs on the initial orders from respected buyers. Typically, a buyer for resale will have a much greater freedom to buy, will be involved in the pricing of the goods purchased, and will be responsible for replenishing depleted stocks. In purchasing for resale, brand names are more important, and standardization less important, than in the industrial purchasing situation.

Buying Performance and Control

Goods purchased for resale typically move more quickly through a firm's logistics system than materials purchased for production. The faster movement of goods creates the need for faster information flow and response times in the former situation. There are no planning buffers such as are created by the production process and the supply inventory in the industrial firm. Thus, the buying function is required to more directly coordinate customer demand with supplier capabilities, and to remain ready to respond rapidly to changes in customer demand patterns. This suggests the importance of control over buying activities.

The basic method of controlling buying for resale is the "open to buy" figure. This designation of the dollar amount which a buyer may be free to commit in purchases stems directly from a store's sales plan and the amount and mixture of merchandise necessary to support the sales plan. Once merchandise is purchased, a buyer regenerates his "open to buy" as the purchased merchandise is sold. Items which prove slow to sell may be "marked down" in order to move them off the shelf and to free "open to buy" dollars for merchandise which offers greater promise of faster, more profitable sales.

Perhaps the two most critical measures of a buyer's performance are the dollars of sales generated from items purchased (compared with plan) and the margin (difference between purchase and sale price) realized on the goods sold. If sales are achieved at the expense of reduced margins, the net result may be a reduction in dollars available to cover the expenses of the wholesaling or retailing operation.

Given the wide responsibility assigned to buyers in a retailing or wholesaling organization, and the special knowledge needed to buy various types of merchandise, it is not surprising that the buying activity may be divided among specialists. For example, a large department store may have 30 to 40 buyers, each responsible for a department within the store featuring a particular kind of merchandise.

GOVERNMENT PROCUREMENT [14]

With a budget of approximately one-fifth of the gross national product of the country, the United States Government is by far the single largest employer as well as purchaser of goods and services, including logistics services. Within the government, the Defense Department represents the largest purchaser of goods, typically weapons and other support systems. Practices implemented by the Defense Department have literally influenced entire industries. For example, when the Department required the use of program evaluation review technique (PERT) scheduling in the administration of projects for which it had contracted, this requirement literally guaranteed the widespread use of the scheduling technique and insured its introduction in other industries not dealing directly with the government.

Procurement is a part of the logistics process in the military. In particular, the military procurement process has been characterized by its development of advanced contracting techniques, and an examination of the way in which price, delivery, and performance can be affected by the proper choice of contract.

Contracting Techniques

Basic contracting techniques employed by the Defense Department include cost-plus-fixed-fee, fixed-price, and incentive contracts.

A cost-plus-fixed-fee contract provides the contractor with a set percentage of initially estimated costs (usually 4% to 6%) for his fee, regardless of the amount by which the actual costs exceed estimated costs.

Under a fixed-price contract, the contractor agrees to produce an item or a service at a fixed price, regardless of the cost.

An incentive contract typically provides bonuses for exceeding performance specifications or for meeting deadlines, and penalties for failing to meet specifications or deadlines. Cost overruns or underruns may be shared by the contractor and the government.

In recent years, the government has turned increasingly to incentive contracts as a means of meeting planning deadlines and reducing the cost of purchased items, at a total saving of about $30 billion per year in the Defense Department alone. Several years ago, Defense Secretary

[14] This section is based on James C. Tanner, "Windfall or Profit," *The Wall Street Journal*, July 22, 1965, pp. 1 and 16.

McNamara estimated that "for every dollar we can shift from CPFF [cost-plus-fixed-fee] to the higher risk arrangements of incentive and fixed-price contracts, we save at least 10 cents." [15]

Trends in government procurement, particularly in contracting, have strongly influenced the organization of the management of logistics activities in aerospace and other industries supplying the government. They have led to the creation of departments with broad responsibilities for procurement, inventory control and scheduling of raw materials and component parts, and even production scheduling. By their very nature these organizations have concerned themselves to a great extent with supply rather than distribution logistics, concentrating on the problem of bringing together the many important components for a weapons or other hardware system, the physical distribution of which is relatively simple. This has led to the creation of organizations which may be regarded as full sisters of physical distribution departments, so-called "materials management groups." Industries in which materials management has attained an important position include those engaged in the management of computers and aerospace products. (24) **Does this suggest other likely candidate industries?** (25) **Which ones?**

PURCHASING, PROCUREMENT, MATERIALS MANAGEMENT, AND LOGISTICS—A SUMMARY

Purchasing is the act of buying, literally signified in most dictionary definitions as the act of paying money for something in the completion of a purchase agreement. Procurement signifies a broader range of activity associated with bringing about the acquisition of a product or service. It involves all of the many steps necessary to bring to a close a successful transaction. Materials management, in addition, deals with a broad portion of the spectrum of logistics activities concerned with supply, including procurement. Relationships among these three activity sets are shown in the context of the "materials cycle," a specific sequence of activities set forth in Fig. 6–5.

The relative roles of purchasing and materials management (physical supply) are further defined in Fig. 6–6. Here, we see that the scope of materials management for supplies, components, and equipment includes purchasing as well as activities of traffic, warehousing, and inventory control. Materials management, or physical supply, in most ways is a mirror image of the other half of a firm's logistics system, that involving physical distribution. And herein lie the seeds of a potential philosophical debate.

[15] *Ibid.*

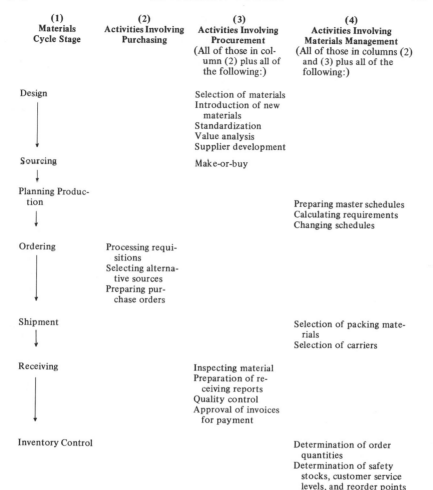

(1) Materials Cycle Stage	(2) Activities Involving Purchasing	(3) Activities Involving Procurement (All of those in column (2) plus all of the following:)	(4) Activities Involving Materials Management (All of those in columns (2) and (3) plus all of the following:)
Design		Selection of materials Introduction of new materials Standardization Value analysis Supplier development	
Sourcing		Make-or-buy	
Planning Production			Preparing master schedules Calculating requirements Changing schedules
Ordering	Processing requisitions Selecting alternative sources Preparing purchase orders		
Shipment			Selection of packing materials Selection of carriers
Receiving		Inspecting material Preparation of receiving reports Quality control Approval of invoices for payment	
Inventory Control			Determination of order quantities Determination of safety stocks, customer service levels, and reorder points and intervals

Fig. 6–5. The "materials cycle" in a firm purchasing to inventory, indicating the relationships among purchasing, procurement, and materials management. Adapted from material presented in Dean S. Ammer, *Materials Management,* Rev. Ed. (Homewood, Ill.: Richard D. Irwin, Inc., 1968), chap. 2.

A good case can be made for not including as parts of a logistics system activities such as buying and selling, which create possession utility. And, in fact, selling is excluded. Why then have we included purchasing? Mainly to ease confusion, strange as that statement sounds.

Materials management, in firms where it has been instituted, has featured a systems approach to purchasing as well as the time-and-place-utility-creating activities of logistics. This philosophy and approach com-

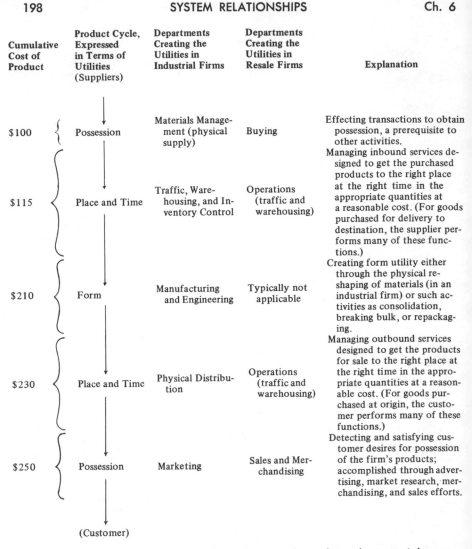

Cumulative Cost of Product	Product Cycle, Expressed in Terms of Utilities (Suppliers)	Departments Creating the Utilities in Industrial Firms	Departments Creating the Utilities in Resale Firms	Explanation
$100	Possession	Materials Management (physical supply)	Buying	Effecting transactions to obtain possession, a prerequisite to other activities.
$115	Place and Time	Traffic, Warehousing, and Inventory Control	Operations (traffic and warehousing)	Managing inbound services designed to get the purchased products to the right place at the right time in the appropriate quantities at a reasonable cost. (For goods purchased for delivery to destination, the supplier performs many of these functions.)
$210	Form	Manufacturing and Engineering	Typically not applicable	Creating form utility either through the physical reshaping of materials (in an industrial firm) or such activities as consolidation, breaking bulk, or repackaging.
$230	Place and Time	Physical Distribution	Operations (traffic and warehousing)	Managing outbound services designed to get the products for sale to the right place at the right time in the appropriate quantities at a reasonable cost. (For goods purchased at origin, the customer performs many of these functions.)
$250	Possession	Marketing	Sales and Merchandising	Detecting and satisfying customer desires for possession of the firm's products; accomplished through advertising, market research, merchandising, and sales efforts.

(Customer)

Fig. 6–6. The relative roles of purchasing, physical supply, materials management, and physical distribution in industrial firms, and buying and operations in firms engaging in resale activities.

plement that of physical distribution management, except for the exclusion of marketing and marketing-related activities from the latter.

We could launch into a long justification for the possible inconsistency. (For example, why is purchasing a more integral systems component of materials management than selling or marketing is of physical distribution management?) But it probably would have little effect on the thousands of practicing managers under all these semantic banners.

SUGGESTED READINGS

ALJIAN, GEORGE W. *Purchasing Handbook,* 2nd Ed. New York: McGraw-Hill Book Co., 1966.
An encyclopedic compilation of contributions by well-known managers and scholars of purchasing. Of special interest may be separate chapters devoted to purchasing internationally and purchasing in Canada, and a discussion of traffic and transportation considerations.

AMMER, DEAN S. *Materials Management,* Rev. Ed. Homewood, Ill.: Richard D. Irwin, Inc., 1968.
Uses the term "materials management" as we have "logistics," particularly for items moving inbound to an industrial or resale enterprise. Among concepts set forth that may be of special interest are the materials cycle source, problems in supplier relations, the measurement of materials management performance, and speculations about the future of materials management.

COMBS, PAUL H. *Handbook of International Purchasing.* Boston: Cahners Books, 1971.
Extends typical discussions about purchasing into the realm of international trade, requiring different knowledge, terms of reference, and decision-making assumptions.

ENGLAND, WILBUR B. *Modern Procurement Management,* 5th Ed. Homewood, Ill.: Richard D. Irwin, Inc., 1970.
Presenting both text and case materials, this book contains a number of cases of particular interest for logistics management, organized around the following topics, among others: purchasing procedure and information systems, determination and control of quantity, some problems in source selection, forward buying and speculation, procurement department reports to management, and appraising procurement department performance.

HEINRITZ, STUART F., and PAUL V. FARRELL. *Purchasing: Principles and Applications,* 5th Ed. Englewood Cliffs, N. J.: Prentice-Hall, Inc., 1971.
Varies from other texts cited here primarily in the great amount of attention that it gives to standardization programs.

LEE, LAMAR J., and DONALD W. DOBLER. *Purchasing and Materials Management.* New York: McGraw-Hill Book Co., 1965.
Relates materials purchasing to various aspects of movement control, traffic, and transportation.

McELHINEY, PAUL T., and ROBERT I. COOK. *The Logistics of Materials Management.* Boston: Houghton Mifflin Co., 1969.
An excellent set of readings including those discussing techniques of managing materials, and elements of a business logistics system.

WESTING, J. H., I. V. FINE, and GARY JOSEPH ZENZ. *Purchasing Management,* 3rd Ed. New York: John Wiley & Sons, Inc., 1969.
Written with the active assistance of the Milwaukee Association of Purchasing Managers, gives some emphasis to newer purchasing techniques with importance for other aspects of logistics: systems contracting, blanket purchase orders, stockless purchasing, and a concise treatment of inventory control techniques used in purchasing.

7

Product Pricing Policies

Five situations illustrate ways in which pricing and logistics problems are interrelated. Before reading this chapter in its entirety, attempt to respond to the questions posed at the end of each situation. We'll find out later what was done in each case.

Several years ago, a manufacturer of soaps and detergents, upon analyzing the relative costs and revenues realized in selling to various customers, found that logistics costs as a proportion of dollar sales dropped rapidly as the size of a given transaction, resulting in a subsequent shipment, increased. The manufacturer's price structure offered quantity discounts for purchases in quantities of 9 cases, 25 cases, 100 cases, and 500 cases. However, many of its sales were in one- or two-case quantities to retail grocery outlets. While its overall costs of logistics in relation to sales were only 12%, comparable costs for one- or two-case orders were found to be 150%. (1) **What steps could be taken, if any, to deal with this situation?**

Recently a manufacturer of paper products entered into a multimillion-dollar contract with a fast food chain to provide expendable items for the chain's customers. The contract price reflected the large dollar value of the contract. However, orders for products under the contract were placed directly with the manufacturer on a weekly basis by each of the chain's 1,500 outlets, creating 75,000 orders per year with an average value of about $70 per order, about one-tenth the size of the manufacturer's average order at the time. On an average shipment, order-processing costs alone approximated 10% of sales dollars. The company's profits on its sales of paper products fell to practically nothing, although sales and production costs as a proportion of sales decreased. (2) **What could the company do?**

A distributor of about 30,000 mill-supply items, upon analyzing the profitability of products groupings in its line, found that profitability varied directly with dollar sales per order, sales per written line on an order, and gross margin (the difference between purchase price and sales price). While the average order size was $40, the figure varied from $18 to $125 for various products categories. Those with sales below the average were found to be unprofitable. The average line item sales value was $16, but varied from $8 to $63. Once again, line item sales below the average were judged unprofitable. Customers typically placed orders containing non-standard items and requiring a special order on the manufacturer. As a result, the distributor was rarely able to fill the complete order at the time it was received. Instead, special items on a given order might arrive from the manufacturer in several shipments over a period of up to 12 weeks. This resulted in frequent communication with both the customer and the manufacturer, as well as duplicated delivery charges for a given order. In addition to the basic cost of about $1 for servicing an order, it was estimated that each subsequent shipment for "back ordered" goods on the same order involved at least $3 in additional costs, not counting the time of the distributor's sales representatives. Although reluctant to change his policies because they reflected those of his competitors, the president of the distributorship was certain that this type of business could not be producing profits on the basis of the 20% margin on sales which the distributor received. (3) **What would you do if you were in his position?**

A manufacturer of wearing apparel sold its products under terms of "$\frac{2}{10}$, net 30 e.o.m." (end of month), meaning that invoices for products which were received by the customer in July, for example, could be paid for up to August 10 (10 days after the end of the month in which the order was placed) to qualify for a 2% discount and were due in full only on August 30. This produced a large peak in customer orders near the end of each month and a large number of requests from company salesmen to schedule shipments (and billing) to make goods available to customers early in the month before payment on the shipment would be due. The practice had increased as competition grew and retail customers had exerted pressures on salesmen to have goods available further in advance of payment. Unfortunately, it had placed an increasing burden on the company's order-processing and shipping sections at the beginning of each month. Staffing was complicated by the fact that 40% of a month's shipments were made during the first four days of each month. The company's operating committee had scheduled the matter for discussion at its next meeting. (4) **What would you recommend to the members of the committee?**

A retailer of fashion merchandise had operated in the traditional manner of the business by displaying new styles, watching what was sold, and attempting to reorder "hot" items. Unfortunately, by the time an item became "hot," it was often difficult to obtain a repeat order, producing shortages of salable merchandise. Other items which were stocked in surplus because they didn't catch on invariably had to be sold at substantial discounts at the end of the three big seasons each year, in order to free up cash for the following season's inventory. The president of the retailing company concluded that there had to be a better way of doing business and was willing to experiment during the coming season. (5) **Could you help him out?**

Logistics is only one of many elements to be considered in pricing decisions. But it can be an important one. Here we will discuss terms of sale and basic types of pricing policies as background for a subsequent consideration of more specific matters such as the establishment of quantity discounts. Finally, we will explore the steps necessary to assess the need for and to implement selected pricing policies.

TERMS OF SALE

Once a price is quoted on a product, a buyer might well ask the following questions: Do I receive a cash discount if I pay for the goods early? Does the quoted price include transportation charges to my warehouse or factory? Am I required to make arrangements to pay the shipping charges, to file claims for damages to goods en route, or to determine the actual shipping charges which apply? Who has control over the selection of the mode and specific carrier for the shipment of the goods? Various elements of a complete statement of the terms of sale typically answer all of these questions. Omission of one or more of these elements can lead to litigation or embarrassment in buyer–seller relationships.

There are three basic elements in a statement of the terms of sale for a given quantity and quality of goods: (1) price, (2) cash discounts and credit terms, if any, and (3) logistics responsibilities.

Price

The most important term of sale is price. All other terms of sale merely aid in the interpretation of the meaning of a price quotation.

Cash Discounts and Credit Terms

It is common practice for a manufacturer or distributor to quote terms of sale which include a statement, for example, of "$2/10$, net 30." This type of statement on the part of the seller makes two stipulations: First, a cash discount of 2% off the quoted price will be allowed the buyer if he pays for his goods within ten days from invoice date; second, the goods must be paid for within thirty days from the date of invoice. These two elements of a statement of mercantile credit are commonly called the cash discount and the net credit period. Although terms of "$2/10$, net 30" are common in many businesses, there are a great number of variations in statements of trade credit.

The size of the cash discount quoted in a statement of trade credit generally depends upon three factors: (1) the cost of the capital needed to carry the trade "loan," (2) custom in certain industries, and (3) competitive factors. First, in regard to cost of capital, consider a situation in which a selling firm computes its cost of capital at 7%. It may quote terms of sale of "$1/10$, net 60." Thus, the 1% discount offered the buyer on payments for goods within ten days of the date of the shipment or the date of the invoice (whichever applies) roughly corresponds to the amount that it would cost the selling firm to carry the buyer's credit for an additional 50 days, or $1/7$th of a year. In this case, the amount and timing of the discount and net credit period correspond roughly to the saving in the cost of capital on the part of the selling firm.

Second, other types of businesses and channels of distribution have operated under mercantile credit terms which have not been varied for many years. Custom plays a large part in keeping terms the same even though changes may be warranted on economic grounds.

Third, the intensity of competition has in some cases necessitated the quoting of cash discounts far in excess of the cost of capital. In these cases, it is hard to distinguish a cash discount from an ordinary price reduction for competitive purposes. Consider the previous example, with terms of "$2/10$, net 30" substituted for "$1/10$, net 60." From the standpoint of the seller in this case, the incremental credit period is 20 $(30 - 10)$ days, or $1/18$th ($20/360$) of a year. The cost of capital for $1/18$th of a year, at the rate of 7%, would be $7/18$% or a little over $1/3$%. And yet, in this example, competitive forces make it necessary for a seller to quote a cash discount totalling $1\frac{2}{3}$ percentage points in excess of its cost of capital. **(6) How was this figure obtained?**

A net credit period is commonly designed to correspond roughly to the period of time in which goods bought for resale can reasonably be expected to be resold. In many businesses, goods bought for resale are expected to "pay for themselves." Goods with potential for rapid turnover, such as grocery products, commonly carry a short net credit period. The net credit period for jewelry, however, could be expected to be relatively long.

Logistics Responsibilities

Buyer and seller must determine the appropriate division of responsibility for matters of logistics, including (1) the point at which delivery is to be taken by the buyer, (2) responsibility for the payment of shipping charges, and (3) control of shipping matters. These responsibilities are often summed up in a statement of "free on board" (f.o.b.) terms.

Point of Delivery to Buyer. The quotation of an f.o.b. point in terms of sale generally indicates the point at which the seller turns over the goods, and responsibility for them, to the buyer. This includes responsibilities for paying for transportation and handling charges, determining the appropriate charges to be assessed, selecting the modes and carriers for transportation purposes, and filing any claims for damages which might occur in transit.

An f.o.b. point can be selected for quotation from many alternatives. Four common quotations are illustrated in Fig. 7–1. Theoretically, a statement of f.o.b. without specific location is incorrect or incomplete. However, in common parlance, the terms "f.o.b." and "delivered" are used to signify roughly whether the terms of sale include payment of

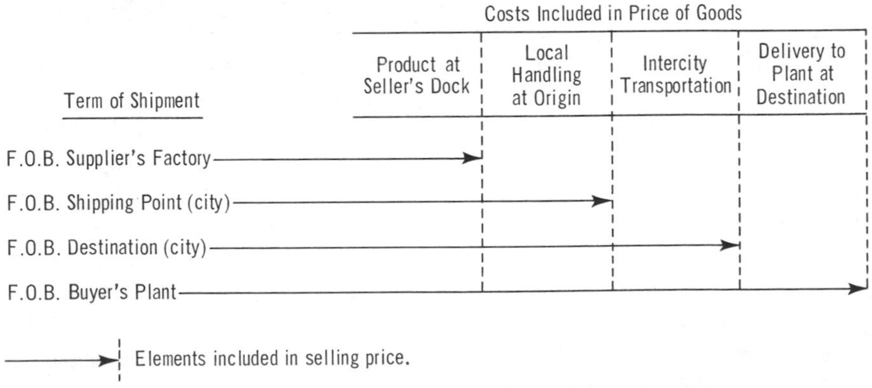

Term of Shipment	Costs Included in Price of Goods			
	Product at Seller's Dock	Local Handling at Origin	Intercity Transportation	Delivery to Plant at Destination
F.O.B. Supplier's Factory	————————→			
F.O.B. Shipping Point (city)	——————————————→			
F.O.B. Destination (city)	————————————————————————→			
F.O.B. Buyer's Plant	——————————————————————————————————→			

————→ Elements included in selling price.

Fig. 7–1. Common quotations of f.o.b. points and responsibility for costs of transportation and handling associated with them.

intercity transportation charges by the seller. In most cases the former does not; the latter does.

Payment of Shipping Charges. Certain additional stipulations may be attached to a basic f.o.b. statement of terms. By means of these stipulations, a seller or buyer can apportion the payment of transportation charges in a manner other than that indicated by the basic f.o.b. statement. For example, "f.o.b. origin, freight allowed" signifies that title to the goods passes at the point at which the carrier picks up the shipment, while transportation charges must be paid by the seller. By means of various "freight allowed" statements, a seller may agree to pay none, a part, or all of the transportation charges on a shipment completely independently of a statement transferring title to the goods.

For example, a shipper desiring to quote a delivered price comparable to that of his competitor might quote "freight allowed" terms from the city cited by the competitor in his terms of sale, a city other than the actual city from which the shipment is made. The amount of freight charges allowed under such terms would result in a delivered cost comparable to that quoted to the buyer by the seller's competition. In other cases, a shipper might wish to limit the transportation charge which he would be willing to pay on a given shipment by stating the maximum that he would be willing to bear. A common quotation is "f.o.b. shipping point, carload freight rate allowed to destination," under which the seller agrees to pay transportation charges up to, but not over, the rail carload rate on any shipment between the two points.

Routing Control. Unless specified to the contrary, f.o.b. terms generally indicate the right of the seller or buyer to route shipments, to the extent that the privilege is granted by carriers of the various modes of transportation. Thus, terms including "f.o.b. origin" designations indicate the right of the buyer to route the shipment. The right of the shipper or receiver to route based on pricing terms has developed largely from custom. Deviations from the general rule occur because of the effectiveness with which one firm is able to route its shipments as contrasted with another. Thus, in the case of a large supplier shipping to a small customer, greater resources for effective routing may exist in the selling firm, thus warranting a stipulation of "f.o.b. shipping point, routing and form of transportation to be selected by shipper."

Regulations governing transportation in the United States place varying emphasis on the right of a shipper to route his freight via the various modes of transportation. Part I of the Interstate Commerce Act specifically designates the shipper's right to route carload traffic by rail. The right is not guaranteed to shippers of LCL shipments, nor in those sections of the Act pertaining to motor carriers, water carriers, and freight forwarders. In air freight transportation, the Civil Aeronautics Act makes no mention of the shipper's right to route his shipments.

In practice, however, a shipper may have a great deal to say about the route his shipment may take. Under any method of shipment, the shipper of freight has a right to tender his shipment to any originating carrier he wishes. Conversely, a receiver of freight might designate to his supplier a mode and carrier to which his shipment should be tendered. For competitive reasons, a carrier will nearly always honor the routing instructions of a shipper or receiver even when not required to do so.

Maximum control over routing may be very important to a firm. Without it, the best laid plans for optimizing a logistics system can be destroyed by a customer's insistence on his right to receive a shipment by a specified route. A firm which ships all or a portion of its product directly from plants or plant-oriented warehouses is particularly vulnerable when it does not have maximum control over routing through the terms of sale which it quotes its customers.

In the situation illustrated in Fig. 7–2, plans recently formulated by Alvarez Electric called for LTL shipments to Syracuse customers from the Pittsburgh warehouse. In the past, both TL and LTL shipments to Syracuse had been made from Columbus. Terms of sale quoted by Alvarez were f.o.b. Columbus. The Syracuse Electric Company had a standing routing request on file with Alvarez' Sales Division: "Ship via Greatway Trucking." Greatway operated between Columbus and Syracuse, charging an LTL rate of $1.75/cwt. for its services between the two cities.

Alvarez' new system called for rail carload shipment from Columbus

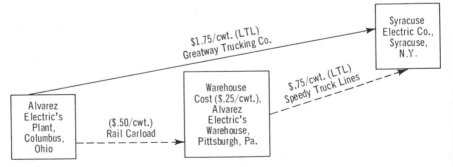

Fig. 7–2. Potential conflicts in supplier's distribution system and customer's specification of originating carrier.

to Pittsburgh at 50¢/cwt., warehousing and handling at Pittsburgh at an estimated cost of 25¢/cwt., and LTL shipment from Pittsburgh to Syracuse for 75¢/cwt., or a total cost of $1.50/cwt. On receipt of a particular LTL order from Syracuse Electric, Alvarez shipped from its Pittsburgh warehouse via Speedy Truck Lines (Greatway did not serve Pittsburgh). Alvarez Electric prepaid the freight from Pittsburgh and billed Syracuse Electric for $1.75/cwt. even though the shipment was not made via Greatway. In a situation like this, Syracuse Electric might well believe it had the right to specify routing of this shipment, at least in regard to originating and delivering carrier. If Syracuse were to specify delivery of Alvarez' shipments by Greatway Trucking, it would penalize Alvarez in terms of delivery time, delivery cost, and the reduction of opportunities for consolidation on shipments to the east from Columbus.

(7) **If you were Distribution Manager for Alvarez Electric in this situation, what would you recommend to your company's top management to avert potential problems of logistics and customer relations?**

This example illustrates one possible penalty of f.o.b. point-of-origin pricing, particularly from the standpoint of the vendor. Another is the inability of the supplying firm to utilize the carriers believed to be most dependable or most helpful in problems requiring tracing (location of shipments en route), rate quotation, or other types of service. Carrier support in obtaining rate adjustments is often conditioned by the degree to which a firm has control over the routing of its inbound or outbound shipments, and can divert freight from one carrier to another.

Other Responsibilities. F.o.b. terms designate the point at which title to a shipment passes from the seller to the buyer. Along with title, other responsibilities pass as well. These include the determination of the appropriate transportation classification and rate under which a product moves and the settlement of claims for damage to the product during shipment. In actual practice, the point of legal transference of these responsibilities may be of minor importance.

Classification and rate determination must be carried out when a product moves for the first time, with a periodic review of such matters thereafter. Individual supplier policy regarding freight claims often overrides "legal responsibility" for such action. For example, it is common practice for many suppliers quoting f.o.b. point-of-origin prices to restore damaged or lost merchandise and file transportation damage claims for customers. A supplier may also issue credit to its customer and collect overpayments of freight charges from carriers when such charges are proven incorrect. These types of services in excess of legal responsibility may be necessitated by competitive considerations.

Comparable Terms in International Logistics. There is a wide array of terminology used to designate logistics responsibilities in terms of sale for international transactions. Among the most important of these is "free along side" (f.a.s.), used in much the same way as f.o.b. "Cost, insurance, freight" (c.i.f.) is used to designate that the freight on the international shipment will be paid by the seller. The relationship between trade terms and legal responsibilities varies *significantly* between domestic and international logistics, however. This subject requires much more space than we can spare for it, but more comprehensive sources of information are readily available.[1]

Cash Discounts and Delivered Pricing

Cash flows resulting from various terms of sale can have a significant impact on company profits. In a majority of sales contracts, the net credit period is no less than 30 days. This is the time period allowed a buyer to pay for his goods and is referred to as trade credit. In contrast, transportation firms are allowed by law to offer only relatively short periods of credit for payment for transportation services.

The credit standing of firms wishing to ship freight on a collect (credit) basis, as opposed to a prepaid basis, first must be reviewed by the carrier. Collect freight bills are generally tendered to the shipper at about the time of delivery of the freight, while prepaid freight bills are presented at about the time a shipment is accepted by a carrier. The Interstate Commerce Commission currently requires railroads to collect freight charges for the performance of their service no more than 120 hours from the time a bill is presented after the origination or delivery of a shipment.[2] A comparable rule for motor carriers requires them to present freight bills no more than 7 days after delivery and collect them no more than 7 days after presentation, thus allowing up to 14 days of "credit." The effect of shipping terms on credit terms offered by both a vendor and a carrier is illustrated in the following example.

An Example. Alvarez Electric and Banshee, Inc., price their goods to land them in Syracuse, New York, for the same total costs to their customers. The same cash discounts and credit terms, $\frac{2}{10}$, net 60, are used by both companies. However, Alvarez sells on an f.o.b. origin

---

[1] For example, see Lawrence P. Dowd, *Principles of World Business* (Boston: Allyn and Bacon, Inc., 1965), especially pp. 344–57, for a discussion of terms of sale used in international commerce.

[2] On a prepaid shipment, the freight bill is presented for payment at the origin point. On a collect shipment, the freight bill may be presented at the origin or destination point. "Collect on delivery" (c.o.d.) shipments require that the receiver pay for freight charges before receiving goods at their destination.

basis, Banshee on an f.o.b. destination basis. Billing and payment procedures and their timing for both Alvarez and Banshee, under the assumptions of rapid and slow collection of individual amounts, are illustrated in Fig. 7–3. The net return to the supplier and net cost to the customer under each of these situations are computed in Table 7–1.

(8) On the basis of the information in Fig. 7–3 and Table 7–1, which customer gets the best deal from a price and service standpoint? (9) Why? (10) What impact does this have on net returns to the supplier? (11) What steps might be taken to correct the situation? (12) What impact might these actions have on supplier–customer relations? (13) What are the chances you might, as the supplier, lose this customer to your competition (either Alvarez Electric or Banshee)?

The relationship between net returns received from point-of-origin and delivered pricing will generally hold for any given set of terms of sale. The differences in net returns in relation to sales in the above example may not at first seem too great. However, on $100,000,000 of annual gross sales, alternative policies could result in a difference of as much as $1,377,000 ($99,000,000 versus $97,623,000) in net returns from sales (see Table 7–2). It should be considered seriously in analyzing pricing policy.

Costs and Logistics Responsibilities. Terms of sale and shipping are sometimes bound by iron-clad industry customs. Or, marketing executives in an individual firm may consider it impossible to alter terms of sale for their products. Whatever the case, it is important that a company's management be informed of comparative costs of transportation and handling incurred under alternative terms of sale that might be quoted to customers. Information which will allow the assessment of effects of sales and shipping terms on company costs and revenues is important. The following information may be useful for such an appraisal:

1. Shipping terms quoted by competing firms
2. Shipping terms quoted by other firms supplying customers with non-competing items
3. A distribution of bills, in dollar amounts, paid on various days from the date of invoice
4. A record of situations in which customer routing requests have interfered with the planned distribution system
5. The cost of claims settlement activities to the company

No one pricing policy is appropriate for every firm. The economics and customs of a particular situation will govern the decision made in regard to pricing policy. Under such circumstances, the costs and bene-

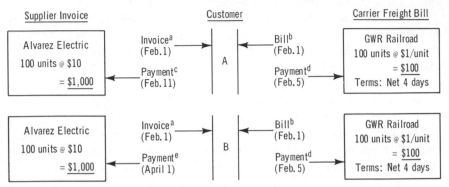

ALVAREZ ELECTRIC
Terms of Sale: F.O.B. Origin, 2/10, Net 60 (Freight Collect)

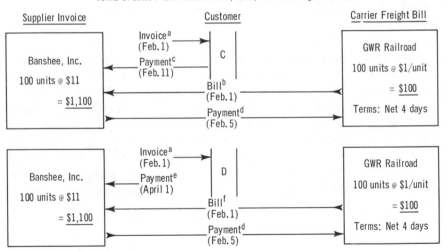

BANSHEE, INC.
Terms of Sale: F.O.B. Destination, 2/10, Net 60 (Freight Collect)

[a] Invoice dated to correspond with estimated date of arrival of shipment.
[b] Presented at the time of delivery.
[c] Payment made 10 days from the date of the invoice.
[d] Payment made 4 days from the presentation of the freight bill.
[e] Payment made 60 days from the date of the invoice.
[f] Presented at the time of shipment.

Fig. 7–3. Billing and payment procedures and time lags under different methods employed by two firms to land goods in Syracuse, New York, for the same "price." To simplify the example in regard to time, a time-in-transit of only one day has been assumed.

fits of various types of terms of sale can only be assessed in relation to the pricing and cash discount practices which govern company sales. In the area of company price policy, this is just one task falling under the responsibility of logistics management.

PRICING POLICIES IN LARGE FIRMS

Pricing policies in large businesses can be divided into two categories: delivered and f.o.b. As a rule, the former are much more popular. Delivered pricing policies meet the needs of sellers to: (1) simplify price-quoting procedures by maintaining "uniform" prices,[3] (2) meet competition by quoting "identical" prices, (3) facilitate fair trade (uniform) retail prices, and (4) maintain maximum control over physical distribution.

Delivered Pricing

The four basic types of delivered pricing systems are those centered around basing-point, zone, single or national, and individual prices. The latter is similar to f.o.b. pricing in effect and will be discussed later in connection with f.o.b. pricing systems.

Delivered pricing systems are differentiated by their use of uniform, as opposed to identical pricing, and the extent to which they are directly or indirectly influenced by transportation and handling costs. The importance of logistics in each of these pricing systems is indicated by the repeated use of the terms "freight absorption," "phantom freight," and "freight allowed or equalized."

Freight absorption refers to the payment of all or a portion of freight charges out of that portion of margin on price theoretically reserved for profit by the seller. It generally occurs when the seller wishes to meet or beat a competitor quoting prices lower than those for which the seller can land his goods at a competitive point of sale. Policies of "freight allowed" or "freight equalized" are more specific means by which a firm practices freight absorption.

Phantom freight is the assessment of freight charges by a seller in excess of those actually incurred in a shipment. It arises when prices are based on freight charges which are higher than those actually incurred by the supplier in accomplishing delivery to the customer.

---

[3] In this discussion, the term "uniform" prices will be used to refer to the prices quoted by one seller to different buyers: the term "identical" prices will be used to refer to the prices quoted by different sellers to one buyer.

TABLE 7-1. Net Supplier Returns and Customer Costs Under Varied Terms of Sale and Customer Payment Periods

Return to Supplier	Cost to Customer

Situation 1. Terms of Sale: F.O.B. Origin, 2/10, Net 60; Customer Payment 10 Days from Date of Invoice

Return to Supplier		Cost to Customer	
Alvarez Electric:		*Customer A:*	
Goods	$1,000.00	Goods	$1,000.00
Less 2% discount	20.00	Less 2% discount	20.00
	$ 980.00	Payment to Alvarez	$ 980.00
Less cost of interest on 10 days'		Plus cost of interest on 50 days'	
credit ($1,000 × 6% × 10/360)*	1.67	credit ($1,000 × 6% × 50/360)	8.33
	$978.33		$ 988.33
		Plus freight	100.00
		Plus interest on freight for 56 days	
		($100 × 6% × 56/360)	.93
			$1,089.26

Situation 2. Terms of Sale: F.O.B. Origin, 2/10, Net 60; Customer Payment 60 Days from Date of Invoice

Return to Supplier		Cost to Customer	
Alvarez Electric:		*Customer B:*	
Goods	$1,000.00	Goods	$1,000.00
Less cost of interest on 60 days'		Plus freight	100.00
credit ($1,000 × 6% × 60/360)	10.00	Plus interest on freight for 56 days	
	$990.00	($100 × 6% × 56/360)	.93
			$1,100.93

Situation 3. Terms of Sale: F.O.B. Destination, 2/10, Net 60; Customer Payment 10 Days from Date of Invoice

Banshee, Inc.:

Goods and freight		$1,100.00
Less 2% discount		22.00
		$1,078.00
Less freight		100.00
		$ 978.00
Less cost of interest on 10 days' credit ($1,000 × 6% × 10/360)		1.67
Less cost of interest for 6 days on freight bill ($100 × 6% × 6/360)		.10
		$976.23

Customer C:

Goods and freight		$1,100.00
Less 2% discount		22.00
		$1,078.00
Plus cost of interest on 50 days' credit ($1,100 × 6% × 50/360)		9.17
		$1,087.17

Situation 4. Terms of Sale: F.O.B. Destination, 2/10, Net 60; Customer Payment 60 Days from Date of Invoice

Banshee, Inc.:

Goods and freight		$1,100.00
Less freight		100.00
		$1,000.00
Less cost of interest on 60 days' credit on goods ($1,000 × 6% × 60/360)		10.00
Less cost of interest on 56 days' credit on freight ($100 × 6% × 56/360)		.93
		$989.07

Customer D:

Goods and freight		$1,100.00

*All interest costs are computed at the rate of 6%/year.

TABLE 7-2. Supplier Returns on Gross Sales of $100,000,000 Under
Varied Terms of Sale and Customer Payment Periods in Table 7-1

Situation and Vendor	Gross Sales	Less Costs Related to Terms of Sale	Net Sales
1. Alvarez	$100,000,000	$2,167,000	$97,833,000
2. Alvarez	100,000,000	1,000,000	99,000,000
3. Banshee	100,000,000	2,377,000	97,623,000
4. Banshee	100,000,000	1,093,000	98,907,000

Basing-Point Policies. The underlying principle of basing-point pricing systems is that customers are charged prices based on a predetermined manufacturing cost plus the transportation costs from one (single basing point) or more (multiple basing points) designated locations. The actual locations at which goods are manufactured, or from which they are shipped, may not correspond to basing points.

As shown in Fig. 7-4, two manufacturers of cornstarch, located at Denver and St. Louis respectively, supply a customer in Louisville, using Kansas City as a basing point. Although the applicable transportation rate from Denver to Louisville is $2.50/cwt., the Denver-based manufacturer charges only $1.75/cwt. (the basing-point rate from Kansas City to Louisville) in order to land his goods in Louisville at a price comparable to his competitor's. He thus absorbs $.75/cwt. of freight costs. In contrast, the St. Louis-based manufacturer charges the applicable basing-point rate from Kansas City to Louisville of $1.75/cwt., but actually incurs only $1.00/cwt. in transportation charges. His price includes $.75/cwt. of phantom freight.

The example discussed above uses a single basing-point system. The principle of a multiple basing-point system is precisely the same. The only difference between the two is found in the quotation of the basing-point rate to a destination from the basing point with the lowest freight rate. The basing-point system was developed by the steel industry, primarily as a means of enabling its members to quote identical prices at various points throughout the United States. According to one authority:

Probably the first group of firms to use it were the members of the Steel Beam Association, a price cartel formed in 1880. The system was only slowly extended to other steel products by various pools and trade associations, until it was more or less generally adopted by the industry under the leadership of the giant United States Steel Corporation.

The next industry to use it was the cement industry. It was probably introduced there by a subsidiary of the United States Steel Corporation, which had become also the largest cement producer in the country. While the steel in-

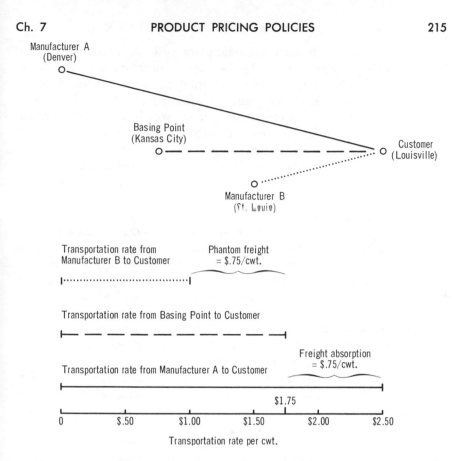

Fig. 7–4. A diagram showing: (1) the applicable transportation rate for cornstarch between St. Louis and Louisville, (2) the basing-point rate charged by both Manufacturers A and B, and (3) the applicable transportation rate for cornstarch between Denver and Louisville.

dustry was the first to adopt the single basing-point system, cement was the first to adopt the multiple basing-point system.

Little information is available about when the system spread to other industries. Single or multiple basing-point systems are known to have been used, temporarily or permanently, for the following products: iron and steel, welded chain, rigid steel conduit, cast-iron pipe, lead, copper, zinc, muriate of potash, gasoline, cement, fire brick, asphalt roofing materials, maple flooring, oak flooring, other lumber products (cedar, hemlock, cypress, pine, fir), wood pulp, sugar, and corn products (corn syrup, corn oil, starch, gluten, feed).[4]

(14) **It is interesting to note that all industries adopting basing-point systems have been those in which transportation costs are an important component in the final delivered price of the product. Why?**

[4] Fritz Machlup, *The Basing-Point System* (Philadelphia: The Blakiston Co., 1949), p. 17.

Arguments put forth against basing-point systems, particularly those based on a single point, were: (1) the manner in which they had to be administered led to exchanges of information among competing firms in violation of antitrust laws; (2) single basing-point systems encouraged customers to order from uneconomic sources, which produced a certain amount of cross-hauling of goods in opposite directions; and (3) the system did not allow price concessions to a customer wishing to purchase on an f.o.b. mill basis. As a result some specific basing-point systems resulting from industry conspiracy or restraint of trade were ruled unlawful in a series of post-World War II court decisions. These decisions affected the corn products, cement, steel, and chain manufacturing industries, among others. The rulings so restricted industry pricing agreements (usually reached through the medium of a trade association) as to make basing-point systems relatively ineffective in practice. An understanding of the nature of basing-point systems is, however, important because of their relationship to other systems of delivered pricing.

Zone Pricing Policies. An individual firm may establish zone prices based on the varying distances between customer location and point of manufacture. Zones are usually created to reflect differences in transportation charges to various groups of locations, under blanket transportation rates. In the absence of blanket freight rates, some customers situated in a zone pay more than average manufacturing costs plus freight rates for transportation to their locations. Others pay less.

Zone pricing systems have been under the close scrutiny of the Federal Trade Commission for some years. Some, considered discriminatory between buyers (i.e., those which charge different delivered prices to competing customers located short distances from each other), have been deemed unlawful. For this reason, zones generally have been designated where wide discrepancies in transportation costs exist between one region and another. For example, firms operating in the eastern United States frequently establish higher prices for the western part of the country, at least until such time as capabilities for producing products on the West Coast are developed by a company or its competitors.

Although zone pricing policies are typical of certain industries, they do not depend upon the organized action of a group of firms. Individual firms can, and many do, quote zone prices.

Single or National Price Policies. Under a single price policy, a firm establishes one price for a particular product in all markets in which that product is sold. In cases where the firm markets its product nationally, such a policy has come to be known as a national price policy.

Single or national price policies have become particularly popular for those types of products sold for ultimate consumption. They make possible market-wide advertising and packaging based on price as well as other promotional material. This type of promotional effort is thought to be reassuring to the consumer who sees a single price printed on the package wherever it may be found.

Single price policies also encourage fair-trade pricing at the retail level.[5] Pricing decisions are simplified by single price policies in that they require the setting or adjustment of a single price on a product on an average-cost basis. In essence, a single price policy is the simplest version of a zone pricing system, in which the entire marketing area for a product is a single zone.

Legal Status. The current status of delivered pricing systems in the American economy has been summed up as follows:

In spite of some apparent conflict in various court decisions and Federal Trade Commission rulings, it appears that delivered pricing practices are legal under a variety of circumstances. *When a seller acts independently and not in collusion with competitors, provided that individual actions of a variety of competitors do not result in a systematic matching of delivered prices,* a delivered pricing plan or policy of freight absorption is apparently legal under any of the following qualifying conditions:

1. If the seller is willing to sell on an f.o.b. basis when a purchaser so requests
2. If the seller maintains a uniform delivered price at all points of delivery (rather than on a zone or basing point basis that results in unequal advantages to different buyers), as when he charges nationwide uniform delivered prices
3. If the seller absorbs freight costs, or some portion of them, in order to meet competition, as when his factory price plus actual freight to destination is higher than the amount a customer would have to pay when procuring the same goods from a competitor
4. If the buyers and/or their customers are non-competitive [6]

Importance for Logistics. All delivered pricing systems, with the exception of those based on blanket freight rates or individual delivered prices, require that either phantom freight or freight absorption be present in a majority of all sales. The theoretical incidence of phantom freight and freight absorption under a zone pricing system is shown graphically in Fig. 7–5; the principle applies to a single or national pricing policy as well.

---

[5] "Fair-trade" or "resale price maintenance" are terms applied to the practice whereby manufacturers set minimum prices below which wholesalers and retailers may not sell.

[6] Theodore N. Beckman, William R. Davidson, and W. Wayne Talarzyk, *Marketing*, 9th Ed. (New York: The Ronald Press Co., 1973), pp. 392–93.

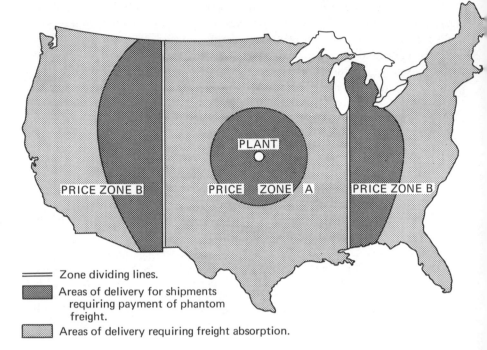

Fig. 7–5. Phantom freight and freight absorption under a zone pricing policy.

The implications and problems of delivered pricing systems for logistics should be clearly understood. They have been used as a means of expanding the geographical market and volume of sales for individual products. But delivered pricing systems are put into effect for other reasons as well. The action may be taken to counteract a delivered pricing policy of a competitor which may place competing products at a comparable price in a company's "home market." Where one item in a product line is priced on a delivered basis, its companion items are likely to be priced identically to allow the distribution of a full product line throughout a firm's market area. As firms grow in size and develop local or regional markets to a near saturation point, they are forced to expand geographic marketing territories if they wish to increase sales volume. A delivered pricing system is the basic method for this type of expansion.

As the average distance between the point of manufacture and the point of resale increases, physical distribution costs per unit of product sold can also be expected to increase. Under a delivered pricing system, particularly single pricing, the price charged for the product in the long run may have to be increased also, if there are insufficient compensating savings in the manufacturing or selling costs.[7]

If delivered pricing systems result in the lengthening of the average distance between consuming markets and a manufacturer's plant and distribution warehouses, where they exist, they can increase problems of control over matters of logistics. Separation of markets and distribution points can lead to increased variability in the level of service offered customers, the dependability of transportation services, and the precision with which production and supply schedules can be drawn up to meet customer demand.

Under these circumstances steps can be taken to improve control. New plants or distribution facilities may be established nearer newly developed markets, or the logistics organization may be decentralized to increase representation in the field.

Under any system of price averaging, such as that employed in most delivered pricing systems, some customers (usually, but not always, those located nearest manufacturing facilities) will "subsidize" others. The transportation cost component of a zone or single price established for a product, just as other components of cost, must be developed on an average basis. That is, dollar amounts of phantom freight and freight absorption must closely approximate each other. Once established, however, imbalance may develop in these logistics cost elements. If more distant markets are developed to a greater extent than closer ones, for example, the amount of phantom freight will not be sufficient to balance out large increments of freight absorption.

F.O.B. and Individual Delivered Pricing Policies

Judicial rulings in support of the Federal Trade Commission in actions against certain types of delivered pricing systems have led a number of firms to adopt either f.o.b. or individual delivered pricing policies. The underlying principle of these policies is that all goods are priced basically from the point of origin, whether that origin be a manufacturing plant or a company warehouse. In such price systems, physical distribution costs will determine the market area to which a firm can price its goods competitively. This is illustrated by the transport isotims shown in Fig. 7–6 for two competing firms.

---

[7] Little evidence exists to support or refute the theory of economies of scale, particularly in manufacturing, beyond some undefined intermediate size of firm in any particular industry. For a discussion of empirical evidence, see Caleb A. Smith, "Survey of the Empirical Evidence on Economies of Scale," in *Business Concentration and Price Policy* (Princeton: Princeton University Press, 1955), pp. 213–38.

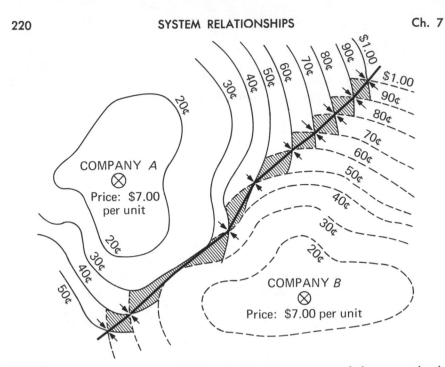

<u>20¢</u>   Shipping distance boundaries at indicated rates per unit (transport isotims

→◄—   Points of indifference in landed price.

———   Theoretical line of indifference, or market boundary.

▓▓▓▓   Areas of indifference in landed price.

Fig. 7–6. Map of transport isotims showing theoretical line of indifference and actual areas and points of indifference in the landed cost of products of two competing companies operating under f.o.b. origin or individual delivered pricing policies.

Hoover has drawn a colorful contrast between market competition under f.o.b. and delivered (with the exception of individual) pricing policies:

The difference between market competition under f.o.b. pricing (with strictly delineated market areas) and under discriminatory delivered pricing is something like the difference between trench warfare and guerilla warfare. In the former case all the fighting takes place along a definite battle line: in the second case the opposing forces are intermingled over a broad area.[8]

Many firms have tried to cope with the economic limitations imposed by pricing policies and geographic location by decentralizing manufac-

[8] Edgar M. Hoover, *The Location of Economic Activity* (New York: McGraw-Hill Book Co., 1948), p. 57.

turing and storage facilities to place them within "competitive range" of major markets. (15) **In what way does this resemble the adoption of a delivered pricing policy involving the discriminatory recovery of freight costs, such as those discussed in the last section?**

Quantity Discounts

In 1936 legislation was passed which was to have a profound effect on the importance of physical distribution costs in establishing quantity discounts on goods. An amendment to Section 2 of the Clayton Act, the legislation that has become known as the Robinson–Patman Act, states in part:

> That it is unlawful . . . to discriminate in price between different purchasers for commodities of like grade and quality . . . where the effect of such discrimination may be substantially to lessen competition or tend to create a monopoly in any line of commerce or to injure, destroy, or prevent competition with any person who either grants or knowingly receives the benefit of such discrimination, or with customers of either of them . . . provided that nothing . . . shall prevent differentials which make only due allowance for difference in the cost of manufacture, sale, or delivery. . . .

Thus the Robinson–Patman Act specifically mentions three major areas of cost which might be used to justify quantity discounts to customers purchasing commodities of like grade and quality: manufacture, sale, or delivery. In actual practice, however, it has been difficult to prove that items sold in quantities of, say, 1,000 units cost less to manufacture per unit than those same items sold in quantities of 10 units. As Davis points out:

> Theoretically, cost savings in terms of manufacturing, delivery, or selling are the grounds for discount defense. But as a practical matter, cost savings in manufacturing have been difficult to defend. Court interpretation of the Robinson–Patman Act has required uniform allocation of overhead costs. And many firms have found it difficult to justify their arbitrary cost allocations For this reason, some firms have abandoned quantity discounts entirely.[9]

Although the logic of the argument that it costs less per unit to sell goods in larger quantities seems sound, records of selling expense have been difficult to allocate on a sale-by-sale basis. This has not precluded attempts to bolster cost defenses with an analysis of sales costs.[10]

For those firms wishing to maintain quantity discount schedules and justify them before the Federal Trade Commission, logistics cost evi-

[9] Kenneth R. Davis, *Marketing Management,* 3rd Ed. (New York: The Ronald Press Co., 1972), p. 826.
[10] For a comprehensive analysis of cost defenses under the Robinson–Patman Act, see Herbert F. Taggart, *Cost Justification* (Ann Arbor: Bureau of Business Research, The University of Michigan, 1959).

dence appears to be the best justification. This is due not only to the reduction in the average cost per unit of goods transported in larger quantities, but also to the detailed documentation which usually accompanies at least transportation activities. Lower rates per unit on shipments of larger quantity are a well-known fact, one that examiners and judges cannot ignore. For some firms wishing to maintain quantity discount pricing schedules, it has become common procedure, in considering quantity discounts suggested by pricing executives, to analyze and approve them in terms of relative logistics costs in handling orders of varying quantities. Because the Robinson–Patman Act allows quantity discounts which are less than, but no more than, justifiable decreases in costs in quantity sales, it has become a task of logistics management to determine whether transportation and handling savings are sufficient to cover the amount of the suggested quantity discount. At least one large manufacturer of goods distributed primarily through grocery outlets goes even one step further. Its logistics management group is empowered to initiate changes in the quantity discount schedule designed both to comply with Federal Trade Commission regulations and to make the prices on various quantities of the firm's goods even more competitive.

Determination of Discount Limits. If the Robinson–Patman Act dictates the upper limit of quantity discount size, how do we determine the lower limit? Although no rule applies to all situations, a general principle can perhaps be stated as follows: A quantity discount should be at least large enough to compensate the buyer for carrying a larger average inventory resulting from a quantity purchase. Consider the following example.

The Nashville Stereo Company is interested in establishing a discount schedule that will encourage its distributors of stereophonic phonograph records to buy in quantities larger than their current average order of two cases each. The records are priced to distributors at about $70 per case. What is the minimum discount needed to encourage them to purchase in lots of ten cases, assuming a relatively constant demand for records throughout the year and average annual sales of Nashville's records of ten cases per distributor?

A simple formula can be devised to provide an approximate solution:

$$D = \frac{\tau(I_n - I_o)}{vS}$$

where

τ = cost of carrying $1 of inventory for one year.[11]

[11] A commonly used figure for many products is .25, representing 25% of the value of the average annual inventory.

I_n = the average value of inventory on hand if ten cases are purchased ($\frac{1}{2}$ the value of the purchase).

I_o = the average value of inventory on hand if two cases are purchased ($\frac{1}{2}$ the value of the purchase).

vS = the dollar cost of goods sold during a year's time (assumed to be an average of all customers).

D = minimum discount required.

Substituting the appropriate information yields the following results:

$$\frac{.25(\$350 - \$70)}{\$700} = \frac{\$70}{\$700} = 10\%$$

This indicates that the minimum amount of discount necessary to encourage purchases in quantities of ten cases is 10%.

Individual firms may deviate widely from "average" performance figures. However, the method provides rough approximations of the minimum discount needed to encourage an alert distributor to increase order size.

Setting Quantity Discounts. The job of setting discounts requires a supplier to balance his own and his customer's needs against regulatory requirements. Consider once again the problem of the Nashville Stereo Company.

A minimum discount of 10% off distributor list price is required to encourage distributors to purchase in quantities of ten vs. two cases of records. Because of the existence of a minimum shipment charge, it costs $10 to ship ten cases (300 lbs.) or $8 to ship two cases (60 lbs.), representing a saving of $3.50 per case, or 5% of sales value, on shipments of ten as opposed to two cases. Savings in packaging for ten cases vs. two amount to about $7.00, or roughly 1% of the total sale. It would be hard indeed to justify a 10% quantity price discount on records to the Federal Trade Commission. A 6% discount would not be enough to induce an alert distributor to buy in larger quantities. Reconciliation of the economic minimum and maximum is impossible in this case.

For other types of goods, reconciliation is possible. The nature of the cost functions involved should be considered for a better understanding of the nature of the decisions which may be reached. The minimum discount function—the statement of the amount of discount needed (stated in percentage of purchase price)—is linear in nature, as shown in Fig. 7-7. If one were to compute the discount needed to encourage the purchase of any quantity of a product with the characteristics of Nashville Stereo's records, the results would fall on line D in the figure.

Transportation rate reductions for shipments in larger quantities follow a "sloping stair-step" pattern when graphed in the manner of Fig.

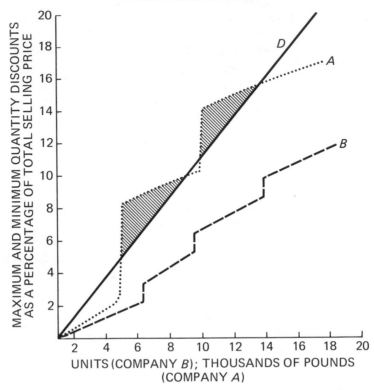

A   Physical distribution cost savings in quantity shipments, Seller *A*.
B   Physical distribution cost savings in quantity shipments, Seller *B*.
D   Increased buyer inventory costs with quantity purchases for both
      Sellers *A* and *B*.
▓   Area of flexibility within which discounts might be quoted, Seller *A*.

Fig. 7–7. Comparison of seller cost savings with buyer cost increases with quantities of sale of increasing magnitude.

7–7. Packing, material handling, and warehousing cost savings may tend to be somewhat more linear. When combined, these factors yield a percentage cost saving function similar to that shown for two companies in Fig. 7–7. Nashville Stereo's cost savings from quantity sales correspond to those for seller *B*. Because they never exceed the minimum discount requirements (*D*), no areas of decision are present; no quantity discount schedule (at least no legally defensible one) can be quoted.

Contrast seller *B* with seller *A*, whose maximum discount function repeatedly intersects with the minimum function because of the difference in the nature of the product sold. The cross-hatched areas in Fig. 7–7 show the two ranges of quotable percentage discounts and quantities within which pricing executives, in consultation with logistics management, might select specific discount schedule points.

At quantities of 5,000 lb., for example, seller A could quote a defensible discount of up to 8% off list price. He would have to offer at least 5% to justify economically the discount to his customers. The quantity discount range defining the "decision zone" at 5,000 lb. would be 5% to 8%. If a quantity discount were desired on orders of 6,000 lb., the decision zone range would be narrowed to two percentage points, 6½% to 8½%. At 10,000-lb. quantities, the range would be expanded again to from 11.4% to 14% off quoted unit prices.

Quantity Discounts and Purchase Contracts. Discounts can be based on the quantity of goods purchased or sold over a period of time, regardless of the number or size of orders placed during the period. This type of discount system is formalized through the vehicle of a purchase (or sale) contract. It eliminates the problem of establishing quantity discounts large enough to encourage increased sales by basing the discount on something other than individual order size.

The purchase contract, from the standpoint of logistics considerations, is a customer-oriented agreement. It requires the customer to estimate his needs over the period of the contract (usually periods of up to one year) and pay the price per unit corresponding to his estimated total order quantity. Deviations in order quantity from pro-forma estimates may result in a final additional assessment or a rebate on all goods sold during the period of the contract. Economies of the seller are difficult to assess under the purchase contract. Chief among these are production scheduling economies and associated benefits resulting from a foreknowledge of quantities likely to be sold and shipped to individual customers. To insure against extreme diseconomies of logistics resulting from a purchase contract, some supplying firms have entered into such contracts only when selling on an f.o.b. point-of-origin basis or when imposing a minimum order quantity on all customers.

Dating and Deal Pricing

Terms of sale often are designed to encourage speculative buying, or buying in advance of normal need, on the part of a customer. Among variations employed for this purpose, price dating and deals are especially important for logistics.

Dating. Under a dating plan, a supplier may ship a product to a customer in advance of need, allowing the customer possession of the product with payment delayed until such time as the product is likely to be sold. For example, O. M. Scott & Sons, a leading manufacturer of lawn care products, offers a dating plan to its distributors under which products with highly seasonal demand on a few weekends in the spring and early summer are shipped to distributors throughout the winter with payment delayed until the beginning of the season.

Dating plans allow suppliers to spread the manufacture and shipping of finished products with highly seasonal demand more evenly over time, thereby reducing inefficient peaks in production and logistics activities. They also reduce the need for storage capacity in a supplier's facilities. They further provide an incentive for the early movement of product closer to the point of eventual need by allowing a customer to build stocks without suffering the financial burden of an investment in inventory. Finally, dating plans often include price discounts for purchases before certain dates, thereby providing an added incentive to the customer to order early and arrange for storing the product in his own facilities. Where this is an important factor, the discount must be sufficient to defray additional costs incurred by the customer. For example, for many types of products, the cost of storage, extra handling, and potential obsolescence of the product may approximate 1% of the value of the product per month. Therefore a supplier seeking to encourage early orders for a product with seasonal demand beginning in April might wish to establish the following dating plan:

Discount	For Orders for Immediate Shipment Received Before:
3%	January 1
2%	February 1
1%	March 1

Under this arrangement the price might be net end of April.

Deals. Deals are special prices quoted on a one-time or limited-period basis. They may be designed to sell obsolete products quickly at the point of ultimate demand, to introduce new products, or to stimulate sales of products whose sales are lagging. Successful deal pricing must take into account buyer economics, particularly in such industries as grocery and drug product manufacture and distribution in which it is used frequently.

A number of food chain organizations have designed guidelines for the consideration of deals by buyers. Features of these models have to be taken into account by vendors (suppliers); the following example demonstrates some common features.

A retail food chain organization, Vi and Cap's Markets, is offered a deal on canned tomato juice which is designed to clear the canner's inventories prior to the new "pack." The product is currently purchased for $4 per case and resold for $5 per case (offering a margin of $1/$5, or 20%), moves at the rate of approximately 2,000 cases per month, and is purchased in carloads of 1,500 cases. Vi and Cap's attempts to maintain an average inventory in its stores equivalent to one week's inventory and an average warehouse inventory equivalent to three weeks of sales, or a total of 2,000 cases.

The canner offers a one-shot deal of $3.25 per case for 10,000 cases or more. Vi and Cap's merchandising management estimates that by reducing its retail price to the equivalent of $4.30 per case and featuring the deal merchandise, it can sell tomato juice at the rate of 6,000 cases per month for one month and 4,000 cases per month until the stock is depleted. There is, however, a 50% chance that the chain's major competitor might take advantage of the same deal, thereby reducing projected sales to 4,000 cases for the first month under the lower price and 2,000 cases per month until the stock is depleted. If Vi and Cap's were not to accept the deal and its competition did, it is estimated that the chain's sales would fall to 1,500 cases per month. Under Vi and Cap's inventory control system, inventories similarly would fall to 1,500 cases.

The chain estimates its inventory carrying costs as 1% of case value per month for interest on investment in the inventory and 1% of case value per month for warehousing and other expenses. While merchandising the deal tomato juice, it is estimated that the average stock of non-deal tomato juice will average half of its normal level, or 1,500 cases.

(16) **Should Vi and Cap's buyer accept the deal?**

In this example there is an equal probability that, while "working off" stocks of deal merchandise, Vi and Cap's inventory position will follow one or the other of these two patterns, with their associated inventory holding costs and benefits:

50% Chance of:

Inventory Level		*Average Monthly Inventory*	
Beginning of March 1	10,000 cases ⎫		
	⎬	Month 1	7,000 cases
End of Month 1	4,000 cases ⎪		
	⎬	Month 2	2,000 cases
End of Month 2	0 cases ⎭		9,000 case months for deal merchandise only

50% *Chance of:*

Inventory Level		*Average Monthly Inventory*	
Beginning of Month 1	10,000 cases	Month 1	8,000 cases
End of Month 1	6,000 cases	Month 2	5,000 cases
End of Month 2	4,000 cases	Month 3	3,000 cases
End of Month 3	2,000 cases	Month 4	1,000 cases
End of Month 4	0 cases		17,000 case months for deal merchandise only

These case months of deal merchandise accumulate costs to Vi and Cap's in the amount of 2% of $3.25, or 6½¢ per case month. A weighted average of the two possibilities suggests an expected carrying charge of 13,000 × $.065, or $845 associated with the deal. In addition, the chain store organization would have to maintain an average inventory of 1,000 cases of non-deal tomato juice, resulting in a weighted average of 3,000 case months at 2% of $4.00, which would be 8¢ per case, or $240. The expected gross margin from the purchase would be $1.05 ($4.30 − $3.25) × 10,000 or $10,500, or $9,415 ($10,500 − $845 − $240) net of inventory holding costs.

Against this, Vi and Cap's would have to compare its expected contribution, net of inventory holding costs, if it did not accept the deal. Under these circumstances, there would be a 50% chance that if the competition did accept the deal and its volume of sales was roughly equivalent to Vi and Cap's, sales would be depressed to 1,500 cases per month for two months and inventories to an average level of 1,500 cases. Assuming that neither competitor accepted the deal, sales would remain at a level of 2,000 cases per month for an equivalent period of four months and inventories at a level of 8,000 (2,000 × 4) case months. The total realized contribution, net of inventory holding costs, would be .5[(3,000 cases × $1 margin per case) − (3,000 case months × $.08 per case month)] + .5[(8,000 × $1) − (8,000 × $.08)], or $5,060.

(17) As merchandising manager for Vi and Cap's, would you accept the deal now? (18) What other factors would you want to take into account in reaching your decision? (19) Could you construct models to compute such guidelines as the necessary buying price, margin, or most desirable purchase quantities for deal merchandise for an organization like Vi and Cap's?

Monitoring Pricing Policies and Logistics Costs

The way in which customers behave in the purchase of a company's products is a direct result of the nature of incentives which reward certain behavior patterns. Pricing incentives are probably the strongest (and most effective) of all factors which influence customer behavior. Both prices and resulting behavior patterns, among other things, influence the profitability of sales.

Other things equal, including price, logistics costs in relation to sales vary inversely (in opposite direction) with such measures as:

1. The size of an order, either in dollar or physical measures
2. The average value per order-line item
3. The length of time a customer may be willing to wait for delivery of his order

These same costs in relation to sales tend to vary directly (in the same direction) with such measures as:

1. The number of line items per order
2. The distance which an order must be shipped
3. The number of shipments required to supply all of the items indicated on an order
4. The severity of the peak, as opposed to normal, requirements for processing orders or effecting shipments during various periods of time
5. The number of points through which an order must be processed
6. The number of points through which an item ordered must pass physically before it reaches the customer

ILLUSTRATIVE PROBLEMS

What about the pricing problems faced by the manufacturer of soaps and detergents, the manufacturer of paper products, the distributor of mill supply products, the manufacturer of wearing apparel, and the retailer of fashion merchandise whose situations were presented at the beginning of this chapter? (20) **Has our discussion suggested alternative actions that these companies might take to resolve their problems?**

In fact, the manufacturer of soaps and detergents instituted a minimum order level of five cases, below which it would not sell. It immediately reduced the number of orders processed by 20% without any significant change in sales.

The manufacturer of paper products, to our knowledge, has done nothing to deal with its problem. Its profit position has not improved.

The distributor of mill supply products took several steps to deal with his problem, including: (1) the elimination of certain lower value items from inventory, (2) instructions to salesmen to concentrate their sales efforts on higher value items and to attempt to sell lower value items in larger quantities, (3) the preparation of sales material highlighting such higher value items, (4) the negotiation of a lower price for one line of relatively unprofitable items upon the discovery that other distributors were experiencing similarly low profits with the line, and (5) the limitation of time granted to manufacturers to explain new products at meetings of the distributor's sales force to only those manufacturing higher value, higher profit items. A check several months after the initiation of these steps indicated that the average sale per line item had risen by about 12% for a particularly unprofitable product family and that a greater proportion of higher value items were being sold.

The manufacturer of wearing apparel dropped the "e.o.m." designation from its terms of sale, thereby eliminating any incentive on the part of customers to play the "calendar game." When this failed to produce immediate results, perhaps because of the difficulties of changing customers' established order schedules, the company instituted temporary sales commission incentives for its salesmen on orders placed for shipment at times other than the first week of each month.

The retailer of fashion merchandise instituted something unheard of in the industry: sales discounts for purchases made during a "pre-display" sale for old customers at the outset of each new season. This provided the retailer with a block of early orders on the basis of which he could gauge the best selling items and place "reorders" for replenishment stocks before his competition depleted manufacturers' supplies. Inventory balance and sales improved immediately.

SUMMARY

In only a few industries, where logistics costs in relation to sales are very great, do logistics factors become the major determinants of pricing decisions. In many others logistics costs can, however, provide a justification for pricing policy. We have seen how creative pricing policies, by inducing distinctly different behavior patterns on the part of supplier and customer alike, can produce savings in logistics costs sufficiently great to enhance the profit performance of both parties.

Our objectives in this chapter have been to: (1) acquaint you with terminology as well as a number of alternative approaches to pricing, and (2) explore the impact of pricing decisions on logistics and vice versa. To the extent that pricing creates constraints on a logistics system, it is important to understand the nature of the constraints if logistics decisions are (1) to be made comfortably within the imposed limits, and (2) to help in the adjustment of the limits themselves from time to time.

SUGGESTED READINGS

BECKMAN, THEODORE N., WILLIAM R. DAVIDSON, and W. WAYNE TALARZYK. *Marketing*, 9th Ed. New York: The Ronald Press Co., 1973.
Offers a complete discussion of current thinking in regard to basing-point and other delivered pricing systems as well as resale price maintenance.

DAGGETT, STUART. *Principles of Inland Transportation*, 4th Ed. New York: Harper & Row, 1955.
Offers a good discussion of the early development and use of group and basing-point rates.

DAVIS, KENNETH R. *Marketing Management*, 3rd Ed. New York: The Ronald Press Co., 1972.
For a discussion of managerial implications of quantity discount quotations and the Robinson–Patman Act.

FAIR, MARVIN L., and ERNEST W. WILLIAMS, JR. *Economics of Transportation*. New York: Harper & Row, 1959.
Updates earlier discussions concerning group rate systems and the effects of rate structures on pricing and interregional competition.

LONGMAN, DONALD R., and MICHAEL SCHIFF. *Practical Distribution Cost Analysis*. Homewood, Ill.: Richard D. Irwin, Inc., 1955.
Discusses the collection of cost data to appraise the relative profits and losses on sales of various quantities as well as other topics related to the identification of costs essential to an effective pricing policy.

MACHLUP, FRITZ. *The Basing-Point System*. Philadelphia: The Blakiston Co., 1949.
This book presents a comprehensive economic analysis of basing-point pricing systems.

8

Customer Service Standards

"In our firm customer service happens, it isn't managed." "If you can't depend on the transportation system for dependable delivery, how can you control customer service?" "Customer service? Ours is good; we ship 95% of all orders within 24 hours after the order arrives at our warehouse." "The customer who yells the loudest gets the best service." These responses in reply to questions concerning the management of customer service are indicative of the growing awareness of the need for managing customer service, the despair with which the problem is approached in many organizations, and possible misconceptions about the nature of customer service.

Awareness of the need for managing customer logistics service is important. Service costs money, suggesting the need for a consideration of the costs in relation to benefits of a service policy.

Further, a customer logistics service program can aid sales, especially in cases where the qualities and prices of competing products are largely indistinguishable. Measurement of the effects of service on sales holds the only potential for the measurement of logistics activities as profit rather than cost centers, for the "total profit" rather than the more typical "total cost" implications of such activities.

Finally, the way in which a service objective is achieved will have an impact on all logistics activities. In particular, it provides the basic inputs for the design of inventory control policies and procedures.

THE SERVICE PACKAGE

A customer service package can be quite complex, including many types of financial, marketing, product, and logistical supporting activities of a non-price nature. We will deal with the latter in some detail after reviewing the total package, the context in which logistical support is carried out.

Financial Support

A well-financed organization may have to provide various forms of financial support to less well-financed customers to whom it wishes to sell its products or services. Customers may desire direct support in the form of loans or equipment financing, as is the case when a soft-drink bottler loans a refrigerated display unit without charge to a retailer's store. As we have seen, less direct financing through trade credit not only is desired, it is expected as the norm in most industries. Terms for the payment of goods received by customers may be extended to allow delays in payment which correspond roughly to the time when the goods likely will be used or resold. As we saw in Chapter 7, a special form of extended credit, typically called a dating plan, is sometimes quoted on products sold on a highly seasonal basis in order to spread orders and shipments over a longer period of time, thus reducing the pressures of seasonal business on order processing, warehousing, and transportation, and encouraging the customer to stock larger quantities of product in anticipation of the selling season.

When all else fails, a supplier may have to place goods with his customers on a consignment basis, agreeing to retain title to the goods until they are used or sold and allowing the customer to return unused or unsold items. For example, competition in the container manufacturing business has forced competitors to store their products, particularly cans, at places where they are used by large customers. The container manufacturer retains title to the goods nearly until the time they are used. While the cans theoretically are sold under contract, the customer is not unwilling to negotiate for the return of unused product. Publishers of books and magazines often agree to accept payment after resale by their newsstand customers. In addition, publishers often allow the return of unsold items from customers who are unable to finance the risk associated with the business.

Price-related financial support may be offered in the form of freight allowances or the payment of freight by the seller on orders exceeding a certain minimum quantity. In effect, the latter is similar to a quantity price discount.

Marketing Support

In simplest terms, a customer wants to be important to his supplier. Aside from the satisfaction provided by feeling wanted, this allows the customer to exert the maximum leverage to obtain concessions, some of which may involve marketing support.

For example, customers may shift the responsibility for all or some of the advertising of a product back to the supplier. Such promotional aids as free samples, point-of-purchase displays, and consultation from the supplier on new methods of improving sales operations may be expected by the retailer or wholesaler. The industrial customer may expect technical information and assistance in the training of his personnel in the use and/or servicing of the product.

Industrial, wholesale, and retail customers like to have information about the market. Information about competitors may comprise part of the marketing data provided by suppliers. At trade levels, there often is an interest in having information about new promotional plans of both the supplier and competitors.

For a vendor's salesman, a buyer prefers a person who is well informed about the products he sells and who takes a personal interest in the buyer's operating problems. He wants a salesman who can do something about improving his sales and operations, either through direct recommendations (which turn out to be right) or through concessions obtained from "the main office." The more productive his contact with the vendor's sales representative, the more frequently a customer may wish him to call.[1]

Product Support

Where product maintenance is important, a supplier likely will be judged in part on the quality of his service program. This includes the warranty offered to ultimate users of the product as well as the quality and convenience of the service and repair network which supports the product. The more complex the product in structure, the more critical its service and repair network. Manufacturers of automobiles and trucks literally have succeeded or failed on the basis of their product support policies and facilities.

Product support relates as well to the nature of the line of products offered by a supplier. Companies not manufacturing a sufficiently

---

[1] For an interesting analysis of what customers want from suppliers, see Bertrand Klass, "What Factors Affect Material Buying Decisions," *Industrial Marketing*, May, 1961, pp. 33–35.

broad line of products may have to purchase items at relatively high cost (and low profit) to fill out their product assortments.

Logistical Support

Logistical support may take on various dimensions to a customer. Included among these are inventory maintenance, order placement, transportation, and material handling.

Inventory Maintenance The customer may want his supplier to maintain as much of the inventory as possible, at least under conditions of stable price levels. He may want his warehouse, if he uses one, to be small in relation to the volume of goods moving through it. In some cases, he may want to eliminate inventories entirely, getting the order from his account and having the supplier ship directly to his customer.

At the retail level, a vendor's or wholesaler's sales representative may be required to take a retail customer's inventory count, rotate his stock, and "dust it."

Above all, a customer is likely to be sensitive to product availability. He will remember a stock-out much longer than an in-stock situation. And this especially is the case during new product introductions or special promotions.

Assistance to the customer in the management of his inventory may be critical if repeated stock-outs are to be avoided. This is important particularly where the task of inventory control is made complex by product lines consisting of many items. For years, drug manufacturers have provided effective inventory control procedures for their distributor–customers. With the increasing capability of computing and communications equipment, suppliers of items ranging from aircraft parts to hardware supplies have made available to their customers programs for the automatic control of inventory, including machine-initiated order placement and inventory replenishment.

Order Placement. In attempting to keep inventory at a minimum, the customer will order as frequently as is reasonable, considering the effect of quantity discounts and his own ordering and holding costs. He may resent limits imposed by minimum acceptable order quantities. He may wait until inventory almost is depleted before reordering, taking the attitude: "I want it yesterday; if I wanted it today, I'd order it tomorrow." He may be influenced by the ease and economy with which he can place his order, possibly by no-charge telephone service, pre-printed order forms, or even a telecommunications device provided by the supplier. He is likely to be impressed by the degree to which he is informed about the progress of his order, particularly when deviations from expected service have occurred or will occur.

Transportation.   The customer may wish to control the selection of the carrier serving him. This preference may result from a desire to obtain any "fringe benefits" (either in terms of service concessions or special favors) he may be able to get from the carrier. Or the customer may feel that his traffic department is more capable in this respect than the supplier's.

When it is profitable for the customer to operate private transportation equipment, he may insist on it regardless of whether private transportation fits in with the logistics system of the supplier. He may want the supplier to file all claims to carriers for loss or damage, especially because shipments typically are more easily traced by the originator of a shipment with his greater access to documents and information related to the shipment. In some cases, the customer may deduct the costs of loss, damage, or shortage from payments to the supplier without obtaining authority for such deductions.

Material Handling.   The customer will want to minimize his investment in material-handling equipment. If he utilizes a system based on a 30″ × 36″ pallet and the supplier uses 40″ × 48″ pallets, the customer may want the supplier to arrange some system for delivering on 30″ × 36″ pallets even if this presents serious problems for the supplier. The customer may request the supplier to load specific parts of shipments together in a truck or rail car so that they can be reshipped directly to a customer's accounts without any sorting or warehousing when the shipment arrives at the customer's receiving dock. He may request the shipment of pallets reflecting the height of the "slots" in pallet racks in his warehouse, or the shipment of pallets containing more than one product-line item or stock-keeping unit (SKU) in quantities reflecting the customer's sales patterns. The customer may also request direct delivery by the supplier to a point other than his warehouse in order to eliminate material handling altogether.

A complete program of financial, marketing, product, and logistical support may well deal with all or most of the problems confronted by a firm's customers. Theodore Levitt has summed up the importance of the service package in this manner:

. . . a truly marketing-minded firm tries to create value-satisfying goods and services that consumers will want to buy. What it offers for sale includes not only the generic product or service, but also how it is made available to the customer, in what form, under what conditions, and at what terms of sale.[2]

[2] Theodore Levitt, "Marketing Myopia," *Harvard Business Review*, July–August, 1960, p. 50.

A number of large firms typically marketing to customers with lesser resources have taken the ultimate step of establishing management programs for customer personnel. Examples include the retail management programs offered by NCR (formerly the National Cash Register Company) to its retailer–customers and the package of management aids and materials made available by International Minerals and Chemicals, Inc., to distributors of its fertilizers and related products.[3]

Logistical support, while only one element of the service package, is basic in nature to the realization of product sales. A concept central to an understanding of logistical support is that of the order cycle.

ORDER AND REPLENISHMENT CYCLES

The order cycle describes the time lapse from the order to the receipt of goods. As shown in Fig. 8–1, it includes the identification of the need for an item; the accumulation of items in, and placement of, the customer's order; order communication to a supply point; order and information processing activities; stock replenishment where necessary; order picking and packing; shipment; and receipt of the order at the point of its origin.

A logistics system comprises one or more replenishment cycles, depending on the number of levels or stages at which inventory is held. The necessity for stock replenishment initiates the replenishment cycle. Order and replenishment cycles are interdependent. The quantity and constancy of customer orders influence the replenishment cycle. However, the order cycle is dependent on the nature of the replenishment cycle both as to the frequency and length of stock-out conditions which affect order cycle dependability.

In a typical two-stage distribution system, such as that shown in Fig. 8–1, an order cycle and an associated replenishment cycle can be thought of as a series of closed loops with demands communicated through each loop in one direction and goods flowing through each loop in the opposite direction. The number of stages (order and replenishment cycles) utilized in a logistics system will vary with the relative volume of sales to a given customer or market area, the nature of the product and product line, and differences between the form in which raw materials are procured and finished goods are manufactured and purchased for final use in a channel of distribution.

Each stage in an order and replenishment cycle can be achieved in a variety of ways. This suggests that the end objectives associated with

---

[3] Bud Reese, "IMC Offers Customer Service to the Nth Degree," *Industrial Marketing*, November, 1961, pp. 96–101.

the performance of the order cycle, synonymous with customer logistics service, can be achieved through a bewildering number of alternative combinations of methods. Before discussing customer logistics service design problems, it is useful to enumerate important alternatives at each step in the order and replenishment cycles. In the discussion which follows, the steps in the order and replenishment cycles are identified with the same numbers and letters used in Fig. 8–1.

Order Cycle

(1) [4] A customer first must identify the need to place an order for an item in his stock. A time lag may arise between the occurrence and identification of the need if the customer does not maintain a continuing or perpetual inventory (requiring a physical review of inventory levels in order to identify the need) or does not update and review inventory requirements on a continuing basis. Computer-controlled inventory systems may provide for frequent updating of inventories, perhaps on an instantaneous, "real time" basis. Much more typical, however, is the daily update of inventories on the computer. A manually controlled system, even though it may provide for a perpetual inventory accounting, more typically provides for less frequent review, perhaps weekly. Under these circumstances, the time lapse between the occurrence and the identification of need for the placement of an order for an item may range from a few hours to a week.

(2) Once the need for an item order is identified, it may be thrown into a pool to allow a sufficient quantity of item orders to accumulate to meet some economic order size. This order size might conform to the minimum quantity needed to qualify for a discount on rates charged for transportation services. More typically at this stage of the distribution system, items may be accumulated to qualify for a quantity price discount which a particular supplier may allow for orders consolidated up to a given weight or value. The delay associated with economic order quantity accumulation may vary a great deal, and in many cases can add a week or more to the order cycle time. Items of critical importance to a customer typically are not subjected to the order accumulation process.

(3) Customers may communicate their orders to a supply point by means of a supplier's salesman, direct mail, telephone, or some other electronic method. The supplier's salesman and direct mail, while they provide "hard copy" (information in writing) at the supply point, probably are the slowest and least dependable of the methods, requiring up to several days (or in the case of the salesman who misplaces the order,

---

[4] These numbers correspond to the numbers in Fig. 8–1.

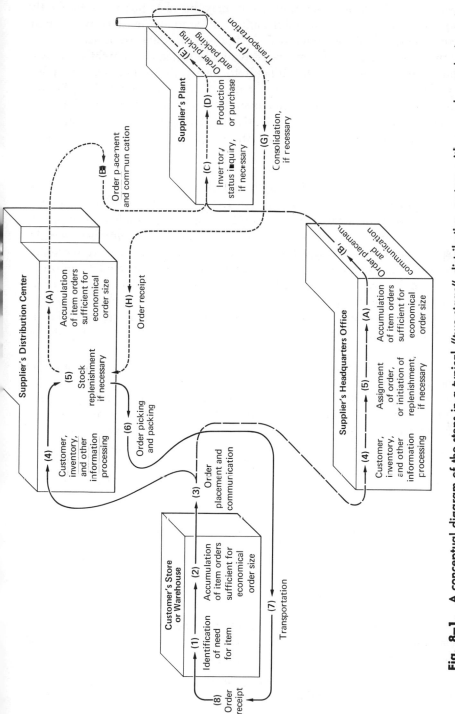

Fig. 8–1. A conceptual diagram of the steps in a typical "two-stage" distribution system with an order cycle (⟶) and related replenishment cycle (··▶), centralized inventory control, and decentralized order processing (--▶).

weeks). Telephone order placement may be fast, but is probably the source of many errors in information. Electronic "hard copy" systems combining telephone, teletype, or high-speed data transmission with written input and output are now available in many different configurations. It may, however, be difficult to justify the installation of such a system between a supplier and any one of his customers unless the volume of information transmitted over the system and the need for accuracy of information are sufficiently great to justify the investment on the part either of the customer or the supplier or both. In cases where the customer and supplier use compatible equipment in the normal course of their business, the incremental cost of establishing a direct link between an information input device already installed at the customer's place of business and an information output device in use by the supplier may be small. More recently, a growing number of suppliers receiving small amounts of information from a large number of sales representatives and customers have turned from telephone transmission to order takers equipped with cathode ray tubes connected to information input devices. As the order is called over the telephone, the order taker can type it up, see it on the cathode ray tube, make necessary corrections, verify the order with the caller, and finally release the information to a computer to initiate a computer-assisted order-filling routine.

Statistics collected by Johnson and Parker from one firm indicate that the time required to transmit an order from the customer to the supplying firm was about 20% of the total order cycle time for rapidly processed orders, but over 75% of total order cycle time for slowly processed orders. In other words, slow order transmittal appeared to be a greater cause of a lengthened order cycle than increases in the time required either to process or to ship orders.[5] Although the results of similar investigations conducted in other firms might yield substantially different results, these findings tend to indicate misplaced emphasis, in some cases, of current efforts to locate stocks in major markets in order to reduce shipping time when order transmittal time is at least as important as other elements in the order cycle.

(4) Upon receipt of the customer's order at the supply point, the supplier may initiate a series of steps including: (a) a credit check for customers not previously approved or for customers ordering in excess of a previously approved credit limit, (b) updating inventory records, if this has not been done independent of the receipt of the order, for items contained on the order received, (c) placing an inquiry on the updated inventory records to determine whether the items ordered are in stock,

---

[5] Richard A. Johnson and Donald D. Parker, "Optimizing Customer Delivery Service with Improved Distribution," *Business Review,* October, 1961, pp. 38–46.

and (d) carrying out any other information processing activities, such as the preparation of sales records, which do not influence directly order cycle activities.

A supplier may be organized to carry out these steps on a centralized or decentralized basis. If the process is centralized, orders must be communicated to the supplier's headquarters office, then subsequently sent to an outlying distribution center. In recent years, some suppliers have redesigned their procedures to allow for the decentralized processing of orders, typically with the elimination of at least one communication and a reduction in time. This, for example, was a significant feature of the plan to create 20 distribution centers to serve the United States, which General Foods Corporation introduced several years ago. Decentralized order processing is assumed in Fig. 8–1.

(5) Orders may contain line items for which there is no stock at the supply point. This situation may initiate a rather complex decision process. The supplier may have the options to: (a) ship available items and back order the rest, thus creating a "split shipment" situation, (b) hold available items until those items found out-of-stock can be replenished, (c) order out-of-stock items from other supply points where they may be found in stock (requiring a decision as to where to direct the first, second, and subsequent inquiries in the system), (d) purchase items found out-of-stock from other sources, even from competitors, or (e) cancel orders for items found out-of-stock. In some cases, the supplier may have no choice. A number of customers, particularly those in grocery products retailing, will no longer accept back orders. Instead they will place the order again as a part of their next order, particularly in cases where weekly order frequency is possible. Of course, in cases where supplier stock-out situations become too frequent, they may elect to place orders with other suppliers. If stock replenishment is necessary, the range of times required for this stage in the process may be great indeed, from several days (required for the transfer of goods from another supply point) up to months (in cases where production for replenishment must be scheduled weeks in advance). The in-stock condition at the supply point, and a supplier's ability to respond to stock-out situations, are the most important determinants of customer service in most systems.

(6) Order picking may be carried out on a semiautomatic or manual basis. A supplier dealing in products typically ordered in single units, such as appliances of a given design, may be able to pack for shipment at the time of manufacture. Suppliers dealing with customers whose orders resemble "grocery lists" of items relatively small in size must maintain extensive picking and packing facilities. Picking and packing times are influenced by such factors as: (a) the degree of automation

and "machine pacing" built into the system, (b) the complexity of customer orders, (c) the size and complexity of distribution facilities from which orders are filled, and (d) the necessity to palletize, depalletize, or transfer goods from a pallet of one size to one of another because of incompatibilities in methods employed by the supplier and his customer or transport company. Relatively small delays in the order cycle result from picking and packing operations. Many suppliers maintain "same day" shipping policies for orders received before some cut-off time, usually at noon or before.

(7) Transportation times basically vary in length with: (a) the size of the shipment, (b) the mode of transportation, and (c) the distance, possibly in that order. Small shipment services, such as those provided by United Parcel Service and the Postal Service, have been relatively fast and dependable over most distances. Truckload shipments are considered by many to be faster and more dependable than carload shipments by rail. However, less-than-truckload (LTL) shipments may be slowest and least dependable of all in many cases. Distance, while a factor in determining the speed and dependability of a shipment, is perhaps of less importance than the size of the shipment or the method chosen for its transportation, especially in recent years with the development of piggyback and air freight transport services.

(8) Typically, a customer is motivated highly to process a shipment quickly upon its receipt, leading to a minimum of delay in the order cycle resulting from such activities. In some cases where the volume of goods received is great, such as at a warehouse serving a chain of grocery stores, the timing of the arrival of the shipment may be critical to its prompt processing. There is a growing trend toward the delivery of orders "by appointment." This has created a number of situations where deliveries tendered before or after the "appointed" time have been refused by the customer, thus adding another element of uncertainty to the order cycle.

(1) **Look over the steps in the order cycle shown in Fig. 8–1. Which ones appear to be largely outside the control of the supplier?** (2) **What does this suggest in terms of the need for cooperation and coordination among the customer, transport carrier, and supplier?**

One step which is a primary determinant of cycle time and variability, stock replenishment, is within the control of the supplier. It can be eliminated if the supplier is willing to stock a sufficiently large quantity of goods at a supply point. Typically, it depends more heavily on other factors such as: (1) the accuracy of demand forecasting methods, (2) the volume of goods sold from the supply point, and (3) the speed with which inventories can be replenished after they have reached a replenishment level. While the steps in the replenishment cycle have many of the same characteristics as those in the order cycle, important differences between the two warrant some attention.

Replenishment Cycle

(A) [6] The replenishment of depleted stocks at distribution centers (warehouses) typically is accomplished by means of truckload or carload transportation services. This may require that items for order be accumulated until their total quantity is sufficient to meet truckload or carload minimums. It can, under circumstances where the volume of product requiring replenishment is low, introduce significant time lags into the replenishment cycle, and is a factor often overlooked when a decision is made to expand the number of distribution points for a product. For example, a distribution center requiring a truckload of product every two weeks for replenishment must hold an order for an item of less than truckload quantity from one to fourteen days before it can be combined with orders for other items to be picked and packed or, in some cases, even released for production.

(B) Order placement and communication is more likely to be managed by means of an automatic reorder system for replenishment purposes. This depends usually on the maintenance of a running or perpetual inventory record with a provision for periodic updating either at each distribution center or sales office on a decentralized basis or at the headquarters office. The updating of the inventory record, to the extent that it delays the recognition of the need for a replenishment order, produces further delay in the cycle. Delays may be minor in cases where punched cards pulled from products shipped from the distribution center are communicated daily by wire to the point where inventory accounting and control takes place and are processed so that records can be updated nightly by computer. Or they can become significant if inventory updating depends on a weekly accumulation of orders placed on a distribution center or an even less frequent physical inventory of items and units in stock at each distribution center.

(C)–(G) Capabilities for inquiring about the status of stock levels may vary a great deal. They may be confined to the facility, plant, or warehouse receiving a replenishment order. Or they may be system-wide, of the type typically maintained at a company's headquarters office or central distribution center. More sophisticated inventory inquiry systems will, through the use of a mathematical programming model or predesignated set of location priorities, also suggest the most logical point from which to replenish an order.

[6] These letters correspond to the letters in Fig. 8–1.

At this point, the procurement or production processes may have to be mobilized to meet a replenishment order. In cases where more than one supplier or plant must be called upon to help fill an order for replenishment stocks, transportation economies may dictate that the stocks be picked, packed, and shipped to a common point for consolidation and final shipment to their destination, the supplier's distribution center. Replenishment shipments, because they move typically in truckload or carload quantities from sources to destinations, usually are not beset with problems of undependable performance by transport carriers to the extent that might be true of customer order shipments in small quantities.

(H) Capabilities for receiving goods at a distribution center, including those for labor, equipment, and facility capacity, may influence the speed with which goods can be taken into stock after they physically arrive at their intermediate destination, the distribution center. Time lags at this stage may depend on the level as well as the variability in volume of product arriving at the facility.

Stages and time lags in a replenishment cycle may depend on whether a replenishment order is designated as "routine" or "rush." A routine order may be placed if a predesignated level of inventory is reached at the distribution center, suggesting the need for replenishment within a period of time compatible with system replenishment cycle capabilities. However, in cases where an actual or imminent stock-out exists, a "rush" designation may allow stage (A) to be circumvented, others to be shortened by various actions, and direct shipment to be made from the supplier's plant to the customer, thereby averting the duplication of effort and time represented by stages (E), (F), (G), (H), (6), and (7).

Order and Replenishment Cycle Profile

The various stages in the order and replenishment cycles are listed in Table 8–1, along with example information drawn from general experience about each stage. Information in Table 8–1 illustrates several points.

When all the stages in an order cycle are taken into consideration, the amount of, and range in, cycle time required to fill a customer demand may be great. Much of this time may be overlooked by the supplier in planning his system. The supplier may have little or no control over several of the stages. Because the ease of measuring performance varies roughly with the degree of control which the supplier may have over each stage, measurement may be relatively difficult for several stages in the order cycle.

TABLE 8-1. Sample Characteristics of Various Stages in an Order Cycle and Related Replenishment Cycle*

Stage	Range of Variation in Time for Completion (Days) in 99% of All Cases	Under Supplier Control?	Relative Ease of Measurement
Order Cycle:			
1. Identification of need for item	1- 7	No	Difficult
2. Order accumulation	1-30	?	Difficult
3. Order placement and communication	1 5	?	?
4. Information processing at supply point	1- 3	Yes	Easy
5. Stock replenishment, where necessary	1-60	Yes	Easy
6. Order picking and packing by supplier	1- 3	Yes	Easy
7. Transportation from supplier to customer	3- 7	?	?
8. Order receipt by customer	1- 3	?	Difficult
Total	15-90		
Replenishment Cycle:			
A. Order accumulation	1-30	Yes	Easy
B. Order placement and communication	1- 2	Yes	Easy
C. Inventory status inquiry, if necessary	1	Yes	Easy
D. Production or purchase	1-90	?	Easy
E. Order picking and packing at supplier's plant or warehouse	1- 3	Yes	Easy
F. Transportation to distribution center	3- 6	?	Easy
G. Consolidation with other replenishment orders en route to distribution center, if necessary	1- 2	Yes	Easy
H. Order receipt at distribution center	1- 2	Yes	Easy
Total	12-100		

*Stages are numbered and lettered to conform with the identification scheme used in Fig. 8-1.

(3) The range of relevant order cycle times represented as a total for the entire cycle is less than the sum of ranges for the individual stages. (You can verify this for yourself by adding up the individual ranges in Table 8-1.) Why?

Consider the following example. The likelihood that various times will be required for the performance of each stage in the order cycle

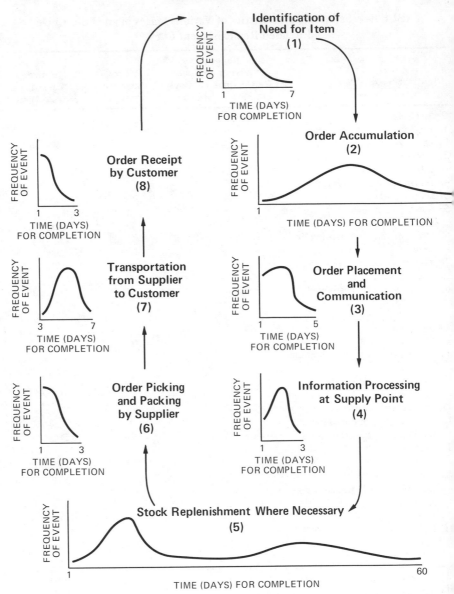

Fig. 8–2. A diagrammatic representation of the frequency distributions of times required to complete the stages in the order cycle for which information is presented in Table 8–1.

is diagrammed in Fig. 8–2. Assume that the probabilities for performance of each stage in the order cycle in a *minimum* amount of time are as follows:

	Time (Days)	Probability of Occurrence
1. Identification of need for item	1	.10 (10%)
2. Order accumulation	1	.05 (5%)
3. Order placement and communication	1	.50 (50%)
4. Information processing at supply point	1	.60 (60%)
5. Stock replenishment, when necessary	1	.01 (1%)
6. Order picking and packing by supplier	1	.60 (60%)
7. Transportation from supplier to customer	3	.05 (5%)
8. Order receipt by customer	1	.80 (80%)
	10	.00000036 (.000036%)

(4) **How did we arrive at an overall probability of .00000036 for our chances of achieving the minimum 10-day order cycle?**

Even if we eliminate stage 5, stock replenishment at the supplier's warehouse, because it is not always necessary, we still find ourselves with a probability of .000036, or 36 chances out of 1,000,000. As indicated in Table 8–1, it is not until we think in terms of 15-day cycle times that we have something worth considering from the standpoint of logistical planning.

The range of times required for stock replenishment at stage 5 in the order cycle does not correspond to the range indicated as a total for all stages in the replenishment cycle in Table 8–1. This is because the replenishment cycle should, in most cases, be initiated before the replenishment stage in the order cycle is reached. That is, the replenishment cycle, while it is interdependent with the order cycle, is carried out in anticipation of certain needs in the order cycle such that stages in both the order cycle and replenishment cycle may be accomplished simultaneously.

Similarly, the ranges of times required for individual cycle stages may overlap to the extent that the activities suggested by each stage overlap. For example, transportation may begin before the picking and packing stage has been completed, particularly in cases where multiple loads or shipments are contained within an order. Or, needs may be transmitted on an item-by-item basis as they arise at the customer's place of business. The order may be communicated and processed to a large degree before the final item demand which triggers a shipment is communicated by the customer to the supplier.

Because of great uncertainties and variations in production and procurement times, replenishment cycle performance may vary a great deal more than order cycle performance.

(5) **Looking once again at Table 8–1, does our assessment of the degree of supplier control at each step of the order cycle conform with the one you drew up earlier?** (6) **In what ways might performance at each step be measured?** (7) **With what degree of ease?** (8) **How**

does this compare with our appraisal in the right-hand column of Table 8–1?

Implications of Order and Replenishment Cycles for Physical Distribution and Materials (Supply) Management

Cycle times represent the extent to which item orders must be initiated in advance of need. The assumption is that stock on hand will be sufficient to meet demands which arise during the cycle time lag required to obtain a replenishment stock of the item. The longer the anticipated cycle time for an item, the larger the required amount of stock on hand at the time the order is placed, termed by inventory theorists the "reorder point."

Because of potential variations in cycle times, reorder points may have to be higher than would be necessary if cycle times could be stated with certainty. Because variations in cycle time cannot be predicted for any one experience, excess stocks result from the "protection" provided by higher reorder points. These stocks, known as "safety stocks," provide protection against the performance uncertainties inherent in an order cycle. We will see later in our discussion of inventory control just how large a reduction in safety stocks may result from customer service standards and controls which reduce variability in order and replenishment cycle times.

MANAGING CUSTOMER LOGISTICS SERVICE [7]

"We provide a 95% service level to customers in our business." This type of response often is recited proudly, sometimes somewhat mechanically, to satisfy an inquiry about customer service. In one case, it may mean, "We meet 19 out of 20 requests for a given item." In another, it may mean, "We replenish our stocks so as to run out during only one out of 20 replenishment cycles." In yet another, it may mean, "We fill 19 out of 20 customers' orders completely." And yet, knowing this, when managers from various companies get together at professional association meetings, they invariably can be found trading meaningless percentage figures to compare non-comparable service policies.

Customer logistics service must be understood to be managed. The definition of service thus takes on importance. Once service is defined, standards can be established, measurement accomplished, implementation carried out, and control exercised.

---

[7] Much of this section is based on James L. Heskett, "Controlling Customer Logistics Service," *International Journal of Physical Distribution,* June, 1971, pp. 140–45.

Importance of Customer Logistics Service Management

A great deal of attention in logistics management is devoted to cost control, as with the so-called "total cost concept" which has gained great attention in recent years. And yet, the bottom-line profit figure on a financial statement may be influenced more markedly by a carefully planned and controlled logistics service program through the impact of service on sales and, more important, on profits. What do we know about this impact? Not much. And the sad fact is that little effort has been made to measure it. The following examples suggest that the impact can be great.

Hutchison and Stolle cite the example of a large retailer, which "determined that when a distribution center was established, sales of white goods (washers, dryers, refrigerators, and so forth) increased immediately by about 15% in the area served, because of the greatly reduced delivery time to customers." [8]

The data processing division manager of the Spiegel general merchandise store chain, in reporting on a new ordering system for handling "will call" business in catalog order stores which increased the ability of the stores to meet promised delivery times of 48 to 72 hours from 30% to 100% of the time, stated:

Initially, the system was installed on an operational breakeven basis, in the interests of improving customer service and as a first step in a long-range order-entry mechanization program. . . . However, additional savings above and beyond the operational breakeven point, in the form of increased sales resulting from fewer cancelled orders, have since become realistically apparent. . . .[9]

An extensive customer service program encompassing a full range of management consulting and coordinated distribution services for purchasers of its products for use in fertilizers was instituted by the International Minerals & Chemicals Corporation. A year later the company reported a 20% increase in sales, a 21% increase in earnings, and the fact that four out of ten customers for IMC fertilizer ingredients had become purchasers of the company's full line of products as opposed to one in ten previously.[10]

Flaks reports on two situations in which logistics systems redesign influenced sales revenues as well as costs. In the first case, a reallocation of plant territories and the expenditure of money for the addition

[8] William M. Hutchison, Jr., and John F. Stolle, "How to Manage Customer Service," *Harvard Business Review*, November–December, 1968, pp. 85–96. See pp. 86 and 87.
[9] "R.A.G.M.O.P. Spells Improved Customer Service," *Distribution Manager*, February, 1969, pp. 31–35, at p. 35.
[10] Reese, *op. cit.*

to existing warehouse facilities operated by a manufacturer were estimated to result in a $200,000 increase in logistics costs, a $1,400,000 reduction in production costs, and a profit increase of $500,000 from an increase in annual sales from $45 million to $50 million. In the second situation, a consolidation of storage points at five distribution centers for a large retail chain with sales of over $1 billion was estimated to produce a $9 million saving in cost of goods sold (including inbound freight costs), a $4 million saving in logistics costs, and an additional $10 million increase in net profit resulting from a $100 million increase in retail sales.[11]

A faulty logistics service program may take its toll in costs as well as foregone sales opportunities. For example, an order involving one or more out-of-stock items often costs at least three times as much to process as one which can be filled completely from stocks held at the order-picking location. Excess costs result from duplicated communications, holding information about incomplete orders on file until all items are in stock or received, delays in billing, and extra service demands on a salesman when a customer receives an incomplete order.

Products found damaged or deteriorated upon delivery may require extra expenses for transportation, reworking, communication, and of course the time of the field sales force.

Considering its importance, the number of firms that have gone about developing a program for controlling logistics service is relatively small. We can, however, learn a great deal from the work that has been done thus far.

A Management Program

A program for managing logistics service requires the definition of such service for an individual industry, company, product, geographic area, or customer. Once the concept of service is defined, standards can be established, measurement accomplished, implementation begun, and control exercised.

Service Definition.   Various ways in which customer logistics service typically is defined, roughly ranked in order of their popularity, are:

1. The elapsed time between the receipt of an order at the supplier's warehouse and the shipment of the order from the warehouse
2. The minimum size of order, or limits on the assortment of items in an order which a supplier will accept from its customers

[11] Marvin Flaks, "A Profit Improvement Approach to Marketing Logistics," in Jerry Schorr, Milton Alexander, and Robert J. Franco (eds.), *Logistics in Marketing* (New York: Pitman Publishing Corp., 1969), pp. 171–210.

3. The percentage of items in a supplier's warehouse which might be found to be out-of-stock at any given point of time
4. The proportion of customer orders filled accurately
5. The percentage of customers, or volume of customer orders, which describes those who are served (whose orders are delivered) within a certain time period from the receipt of the order at the supplier's warehouse
6. The percentage of customer orders which can be filled completely upon receipt at a supplier's warehouse
7. The proportion of goods which arrive at a customer's place of business in salable condition
8. The elapsed time between the placement of an order by a customer and the delivery of goods ordered to the customer's place of business
9. The ease and flexibility with which a customer can place his order

Companies may employ more than one of these measures, although one typically prevails in the individual minds of most marketing and logistics executives. Just which one may depend on the orientation of the company.

The definitions near the bottom of this list almost never are employed today on a regular basis, perhaps because they present greater measurement and control problems. And yet they are customer-oriented definitions, in contrast to supplier-oriented definitions appearing at the top of the list. From this it should be reasonable to conclude that a problem of some importance in the management of customer logistics service will be that of introducing and maintaining customer-oriented rather than supplier-oriented programs.

What is important from the customer's point of view? Is it the immediate availability and shipment of a complete order? Is it merely the knowledge of when and if an order will arrive? Is it the flexibility with which he can place his order? Or is it the policy which determines whether the customer or his supplier will pay for transportation of emergency shipments? Many companies don't know because they've never asked their customers. Those who do, for example, are continually surprised by the fact that most customers express a greater need for *dependability* than for speed in response to their orders.

From the supplier's viewpoint, costs associated with certain types of service failures may suggest appropriate definitions.

Service definitions should be relevant, offer some basis for continuing measurement, and be as few in number as possible. This will require a manager to rank service matters in terms of their importance and to concentrate on those few that have the most meaning.

Establishment of Standards. Many executives point with pride to their companies' policies of shipping orders within 24 hours of their receipt at a company warehouse. Others cite the fact that at any one time at least 95% of their companies' product-line items can be found in stock. At least one major grocery products manufacturer claims that at least 98% of its customers receive their goods within 72 hours of the time orders are received at the manufacturer's distribution centers and within four hours of a prearranged delivery time. What factors influence companies in establishing such standards for customer logistics service?

Economics. Perhaps first and foremost are economic considerations. Service usually costs money. A policy of processing and shipping all orders within 24 hours of their receipt at a company's warehouse precludes any workload smoothing from day-to-day. As a result, labor and equipment must be provided every day to meet the maximum possible volume of orders, a policy that results in costs higher than those under more flexible policies permitting lower levels of service. While there are a number of system components and methods which can be combined to meet any customer service standard, these alternative methods decline in number and are more expensive as standards reflect higher (faster and/or more dependable) levels of service.

Any service standard can be translated either directly or indirectly into a cost. One example of a manufacturer's attempt to translate the coverage of item demands placed on its distributors by their retail customers is shown in Fig. 8–3. The table in Fig. 8–3 is prepared in advance by the Corning Glass Works to allow each distributor–customer to select an automatic replenishment policy which will satisfy item availability standards of that distributor, produce an acceptable order frequency, and result in a reasonable cost, reflected indirectly as the level of inventory necessary to support each item availability level and order frequency. (9) **How do you explain the relationships shown in Fig. 8–3?**

Hill cites an example drawn from data resulting from his experiences, to point up the impact of service level on cost. Defining service level as "the percentage of products available for shipment to customers on the day an order is received," he presents an example in which a 75% service level at a single supply point (warehouse) must be supported by $211,000 in inventory, a 90% level by almost twice as much inventory, $402,000, and a 97% level of customer service by $620,000 in inventory. In his example, for which service-industry cost relationships are not unusual, the company chose to compromise between service and cost by electing a 90% service level.[12]

---

[12] W. Clayton Hill, "Distribution Systems Management: Key to Profits in the Sixties," in *Marketing Precision and Executive Action*, Charles H. Hindersman (ed.) (Chicago: American Marketing Association, June, 1962), pp. 121–38, at p. 130.

Nature of the Environment.   Environmental considerations may take into account customer and competitor behavior. What is the impact of customer inventory management policies? Do they allow for adequate replenishment cycle times?   Or do they by accident or design produce the need for rapid response time, service that must be provided through the decentralization of supplier stocks, the frequent use of premium transportation methods, or some other means?

One firm manufacturing a line of cleaning products found that its industrial customers, largely other manufacturing companies, had storage space sufficient to house sizable inventories and anticipated their demands by means of systematic inventory management programs. Institutional accounts, such as restaurants, not only did not have space to store inventories of cleaning products, but also relied typically on informal ordering procedures that often were not initiated until the customer had actually run out of product.   This company's institutional accounts clearly required a higher level of customer logistics service than its industrial accounts.   By the same token, retailers as a group may require higher levels of service than wholesaler customers.   Or smaller accounts may require higher standards of service than larger accounts.

Competitors' service policies, whether they are carefully set or not, can be an important influence on the level of service established as standard. Research suggests that competitors' physical distribution service levels can have considerable influence on sales results. An experimental study, later supported by field research, indicated that selected wholesalers of convenience goods: (1) did not distinguish between differences in logistics service levels provided by competing manufacturers in planning and executing orders for the replenishment of their stocks, (2) as a result, experienced a higher rate of stock-out conditions on line items for which poor service was provided (as measured by the length and variance in cycle times), and (3) sold more than usual of the competing product when a product line was found to be out-of-stock.[13]

Nature of the Product.   Several product characteristics have a direct effect on the level of customer service which a firm would want or could afford to provide. They include the customer's willingness to substitute one product source or brand for another, physical characteristics of the product itself, and its pattern of demand.

---

[13] James L. Heskett, "Predictive Value of Classroom Simulation," in William S. Decker (ed.), *Emerging Concepts in Marketing* (Chicago: American Marketing Association, 1963), pp. 101–15. A follow-up field study of actual business decisions offered confirmation of laboratory findings. For some results of this work, see John L. Rider, *An Evaluation of the Predictive Value of Observational Gaming,* an unpublished Master's thesis deposited in the library of The Ohio State University, 1963.

% OF RETAIL CUSTOMER ORDER-FILL BY DISTRIBUTOR	ANNUAL INVENTORY TURNOVER FOR DISTRIBUTOR (ANNUAL SALES ÷ AVERAGE INVENTORY)	AVERAGE DISTRIBUTOR INVENTORY

IF DISTRIBUTOR ORDERS EVERY 2 WEEKS FROM CORNING

% OF RETAIL CUSTOMER ORDER-FILL BY DISTRIBUTOR	ANNUAL INVENTORY TURNOVER	AVERAGE DISTRIBUTOR INVENTORY
99.50%	6.80x	$24,052
99.20	7.16	22,910
99.00	7.33	22,373
98.00	7.93	20,560
97.00	8.48	19,351
96.00	8.88	18,478
95.00	9.21	17,806
94.00	9.53	17,202
92.00	10.13	16,194
90.00	10.66	15,389

IF DISTRIBUTOR ORDERS EVERY 3 WEEKS FROM CORNING

% OF RETAIL CUSTOMER ORDER-FILL BY DISTRIBUTOR	ANNUAL INVENTORY TURNOVER	AVERAGE DISTRIBUTOR INVENTORY
99.50%	6.26x	$26,208
99.20	6.57	24,957
99.00	6.73	24,369
98.00	7.33	22,382
97.00	7.79	21,058
96.00	8.16	20,102
95.00	8.47	19,386
94.00	8.77	18,704
92.00	9.32	17,600
90.00	9.81	16,717

IF DISTRIBUTOR ORDERS EVERY 4 WEEKS FROM CORNING

% OF RETAIL CUSTOMER ORDER-FILL BY DISTRIBUTOR	ANNUAL INVENTORY TURNOVER	AVERAGE DISTRIBUTOR INVENTORY
99.50%	5.69x	$28,823
99.20	5.97	27,472
99.00	6.11	26,836
98.00	6.64	24,691
97.00	7.05	23,260
96.00	7.38	22,227
95.00	7.65	21,433
94.00	7.92	20,717
92.00	8.40	19,523
90.00	8.83	18,572

Fig. 8–3. Sample print-out from the Customer Inventory Management Service (CIMS) provided by the Consumer Products Division, Corning Glass Works, to its distributor customers contemplating the use of Corning's automatic system for the replenishment of distributor stocks. *Source:* Consumer Products Division, Corning Glass Works.

% OF RETAIL CUSTOMER ORDER-FILL BY DISTRIBUTOR	ANNUAL INVENTORY TURNOVER FOR DISTRIBUTOR (ANNUAL SALES ÷ AVERAGE INVENTORY)	AVERAGE DISTRIBUTOR INVENTORY
IF DISTRIBUTOR ORDERS EVERY 5 WEEKS FROM CORNING		
99.50%	5.23x	$31,373
99.20	5.48	29,929
99.00	5.61	29,250
98.00	6.08	26,956
97.00	6.45	25,427
96.00	6.74	24,322
95.00	6.99	23,473
94.00	7.22	22,708
92.00	7.65	21,434
90.00	8.03	20,415
IF DISTRIBUTOR ORDERS EVERY 6 WEEKS FROM CORNING		
99.50%	4.82x	$34,003
99.20	5.05	32,471
99.00	5.17	31,760
98.00	5.59	29,318
97.00	5.92	27,696
96.00	6.18	26,524
95.00	6.40	25,623
94.00	6.61	24,812
92.00	6.99	23,461
90.00	7.33	22,379

Fig. 8–3. Continued.

Substitutability. Product substitutability at all levels in a channel of distribution will determine the degree of care with which a seller regards his customer service policy.

Results of a survey conducted recently by *Progressive Grocer* magazine which are reported in Fig. 8–4 indicate a great deal of variability in customers' tendencies to substitute various competing products for one another. (10) **Are these results what you might have expected?** (11) **How might you explain them?**

In industrial goods markets, factors such as the standardization of specifications and the expiration of patent rights to products and processes have increased the prevalence of goods or brands being substituted for others.

Physical Characteristics. Of primary importance among a product's physical characteristics are: (1) its ability to bear the cost of high-priced premium customer logistics service, and (2) the risk of storing it.

| | Per Cent of Customers Who Would[a] | | | | | | | | | | | | | | |
| Product | Buy Elsewhere[b] | | | | | Switch Brands[b] | | | | | Buy Later at Same Store[b] | | | | |
	#1	#2	#3	#4	#5	#1	#2	#3	#4	#5	#1	#2	#3	#4	#5
Margarine	17%	18%	26%	36%	·17%	58%	46%	66%	27%	52%	25%	36%	10%	45%	33%
Cigarettes	75	82	81	83	80	10	4	17	17	5	15	14	2	8	15
Gelatin	13	11	27	10	21	61	50	60	40	49	26	42	13	60	32
Liquid starch	6	9	27	11	28	50	39	54	44	53	44	52	19	56	19
Hand soap	30	21	33	45	30	43	43	53	36	49	26	36	15	27	23
Toothpaste	39	36	63	60	43	52	40	28	30	36	9	24	10	20	21
Cereal	30	28	28	20	24	61	59	58	30	57	9	17	15	60	20
Dog food	61	62	39	25	41	39	38	50	50	44	—	—	11	50	19
Baby food	40	60	48	20	59	40	33	46	40	33	20	7	9	60	7
Deodorant	59	54	67	56	58	36	19	25	33	26	5	27	10	22	16
Shampoo	61	54	66	67	57	26	21	27	33	23	13	25	8	17	20
Regular coffee	46	48	36	27	36	32	28	57	18	33	23	28	6	64	33
Catsup	30	7	26	40	19	57	59	67	40	63	13	35	8	30	19
Mayonnaise	52	7	39	22	27	26	55	51	22	59	22	41	13	67	14
Instant coffee	33	14	44	11	29	52	36	53	33	50	14	55	4	67	23
Canned tuna	30	19	22	9	18	52	56	67	46	53	17	26	12	55	29
Canned peaches	9	10	11	9	18	73	52	81	36	55	18	38	8	64	27
Peanut butter	17	18	26	20	27	67	46	61	50	58	17	36	14	40	18
Jam	9	21	15	36	21	77	48	77	27	64	14	31	8	46	16
Tomato juice	27	15	17	11	17	68	56	76	44	66	5	30	7	56	17
Toilet tissue	26	28	24	25	22	65	52	63	33	61	9	21	13	50	18
Facial tissue	22	19	19	—	19	70	52	67	33	64	9	30	14	78	19
Aluminum foil	17	18	13	33	15	78	46	80	33	68	4	36	8	44	19
Salad oil	26	11	24	38	20	57	50	67	38	62	17	39	10	38	20
Solid shortening	13	12	27	18	20	65	35	65	50	56	22	54	8	46	27
Canned soup	32	14	33	25	25	46	45	51	33	50	23	41	17	50	25
Canned milk	20	14	15	30	13	70	43	77	30	68	10	43	8	50	20
Canned corn	27	7	18	9	19	55	65	73	55	57	18	31	10	46	24
Canned green beans	18	11	17	29	19	64	61	78	57	57	18	32	6	29	24
Laundry detergents	46	36	51	50	52	38	29	43	30	23	17	43	9	30	27
Waxed paper	13	12	13	20	14	78	65	74	40	73	9	23	13	50	14

[a] Out-of-stock, a big problem to supermarket operators, is also a big factor in the minds of consumers when selecting a favorite store. In answer to a question about how they would react to an out-of-stock situation on their favorite brands of 31 types of grocery products, they show some interesting unanimity of opinion. A dominant percentage of customers in all neighborhoods say they will go to another store to buy their favorite brands of cigarettes, coffee, deodorant, dog food, laundry detergent, and shampoo. High-income shoppers and Negroes show strong brand loyalty to toothpaste. Young marrieds and small-town customers will go out of their way to get their favorite brands of baby foods.

In nearly all but the few categories mentioned above, better than half the customers in all neighborhoods say their reaction to an out-of-stock situation on their favorite brand would be to choose a substitute.

The percentages sometimes add up to more than 100 per cent due to the fact that some respondents checked "buy elsewhere" and "buy later at the same store," indicating that they would do one or the other but will not switch brands.

[b] Key to store neighborhood numbers: #1 = young married, #2 = blue collar, #3 = high income, #4 = Negro, #5 = small town.

Fig. 8–4. Selected results of *Progressive Grocer* survey of how different types of customers say they would react to stock-outs on favorite brands. Source: *Progressive Grocer: The Magazine of Super Marketing*, Vol. 47, October, 1968.

In Chapter 2 we said that the dollar density of a product determines its ability to bear the cost of high-priced transportation. This factor also influences inventory holding costs, but inversely to movement costs. Machine tools, for example, have high dollar densities. In general, machine tools, especially replacement parts, can bear high movement costs. On the other hand, inventory holding costs for machine tools can be great in absolute amounts. This combination of factors will encourage a firm dealing in such products to maintain low inventories and utilize faster methods of transportation and material handling. At the same time, the firm's order cycle may include a relatively high proportion of time for replenishment activities, because it may produce and store very little product in anticipation of orders.

Refined lead, with its moderate dollar density but extremely high weight density, might be stored in quantity at various points in order to conserve movement costs and accommodate the refining schedule. It would not likely be moved rapidly from point to point to meet customer service demands. Orders for lead may be required some time in advance, not so much to provide for production and replenishment activities as to allow for a slow, economical movement and storage pattern.

The characteristics of goods refer not only to weight and value, but also to the ease and risk of storage. This has a marked influence on customer service. The distribution of wet yeast, for example, is highly regulated by the government because of its tendency to deteriorate rapidly. To insure supplies of fresh yeast on grocers' shelves, a manufacturer maintains daily or thrice-weekly deliveries to his customers. An autumn line of cruise fashions is nearly worthless if made available at any time (even the following season) after the cruise purchases. In these situations, where a stock-out can result in a considerable quantity of almost certainly unrecoverable sales losses, customer service standards will be set at relatively high levels, a result not so much of a firm's desire to serve, but of its need to do so.

Pattern of Demand. Customer service standards are much more difficult to comply with during periods of peak, as opposed to periods of slack, customer demand. It is precisely during peak demand periods that customer service, as evidenced by the availability of the product, may be most important.

Some products are demanded only during certain seasons. Sales lost because of a stock-out in umbrellas during a rainy season cannot be recovered until the next similar season, if then.

Demand may take on short-run patterns generally related to salesmen's incentives, ultimate consumer demand patterns, and inventory tax levies. Many firms with monthly sales incentive periods receive 40% of their orders in the last week of the month, the result of salesmen's desires to "catch up" on placing their orders and speed their own compensation by 30 days.

A wholesaler of grocery products is likely to encounter heavy demand from retailers just prior to the weekly bulge of retail sales corresponding to wage payment dates for the consumer. These may be weekly, resulting in most communities in a midweek peak of wholesaler deliveries. Where weekend closings are common, Monday may present another peak in retail demand.

To reduce property taxes on inventories, buyers and sellers alike may arrange to have goods in transit at certain dates during the year. This reduces the amount of goods in stock for both without interrupting the supply cycle. At the same time, it places a periodic burden on the supplier to meet fluctuations in demands of customers caused by this type of disturbance in the supply process.

In establishing customer service standards, managers often unintentionally overlook the need for differentiated standards for various major groups of items in the product line. For example, high-volume items in the line will, if stocked-out, produce many more back-order situations than stock-outs on low-volume sales items, perhaps requiring a 99% line-item fill rate for high-volume items and a 95% line-item fill rate for low-volume items.

Nature of Demand. At the level of the ultimate consumer, marketing men have distinguished the nature of products on the basis of the manner in which the customer regards them in contemplating a purchase. In this respect, convenience items are those frequently purchased in small quantities at many retail outlets. Shopping goods are those which customers buy only after visiting several stores, comparing qualities and prices, and pondering their decision. Specialty items are bought at exclusive, or widely spaced, outlets; they are purchased at lengthy intervals, without extensive product comparison between stores.

In general, a consumer is more willing to substitute one brand of convenience or shopping goods for another (given the absence of the first in the market) than he is to substitute one brand of specialty goods for another. This may require an intensive distribution strategy for the manufacturer, with emphasis on obtaining distribution through as many retail outlets as possible. In contrast, a manufacturer of specialty goods may be able to distribute his product through relatively few retail outlets, possibly under an agreement which provides each with an exclusive sales territory. Thus, the emphasis upon all types of customer logistics service is perhaps greatest among firms marketing convenience or shopping goods. This is one reason why the grocery products industry has been a leader in emphasizing all forms of customer logistics service.

Customer expectations vary with the type of item ordered. The president of a retail discount department store chain, in discussing his customers' expectations of availability for major household appliances, commented that customers expected standard items such as white, 16-cubic-foot, right-hand-door refrigerators to be deliverable to their homes within 48 hours of their purchase. In sharp contrast, most customers were prepared to wait as long as *six weeks* to get delivery on a refrigerator unit of exotic color, non-standard size, or with a left-hand door. (12) **Why were they willing to wait?** And yet, how many refrigerator and other manufacturers treat all units alike for purposes of measuring and controlling customer service?

It is costly to maintain a high level of customer logistics service for all products, all customers, and all geographic areas. And it most likely is unnecessary.

Once standards are determined, a statement of logistics service policy for customers can be developed. Gustafson and Richard cite an example of a customer logistics service policy for an industrial repair parts company: [14]

GENERAL STATEMENT

We guarantee our customers service that is timely, dependable, convenient, and understandable. We will devise an individual plan for each customer to guide us in our service to him. Specific levels of individual services are detailed under the following four headings: time, dependability, communication and convenience.

A. *Time*

(1) Order-cycle time (defined as the time taken from the submittal of an order from a customer to receipt of the merchandise) will be developed with each individual customer within prescribed limits. Typically, this will be five days in metropolitan areas and ten days in rural areas.

(2) Emergency orders have priority and will be specially processed so that a minimum amount of time elapses. In most cases this should be same-day or next-day shipment.

(3) Invoices will be mailed one day after merchandise has been shipped.

(4) Credit memoranda will be issued the day after approval has been made. The approval process should not exceed a week and covers damages, return goods, order filling and shipping errors.

B. *Dependability*

(1) The order-cycle times developed for each customer will be met with dependable regularity (95% of the time) with an allowable tolerance of plus or minus a day.

(2) Order filling accuracy should be at the 99.5% level or better.

(3) Stock-outs should not exceed 1% of all items stocked.

[14] John F. Gustafson and Raymond Richard, "How to Establish Yardsticks for Customer Service," *Transportation & Distribution Management*, July, 1964, pp. 35–37. See pp. 35–36.

(4) Back orders will be handled according to customers' desires (cancel all back orders, ship immediately, ship with next shipments, etc.).

C. *Communication*

(1) A special function has been designated responsible for all customer/company communications on physical distribution services—the sales order service department. Such important topics as order status, complaint handling, notification of delays, etc., will be handled by this department. The customer will be able to depend on getting answers from this contact point. All contacts will be done by courteous, intelligent, knowledgeable and service-oriented individuals.

(2) Salesmen's communications on distribution services will also be handled by the sales order service department.

(3) Invoices, order forms, and other means of written communications will be designed to provide the kind of information customers need and in the form they desire it.

(4) All policies pertinent to customer service will be explained in an easy reference guide given to the customer.

D. *Convenience*

(1) During the course of working out an individual plan for each customer on desired standards for order-cycle time, other services should be determined also. These include order submittal, shipping and loading instructions, delivery instructions, invoicing instructions, back-order procedures, and other pertinent customer considerations.

(2) The only information source on customer services will be the sales order service department. Customer contacts will be courteous, prompt, and made by knowledgeable individuals.

Measurement. Measurement of logistics service performance must be consistent with definitions used for customer service standards, current, and carried out at reasonable cost. It varies in difficulty with the scope of the customer service cycle being measured.

Unfortunately, customer service standards are defined too often in terms of what can be measured rather than what is relevant to the performance of a logistics system. For example, it may be convenient to measure the proportion of orders picked, packed, and shipped within 24 hours of their receipt at a supply point. However, this measure provides information about only a small and relatively unimportant element in the order cycle. A management deluded into thinking that it has measured customer service adequately with such information perhaps would be better off not collecting it at all.

An excellent example of this problem was a manufacturer of industrial expendables with a policy of filling 95% of all individual line items appearing on customer orders from stock. In fact, company executives cited computer-generated information indicating that inventories were being controlled in such a way that the standard was being met. Continued customer complaints led to an investigation and the discovery that an average order contained approximately four line items. Thus, if all items appeared on orders with about the same frequency, one out of every five orders (totalling 20 line items × 95% line-item coverage) would contain an out-of-stock item. The 80% order-fill rate produced by a 95% item-fill policy was not acceptable to many of the company's customers. (13) **What would the order-fill rate under these assumptions have been if an average order contained 10 line items?**

Interestingly, in terms of cost to the manufacturer in this case, unfilled orders were a more significant indicator of back-order costs than unfilled line items. From the standpoint of *both* the supplier and his customer, an order-fill measure was more relevant.

Customer-oriented standards of service are often most relevant to service program design efforts. Their measurement requires the cooperation of both customers and carriers in providing information about the speed, dependability, and condition in which goods arrived after they were ordered. Realistically, three dates can be found for every order: (1) the date of the order, (2) the date on the bill of lading indicating order shipment, and (3) the date on a dock receipt signed by the customer at the time of delivery. Two are often available in the supplier's files. The third will be held by the carrier and/or the customer receiving the shipment. While these dates do not circumscribe the order cycle as we have defined it, they provide the most complete and readily available information for the time and effort expended.

Customer and carrier cooperation can be obtained for measurement purposes, particularly if the effort is well-defined and conducted on a current basis. After all, if such measurement can lead to improved performance, the customer should be convinced of the value of measurement. If the carrier values the business he receives, he should be willing to assist in the monitoring effort as a part of the service package he provides.

The costs of carrying out an audit of many of the stages in an order cycle often require that such work be accomplished with a (small) sample of orders pulled from the supplier's files, possibly those received from a small number of customers. As in any statistical sampling process, care must be exercised to insure that an adequate and unbiased sample is obtained.

Requested information is much more likely to be obtained if it is solicited on a current basis. Requests for information about shipments tendered to carriers should be made of the carrier's representatives at the time the shipment is initiated. Information requested of customers may be obtained by means of short response forms attached to the shipment or invoice for completion and return to the supplier. Such forms typically are useful only for determining the date of the receipt of the shipment and the condition in which goods arrived at their destination.

More complex information may be obtained on a periodic basis by salesmen or other representatives of the supplier's organization. Information pertaining to preselected customer orders may be more precise and less biased than that volunteered by the customer on a non-systematic basis.

An alternative to the sampling of documents for fixing service levels is a poll of customers' attitudes toward a company's and its competitors' logistics service. As Hutchison and Stolle point out, "Companies spend large sums of money interviewing customers to determine their attitudes toward *products*—but their feelings concerning service are neglected." [15] Unfortunately, such "popularity" polls are influenced by many non-logistics factors. For example, experience with one such customer poll indicated the customers' reactions to logistical service varied directly with their relative perceptions of suppliers' salesmen, trade advertising and promotion, pricing policies, and product quality.[16]

Without a systematic collection of information, organizations are prone to manage customer service by the "half-deaf ear to the ground" approach, relying on customer complaints as the measure of service. This approach delegates responsibility for an important element of business to the customer. Customers may not perceive differences in service provided by competing suppliers in sufficiently accurate terms to be reliable sources for control information. Their reactions, if not structured, tend to be based on the most recent experience or most flagrant violation of expected performance. The systematic collection of information from a sample of customers on a continuing basis can help avert the problem.

Implementation. Even after considering the elements discussed at some length above, a program of customer service management, no matter how well designed, may founder in implementation because of a tendency to overlook certain obvious elements of an effective program. Several elements which seem to us to be most commonly overlooked are discussed here as representative of a much longer list of possible pitfalls.

Failure To Consider Human Aspects of the System. Customers are human. It is increasingly easy in a machine age to overlook this fact. Several companies have encountered adverse customer reaction to the installation of a central order-processing facility requiring communication by long-distance telephone, even when the calls can be made toll-free. Even though goods continued to be shipped in such cases from the same decentralized supply points, customers were found to prefer dealing with

[15] *Op. cit.*, p. 89.
[16] *Ibid.*, p. 92.

supplier account representatives (order takers) located closer to them. In some cases, suppliers have created telephone switching systems that allow them to make the customer feel he is dealing with an account representative "close to home" when in fact his order is received and processed centrally.

Failure To Establish Procedures for "Non-Standard" Situations. Many companies operate as if back orders, for example, never occur, even though few companies are immune from that plague. They fail to establish a routine for dealing with back-order situations. As a result, such matters are handled in non-routine, expensive ways. The worst problem resulting from back orders, for example, is the costly excess of duplicated stock checking and communication effort which they can produce. One manufacturer of automotive parts estimated recently that 85% of the capacity of its phone lines was consumed by communications resulting from back orders, a load which at times interfered with major functions of the company. Another manufacturer of home and industrial tools generates two back orders for every order received and yet is able to handle the resulting load without a major disruption to its other operations. Problems resulting from "non-routine" occurrences can be dealt with by: (1) limiting alternatives open for resolving back-order or other "non-standard" situations, (2) providing specific routing for messages and product, or (3) issuing procedures designed to assign all responsibilities for resolving "non-standard" situations to a separately identified group of specialists, i.e., "trouble-shooters" or "expediters."

Failure To Invest Sufficient Time and Effort in Communicating Program to Customer. Typically, both benefits and penalties for customers and suppliers alike result from any change in customer logistics service programs. For example, economies and other benefits can result to both customers and suppliers if customers can be regimented to a degree in their behavior. Fixed order dates or deadlines can create significant opportunities for system economies through the pooling of shipments and the evening of order processing loads. However, if only the restrictions and not the benefits are perceived by the customer, such plans may be difficult or impossible to implement.

Adverse customer reaction to most system innovations can be traced to a failure to orient the customer to the advantages he may receive from the innovation and the ease with which his personnel can adapt to it. The time and money required to communicate a change in the logistics service program to customers may represent the most important investment that a supplier may make to insure the success of an otherwise well-designed program.

Control. "We checked transit times several years ago and found them to be satisfactory." "We don't get many service complaints; therefore, we assume we're doing all right." These types of comments are often made in response to inquiries about customer service control efforts. And while customer service may be controlled under the philosophy that it is a byproduct of the system, such an approach may overlook opportunities for gaining competitive advantages.

We discussed earlier the study in which wholesale distributors of drug, tobacco, and candy products failed to distinguish in their inventory control programs between suppliers providing good and poor service, and the higher levels of stock-out conditions which this produced for products on which poor service was offered. In a follow-up to that study, specific inquiries placed with customer or marketing service managers at manufacturing companies whose products were involved in the study led to three conclusions: (1) there was little relationship between the proximity of a manufacturer's supply point to his customer and the transit time required for a shipment between the two points, (2) there was no perceivable relationship between service levels (cycle time lags) actually provided and those which the manufacturers' managers thought were being provided, and (3) there was little knowledge about the comparative service provided by manufacturers of directly competing products.[17]

Logistics service control can be incorporated as part of a broader program for controlling all aspects of logistics management. Specifically, once the appropriate measures and standards of performance are established, information about them should be reported up through the organization, they should be taken into account in evaluating performance, and they should form the basis for corrective action which, when possible, has been planned in advance as a part of the program.

At a given distribution center or at the corporate level, a company may employ periodic reports indicating items such as:

1. Proportion of line items shipped vs. ordered
2. Proportion of orders filled completely within a certain time after their receipt, with a tabulation of reasons for non-performance
3. Proportion of emergency orders in the total processed
4. Proportion of air freight (or other premium transportation) costs in total transportation costs in a warehouse region or on a corporate-wide basis
5. Sampled customer replenishment cycle times
6. Transit times and their variability between given points, by carrier

---

[17] Paul R. Stephenson, *Manufacturers' Physical Distribution Service Knowledge and Penalties: An Experimental Analysis,* unpublished Master's thesis deposited in the library of The Ohio State University, 1963.

In using such measures to evaluate individual performance, care must be taken to insure that an individual so measured has a reasonable amount of control over the measure used. Further, it is important that he have continuing knowledge of his performance ratings as well as information about how to improve his performance levels. Finally, the most effective programs involve the individual in establishing his own standards of performance, most often up to a year in advance.

Control detached from corrective action and future planning is like a broken electrical circuit. The mere existence and knowledge of a system of service measurement and control often will influence performance. This, in combination with the development of explicit procedures for coupling the control program with appropriate corrective actions will contribute to an effective program.

SUMMARY

A customer may require financial, marketing, product, and logistical support. This discussion has concentrated on the latter. Logistical support may be measured in terms of product availability at the time, at the place, and in the quantities desired; relative freedom in the manner and timing with which orders can be received from customers for processing; the condition in which ordered goods are delivered to customers; and the speed and dependability with which items ordered can be made available to the customer.

This latter feature of customer service can be treated in terms of the order cycle and one or more levels of replenishment cycles.

The concept of the order cycle is one of the most basic concepts for logistics management, and provides a foundation for an understanding of forecasting and inventory theory, to be discussed in Part IV.

The effective management of customer logistics service requires that service be defined, standards for its management established, measurement be carried out, care be taken in program implementation, and a program for control initiated.

The ultimate test of any such program is its relevance to the overall goals of the company, customer needs, and competitive behavior, as well as the manner in which those needs might vary by customer, product line, individual products, geographic territory, and point in time.

SUGGESTED READINGS

At the time we prepared the first edition of this book, there literally was nothing in print regarding customer service standards for logistics management. In the intervening years, several sources have appeared, of which the following may be of special interest.

FLAKS, MARVIN. "Profit Improvement Approach to Marketing Logistics," in JERRY SCHORR, MILTON ALEXANDER, and ROBERT J. FRANCO (eds.). *Logistics in Marketing*. New York: Pitman Publishing Corp., 1969.
Discusses customer service, sales, and profit improvements in the context of the logistics system design effort.

GUSTAFSON, JOHN F., and RAYMOND RICHARD. "Customer Service in Physical Distribution," Parts I through V, appearing in the following issues of *Transportation & Distribution Management:* April, 1964, pp. 19–21 and 24; May, 1964, pp. 34–37; June, 1964, pp. 34–37; July, 1964, pp. 35–37; and August, 1964, pp. 31–34.
Presents a comprehensive treatment of various aspects of managing customer service, including the determination of levels of required service, assigning organizational responsibilities for setting customer logistics service standards, and the control of performance.

HUTCHISON, WILLIAM M., JR., and JOHN F. STOLLE. "How to Manage Customer Service," *Harvard Business Review*, November–December, 1968, pp. 85–96.
Sets forth basic principles for the design of customer-oriented logistics service standards, and includes experiences of a company which designed, tested, and implemented a program encompassing such standards.

MEAD, RICHARD R. "The Time Dimension and the Order Cycle," in DAVID McCONAUGHY and C. JOSEPH CLAWSON (eds.). *Business Logistics—Policies and Decisions*. Los Angeles: Research Institute for Business and Economics of the Graduate School of Business Administration, University of Southern California, 1968.
Comments on the importance of time as a variable in customer service, the need for dependability of service, and the way in which parties to a transaction can control the level and variability of times required to perform various activities in an order cycle.

PART FOUR

LOGISTICS SYSTEM DESIGN

This section of the book is a reaction to the typical article about logistics system design which attempts to set forth a technique for solving a design problem in a format that cannot possibly allow the author to explore his subject. As a result, the effort lacks authenticity. The reaction of a friend of ours sums up our impression: "It sounds great; now what the devil do I do with it?"

To obtain the proper context for system design work, it is necessary to become intimately familiar with an organization's current practice. We have elected to use one company example throughout Part Four. By the time we are finished, you will be tired of hearing about the Warren G. Wonka Manufacturing Company. But you will know a great deal about a company, its logistics problems, and approaches to system design that can deal with these problems.

Chapter 9 has dual purposes, to familiarize you with the Wonka Company and to illustrate an approach to a logistics system audit designed to provide necessary background information in a systematic manner.

Chapters 10 and 11 explore the basics of inventory theory and more practical inventory management programs. Inventory management really is what logistics is all about, even though only a little over a third of all logistics costs are directly concerned with the storage and handling as opposed to the transportation of inventory. This argues for the inclusion of all costs in the design of inventory management models, a topic we take up late in Chapter 11.

Chapters 12 and 13 deal with the location of facilities and, more important, of inventories. Again, we first explore the theory of location and economic development, then relate it directly to problems experienced by the Wonka Company.

Chapter 14 allows us to continue our exploration of inventory management along the time dimension, and of ways in which more effective allocation and scheduling of production and product movement can contribute to improved performance.

Although it provides the basis for the design of the physical aspects of a logistics system, we discuss logistics information flow and the design of the information subsystem as the final element in logistics system design in Chapter 15. This ordering of material results from our intent to overcome the inherent dullness of discussions about information flow by first developing an understanding of the need for, and role of, information in a logistics system.

Chapter 16 is an attempt to bridge the almost complete lack of communication between theorists (and managers, for that matter) dealing in inventory control and location problems. Here we set forth guidelines for comprehensive system design. The objective of the chapter is to place in perspective system elements and design techniques.

There are several important things to remember as you read this section. We intend to explain concepts in sufficient detail that you can reconstruct our figures or, better yet, develop some of your own. Keep in mind, however, that in a computer age you may, as a manager, never be asked to carry out what appear to be at times forbidding computational tasks. To the extent that you may be asked to approve plans based on techniques described in this section, you will want to acquire at least a working understanding of such techniques, including their strengths and weaknesses.

It is unrealistic to treat matters of system design in sequence and impossible to deal with them simultaneously. Part Four is the compromise resulting from this dilemma.

9

The Logistics System

Before determining what a logistics system should be, we need to find out what it is. The system audit is the vehicle for such information gathering. Here we are interested in the elements of such an audit as well as techniques for performing the audit.

There are any number of ways of describing a logistics system, and the terms employed are quite confusing. In our endeavor to clarify system descriptors, the Warren G. Wonka Manufacturing Company, Inc. will provide us with a continuing illustration, not only in this chapter but throughout the chapters dealing with logistics system design.

SYSTEM REVIEWS

The collection of system reviews provides an organized method of conducting a logistics system audit. Just as we use different perspectives in drawing blueprints for a three-dimensional structure, each review offers a basically different way of looking at the system. Those we will discuss can be viewed in three categories, concerning management views, system outputs, and system inputs. Our intention here is to suggest the range of information useful for a system analysis. Some of the following information is useful for orientation purposes only; the remainder will be used directly in our analysis of the logistics system employed by the Wonka Company.

Top Management Review of Objectives, Scope, and Constraints

At the outset of the auditing process, it is important to elicit top management views regarding the objectives of logistics activities as well as perceptions of the nature of the system design and management task. This information, obtained through interviews, not only provides guidelines for further efforts but alerts top management personnel to the auditing activity and forces them to consider, in many cases for the first time, issues regarding interrelated activities which a logistics system comprises.

We have assumed that the audit of the Wonka Company's logistics system was performed by a consultant to the Company. However, it could just as well have been carried out by personnel within the company who are capable of assuming the independent point of view essential to a successful audit. Such individuals might include the corporate director of logistics in a decentralized, divisionalized corporation (with review at the divisional level) or a representative of the company's control group with a functional interest in logistics activities.

Our consultant's interview with Warren G. Wonka, President of the Company, was not totally successful, as you might conclude from the following excerpts from the conversation. It was, however, typical in many respects, and was of course supplemented by similar interviews with members of Wonka's top management team.

After the usual short exchange of pleasantries, Wonka zeroed right in on the purpose of the visit. "As you might guess, we're expecting great things from your analysis of our transportation and warehousing. I guess you call it the logistics system. George Dalton [the Company's Distribution Manager] tells me that you begin by performing a system audit. Just what is the purpose of such an audit? It sounds a bit academic to me."

Interviewer: "The audit is a special way of describing the existing logistics system which the Company uses. In order to improve upon it, you have to know what you've got now. In order to measure improvement against a possible plan, you have to have the type of benchmark which we feel the audit provides."

Wonka: "How do you know our logistics activities need to be surveyed?"

[(1) **At this point, what would your reply be if you were the interviewer?**]

Interviewer: "How long has it been since you've systematically collected information about logistics activities as an interrelated system of parts?"

Wonka: "I'm not fully certain what you mean, but I can't recall that we ever have done anything like that."

"With the changes in transportation and warehousing technology, improvements in techniques for such activities as inventory control, increased capability of computers, and shifts in Company markets and the prices the Company pays for logistics services, I think it is safe to say that this in itself is justification for the current audit."

"I take it that you assume that all of these matters are associated with logistics."

Interviewer: "In various companies. However, I would like to get your views. Just what do you regard as the scope of the logistics system in this Company?"

[(2) **Would you expect this question to elicit a useful response from the President? (3) Why?**]

Wonka: "Well, as you know we are engaged in the manufacture of levelors for the consumer market, which we reach by means of nearly 600 company salesmen selling both direct to individual homes and to retail hardware and lumber outlets. Critical factors in selling to this market include the availability of units when and where they are needed. Here, inventory balance on a geographic basis is important. And we can save a pile of money shipping in carload lots from our plant to our fifteen DC [distribution center] locations. Because of the importance of service and the need for parts replacement from time to time, parts distribution is both a headache and an extremely important element of our business. . . ."

"Could you give an idea of what you regard as the range of activities which logistics encompasses in this Company?"

"I suppose the simplest answer would be to say those activities for which George Dalton is responsible."

[(4) **Would you accept this as a response? (5) What would your next comment or question be? (6) How could you begin making this valuable time count?**]

Interviewer: "Perhaps we can get a better idea of this after we get into the audit. It would, however, help me a great deal to determine what you feel are the most important objectives of the work we are about to engage in."

Wonka: "Isn't that your job? Just like a consultant; he borrows your watch, then tells you what time it is. [Smiling, fortunately.] Naturally, we'd like to realize the greatest possible increase in company profit from your work."

"All right. But perhaps we can get more specific. Logistics in many companies involves the trading of some costs for others. The costs of customer service and lost sales are two such costs. At the present time, would you place greater emphasis on achieving lower logistics costs or better customer service?"

"We'd like to get the greatest amount of customer service for the least cost."

[(7) Is this a useful response? (8) Where would you go from here as the interviewer?]

Interviewer: "Assuming that you could achieve one result only by compromising on the other, where would you place the emphasis?"

Wonka: "You don't give up easily, do you? My current concern, and I suppose my greatest concern for the foreseeable future, is in increasing the profitability of our existing sales base as well as future sales. As you know, our recent performance hasn't been what you would call outstanding. If we can cut costs significantly, even if it means cutting back a bit on service, I suppose I'd go for it."

A further fifteen-minute discussion produced impressions tabulated by the interviewer in the first column of Table 9–1.

Interviewer: "Let's direct our attention for a few moments to possible directions which a system design effort might take. This is perhaps a better way of approaching the matter of acceptable scope for the study and will give me some idea of what you regard as the kinds of recom-

TABLE 9-1. Top Management Views Regarding the Objectives of a Logistics System Review Effort, as Perceived by Interviewer, Warren G. Wonka Manufacturing Company

	Executive and Priorities*				
	President	VP, Marketing	VP, Finance	VP, Mfg.	Distribution Manager
Objectives of the Effort:					
Greatest service at least cost	1	1	1	1	1
Maximum profit	1	1	1	1	1
Improved customer service with no increase in logistics cost	2	1	2	2	1
Reduced costs for logistics with no change in customer service	1	2	1	1	1
Reduced costs for logistics with selective reductions in customer service	2	3	2	1	2
Goals:					
Logistics cost reduction of	10%	0–5%	10%	15%	10%
Customer service change	None	Item-fill improvement of 85% to 95%	None	None	Four-day response time on 95% of orders

*Priorities are rated so that 1 = high priority, 2 = moderate priority, and 3 = low priority.

mendations that possibly could be implemented as a result of this study."

Wonka: "Look, I'd buy almost anything if you can persuade me that the economic benefits are great enough."

"It's that word 'almost' that worries me. But you've brought up an important point. What is the cut-off point for ROI [return on investment] on projects involving capital investment at the moment?"

Wonka: "About 30% before tax, although that's a throw-back to better days. As you know, we only managed to earn about 16% before taxes on our stockholder's investment last year."

"Now about the 'almost anything.' If, for example, we were to come up with a recommendation that different methods of transportation be employed, would you feel that this is something that we should be commenting on?"

"Definitely."

"What would be the chances of implementing such a recommendation?"

"Very good, as far as I'm concerned. George Dalton might, however, want to argue the point with you."

For the next fifteen minutes, the interview dealt with other matters regarding scope and limitations listed in Table 9–2.

Interviewer: "Would you regard it as logical that we might recommend a new plant location as a result of our study?"

Wonka: "I might think that you would be stepping outside the bounds of the scope I have in mind for your work. What are the chances that you would be able to comment on plant location?"

"Pretty good. It's almost a byproduct of the DC location analysis that we discussed a few minutes ago. Would your management committee consider acting on a proposal to relocate the plant?"

"Anything's possible, although you'd have to make a strong case for it. Hans Roberts, our Vice President of Production, would be opposed to such a proposal under almost any circumstance. He was the strongest supporter of our Cleveland plant expansion five years ago."

At the end of an hour, the interview ended with an expression of strong support from the President.

These questions and responses, of varying value, are only suggestive of those that might result from this stage of the audit process. Based on this interview and others (results of which were tabulated by the interviewer in the form shown in Tables 9–1 and 9–2), it was possible to begin a more detailed audit of Wonka's logistics system with at least a general knowledge of the way in which Company principals viewed the objectives and scope of, and the limitations on, a system redesign.

(9) **What initial actions, if any, does the information in Tables 9–1 and**

TABLE 9-2. Top Management Views Regarding Scope of, and Limitations on, Logistics System Review Effort, as Perceived by Interviewer, Warren G. Wonka Manufacturing Company

	Extent of Agreement With Statements by Executive*				
	President	VP, Marketing	VP, Finance	VP, Mfg.	Distribution Manager
I believe the review should provide guidance for:					
1. Selection of new carriers, transport methods	5	5	5	5	5
2. Altering warehouse service territories	5	5	5	5	5
3. Altering plant service territories	5	5	5	3	5
4. Instituting new controls over logistics activities	5	5	5	5	5
5. Changing warehouse locations	4	2	4	4	5
6. Altering the level of customer service	4	5	4	4	4
7. Selecting new supply sources	2	1	3	1 (circled)	3
8. Creating new inventory control system	3	2	2	2	3
9. Implementing a new production planning procedure	2	3	2	1 (circled)	3
10. Changing pricing structures	3	1 (circled)	3	2	4
11. Selection of a new computer	1	1	1 (circled)	1	1
12. Selection of a new communication method	2	2	3	2	3
13. Eliminating least profitable customers	3	1	3	2	3
14. Eliminating least profitable sales territories	1 (circled)	1 (circled)	1 (circled)	2	2
15. Changing plant locations	1	3	1	1 (circled)	3
16. Altering terms of sale	2	1 (circled)	2	2	3
17. Changing order-processing procedures	3	4	4	1	3
18. Crediting new billing and collection procedures	1	1 (circled)	1 (circled)	1	2
19. Reorganizing for logistics management	4	3	4	3	4
20. Other	–	–	–	–	–

*Responses were graded as 5 = strongly agree, 4 = agree, 3 = neutral, 2 = disagree, 1 = strongly disagree; circled responses indicate limitations which would preclude such recommendation from being implemented.

9–2 suggest be taken by our consultant? (10) How valuable for guidance in carrying out the study are the objectives on which there is
agreement about priority?

This first stage of the system process is a highly critical one. It provides an indication of: (1) the knowledge of, and support for, the
proposed system redesign effort on the part of the Company's top management, (2) the differences in views regarding the objectives and
scope of the effort, and (3) the ease with which eventual recommendations might be implemented. It might be carried out prior to submitting
a proposal or subsequent to an agreement regarding a proposal about
which there appears to be differences of opinion.

(11) At this stage, what would you do if you found the President of
the Company totally uninformed and relatively disinterested in a study
aimed at appraising the design of the Company's logistics system?
(12) Assuming you found differences of opinion among top executives about the scope of such a study, would you attempt to resolve
them at this stage? (13) How?

SYSTEM OUTPUT REVIEWS

System output reviews include those which describe the physical configuration of the system, raw material and product characteristics, markets
and competition, flows of communication and product, costs, and executive
concerns. Although they can be prepared in any order, we have found
that the order listed here provides a logical progression in which each
review builds on the one before it. Output reviews may be organized
around divisions, major product categories, major market categories, or
other bases, depending on the nature of the business being surveyed.
In the case of the Wonka Company, it appeared most logical to organize
the reviews around two product groups, machines and parts. For purposes of simplification, we will limit our discussion for the most part to
the review of the logistics system for machines.

Physical Configuration of the System

Information useful in constructing a description of the system's physical
configuration includes the following: (1) locations of major sources of
raw materials, plants, distribution centers, and major markets, (2) the
volume of each major product category shipped to and from every location,
perhaps during the preceding year, (3) methods of transportation employed between each pair of locations identified previously, expressed in
terms of not only mode but typical shipment weight distributions and

shipment composition (numbers of product-line items, orders, or pieces), perhaps also during the preceding twelve months, (4) shipments (sales) from each inventory location and average inventories and product-line items held in stock there, and (5) production, shipment, or storage capacities for each inventory location, with the first two of these items identified in terms of one-week or one-month periods of time.

Questions of this sort yielded the information about the Wonka Company shown in Fig. 9–1 and Table 9–3. Although this information is of use in later stages of a system analysis, the process of analysis can begin at this point. For example, if our consultant has collected information about product inventory levels and throughput on a consistent basis (that is, totally in terms of cost dollars, product weight, or even sales dollars), we can construct turnover ratios for each location. This information, when graphed as in Fig. 9–2, offers an early indication of the consistency of results obtained by means of the Company's inventory control system, particularly at distribution centers.

(14) **What does the slope of the line which best fits the plotted points in Fig. 9–2 tell our consultant? (15) What are possible implications for facilities falling below or above the line?** We will be better able to deal with these questions after we have studied inventory control in greater detail. The graph is introduced here to emphasize the point that the system audit and analytical effort need not be carried out on a totally sequential basis.

Product Line

There are several points in a system audit at which the entire effort can be jeopardized by an overabundance of information. The product-line review is one of them. Whenever we approach one of these critical points, it is important not only to test the relevance of each available piece of information, but also to sample data, where possible, to reduce the burden of information collection and storage for both the analyst and the organization being audited.

At Wonka, it was possible for our consultant to collect detailed company-wide data for a sample of 10 out of 40 machine items, as shown in Table 9–4 (page 281). But it was necessary to restrict the sample even further for the more than 5,000 types of parts used and sold by the Company. On the basis of this information, the concentration of Company sales and the inventory turnover rate for each item could be described in the form shown in Fig. 9–3. Here we see that about 80% of unit sales of levelor machines were concentrated in only 20% of the items in the sample (two of the ten). This item sales frequency distribution is more or less typical of most companies. (16) **At this point, can you speculate**

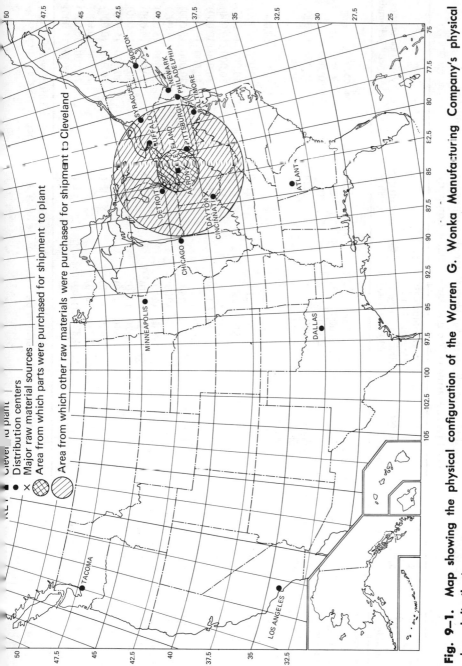

Fig. 9–1. Map showing the physical configuration of the Warren G. Wonka Manufacturing Company's physical supply and distribution system.

TABLE 9-3. Important Annual Shipment Patterns for Raw Materials, Components, and Finished Machines and Parts, Warren G. Wonka Manufacturing Company

Commodity	Origin–Destination[a]	Annual Shipments in Pounds of Gross Shipping Weight[b] (000's omitted)		Primary Method of Shipment[b]	Typical Quantities Shipped[b] in Pounds
Raw Materials:					
Sheet and bar steel	Pittsburgh–Cleveland	14,000		TL	45,000
Rubber beltings	Akron–Cleveland	3,000		TL	30,000
Container stock	Dayton–Cleveland	4,500		TL	30,000
Parts	100-mile radius–Cleveland	16,000		TL; LTL	40,000 (1,000)
Other	300-mile radius–Cleveland	3,000		LTL	None
	Cleveland (plant)–Cleveland (distribution center)	640	(200)	(LTL)	(8,000)
Finished Product:	Buffalo	720	(210)	TL (LTL)	30,000 (4,000)
	Syracuse	510	(180)	TL (LTL)	30,000 (3,500)
	Boston	1,750	(520)	TL (LTL)	30,000 (10,000)
	Newark	3,730	(1,100)	TL (TL)	30,000 (30,000)
	Philadelphia	1,620	(500)	TL (LTL)	30,000 (10,000)
	Baltimore	870	(250)	TL (LTL)	30,000 (5,000)
	Pittsburgh	640	(200)	TL (LTL)	30,000 (4,000)
Cleveland to	Cincinnati	820	(240)	TL (LTL)	30,000 (5,000)
	Detroit	1,430	(420)	TL (LTL)	30,000 (8,000)
	Chicago	2,520	(750)	TL (LTL)	30,000 (15,000)
	Minneapolis	870	(230)	TL (LTL)	30,000 (5,000)
	Atlanta	1,620	(500)	CL (LTL)	70,000 (10,000)
	Dallas	2,780	(820)	CL (TL)	70,000 (30,000)
	Los Angeles	4,820	(1,200)	CL (TL)	70,000 (30,000)
	Tacoma	920	(270)	CL (LTL)	70,000 (5,000)

[a] All shipments to Cleveland inbound from raw material sources; all shipments from Cleveland outbound to distribution centers, with an additional 1,120,000 pounds of machines (4.2% of the total) and 670,000 pounds of parts (8.0% of the total) shipped directly from the plant to customers via package shipment services.

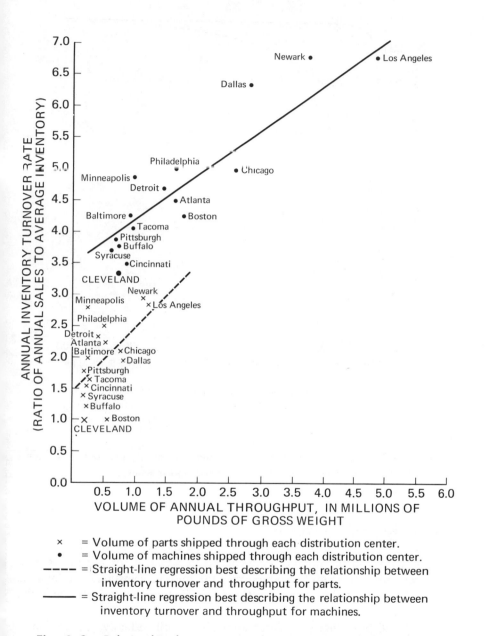

x   = Volume of parts shipped through each distribution center.
•   = Volume of machines shipped through each distribution center.
---- = Straight-line regression best describing the relationship between
        inventory turnover and throughput for parts.
——— = Straight-line regression best describing the relationship between
        inventory turnover and throughput for machines.

Fig. 9–2. Relationship between inventory turnover and throughput for
parts and machines at the Wonka Company's distribution center.

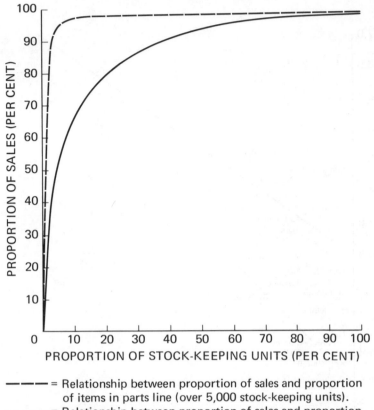

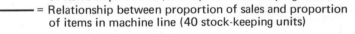
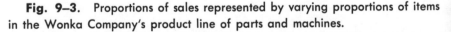

---- = Relationship between proportion of sales and proportion
of items in parts line (over 5,000 stock-keeping units).
——— = Relationship between proportion of sales and proportion
of items in machine line (40 stock-keeping units)

Fig. 9–3. Proportions of sales represented by varying proportions of items
in the Wonka Company's product line of parts and machines.

on how our consultant could make use of this information in redesign-
ing Wonka's logistics system?

Data of the type contained in Table 9–4 allow us to relate inventory
turnover rates to the number of locations at which items are maintained
in stock, the number of production runs and replenishment shipments
scheduled during the course of the preceding twelve months, and the
seasonality of item sales. The cube, weight, and value per unit for each
product will prove useful in later analysis as well. Finally, the combination of transportation methods and number of stock points can be related
to the volume of sales for each item in order to allow an appraisal of
the extent to which the system accounts for, and adjusts to, differences
in product characteristics.

TABLE 9-4. Logistical Characteristics for Levelor Product-Line Items, Warren G. Wonka Manufacturing Company

	Items Representing 81.0% of Unit Sales		Items Representing 17.6% of Unit Sales			Items Representing 1.4% of Unit Sales				
Line item number	122L	132L	14V	13V	44V	2M	3M	4M	5M	8M
Size (in horsepower)	2	5	15	25	50	70	90	120	160	200
Manufacturing cost	$60	$45	$95	$145	$400	$400	$500	$550	$600	$1,050
Selling price after retail margins and salesmen's commissions	$90	$70	$140	$220	$600	$600	$750	$975	$900	$1,575
Annual units sold	92,900	79,500	28,500	7,450	1,700	1,375	775	525	208	125
Units shipped from distribution centers (DC's)	92,900	79,500	28,500	7,450	1,550	1,175	400	430	10	15
Number of stock points (including plant DC)	16	16	16	16	16	16	16	16	8	16
Average inventory during year	12,700	14,200	7,300	2,700	320	720	130	430	40	60
Method of transport:										
From plant to DC	TL, CL									
From plant to customer	LTL, TL, CL									
From DC to customer	LTL, TL									
Item weight (packed), lbs.	36	25	50	85	155	195	230	290	380	470
Item weight (unpacked), lbs.	30	21	43	75	135	173	205	245	335	405
Item cubic dimension, cu. ft.	3	4	8	12	23	27	33	35	53	53
Number of scheduled production runs per year (plant)	24	24	24	24	24	12	12	6	6	6
Number of replenishment shipments per year (average per DC)	52	52	46	43	32	12	12	12	8	8
Maximum weekly demand	3,375	3,310	800	260	44	46	20	14	8	7
Minimum weekly demand	1,700	1,670	390	130	25	22	10	8	0	0

Raw Materials and Components

A similar set of information was collected for raw materials and components used in the manufacture of levelors. Wonka fabricated only a small portion of the parts for its machines, purchasing about 80% of such components from suppliers. Nearly all of these suppliers were located within a 100-mile radius of the Cleveland plant. All metalworking required for the fabrication of metal housings for the levelors was, however, done in Wonka's plants.

In quantity, the more important items shipped to Wonka's plant, other than parts, included sheet and bar steel, rubber belting, and cardboard container stock. However, the procurement and inbound scheduling of component parts consumed most of the time of the Company's Purchasing Department.

Information concerning the four most important categories of raw materials and components, representing more than a thousand stock-keeping units used by the Company in manufacturing its products, is shown in Table 9–5.

TABLE 9–5. Logistical Characteristics for Important Categories of
Components and Raw Materials Used in the Manufacture of
Levelors by the Warren G. Wonka Manufacturing Company

	Components	Sheet and Bar Steel	Rubber Belting	Cardboard Container Stock
Unit of measure	Hundred pounds	Ton	Hundred pounds	Hundred square feet
Annual usage (in units)	157,000	20,000	15,000	95,000
Cost per unit	$340	$280	$95	$4.50
Number of sources of supply	300	2	4	2
Number of stock-keeping items	1,010	22	18	6
Average inventory during year (in units)	11,500	1,500	1,500	11,000
Method of inbound transport	LTL	TL	TL, LTL	TL, CL
Average unit weight (lbs.)	100	2,000	100	10
Average unit cube (cu. ft.)	4	40	20	4
Number of orders, shipments per year	15,000	26	26	26
Maximum weekly usage (in units)	6,000	500	510	3,500
Minimum weekly usage (in units)	2,200	210	210	1,300

Markets

This portion of the audit was intended to pinpoint the location of demand by type of customer and the manner in which customers purchased products from Wonka. Specifically, our consultant was interested in: (1) the size (in shipping weight), frequency, and complexity (in terms of numbers of line items) of customer orders, (2) the importance of availability as opposed to other factors in the customer's purchase decision, (3) acceptable service levels, based on perceptions of customer expectations, (4) seasonal patterns of sale by product or customer groups, (5) typical terms of sale in selling each product group, and (6) the nature of actual or potential competition.

Information regarding Wonka's markets for both parts and machines is shown in Table 9–6. Because much of the information was not available at the time of the audit, estimates for many of the items of information were based on samples of 100 orders each for levelors and parts, selected systematically from files containing such documents for the preceding twelve months.

(17) Looking at Table 9–6, which do you think are the most significant pieces of data for a subsequent appraisal of Wonka's logistics system? (18) Why?

Service

Measures of customer service discussed in Chapter 8 make up the guts of the service review. For each such measure, data can be collected regarding actual performance, performance goals, expected performance by various involved executives and marketing personnel, and performance in relation to competition.

Because of the wide range of possible measures, those that have the greatest applicability for the company's marketing and distribution needs should be selected. For example, in Wonka's case, it might have been possible to measure the length and variability of order-cycle time (the time lapse between the customer's realization of need for more stock, or more realistically the point in time at which he placed his order, and his receipt of goods in usable condition) for line items or complete orders, the item-filling or order-filling capability on demand at both Wonka's DC's and plant, and the percentage of shipments on which damage or pilferage was experienced. Such measures could be made by DC, by customer or type of customer, or by product or type of product.

(19) Knowing what you know now about Wonka's business, which measures of service would you select? (20) Why?

TABLE 9–6. Information Regarding Markets for Machines and Parts,
Warren G. Wonka Manufacturing Company

	Machines	Parts
Per average order:[a]		
Dollar value	$1,800	$350
Weight (in pounds)	640	50
Number of line items	4	10
Factors in ultimate purchaser's decision		
to buy (on a scale of 1 = important		
to 5 = not important):[b]		
Convenience	4	2–5
Availability	3	1
Price	2	3–5
Design	1	1
Other	n.a.	n.a.
Service levels acceptable to customer:[c]		
Order cycle time (from order to		
receipt of goods)	7 days	5 days
In-stock rate (for units ordered)	90%	99%
In-stock rate (for line items ordered)	90%	99%
Complete order in-stock rate	80%	95%
Seasonal patterns of sale:		
Peak sales (months of the year)	May, June, December	May through September
Low sales (months of the year)	January, February	October through April
Typical terms of sale:	Delivered; 2%, 10 days;	Delivered; 2%, 10 days;
	net 60 days; 10%	net 30 days
	discount on 10 units	
	or more[d]	
Nature of competition:		
Share of market for Wonka	15%	10%
Number of major competitors	4	15
Share of market for largest		
competitor	20%	10%
Trend in Wonka's share of market	Up	Constant

n.a. = not available.
[a]Obtained by sampling systematically 100 orders each for machines and parts.
[b]Based on interviews with Wonka's sales managers.
[c]Based on interviews with Wonka's sales managers, a sampling of salesmen, and a sample of customers.
[d]Interpreted as delivered to the customer's place of business, with a 2% discount for payment within 10 days of the invoice date (typically a date sometime after that of actual shipment from the plant or one of the distribution centers), with the entire amount billed expected to be paid within 60 days of the invoice date, and an additional 10% discount on orders of 10 or more levelors.

In Wonka's case, our consultant decided that it would be necessary to measure service in terms of both machines and parts, and further that it would be useful to segment both categories into frequently purchased, high-priority items (such as the 122L levelor or the basic clutch mechanism) and less frequently purchased, low-priority items (such as the model 2700H levelor or handle-bar covers).

Time and cost considerations limited the initial survey to item- and order-fill rates within varying lengths of time from order receipt. This information was obtained by sampling 50 orders and related shipping information at each of Wonka's DC's and the plant. Selected information from this survey is shown in Table 9–7. It may suggest problem symptoms to you. (21) **What are they?** (22) **What are possible causes of these symptoms?** (23) **How serious do you think each symptom may be?**

In order to assess the implications of the information in Table 9–7, it was decided that an effort should be made to make an objective appraisal of Wonka's level of customer service in relation to its competition. Past experience warned our consultant of the possibilities for bias in this type of appraisal. With this in mind, he had to choose between interviews with distributors, interviews with Wonka's sales and distribution personnel, and a sampling of distributors' documents reflecting Wonka's performance against that of its competitors. (24) **Placed in the position of our consultant, which would you choose?** (25) **Why?**

It was decided to interview salesmen and attempt a sampling of distributor documents. Salesmen who were interviewed consistently rated the Company's service, in terms of speed, dependability, availability, and damage-free delivery, lower than that of its competition. Information in the files of the only two of Wonka's 50 distributors who were willing to submit to the sampling process suggested that order-cycle times and item- and order-fill rates did not vary significantly between Wonka and three of its competitors from whom these particular distributors purchased their inventories.

(26) **What is the value of this information?** (27) **As the consultant in this situation, would you disseminate it to the distributors who supplied it?** (28) **With their permission, to other distributors?** (29) **To Wonka's personnel?** (30) **If so, to whom?** (31) **Why?**

Time-Flow Diagram

A time-flow diagram portrays a company's logistics system in terms of the time relationships between events which take place in the system. This emphasizes not only the service response time which a system is capable of providing, but also duplications and bottlenecks in the design of the system itself.

Relevant events in the logistics process can be grouped into time cycles, as shown for the Wonka Company in Fig. 9–4. The order and replenishment cycles are similar to those described in Chapter 8. In addi-

TABLE 9–7. Item- and Order-Fill Rates Within Various Time Periods from Receipt of Order, Warren G. Wonka Manufacturing Company*

	Machines			Parts		
	High-Volume, High-Priority Items	Low-Volume, Low-Priority Items	All Items	High-Volume, High-Priority Items	Low-Volume, Low-Priority Items	All Items
Percentage of Order-Line Items Shipped Within:						
24 hours	4%	7%	5%	20%	30%	22%
48 hours	29	35	30	58	50	57
72 hours	63	75	65	79	60	77
96 hours	72	85	75	88	72	87
7 days	76	87	78	94	80	92
10 days	80	87	81	97	85	96
30 days	93	88	92	99	90	99
Percentage of Orders Shipped Completely Within:						
24 hours	n.a.	n.a.	15%	n.a.	n.a.	12%
48 hours	n.a.	n.a.	29	n.a.	n.a.	27
72 hours	n.a.	n.a.	58	n.a.	n.a.	37
96 hours	n.a.	n.a.	69	n.a.	n.a.	43
7 days	n.a.	n.a.	77	n.a.	n.a.	68
10 days	n.a.	n.a.	91	n.a.	n.a.	80
30 days	n.a.	n.a.	99	n.a.	n.a.	92

n.a. = not available.

*Based on a sample of 50 orders and related shipping documents from the files of the company.

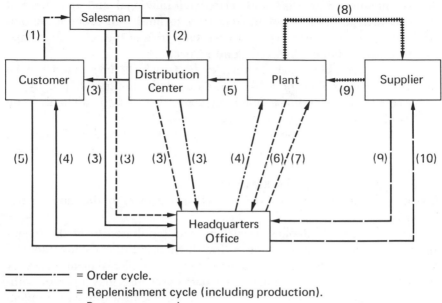

Fig. 9–4. Time-flow diagram for the Wonka Company's logistics system, including two-stage distribution, single-stage supply, decentralized distribution and order processing, and centralized inventory accounting, inventory control, and billing and payment. The various flows of information and product are numbered in the approximate order in which they occur.

tion, we see inventory update cycles for both finished product and raw materials, beginning with the actual depletion of the inventory at distribution centers and plants, respectively, and ending with the recording of such depletions at Company headquarters. The procurement cycle begins with the realization of need for raw materials on the part of production and procurement personnel (assisted by centralized inventory accounting) and ends with the receipt of raw materials in good condition at the plant when they are needed. The billing cycle begins with the creation of an invoice at the manufacturer's headquarters and ends with the receipt of payment in full for goods shipped, also at Company headquarters.

Where it is advisable to do so, a time-flow diagram can be constructed by sampling related documents: (1) to measure results for a substantial number of orders at each stage in the logistics system and (2) to follow a small number of product and related informational and transactional flows through the entire system from start to finish. In order to accomplish either of these tasks, we must have some idea of the relevant internal events which influence logistics performance.

Easily measurable events in each cycle, to which times often can be assigned, are presented in Table 9–8, along with results obtained by reconstructing time lags for a sample of 490 orders drawn randomly from the Wonka Company's files for a recent period of time.

The logistics system diagrammed in Fig. 9–4 can be referred to as encompassing a two-stage (two levels of inventory, warehousing, and transportation) distribution and a single-stage supply system. It embodies decentralized inventory location and order processing and centralized inventory accounting and control as well as customer billing and vendor payment.

The time-flow terminology used here may be altered to fit the operations of a company. For example, a firm distributing directly to customers from plants on a to-order basis will have no replenishment cycle. A wholesaling organization selling from one warehouse may operate without an internal (plant-to-warehouse or warehouse-to-warehouse) replenishment cycle. A retail food chain with company-operated warehousing will regard the order cycle as the link between customers and the retail store, the replenishment cycle as a link between a store and its warehouse, and the procurement cycle as the process of supplying the warehouse from vendors.

Time-flow measurements often can yield revealing information about the way in which a logistics system really functions. Difficulties in obtaining them arise because time cycles in the system: (1) sometimes transpire sequentially, sometimes concurrently, (2) are interdependent and greatly affected by "linkage," and (3) may vary widely for different combinations of facilities, different products, and different customers at different points in time.

(32) **Looking at Fig. 9–4 and Table 9–8, can you surmise which of the cycles occur sequentially, and which concurrently?**

A properly functioning replenishment cycle in most companies is one which rarely creates a delay, for want of product at distribution centers, in the very critical order cycle. This may be the case regardless of the length or dependability of the replenishment cycle, if precautions are taken to anticipate slow or undependable replenishment times.

This anticipation represents the all-essential "linkage" between cycles and is an important element in a time-flow analysis. For example, a company with a distribution center reorder point (representing linkage) equivalent to five days' sales for a given stock-keeping unit and a replenishment cycle of 10 to 15 days for the same unit will experience ware-

TABLE 9–8. Frequency of Time Delays in Order-Processing System, Sample of 490 Orders, Warren G. Wonka Manufacturing Company

Days	Number of Orders With Days Between:*			
	Receipt of Order at, and Shipment from, Distribution Center	Shipment from Distribution Center and Receipt of Order in Cleveland from Salesman	Receipt of Order and Receipt of Bill of Lading in Cleveland from Salesman and Distribution Center, Respectively	Receipt of Bill of Lading and Invoicing in Cleveland
-36	-	1	-	-
-26	·	1	·	·
-17	-	1	-	-
-16	-	1	-	-
-13	-	1	-	-
-11	-	1	-	-
-10	-	2	-	-
- 9	-	-	1	-
- 8	-	1	-	-
- 7	-	2	1	-
- 6	-	-	2	-
- 5	-	5	4	-
- 4	-	4	7	-
- 3	-	12	14	-
- 2	-	12	32	4
- 1	-	15	43	19
0	113	54	182	44
1	180	69	50	150
2	74	103	55	106
3	40	83	40	60
4	20	36	24	40
5	20	35	17	19
6	10	19	4	15
7	8	6	3	11
8	5	7	2	9
9	7	12	1	4
10	1	1	1	-
11	2	3	1	4
12	-	1	-	2
13	1	2	1	-
14	2	-	2	-
15	1	-	-	-
16	1	-	-	-
17	-	-	1	-
18	1	-	-	1
19	1	-	-	-
20	1	-	-	-
22	-	-	-	1
25	1	-	-	-
28	-	-	1	-
30	-	-	-	1
38	-	-	1	-
39	1	-	-	-
	490	490	490	490

*Note that the time segments described are not mutually exclusive.

house stock-outs and order-cycle delays. Another with a 30- to 40-day replenishment cycle, but with warehouse reorder points set at 40 days' worth of sales, will have a slower replenishment cycle but excellent linkage, resulting in no order-cycle delays for replenishment purposes.

Conditions under which logistics activities are managed vary from location to location, product to product, customer to customer, and time to time. Where they are significant, they will influence the information gathering process for a time-flow analysis. For example, an average or range of performance times constructed from data produced by two products with distinctly different characteristics will mean nothing.

At this stage in the system audit, the time-flow diagram may have more conceptual than practical value. It is useful to diagram events to understand their sequence and relationships. The collection of information about the amount and range of elapsed times for each event or cycle of events, because of its complexity, may be deferred to such time as there is a need to explore possible bottlenecks or problem causes.

(33) Does the information presented in Fig. 9–4 and Table 9–8 suggest any potential problems to you? (34) Based on this information, would you want to do some further sampling? (35) Of what? (36) Where? (37) How?

Costs

A company-wide or divisional profile of functional costs logically associated with logistics activities can: (1) further contribute to an awareness of system scope and importance, (2) point up weaknesses in cost accounting and reporting conventions within an organization, and (3) suggest broad areas of activity for future analysis. The documentation of more specific cost items and relationships will prove useful for detailed system analysis.

Functional logistics costs in many companies today have to be constructed from generic accounts. The experience at the Wonka Company was typical in this regard. For example, labor costs for each facility were counted and reported in a "facility statement." In statements prepared for distribution center facilities, this was sufficient for initial measurement needs. However, in the plant facility statement, it was impossible to obtain that portion of labor costs incurred in the handling of raw materials, work in process, or finished product. These costs could only be estimated by reconstructing the manning requirement for the plant warehouse and assigning a cost per man for wages and fringes. Similar problems were encountered in determining costs of supervision, material-handling equipment maintenance, equipment depreciation, various space costs for warehousing, and other logistics costs incurred at the plant.

Cost information may have to be constructed from a variety of sources. For example, inventory carrying cost calculations require statements of the value of the average inventory on hand, often maintained by the inventory control or corporate accounting groups, as well as top management opinions about the proper cost to assign for money invested in the inventory. Costs of private transportation or warehousing activities shared by two or more company divisions may be obtained only from divisional reports, and may be interpreted only in terms of the rules used for charging costs internally to each division (so-called transfer pricing guidelines).

For these reasons, it is often useful to elicit cost information from as many independent sources as possible within an organization, carefully document each source on an item-by-item basis, then attempt to arrive at useful estimates and a reconciliation of often confusing figures by exploring the assumptions with which each estimate was prepared. Above all, it is unrealistic to assume that a single figure is associated with a given cost item by all interested parties in an organization.

Cost statements for Wonka's logistics operations are presented in Table 9–9. (38) Based on your general knowledge of logistics cost relationships, could you formulate any initial impressions from these figures? (39) Do they suggest to you areas for further and closer analysis?

Executives' Concerns

In the course of the audit process, our consultant collected a catalog of executive concerns about logistics system performance. While past experience suggested that many of these would not be substantiated by fact, he knew it was too early in the study to ignore any of them. Among the more frequently expressed concerns were: (1) the increasingly frequent stock-outs at distribution centers with accompanying order "splits" between distribution centers and the plant, or LTL orders shipped entirely on a "rush" basis from the plant, (2) the large amount of "dead" inventory thought to exist in distribution center inventories, (3) rapidly rising small-shipment transportation costs, encountered typically on split shipments, (4) poor distribution center management and service, and (5) a general lack of communication between groups managing interlocking elements of the system.

Plant LTL shipments were caused by orders for items either not normally carried, such as new products, or items which were out of stock temporarily at distribution centers. As a result, shipments were often split, with the item not in stock sent directly from the plant and the balance of the order sent from the distribution center. At other times the

TABLE 9–9. Logistics Cost Trends, Warren G. Wonka Manufacturing Company*

Cost Item	Percentage of Logistics Costs, Two Years Previous	Percentage of Logistics Costs, Current Year	Approximate Dollar Costs, Current Year ($000)
Physical Supply:			
Raw material transport (including estimated vendor costs):			
Parts	3.8%	3.7%	$ 704
Other raw materials	.8	.8	150
Warehousing ($1.50/sq. ft./year)	2.4	2.3	450
Material handling (50¢/ cwt. in and out of plant warehouse)	1.0	1.0	200
Inventory carrying:			
Raw material at plant (10% of value)	3.0	2.9	550
Work in process at plant (10% of value)	2.6	2.5	475
Procurement:			
Salaries and fringes	1.0	1.0	183
Overhead	.5	.5	87
Total physical supply	15.1%	14.7%	$ 2,799
Physical Distribution:			
Transportation:			
Primary (plant to DC's)	10.1%	6.9%	$ 1,317
Secondary (plant and DC's to customers)	12.8	7.7	1,485
Warehousing (16 DC's)	12.2	12.6	2,454
Packing	4.0	3.3	628
Inventory carrying:			
In-transit stocks	2.6	2.6	496
Cycle and speculative stocks	16.3	16.8	3,240
Safety and dead stocks	10.2	16.4	3,170
Order processing:			
Complete orders	5.1	4.9	944
Partial orders (containing back-ordered items)	6.2	8.6	1,657
Total physical distribution	79.5%	79.8%	$15,391
Management of Logistics Activities	5.4%	5.5%	$ 1,105
Total, All Logistics	100.0%	100.0%	$19,295

*Logistics costs represented 9.9% of dollar sales in the current year, 9.4% of dollar sales in the previous year, and 9.0% of dollar sales two years previously.

entire order was relayed to the plant because the customer, typically a service center, insisted on receiving the order in one shipment.

LTL shipments made directly from the plant to customers had increased significantly for Wonka in recent months. A study by the Company's Controller, James Webb, indicated that they had increased 25% in a recent month compared to the same month a year earlier, reaching a figure of 1,350, of which 450 were thought to be portions of split shipments. Further, the average weight of an LTL shipment from the plant directly to customers had declined from 380 pounds to 340 pounds.

As a result, our consultant requested an analysis of documents regarding 100 orders placed with distribution centers, involving approximately 750 line items, on which it appeared that there were 150 line items shipped from sources other than the designated distribution center. Reasons appeared to be: (1) out-of-stock conditions at the respective distribution centers for 94 items, (2) out-of-stock conditions at the plant for 19 items, (3) typically new items not carried at the distribution center for 33 items, and (4) items lost in transit and replaced from an alternate source on an emergency basis for 2 items. Roughly half of the 150 items eventually were shipped from the plant and the other half from distribution centers, at the request of either ordering salesmen or distribution center personnel at the out-of-stock facility.

Wonka's computer had been programmed to observe actual sales data, forecast expected demand, monitor field inventory levels, calculate target inventories, make up replenishment stock orders for distribution centers, and prepare a variety of management reports which would assist inventory planning and control. The task of design was assumed largely by representatives of the computer manufacturer. An immediate result from the implementation of the new system was a $700,000 increase in the value of inventory. This was in contrast to the $500,000 reduction which had been expected. (40) **Should the initial increase have been a surprise?** (41) **Why?**

Recently, the Cleveland office had been receiving a growing number of complaints about inadequate inventories and slow customer deliveries. Nevertheless, computer reports indicated a rapid growth in the amount of dead stock (composed of items with no sales from a distribution center over a year's time) at both distribution centers and the plant.

Small shipments, often resulting from the splitting of an order, were subject to minimum freight charges, regardless of size, below about 300 pounds. Minimum charges were the most rapidly rising of all transportation rates. A study of shipments subject to minimum charges from the plant during comparable 60-day periods in the past two years indicated that while the number of such shipments had risen 5.6% from 1,289 to 1,361, the size of the average minimum charge paid rose 13.9% from $4.17

to $4.75. Thus, payments for freight charges on minimum shipments as a proportion of total freight charges paid on shipments out of the plant had risen in a year's time from 13.6% to 20.7%.

Although there was no way of measuring it exactly, it was the opinion of several members of Wonka's management that the quality of service provided by many of the Company's distribution centers varied directly with the volume of business which the Wonka account represented. Several warehouses with which Wonka had maintained good relations had asked the Company to move its products. In these cases, Wonka executives concluded that the Company did not provide the warehousing company with sufficient revenues to warrant servicing its account.

SYSTEM INPUT REVIEWS

An audit of system inputs primarily involves an examination of those arrangements, procedures, and policies used in the operation, appraisal, and maintenance of the system. It includes a description of organizational responsibilities and relationships as well as an audit of relevant procedures and policies employed in the management of marketing and sales activities, order processing, forecasting, inventory control, transportation, warehousing and warehouse location, packaging and material handling, production planning, and procurement.

Organization

Action and advisory responsibilities for logistics and logistics-related activities at the Wonka Company were arrayed against the Company organization chart, presented in Fig. 9–5. Action responsibilities were defined as those for which the individual in question had action authority and for which he was held accountable. Advisory responsibilities were those for which an individual was held accountable to provide supporting analysis and advice to those with action responsibilities.

(42) What are your first impressions in looking at Fig. 9–5? (43) How might certain organizational relationships that you see there affect Company performance?

Marketing

Marketing policies had remained remarkably stable since the time Warren Wonka's uncle had produced the first levelor in his garage on

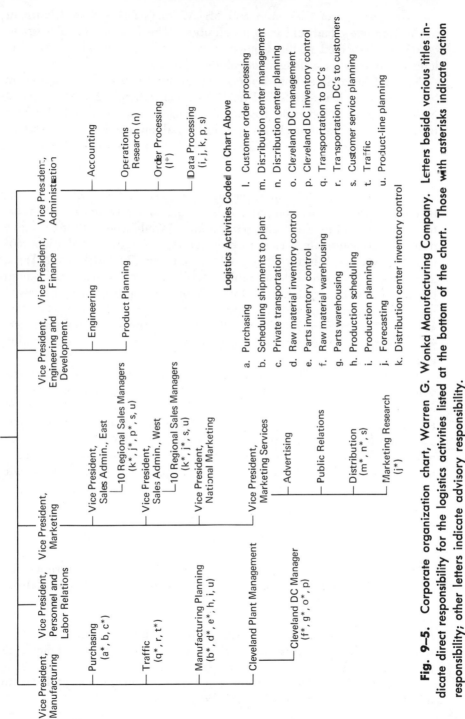

Fig. 9–5. Corporate organization chart, Warren G. Wonka Manufacturing Company. Letters beside various titles indicate direct responsibility for the logistics activities listed at the bottom of the chart. Those with asterisks indicate action responsibility; other letters indicate advisory responsibility.

Logistics Activities Coded on Chart Above

a. Purchasing
b. Scheduling shipments to plant
c. Private transportation
d. Raw material inventory control
e. Parts inventory control
f. Raw material warehousing
g. Parts warehousing
h. Production scheduling
i. Production planning
j. Forecasting
k. Distribution center inventory control
l. Customer order processing
m. Distribution center management
n. Distribution center planning
o. Cleveland DC management
p. Cleveland DC inventory control
q. Transportation to DC's
r. Transportation, DC's to customers
s. Customer service planning
t. Traffic
u. Product-line planning

the western edge of Cleveland and Mr. Wonka's father, now Chairman of the Company, had sold it to a neighbor. The Chairman's sales orientation was reflected in the Company policies, even though he was no longer active in the management of the Company.

Nearly 600 salesmen sold Labrsaver Levelors door-to-door, calling on both individual households and business organizations. Twenty regional managers were responsible for selling machines to some 3,000 larger business accounts and machines and parts to about 300 designated service centers, typically retail hardware and lumber outlets that were willing to maintain repair shops, a minimum parts supply, and a qualified Wonka-trained repairman on duty.

In addition, regional managers were responsible for reviewing territory sales forecasts and computer calculations of safety stock and inventory levels for all machine and parts items. Wonka could afford to have its own warehouse supervisors in only the eight largest distribution centers: Los Angeles, Newark, Dallas, Chicago, Boston, Philadelphia, Atlanta, and Detroit. In each of these public warehouses, office space was rented for the supervisor (paid directly by the Wonka Company), who reviewed inventory records, traced orders, and provided general trouble-shooting support. For the remainder of the distribution centers, regional managers were assigned the responsibility for providing control over distribution center services.

All salesmen were paid on a straight commission basis—20% of the value of all machines for which they wrote orders. They received no commission on parts, and sold very few except as extras at the time of the original machine sale. Commissions were paid monthly on all orders for which invoices were mailed by the last "accounting" day of each month. Commissions ranged from $5,000 to $30,000 per year per salesman. In return, salesmen were expected to provide their own automobile and pay all of their own travel, telephone, and other sales expenses.

Regional managers received salaries of $15,000 per year and typically averaged another $17,000 per year from the 1% sales commission that they received for all machines and parts sold to larger accounts and service centers.

The commission compensation policy created substantial turnover on Wonka's sales force. Salesmen were hired at the rate of about 200 per year in order to produce a net gain of about 50 per year in the size of the sales force. This in turn created a rapidly changing product mix for a given sales territory, resulting from individuals' preferences in selling alternate products for a given application. It was difficult to predict these changes over short periods of time.

(44) How would you expect these sales management policies to affect logistics performance? (45) Why?

Mr. Wonka's father held the personal belief that the Company's unique direct sales approach as well as its unusually strong emphasis on service, including both immediate availability of the Company's complete line of machines and parts as well as the high quality of service offered by its service centers, had enabled it to survive both depression and periods of severe competition from discounters selling other brands of levelors.

The Company sold its machines to ultimate users at the same price both on a direct sales basis and through service centers. Both salesmen and service center operators were policed carefully to insure a continuance of this policy. Products were priced to yield a margin equivalent to 50% of the direct costs of manufacturing (primarily labor and materials) after deducting the 20% commission to salesmen on machines and the 20% and 40% margins to service center operators on sales of machines and parts, respectively. All costs of advertising, sales administration, logistics, research and development, manufacturing overhead, and general administration and overhead were charged against this margin figure.

There was no specifically stated policy for customer service in the Company. However, a stock-out on any machine item and all but the parts items for discontinued machines at a distribution center triggered an immediate tracing and replenishment effort, and resulted in extra sales time devoted to an individual customer. The time required for this type of activity resulted in estimates of sales costs ranging from $5 to $25 per back-order. However, a question was raised in our consultant's mind about whether these costs should be factored into the system analysis because of the fact that costs incurred by salesmen were not charged to the Company.

Under the aggressive leadership of the Vice President of Sales, Richard Markham, an ambitious program of new product development and introduction was instituted. Within the past two years, the number of separate items in the line nearly had doubled, with many levelor models having similar capabilities. The sales of new products were highly unpredictable. While the Company had not had a new product failure on a national basis, sales success in individual distribution center territories varied a great deal, depending upon: (1) the effectiveness with which it was introduced to the salesmen, (2) the number of demonstration units which were made available to salesmen, and (3) the speed with which distribution centers were able to obtain stocks with which to fill orders.

A number of alternative policies for introducing new products had been debated in recent years. Marketing executives generally felt that the nation-wide simultaneous introduction of new products was essential to the morale of the field personnel and the effectiveness of the introduction.

There were debates as well over the current policy of not stocking a new product at a distribution center until three orders had been received for it. Distribution department personnel complained that even under this policy dead stocks of new products developed at various distribution centers. Marketing personnel replied that by the time customers placing firm orders necessary to get the new product into stock at a distribution center finally received shipment, they often had changed their minds about purchasing a Labrsavr Levelor.

Order Processing System

The Company received about 20,000 orders per month. They arrived by telephone, mail, or personal delivery at the distribution centers or the plant, placed directly by customers or by salesmen. The distribution centers and the plant, upon filling the orders, mailed copies of bills of lading (shipping documents) to Cleveland, where the information was punched on five-track computer tape and the inventory accounts at the distribution centers and the plant updated accordingly by computer.

As distribution center inventories were "debited," weights and other information for necessary replacement stocks for all items were recorded. When accumulated weights reached minimum quantities specified for plant-to-DC shipments, stock orders for shipment from the plant were prepared for each distribution center on the basis of forecasts, target inventory levels, and the monitored inventory levels available.

Inventory Control Program

Until several years previously, the stocks maintained in distribution centers had been controlled by the salesmen in the field. They ordered products for inventory at the distribution centers from which they drew stock, and they were held responsible for the freight costs of returning dead stocks back to the plant. Problems of accounting and disputes with field sales personnel over causes of dead stock situations convinced management to establish a centralized computer system to control inventory. In addition, executives at headquarters felt that only a computer-based system would be capable of handling the growth in sales volumes and product lines which was anticipated.

Forecasting

From the records of historical sales by product, item, and distribution center, the computer was able to forecast the expected demand for each item in each distribution center territory. This was done using an exponential smoothing model, whereby correction was made gradually for changes in levels of demand according to a procedure which will be discussed in detail in Chapter 11. Upon their preparation by the computer, stock orders resulting from this forecasting model were reviewed by regional sales managers, who could introduce "override" forecasts and orders to reflect knowledge they possessed about future demand which differed from recent demand patterns.

Transportation and Warehousing

Most shipments of raw materials and finished products were moved by methods outlined in Table 9–3. Major considerations in the selection of these methods were the cost of the transportation service combined with costs of claims and losses resulting from damage. Rates paid for for-hire transportation services for raw materials, parts, and machines are graphed in Fig. 9–6. (46) **How would you describe the rate relationships shown there?**

Storage capacity at the plant, amounting to 100,000 square feet, was well utilized. As a result, none other than shipments designated as "emergency" by sales personnel were shipped from the plant direct to customers. Further, the Cleveland plant facility did not have sufficient storage and order-picking space to serve as a distribution center. Consequently, the Cleveland distribution center was operated out of a facility located two miles from the plant.

The Purchasing Department scheduled its inbound shipments in such a way that the supply of raw materials and parts for production rarely fell below three weeks' worth. This had been reduced recently from a four-week policy. Further, it had adopted the policy with certain important suppliers that they maintain certain quantities of parts in their warehouses reserved for Wonka. In some cases, Wonka had extracted this concession at no difference in price by threatening to buy elsewhere, even though it was thought to cost suppliers 1% to 1½% per month of the value of product held in vendors' inventories in this fashion. This again helped conserve plant warehouse space at Cleveland.

Located in an older, more fully developed section of the city, Wonka's plant site provided no opportunity for expansion.

Material Handling and Packaging

All levelor units were packed in cartons with styrofoam bracing, a far cry from the wood crates that had been used at one time. Small items

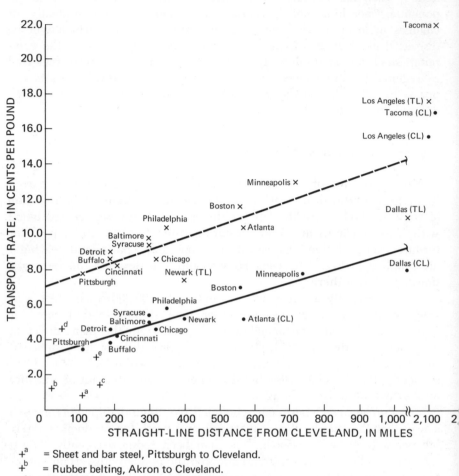

+^a is written as below in the legend.

+ᵃ = Sheet and bar steel, Pittsburgh to Cleveland.
+ᵇ = Rubber belting, Akron to Cleveland.
+ᶜ = Container stock, Dayton to Cleveland.
+ᵈ = Parts, 100-mile radius to Cleveland.
+ᵉ = Other raw materials, 300-mile radius to Cleveland.
× = Finished parts, Cleveland to distribution centers.
• = Machines, Cleveland to distribution centers.
— — — = Straight-line regression for transport rates on parts, LTL unless otherwise noted.
———— = Straight-line regression for transport rates on machines, TL unless otherwise noted.

Fig. 9–6. Transportation rate relationships for products shipped by the Warren G. Wonka Manufacturing Company.

were then placed on pallets in multiple unit quantities for handling by lift truck. Larger items were handled directly by a clamp lift truck at the factory. Distribution centers which did not have clamp lift trucks had to place even the larger units on pallets for handling by regular lift truck. Depending on their size or fragility, parts were either boxed or sacked. Wonka's policy of associating its name with all part items required that those from vendors be repackaged upon receipt. Small part orders, typically for "emergency" shipment, were shrink-wrapped with plastic to a cardboard backing and shipped by parcel service.

Production Planning

Wonka's plant had three assembly lines on which small, medium, and large items were scheduled for production on a "cycle" basis.

Economic order quantities determined the quantities and frequency of production runs. Order quantities were adjusted upward, where necessary, to allow the production of certain items on every other or every third production cycle, for example. Annual nation-wide forecasts of demand for each item were used for determining quantities. Examples of the frequency with which various items were produced, suggesting the size of production runs for selected items, are shown in Table 9–4.

The sequence of items assembled in an assembly line "cycle" had been designed to minimize the costs of changing over the line for the production of the next item.

Production runs were adjusted, for quantities in excess of economic order quantities, to meet 150% of the expected demand between production runs. This provided a safety cushion of plant stocks in proportion to the size of their respective production runs and provided an easy-to-follow rule of thumb.

The Cleveland plant was operated on a two-shift basis the entire year. It was estimated that the rate of production represented about 75% of two-shift capacity. The third shift was used for clean-up, material handling, and maintenance by a skeleton crew. For this reason, and because Company personnel policies were oriented to a constant work force size with no lay-offs, a third shift for production had not been considered seriously by the Company to meet seasonal demands.

As a result, the basic production plan was laid out on an annual basis, taking into account the fact that the plant was closed for two weeks each July. Production cycles and quantities varied significantly only for new items for which patterns of demand had not been established. Peaks and valleys in item demands were absorbed by distribution center stocks. This placed particular importance on the correct allocation to distribution centers of stocks coming off the production lines. Unfortunately, at times products had to be shipped in advance of orders for distribution centers in order to clear the plant warehouse floor for basic stocks of other items.

Procurement

Procurement policies of importance for logistics include guidelines for making or buying products, determining when and where to buy, and coordinating with traffic department personnel regarding the purchase of product quantities to take maximum advantage of transportation rate breaks as well as quantity discounts and the potential for consolidating small inbound shipments from vendors located near one another.

Constant production activity simplified the scheduling for buying and for shipments inbound to the Cleveland plant. Much of the time of Wonka's four-man Purchasing Department was spent in evaluating alternative suppliers of machine components and in obtaining cost estimates for the production of components for new models. This process involved the manufacture of one or more prototype pieces by Research and Development, the preparation of specifications for their mass production, the distribution of prototypes to Wonka's plant engineer and to reliable suppliers for cost estimates, and the collection and comparison of estimates. Because of the limited capacity and capability of Wonka's parts manufacturing operation, decisions to produce the item "in house" were made only when the "in-house" operation could (1) make the item and (2) make it for direct costs (labor and materials) of less than 50% of the price quoted by an outside vendor.

Other things equal, the Purchasing Department favored suppliers located nearest the Cleveland plant. The primary reason given for this policy was to allow for easier contact and closer coordination between Wonka and the supplier. Purchasing personnel made an effort to visit each of Wonka's 300 suppliers every year.

In addition to the 12-month production projection, the Purchasing Department received a monthly 90-day projection of firm production needs against which purchases could be made. With this in hand, inbound shipments were scheduled to achieve the following objectives:

1. On items on which the production line was dependent, a minimum of three weeks' stock at all times and no stock-outs.
2. On supplies of a less critical nature, a minimum of three weeks' stock at all times and no more than one stock-out per year per item.

The frequency of purchase depended on the nature of the item. Commodities such as sheet and bar steel were bought on a standard contract basis, with the final quantity price discount determined by the total amount purchased over the period of the contract. Under the terms of the contract, a truckload shipment from the supplier was made periodically unless the vendor was notified seven days in advance of any changes in this schedule. For certain high-value components, orders were written in advance of each production run on which they were used. Of the tonnage inbound to the Cleveland plant, approximately 20%, or 4,000 tons, moved in LTL shipments averaging about 1,000 pounds each.

Our consultant found that in fact there was little coordination between the Purchasing and Traffic Departments at Wonka. Purchasing personnel explained this by reminding him that vendors typically handled traffic matters in accordance with Wonka's policy of purchasing on a delivered basis. As one put it, "Our vendors are most familiar with the best way to have their products handled. We like to keep the responsibility on their shoulders." Counterparts in the Traffic Department generally were familiar with neither the quantities in which inbound raw materials and components were moved nor the specific locations from which such shipments originated.

SUMMARY

We have covered a wide range of topics and a great deal of information in our audit of the Wonka Company's logistics system. Yet every type of information surveyed in our case example has potential significance for the performance and analysis of the Company's logistics system. The basic problem of the analyst is to sort out pieces of information, particularly those that relate system outputs to inputs, those that are of the greatest significance, and those that represent opportunities for the greatest improvement in system performance. This is the concern of the chapters in Part Four.

You may feel that you need additional information in order to pinpoint the greatest areas of opportunity for improving Wonka's logistics system. All to the good. In fact, it would be useful to jot them down. An effective analyst must identify errors of omission as well as those of commission.

At this point in an analysis, it is typical to experience confusion, a feeling of being overwhelmed by facts. A knowledge of analytic techniques to be discussed in the succeeding chapters will help clear the air. But perhaps most important of all is common sense, a feeling for system relationships that transcends and points the way for analysis. It is time to step outside the Wonka Company's system and review it as objectively as possible. (47) **What types of problem symptoms do you see cropping up in the data collected in the audit, particularly that discussed under** the heading of system outputs? (48) What possible causes are suggested by the description of inputs? (49) Can you begin to develop some feeling for the general nature of actions which might be taken to deal with these causes? (50) Or areas of further analysis which may help provide direction for potential actions?

SUGGESTED READINGS

Bowersox, Donald J., Edward W. Smykay, and Bernard J. LaLonde. *Physical Distribution Management,* Rev. Ed. New York: The Macmillan Co., 1968.
Contains one of the few discussions of distribution system audits.

Hessler, Kenneth W. "Assignment—Design and Phase-in a New Distribution System," in Norman E. Daniel and J. Richard Jones, *Business Logistics.* Boston: Allyn and Bacon, Inc., 1969.
An interesting case study of the design process for a logistics system. Of particular interest is the designation of the problem and the establishment of the objectives of the analysis.

Magee, John F. *Industrial Logistics.* New York: McGraw-Hill Book Co., 1968.
Concepts useful in identifying and describing logistics system structure are discussed along with various aspects of the design of, and organization for, studies of logistics activities.

Turner, Michael S. V. *Freight Transport Planning and Control.* London: Business Publications Limited, 1966.
The first chapter of this book argues for the use of the specific evaluation (S.E.) of pre-defined alternatives as opposed to operational research techniques in analyzing a less limited number of alternatives associated with complex logistics problems. Subsequent material discusses the nature of questions to be posed prior to an analysis of marketing, transport and handling, storage and stock, and packaging activities.

10

Theory of Inventory Control

When is a refrigerator not a refrigerator? In terms of logistics, when it is in Pittsburgh at the time it is desired in Houston. When it is yellow instead of the desired coppertone. When it is ten cubic feet in size rather than some other desired size. When it is crated in a warehouse at the time it is needed for display in a retail store. In short, utilities are created in goods when they are at the right place, at the right time, and in the type and quantity desired. The theory of inventory control concerns itself largely with the last two of these three matters.

Throughout the discussion of inventory management we will refer to stock-keeping units (SKU's), SKU inventories, stock-keeping unit locations (SKUL's), product line, and total inventory.

Stock-keeping units may be described separately because they differ from others in shape, size, color, fragrance, strength, or other characteristics. When we speak of an SKU inventory we will mean the stock of an individually described SKU. An SKU inventory is composed of any number of units. A stock-keeping unit location is a stock-keeping unit inventoried at one location; one stock-keeping unit may have any number of stock-keeping unit locations. One or more SKU's make up a product line, and the sum of units in all SKU's and at all SKUL's make up the total inventory for a company.

THE NATURE OF INVENTORY

Inventories can be categorized into cycle, in-transit, safety, speculative, and dead stocks, signifying the reasons for which they are accumulated and held.

Cycle stocks are those required to meet the basic demand for stock-keeping items under conditions of certainty, that is, in situations in which we can predict demand and replenishment times perfectly. Such stocks are shown in Fig. 10–1.

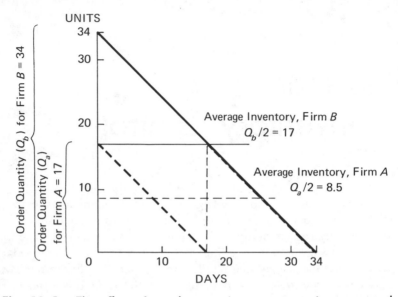

Fig. 10–1. The effect of reorder quantity on average inventory on hand for two firms (A and B), assuming a constant depletion (demand) rate.

In-transit stocks are those en route from one inventory location to another. They may be considered as a part of cycle stocks, although they are not available for sale and subsequent shipment until their arrival at destination.

Safety stocks are those accumulated and held in excess of cycle stocks because of uncertainties in either demand for a stock-keeping item or the time required for its replenishment in stock.

Speculative stocks are created for reasons other than meeting current demand. Production economies may suggest that goods be produced other than when they are demanded in order to maintain the workload and working force at a constant level. Goods produced seasonally, such as canned produce, may be consumed on a year-round basis. Inventories may be accumulated in anticipation of price increases or strikes.

Dead stocks usually are identified as those for which no demand has been registered for some specified period of time. They may be obsolete on a company-wide basis or only for a single inventory location.

MANAGEMENT OF INVENTORY UNDER CERTAINTY

The problem of determining inventory policies would be relatively easy if, for example, customers buying items from a manufacturer organized their buying so that they purchased an equal amount of all items every day of the week. It would be simplified still further if the time required to schedule and accomplish production to replenish stocks of the item was known and constant. Under these conditions, we could implement a time-tested formula for determining the proper amount of each item to order from our production line and when, in terms of the amount on hand, to reorder. While these conditions never prevail completely, there are times when models developed for this set of conditions can be useful.

Determination of Order Quantity

There are two major influences on the decision regarding the quantity of product to order to accommodate demand. The first is the cost of placing an order. The second is the cost of carrying inventory. Because the cost of placing an order (or the cost of setting up a manufacturing run) is assumed to be constant regardless of the size of the order or run, order cost per unit will decrease as the order size increases. However, as order size increases, it will take longer to deplete the quantity ordered. Further, the average amount of inventory on hand over the cycle from depletion to replenishment to depletion again will be greater, assuming a constant rate of depletion. This is illustrated in Fig. 10–1. Under assumptions of fixed and known demand, information in Fig. 10–1 suggests that any change in the average level of inventory on hand will be half as much, in units, as the change in reorder quantity.

In a given situation, we thus have the alternatives of ordering varying amounts. The more we order each time, the larger the average amount we will have on hand and the higher our inventory carrying charges (interest on investment, warehousing, insurance, property, taxes, and obsolescence or damage) will be. However, the more we order each time, the fewer the orders we will need to place to procure a given amount of product. Thus, our ordering costs should be reduced. Under these conditions, the relative costs of carrying and ordering inventory vary inversely.

This relationship, and the rationale for basic inventory theory, can be demonstrated intuitively by the following example drawn from the experience of the Warren G. Wonka Manufacturing Company, with item 5M. The manufactured cost of item 5M is $600, the cost of carrying a unit in stock for a year is about 25% of this amount, or $150, and the cost of placing an order (tooling up for a manufacturing run on item 5M) is $100. We may assume that demand is constant at 4 units per week.

Clearly, we could follow many strategies for managing the inventory of item 5M. They might vary from placing one order for a year's supply (4 units per week × 52 = 208 units) to placing 208 orders for one unit each. The economic consequences of several strategies are shown in Table 10–1. The lowest total cost is produced by placing 12 orders for

TABLE 10–1. Inventory Carrying and Ordering Costs for Various Strategies for Ordering Item 5M, Warren G. Wonka Manufacturing Company

Current Annual Demand	Number of Orders	Units Per Order	Average Inventory On Hand (Units)	Average Value of Inventory On Hand	Annual Inventory Carrying Costs	Annual Ordering Cost	Annual Total Cost
208	2	104	52.0	$31,200	$7,800	$ 200	$ 8,000
208	8	26	13.0	7,800	1,950	800	2,750
208	12	17	8.5	5,100	1,275	1,200	2,475*
208	16	13	6.5	3,900	975	1,600	2,575
208	104	2	1.0	600	150	10,400	10,550

*Lowest annual total cost among alternatives shown.

17 units each. Notice the nature of inventory carrying and ordering or setup costs under alternative strategies. These costs are graphed in Fig. 10–2.

This same problem can be represented mathematically by stating total costs in the following manner:[1]

$$C = \frac{Qvr}{2} + \frac{AS}{Q}$$

where

C = total inventory management cost (in dollars)
Q = the quantity ordered (in units)
v = average cost or value, per unit, of product (in dollars)
r = the annual inventory carrying charge (as a percentage of product cost or value)
A = the ordering or set-up cost (in dollars per order or set-up)
S = the annual demand or usage of the product (in units)

---

[1] Symbols used in this discussion have been selected to correspond to those in current usage, typified by the notation in Robert Goodell Brown, *Decision Rules for Inventory Management* (New York: Holt, Rinehart and Winston, 1967). For convenience, all symbols used in this and the following chapters have been grouped in Appendix A at the end of the book.

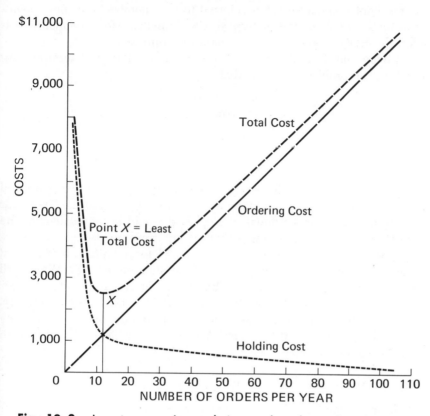

Fig. 10–2. Inventory carrying, ordering, and total costs for various strategies for ordering item 5M, Warren G. Wonka Manufacturing Company.

Here, $Qvr/2$ is just another way of stating annual inventory carrying costs as one-half the quantity ordered ($Q/2$) times the unit value or cost (v) times annual inventory carrying charges (r). Similarly, AS/Q states annual ordering or set-up costs in terms of the number of orders per year (S/Q) times the cost per order or set-up (A).

From the formula for total cost, we can derive a formula for the optimum value for Q (Q^*) by setting C equal to a minimum value, zero, taking the first derivative of the cost equation, and solving for Q.[2] Doing this, we obtain:

$$Q^* = \sqrt{\frac{2AS}{rv}}$$

[2] So-called optimums will be designated by an asterisk (*) in addition to the regular symbol. For a complete listing of terminology used in this and subsequent chapters regarding inventory control, see Appendix A.

The resultant formula for Q^* is referred to by a number of names, including Camp's formula or the Wilson lot size formula. Most commonly, it is called the EOQ (economic order quantity) formula.

Applying this formula to the information used in our intuitive approach to the problem, we find that:

$$Q^* = \sqrt{\frac{2(208)(\$100)}{.25(\$600)}},$$

$$Q^* = \sqrt{\frac{\$41,600}{\$150}} = \sqrt{277} = 16.7 \text{ units}$$

Because it would be impossible to order part of a unit in this situation, the optimum order quantity would equal 17 units, just as we happened to calculate by means of our previous "cut and try" approach. Thus, our solution for the example shown in Fig. 10–2 would be equivalent to the quantity indicated by dropping a vertical line from point X.

Before proceeding to more complex model formulations, it is helpful to check out our model from an intuitive standpoint. (1) **What will happen if we increase either of the values in the numerator of our model (A or S)? (2) Is this what we would expect? (3) Similarly, what effect would an increase in the values in the denominator (r or v) have on our order quantity?** This is a useful exercise to employ with all of the models we may consider.

Determination of Order Point

The order point should correspond to customer demand during the period required to obtain an order of the size placed. Under conditions of certainty this can be calculated as a function of daily demand and the number of days required to replenish our supply. Stated another way, it is usage or demand (x) during the order cycle. Because we can assume we know what this will be, we can order our shipment to arrive in stock sometime after the last unit in stock has been purchased but before customer demand results for the next unit.

If it required two weeks to make an order of model 5M levelors at the plant, and units in the order became available as a batch on the last day of the two-week production cycle, eight units (12 operating days × an average demand of ⅔ unit per day) would represent our reorder point (P), the quantity necessary to cover usage until receipt of the next lot.

Contrasts Between Inventory Control in Distribution and Production

The preceding example was based on information typical of the inventory control process at the Cleveland plant. This differed greatly from the information appropriate to the management of inventory at the Pittsburgh distribution center (DC), for example.

First, instead of a setup cost of $100 per order which we used for the Cleveland plant, the cost of placing an order at the Pittsburgh DC might be as low as $2 per order. The only costs involved at Pittsburgh are the clerical costs of preparing and mailing the order. If our order for 5M's appears as only one line item on an order including other models, the allocated cost of ordering 5M's may be very low.

Second, our ordering procedure may be based on the assumption that we can obtain 5M's from Cleveland only five operating days after we place our order. This would require that the Cleveland plant have sufficient stocks to meet our orders.

Third, our inventory value per unit for 5M's at Pittsburgh is 5% ($30 per unit) higher than it is at the Cleveland plant. This reflects the picking, handling, and transportation expense incurred in getting the product from Cleveland to Pittsburgh.

Fourth, our inventory carrying charge factor at Pittsburgh is set at 30% of the average value of inventory on hand over the year. This represents the greater risk of obsolescence (and the potential for subsequent reshipment back to Cleveland) associated with committing 5M's to an outlying distribution center rather than holding them at the more central Cleveland DC.

Because all of our demand for the period in question is expected to arise at Pittsburgh, this figure will not be changed in our calculation.

Using inputs appropriate for Wonka's Pittsburgh DC, we find that an EOQ for Pittsburgh should be two units, and the reorder point three units, for the period of time under consideration. (4) **Review your understanding of the preceding discussion by computing these values yourself.**

Formula Application

In the examples above, demand has been stated in terms of units (instead of dollars of sales), and the length of the period under consideration was a year in each case. Sometimes other units of measurement may be more appropriate. Whatever units are used, it is important to be consistent in the use of measures. This requires an expression of order quantity and demand rates in common terms, either in dollar amounts or units. In addition, measures of the cost of carrying a unit of inventory, the total demand, and the number of orders required should all be stated in terms of the same period of time, whether it be a year a month, or some other period of time.

MANAGEMENT OF INVENTORY UNDER UNCERTAINTY

Typically, we will not know for sure what demands may develop for our product. Only by chance will our inventories match the demands placed upon them. Further, order-cycle times are not constant. Communication and transportation times vary from one experience to the next. It may take longer to assemble the items in one order than it does those in another. The relationship, in days, between the occasion of an order and the scheduled production run from which the order must be filled will vary. (Remember Fig. 8–2?)

The combination of these factors may produce great variances in the demand during an order cycle. Under the circumstances, our alternatives range from maintaining (safety) stocks in excess of those we would maintain to meet average and constant demands under certain replenishment conditions to suffering the potential loss of sales because of stock-out conditions at a distribution warehouse or assembly-line shut-downs because of stock-out conditions at a plant.

A new cost trade-off is introduced into our inventory management problem, that of inventory holding cost vs. stock-out cost. It is represented diagrammatically in Fig. 10–3. Here, the cost trade-offs we have been dealing with under conditions of certainty are bounded by solid lines. The expansion of our problem under conditions of uncertainty is represented by the entries bounded by broken lines. It will be helpful to return to Fig. 10–3 at several points during our discussion.

Because of uncertainties about demand during the order cycle, our emphasis shifts in most inventory management situations dealing with uncertainty from the order quantity to the order point calculations. Order quantity will be important to the extent that it influences the number of orders and hence the number of times that we must expose ourselves to potential stock-out conditions at the tag end of each order cycle. However, it is the point (in terms of units) at which we place our order which will be the primary determinant of our ability to fill product demands while we are awaiting the availability of the order. We will use information drawn from Wonka's Pittsburgh distribution center to illustrate the following concepts.

Establishment of Usage Probability Levels

It is likely that Wonka's Pittsburgh distribution center, which has a sales forecast of 16 units per accounting period (four weeks) will encounter some days on which it sells nothing and others on which it receives orders for several units of item 5M. An analysis of past sales records for

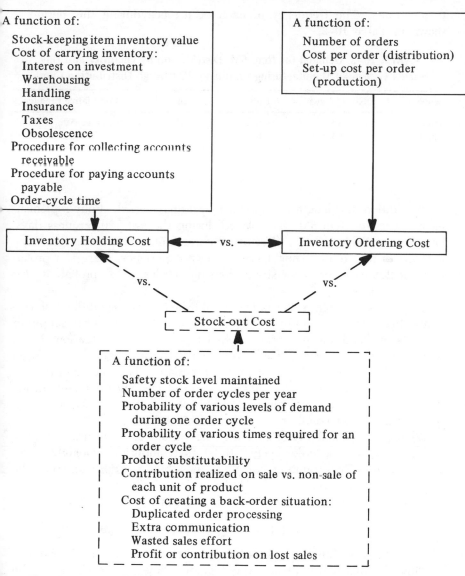

Fig. 10–3. Trade-offs typically represented in inventory control theory.

120 business days [3] during a period comparable to that under consideration indicates that the range of daily orders during this period has been from

---

[3] Business days are sometimes represented by the term "O-days," meaning operating days as differentiated from calendar days which include non-business days. All inventory management is assumed to deal with O-days, except for cases involving inventory in transit which generally moves every day, thus requiring measurement in terms of calendar days or translation into comparable O-days.

0 to 2 units. The frequency of each occurrence during this period is shown in Table 10–2.

TABLE 10–2. Demand for Item 5M, Distribution by Quantity and Day, Warren G. Wonka Manufacturing Company, Pittsburgh Distribution Center

Demand	No. of Days	Units	Frequency	Cumulative Frequency
0 units	60	0	50%	50%
1 unit	40	40	33	83
2 units	20	40	17	100
Total	120	80	100%	

In addition, the length of the order cycle has varied. Four replenishment orders for item 5M were placed during the last 120 business days. One was available six days after order placement, two more in five days, and one in four days. Thus, based on past experience, there is a probability of 25% each for either six- or four-day cycles, a 50% probability for one of five days.

If we were to follow the policy established under conditions of certainty, that of ordering in quantities of two units each time the supply of item 5M on hand and on order reached three units, the situation shown in Fig. 10–4 could occur. Here we see that Wonka would have been required to back-order item 5M on two occasions. The minimum reorder point of three units was not sufficient to meet customer demand during the time required for replenishment of stock. In other words, usage exceeded the reorder point, or $x > P$, on two occasions.

What is the probability of encountering various levels of usage, p ($x =$ 0 to 12), during the order cycle? Rules for computing probability provide the basis for counting up these possibilities. For example, the chances of encountering a six-day order cycle and six straight days during each of which demand is 2 units of item 5M can be calculated as follows:

$$p(x = 12) = .25(.17)(.17)(.17)(.17)(.17)(.17) = .000003946$$

That is, the probability of encountering a demand of 2 units in a day is roughly 17%, that of 4 units in two consecutive days, 17% × 17%, etc. The likelihood of encountering an order cycle of six days is 25%. Multiplying all of these probabilities, we arrive at an estimate that the p ($x = 12$) in this case would be about four chances in a million. Common sense would tell us that, except for the situation in which the cost of a stock-out per unit (π) is great it would not be necessary or desirable to prepare for the circumstance, $x = 12$.

What about $x = 11$? The situation, $x = 11$, could be accomplished by receiving orders for 2 units on each of five days and for 1 unit on the sixth of a six-day cycle of O-days. Since there are six different patterns in

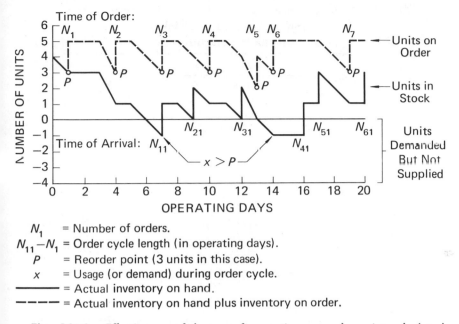

N_1 = Number of orders.
$N_{11}-N_1$ = Order cycle length (in operating days).
P = Reorder point (3 units in this case).
x = Usage (or demand) during order cycle.
——————— = Actual inventory on hand.
– – – – = Actual inventory on hand plus inventory on order.

Fig. 10–4. Effectiveness of the use of an optimum reorder point calculated on the basis of certainty while operating under conditions of uncertainty, Warren G. Wonka Manufacturing Company, Pittsburgh Distribution Center.

which this level of x could be encountered, the probability of the basic pattern is multiplied by 6:

$$p(x = 11) = 6[.25(.33)(.17)(.17)(.17)(.17)(.17)] = .0000459$$

Here there is a 33% chance of encountering a demand of 1 unit on any one of the six days of the cycle. In order to have $x = 11$, a demand for 2 units daily must be encountered on the other five days of the cycle. This level is likely to be found fewer than 5 out of 100,000 times. Continuing in this fashion, the table of probabilities for various values of x could be constructed. This is shown in Table 10–3.

Notice how, when the information in Table 10–3 is graphed, as in Fig. 10–5, it corresponds to a bell-shaped, or normal curve. This is often the case when fluctuations of values about a mean value of usage are random in nature. More will be said about this later.

A Fixed Order Point, Fixed Order Quantity Model

One basic approach to inventory control under uncertainty is similar to the EOQ model for conditions of certainty which we considered earlier.

TABLE 10–3. Probabilities for *x* for Item 5M, Accounting
Periods 12, 13, 1, 2, and 3,
Warren G. Wonka Manufacturing Company

x	p(x)	P(x)*
12	.0000	–
11	.0000	.0000
10	.0005	.0000
9	.0027	.0005
8	.0104	.0032
7	.0305	.0136
6	.0727	.0441
5	.1332	.1168
4	.1984	.2500
3	.2230	.4484
2	.1919	.6714
1	.1016	.8633
0	.0351	.9649
Total	1.0000	

*Cumulative probability of more than *x*.

Under this concept, our order will be triggered when the inventory on hand and on order reaches a predetermined minimum level sufficient to meet specified levels of demand during the order cycle. An economic order quantity will be ordered. And orders will be placed intermittently, whenever demand is sufficient to draw our available supply down to the order point.

Determination of the Order Point. In order to adjust the order point effectively to accommodate uncertainty, it must be assumed that future demand can be predicted, subject to certain random differences between predicted demand and the actual demand which will be encountered. For purposes of discussion, we will assume that our predicted demand for item 5M in the Wonka case is as described previously and as shown graphically in Fig. 10–5. While a quantity between 9 and 10 units describes nearly all of the demands which we might encounter during an order cycle, theoretically it would be possible for us to face 12 units of demand.

Clearly, if we wished to eliminate all possibility of a stock-out situation on item 5M during the period under consideration, we would reorder when our stock on hand and on order reached 12 units. This policy would appear to be too cautious and expensive, based on our prior knowledge. The underlying principle of the calculation for reorder point under uncertainty is that we should continue to add units to our order point (and hence to our average inventory) until the additional cost of adding

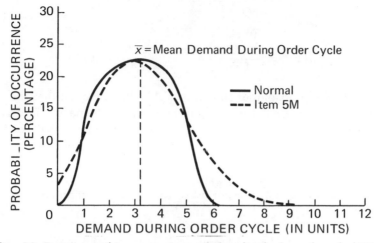

Fig. 10–5. A graphic comparison of the distribution of probabilities for usage of item 5M and a normal distribution of probabilities.

a unit equals the savings resulting from this action. Setting the cost of carrying an additional unit, rvQ/S, equal to the cost and likelihood of encountering a stock-out, $p\ (x > P)\ (\pi)$, results in a formula for determining the optimum probability of a penalty of given size which can be tolerated in an order situation:

$$p(x > P)^* = \frac{rvQ}{\pi S}$$

For example, checking back on the situation involving item 5M in the Wonka inventory, we must arrive at some estimate of a value for the stock-out penalty (π). In this case, our investigation shows that the extra clerical cost of a back order approximates $10 per unit. The probability of losing a sale during a stock-out on item 5M is about one-half of the expected excess of demand over available supply, or $\frac{1}{2}E\ (x > P)$; in other words, customers will shift their purchase to another brand of levelor about 50% of the time when item 5M is desired but not available. Because profit on a sale of a 5M is $90, the profit penalty per unit on a stock-out will be estimated at $45. Thus $\pi = \$10 + \$45$ or $55.

To provide a starting estimate for Q, we could use our estimate of 2 units obtained above, under the assumption of conditions of certainty. Using an annual rate of 30% for r and a value of $630 for v ($600 per unit manufactured cost plus $30 per unit for picking, handling, and transportation from Cleveland to Pittsburgh), we can compute a value for $p\ (x)^*$, the optimum cumulative probability of a usage rate higher than the quoted figure for x. Once again, we annualize our demand rate at 208 units per year for the period of time in question and obtain:

$$p(x)^* = \frac{rvQ}{\pi S}$$

$$p(x)^* = \frac{.30(\$630)(2)}{\$55(208)} = \frac{\$378}{\$11,440} = .0330$$

Referring to the probabilities shown in Table 10–3, we see that the value .0330 is satisfied by a point somewhere between $x = 6$ and $x = 7$. In other words, if we set P equal to 7, we will be prepared to meet that portion of possible demand during an order cycle that will prove most profitable to the firm.

For any order point, the expected stock-out cost per order cycle, $E(s)$, for a number of cycles over a period of time can be computed as:

$$E(s) = \pi \left[\sum_{x = P + 1}^{x_{max}} (x - P)p(x) \right]$$

That is, the sum of the probabilities of various levels of usage during order cycles occurring in excess of $P = 7$ (or 8 through 12 in the situation involving item 5M) are multiplied by the stock-out penalty to arrive at the expected stock-out cost under the assumed policy. In the example:

$$E(s) = \$55[5(.0000) + 4(.0000) + 3(.0005) + 2(.0027) + 1(.0104)] = \$55(.0173) = \$.95$$

Having found the value of the expected stock-out cost under an assumed policy for P, we can compute an order quantity for item 5M for our Pittsburgh warehouse.

Determination of Optimum Order Quantity. Our previously developed model for EOQ under conditions of certainty allowed us to trade inventory holding costs against ordering costs. To this model, all we need do to take into account conditions of uncertainty is add stock-out costs, essentially as another element of ordering costs. We must take into account the cost resulting from expected back-order penalties, $E(s)$, as well as ordering activities, A, both multiplied by the number of orders per period under consideration, S/Q, or $S/Q[A + E(s)]$.

The cost of carrying inventory under a given policy can be represented by inventory carrying cost per unit (rv) multiplied by the average quantity on hand under conditions of certainty ($Q/2$) plus the extra amount accumulated because of the excess of the order point (P) over the average usage during the order cycle ($\bar{x}$) which would exist where P purposely is set greater than the average usage during the order cycle ($\bar{x}$) in order to compensate for uncertainty in x for any given cycle. Thus, the extended formula for the total cost of a given policy would appear as:[4]

$$C = \frac{S}{Q}[A + E(s)] + rv\left[\frac{Q}{2} + (P - \bar{x})\right]$$

If the order point (P) is assumed constant and independent of the order quantity (Q), then the expected usage in excess of the order point, $E(x > P)$, is a constant. Setting the above equation equal to a minimum cost (C) of zero, and taking the first derivative of the cost equation, we obtain as a result a formula for determining optimum order quantity:[5]

$$Q^* = \sqrt{\frac{2S[A + E(s)]}{rv}}$$

In the Wonka case:

$$Q^* = \sqrt{\frac{2(208)(\$2.00 + \$.95)}{.30(\$630)}} = \sqrt{\frac{\$1,227.20}{\$189.00}} = \sqrt{6.5} = \text{about } 3$$

This value of Q^* does not correspond to the one assumed earlier in our computation of order point, requiring a recalculation of P using an assumed value of 3 instead of 2 for Q, thus producing the following recomputed value for $p(x)^*$:

$$p(x)^* = \frac{rvQ}{\pi S} = \frac{.30(\$630)(3)}{\$55(208)} = \frac{\$567}{\$11,440} = .0494$$

Thus, our new suggested value for P, referring to Table 10–3, would fall near 6. The assumption of $P = 6$ would create a new value for stock-out cost, $E(s)$:

$$E(s) = \$55[6(.0000) + 5(.0000) + 4(.0005) + 3(.0027) + \\ 2(.0104) + 1(.0305)] = \$55(.0614) = \$3.38$$

[4] The formula developed here is one which assumes that sales are delayed, not lost, in a back-order situation for purposes of calculating carrying costs. In most situations, the differences in results obtained from this formula and one which assumes sales lost under back-order conditions are slight. As we will see later, the factor for $P - \bar{x}$ drops out for most problem formulations.

[5] The result is derived as follows:

$$\frac{d(C = 0)}{dQ} = \frac{d(vS)}{dQ} + \frac{S}{Q}\frac{d}{dQ}[A + E(s)] + [A + E(s)]\frac{d}{dQ}\frac{S}{Q} + \\ \frac{d}{dQ}[rv(P - x)] + \left(\frac{Q}{2}\right)\left(\frac{d}{dQ}\right)rv + rv\left(\frac{d}{dQ}\right)\left(\frac{Q}{2}\right);$$

then $\quad 0 = 0 + 0 - \frac{S}{Q^2}[A + E(s)] + 0 + 0 + \frac{rv}{2}$,

so that $\quad \frac{rv}{2} = \frac{S}{Q^2}[A + E(s)]$,

and $\quad Q^* = \sqrt{\frac{2S[A + E(s)]}{rv}}$

This would necessitate recomputations of Q and P until the values for both stabilize. In the Wonka example, these values stabilize at $Q = 4$, $P = 6$. (You might wish to verify this for yourself.) In other words, when our quantity on hand and on order reaches 6, we should order 4 more. Under these rules, it is quite possible that at times we might have more than one order in process.

A Fixed Order Interval Model

A second basic approach to inventory control is one in which we compare available stocks with forecasted demand levels and place orders only at certain regular, specified times. Unless our demand is realized in increments of one unit and our order intervals are extremely short, the actual order point (in terms of quantity of product on hand and on order at the time the order is placed) may vary. In addition, we may or may not order in fixed quantities. Most likely, we will not. Instead, we will order a quantity necessary to bring our stock on hand and on order up to a level sufficient to satisfy some specified level and variability of customer demands over the period which will pass before we have a chance to order stock again and receive it physically into our inventory. In other words, each order represents our only chance to provide for the succeeding order interval plus the order cycle following our next order. This quantity can be termed an "order up to level" or a max value. We will designate it with the letter W.

What is our order interval? If we project sales of about 640,000 pounds of all models of our product through the Pittsburgh DC during the next year, this would mean about 21 truckloads of freight at a minimum of 30,000 pounds per truckload. Stated another way, if there was no seasonality in our sales at Pittsburgh, we would ship a truckload every 2½ weeks, or every 15 operating days. If the average order cycle remained five days, the period of time for which we would have to provide inventory coverage with our W level typically would be 20 operating days, with a range from 19 to 21 operating days.

Determination of Max (W) Value. The similarity of actual probabilities of usage resulting from random fluctuations from mean usage, shown in Fig. 10–5, allows us to assume a normal distribution for values of x. A basic measure of deviation from the mean (average) value in a normal distribution is called a standard deviation. By definition, one standard deviation (σ) above and below the mean will include about 68% of all possible usage levels. Two standard deviations above and below ($\pm 2\sigma$) the mean include about 95% of all occurrences, and three above and below

($\pm 3\sigma$) include more than 99.7%. Specific percentages represented by various numbers of standard deviations above the mean are presented in Appendix B.

To calculate the value for a standard deviation of values of x in our example, we must first determine the magnitude of σ both in the length of the reorder cycle (assuming that the order interval is fixed) and the level of daily demand. This is carried out in Table 10–4.

Thus, we have a situation in which the nature of one order interval and one order cycle is 20 (15 + 5) days in average length, with a standard deviation from average of .709 days. Daily demand averages .67 of a unit, with a standard deviation from average of .747 of one unit. Given this information, it can be shown that the standard deviation of usage during the order interval plus the order cycle is:

$$\sigma_x = \sqrt{\bar{t}\,\sigma_{oc}^2 + \bar{x}_d^2\,\sigma_{dd}^2}$$

where

$\bar{t}$ = average length of order interval plus order cycle
σ_{oc} = the standard deviation in order interval and order cycle lengths
$\bar{x}_d$ = average usage per day
σ_{dd} = the standard deviation in daily demand rates

Thus,

$$\sigma_x = \sqrt{20(.709^2) + (.67^2)(.747^2)}$$

$$= \sqrt{11.06} = 3.3 \text{ units}$$

That is, there is a 68% chance that usage during one order interval plus one order cycle will fall in the range of 20(.67) $\pm$ 3.3 units, or 10.0 to 16.6 units. The normal curve for this problem, showing ranges of usage for all levels of probability, is shown in Fig. 10–6.

Therefore, we say that a beginning inventory on hand and on order of 16.6 units (actually 17) will be sufficient to meet usage levels likely to be encountered in 84% (all quantities of less-than-average usage plus 34% of more-than-average usage levels) of all combined order interval–order cycle periods encountered for item 5M in the periods under consideration.

What is the optimum probability of a stock-out to provide for in our W quantity? The previous formula

$$p(x > W)^* = \frac{rvQ}{\pi S}$$

used as the formula for determining elements of a fixed order quantity policy can be used to assess probability in this type of case. Because N, the number of orders placed during a given period, has been determined

TABLE 10–4. Calculation of Standard Deviation of Order Cycle and Daily Demand, Item 5M, Warren G. Wonka Manufacturing Company, Pittsburgh Distribution Center

		Order Cycle		
Days	Frequency (f)	Deviation from Mean (d)	d^2	fd^2
19	1	1	1	1
20	2	0	0	0
21	1	1	1	1
	$N = 4$			$\Sigma fd^2 = 2$

Standard deviation $(\sigma) = i\sqrt{\dfrac{\Sigma fd^2}{N}}$, where N = total of the various frequencies, and i = the size of the class interval (1 day in this case).

Standard deviation of order cycle = $\sigma_{oc} = 1\sqrt{2/4} = 1\sqrt{.5} = .709$

		Daily Demand		
Amount (units)	Frequency (f)	Deviation from Mean $(d)*$	d^2	fd^2
0	3	2/3	4/9	12/9
1	2	1/3	1/9	2/9
2	1	1-1/3	16/9	16/9
	$N = 6$			$\Sigma fd^2 = 30/9$

Standard deviation of daily demand = $\sigma_{dd} = 1\sqrt{\dfrac{30/9}{6}} = .747$

*The mean daily demand = 2/3 unit per business day.

already, it can be substituted into the above formula for the unknown Q. Previously, we saw that

$$Q = \frac{S}{N}$$

Substituting S/N for Q in the formula for $p(x > W)*$, we obtain

$$p(x > W)* = \frac{rv}{\pi N}$$

Using previously discussed values, plus the value of 21 for N, the number of orders to be placed in a year, we find that:

$$p(x > W)* = \frac{.30(\$630)}{\$55(21)} = \frac{\$189}{\$1,155} = .164$$

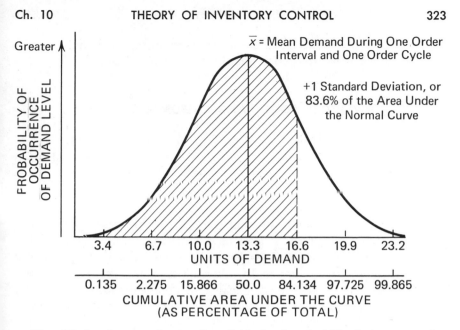

Greater

PROBABILITY OF OCCURRENCE OF DEMAND LEVEL

$\bar{x}$ = Mean Demand During One Order Interval and One Order Cycle

+1 Standard Deviation, or 83.6% of the Area Under the Normal Curve

| 3.4 | 6.7 | 10.0 | 13.3 | 16.6 | 19.9 | 23.2 |

UNITS OF DEMAND

| 0.135 | 2.275 | 15.866 | 50.0 | 84.134 | 97.725 | 99.865 |

CUMULATIVE AREA UNDER THE CURVE
(AS PERCENTAGE OF TOTAL)

Fig. 10–6. Ranges of usage for all levels of probability during one order interval and one order cycle, item 5M, Wonka Manufacturing Company, Pittsburgh Distribution Center (shaded area refers to the example on page 320).

From the table of areas of the normal probability distribution, presented in Appendix B, we locate the complementary value for .164. In other words, if we wish to permit a 16.4% chance of a back-order situation during a given order interval–order cycle period, we must make sure that enough stock is on hand to meet 33.6% of the values for usage which exceed average usage, the proposition indicated by the shaded area in Fig. 10–6. This occurrence is represented by about one standard deviation above the average usage (from Appendix B; check it out). Thus:

$$W = \bar{x} + 1\sigma$$
$$= 20(.67) + .98(3.3)$$
$$= 13.3 + 3.2 = 16.5 \text{ units, or 16 or 17 units}$$

If, at the beginning of an order interval, the amount of stock of item 5M on hand or on order (q) is 5 units, then:

$$Q = W - 5$$
$$= 16 - 5$$
$$= 11 \text{ units}$$

The order quantity would be 12 units. Similarly, if the stock on hand and on order was 2 units, the order quantity would be 14 units.

INVENTORY POLICY AND CUSTOMER SERVICE

In a fixed order interval model, we can increase the max (W) value, thereby reducing the likelihood that we will run out near the end of an order interval plus its subsequent order cycle (in our example, 20 operating days). For each unit that we raise W, we will add one unit to our average inventory. The levels of W at which our inventory carrying costs increase at the same dollar rate that our costs of lost sales (back-order costs) decrease typically will describe the alternative policies involving the lowest total penalty costs. In Table 10–5, the value of W producing the lowest total penalty cost is 16, differing from the precise value we computed previously, 16.5 units, because of approximations.

Similar computations can be made for the determination of the order point under a fixed order point type of model.

Consider the implications of the information in Table 10–5 for statements describing customer service standards. In Chapter 8, we said that customer service policies most often are stated in terms of the percentage of potential unit sales or orders which are fully satisfied. Perhaps the most often quoted figure for customer service is a 95% unit fill rate (synonymous with a 95% line item fill rate only when all orders are for one unit each). In the case of item 5M in Wonka's line (as shown in column 4 of Table 10–5), we can see that a 95% unit fill rate would produce higher total costs than one of 98%. However, even the latter level of customer service would still allow us to run out of stock to some degree on 21.2% of the order cycles for item 5M. Assuming 21 (312 operating days per year ÷ 15 operating days per order interval) orders per year for the item, we would expect to run out of 5M's about four times per year. Our penalties for having more than optimum quantities for W would be somewhat less severe than those incurred for having lower-than-optimum W levels. (5) Why is this the case?

REVIEW OF RESULTS, BASIC MODELS

By reviewing results of the application of our fixed order quantity and fixed order interval models to Wonka's Pittsburgh inventory problem for item 5M, we can gain some further insight into the implications of these policies.

Fixed Order Interval Inventory Policy, Item 5M, Wonka Manufacturing Company, Pittsburgh Distribution Center

(1) Max (W) Value (Units)	(2) Percentage of 21 Order Cycles Stocked Out, $p(x > W)$[a]	(3) Percentage of Potential Units of Sale Stocked Out[b]	(4) Average Inventory (Units)[c]	(5) Cost of Lost Sales[d]	(6) Inventory Carrying Charge[e]	(7) Total Cost[f] [(5)+(6)]
10	75.8%	18.8%	3.6	$2,150	$ 680	$2,830
11	65.5	15.7	3.8	1,791	718	2,509
12	54.0	12.2	4.3	1,398	813	2,201
13	42.1	9.4	4.9	1,072	926	1,998
14	30.9	6.2	5.7	710	1,078	1,788
15	21.2	3.8	6.7	434	1,267	1,701
16	13.6	2.1	7.7	242	1,456	1,698[g]
17	8.1	1.3	8.7	148	1,645	1,793
18	4.5	.7	9.7	80	1,834	1,914
19	2.3	.3	10.7	34	2,023	2,057
20	1.1	.1	11.7	12	2,212	2,224
21	.5	.04	12.7	4	2,401	2,405
22	.2	.01	13.7	1	2,590	2,591
23	.1	.005	14.7	1	2,779	2,780

[a]Drawn directly from Appendix B, assuming an average demand per order cycle of 13.3 units and a standard deviation (σ) of 3.3 units (or 1 unit = .30). For example, if $W = 10$, the probability of x (demand) being 11 units or more can be read from Appendix B as the percentage (25.8% or .2580) associated with the number of standard deviations equivalent to the difference between average demand (13.3 units) and 11 units (2.3 units = .70) plus all occurrences of above-average demand (50%).

[b]Computed by calculating a weighted sum of stock-outs resulting from all possible demand levels in excess of W, using Appendix B; for example, for $W = 10$, the weighted sum =

$$\sum_{x=11}^{x=23} p(x > W)$$

The results of these calculations were then divided by the average demand per order cycle, 13.3 units, to arrive at the percentage in column (3).

[c]Verify these levels for yourself.

[d]Based on the multiplication of the percentages listed in column (3) × 208 units of expected sales during the year × $55(\pi$, or the estimated cost per unit of a stock-out), with the result rounded to the nearest dollar.

[e]Computed on the basis of a $630 value per unit (production plus transportation costs) × 30% annual carrying cost, with the result rounded to the nearest dollar.

[f]Not including ordering costs (assumed not to vary for a fixed order interval model).

[g]Alternative producing the lowest total penalty costs.

We would expect to have an average of 2.7 units of stock on hand at the end of order cycles under the fixed order quantity model and 2.7 (16 − 13.3) on hand at the end of order intervals plus their respective order cycles under the fixed order interval model. This is safety stock. Take another look at Fig. 10–4. Notice the impact that 2.7 units of safety stock (essentially, added below the zero inventory level) would have on Wonka's ability to serve its customers during the period of time portrayed there.

Average inventories under the two models would be 4.7 units (6.7 + 2.7/2) and 7.7 units (72.7 + 2.7/2), respectively. (6) **Verify this for yourself.** Thus, safety stocks would represent 57% of the average inventory for the fixed order quantity model and 35% of the average inventory for the fixed order interval model, perhaps reflecting the more frequent orders and risk of stock-out under the former policy (with 2½ times the orders that the latter policy requires).

An optimal fixed order quantity policy would have us run out of stock on 21.2% of all order cycles, about four times per year, and fill 98% of potential unit demand. The optimal fixed order interval policy would produce the same results, except that we would expect to run out of stock only about twice per year.

If you would like to work through the inventory model once more, try this problem. (7) **What would be the impact on total inventory costs for item 5M at Pittsburgh if the volume increased sufficiently to allow weekly truckload shipments from Cleveland, under the assumption that it costs us $2 to place an order for 5M's as part of a larger order?** (8) **Putting it another way, how much additional, if any, would you be willing to pay in freight costs in order to obtain 52 deliveries per year instead of 21? Which inventory model would you recommend to Wonka under these conditions?**

CONCLUSION

It is safe to say that no two inventory control models in actual use are alike. If they do not vary in structure, at least they vary in the nature of the inputs used for computational purposes. Differences in terminology and symbolism further confuse anyone attempting to invade the mysterious and often private world of the inventory controller (particularly the green eye-shade variety). Much of the confusion can be credited to academicians and authors, each of whom uses private symbols and definitions for a world already redefined many times by his predecessors. For these reasons, it is useful to review the basic structural

TABLE 10–6. Basic Features of Q and P Inventory Models

Inventory Control Model Element	Form Assumed by Model Element in Each Type of Model*	
	Q Model	P Model
Order point (P)	Fixed	Variable
Order quantity (Q)	Fixed	Variable
Order interval (R)	Variable	Fixed

*Types of basic alternative models are coded as follows: Q = fixed order quantity models, P = fixed order interval models.

forms that describe all formal inventory control models.

The order point (P), order quantity (Q), and order interval (R) may take on fixed or variable values, thereby in combination describing the basic models available for inventory control purposes. These elements are listed in Table 10–6, along with notations indicating elements typically associated with each type of control model.

Names assigned to model types vary, according to the authority consulted. EOQ models, or Q models, or two-bin (one bin containing the order point quantity and the other containing units in excess of the order point quantity) or fixed order quantity models are based on a fixed order quantity, fixed order point, and a variable order interval. Models variously called P or fixed order interval models have fixed order intervals, variable order quantities, and variable order points.

It should be noted that there is basic disagreement about inventory model classification among experts. For example, if we encounter one unit of demand at a time and our fixed order interval is such that no more than one unit of demand occurs during the order interval, then we would in fact have a fixed order point. If the difference between the expected stock on hand at the end of an order interval–order cycle and the operating level (also called the max level, or the "order up to" level) was equivalent to an economic order quantity, then we would have a fixed order quantity, in fact an EOQ. Further, if stocks on hand are reviewed periodically on a fixed schedule, but actually ordered less frequently whenever an order point is encountered, don't we in fact have a variable order interval?

Inventory control models incorporating features of both Q and P models are perhaps most popular in actual practice. The most common of these, termed by Buffa the "optional replenishment" model, is also called the S,s and min–max model.[6] The S,s model incorporates a fixed order

[6] Elwood P. Buffa, *Production-Inventory Systems* (Homewood, Ill.: Richard D. Irwin, Inc., 1968), p. 98.

point with a fixed order interval system. If the fixed order point is not reached at the time of the review, no order is placed. The fixed order point (min value) may be determined by subtracting a quantity from the max value which represents an efficient purchasing quantity (for example, one which qualifies the buyer for a quantity discount) or an efficient shipping and handling quantity (a case, a pallet quantity, or a truckload).

This allows orders to be placed in efficient quantities and reduces costs resulting from the frequent placement of small orders. However, where stock-out costs are significant, the amount of safety stock under an "optional replenishment" or S,s model may have to be increased to guard against the possibility that the level on hand at the time of a review may be slightly above the order point, thereby raising the necessary coverage to two order intervals plus the order cycle.

Of greater importance to a logistics manager is the result produced by the inventory model in actual application, not what it is called or how it is categorized. Having briefly explored the basic theory behind inventory models without looking into the countless model variations designed to accomplish a variety of specific objectives, we will next consider how the models can be selected and implemented as elements of a logistics system.

SUGGESTED READINGS

BROWN, ROBERT G. *Decision Rules for Inventory Management*. New York: Holt, Rinehart and Winston, 1967.
    This book, written almost like a novel (including an implied love story), is the result of a wealth of practical experience on the part of the author. Calling upon a number of examples centered around a richly described company case situation, Brown lays out a "how-to-do-it," including both managerially oriented memoranda and technical notes, for a wide range of inventory control techniques oriented to procurement and distribution as well as production. This is easily the most readable of all comprehensive treatments of inventory control.
BUCHAN, JOSEPH, and ERNEST KOENIGSBERG. *Scientific Inventory Management*. Englewood Cliffs, N. J.: Prentice-Hall, Inc., 1963.
    Presents an excellent treatment of inventory control techniques as well as many examples of applications in various industries.
BUFFA, ELWOOD S. *Production-Inventory Systems*. Homewood, Ill.: Richard D. Irwin, Inc., 1968.
    As the title suggests, this book concentrates on inventory and production control techniques. It does an effective job of relating inventory models to the production system in which they are employed. Limited emphasis is placed on inventory control for distribution applications.
FETTER, ROBERT B., and WINSTON C. DALLECK. *Decision Models for Inventory Management*. Homewood, Ill.: Richard D. Irwin, Inc., 1961.

Presents a series of theoretical formulations interspersed with computations based on running examples which clarify many of the underlying principles of inventory management.

PRITCHARD, J. W., and R. H. EAGLE. *Modern Inventory Management.* New York: John Wiley & Sons, Inc., 1965.
This is a carefully written, well-illustrated book which presents its complex subject in a clear manner requiring only a knowledge of algebra. The relationship of inventory models to customer service objectives is covered especially well.

STARR, MARTIN K., and DAVID W. MILLER. *Inventory Control: Theory and Practice.* Englewood Cliffs, N. J.: Prentice-Hall, Inc., 1962.
A thorough treatment of the theory of inventory control and the design of inventory studies, decision procedures, and operating methods.

11

Inventory Program Management

An inventory model is only one element of an inventory management program. The design of such a program is of major strategic importance. It requires that we bridge the gap between inventory theory and inventory management. The logistics manager, while he may be no expert on the subject of inventory control, should be in a position to (1) encourage his staff to think of the inventory management program in much broader terms than traditionally are assumed, and (2) represent top management views and objectives in the appraisal and redesign of the program.

Elements of a broad-based inventory management program are outlined in Fig. 11-1. They include the determination of management goals, assessment of basic business needs, design of the inventory control model, design of a forecasting model to provide demand inputs, design of a program for other inventory model inputs, establishment of inventory contingency procedures, testing for internal compatibility of program elements, and testing for the compatibility of the program design with business requirements external to the program itself. Once again, our friends at the Wonka Manufacturing Company provide us with a specific example.

DETERMINATION OF MANAGEMENT GOALS

Management goals for logistics activities generally concern customer service and cost. In discussing management goals with Mr. Wonka at

I. Determination of management goals

II. Assessment of basic business needs

III. Design of inventory model, such as:

$$Q* = \sqrt{\frac{2S\,[A + E(s)]}{rv}}$$

$$p(x)* = \frac{rvQ}{\pi S} = P$$

$$E(s) = \pi \left[\sum_{x = P + 1}^{x\,max} (x - P)\, p(x) \right]$$

IV. Design of forecasting model (for S, above)
    Trend seasonal

V. Design of program for other inventory model inputs:
   A = order cost (source: Accounting)
   π = stock-out cost (source: Marketing Management)
   r = inventory carrying cost (source: top management)
   v = unit cost of product (source: Accounting)
        order interval and order lead time

VI. Establishment of inventory contingency procedures

VII. Design of remaining program elements
     Computational device
     Update cycle
     Program review procedures

VIII. Testing for internal compatibility

IX. Testing for external compatibility

Fig. 11–1.   Elements of an inventory management program.

the outset of the appraisal process for Wonka's logistics system, our consultant learned about Wonka's concern for obtaining greater profits from existing sales at the possible risk of some deterioration in the company's service to customers. Further interviews with George Dalton, the Distribution Manager, indicated that a basic service objective was to be able to fill 90% of all line-item orders for machines within four days of the time they might be placed with any one of the Company's distribution centers. Dalton suggested that these goals might be reviewed and possibly lowered, depending on the results of the system review. In his words, "I'm not sure that our management has sufficient information about the implication of service policy alternatives for costs on which to base a decision about service goals. This may be an important result from your work."

ASSESSMENT OF BASIC BUSINESS NEEDS

Economic order quantities for manufacturing purposes were computed on the basis of production economics, including set-up costs of the type suggested for item 5M in Chapter 10. The importance of producing in economic lot sizes dictated the use of a Q model at the factory.

Similar obvious economies of replenishing distribution centers, where possible, in pallet-size quantities for machine items, case-size quantities for parts, and truckload or carload quantities for total shipments were assumed by the consultant to have a great influence on EOQ's, replenishment points, and order intervals for shipments from a plant to a distribution center.

The computational capacity which the Company was willing to make available for inventory control purposes suggested that it would be possible, given the size of the Company's product lines and the budget for computer and communications, either to: (1) assign personnel to each distribution center to manage inventory on a manual, decentralized basis, or (2) continue the current practice of communicating information to a central point (Cleveland) by mail to facilitate centralized control of inventories and the automatic replenishment of DC's. A third alternative requiring considerably more provision for communication would be to communicate nightly by teletype or other means to Cleveland the inventory status of each DC. Finally, a real-time system of continuous communication and updating of central files could be implemented for a significant increase in both communication and computing costs. In any event, Company personnel would be stationed at each distribution center to accept orders and handle "inside" customer relations.

DESIGN OF INVENTORY MODEL

A review of the advantages of each of the basic philosophies of inventory control provided an opportunity to assess the approaches which could be employed at the Wonka Company.

P Model Features

A *P* (fixed order interval) model for inventory control at Wonka's distribution centers would allow the plant to ship to certain DC's each day of the week, thereby evening the work load for plant shipping personnel. For slower moving items, it would allow distribution center personnel to review a subset of all item needs each day during a cycle of perhaps a month in which all needs would be reviewed with a constant expenditure of effort. Clearly, it would facilitate shipment and vehicle scheduling for shipments from Cleveland to DC's. And it would facilitate larger, more economical, less frequent shipments.

Q Model Features

A *Q* (fixed order quantity) replenishment model theoretically would result in optimum holding and ordering costs at DC's, although it might require uneconomic shipments of various items on a given day. If adjusted to case, pallet, or vehicle quantities, the *Q*'s for various items could represent the most economic handling or shipping quantities for individual items. With shipments geared to orders triggered by calculated order points, less safety stock might be required for some items under a *Q* model.

S,s Model Features

The *S,s* (fixed order interval, fixed order quantity) model would offer some of the features of both the *P* and *Q* models. However, it would require reorder points in excess of demands during the order interval plus the order cycle for items for which stock-out penalties were high. Consequently, it could result in high safety stock levels.

Plant Inventory Control at Wonka

Machine production at the Wonka plant in Cleveland was cycled about every two weeks, or 24 times per year. The decision to include the assembly of a particular levelor model in a production cycle was prompted by the relationship of the units on hand to the number which could be expected to be ordered for DC's during the following two weeks. Standard production runs were based on EOQ calculations. Both the timing and quantity of production orders for a given SKU were influenced by: (1) the general level of demand for other items, (2) the knowledge of unusually heavy upcoming demand, and (3) the critical nature of the item. These factors were taken into consideration intuitively by the Manager of Manufacturing Planning at the Cleveland plant.

(1) **How would you categorize this model in theoretical terms?**

Distribution Center Inventory Control

In replenishing distribution center stocks, target inventories were set from predictions of maximum demand. The two targets for each item were called max and min levels, representing maximum and minimum units desired at the distribution center. Max and min levels were calculated from max and min ratios which accounted for various order-cycle time lags encountered in replenishing distribution center inventory. Six time lags were identified; they are shown in the table below, with typical values for a sample distribution center:

Type of Time Lag	Max, in Days	Min, in Days
1. Invoicing lag, reflecting difference in date of actual distribution center shipment and invoicing	5	—
2. Days to accumulate stock order in computer	12	—
3. Traffic Department order processing	3	3
4. Production of stock order at plant	6	6
5. Time in transit	5	5
6. Contingencies	5	5
Totals	36	19

Thus, assuming 20 working days a month, a max value of $36/20 = 1.8$ months and a min value of $19/20 = .95$ month would be calculated for the example distribution center. Multiplications of the predicted months' maximum demand figures by the max and min figures yielded a range in the number of units desired at each distribution center. The predicted maximum demand figure calculated in this manner (max, in months × predicted maximum demand per month) was reduced by the sum of inventories on hand, in transit, and on order on a daily basis. The remainder was then the amount to be shipped for that item if a stock order was generated on that day. These differences were summed up, and if the total weight of all such units required was equal to or greater than the shipping weight established for a warehouse (e.g., a 40,000-

pound truckload or a 60,000-pound rail carload), a stock order was prepared by the computer, listing all the products and the number of units required.

Even if the sum of the weights tabulated each day was less than the established cumulative shipping weight, a report was generated daily showing all items where the available inventories were below min target levels. This "below min" report was occasionally the basis for an LTL exception order to be shipped from the plant to a distribution center, depending upon whether the traffic personnel who monitored the figures were willing to authorize such a shipment. No clear decision rules were described for cases encountered in the "below min" reports.

Max and min values were estimated for each distribution center, basically depending on the distance between the distribution center and the plant and the method of transportation used for shipping stock orders. This could create problems if the traffic department failed to communicate a change in shipping policy. For example, in recent months, the traffic department had begun supplying some distribution centers by rail instead of truck, with an increase in transit time over that experienced with trucking methods. In several instances, excessive stock-out conditions at the distribution center had baffled the Data Processing Manager, William Granger, until he discovered almost by chance that the assumption regarding transit time used in the computer inventory model for these distribution centers was incorrect.

The rule of thumb for returning stock to the plant was that if it had been stored at a distribution center for at least a year and there had been no sales locally or at any other distribution center, it would be returned. Locally dead stock would be transshipped to another distribution center or to the customer in another distribution center's territory where there was a demand for the product. This was done only when the quantity to be transshipped amounted to 1,000 pounds or more.

Twice a year a report was issued listing dead stock by distribution center and item. It was estimated that at any one time 10% to 12% of the total inventory was dead.

(2) **Theoretically, what family of inventory models does Wonka's distribution center replenishment model belong to? (3) Do the plant and distribution center models meet the needs of each operation? (4) Why?**

DESIGN OF A FORECASTING MODEL

Wonka's Marketing Research Manager felt that his previous decision to implement a statistical model to forecast distribution center shipments to customers was justified by the results of a survey of a wide variety of forecasting techniques by several expert practitioners who concluded, "At the present time, most short-term forecasting uses only statistical methods, with little qualitative information." [1] Our experience supports this judgment, and suggests that statistical techniques with manual revisions to reflect changes in the external environment that affect short-term sales will continue to be the most effective means of obtaining forecasts of sufficient accuracy for inventory control purposes. Such techniques are easy to understand and develop. They are based on the usually valid philosophy that in the short-term future, sales will continue as they have in the short-term past. And, perhaps most important, they are economical when the number of stock-keeping unit locations (SKUL's) for which forecasts must be prepared is great.

Relevant statistical forecasting techniques include the moving average, exponential smoothing, and adaptive techniques. Each can be viewed as encompassing slightly different sets of variables which represent the means by which the forecasting model can be tuned, like a television set, to produce the best results. There is no method for optimizing the fine tuning result. As we shall see, it must be carried out through the application of common sense and a persevering attitude toward trial and error.

Moving Average

This forecast is the result of the sum of actual demands realized for an item in the most recent "x" weeks, for example, divided by "x." Sales forecasts based on two- and five-period moving averages for items 122L and 2M at the Pittsburgh distribution center are shown in Table 11–1, along with actual sales for each. (5) **Which number of periods (the tuning knob in this technique) appears to produce the most accurate results? (6) Why? (7) Calculate the forecast for each item for period 12 under both the two- and five-period moving average. Which is greater? (8) Why?**

The moving average technique requires a great deal of memory capacity, whether used in manual or computerized form. After all, if you have to hold five items of information in memory in order to calculate a five-period moving average forecast for each item held in stock at each location, the total memory requirement for the entire line may be very costly. Further, it may be desirable to add a tuning knob (variable), one which allows us to weigh recent experience more (or less) heavily than

[1] John C. Chambers, Satinder K. Mullick, and Donald D. Smith, "How to Choose the Right Forecasting Technique," *Harvard Business Review*, July–August, 1971, pp. 45–74.

less current sales experience. Exponential smoothing, really just a special case of a moving average, meets these needs.

Exponential Smoothing

Exponential smoothing updates each new forecast on the basis of only three pieces of information: the difference between the actual and forecast demand for the most recent accounting period multiplied by the weight to be applied to the difference. The result is either added to, or subtracted from, the previous forecast to produce a forecast for the next period. The weight is called the alpha factor.

Notice in Table 11–2 how the calculation of the forecast for the next period is self-contained on each line of information. Compare this with the five items of information stored from previous periods on which the five-period moving averages in Table 11–1 were calculated. (9) **In Table 11–2, which of the alpha factors used for items 122L and 2M produces the best results? (10) Why? (11) Does this suggest the possible test of further alpha factors for either of the items?** Select one and try it just as the designer of a forecasting model would be required to do. Before doing this, you might calculate the forecast for period 12 for each item using both a .1 and .2 alpha factor. **(12) Which produces the highest forecast? (13) Why?**

Moving averages have a tendency to lag actual changes in sales levels. Although the amount of this lag may be controlled to some extent by the number of weeks included in a moving average or the alpha factor used in an exponential smoothing model, it cannot be eliminated. In cases where there are systematic changes in sales levels caused by a basic upward or downward sales trend or a consistent seasonal pattern year after year, adaptive forecasting methods taking trends or seasonal factors or both into account may produce much more accurate results.

Adaptive Techniques

Adaptive forecasting models anticipate sales based on past trend or seasonal patterns. Calculations for these patterns may vary endlessly. In Table 11–3, for example, we have based a trend calculation on a comparison of sales during the most recent 13 accounting periods with those for the previous 13 accounting periods, using the ratio as the basis for estimating sales during the next 13 accounting periods. This assumes that our trend is relatively stable and will continue. For situations where trends are less stable, they could be based on year-to-year comparisons of shorter sales periods.

Item 122L			
(1) **Accounting** **Period**	**(2)** **Sales**	**(3)** **Forecast on** **Two-Period** **Moving Average**[a]	**(4)** **Deviation:** **Sales (2) −** **Forecast (3)**
9	490	470[b]	+ 20
10	580	480[b]	+100
11	570	535	+ 35
12	680	575	+105
13	740	625	+115
1	300	710	−410
2	350	520	−170
3	320	325	− 5
4	390	345	+ 45
5	550	355	+195
6	670	470	+200
7	480	610	−130
8	470	575	−105
9	500	475	+ 25
10	580	485	+ 95
11	600	540	+ 60
12	n.a.	n.a.	n.a.
Total, periods 1 through 11			1,440[c]

(5) **Mean Absolute** **Deviation (Last** **Five Periods)**	**(6)** **Forecast on** **Five-Period** **Moving Average**[d]	**(7)** **Deviation:** **Sales (2) −** **Forecast (6)**	**(8)** **Mean Absolute** **Deviation (Last** **Five Periods)**
156[b]	498[b]	− 8	135[b]
151[b]	525[b]	+ 55	117[b]
115[b]	535[b]	+ 35	73[b]
102[b]	570[b]	+110	87[b]
75	585[b]	+155	72
153	612	−312	133
167	574	−224	167
161	528	−208	202
149	474	− 84	196
165	420	+130	192
123	382	+288	187
115	456	+ 24	147
135	482	− 12	108
131	512	− 12	93
111	534	+ 46	76
83	540	+ 60	31
n.a.	n.a.	n.a.	n.a.
131[e]		1,400[c]	127[e]

n.a. = not available.

[a]Computed as follows: The forecast for period 11 = sales for periods 9 + 10 divided by 2.
[b]Calculations are based on previous results for periods not ,shown in the table.
[c]This figure represents the mean absolute deviation (MAD) for periods 1 through 11,
computed by adding figures for those periods after removing the signs.

and Five-Period Moving Averages, Pittsburgh Distribution Center

Item 2M

(1) Accounting Period	(2) Sales	(3) Forecast on Two-Period Moving Averages [a]	(4) Deviation: Sales (2) − Forecast (3)	(5) Mean Absolute Deviation (Last Five Periods)	(6) Forecast on Five-Period Moving Average [d]	(7) Deviation: Sales (2) − Forecast (6)	(8) Mean Absolute Deviation (Last Five Periods)
9	10	7[b]	+3	3.6[b]	7[b]	+3	3.2[b]
10	2	7[b]	−5	3.5[b]	8[b]	−6	3.3[b]
11	9	6	+3	3.6[b]	6[b]	+3	3.2[b]
12	8	6	+2	3.5[b]	8[b]	0	3.3[b]
13	4	9	−5	3.6	7[b]	−3	3.0
1	11	6	+5	4.0	7	+4	3.2
2	3	8	−5	4.0	7	−4	2.8
3	9	7	+2	3.8	7	+2	2.6
4	7	6	+1	3.6	7	0	2.6
5	2	8	−6	3.8	7	−5	3.0
6	11	5	+6	4.0	6	+6	3.4
7	5	7	−2	3.4	6	−2	3.0
8	13	8	+5	4.0	7	+5	3.6
9	7	9	−2	4.2	8	−2	4.0
10	7	10	−3	3.6	8	−3	3.6
11	5	7	−2	2.8	9	−2	2.8
12	n.a.	n.a.	n.a.	n.a.	n.a.	n.a.	n.a.
Total, periods 1 through 11			39[b]	3.6[e]		35[e]	3.2[c]

[d] Computed as follows: The forecast for period 1 = sales for periods 9 + 10 + 11 + 12 + 13 divided by 5.

[e] This figure represents the average of the mean absolute deviation (MAD) for periods 1 through 11.

TABLE 11-2. Sales Forecasts Based on Exponential
Warren G. Wonka Manufacturing Company,

Item 122L

(1) Accounting Period	(2) Sales	(3) Forecast with .1 Alpha Factor[a]	(4) Deviation: Sales (2) − Forecast (3)
13	740	575[b]	+165
1	300	592	−292
2	350	563	−213
3	320	542	−222
4	390	520	−130
5	550	507	+ 43
6	670	511	+159
7	480	527	− 47
8	470	522	− 52
9	500	517	− 17
10	580	515	+ 65
11	600	522	+ 78
12	n.a.	n.a.	n.a.
Total, periods 1 through 11			1,318[b]

(5) Mean Absolute Deviation (Last Five Periods)	(6) Forecast with .2 Alpha Factor[c]	(7) Deviation: Sales (2) − Forecast (6)	(8) Mean Absolute Deviation (Last Five Periods)
120[b]	610[b]	+130	130[b]
124[b]	636	−336	129[b]
136[b]	569	−219	145[b]
148[b]	525	−205	180[b]
204	484	− 94	197
180	465	+ 85	188
153	482	+188	158
120	520	− 40	122
86	512	− 42	90
63	504	− 4	72
68	503	+ 77	70
52	518	+ 82	49
n.a.	n.a.	n.a.	n.a.
120[e]		1,372[d]	125[f]

[a]Computed as follows: The forecast for period 1 = actual sales for period 13 less the forecast for period 13 multiplied by the alpha factor (.1), with this amount added to, or subtracted from, the forecast for period 13.

[b]Calculation based on previous results for periods not shown in the table.

[c]Computed as follows: The forecast for period 1 = actual sales for period 13 less the fore-

Smoothing Method, Using Alpha Factors of .1 and .2,
Pittsburgh Distribution Center

Item 2M			
(1)	(2)	(3)	(4)
Accounting Period	Sales	Forecast with .1 Alpha Factor[a]	Deviation: Sales (2) − Forecast (3)
13	4	7.0[b]	−3.0
1	11	6.7	+4.3
2	3	7.1	−4.1
3	9	6.7	+2.3
4	7	6.9	+ .1
5	2	6.9	−4.9
6	11	6.4	+4.6
7	5	6.9	−1.9
8	13	6.7	+6.3
9	7	7.3	− .3
10	7	7.3	− .3
11	5	7.3	−2.3
12	n.a.	n.a.	n.a.
Total, periods 1 through 11			31.4[d]

(5)	(6)	(7)	(8)
Mean Absolute Deviation (Last Five Periods)	Forecast with .2 Alpha Factors[c]	Deviation: Sales (2) − Forecast (6)	Mean Absolute Deviation (Last Five Periods)
2.7[b]	7.2[b]	−3.2	3.9[b]
2.7[b]	6.6	+4.4	3.9[b]
2.3[b]	7.5	−4.5	3.9[b]
2.7[b]	6.6	+2.4	3.5[b]
2.7	7.1	− .1	2.7
3.1	7.1	−5.1	3.1
3.2	6.1	+4.9	3.2
2.7	7.1	−2.1	2.7
3.6	6.7	+6.3	3.5
3.6	8.0	−1.0	3.7
2.7	7.8	−1.8	3.0
2.2	7.4	−2.4	2.5
n.a.	n.a.	n.a.	n.a.
2.9[e]		35.0[d]	3.2[e]

cast for period 13 multiplied by the alpha factor (.2), with this amount added to, or subtracted from, the forecast for period 13.

[d]Figures in this column were added after the sign was removed.

[e]This figure represents the mean absolute deviation (MAD) for periods 1 through 11, computed by adding figures for these periods and dividing the result by 11.

TABLE 11-3. Sales Forecast Based on Trend Seasonal Forecast,

Item 122L			
(1)	(2)	(3)	(4) Sales Last 13 Periods Compared to Sales Previous 13 Periods[a]
Accounting Period	Sales	Sales for Last 13 Periods	
13	740	6,130	1.11
1	300	6,170	1.10
2	350	6,220	1.11
3	320	6,270	1.12
4	390	6,240	1.10
5	550	6,340	1.12
6	670	6,380	1.11
7	480	6,420	1.10
8	470	6,470	1.11
9	500	6,520	1.11
10	580	6,570	1.11
11	600	6,630	1.12
12	n.a.	n.a.	n.a.

(5) Period Sales, as Proportion of Annual Sales, Last Three Years[b]	(6) Forecast on Trend Seasonal Basis[c]	(7) Deviation: Sales (2) − Forecast (6)	(8) Mean Absolute Deviation (Last Five Periods)
.11	715	+25	41.0[f]
.05	340	−40	41.0[f]
.06	407	−57	42.6[f]
.05	348	−28	47.6[f]
.07	475	−85	47.0
.08	559	− 9	43.8
.09	633	+37	43.2
.07	491	−11	34.0
.07	499	−29	34.2
.08	575	−75	32.2
.08	579	+ 1	30.6
.09	662	−62	35.6
.10	n.a.	n.a.	n.a.
Totals 1.00		434[d]	39.5[e]

[a]This represents the trend measurement used in this particular model.

[b]Calculated by adding the sales for a given accounting period for each of the past three years and calculating the proportion of total sales for the three-year time span that this represents, thus accounting for the seasonal factor.

[c]Calculated for period 1, for example, by multiplying the sales for the last 13 periods

Warren G. Wonka Manufacturing Company, Pittsburgh Distribution Center

Item 2M

(1) Accounting Period	(2) Sales	(3) Sales for Last 13 Periods	(4) Sales Last 13 Periods Compared to Sales Previous 13 Periods[a]
13	4	87	1.05
1	11	92	1.06
2	3	85	1.05
3	9	86	1.06
4	7	88	1.05
5	2	86	1.07
6	11	93	1.07
7	5	90	1.06
8	13	97	1.07
9	7	96	1.06
10	7	94	1.06
11	5	92	1.05
12	n.a.	n.a.	n.a.

(5) Period Sales, as Proportion of Annual Sales, Last Three Years[b]	(6) Forecast on Trend Seasonal Basis[c]	(7) Deviation: Sales (2) − Forecast (6)	(8) Mean Absolute Deviation (Last Five Periods)
.07	6	−2	2.4[f]
.09	8	+3	2.2[f]
.06	6	−3	1.8[f]
.08	7	+2	2.2[f]
.08	7	0	2.0
.08	7	−5	2.6
.06	6	+5	3.0
.10	10	−5	3.4
.09	9	+4	3.8
.08	8	−1	4.0
.07	7	0	3.0
.07	7	−2	2.4
.07	n.a.	n.a.	n.a.
Total 1.00		30[d]	2.8[e]

[column (3)] at period 13 by the trend measurement for period 13 [column (4)] by the seasonal factor for period 1 [column (5)].

[d]This figure is the sum of deviations, without regard to sign, for periods 1 through 11.

[e]This figure represents the mean absolute deviation (MAD) for periods 1 through 11, computed by adding figures for those periods and dividing the result by 11.

[f]Calculation based on previous results for periods not shown in table.

We have combined trend and seasonal factors in Table 11–3 by projecting sales for future accounting periods on the basis of the preparation of the sales achieved during that accounting period during the previous three years. Compare results for items 122L and 2M achieved by all of the methods shown in Tables 11–1, 11–2, and 11–3. (14) **How do the results achieved by the trend seasonal (adaptive) technique compare with others? (15) Why?**

Adaptive techniques require larger computer storage and greater computational time, in most cases, than moving average methods of statistical forecasting. In a wide product line with SKUL sales affected by a number of factors, it may be most economical to use adaptive techniques only for those items for which they produce the greatest improvement over other techniques. (16) **With this in mind, what would you recommend concerning forecasting techniques for items 122L and 2M?**

Trend smoothing and curve fitting represent additional extensions of adaptive techniques. In our example, they would be applied by first "de-seasonalizing" sales information by accounting period by multiplying sales for recent accounting periods by the respective seasonal factor for each. Straight lines or curves producing the best fit between the resulting "regression line" and actual sales points could be calculated and extended into the future. We accomplished the same result in Table 11–3 by comparing sales on an annual (13 accounting periods) basis.

Forecasting for DC Replenishment at Wonka

From the records of historical sales by product, item, and warehouse, the computer was able to forecast the expected demand for each SKUL maintained by the Wonka Company. This was done using an exponential smoothing equation, whereby correction was made gradually for changes in levels of demand according to the following formula:

$$\text{Forecast} = \text{Old Average} + \text{Alpha (Newest Demand} - \text{Old Average)}$$
$$= \text{Old Average } (1 - \text{Alpha}) + \text{Newest Demand (Alpha)}$$

Under this formula, Alpha could assume any value between 0 and 1. Each forecast period used an old average which was the previous period's forecast. The newest demand was the most recent actual demand figure. In the Wonka system, an Alpha equal to 0.15 was established for all products and territories, although the system had provision for the manual insertion of any value for any item.

A correction was then added to the forecast figure for each item to provide safety stocks to account for variations in demand. This correction was defined as some percentage of the mean absolute error or deviation (MAD) (expressed in units for each item) of the forecast. MAD was calculated in the following manner:

Old Forecast − Newest Demand = Absolute Error
Old Mean Absolute Error
  (1.0 − 2 Alpha) +
  (2 Alpha × Current Error)   = New Mean Absolute Error or MAD
         Safety Stock = Service Percentage × MAD

The service percentage used in all cases was 0.98. In this way a predicted maximum demand was calculated as the forecast demand plus 98% of the value for the mean absolute deviation for each item at each DC during the forecast period. A new forecast was prepared for each DC every 30 days; the periods were staggered (forecasts for five of the DC's every 10 days) to balance the production load on the Cleveland plant.

An example showing the actual calculations resulting from Wonka's forecasting method is presented in Table 11–4. (17) **What changes, if any, would you make in Wonka's forecasting model? (18) Why?**

Need for Adaptation to Inventory Program

Forecasting is a "science" that is based on heuristic, or trial and error, approaches to model building. This produces the great danger that we might become involved in an endless search for the best method for each specific SKUL under various sets of circumstances. At the other extreme, many firms treat all products and markets alike for statistical forecasting purposes. In order to fit forecasting policy and specific models to the needs of both the product line and the inventory model with which they are to be employed, it is necessary to have some feeling for the impact of forecasts on inventory management results.

Forecasting Models and Inventory Management Results

The actual level of demand forecast for a future period may affect the economic order quantity used to replenish an item. The accuracy of the forecasting method will influence the amount of safety stock required to support a specified level of SKUL availability (customer service). (19) **Which of these do you think is more important from a total cost standpoint? (20) Are these considerations more important in connection**

TABLE 11–4. Example of Forecasting Calculations Under Current Procedures Employed at the Warren G. Wonka Manufacturing Company

Forecast Procedure	Time Periods				
	1	2	3	4	5
a. Actual demand (in units of demand per time period)	30	35	25	20	10
Computation:					
b. Old forecast of base demands (in units of demand per time period)	20	21.5	23.5	23.7	23.1
+					
[c. Alpha	.15	.15	.15	.15	.15
×					
d. New absolute error (a − b)]	10	13.5	1.5	−3.7	−13.1
=					
e. New forecast of base demand	21.5	23.5	23.7	23.1	21.1
[f. Old mean absolute deviation (from previous period)	6	7.2	9.0	6.8	3.7
×					
g. 1.0 − 2 Alpha]	.70	.70	.70	.70	.70
+					
[h. New absolute error (a − b)	10	13.5	1.5	−3.7	−13.1
×					
i. 2 Alpha]	.30	.30	.30	.30	.30
j. New mean absolute deviation (MAD)	7.2	9.0	6.8	3.7	−1.3
×					
k. Service percentage (arbitrarily set)	.98	.98	.98	.98	Not available for negative values
=					
l. Safety stock	7.1	8.8	6.7	3.6	—
m. New forecast of base demand + safety stock (e + l)	28.6	32.3	30.4	26.7	21.1

with the use of P or Q inventory models? (21) Why? We will see a bit later how sensitive total cost results are to various kinds of inaccuracies in forecasts and other data inputs for inventory management purposes.

Clearly, this is an area in which simulation software provided by computer manufacturers or prepared "in-house" will aid in the analysis of interrelationships between forecasting and inventory models in specific situations.

DESIGN OF PROGRAM FOR OTHER INVENTORY
MODEL INPUTS

In addition to demand estimates, we have seen that inventory models require estimates of order placement or set-up costs, stock-out costs, inventory carrying costs, the unit costs of the product items under management, and relevant lead times for inventory replenishment. This is where the fun starts, for there are many ways, many of them highly subjective and all justifiable on some basis, for measuring these inputs.

Order Placement or Set-Up Costs

We encounter order placement costs at the distribution center and in the purchasing function. The equivalent type of cost in the production process is the cost of setting up a machine or a production line to produce an item to fill an order or to replenish inventories at the plant. Still another type of cost, that of filling customer orders as they are received at a distribution center or a plant warehouse, does not become relevant until we discuss stock-out costs.

Order placement costs in the replenishment of a distribution center from a plant warehouse may include wages and fringe benefits for time actually spent in order preparation and inventory review, the cost of communicating the order, and wages and fringe benefits in the selection and packing of the order at the plant warehouse.

Purchase orders again involve costs of inventory review and order preparation and communication. Other costs associated with the order, however, typically are incurred by the supplier.

Some companies, particularly where orders containing few line items are the rule, collect all order-processing costs and divide them by the total number of orders placed, to obtain a full average cost per order. Others approach the problem by estimating the cost to prepare standard order information which has to be entered regardless of line item composition, multiply this by the number of orders processed, then allocate the remaining costs to the number of line items entered on all orders. This approach produces a fixed cost per order and a variable cost by line item.

At Wonka, time measurements produced an estimate of about $10 per order in costs to assemble header information in preparation for the entry of specific line items at a typical distribution center. Total costs allocated to the ordering of machine inventories at the Pittsburgh warehouse were $850 per year. Given a total fixed cost of $170 ($10 × 17 orders per year), it was estimated that variable costs totalled $680. An average order from the Pittsburgh distribution center contained twenty line items, making a total of 340 line items for the year, or about $2 in incremental costs per line item.

While some debate developed about whether the full cost of $50 per order ($10 in fixed costs + $40 in variable costs) or the incremental cost of $2 per line item should be used in the inventory control model, it was decided that fixed costs would be incurred regardless of the number or size of line items and that the line-item cost was most relevant to the cost of that item. Those arguing for the total cost figure maintained that the use of incremental costs would produce very small economic order quantities for certain items. It was agreed that if this resulted in the repeated shipment of "onesies and twosies" from the plant to a distribution center, a minimum line-item order size would be instituted, regardless of the computed economic order quantity.

Machine or production line set-up costs may register over a wide range of values, depending on the sequence in which products are made, the relative complexity of the machine tools required for the production process, the need for time-consuming machine shutdowns for change-over, and the degree to which capacity (restricted by such shutdowns) is needed. Industrial engineers called in to help provide estimates at Wonka recommended that an average cost of $100 per set-up might be used.

Purchase order placement costs, composed of an allocated portion of the labor, communication, and overhead expenses of the purchasing department, were divided between contract purchases, involving periodic standard shipments, and other orders, requiring preparation each time an order was placed. Only the latter were relevant for inventory control over raw materials.

Contract purchases involved a large negotiating expense per contract. Once agreed to, however, shipments under contract purchases were received periodically without the placement of an order. The only incremental expense involved in contract purchasing was a review of stocks to determine whether the shipping schedule or quantities should be changed. Further, none of these expenses influenced the quantity for which the contract was written.

Remaining costs allocated to non-contract purchases produced a total cost per order of about $60. Because purchase orders rarely involved more than one or two line items, no attempt was made to establish an incremental cost per line item.

Stock-Out Costs

"Hard" stock-out costs which are most easy to measure include the costs of duplicate order processing, extra communication (often at the company's expense), and LTL transportation costs where a routine order might have moved at a truckload rate. It is not unusual to find these costs amounting to three times those for the processing of a routine order involving no stock-out items.

The "soft" costs almost never considered and nearly impossible to measure are those of lost selling time (if sales representatives, as the result of a stock-out, must "hand-hold" to maintain customer goodwill) and foregone profit, or more appropriately, contribution on lost sales. In many situations, the "soft" costs exceed the "hard" ones, particularly for products for which substitutes are readily available to the buyer.

The problem of estimating "soft" stock-out costs is further complicated when the stock-out occurs at a stage once or twice removed from the ultimate sales point. For example, what is the impact on ultimate sales of the inability of Wonka's plant warehouse to ship an item ordered by the Pittsburgh distribution center (and to remain unable to ship it for varying lengths of time)?

Lost sales, too, are a function of consumer buying behavior. There is some evidence, for example, that consumers are more willing to substitute a popular model in one company's product line for that in another's than they are to do so for less popular or non-standard items. They have higher expectations regarding product availability for standard or popular items as opposed to non-standard or less common items (slow movers). This suggests that the cost of lost sales resulting from the substitutability of competing items varies by item.

An ingenious way has been suggested to estimate costs of lost sales by attaching probabilities and costs to: (1) the loss of an item sale, (2) the loss of an order, and (3) the loss of a customer as a result of the inability to supply an item when ordered.[2] This can produce a considerably higher cost than other methods. (22) **When can it be most easily justified?**

"Soft" stock-out costs often are put aside for inventory management purposes, particularly at distribution centers. Nevertheless, Wonka's marketing orientation led to the inclusion of a "lost sales factor" of the company's average profit on 50% of the items demanded by customers but not supplied by the distribution center because of a stock-out. (23) **What do you think of this?**

Stock-out costs in the procurement process vary even more drastically. Compare, for example, the cost of being out-of-stock on a component needed in the production process as opposed to floor cleaning compound. Often, the cost of a stock-out for a production component is so great that it precludes any stock-outs.

[2] Donald J. Bowersox, Edward W. Smykay, and Bernard J. LaLonde, *Physical Distribution Management*, Rev. Ed. (New York: The Macmillan Co., 1968), p. 212.

Inventory Carrying Costs

Major inventory carrying cost categories are those associated with (1) the investment in inventory, (2) warehousing, and (3) spoilage or obsolescence.

Many executives are surprised by the high cost of carrying inventory. The most commonly quoted figure for these costs is approximately 25% of the average value of inventory on hand over the course of a year. Cost figures vary from firm to firm and from product to product, but it would not be surprising to find current inventory carrying costs in a company falling within the following ranges: costs associated with the investment in inventory, 8% to 20% of the average value of inventory on hand over a year's time; warehousing, 3¾% to 9% (3% to 6% for storage, ½% to 2% for property taxes, and ¼% to 1% for insurance); and spoilage or obsolescence, 0% to 30%.

An informal poll conducted in 1959 led Holbrook to report:

> Thus far, I have found more than a third of the individuals polled did not know what their company's average inventory carrying cost is; of them, many observed that their companies simply do not use such a figure. . . . Among those who report that they do use such a figure in their work, the answers range from 12 percent to 35 percent.[3]

The implementation of computer-oriented inventory control programs in many firms, large and small, probably has increased knowledge and awareness of inventory carrying costs a great deal in the intervening years.

Investment in Inventory. The debate which developed at the Wonka Company illustrates several bases for assessing the cost of investment. Perhaps the simplest and easiest to document is the use of a cost comparable to the prime lending rate, a cost which in recent years has ranged from 6% to 8½%. It was this cost factor that was advocated by the head of Wonka's Accounting Department. The Vice President, Finance, fully aware that the effective cost of money to the Company was made up of a weighted average of the cost of both debt and equity, felt that the cost should be represented by a figure twice the prime interest rate.

At this point, Mr. Wonka himself entered the debate by asserting that money invested in inventory should earn at the same rate as the return on the stockholders' investment. When informed by the Vice President, Finance, that this was a relatively low 16%, Mr. Wonka replied, "I had

[3] John B. Holbrook, "A Simple Tabular Method for Determining Economic Order Quantities," in *Managing the Materials Function* (New York: American Management Association, 1959), AMA Management Report No. 35, pp. 65–66.

in mind the figure representing what it should be, not what it is. It should be our cut-off point for capital investment, 30% before taxes."

(24) **How would you resolve this?** Remember, inventory costs represent just one more knob on the control panel.

In cases where a concerted attempt is being made to reduce inventory levels by means of this control, there may be no relationship between real and assessed costs. At a time several years ago when plant managers in the U.S.S.R. were thought to be hoarding raw materials in order to meet production quotas, several Russian economists were reported to have recommended that: (1) the managers be evaluated on a cost basis as well as on their ability to meet quotas and (2) they be assessed a cost penalty of 50% of the average annual value of raw materials on hand at each plant.

At Wonka, the Executive Committee settled on a temporary inventory carrying cost rate of 14%, a figure close to twice the prime rate and the company's earnings rate before taxes on all assets available to it. This decision was based in part on the assurance of the Vice President, Finance, that funds currently were not in short supply and that the competition for available funds for capital spending projects was not great. The Committee agreed to review the situation every six months.

Warehousing. Relevant warehousing costs associated with inventory holding include storage (facility), property tax, and insurance costs, not the costs of handling product into and out of a warehouse facility. Each of the cost elements varies by location.

Where owned or leased facilities are used and company personnel constitute the warehouse work force (particularly office and supervisory personnel more likely to be charged to storage), costs may have to be imputed from company records. Further, unless capacity limits are being tested, the incremental cost of storing extra inventory may be very little. When capacity limits are reached, the incremental cost then becomes very high.

In cases where public warehousing is used, bills paid for storage services provide the basis for documenting storage costs. Great differences in such charges are assessed by public warehousemen from one city to the next and even within the same city.

At Wonka, storage, property tax, and insurance costs were accumulated and prorated to the average amount of inventory on hand during the year at all warehouses. They amounted to 4%, 1.5%, and .5% of the average value of inventory on hand, respectively.

Spoilage or Obsolescence. Costs of spoilage or obsolescence are elusive and vary greatly with the type of product under consideration.

Although spoilage is not difficult to identify, when is a product obsolete? When it has been superseded by another item in the product line, even though it continues to sell in reduced quantities, or when it has not been sold from a distribution center's inventory for some time, even though it continues to be sold in other distribution center territories? Most firms identify obsolete merchandise, or perhaps more accurately "dead stock," in terms of the frequency of orders for such items. For example, an item for which no order has been received at a distribution center for perhaps 90 days is considered in some companies to be dead and a candidate for reallocation to other distribution centers that are shipping it.

Thus, costs of spoilage or obsolescence may range from those associated with the total loss of the product (as with perishable produce) to the reworking of product (as with powdered soap products) to the reallocation of product from one distribution point to another. In the case of total loss, it is not only the product but the associated transportation and storage "invested" in the product which is lost. In a rework situation, costs incurred are those of extra transportation (two extra shipments, back to and away from the plant), potential loss in rework, the cost of rework itself, extra storage, and possibly customer badwill. Reallocation generally allows "dead stock" to be sold at full price, but requires above-normal transportation and storage expense. One large firm manufacturing a wide line of products assigns obsolescence factors ranging from 0% to 30% of the average value of inventory over the year to its product families.

The total costs of damaged stock and the inter-warehouse transfer of units held in stock for some time at Wonka's distribution centers constituted 10% of the value of product on hand during the preceding year, the figure for obsolescence factored into DC inventory costs. Half of this amount was charged to inventories held in Cleveland. (25) **Would you agree with the method of estimating these costs at Wonka?** (26) **Why?**

Inventory models, such as those we considered in Chapter 10, assume a single factor for inventory carrying costs (r), which varies with the value, per unit, of the product under consideration. We have seen that while some of Wonka's inventory carrying costs included in r do vary with the value of the product, warehousing costs varying with the location of the inventory constitute 20% of r while spoilage or obsolescence costs largely related to characteristics of the product other than its value amount to 33% of the total for r.

This argues, where possible, for the assessment of inventory carrying cost factors on a location-by-location and product-by-product basis to minimize penalties resulting from the application of model norms to products deviating from the norms assumed in the model. Although such specific SKUL analysis is becoming more feasible economically for companies which have acquired third-generation computers, Wonka's computing capacity did not permit the economical accomplishment of such detailed analysis.

Inventoried Cost Per Unit of Product. The inventoried cost per unit for products purchased from outside vendors includes the purchase price and the cost of inbound transportation. For products produced within the company, standard manufacturing costs often are used to establish the inventoried value of finished products. To this must be added the cost of transportation to subsequent distribution points where other inventories may be located. Thus, item values for a given product at distribution centers will be greater than those at plants.

It would seem, then, that we have found at least one inventory model input about which there is little debate. But wait. At least one leading European manufacturer takes as its product value for control at its distribution centers only the incremental value added to the product by moving it from a plant warehouse to a distribution center. (27) **What is the rationale for this? (28) What effect would it have on order quantities?**

Order-Interval and Order-Cycle Times

Order intervals, in manufacturing operations where P models are used, depend upon the scheduled frequency of manufacture. At a distribution center, they are more sensitive to product-line demand, varying inversely with it. A heavy sales season each year, for example, may permit the order interval at a distribution center to be reduced by the increased frequency with which the distribution center assembles orders sufficient for a carload or truckload shipment from the plant.

Factors influencing order-cycle times were discussed in Chapter 8. Of interest to us here is the fact that cycle times exhibit more severe random variations than order intervals, and often exhibit trends only over long periods of time. Of course, they will vary to a degree with the distance between distribution center and plant and the mode of transportation used.

As a result, order-interval times can be estimated periodically by measuring only a small number of present order intervals at each facility at which stock is replenished. Order-cycle times, however, may require estimates based on larger samples of actual experiences at each replenishment point and two sets of conditions: one imposed when the replenishment procedure is dependent on production and another when there is a buffer or back-up stock from which to draw at a plant warehouse.

As we have seen, order intervals varied from one to three weeks at Wonka's distribution centers. Order-cycle times, on the other hand, ranged from four days for items held in stock at the plant up to four weeks for items for which replenishment had to be obtained directly from production.

Testing the Sensitivity of Results to Model Inputs

The difficulty of obtaining some types of inventory model inputs, and the wealth of equally defensible bases for estimating others, may seem discouraging. One encouraging note, however, is that the impact of even large variations in most inputs is relatively small, both in terms of resulting inventory carrying and ordering costs, and in terms of the customer service variations caused by the failure to identify inputs accurately. This suggests that the relative importance of the accuracy of each input be tested so that management can concentrate on establishing and updating the one or two inputs that are found most critical.

For illustrative purposes, assume that the conditions existing in the example shown for item 5M in Table 10–5 (page 325) are true conditions. However, Wonka Company analysts fail to assess various demand and cost inputs accurately. Information in Table 11–5 indicates the consequences, in terms of excess inventory or added stock-out conditions, of various potential differences between assumed and actual experience.

Situations 3, 4, 5, and 6 in Table 11–6 show what would happen if the variation in order-cycle and order-interval times was underestimated by 50%, if the inventory carrying cost factor was underestimated by 50%, if the stock-out cost penalty was underestimated by 50%, and if the order cost was overestimated by 50%, respectively. Variations in total costs from the optimum resulting from these inaccurate inputs range from 0% to about 13%.

In contrast to this low level of sensitivity, inaccurate forecasts of demand under a fixed order interval system produce rather large cost variances. (29) **Does this seem logical to you?** (30) **Why?**

In the example cited, if demand were underestimated by 50%, both in terms of its level and variation, the resulting low level of inventory carrying cost would be offset several times by the large number of sales lost because of stock-out conditions. The resulting total cost would be more than twice that realized under an accurate forecast. In contrast, if demand were overestimated by 50%, as in situation 2 in Table 11–5, we would incur almost no stock-outs but would be penalized in terms of excessive inventory carrying costs. However, notice that, within the range of inaccurate demand inputs and cost inputs we have considered

TABLE 11-5. Sensitivity of Inventory Management Costs to Differences Between Expected and Actual Operating Conditions, Using a Fixed Order Interval Inventory Model, Item 5M, Warren G. Wonka Manufacturing Company[a]

Anticipated Experience	Actual Experience	Stock-out Cost	Carrying Cost	Total Cost	Deviation from Total Costs Resulting from Accurate Prediction of Actual Experience[b]		
					Stock-out Cost	Carrying Cost	Total Cost
1. Demand = 2 units/wk. = .33 unit/day	Demand = 4 units/wk. = .67 unit/day	$3,316	$ 567	$3,883	+$3,074	−$ 889	+$2,185
2. Demand = 6 units/wk. = 1 unit/day	Demand = 4 units/wk. = .67 unit/day	0	3,346	3,346	−242	+1,890	+1,648
3. Order interval + order cycle = 20 days, σ = .355 day	Order interval + order cycle = 20 days, σ = .709 day	434	1,267	1,698	+192	−189	+3
4. Inventory carry cost factor = .15	Inventory carry cost factor = .30	80	1,834	1,914	−162	+378	+216
5. Stock-out cost penalty = $27.50/unit	Stock-out cost penalty = $55.00/unit	434	1,267	1,701	+192	−189	+3
6. Order cost = $3.00	Order cost = $2.00	242	1,456	1,698	0[c]	0[c]	0[c]

[a] As computed by means of the model discussed on pp. 320 through 324.

[b] Total costs resulting from the accurate prediction of actual experience are shown in Table 10-5 as $1,698, made up of $242 in stock-out costs and $1,456 in inventory carrying costs.

[c] Because the number of orders is imposed by external factors in this case, no cost deviations result from an inaccurate assessment of ordering costs.

TABLE 11-6. The Inventory "Whip-Saw" Effect in a Channel of Distribution

Channel Member	No. of Companies[a]	Period Demand (Units)	Ending Inventory (Units)	Minimum Value (Units)[b]	Maximum Value (Units)[b]	Order Quantity (Units)[c]	Change in Demand from Last Period	Change in Order Quantity from Last Period
				Period 1				
Retailers	9	10	10	10	20	10	0%	0%
Wholesalers	3	30	30	30	60	30	0%	0%
Manufacturer	1	90	90	90	180	90	0%	0%
				Period 2				
Retailers	9	11	9	11	22	13	+10%	+30%
Wholesalers	3	39	21	39	78	57	+30%	+90%
Manufacturer	1	171	9	171	342	333	+90%	+270%
				Period 3				
Retailers	9	11	11	11	22	11	0%	-15%
Wholesalers	3	33	45	33	66	21	-15%	-63%
Manufacturer	1	63	279	63	189	0	-63%	-100%

[a]All companies use a fixed order interval, min–max inventory model and place orders at the end of each period.

[b]Adjusted on the basis of each demand period to reflect new period demands, with min value equal to one period's demand (including order-cycle coverage and safety stock) and max value equal to two periods of demand (including order-cycle coverage and safety stock).

[c]Order-cycle time equals approximately one-half period.

here, overestimating demand produces less severe penalties than underestimating demand, in this case a total cost about double that of the optimal result. (31) Why is this the case? (32) Would it apply in all inventory control situations? (33) Why?

Potentially severe penalties from inaccurate demand inputs are a characteristic of fixed order interval inventory models, and perhaps explain the emphasis which has been placed on demand forecasting as opposed to efforts to estimate other cost inputs more accurately. Because the magnitude of penalties due to inaccurate demand inputs is caused mainly by the long time period for which inventory coverage must be provided (an order cycle and an order interval), they potentially are much less severe with the use of a fixed order quantity model in which demand must be covered only for the length of the order cycle.

Further, Brown has demonstrated in a general case that when sales are overestimated by 100% in an EOQ (Q) model, the resulting EOQ is about 40% greater than it should be. But when inventory carrying cost increases are offset by reduced ordering costs, the total annual costs increase by only 6% over the total obtained by using accurate demand inputs.[4]

The relative insensitivity of results to inputs which we have measured by example should not destroy our perspective on inventory control models. Remember, we are comparing results obtained by the use of optimum and non-optimum inputs within the framework of a commonly accepted inventory model.

Because of the relative insensitivity of results to inputs other than demand forecasts, particularly in a range of values around those producing an optimum, EOQ's, order points, and order intervals may be adjusted to reflect opportunities for saving costs which are external to most inventory control models. This suggests that we consider the place of the inventory control model in the overall logistics system, and select control models and elements which are compatible with the overall makeup and mission of the logistics system.

ESTABLISHMENT OF INVENTORY CONTINGENCY PROCEDURES

Inventory theory is not very helpful when it comes to dealing with the question of what to do when a stock-out occurs or is imminent at a distribution center. The assumption is often made that a replenishment order can be expedited from a plant warehouse. When that source is exhausted, under what conditions do we (to the horror of the plant manager) reschedule the production process, wait for the plant to produce

---

[4] Robert G. Brown, *Decision Rules for Inventory Management* (New York: Holt, Rinehart and Winston, 1967), p. 16.

our order according to its previously set schedule (to the horror of the distribution center manager), or replenish the stock-out from another distribution center (to the horror of the traffic manager)? The task is the unpleasant one of determining the least of various possible evils.

This problem borders on those of inventory location strategy and production planning, which we will take up later. However, it requires that procedures be established for dealing with routine contingencies.

Our discussion up to this point has assumed an orderly, if uncertain, inventory management pattern. A number of questions arise when a stock-out is imminent or actually occurs. Among the more important are: How do we anticipate a possible stock-out condition? If a stock-out occurs in spite of our efforts, how do we determine the need for expediting? The source (plant or another distribution warehouse) from which the shipment should be made? And if stock-outs are likely, or do, occur, at more than one distribution point, how do we establish priorities for meeting inventory needs at one or the other or both? How do we allocate available stocks to the needy distribution points? Conversely, how do we determine that one distribution point has too much stock in a given SKU and can be regarded as a source for other distribution centers in the system for that SKU?

Anticipation of Possible Stock-Out Conditions

As we have seen, the amount of goods on hand and on order, when compared with the rate of customer demand and the relative speed and dependability with which replenishment orders can be filled, determines the likelihood of a stock-out condition as well as the need to initiate a replenishment order.

In many companies, the speed with which replenishment orders from a distribution center can be filled from a plant depends on whether the item is held in stock in sufficient quantities to accommodate the order (creating a distribution of short replenishment cycle times) or whether an order for the replenishment quantity (or more) has to be placed on the plant (creating long replenishment cycle times). The situation can produce a replenishment cycle experience of the sort shown in Fig. 11–2. One alternative for dealing with the problem is to maintain reorder points, and therefore safety stocks, at distribution centers sufficiently high to accommodate possible stock-out conditions at the plant. A more acceptable alternative for companies with sufficient computing capacity is to project distribution center replenishment orders for the period ending with the next scheduled production output of the item to determine those

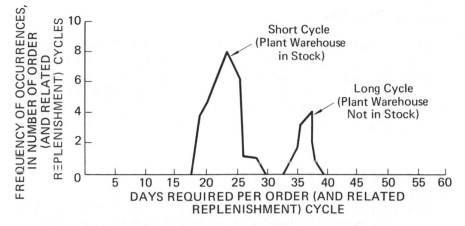

Fig. 11–2. Distribution of order (and related replenishment) cycle times for a sample of orders for an SKU placed on a plant warehouse by distribution centers, showing the performance pattern created by in-stock and stock-out conditions at the plant warehouse.

items that warrant rescheduling in the production process or expedited shipment once production occurs. This leads to the question of expediting plant output.

Determination of Need for Expediting

The need for expediting may be influenced by the relative popularity of the item for which a stock-out is likely, the cost of providing expedited as opposed to typical service, and the possible penalties of not providing expedited service. The complexities of these considerations require some simplification. For example, in a company where special emphasis is placed on the ability to fill orders at distribution centers, the projected sales volume for each SKUL might be translated into order entries, with a cost assigned to the failure to fill an order entry. The total cost of expected unfilled order entries (stock on hand plus due-in less promised-out, compared to demand during the expected replenishment cycle) could be computed for SKUL's for which stock had fallen below an absolute minimum number of days of demand. Where this cost might be reduced by more than the cost of expedited shipment, such shipment could be accomplished from either a plant or another DC. In cases where the sum of such costs for an SKU at all DC's exceeded the cost of rescheduling production, the rescheduling could be implemented.

Sourcing Decisions

Before rescheduling production, however, it may be desirable to compare the economics of the decision to reschedule with one which might avert rescheduling by making the replenishment shipment from another distribution center. This might be considered in cases where the second distribution center might have the desired EOQ in its "excess" stock. Excess can be determined in a variety of ways, but in many companies it may represent anything in excess of the amount that might be sold in the next six months at the current rate of sale. In a well-controlled inventory program, excess stocks typically occur only in cases where expected demand drops rapidly or is never realized.

Where excess stocks exist, the comparative economics of having them "cross-hauled" to another distribution center will include a comparison of small-shipment cross-hauling costs less the reduction in stock-out costs, as opposed to the costs of shipment to the plant warehouse for subsequent reshipment in a larger sized shipment to the first distribution center less the reduction in stock-out costs from that action. Both of these alternatives then would have to be compared with the economics of delaying shipment until the product becomes available at the plant. This latter alternative would produce transportation cost savings resulting from the avoidance of having to replenish "excess" stocks after they are shipped from one distribution center to another while incurring higher expected stock-out costs.

Allocation of Stocks Between Needy Distribution Points

It can be shown mathematically that under conditions where the quantity on hand at the plant warehouse, for example, is not sufficient to meet distribution center orders or potential needs before the next plant output, the least-cost approach to the problem is to allocate the product in such a manner that all distribution centers have their stocks brought up to roughly the same levels, stated in terms of weeks of demand. This computation has been made, however, under conditions where no additional shipments are assumed to be needed as a result of the decision. Further, it assumes a constant estimated cost per stock-out. Under circumstances where customers will settle for nothing less than their full order, this may become a determining factor in the final decision.

These are indicative of the types of contingency procedures which are useful in a fully developed inventory management program. (34) **Does it appear to you that contingency procedures in general are easier to administer under centralized or decentralized inventory management programs?** (35) **Why?**

At the Wonka Company, those assigned the responsibility for inventories at DC's had the authority to make sourcing decisions. This created a number of problems:

1. It sometimes required contact with several other distribution centers before one was found with adequate "surplus" stocks.
2. Contacts were made with "buddy" distribution center managers rather than those whose replenishment shipment would produce the lowest transportation cost.
3. In the absence of any definition of what "surplus" stock was, distribution center managers would help each other out, then find out that they had shorted themselves on the very items crosshauled between distribution centers.

(36) **Knowing what you do about the Company, what would you suggest as possible methods of dealing with these problems?**

DESIGN OF REMAINING PROGRAM ELEMENTS

The remaining elements of an inventory management program include the computational device, the update cycle, and the program review procedures.

The Computational Device

Basically, the choice of computation devices these days can be described in terms of the proportion of the task committed to machine (the computer) or man. The most effective systems today are designed to capitalize on the advantages of each.

The computer, of course, offers the basic advantages of low-cost, accurate handling of complex computations. Where model inputs, such as forecasts of demand, must be updated frequently and the size of the product line is large, the computer may be the only way to implement the use of a comprehensive inventory model. Complex inventory contingency procedures, considered earlier, may also suggest the use of the computer. Finally, it offers the advantage of frequent, low-cost review of all of the inventory records.

In contrast, manual inventory systems may work well if it is important to update inventory records at the time of the transaction. Under a computer-oriented system, this is possible only if the computer, or some portion of it, is dedicated to the system to provide a "real-time" update capability (changing records as the transactions occur). Dedicating computer capacity, up to now, has been an expensive proposition. Further, manual systems are useful in situations where demand is so erratic that a computer-driven model cannot anticipate demand sufficiently well to be effective. This is particularly true for newly introduced products with no demand history or for products which fall seasonally into the "dead stock" category, but for which seasonal demand remains. In several companies, items stocked only at one warehouse, essentially for the convenience of one or a few customers, are managed manually by the personnel at that warehouse who may be in closer contact with the customer and more sensitive to his ordering intentions.

The Inventory Update Cycle

As we have seen, the inventory update cycle is represented by the time difference between the receipt or withdrawal of stock and the respective increment or decrement of the records on which stock balance is maintained. In this case, "withdrawal" may mean any action that reserves stock for a specific customer and makes it unavailable for sale to others.

Clearly, the length of the update cycle determines the accuracy of the recorded inventory balance and the decisions based on this figure. In some cases, it requires that extra inventory be maintained to provide an additional buffer for inaccurate inventory balances. For example, in both the Q and P models, a five-day lag in recording inventory withdrawals may mean that five extra days of sales need to be included in the order-cycle estimate. Clearly, an investment in faster communication services can be offset by inventory savings. When taken into account, it should produce an incentive to shorten update cycles.

Consider another problem typical of many distribution centers. The update cycle for receipts is different from that for withdrawals. On a replenishment shipment from a plant, an average transit time is assumed, at the end of which the inventory of the distribution center is credited with the receipt. This is a convenient method, but it sometimes produces a credit even before receipt of the inventory. In contrast, shipments from the center are not recorded until reported, perhaps several days later. Where frequent inventory receipts and withdrawals are common, the adverse effects of the inventory update cycle can be reduced if delays for both receipts and withdrawals roughly are the same.

Program Review Procedures

The statistical preparation of demand inputs and the day-to-day replenishment of inventory levels according to a planned program are parts of the process which Anthony calls operational planning: [5]

. . . where rules are devised that prescribe the action that is most efficient under a given set of circumstances.

The task of reviewing the forecasting model, the inventory model, the judgmental inputs required by each, and the inventory management program itself, are those encompassed by a higher level of management responsibility termed by Anthony "management control." He defines management control as: [6]

. . . the process by which managers assure that resources are obtained and used effectively and efficiently in the accomplishment of the organization's objectives.

A formal program for management review is the most essential element of an effective inventory management program.

The frequency of review will depend on the degree to which conditions influencing each element to be reviewed might change. Changes in the nature of product demand characteristics, brought on by a change in the market and its usage of items in the product line, might warrant a change in forecasting methods. More typically, signals can be built into the model, in the form of methods for measuring actual against forecast demands, in order to kick out those items for which the model appears to be ineffective. Provision can be made for estimating demand for these items on a manual basis. A review of forecasting model results might be conducted quite frequently. Model reviews would be required only on an as-needed basis, hopefully not very frequently. Much the same is true for the inventory model.

Judgmental inputs required by the inventory model may be reviewed with varying frequencies. For example, the cost of money invested in inventory as a part of the inventory carrying cost assumption did not vary greatly for many years prior to 1968. Since that time, it has become a highly variable input, requiring review perhaps every six months. Order-processing costs, influenced by trends in labor and communication costs and the relative complexity of orders, may be more stable, requiring an annual review. Stock-out costs, because they reflect in part the substitutability of one product for another, may have to be reviewed on a product

---

[5] Robert N. Anthony, *Planning and Control Systems* (Boston: Division of Research, Graduate School of Business Administration, Harvard University, 1965), p. 70.
[6] *Ibid.*, p. 17.

family basis, on a schedule to conform with the product life cycle of the family. That is, a newer product with fewer substitutes and greater customer loyalty may have a lower back-order cost than one which has a growing amount of competition from alternative products.

Finally, questions of broader significance may be raised from time to time, depending on the performance of the existing management system and the constraints imposed by general management. For example, the consequences of alternative strategies involving inventories can be estimated by means of the same models employed for existing inventory management purposes. Goal sets that may be inconsistent, undesirable (in terms of high carrying costs or inferior customer service levels which they might produce), or even impossible to achieve can thus be identified in advance and avoided.

The problem with most inventory management programs is that they are out-of-date. Clearly, if program review is to be accomplished, responsibility for it must be set forth explicitly. Hupp has argued persuasively that such responsibility should be assigned to someone in top management ranks.[7]

TESTING FOR INTERNAL COMPATIBILITY

There are certain dimensions along which it is useful to check an inventory management program for internal compatibility. Several examples serve to illustrate directions this stage may take.

The forecasting period should roughly conform to the time periods of greatest concern in the inventory model. For example, if the order point is of great concern in the inventory model because it provides various levels of coverage during an order cycle, and the typical order cycle is no more than two weeks in length, an estimate of demand for the next two weeks is a much more useful output from the forecasting model than one which produces an estimate based on $\frac{1}{13}$ of a computed demand for the next six months. (37) **Review Wonka's method of estimating demand on this basis, described earlier in this chapter. What is your conclusion?**

In contrast to this, production planning may require a firm knowledge of demand three months in advance, thus requiring a different output from the forecast.

The nature of the inventory model will influence the computational device used to execute it. If the number of SKUL's is not too great, manual methods of computation and review may be adequate for use

[7] Burr W. Hupp, "Inventory Policy is a Top Management Responsibility," *Handling & Shipping*, August, 1967, pp. 47–49.

with a fixed order interval model in which a portion of the product line can be reviewed on each of several days in rotation, thereby reducing the peaks and valleys in order review and placement activities.

In contrast, a fixed order quantity model may be more difficult to manipulate by manual means unless it is used in connection with a visual, two-bin method of control (with an order triggered by the emptying of the first bin, and the order size determined by the capacity of a bin) typical of some inventories of small parts and expendable items.

The importance of internal compatibility between the inventory model and inventory update cycle as elements in the management program can be illustrated by the following two situations.

A large wholesaler of sewing notions, distributing a wide line of products through eight owned distribution centers, maintained no perpetual (running) inventory records, either by means of computer or manually. Instead, warehouse personnel took most of one day each month to count all inventory and, later that same day, placed all orders for delivery from the factory during the following month. This fixed order interval process permitted the placement of twelve orders per year as well as fill-in orders for items for which demand forecasts proved too low (of particular importance for style items in the line, basically consisting of the fashion colors for the coming season).

A manufacturer of packaged chemical products maintained a perpetual inventory record on a computer at its company headquarters, employing an automatic warehouse replenishment system using a min–max model. Warehouses would ship goods ordered by customers, then mail notification of the shipments to headquarters. Salesmen also wrote up orders and mailed them to headquarters. When matching documents from the salesmen and the warehouse were received and checked, the billing procedure began. After the customer invoice was prepared, the warehouse inventory records were adjusted to reflect the shipment and sale. (Note that this system closely conformed to the one employed at Wonka.)

(38) Which of these systems do you feel was made up of elements with the greatest internal compatibility? (39) Why? (40) How might either be improved?

TESTING FOR EXTERNAL COMPATIBILITY

To what extent does the inventory management program, regardless of the internal compatibility of its elements, take into account (1) important determinants of company performance, and (2) channel inventory management behavior?

Company Operating Characteristics

Company operating characteristics to which an inventory management program should be responsive may be as diverse as, among others, restricted capacities, opportunities for savings from purchasing discounts and volume transport rate reductions, and the relative expense of managing the inventories of various SKUL's.

Capacity Constraints. As an example, set-up costs are an important element of a production planning decision. Where production capacity constraints are severe, we may find the minimum cost objective of inventory management to be influenced heavily by set-up cost or loss of downtime due to set-ups. The quantity ordered in relation to demand is a direct determinant of the number of times during a given period that set-up costs are incurred. Therefore, Q (fixed order quantity) models most directly satisfy the minimum cost objective when set-up costs are important and cannot be reduced by a sequencing of items to be produced. At times such as these it may be necessary to impose an allocation device.

Similarly, the incremental inventory carrying cost at a warehouse which is filled to capacity may be very great, especially if it is important to maintain inventory in one facility for control purposes. At such times, the carrying cost factor provides at least a crude method for reducing all inventories at the facility, assuming that some sales activity is taking place.

Quantity Purchase Discounts and Volume Transport Rates. Where there are significant opportunities for discounts for purchasing goods in minimum quantities, the inventory control model should take them into account. The same is true in the case of volume transport rates.

The following formula can be used to calculate the relative desirability of ordering or handling goods in sufficient quantity to take advantage of a quantity purchase discount (on one or a group of items), a minimum weight break in a transportation tariff, or cost savings from handling goods in, for example, pallet quantities: [8]

$$Q_1 = \frac{2dS}{r} + (1 - d) \ Q_o$$

where

$Q_1 =$ the maximum quantity that can economically be ordered to qualify for a discount on unit cost

[8] The derivation for this formula can be found in Brown, *op. cit.*, pp. 205–6.

d = the fraction by which the price will be reduced from the existing price if a larger quantity is ordered

S = annual usage, in units (pieces, pounds, or dollars)

r = carrying charge, expressed as a percentage of the value of the average quantity on hand over a year's time

Q_o = economic order quantity based on the current price

An example from Wonka's Pittsburgh distribution center operation illustrates the use of the formula. The annual throughput of levelors and parts at Pittsburgh represents about 640,000 pounds with an average manufactured value of about $4.00 per pound. Currently, this quantity is being shipped in 17 truckloads of 40,000 pounds each, under a 40,000-pound minimum rate of $2.00 per cwt. If we were to estimate a theoretical EOQ for this situation, using the basic formula for certain conditions discussed in Chapter 10, an inventory carrying cost factor of .30, and an order cost of $50 per order, we would come up with an EOQ of about 4,600 pounds per shipment. The LTL rate to ship in this quantity from the plant is $5.50 per cwt. (41) **On the basis of the formula cited above, should we be shipping in quantities comparable to truckloads of EOQ's?**

There are a couple of things to note in using this formula. First, no matter by what amount Q_1 exceeds the amount needed to obtain the price or cost discount (40,000 pounds in the above example), it will be most economical to ship the minimum amount, regardless of the difference. Of course, if there are several discount levels and the economics favor our taking advantage of the first, we will want to test to see if we can qualify for the second and succeeding ones. However, in further testing, the base price (upon which it is calculated) and the existing EOQ (Q_o) become those associated with the quantity discount for which we have already qualified.

Try this one. A pallet quantity of Item 7M motors is 24. Each one weighs about 60 pounds and has a value of $150. Our annual demand for this item at Pittsburgh is about 1,000 and the line item cost of placing an order is $2.00. It costs approximately $2.00 per motor to handle and transport them in pallet quantities and approximately $4.00 per motor if we handle them loose. (42) **What should we do?** (43) **How low could the annual demand (and Q_o) fall before we would be better off shipping and handling this item loose?**

You may wish to compare your results with those of the warehouse manager of a large eastern grocery chain who was confronted continually with incoming grocery products in partial-pallet quantities. Because his warehouse was equipped with pallet racks permitting the full use of vertical space, partial-pallet quantities greatly reduced the capacity of the warehouse at a time when space was becoming critically short. Upon investigation, it was found that buyers for the chain were buying on the basis of economic order quantities for which computations did not take account of handling and storage economies of purchases in pallet-sized quantities. A calculation of cost implications suggested that when economic order quantities constituted more than 40% of a pallet quantity, in most cases the pallet quantity should be ordered.

Similarly, many grocery chains have adopted the policy of not restocking store shelves in quantities of less than one case, even though this has set a minimum (about 1½ cases of merchandise) on the shelf space devoted to any one item displayed in the store. The costs of handling quantities of less than one case are prohibitive.

Expense of Inventory Management Itself. The expense of managing inventories of low-volume SKUL's can become a burdensome element of cost. For such items, requiring relatively infrequent orders, the ordering and order-picking costs may be reduced significantly through the use of the fixed order quantity model.

However, many companies have turned to ABC analysis to provide the basis for devoting different amounts of attention to various SKUL's and concentrating on the SKUL's that are of greatest importance to the company. Basically, this involves arraying SKUL's in terms of their sales volume or units sold, then: (1) developing the most carefully designed inventory programs for perhaps the top 10% of all SKUL's, so called "A" items, or (2) establishing the highest customer service standards for the "A" items, on the assumption that these are the items customers will expect the company to have in stock.

For example, referring back to Table 9–3, it stands to reason that customers would not expect the same in-stock rate for levelor models 122L and 2700H in Wonka's product line. In this case, we probably wouldn't want to neglect the control of inventory for the 2700H, because of its relatively high value. However, the ABC approach might be valid for the Company's parts inventory.

There are several reasons for basing an ABC program on the frequency with which various items appear on customer orders rather than their absolute sales volume, either in units or dollars. To the extent that order-fill rates are both a measure of customer service and significant determinants of logistics costs, they provide better indicators of the need for management attention.

Channel Inventory Management Behavior. Performance problems in a channel of distribution may be caused by the management of inventory at several levels in a distribution channel or within an organization without adequate communications between the levels. Independently managed inventories typically will create a "whip-saw" effect in a channel, as illustrated in Table 11–6. Here we see during Period 2 that the combination of rising expectations resulting from an actual 10% increase in sales at the retail level and a coincident adjustment of min and max values based on this increase can result in a 270% increase in orders on the manufacturing plant at the end of this channel. Then during Period 3, even if the 10% sales increase is maintained, orders fall off by 15% at the retail level, 63% at the wholesale level, and dry up completely at the plant level. At this point the channel is glutted from its overreaction in Period 2. The linkage of inventory management programs with even a fraction of the responsiveness of these can create problems for the manufacturer at the end of the "whip-saw." This is an extreme example, but the problem is typical of all multistage inventory systems.

In this case, management may have the choices of: (1) altering the forecasting model to disregard certain short-term demand changes, (2) instituting a program for single-stage (centralized) inventory management, assuming that two or more stages can be brought under the control of a single group, or (3) instituting a form of direct communication which might provide accurate estimates of demand at the point of ultimate sales rather than at the place of business of an intermediary in the channel with whom the manufacturer might deal.

SUMMARY

The core of an inventory management program is composed of an inventory model, forecasting model, contingency procedures, computational device, update cycle, and program review procedures. In an effective inventory management program these elements not only are internally consistent, but their design is responsive to management goals, basic needs of the organization, and affairs of the organization external to the program. Further, through periodic appraisal and review, the program reflects changes in these goals, needs, and external affairs.

Among the practical comparative advantages of a program utilizing a fixed order quantity (Q) inventory model are: (1) it provides for packaging, shipment, handling, or manufacture in constant, efficient quantities, (2) it requires inventory coverage only during the order cycle, not for the order interval as well, (3) it produces low ordering and picking costs for especially slow-moving items, and (4) it fully reflects the importance of set-up costs, making it particularly useful for production control where these costs tend to be more important. An inventory program built around the use of a Q model typically produces results less

sensitive to forecasting results. However, its computational requirements
and need for continuing review may require its use in conjunction with
a computer, particularly for product lines with many SKUL's.

On the other hand, an inventory management program centered around
a fixed order interval (P) model: (1) allows for the combined ordering
of many items supplied from the same source, thereby reducing ordering
and order-picking costs per line item, (2) facilitates shipping in multi-
SKUL shipments, producing higher-volume shipments moving at lower
transportation rates, (3) is particularly effective for items for which the
cost of a stock-out is low, and (4) is useful when demand is registered
in large increments, requiring replenishment orders of widely varying
sizes to maintain a constant inventory target (max value). A P model
will, however, place greater demands on the forecasting model because
of the need for coverage (and an accurate forecast) for both the order
interval and the order cycle. It is relatively easy to manage, and is used
often in conjunction with manual control.

All inventory management programs: (1) are relatively insensitive to
inaccuracies in other than demand forecasts, (2) benefit from accurate
knowledge of actual inventory levels (through timely update cycles) at
the time inventory levels are viewed, and (3) require a periodic review
of important inputs, particularly for the management of critical, high-
volume, frequently ordered items in the product line.

In discussing inventory management programs, it is tempting to become overly critical about the design process. Remember one thing.
We have compared features of various inventory management programs
as we explored the design process in this chapter. We did *not* compare
the use vs. the non-use of a program. *Our discussion suggests that the
decision to institute the use of an inventory management program is more
important than the choice of the particular program elements.* The inquiries produced in assembling inputs for the design of any program
will likely be of much greater value to the practicing executive than
philosophical debates about which of several programs is best.

SUGGESTED READINGS

Please refer to those listed at the end of Chapter 10, especially the book
by Brown.

12

Location Theory

Every industrial or commercial location is unique. This means that in relation to markets or sources of goods, it has certain geographic limits, or barriers, imposed by space and time. These limits are measured in units of miles and minutes as well as units of cost.

A foremost theorist in the field of economics of location viewed the problem with mixed feelings and somewhat philosophically as follows:

> If everything occurred at the same time there would be no development. If everything existed in the same place there could be no particularity. Only space makes possible the particular, which then unfolds in time. Only because we are not equally near to everything; only because everything does not rush in upon us at once; only because our world is restricted, for every individual, for his people, and for mankind as a whole, can we, in our finiteness, endure it all . . . and even within this little world, we are familiar with not more than its innermost circle. Depth must be bought with narrowness. Space creates and protects us in this limitation. Particularity is the price of our existence.[1]

As we will see, area development is the *cause* of many location decisions. At the same time, it is the *result* of many decisions made by individuals (representing themselves, their businesses, their governments, and other entities) to locate in a given area. Thus it is unreasonable to divorce location theory and area development.

An understanding of some of the basic concepts of location theory can help to relate the various elements of logistics systems which have been discussed earlier, and can provide a better perspective for viewing reality. It should also foster an appreciation of the magnitude of the job facing

[1] August Lösch, *Die Räumliche Ordnung der Wirtschaft* (Jena: Gustav Fischer Verlag, 1940), translated from the second revised edition (1944) by William H. Woglom with the assistance of Wolfgang F. Stopler, *The Economics of Location* (New Haven: Yale University Press, 1954), p. 508.

geographers, economists, sociologists, and other students of the problem in formulating a general theory of location. Most important, it can provide an acquaintance with the shortcomings of existing theory.

Location theory serves as a guide in analyzing economic development trends throughout history. In terms of the future it serves as a basis for predicting rates and types of economic development. Efforts to develop location theory have not been confined to the ivory tower. Lösch, for example, recognized that "Many manufacturers as well as wholesale and retail dealers have expanded their market areas excessively. They ship too far at a loss." [2] He thereby related theory to actual business situations.

The purpose of this chapter is to explore reasons why economic development takes place where it does, with special reference to the influence of, and importance for, logistics. For example, what effect does proximity to an urban community have on agricultural land use? What effect do the relative positions of a plant site, its raw materials sources, and its markets have on a firm's landed costs? [3] Why are plants grouped as they are? What determines the market area of a given production site? How does competition influence plant location and market area?

It would be inappropriate here to knit together all of the previous work which has been done in location theory, even if this could be accomplished. We will present important "cornerstone" pieces of this work, citing those writers currently trying to assemble and build upon the theoretical work of their predecessors. It is not entirely fair to those working in the field to extract and discuss briefly only a portion of their work, and the reader should realize that these are only some of the interrelated ideas which make up location theory.

FOUNDATIONS OF LOCATION THEORY [4]

To form a theory of general application, strict assumptions must be imposed upon almost all aspects of the subject at the outset. As the theory is developed and verified, and as new techniques of analysis are devised, assumptions may be relaxed one by one. Although progress is being made, many of the restrictive assumptions of location theory still remain with us today.

---

[2] *Ibid.*, p. 396.

[3] Landed cost is the total cost expended to gain possession of a given item at a given place.

[4] Basic studies in location theory often refer to costs of movement by the simpler, if misleading, term "transportation." Wherever the term "transportation" is used throughout the remainder of his chapter, the term "logistics" can usually be substituted for it.

Thünen's "Isolated City State"

The earliest formal work in the field of location theory bearing directly on the influence of transportation on location was done by Johann Heinrich von Thünen early in the nineteenth century.[5] Thünen visualized an isolated city state situated in a limitless plane of equal fertility. He then attempted to speculate on the use of land surrounding the isolated city state for agricultural purposes.

Assuming a constant transportation rate for a given weight and distance, Thünen reasoned that those products with a low dollar weight factor, i e., a low value per pound, would be cultivated nearest the city because of the burdensome nature of transportation charges on such products. He hypothesized that "the value of produce at the place of production decreases with the distance of the place of production from the market." [6] In other words, the value of a product at the point of production is equivalent to market value less the cost of transportation from point of production to market. He concluded that, other things being equal, transportation costs are substitutes for rent costs.

Thünen recognized that land has a commercial value only if it can be used directly or indirectly to produce a product that can be sold in a commercial market, and that this depends not only on its intrinsic fertility but also on its location relative to a market, that is, upon production capacity and logistics. Every crop has a rent-paying capability called a bid rent, which is equal to the market price for its yield per acre less production and transportation costs. A farmer at a given distance from a market chooses the crop with the highest bid rent. Under assumptions of equal fertility and equal transportation cost in every direction, land use rings are formed around the market. Growers of crops with lower transport costs are able to locate at distances further from the market. As you move away from a market, eventually the bid rent of all crops is reduced to zero by transport cost increases, and the outer boundaries of the system are established.

The model provides a farmer with a rationale for choosing between different crops. If he wishes to maximize profits, he chooses to grow the crop with the highest bid rent. This offers some insight into the existence of farm regions such as the corn belt. Independent farmers, making their own choices about which crops to raise, end up making the same crop choice because that is the crop with the highest bid rent for

[5] Johann Heinrich von Thünen, *Der Isolierte Staat in Beziechung auf Landwirtschaft und Nationalökonomie,* 2nd Ed. (Rostock: 1842), English edition available entitled *Von Thünen's Isolated State,* translated by C. M. Wartenburg and edited by Peter Hall (Oxford: Pergamon Press, 1966).
[6] *Ibid.,* p. 37.

that location. Thünen's analysis also indicated that intensity of land use increases nearer the market. That is, if the value of land is high due to its nearness to market and transportation costs are low, it pays to work land more intensively by applying more fertilizer or field labor. This is a balancing of the marginal utility of factor inputs. The result is generally observable. Near large population centers yields are generally higher and those crops which respond best to intensive inputs predominate.

Thünen also noted some interesting effects of logistics on land use arrangement. If transportation costs are lower along certain routes, rents in the vicinity of these improved paths will be higher at a given distance from the market than in other directions. Given a constant demand, land use rings will be stretched in these favored directions and contracted in other directions. Slightly more produce will reach the market at slightly lower prices.

There is a generality gained from the very simplicity of Thünen's analysis. He wrote for another time, when horse-drawn wagons and ox carts brought farm products to town. Yet his notions of the substitutability of bid rents and logistics costs, of marginal substitutions causing greater intensity of land use in high rent areas, and of the interdependence of commercial land uses apply in many situations in different societies and times. In a very general way the theory offers insight into modern urban land use patterns where changes in intensity of land use are closely related to modifications of the transportation system.

Weber's Transport Orientation

Thünen's theory had to do with organizing production in a region surrounding a single market point. Alfred Weber's theories dealt with raw material and production points serving multiple markets in the region.[7] He assumed that certain materials used in manufacture would be available everywhere in his economy, paralleling Thünen's assumption that all resources (in the form of soil fertility) were constantly available. Weber's omnipresent materials, which we might consider as air and water, for example, were called "ubiquities." Other materials limited to certain locations were referred to as "localized" materials, such as mineral deposits.

Weber also classified materials from the standpoint of the part they played in the manufacturing process, in order to determine their importance for transportation (logistics). Those materials which entered into

[7] This section, unless otherwise indicated, is based on Alfred Weber, *Über den Standort der Industrien*, translated by C. J. Friedrich as *Alfred Weber's Theory of the Location of Industries* (Chicago: University of Chicago Press, 1929), pp. 37–94.

the final product without a loss in weight were called "pure" materials; these ranged from raw materials, which entered a portion of their weight into a finished product, to fuel, which added nothing to the weight of the product. Equipped with these definitions, Weber attacked the problem of a firm's decision of where to locate between a source of raw materials and a market, as indicated by points A and B, in Fig. 12–1.

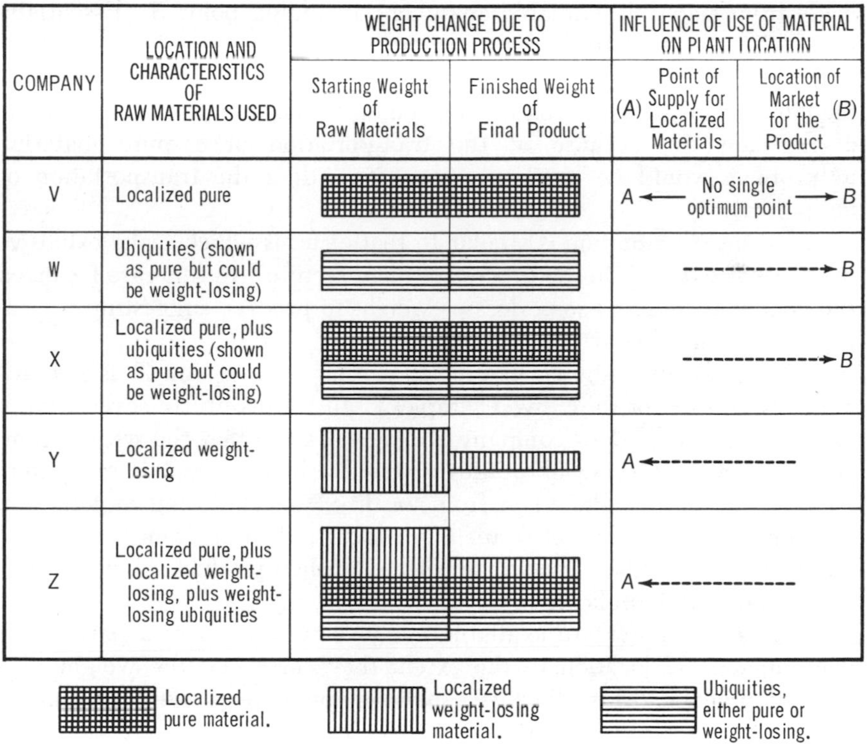

COMPANY	LOCATION AND CHARACTERISTICS OF RAW MATERIALS USED	WEIGHT CHANGE DUE TO PRODUCTION PROCESS		INFLUENCE OF USE OF MATERIAL ON PLANT LOCATION	
		Starting Weight of Raw Materials	Finished Weight of Final Product	(A) Point of Supply for Localized Materials	Location of Market for the Product (B)
V	Localized pure			A ⟵ No single optimum point ⟶ B	
W	Ubiquities (shown as pure but could be weight-losing)			----------------⟶ B	
X	Localized pure, plus ubiquities (shown as pure but could be weight-losing)			----------------⟶ B	
Y	Localized weight-losing			A ⟵---------------	
Z	Localized pure, plus localized weight-losing, plus weight-losing ubiquities			A ⟵---------------	

Localized pure material.   Localized weight-losing material.   Ubiquities, either pure or weight-losing.

The width of the bars indicates the relative weight of the materials used in making the product.

Fig. 12–1. Examples of five firms using different types of materials in their products, showing the directional pull of plant location toward raw material sources or markets.

Assuming equal costs of transportation for equal weights of raw materials and finished products hauled a given distance, company V in Fig. 12–1 would gain no advantage by locating its plant at A or at B, or at any particular point in between. The cost to haul its pure raw materials would be the same as for its finished product. Oil refineries, at which crude oil is directly converted into various products during the refining process, are examples of this type of situation. In this regard, it is interesting to note the lack of noticeable concentration of refineries near oil fields or markets. Although greater compatibility of pipeline operations with larger shipments of crude, as opposed to finished products, tends to favor market orientation of refineries, field refineries are feasible as well.

Company W, utilizing ubiquities only, would have everything to gain by manufacturing only at the point of consumption, given a product made from materials available anywhere, including point B. Essentially this is the nature of the soft-drink bottling industry.

The optimum point of production for company X is at B also. Although its transportation costs would be much more important than those of company W, because of the transportation of a pure material, its problem would be much the same (avoiding the transportation of ubiquities).

Company Y's situation is similar to that of firms which make extensive use of localized fuels in the process of manufacture. In this case localized raw materials undergo some loss of weight in process, suggesting a location for production at point A.

The last situation shown in Fig. 12–1, that of company Z, is perhaps the most realistic of these five examples. Most firms utilize several types of raw material, as does company Z. Here we see that the weight component of weight-losing ubiquities in the finished product is more than balanced by the weight taken from localized weight-losing materials in the same process. The net result is a weight reduction from the total of raw material weights to the weight of the finished product. A plant location at point A is indicated.

Because ubiquities are available everywhere, they play a part in the determination of location to the extent they enter into the weight of a finished product. This effect is usually to promote market location, as in the case of soft-drink bottling plants. In this industry, the weight of the product mostly is composed of water; consequently every market of any size has at least one soft-drink bottling plant. Localized materials, on the other hand, control location not only by the degree to which they enter into the weight of finished product, but by the extent to which they are localized. To describe the control which is exerted by the relative weights of raw materials and finished product, Weber formulated a "material index": *the proportion of the weight of localized raw materials to the weight of the finished product.* Upon this idea of a material index, he based three theorems:

1. All industries whose material index is not greater than one . . . lie at the place of consumption.
2. Pure materials can never bind production to their deposits.

3. Weight-losing materials, on the other hand, may pull production to their deposits. For this to happen, however, it is necessary that the material index . . . [for any one source location] . . . be greater than one, and that . . . [its] portion of the material index be equal . . . [or greater than half of the sum of the material indices for all raw material sources and the market].[8]

(1) What are the material indices for the companies whose production processes are illustrated in Fig. 12–1? (2) Which of these companies does the Wonka operation most closely resemble? (3) Why? (4) Does it explain the company's selection of plant locations? (5) Why?

The Nature of Transfer Costs [9]

The dominant characteristic of transportation rates is that they are tapered. That is, a given weight is charged smaller increments per mile as the distance of a shipment increases. (For example, see the graph of rates paid by Wonka, in Fig. 9–6.) Hoover has shown that this characteristic of the transportation rate structure tends to encourage firms using only pure materials (like company X in Fig. 12–1) to locate either at raw material sources or at markets.[10]

Procurement and distribution costs (with only transfer costs graphed) for a firm locating at any point between points A and B in Fig. 12–2 will taper with the transportation rate schedule. Here it is assumed that one material or combination of pure materials is available at the source. AC represents the cost of handling at the source. As the firm locates nearer the market, point B, its total procurement costs, in the form of handling and transportation, will rise but at a lessening rate. Costs of handling at, plus transportation costs to, the destination behave in the reverse fashion, rising as the firm locates away from point B. As shown by line EF, total transfer costs will be minimized at either the source or the market.

As Hoover correctly noted, transit privileges may cancel out the advantages of locating at any particular point between A and B. Transit privileges would tend to equalize freight charges between A and B in Fig. 12–2, regardless of the particular location of plant facilities between them.

---

[8] *Ibid.*, p. 61.

[9] Costs incurred in moving raw materials and finished products from one terminal (or node in the logistics system) to another. For a complete discussion of the importance of transfer costs, see Edgar M. Hoover, *The Location of Economic Activity* (New York: McGraw-Hill Book Co., 1948), pp. 26–66.

[10] *Ibid.*, pp. 29–40.

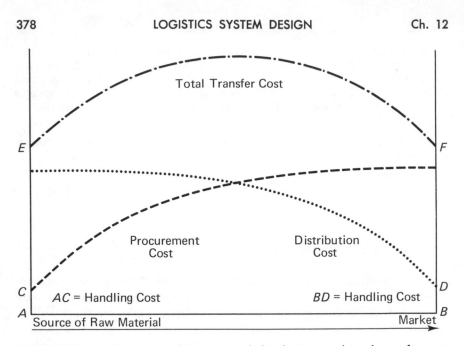

Fig. 12–2. Costs of procurement and distribution, and total transfer cost, for locations on a direct route between A and B.

Multiple Sources and Markets

The next logical step was to develop the theory of facility location to take into account the more realistic situation of multiple sources of incoming products or multiple markets for outgoing products.

Weber approached the problem in the abstract sense by constructing triangles encompassing three points—two sources of raw materials and one market. The problem was to select an optimum location for a producing facility in relation to these three points.

Consider three plants producing three different products, each product using the same weights of localized raw materials, but having different finished product weights. Locational factors and statistics for each are shown in Fig. 12–3. A point equidistant from each of the raw material sources and the market can be selected as a tentative location, a first approximation from which the optimum location will be determined. This is shown as P in Fig. 12–3. In each case, the optimum location will be influenced by the relative weights of raw material inputs of localized raw materials from points R_1 and R_2. It will also be influenced by the resulting weight of the finished product.

Finished product weight is influenced by two factors: (1) the amount of weight of raw materials which is lost in the production process, and

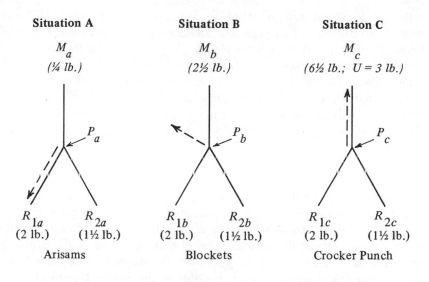

Situation A	Situation B	Situation C
M_a	M_b	M_c
(¼ lb.)	(2½ lb.)	(6½ lb.; U = 3 lb.)
P_a	P_b	P_c
R_{1a} R_{2a}	R_{1b} R_{2b}	R_{1c} R_{2c}
(2 lb.) (1½ lb.)	(2 lb.) (1½ lb.)	(2 lb.) (1½ lb.)
Arisams	Blockets	Crocker Punch

R_1 and R_2 = Locations of raw material sources. The weight of raw material to be used in each unit of finished product is indicated in parentheses.

M = Location of the market for the finished product. The weight of raw material to be used in each unit of finished product is indicated in parentheses.

U = Ubiquitous raw material added during the production process, per unit of finished product.

P = Starting point for plant location analysis.

$- - \rightarrow$ = Direction of "pull" toward the optimum plant location.

Fig. 12–3. Three situations showing the influence of varying weights of raw materials and finished products on plant location decisions.

(2) the weight of ubiquitous material, if any, which is added during the process. The weight loss of $3\frac{1}{4}$ lb. experienced in the production of Arisams is great. The weight loss of one pound experienced in making Blockets is much less. There is actually a net weight gain in the process of making Crocker Punch, due to the addition of a great amount of ubiquitous material, perhaps water. In the following discussion, transportation costs are assumed to correspond directly to the weight of goods moving over any segment of the system under consideration.

Weber's theory can once again be applied to the situation in question. If we computed the materials index for Arisams, we would find it to be $14[(2 + 1\frac{1}{2}) \div \frac{1}{4}]$. Recalling Weber's theory, a result in excess of 1 would indicate that location in the market would not be feasible.

In order to determine whether location at any one of the raw material sources would be desirable, location weights for each source and destination could be computed. Location weights would consist of the respective ratios of localized raw material to finished product weight for each source. In the case of Arisams, the location weight for source R_{1a} would be 8 $(2 \div \frac{1}{4})$, and for source R_{2a}, 6 $(1\frac{1}{2} \div \frac{1}{4})$. In the case of the market, it would always have a location weight of 1 $(\frac{1}{4} \div \frac{1}{4})$. In situations where the location weight of any one source of raw materials is greater than the sum of the weights for other sources and the market, production will gravitate to that source, as in the case of Arisams, where the weight for R_{1a} is 8, greater than the sum of weights for the other points in the system $(6 + 1 = 7)$.

Common sense would tell us that if we were to tie three strings of equal length together in the middle of a round table, running each to the edge of the table in the relationship shown in Fig. 12–3, then attaching at the end of each a weight proportional in size to the material weight of M_a, R_{1a}, and R_{2a} for Arisams, the weight for R_{1a} would pull the other two over the edge of the table at a point corresponding to R_{1a} in the figure. The same situation would prevail in the making of Crocker Punch, except that the relatively heavy weight of the finished product would suggest a plant location in this case at the market. The rule is simply that if the weight at any one nodal point exceeds the sum of the other two, the least-cost location will be at that point.

In the case of Blockets, the materials index is $1.4[(2 + 1\frac{1}{2}) \div 2\frac{1}{2}]$. However, no one raw material or finished product has a location weight in excess of the sum of the others. The point of production will be found to lie at none of the points R_{1b}, R_{2b}, or M_b. The point will be pulled from P_b, however, in the direction which will reduce the distance that the heaviest product would have to be carried. This will be done at the expense of some increase in distance for the other two. At the point where nothing further is to be gained by "trading-off" increased transportation expense for R_{1b} and R_{2b} for decreased expense from M_b to P_b, the least-cost location for a plant will have been reached.[11]

The examples shown in Fig. 12–3 assume an equal transportation charge for a given weight carried a given distance, regardless of the nature of the product. In reality, this does not exist. However, weights used in the examples could be adjusted to reflect comparative transportation charges on R_1 and R_2, and the finished product in each case. Because finished products are generally worth more than the sum of their component materials (and transportation charges are to some degree based on the value of the product being transported) we might conclude that the relative weight of the finished product in each of the cases shown in Fig. 12–3 should be increased to reflect this fact. This would have

[11] For a mathematical determination of the point of least transportation costs, see Friedrich, *op. cit.*, pp. 227–40. Regional scientists generally regard Weber's solution as misleadingly simple and of limited value in actual problems.

the effect of drawing production sites closer to markets, an industry-location practice which has long been ascribed in part to value-of-service characteristics in the transportation rate structure.

Another assumption of the discussion has been that a non-tapering, perfectly patterned transportation rate structure exists in relation to the distance a product is carried. As Hoover has pointed out:

Actual distance costs are of course not proportional to airline distance. Transfer is canalized along established routes and is much cheaper and quicker on some routes than on others. Along any one route, the rates are lower per ton-mile for longer hauls and for hauls between important and competitive terminals. The progression of transfer costs along a route is stepwise rather than continuous. Finally, there are innumerable special exceptions and localized advantages in any actual rate structure, involving still further departures from the direct distance relation.[12]

(6) **Using weights to represent estimates of transportation costs, once again evaluate Wonka's plant location in terms of Weber's rules. What do you find?**

Production Cost Differentials

To expand the formulation of theory governing the location of business activity, consider the case of Blockets described above. First, isotims (lines of equal transportation cost from a common origin) could be drawn around both raw material sources and the market for the makers of Blockets in Fig. 12–3. This has been done in Fig. 12–4. The width of the rings around each point corresponds to the relationship between weights of R_{1b}, R_{2b}, and F_b for Blockets. In other words, the heavier raw material, R_{1b}, costs more than raw material R_{2b} to transport a given distance. Therefore, its transport cost isotims are more closely spaced than those for R_{2b}. In turn, the finished product, F_b, is heavier than either of the raw materials and its transport cost isotims are the most closely spaced.

Drop a pencil point at any spot on Fig. 12–4, designate it as a production location, and you will be able to translate that point into a total cost to haul raw materials to it from R_{1b} and R_{2b} and finished product from it to market M_b. As we have said, one point on Fig. 12–4 will have the lowest total transportation cost characteristics. This point is designated as X. Rings, called "isodapanes" by Weber, can then be plotted out from X, representing successively higher total costs of transportation.

Next, consider two possible production sites alternate to site X, each with widely differing cost structures, possibly due to wage differentials

12 Hoover, *op. cit.*, pp. 51–53.

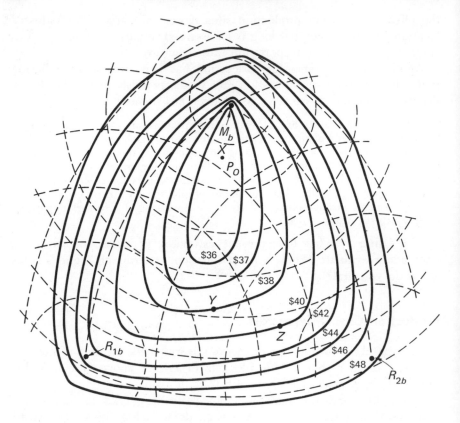

--- = Isotims. Each isotim around points R_{1b}, R_{2b}, and M_b represents \$4 of
transport cost per Blocket.

⸺ = Isodapanes. Values for each represent the total transportation costs from
any point on a given isodapane to points R_{1b}, R_{2b}, and M_b.

Fig. 12–4. A construction of isodapanes showing the interrelated influence of transportation and production costs on the selection of a production
site. (Each isotim around points R_{1b}, R_{2b}, and M_b represents \$4 of transport
cost per Blocket.)

or other factors. We will call them points Y and Z. Assume that production costs at points X, Y, and Z are \$62, \$58, and \$55, respectively.

A comparison of the sum of transportation costs (as indicated by the
value of the nearest isodapane) and production costs at each site will
indicate the site which offers the lowest overall potential for combined
production and transport costs. In this case, the overall cost at point Z
will be \$1 less (\$40 + \$55 = \$95) than at point Y (\$38 + \$58 = \$96),
and \$3 less than at point X (\$36 + \$62 = \$98). After weighing the costs

of production and transportation, point Z would probably be selected as the optimum site under particular conditions.

Agglomeration

The output of a point can be expanded by the decision of a single company to increase the size of its producing facility at that point (and thereby take advantage of economies of scale). It also may be expanded by the decision of two or more companies to relocate at a common point to benefit mutually.

Forces attracting competing and non-competing enterprises to a common location can be called agglomerating forces. More specifically, they can be identified as desires or needs on the part of firms to adjust to uncertainty, share facilities and institutions, and share functional contacts. Competing firms may reduce customer uncertainty by locating where customers "shopping" for competing products can expect with high probability that satisfactions will be obtained. The sharing of facilities and institutions is often undertaken by non-competing, perhaps complementary, firms desiring to share building overhead, police and fire protection, streets, and other social overhead investments, none of which any one could provide for itself. Finally, competing and non-competing firms may share customers to save them time and travel, share specialized business services which can be supported only when a sufficient volume of business demand is generated, or share benefits of pooled and competing resources such as a labor pool, lower rates from increased transportation competition to and from the location, political pressure group concessions resulting from location size, and joint commercial promotions.[13]

Despite the difficulties which formal economic theory has had in explaining the phenomenon, the tendencies for agglomeration are everywhere apparent. One of the most striking examples in recent years has been the concentration of electronic products manufacturers around Los Angeles, San Francisco, Boston, and in the Minneapolis–St. Paul area. There are many reasons for a firm's decision to "join the pack" of competing or non-competing firms located at or around a particular point. Weber early attempted to picture the economic reasons for this tendency by utilizing isodapanes.

Conceptually, forces of agglomeration can be treated much as production economies at various sites in relation to appropriate isodapanes, as shown in Fig. 12–4. At the same time, it is important to note that "deglomerating" forces such as rising labor costs (with increased de-

[13] We are indebted to Prof. John N. Nystuen, University of Michigan, for this classification of underlying forces of agglomeration and for his general editing of this chapter.

mand for labor) may accompany the advantages of agglomeration. When it is used, therefore, the term agglomeration refers to the net advantages which can be gained by a sharing of common location by various enterprises.

NETWORK ANALYSIS

Location theory concentrates on the causes and nature of economic activity at a specific location. Network analysis, on the other hand, is concerned with: (1) the manner in which centers of activity are connected, (2) the economics of network construction, and (3) the interrelationships between network connectivity and economic development at a given location. Practical applications of such analysis include the establishment of priorities for building roads, for example, to meet various objectives of: (1) raising by a maximum amount the degree of connectivity between towns, (2) contributing the maximum amount to the economic development of communities represented by network nodes, or (3) providing the shortest travel time for the greatest number of people living in the area served by the network. Other successful applications include the determination of the route for the construction of the least costly pipeline to collect crude oil from a number of producing points.

Many of the concepts of network analysis have been adapted from electrical engineering, in which the analysis of networks, in the form of electrical circuits, comprises a substantial body of knowledge. We can provide only an introduction to some of the concepts here.

Graph Theory [14]

The degree of connectivity, or the extent to which nodes are connected in a network, can be measured by a number of concepts falling under a body of knowledge called graph theory. One such concept is the beta (β) index. The β index is the ratio of the number of routes (e) to the number of vertices or nodes (m) in a system, or:

$$\beta = \frac{e}{m}$$

(7) Calculate β for networks A, B, C, and D in Fig. 12–5. (8) How does β vary with what appears to be the development of the network? (9) What might you want to know, in addition to β, about a network?

[14] A well-written introduction to graph theory and its use in transportation analysis is presented in K. J. Kansky, *Structure of Transportation Networks* (Chicago: Department of Geography, University of Chicago, 1963), Research Paper No. 84.

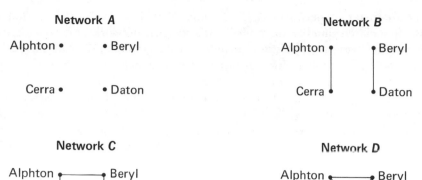

Fig. 12–5. Four stages of network development and connectivity.

Another measure of network connectivity relates actual to maximum connectivity. Maximum connectivity is defined as a route between each pair of nodes which does not pass through a third node, comparable to "non-stop" airline service as opposed to "direct" service (one aircraft making one or more stops en route). It is possible to deduce a general formula for computing the number of routes needed to connect all pairs of network nodes by considering again the simple network of four nodes (m) shown in Fig. 12–5. All possible ways of connecting these four nodes can be shown in a 4×4 matrix of origins and destinations, or 4^2 (m^2) or 16 possible routes. But when arrayed this way, it becomes clear that we are not interested in the four routes in the matrix which link nodes to themselves (equivalent to m, the number of nodes on the network). And unless we are concerned with one-way routes, we aren't interested in whether a route connects node A to node B as opposed to node B to node $A;$ we are interested in one-half of the remaining nodes shown in the matrix. This is a number represented by $\frac{1}{2}(m^2 - m)$, the maximum number of routes providing "non-stop," two-way linkage between m nodes on a network. The actual number of routes on a network can be compared to the maximum number to form an index of connectivity, a number ranging from 0 to 1. (10) **What is the index of connectivity for networks A, B, C, and D in Fig. 12–5?**

The *diameter* of a simple graph (network) is the number of point-to-point routes in the shortest path between the nodes in the network that are farthest apart. The *central place* on the graph is the node that has the lowest associated number, defined as the maximum number of routes required to reach the furthest node on the network from the node for which the associated number is being determined. (11) **Compute** the diameter of networks *A, B, C,* and *D* in Fig. 12–5. (12) **What is the associated number for node Cerra in each network (or, considering it another way, at each stage of network development)?** The hierarchy of associated numbers for various nodes in a network defines the centrality or the remoteness of each node.

There is a simple measure of connectivity, referred to as *local degree,* for nodes on the network. In this case, *m* is always 1 and the beta (β) index for local degree for the node is merely the number of network routes leading to or from the node. (13) **What is the index of local degree for node Cerra in the networks shown in Fig. 12–5?**

Regional scientists in a variety of situations have established direct relationships between local degree (the connectivity of the node), economic activity at the node, and traffic flow to and from the node. However, the reliability of such measures has depended on the proper identification of relevant network properties. (14) **What results would you predict for a study that attempted to relate the level of economic activity in New York City to its position on a network described only by the railroad network of the United States? (15) Why? (16) Do you see any possible uses of graph theory by highway designers? (17) By economists for city Chambers of Commerce? (18) By logistics system planners?**

Network Design and Performance

The design of all but the simplest of networks by analytic methods still defies mathematicians. For example, if we wish to link points R_{1a}, R_{2a}, and M_a in Fig. 12–3 with the shortest network of roads, we know that if the interior angle (the angle formed by lines connecting any one point with the other two) is more than 120°, the shortest network is two straight lines connecting that point with the other two (not connecting the other two directly).

Where all interior angles are less than 120°, the shortest network is formed by finding a fourth point *D* (similar in concept to P_a in Fig. 12–3) at which the other three points can be linked directly by three straight lines forming angles of 120° between them, as shown in Fig. 12–6. This assumes, of course, that the cost of constructing roads is roughly constant over the area shown in Fig. 12–6. (19) **What is the difference in the nature of this assumption from that in situation A of Fig. 12–3? (20) What is the difference in objectives for each of the problems? (21) How would you expect this to affect the location of** P_a **in Fig. 12–3 as opposed to point** *D* **in Fig. 12–6?**

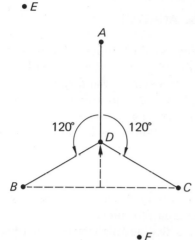

Scale: 0 5 10 15 20 Miles

Fig. 12–6. Determination of the shortest network route linking nodes A, B, and C.

The problem of designing a network to connect more than a small number of points has to consider the creation of various numbers of nodes such as D in Fig. 12–6. The location of any one of these nodes can be accomplished by rules similar to our 120° rule above. However, the simultaneous location of two or more such "cross-road" nodes in the optimal manner has not yet been solved mathematically. The way in which you might link nodes A, B, C, E, and F in Fig. 12–6 by a network of minimum total length, by trial and error, is the way a computer would do it at this stage of development in network design techniques. (22) **Give it a try. What length of network do you come up with, measured in units shown in Fig. 12–6?** (23) **How many nodes does it have?** (24) **Where are they?**

Network design is further complicated by the possible differences in objectives between those who build the network as opposed to those who use it. (25) **If you were planning to transport goods in equal quantities among points A, B, and C in Fig. 12–6, but did not expect to have to pay for the construction of the network, what type of design would you recommend?** (26) **What would you do if you were a sophisticated highway planner wishing to take both construction and user costs over time into account?**

Shortest route problems are of particular importance to those planning delivery or sales routes to accomplish an objective for route coverage with a minimum of travel. We will consider such problems and approaches to them in Chapter 14.

TRADING AREA ANALYSIS

The decision by a potential customer to do business at one location as opposed to another is influenced only in part by the ease with which the transaction can be accomplished, a function of the distance between the customer's home, for example, and the other locations. At least one other important consideration is the customer's assessment of the likelihood of successfully completing his transaction at each location. This is true especially for goods sold at retail, so-called consumer goods, and it has given rise to a family of techniques intended to help define trading areas and the strength of "gravitational pull" which competing trading areas can exert to overcome inertial forces or "friction" created by distances between trading areas and potential customers.

Reilly, in an early effort to inject scientific analysis into marketing planning, formulated a "law of retail gravitation," stated in this manner:

> Two cities attract retail trade from an intermediate city or town in the vicinity of the breaking point, approximately in direct proportion to the populations of the two cities and in inverse proportion to the square of the distances from these two cities to the intermediate town.[15]

Reilly defined a breaking point as the point on a line between two competing trading centers which delineated the relative area over which each trading center would have retail trade influence. Converse and Huegy interpreted this concept in terms of the following formula: [16]

Breaking point between A and B, in miles from $B =$

$$\frac{\text{Distance between } A \text{ and } B}{1 + \sqrt{\dfrac{\text{Population of town } A}{\text{Population of town } B}}}$$

(27) Assuming that the population of City B in Fig. 12–6 is 50,000, the population of City C 100,000, and the distance between cities B and C 40 miles, where on the line connecting the two cities would you expect the trading influence of City B to end? (28) Using this concept, would you speculate on the relative proportion of purchases made outside of City F by its residents in City C as opposed to City B, assuming that the distance between Cities F and C is about 13 miles and the distance between Cities F and B about 32 miles? (29) Would the proportions vary with the size of City F? (30) Why? (31) How?

The law of retail gravitation resulted from the measurement of the

---

[15] William J. Reilly, *The Law of Retail Gravitation* (New York: The Knickerbocker Press, 1931), p. 9.

[16] Paul D. Converse, Harvey W. Huegy, and Robert V. Mitchell, *Elements of Marketing*, 6th Ed. (Englewood Cliffs, N. J.: Prentice-Hall, Inc., 1958), pp. 29–30.

sales of leading stores in larger cities in Texas, house-to-house interviewing to determine consumer buying habits, and retail stock checking
to determine the size and breadth of assortments carried for various
products.[17] (32) **How well do you think it could be adapted to the
problem of determining retail trading areas for competing shopping centers? (33) Competing stores selling home furnishings such as rugs,
draperies, and major items of furniture? (34) Competing cigarette and
candy counters? (35) Why?**

Business researchers, uncomfortable with the assumption that an in
visible line separates individuals shopping at either of two competing
retail outlets, have concentrated on the definition of primary, secondary,
and tertiary (marginal) trading areas for competing retail operations.
Estimates of the shape of such areas are based not only on the distance
between the seller's location and that of the prospective buyer, but also
on such factors as the type of goods being sold, the location of competing outlets, the buyer's economic capacity to buy, the buyer's life style,
and any natural barriers to movement within the potential trading area.
(36) **In measuring distance in such analyses, would it be more appropriate to measure it in miles or minutes? (37) Why?**

The assumption implicit in this approach is that a store, for example,
will obtain the highest proportion of the total purchases of a given type
of product in its primary trading area and lesser proportions in its secondary and tertiary trading areas. Huff has formalized this into a series
of models based on the probability that consumers will shop at one of
two or more competing retail outlets, based in part on their location in
relation to such outlets.[18]

Assumptions regarding the "gravitational pull" of different types of
products, services, and stores have led marketing organizations to develop various strategies for disseminating their companies' goods and
services. For example, manufacturers selling through only a few dealer-
ships with large, well-defined exclusive sales territories for each assume
that the gravitational pull of their product is great and that customers
will travel some distance to shop for, and perhaps buy, it. (38) **What
types of products with which you are familiar fit into this category?**
Other companies may employ a selective distribution policy under which
a few competing outlets in each market are permitted to sell their products. Yet others may develop an intensive distribution strategy in which
every possible outlet is recruited for the sale of their products. (39)
What are characteristics of products that fit this latter category?

[17] For a description of this work see William J. Reilly, *Methods for the Study of
Retail Relationships* (Austin: University of Texas, 1929).
[18] See David L. Huff, "A Probabilistic Analysis of Consumer Spatial Behavior,"
in William S. Decker (ed.), *Emerging Concepts in Marketing* (Chicago: American
Marketing Association, 1963), pp. 443–61.

INPUT–OUTPUT ANALYSIS

Input–output analysis is a means of determining the change in sales of one product, say steel, based on measurements of the amounts of steel which have gone recently into the products of other industries for which sales forecasts have been made.

The first application of input–output analysis developed by Leontief [19] was in the examination of the economic interrelationships between segments of the economy. Among other things, this permitted more accurate projections of the impact that an expansion or contraction in one segment of the economy, perhaps an industry, would have on suppliers of goods and services to that segment or industry.

Isard utilized this basic tool of econometrics in an attempt to formulate a more general theory of location and procedures for the application of theory to practice. He viewed the problem of regional and interregional analysis in a general sense, comparing the purchases and output, in monetary values, for relevant industries in two or more regional or national economies. One purpose was to develop a rationale for interchange of products between the economies and to predict the success of any type of economic activity in a new location. For example, Isard viewed the output of a company or industry as the sum of "functional" inputs such as manufacturing labor, transportation, and materials. In this type of analysis the problem of optimizing location (and thereby costs) becomes one of trading-off one type of input for another. For example, savings in manufacturing labor at a particular point may far outweigh extra costs of transportation incurred in bringing raw materials in. Thus, a portion of labor input is "traded" for a quantity of transportation input. This technique of analysis leads logically to the use of other graphic and mathematical approaches to the problem.[20]

There are two serious problems with input–output analysis which are evident when the method is used for regional analysis. The technique assumes that changes in volume will not affect the proportionate contribution to an industry from every other industry and further, if the model is to be used to forecast future conditions, that these coefficients of exchange will remain unchanged over time. Technological and orga-

[19] Wassily W. Leontief, *Studies in the Structure of the American Economy* (Fair Lawn, N. J.: Oxford University Press, 1953).

[20] See the following sources, all published at New York and Cambridge by John Wiley & Sons, Inc., and The Technology Press of the Massachusetts Institute of Technology, respectively:

Walter Isard, *Location and Space-Economy* (1956), pp. 172–88;

Walter Isard, Eugene W. Schooler, and Thomas Vietorisz, *Industrial Complex Analysis and Regional Development* (1959);

Walter Isard, *Methods of Regional Analysis: An Introduction to Regional Science* (1960).

nizational change occurs all the time, and therefore the method can be used for only short-run forecasts. The second problem is that the method requires detailed empirical data. Information on direct interaction between all types of industry is required. If the study is detailed, it requires a large amount of data. It is therefore expensive to operate. The two problems combined have meant that not many regional input–output models have been operated even though the method is theoretically more satisfactory than commonly used regional forecast models.[21]

LINEAR PROGRAMMING IN NETWORK DESIGN

Linear programming provides the basis for the systematic linking of supply and demand points to obtain a least-cost combination. The procedure requires a knowledge of current and prospective market locations. Quantitative limits on sources of supply and projections of quantities of demand, market by market, must also be known. Possible fixed facility locations must be considered after discarding obviously impossible alternatives. Transportation rates, weighted to correspond to the relative importance, in terms of volume, of incoming and outgoing materials, are a necessary element of the analysis. Other constraints may be imposed on the problem, such as the existence of other producing units in a network, with the attendant problem of market definition (and sometimes protection) for facilities in which large amounts of money already have been invested.

This technique has been adapted by Ford and Fulkerson in the development of some of the most advanced techniques for network design.[22] We will discuss linear programming in greater length later, at that time considering the limitations and strengths of the method.

INFLUENCES OF LOGISTICS ON ECONOMIC DEVELOPMENT

We have discussed the effects of transportation (logistics) on the location decision in the general sense. Once made, the original location decision also can be modified by logistics considerations.

A variation of Thünen's transportation cost belts can be used to specu-

[21] For examples, see Daniel H. Garnick, "Disaggregated Basic-Service Models and Regional Input–Output Models in Multiregional Projections," *Journal of Regional Science*, April, 1969, pp. 87–100; W. H. Miernyk, *The Elements of Input–Output Analysis* (New York: Random House, 1965); G. Rey and C. B. Tilanus, "Input–Output Forecasts for the Netherlands, 1949–1958," *Econometrica*, July, 1963, pp. 454–63; Wesley H. Long, "An Examination of the Linear Homogeneity of Trade and Production Functions in County Leontief Matrices," *Journal of Regional Science*, April, 1969, pp. 47–67.

[22] L. R. Ford, Jr., and D. R. Fulkerson, *Flows in Networks* (Princeton, N. J.: Princeton University Press, 1962).

late on the area which a firm might supply from a given point of storage or production. Consider the situation of three competing firms, shown in Fig. 12–7. Each has a plant located equidistant from the other two.

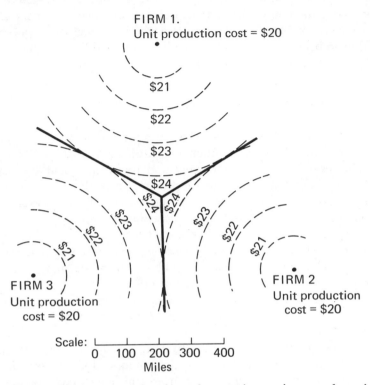

FIRM 1.
Unit production cost = $20

$21

$22

$23

$24

FIRM 3
Unit production
cost = $20

FIRM 2
Unit production
cost = $20

Scale:
0   100   200 300   400
Miles

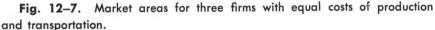

Fig. 12–7. Market areas for three firms with equal costs of production and transportation.

Each experiences the same production cost per unit ($20), and transportation costs per unit are constant and equal for all firms ($.01 per mile per unit). The latter is indicated by the cost belts radiating from each production site. In this case, boundaries of the markets served by each plant (assuming completely rational economic behavior and a price policy which charges a price based on production cost plus cost of transportation to any given point) will be delineated by points at which the price charged by any two or more of the firms is the same. Theoretically, all of these points are situated at the intersection of comparable cost belts of two or three firms. By connecting these points, market boundaries are formed.

Influence on Market Boundaries

Decreased costs of transportation for one firm in comparison with another will enlarge the market territory of the first at the expense of the second. This is the relationship shown for the three firms in Fig. 12–8. A combination of lower logistics costs, production costs, or both

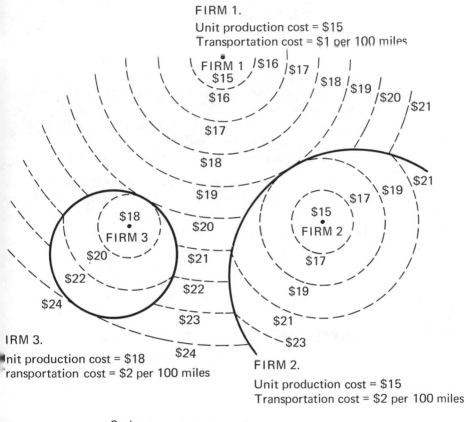

Fig. 12–8. Market areas for three firms having unequal costs of production and transportation.

can result in a greatly increased market area for one firm at the expense of another. Thus, firm 1 benefits in this manner at the expense of firm 3 in Fig. 12–8, enlarging its market area to encircle completely a small area surrounding firm 3's plant. (40) If the diagram were extended further, would firm 1's market area also eventually encircle firm 2's? [23]

Isard offers a formula for the determination of the point at which a theoretical market boundary will fall between two competing fixed facilities.[24] It requires a knowledge of production or landed costs at the two competing points, the transportation rate per unit of distance paid by each competing firm, and the distance between competing fixed facilities. It is stated as:

$$p_1 + r_1 d_1 = p_2 + r_2 d_2,$$

where

p_1 and p_2 are the production or landed costs of two firms, 1 and 2, respectively, at competing fixed facilities;

r_1 and r_2 are the transportation rates per unit per mile paid by firms 1 and 2, respectively;

d_1 and d_2 are the distances between the market boundary line and firms 1 and 2, respectively; and

$d_1 + d_2$ is the distance between facilities of firms 1 and 2.

Assume a production cost of $20 per unit for two competing firms. Assume further that the transportation rate is $.10 per mile per unit for each and the distance between the firms' facilities is 100 miles. Where will the boundary fall between them? Common sense is verified by the formula, which indicates:

$$20 + .10 \, d_1 = 20 + .10 \, d_2 \quad \text{and} \quad d_1 + d_2 = 100$$
$$.10 \, d_1 = .10 \, d_2$$
$$d_1 = d_2$$
$$d_1 - d_2 = 0$$

Adding simultaneous equations:

$$
\begin{aligned}
d_1 - d_2 &= 0 \\
+ \, d_1 + d_2 &= 100 \\
\hline
2d_1 \quad &= 100 \\
d_1 \quad &= 50 \\
d_2 \quad &= 50
\end{aligned}
$$

(41) What would be the case where both firms simultaneously lowered their production cost to $15, but firm 1 negotiated a favorable rate of $.08 per mile per unit for the transportation of its product?

(42) Based on information presented in Chapter 9, could you con-

---

[23] A full description of a method for determining non-overlapping market areas is found in C. D. Hyson and W. P. Hyson, "The Economic Law of Market Areas," *Quarterly Journal of Economics*, May, 1950, pp. 319–24.

[24] Based on the formula stated by Isard, *Location and Space-Economy, op. cit.,* p. 147.

struct a map similar to that in Fig. 12–8 for the Wonka Company? (43) What meaning would it have?

Blanket Transportation Rates and Pricing Policy

Implicit in the development of Figs. 12–7 and 12–8 are two assumptions: (1) that customers will purchase from the firm offering the lowest price, and (2) that producers will price their product at an amount based directly on the costs of production and transportation. You may argue, and rightly so, that in actual practice these assumptions are commonly violated by uniform delivered pricing policies. The point is granted. But even under these circumstances, the diagrammatical approach shown here will serve to demonstrate two things: (1) the points from which a firm with several distribution points can most economically serve a given territory, and (2) those sales which are profitable and those which are not when made from a given point on a delivered price basis.

It is likely that blanket transportation rates, discussed earlier, directly contribute to delivered uniform pricing policies. By discontinuing incremental charges for additional distance beyond certain "gateways" to blanket rate areas, transportation firms (transfer media) allow uniform delivered prices to conform more directly to cost.

Transportation and Economies of Scale

Figure 12–8 fails to show clearly the interrelationship between costs of transportation and production costs associated with a reduction or increase in the former. Decreases in transportation costs in relation to competition allow a firm to expand its market territories, providing the differential can be maintained. Market territory expansion allows it to produce more at a given location. This may offer economies of scale in the production operation. These economies, in turn, may allow a company to expand further the market territory served from the plant. In cases such as this, transport cost advantages can create a self-reinforcing chain of events.[25]

Dynamics of Logistics and Location

Much of the work concerning dynamic location theory has centered around the division of a linear market (that is, all customers located on

[25] For a graphical explanation of this phenomenon, see Isard, *Location and Space-Economy, op. cit.,* pp. 148–51.

a straight line between two competing suppliers) under varying assumptions as to the relative ability of firms to relocate, the ability to compete with prices, the number of competitors, the elasticity of demand in relation to price, and others.[26]

You can explore these theoretical concepts by drawing a line representing a market of 100 units of sales (one unit of sale per unit of distance on the line), a cost of logistics of one dollar per unit of distance between a producing and consuming point, and a contribution of $50 per unit of product manufactured and sold. **(44) Where would a company enjoying a monopoly position locate its plant in this market? (45) Where would its first competitor, enjoying similar economics, locate its plant? (46) Assuming that it costs $500 to relocate a plant, where would these competitors relocate their plants in alternating "moves," in order to maximize their contributions?** You can devise a series of "games" that approximate reality to a greater and greater extent by, among other things: (1) increasing the number of competitors, (2) introducing both fixed (unvarying with volume) and variable (with volume) costs of production, and (3) expanding the competition "space" to two dimensions.

INFLUENCES OF LOCATION ON LOGISTICS

Economic development and the development of facilities to transport and handle goods take place simultaneously and are in large measure interrelated. We shall couch the second phase of our discussion in terms of national and regional economic development, using specific examples and statistics to illustrate various points.

Central Place Theory

Much of the thinking about current area development is based on the provocative work done by Christaller and by Lösch.[27] Both men carried out detailed studies of the nature of the way in which areas develop, Christaller in Southern Germany and Lösch in both Germany and the United States. Their work has formed the basis for a "central place

---

[26] For early examples of situations of progressively relaxed restrictions see Harold Hotelling, "Stability in Competition," *Economic Journal*, March, 1929, pp. 41–47; Abba P. Lerner and H. W. Singer, "Some Notes on Duopoly and Spatial Competition," *Journal of Political Economy*, April, 1937, pp. 145–86; Arthur F. Smithies, "Optimum Location in Spatial Competition," *Journal of Political Economy*, June, 1941, pp. 423–39; and Gardner Ackley, "Spatial Competition in a Discontinuous Market," *Quarterly Journal of Economics*, February, 1942, pp. 212–30.

[27] Walter Christaller, *Die zentralen Orte in Suddeutschland* (Jena: Gustav Fischer Verlag, 1933), and Lösch, *op. cit.*

theory." [28] Two major theses of this work are that: (1) centers of economic activity organize themselves in a regular, symmetrical pattern, with each level of activity being spaced differently according to its magnitude and the number of competing firms, and (2) an area, once it has acquired a certain range of economic activity, enters into a state which Lösch has called "location equilibrium," a condition best described as one in which separate communities have developed to a point where no one community has a locational advantage that would return "extraordinary profits" to it.

Central place theory [29] hypothesizes that, other things being equal, in a competitive economy firms will tend to locate in a regular pattern in order to: (1) maximize the size of the economical market area for any one producing location, and (2) reduce extraordinary profits that one firm might otherwise enjoy at the expense of another because of its location.

Fortunately or unfortunately, other things are never equal. Certain points offer special attractions for a given type of economic activity. Also, as pointed out earlier, the transportation rate structure is not constructed on a regular or even, at times, a rational basis. For these reasons, most of Lösch's measurements, and those of others, were deliberately made in carefully selected, fully developed environments characterized by regularity of urban locations and land use.[30]

Lösch reasoned that the demand for a firm's product was a function of delivered (production plus logistics cost) price. At a point sufficiently distant from a manufacturing point, demand would disappear altogether. He then concluded that:

The [total] demand of the curtailed sales area [of given constant size] is greater when it is circular in form. But per unit of area of the market region, the demand of the small circle, not that of the large circle, is greatest because in the latter case the average for the area is reduced by the small demand near the limits for shipment. The average demand in the small circle is obviously greater than any polygon of equal area. But because circles leave empty corners, the demand per unit of the entire area in the case of the hexagon exceeds not only that of a square and a triangle, but even that of a circle. In other words, among all the possibilities of realizing the same total demand, the most land is required with a triangle, and the least with a regular hexagon.

[28] For two excellent developments of early work, see Brian J. L. Berry and William L. Garrison, "The Functional Bases of the Central Place Hierarchy," *Economic Geography*, April, 1958, pp. 145–54; and E. Ullman, "A Theory of Location for Cities," *American Journal of Sociology*, May, 1941, pp. 853–64.

[29] The terms "central place," "urban place," "place," and "city" are often used interchangeably in this context.

[30] Iowa, for example, has been a favorite proving ground for advocates of central place theory. See Edwin N. Thomas, "Toward an Expanded Central Place Model," *Geographical Review*, July, 1961, pp. 400–11.

The honeycomb is therefore the most advantageous shape for economic regions.[31]

For logistics, the significant theme in central place theory is the notion of the efficiency of a system of nested market areas and the corresponding hierarchy of towns and cities of different sizes in a region. Activities which draw people long distances and/or require a large market to operate are located in big cities. At the opposite end of the scale are convenience-goods firms such as gas stations, corner grocery stores, and drug stores. They are distributed in a pattern very similar to the distribution of people because, in the first place, people will not travel far to obtain their goods or services and, secondly, they can reach a threshold of business (profit point in volume of sales) with a small number of customers. The result is a hierarchy of centers of business activities. Another example of this phenomenon is the hierarchy of the central business district, regional shopping centers, and neighborhood shopping centers of a large metropolis.

Attempts have been made to apply central place theory in a number of ways. At the local level, measurements have been taken to determine the size of community which fosters certain types of enterprise, essentially minimum population requirements. At the regional level, investigations designed to test the hypothesis that areas enter into a state of equilibrium are being conducted.[32] Of immediate concern to us is the meaning which economic development, of whatever pattern, has for logistics.

From a logistical point of view the choice of size of a city in which to locate a facility will reflect the threshold size of the activity and the transportation cost of the distribution stage to the next level in the hierarchy. **(47) Does this suggest a manner in which a firm distributing its products nationally might organize its distribution system? (48) Why?**

Current Trends

What is the nature of economic development, and what significance does it have for logistics? Statistics for the United States can be used to illustrate pertinent points in this respect.

Growth of Area Population and Economic Development. The most striking example of area development in the United States in recent years has been the development of the West Coast. Figure 12–9 indicates that

[31] Lösch, *op. cit.*, p. 112.
[32] A good summary of central place theory applications as well as other analyses of regional market organization is found in Brian J. L. Berry and Frank E. Horton, *Geographic Perspectives in Urban Systems* (Englewood Cliffs, N. J.: Prentice-Hall, Inc., 1970). Also see Brian J. L. Berry, *Geography of Market Centers and Retail Distribution* (Englewood Cliffs, N. J.: Prentice-Hall, Inc., 1967).

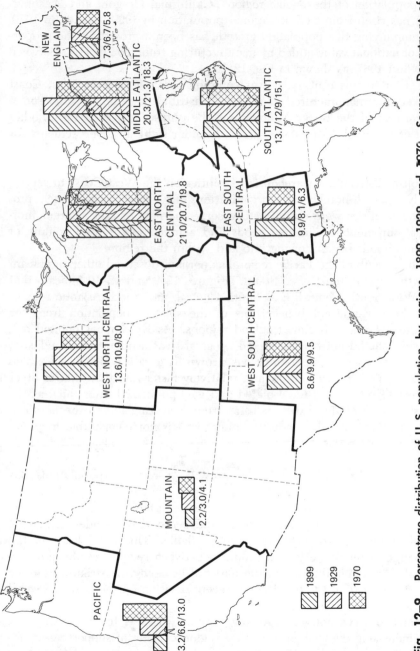

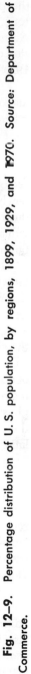

Fig. 12-9. Percentage distribution of U. S. population, by regions, 1899, 1929, and 1970. Source: Department of Commerce.

the population of the Pacific region (California, Oregon, and Washington) has risen from 6.6% of national population in 1929 to 13.0% in 1970. Accompanying this population growth has been a growth in the proportion of national value added by manufacturing from 6.0% to 11.3% between 1929 and 1967, as shown in Fig. 12–10.

Earlier in this century, it was common practice to serve West Coast markets for manufactured goods from distribution points located somewhere east of the Rocky Mountains. The phrase, "prices slightly higher west of the Rocky Mountains" was a familiar sight in advertisements for finished products.

The increasing volume of demand enabled many Eastern suppliers to establish distribution warehousing facilities on the West Coast to service newly opened branch sales organizations. In many cases, branch producing facilities were established to serve the new market. Larger individual shipments of finished goods and a much larger total volume of finished goods began flowing into and within the region.

The growth of the Pacific region has perhaps obscured other significant growth areas in the United States. Figures 12–9 and 12–10 indicate that the West South Central, East South Central, and South Atlantic regions have been significant beneficiaries of the shift of population from the Middle Atlantic and New England regions. As Hoover has pointed out, the shift should not be interpreted necessarily as a migration of industry. The population of the country has grown at a rate which has enabled one region's industry to grow at a relatively faster rate than that of other regions. Except for a few isolated and well-publicized cases, such as the physical shift of the textile industry from New England to the South in the past three decades, industry "migration" is not comparable to population migration.[33]

Regional Self-Sufficiency. The growth of regional populations has created local markets able to support increasing numbers of those industries in which economies of scale are important. As a consequence, regional self-sufficiency increases in the sense that broader ranges of locally produced products are made available. This trend leads to the exchange of more specialized products between regions, establishing regional trading equilibrium in the national economy. A striking example of the existence of the trend is the recent decision on the part of several publishers of national newspapers and magazines to publish regional editions to serve not only growing regional markets for readership but also increasing numbers of firms in a region capable of supporting a substantial regional advertising program. And this in an industry where manufacturing (i.e., printing) economies of scale are tremendous.

33 Hoover, *op. cit.*, pp. 148–51.

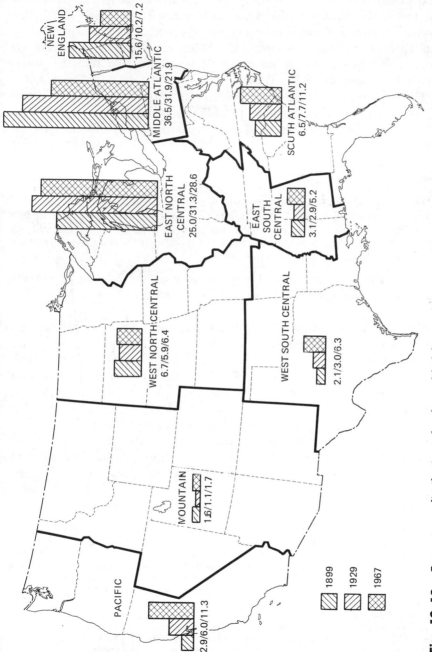

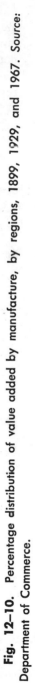

Fig. 12–10. Percentage distribution of value added by manufacture, by regions, 1899, 1929, and 1967. Source: Department of Commerce.

Regional self-sufficiency is likely to continue to change the pattern of logistics in the United States. One might foresee a decrease in the distances over which finished products are transported as the movement of goods within regions increases. **(49) What effect might increasing regional self-sufficiency have on transportation costs and rates for interregional movements? (50) Why?**

This same market "magnetism" which has attracted industry to growing regions is likely to continue to pull producing facilities away from raw material sources.[34] This does not necessarily mean that the average distance any single raw material or finished goods component will have to move to reach a processing point will increase. As has been pointed out:

> The chain of processing between raw materials and final products has been growing longer and longer. The tendency of any plant in the chain to use materials which are already processed has continued to grow. As a result, in increasing degree, plants hold down their freight-in costs by locating near other plants—not near a raw material source.[35]

(51) What impact would this trend have on the relative proportion of logistics costs in the final value of a product? (52) Why?

National Development. The characteristics of an economy are derived from those of its regions. Considering this, it is not surprising that the economy of the United States has undergone slow, but inexorable, changes throughout its history. These changes, based on the general economic standard of living, can be compared directly with the developmental changes which take place in a region over a period of time.

The agricultural phase through which the United States passed is far behind us. For the past eighty years, location theorists and regional economists have concerned themselves primarily with the location and development of extractive and manufacturing industries. A more recent phase, one characteristic of a highly developed society, is a noticeable shift in the relative importance of the manufacturing and trade and ser-

[34] The assumption that basic industry location in this country has been tied to raw material sources might well be more closely examined. There is a great deal of evidence, for example, that even an industry such as the iron and steel industry has always been "market" oriented to the extent that its producing facilities have located at points strategic to markets which also offered one or more of the raw materials necessary for steel production. As more desirable raw material sites are exhausted, the locations of producing sites for basic industry are following the market, not the raw material sources.

[35] Benjamin Chinitz and Raymond Vernon, "Changing Forces in Industrial Location," *Harvard Business Review*, January–February, 1960, p. 130. Several reasons might be advanced for this trend: (1) the increasing technology, and resulting increasing number of processes requiring plant sites, needed to produce more complex products, and (2) the lessened raw material source "pull" exerted by some of the richest mineral deposits, now largely depleted.

vice activities in the economy. Figure 12–11 shows relative trends in employment in the major categories of activities.

Employment in agriculture and the extractive industries reached a high point as a proportion of total employment sometime in the nineteenth century, probably just before the Civil War. By 1870, as shown in Fig. 12-11, it was already on its way downward. Manufacturing employment reached a proportionate peak in 1920 in relation to trade and service employment. Since then the latter two have been increasing in impor-

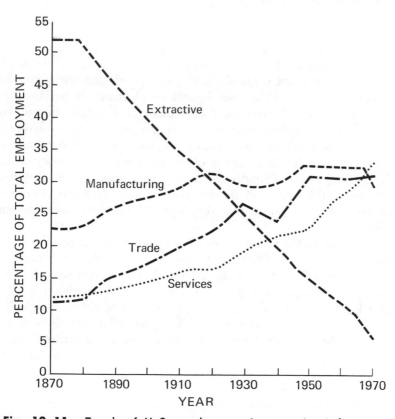

Fig. 12–11. Trends of U. S. employment in extractive industries, manufacturing, trade, and services, 1870–1970. Each category is stated as a percentage of total employment. Extractive occupations include agriculture, forestry, mining, and fishing. Manufacturing occupations include manufacturing and contract building construction. Trade occupations include retailing, wholesaling, finance, insurance, real estate, and transportation. Service occupations include education, other professions, domestic services, personal services, and government. Totals do not include persons in military service. *Source:* Department of Commerce, Office of Business Economics, *Survey of Current Business.*

tance. The trends shown in Fig. 12–11 require careful interpretation, because they contain no weighting of the relative "income-generating" power per person employed in each of the categories over a period of years. One would suspect, for example, that the growth of automation in manufacturing has increased the generating power per person employed even if it has perhaps led to a levelling-out of total employment. Employment statistics instead of income statistics were used to show long-run trends, because of the absence of detailed figures for income on a national level before 1930.

A second major trend in the development of our economy has been the pronounced shift to a customer-oriented business philosophy. This philosophy has placed a good deal of emphasis on the importance of giving the customer what he wants, when he wants it, and in the necessary quantities. It is not confined to the service of ultimate consumers, those who consume for their own benefit or pleasure. It has been extended backward slowly through the channel of logistics. Recent emphasis in retailing management has been placed on the reduction of inventories to increase turnover ratios. Retailers placing emphasis on inventory control have shifted many of the problems of inventory control onto the wholesalers who supply them. In many cases, wholesalers have passed some of this increased burden back to manufacturers, thus continuing the series of repercussions that were begun at the ultimate consumer level.

A third major factor based on the level of national development can be referred to as the "technology of material." Manufacturers have attacked the "barriers" of location by utilizing lighter weight materials in a wide range of products. The post-war emergence of aluminum, plastics, and other light materials has enabled manufacturers to increase the dollar-weight factor of goods produced.[36] (53) **What effect would you suppose that this has had on the average density of manufactured goods? (54) Or on the importance of cubic capacity of equipment designed for various carriers in the transport industries?**

Taken in the sum, what importance do these national developments have for the logistics system of this country? The recent emphasis on services, on customer orientation, and on improved technology of materials has challenged the flexibility and adaptability of various systems of logistics. All three developments should contribute to a trend of generally lower weights for shipments.[37] The first two developments (customer orientation and shifting of inventory position) have resulted in

[36] The dollar-weight factor is the ratio of dollar value to a given amount of weight for any product.
[37] The most comprehensive information available on this question, supplied by the 1963 and 1967 *Census of Transportation,* provides little indication of trend.

generally smaller shipments and "tight" inventory policies of customers at various levels in economic channels. The third factor (materials technology) has reduced the weight of shipments without, in many cases, influencing their cubic size. This will continue to influence the design of logistics systems in the economy to accommodate lighter, bulkier shipments.

INTERRELATIONSHIPS BETWEEN AREA DEVELOPMENT
AND LOGISTICS—A CASE EXAMPLE

Does the development of logistics facilities and services follow economic growth? Or is the relationship reversed? These questions have been asked since the world's first trade routes were developed, for they have been critical for decisions concerning trade and development, particularly to countries with far-flung empires. We will dodge the argument, adopting the position that the two developments are so interrelated as to be impossible to sort out.

As areas, either cities or limited regions, develop economic activities of a somewhat specialized nature, they generate new demands for raw materials, supplies, and consumer goods just as they develop their capacities to trade with other areas. Increased interchange by an area with its neighbors encourages at least three developments: (1) the growth of freight volume which permits the use of more economical means of handling shipments, (2) an increase in the quantity and variety of available transportation services and material-handling (warehousing) firms, as well as an increase in competition, and (3) changes in the structure of the logistics network to facilitate and serve the development of important areas of economic activity.

Regional development results in decreased costs of transportation to and from cities and regions of larger size. Generally speaking, transportation charges have been adjusted to reflect the nature and quantities of the materials flowing to and from each region. This, in turn, may influence the further development and concentration of economic activity in those areas. A case example provides an opportunity to explore the interrelationship further.

The United States currently is witnessing a dramatic example of the third major type of development affecting logistics listed above, the improvement of facilities for more efficient transportation through the construction of the world's most extensive network of high-speed highways. This effort already has produced significant reductions in the line-haul costs of motor carriers, indirectly affecting most domestic freight transportation rates, as well as the more highly publicized reduction in deaths from highway accidents.

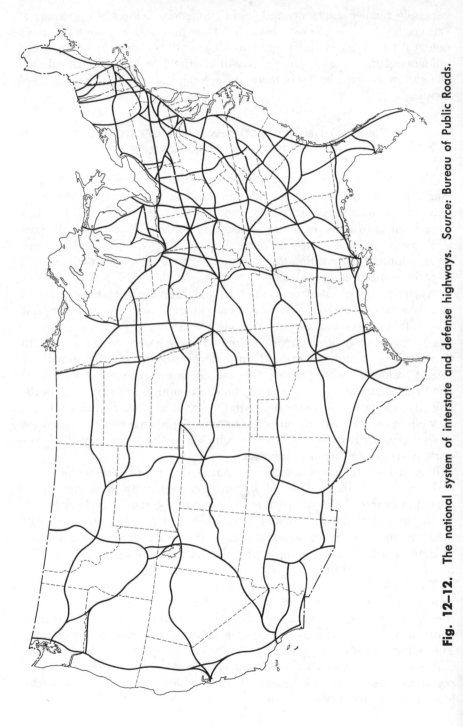

Fig. 12–12. The national system of interstate and defense highways.   Source: Bureau of Public Roads.

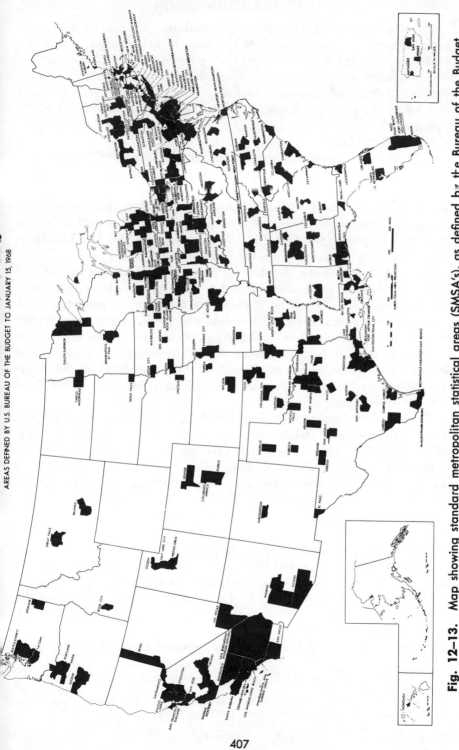

AREAS DEFINED BY U.S. BUREAU OF THE BUDGET TO JANUARY 15, 1968

Fig. 12–13. Map showing standard metropolitan statistical areas (SMSA's), as defined by the Bureau of the Budget.
Source: Department of Commerce.

Existing regional development influenced the structure of the interstate highway system network. At the time it was planned, it was designed to serve 182 of the 199 cities with populations of 50,000 or more.[38] When completed, it will connect 42 of the 48 state capitals (excluding Juneau, Alaska, and Honolulu, Hawaii). Apropos of our earlier discussion, notice the regularity, as suggested by Lösch, of points of intersection (particularly within major regions) on the interstate highway system, shown in Fig. 12–12.

(55) Regional science suggests that greater accessibility may contribute to the economic growth of a community in relation to others. Looking at Fig. 12–12, and relating it to the map identifying standard metropolitan statistical areas (SMSA's) in Fig. 12–13, how would you assess the differential benefits to various communities provided by the Interstate Highway System? (56) Which cities do you feel benefitted most, relatively speaking, from the system? (57) Why?

(58) Waterloo, Iowa, located in northeast Iowa, was one of the largest cities most perfectly bypassed by the system. As an economist advising the City Council of Waterloo at the onset of construction of the interstate system, what effects would you predict for the community as a result of this situation? (59) What advice would you give them?

(60) In general, how would you expect the location of regional and logistics activity to change as a result of the construction of the Interstate Highway System? Consider one indicator, the trend in the location of warehousing activity.

A survey conducted in 1965 by *Handling & Shipping* magazine pinpointed the locations chosen by manufacturers for nearly 500 new distribution centers, operated in both privately owned and public space, between 1960 and 1965.[39] One conclusion from this survey was that locations for distribution centers were becoming more diversified. While a large proportion of such centers was being located in the largest standard metropolitan areas, less well-known centers of economic activity like Cozad, Nebraska, were appearing on the list in increasing numbers.

Further, a weighted analysis of the data indicated by the *Handling & Shipping* survey suggested that only 49.3% of the new space reported in the survey was located in the 35 largest standard metropolitan statistical areas (SMSA's), as shown in Table 12–1. This was far below the aggregate proportion of all general public warehousing space, 61.6%, located in the same 35 SMSA's, reported in the 1963 *Census of Business*. However, a similar calculation of data reported in the 1967 *Census of*

---

[38] H. E. Hilts, "Planning the Interregional Highway System," *Public Roads*, June, 1941, pp. 69–96.

[39] Kenneth Marshall and John Miller, "Where Are the Distribution Centers Going?," *Handling & Shipping*, November, 1965, pp. 37–45.

TABLE 12-1. Trends in the Concentration of General Public Warehousing Activity in the United States

	Proportion of Square Footage for Each Year				Proportion of New Distribution Centers, H & S Survey
Standard metropolitan area groupings	1954[a]	1958[a]	1963[a]	1967[a]	1960-1965[b]
35 largest SMSA's	51.5%	60.2%	61.6%	51.3%	49.3%
Remaining SMSA's with population over 250,000[c]	18.2%	19.6%	21.5%	20.3%	15.6%
Remainder of United States	30.3%	20.2%	16.8%	28.4%	35.1%
Total percentage	100.0%	100.0%	100.0%	100.0%	100.0%
Total square footage (in millions)	108.3	119.3	129.2	186.5	22.3[d]

[a]Based on information contained in the *Census of Business* for the appropriate years.

[b]Based on information contained in Kenneth Marshall and John Miller, "Where Are the Distribution Centers Going?," *Handling & Shipping*, November, 1965, pp. 37–45.

[c]Limited to SMSA's with population over 300,000 in 1958.

[d]Estimated on the basis of size distributions reported by Marshall and Miller, *op. cit.*, p. 42.

Business, also shown in Table 12–1, indicated the concentration of space in the largest SMSA's had fallen to 51.3%. In the few short years between censuses, a previous trend may have been reversed. **(61) Would you have expected this? (62) How would you explain it?**

In Table 12–2, we see that among the largest SMSA's, those of Paterson–Clifton–Passaic (New Jersey), Philadelphia, and New Orleans have the highest concentration of general public warehousing space per capita. However, SMSA's with much higher concentrations include Jersey City, Salt Lake City, Jacksonville, and Charlotte (North Carolina). **(63) How do you explain this?**

Relating the number of new distribution centers recorded in the *Handling & Shipping* survey to SMSA populations, we find that the largest SMSA's with the highest number of new centers per million of population during the period of 1960 to 1965 were Atlanta, Dallas, Kansas City, Denver, Portland, and Columbus. **(64) Is this and the information in the previous paragraph consistent with what you expected on the basis of your analysis of Fig. 12–12 and 12–13? (65) Why? (66) What other factors may have influenced these trends?**

SOME CONSIDERATIONS FOR THE FUTURE

As a means of summing up, it is important to note some of the basic trends in location, economic development, and logistics which will affect their interrelationships.

TABLE 12-2. Trends in Concentration of General Public Warehousing Activity in the United States

Standard Metropolitan Statistical Area	Per Capita Square Footage of Warehouse Space		Percentage Change, 1967 vs. 1958	New Private and Public Distribution Centers Per Million People Established Between 1960 and 1965, *Handling & Shipping Survey*[c]
	1958[a]	1967[b]		
Largest SMSA's:				
New York	.96	1.03	+7%	.6
Los Angeles–Long Beach	.55	.71	+29	4.2
Chicago	1.22	1.65	+35	3.9
Philadelphia, Pa.–N. J.	2.06	1.36	−34	1.9
Detroit	.53	1.05	+98	2.7
San Francisco–Oakland	1.17	.63	−46	5.7
Washington, D. C.–Md.–Va.	.37	.13	−65	1.0
Boston	1.45	1.37	−6	3.1
Pittsburgh	.55	.57	+4	1.7
St. Louis, Mo.–Ill.	1.09	1.57	+44	2.4
Baltimore	.62	.90	+45	1.2
Cleveland	1.58	1.60	+1	5.3
Houston	1.28	1.87	+46	6.5
Newark	.97	1.93	+99	2.4
Minneapolis–St. Paul	1.86	1.89	+2	4.7
Dallas	1.39	1.61	+16	17.6
Seattle–Everett	1.08	1.21	+12	6.3
Anaheim–Santa Ana–Garden Grove	N.I.d,e	.00	?	.0
Milwaukee	.81	.92	+14	1.6
Atlanta	1.25	2.41	+93	18.8
Cincinnati, Ohio–Ky.–Ind.	.50	.29	−42	3.1
Paterson–Clifton–Passaic, N. J.	2.20	2.22	+1	3.4
San Diego	N.I.d,e	.00	?	1.0
Miami	.61	.89	+46	2.1

Kansas City, Mo.-Kans.	1.92	2.69	+40	9.2
Denver	.29	1.34	+356	8.6
San Bernardino-Riverside-Ontario, Calif.	.10	.00	-100	.0
Indianapolis	1.19	1.58	+33	1.1
San Jose	.47[e]	D.W.[f]	?	.0
New Orleans	2.06	.80	-61	3.3
Tampa-St. Petersburg	.47	1.07	+127	2.6
Portland, Ore.-Wash.	1.38	1.86	+35	8.5
Phoenix	D.W.[f]	.43	?	3.0
Providence-Pawtucket-Warwick, R. I.-Mass.	D.W.[f]	.76[e]	?	2.4
Rochester	1.02	.57[e]	-45	.0
Dayton	D.W.[f]	.84[e]	?	.0
Other SMSA's With High Concentration:				
Jersey City	4.87	6.54	+34	9.9
Jacksonville	1.41	3.60	+155	15.4
Salt Lake City	.85	3.62	+326	4.5
Charlotte, N. C.	3.49	5.00	+43	9.5
Weighted Average of 35 Largest SMSA's	1.02	1.14	+12	3.3
Weighted Average of Remainder of U. S.	.44	.76	+73	2.1
Weighted Average of Entire U. S.	.67	.91	+36	2.6

[a] 1958 *Census of Business*, Vol. III, *Wholesale Trade Summary Statistics* (Washington, D. C.: Department of Commerce, Bureau of the Census, 1961), pp. 10-19 and 10-20, with comparisons made to *1960 Census of Population* results.

[b] 1967 *Census of Business, Public Warehousing* (Washington, D. C.: Department of Commerce, Bureau of the Census, 1970), pp. 9-28 and 9-29, with comparisons made to *1970 Census of Population* results.

[c] Kenneth Marshall and John Miller, "Where Are the Distribution Centers Going?," *Handling & Shipping*, November, 1965, pp. 37-45. This study reported results of a survey of all of the largest 1,000 companies with Standard Industrial Classification numbers 10 through 14 (mining) and 19 through 39 (manufacturing). Of 852 companies surveyed, 357 or 41% supplied information about 467 new distribution centers. The ratio computed in each case is the number of distribution centers per million people in the SMSA according to the *1960 Census of Population*.

[d] Not included among SMSA's with 250,000 or more in population in 1960.

[e] Not included among the 35 largest SMSA's.

[f] Data withheld to preserve the confidentiality of information.

We have termed costs of transportation, and in a broader sense logistics, as barriers to the development of supply sources, markets, and regions. In practice, costs of logistics impose an important restriction on supply and market area definition. In a survey performed several years ago, 50% of the firms polled indicated that between 1955 and 1960, because of excessive logistics costs, they had to withdraw from markets previously served.[40]   In spite of the common practice of pricing goods at a uniform level designed to be competitive in remote markets, many firms apparently do feel the presence of the logistics barrier from time to time.

(67) A desirable long-run goal is to decrease total costs of performing a given unit of business. Assuming that it might be possible to do this by reducing the importance of logistics costs, in relation to those of production and marketing, what would be likely to take place?

Consider a counteracting trend which, at the same time, will make the job of reducing the relative importance of logistics more difficult and tend to draw a firm from its markets. Many years ago it was suggested by Weber:

> . . . in any given industrial process it is the proportion of the weight of the ubiquities used to the weight losses of localized materials which gives the basic answer to the question of whether the particular industry settles at the places of consumption or moves to the material deposits.
> . . . development will, as it concentrates population, produce an ever-increasing demand for the available amount of ubiquities. In consequence, unreproducible ubiquities will be used up at certain places, and reproducible ubiquities will be in such demand at many places that the demand will exceed the local output. . . . This means that the development, insofar as it signifies concentration of population, continuously diminishes the share of ubiquities in production and substitutes localized materials in their place.[41]

This development, Weber concluded, would tend to separate production activities from their markets. A current example of the threat of exhaustion of a ubiquity is water. It is possible that, given a great enough economic and population development with less rapid introduction of ecologically sound practices and technological development of improved water-processing facilities, water could become, to selected areas, a localized material requiring transportation from one place to another. This trend would tend to divorce heavy users of water from certain of their markets, drawing them nearer plentiful supplies of water.

A concurrent, but contrasting, problem is illustrated by the steel industry in this country. Some desirably located deposits of localized materials such as iron ore are being exhausted, requiring the development of less desirably located deposits. This trend has lengthened the total

[40] "Better Transportation Is Up to Management," *Dun's Review and Modern Industry*, June, 1958, pp. 64–65.
[41] Friedrich, *op. cit.*, pp. 73–74.

supply line of many steel companies unable to locate at great distance from their markets.

These developments may tend to divorce the location of some industrial activities from either markets or sources of raw materials. At the same time, they will impose a heavy burden on such firms to develop better systems of logistics to counteract unfavorable locational trends.

SUGGESTED READINGS

ABLER, RONALD, JOHN S. ADAMS, and PETER GOULD. *Spatial Organization.* Englewood Cliffs, N. J.: Prentice-Hall, Inc., 1971.
Offers an interesting, comprehensive introduction to a variety of concepts explaining the spatial arrangements of economic activity.

BECKMANN, MARTIN. *Location Theory.* New York: Random House, Inc., 1968.
This lucid little book deals with most of the matters covered in this chapter and, as well, offers mathematical explanations for these phenomena. Of particular interest is a final chapter reviewing the locational effects of economic growth.

DEAN, ROBERT D., WILLIAM H. LEAHY, and DAVID L. MCKEE (eds.). *Spatial Economic Theory.* New York: The Free Press, 1970.
A collection of classic articles on the subject.

ISARD, WALTER. *Location and Space-Economy.* New York: John Wiley & Sons, Inc., 1956.
For an approach to general location theory utilizing principles of econometrics which offer the greatest promise for future work in the field (and upon which subsequent methods and projects of regional analysis have been developed by Isard).

KARASKA, GERALD J., and DAVID F. BRAMHALL (ed.). *Locational Analysis for Manufacturing.* Cambridge, Mass.: The M.I.T. Press, 1969.
This collection of readings contains several dealing with the variation of transportation costs over space and empirical results of observations of actual plant location decision processes.

SAMPSON, ROY J., and MARTIN T. FARRIS. *Domestic Transportation,* 2nd Ed. Boston: Houghton Mifflin Co., 1971.
Provides a profile of major routes and commodity movements in U. S. transportation, and a review of location theory and transportation cost relationships.

SMITH, DAVID M. *Industrial Location.* New York: John Wiley & Sons, Inc., 1971.
A comprehensive synthesis of the contributions of geographers and economists to industrial location problems. Part Five deals with several of the more recent approaches to industrial location, including correlation and regression analysis, linear programming, and input–output analysis.

THOMPSON, WILBUR R. *A Preface to Urban Economics.* Baltimore: The Johns Hopkins Press, 1965.
An excellent treatise on the application of locational analysis to the practical problems of cities. In particular, the role of transportation in urban land development is emphasized, and interactions between transportation systems and land use, local public economy, and unemployment and poverty are discussed.

13

Inventory Location
Strategy

Talk of location strategy typically concerns fixed facilities, bricks and mortar. This really puts the means, the building or other storage site, before the end objective, the positioning of inventory on an economically rational basis. Instead, we will consider a variety of fixed facility location problems under the heading of inventory location strategy.

Inventory location strategy is much like shooting at a moving target. Production, warehousing, and transportation costs assumed in an analysis change. Markets and sources of raw materials change. If we shoot directly at the target (use current costs, activity levels, and other measures), we stand a good chance of firing behind it (arriving at an outmoded result before the resulting system is implemented). If we fire too far ahead of the target (design a system on long-range forecasts), chances are excellent that the target will change its course (costs and markets will shift) and we will miss just as badly. So timing is an important element of location strategy. Commitment to long-term constraints is another.

Once determined, the locations of a firm's plants or warehouses invoke definite constraints on the logistics system for varying periods of time. To speak of the long run in regard to these constraints might in many instances imply a time period of fifteen to twenty years, or longer. On the other hand, it is possible to make arrangements for public warehousing of goods on very short notice and to terminate those arrangements on equally short notice. In this case the long run might involve only a month, while the short run would refer to day-to-day operations and decisions concerning the goods stored in such facilities.

We have made the inventory location decision sound like a terrifying one. In practice, decisions must be made. And there are a number of tools for determining the logistical implications of inventory locations. These quite likely constitute the most widely and successfully applied body of operations research techniques in industry today.

By means of a set of examples, we will attempt to accomplish several objectives. Concurrent with our assessment of the role logistics plays in the development of location constraints, we shall: (1) explore in a realistic manner the development of a logistics location strategy, (2) describe one or more methods for appraising each step in a system development, (3) suggest the types of information needed for proper analysis and the means of collecting it, (4) review shortcomings of the methods of analysis discussed, and (5) consider alternatives other than relocation at every possible opportunity.

THE ROLE OF LOGISTICS IN INVENTORY LOCATION STRATEGY

The importance of logistics considerations in inventory location strategy will vary from firm to firm. In any event, the final decision will be made on the basis of factors in addition to those of logistics. For example, an examination of any one of the many plant location checklists will reveal this. One of the most comprehensive, for example, lists total transportation costs as one of six major cost categories contributing to the final decision. Of nineteen major factor categories listed, only two deal directly with matters of logistics.[1] Nevertheless, it is often the responsibility of logistics management to inform those making the final decision of the transport and other cost implications of various plant location alternatives.

In contrast, logistics factors are of great importance in warehouse location. The location of warehouse facilities will determine how fast, and at what cost, the firm's production line or its customers can be served from supply sources. Nearly all costs affected by the decision are logistics costs. For these reasons, logistics management often plays a prominent role in deciding matters of warehouse location.

[1] See Appendix D in *Techniques of Plant Location,* Studies in Business Policy No. 61 (New York: National Industrial Conference Board, 1953), pp. 43–48. The nineteen major factor categories mentioned are location, character of surrounding territory, population statistics, civic administration, climate, cost of living (per capita), labor, transportation facilities, power and fuel, water, data on present manufacturing concerns, industrial legislation, financial data, eductional, recreational and civic data, special inducements, building costs, available industrial properties, and sites.

THE NATURE OF THE PROBLEM

Those writing about the location of logistics facilities invariably are tempted to discuss the problem in terms of a grand, sweeping redesign.[2] Among the questions asked might be: Given the opportunity to relocate our 10 plants and 90 warehouses, where would we put them? How many would we continue to use? There are few firms that can afford to devote any serious amount of time to these types of questions. Even if they spent the money to find the answer, it is doubtful that they would be able to carry out all resulting recommendations before they became obsolete.

The hard fact remains that the relocation or installation of fixed facilities, especially plants, is an expensive proposition. A more realistic approach to the problem might be: Given a projected demand pattern for our products ten years from now, how can we locate new facilities as they are needed to prepare ourselves for it? This approach is piecemeal in character. A warehouse is opened here; two are closed there. A plant is opened at another place. These changes are more effectively made if they are part of a long-range plan. But the plan is not realized overnight, nor may it retain its validity for the full period of its projected existence. Remember our moving target?

The optimum plant or warehouse location has never been found. Any quantitative technique developed to date that purports to provide an optimum location is naïve. However, this assertion does not preclude the use of an organized approach to the problem of location strategy that will suggest the direction in which location planning should proceed.

OPTIMIZING TECHNIQUES

Single Inventory Problem—Center-of-Gravity Approach

The center-of-gravity approach, for all its limitations, still stands as a basic approach which, in its simplicity, offers the best vehicle for estimating a good single inventory location. Just as the best auto polish is said to be the one the customer will use most often (the easiest to apply), so it is likely that center-of-gravity analysis may well offer the best opportunity for use by management.

The Method. The center-of-gravity method is based on the principle that however weights may be distributed on a flat surface, a point can be found on which the flat surface can be balanced. This will represent

[2] For one of the most interesting discussions dealing with the relocation of distribution warehouses, see Harvey N. Shycon and Richard B. Maffei, "Simulation—Tool for Better Distribution," *Harvard Business Review*, November–December, 1960, pp. 65–75.

the point on the surface from which the sum of distances to all of the weights, multiplied by the weights themselves, is at or near a minimum. It is the point which potentially offers low transportation costs for the nodal points (weights) and the network connecting them to the center of gravity.

We need not go to the trouble of finding a board and measured weights to use the approach. A simple calculation enables us to locate the center of gravity. To determine the center of gravity for the points and weights shown in Fig. 13–1, for example, we must first calculate the weighted center on the x axis by:

1. Weighting each activity point (node) by multiplying the weight at the point by the number representing the X coordinate at its location (.5 × 50; 2.5 × 150; .5 × 100; and 2.5 × 100 for points A, B, C, and D, respectively, in Fig. 13–1)
2. Adding all weighted coordinates (25 + 375 + 50 + 250 = 700)
3. Dividing the result by the sum of the weights themselves, or 700 ÷ (50 + 150 + 100 + 100) = 1.75, to obtain the coordinate for the center of gravity on the X axis
4. Locating the computed X coordinate on the map

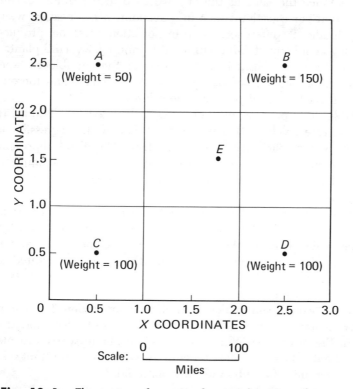

Fig. 13–1. The center of gravity for weights on a plane.

The same procedure would then be carried out for the Y axis. (You can do this.) (1) **The result for the example is shown as point *E* in Fig. 13–1. Does it agree with the results of your computation?**

An Example.   A question was raised at the Warren G. Wonka Manufacturing Company about sites other than Cleveland for the Company's only manufacturing plant. Significant increases in sales would require expansion of the 60-year-old facility. And sales patterns had shifted southward and westward from the Northeast as the Company began to emphasize a national sales effort.

A center-of-gravity analysis was performed to provide a rough estimate of the suitability of the Cleveland plant site from a transportation standpoint. Three major information inputs were used: (1) the map of inventory locations arrayed on the grid shown in Fig. 9–1, page 277, (2) estimates of the variability of transportation costs with distance for raw materials and finished products, presented in Fig. 9–6, on page 300, and (3) information regarding volumes of movement presented in Table 9–3, on page 280.

The procedure used for calculating the Company's logistics center of gravity is much the same as the one we used in the simple example. It required that our consultant take into account in his location weightings certain significant differences in transportation rates on product categories moving inbound to and outbound from the Cleveland plant. These weightings were established on the basis of the variable cost per mile of transporting inbound raw materials on the one hand and the outbound mixture of machines and parts on the other.

Variable costs of transportation were calculated by dividing the difference in rate levels at two points on either of the regression lines in Fig. 9–6 by the difference in distance from Cleveland represented by the two points. For example, the variable cost per mile to ship machines was calculated by subtracting the transportation cost for a 300-mile shipment (4.8¢ per pound) from that for a 500-mile shipment (6.0¢ per pound) and dividing by 200 miles to produce a per-pound variable cost of .006¢ per mile. Similar calculations for parts produced an estimate of .007¢ per mile. Because the proportion of machines and parts moving to each distribution center was roughly the same, a weighted average of about .0063¢ per mile was obtained for the mix of products moving out from Cleveland.

(2) **How would you make a similar computation for components and raw materials moving inbound to Cleveland, also plotted on the graph in Fig. 9–6? (3) What result do you obtain when you make the computation? (4) How does it compare with our consultant's estimate of .003¢ per mile for inbound raw materials?**

TABLE 13–1. Calculations for the Longitudinal (East–West) Coordinate for the Logistics Center of Gravity for Wonka's Manufacturing Plant

(1) Centers of Activity	(2) Quantity of Items Moving Inbound to Centers of Activity (in Millions of Pounds)[a]	(3) Transport Cost Weighting (in Thousandths of Cents per Mile)[b]	(4) Total Weight for Center of Activity [(2) × (3)]	(5) Longitudinal Map Coordinate[c]	(6) Total Weighting for Center of Activity [(4) × (5)][d]
Cleveland plant	40.5	3.0	121.5	81.25	9,900
Distribution Centers:					
Cleveland	.8	6.3	5.0	81.25	410
Buffalo	.9	6.3	5.7	78.75	446
Syracuse	.7	6.3	4.5	76.25	336
Boston	2.3	6.3	14.5	71.25	1,032
Newark	4.8	6.3	30.3	74.00	2,235
Philadelphia	2.1	6.3	13.2	75.00	993
Baltimore	1.1	6.3	6.9	76.25	528
Pittsburgh	.8	6.3	5.0	80.00	403
Cincinnati	1.1	6.3	6.9	84.00	582
Detroit	1.9	6.3	12.0	82.75	990
Chicago	3.3	6.3	20.8	87.75	1,820
Minneapolis	1.1	6.3	6.9	93.00	645
Atlanta	2.1	6.3	13.2	84.00	1,109
Dallas	3.6	6.3	22.7	97.50	2,210
Los Angeles	6.0	6.3	37.8	118.00	4,460
Tacoma	1.2	6.3	7.6	122.50	925
Totals			334.5		29,024

Weighted center of gravity for longitudinal (east–west) coordinate = 29,024/334.5 = 86.6

aFrom Table 9–3.
bCalculated from information in Fig. 9–6.
cFrom Fig. 9–1.
dAll calculations in this table represent slide-rule approximations.

Armed with this information, our consultant made the calculation shown in Table 13–1 to obtain the longitudinal (east–west) coordinate for the center of gravity of Wonka's transportation network, 86.6 as measured on the map shown in Fig. 9–1. You might wish to test your understanding of the procedure by calculating the latitudinal (north–south) coordinate. (5) **How did your figure compare with that of 39.9 measured on the map shown in Fig. 9–1, obtained by our consultant?**

Tracing the longitudinal and latitudinal coordinates to a point on the map shown in Fig. 9–1, our consultant found that they converged at a point near Indianapolis, Indiana. Knowing this location, he then prepared an estimate of annual transportation costs to and from this point, based on information graphed in Fig. 9–6. This is presented in Table 13–2. The result, $4,919,900, compared with the calculated current annual cost of $4,476,500 for the operation of the plant in Cleveland, suggested that, instead of savings, additional costs would result from a move from Cleveland to Indianapolis. (6) **Why do you think he obtained this seemingly contradictory result?**

(7) **As a result of our analysis, would you recommend that further effort be undertaken to sharpen the estimates made by means of the center-of-gravity approach?**

For example, you could make a good case for using individually calculated weightings for each location in this situation, particularly given the rather large deviations from the regression lines in Fig. 9–6 for: (1) locations more distant from Cleveland and (2) locations for which lower-cost methods of transportation (truckload for parts, carload for machines) are employed. If this were to be done, individual weightings could be established for each location by deducting the fixed portion of the total expense (indicated by the point at which each regression line intersects with the left-hand edge of the graph in Fig. 9–6) from the actual rate to each point. (8) **What result would this more detailed analysis produce in terms of location and total transportation cost differential between operations at Cleveland and a proposed new site?** (9) **Is the difference in result in this case sufficient to warrant the extra analysis?**

(10) **Would your view regarding further analyses change if you found that, within a radius of 400 miles of Cleveland, parts and other raw materials could be regarded as ubiquitous materials, available within a radius of the new location similar to that of the existing one?** (11) **What would you have to do to find out?**

(12) **Would your view regarding a proposed move, and the analysis necessary for the decision, change if, in addition to the conditions set forth above, all of the Company's sales growth over the next five years**

TABLE 13-2. Calculation of Estimated Comparative Transportation Costs to and from Actual Cleveland and Hypothetical Indianapolis Plant Locations

Commodities	Cleveland		Indianapolis	
	Rate/Cwt.	Annual Cost	Rate/Cwt.	Annual Cost
Inbound:				
Sheet and bar steel	$ .80	$ 112,000	$ 1.75	$ 245,000
Rubber beltings	.60	18,000	2.00	60,000
Container stock	.70	315,000	.70	315,000
Parts	4.20	671,000	6.00	960,000
Other items	3.00	90,000	3.90	117,000
Total inbound		$1,206,000		$1,697,000
Outbound finished product to:*				
Cleveland	$ 4.20	$ 35,300	$ 6.40	$ 53,800
Buffalo	6.40	59,500	7.40	68,800
Syracuse	6.40	44,100	8.40	58,000
Boston	7.80	177,000	9.80	222,000
Newark	6.80	328,100	8.60	416,000
Philadelphia	6.40	135,800	8.20	173,900
Baltimore	6.40	71,600	7.80	87,400
Pittsburgh	5.00	42,000	6.60	55,500
Cincinnati	5.80	61,500	5.00	53,000
Detroit	6.00	111,000	6.20	114,600
Chicago	6.80	222,100	5.50	180,000
Minneapolis	9.00	99,000	7.60	83,600
Atlanta	8.20	174,000	7.20	152,500
Dallas	11.60	417,500	9.50	342,000
Los Angeles	17.90	1,079,000	16.00	963,000
Tacoma	17.90	213,000	16.70	198,800
Total outbound		$3,270,500		$3,222,900
Total inbound and outbound		$4,476,500		$4,919,900

*Calculated on the basis of a composite rate falling between the rate distance regression lines shown in Fig. 9-6, approximately 1/3 of the distance above the regression line for transport rates for machines.

was expected to be represented by a doubling of sales in the territories served by the Dallas, Los Angeles, and Tacoma distribution centers?

Limitations.   The center-of-gravity technique has some rather obvious limitations. First, to retain its simplicity it assumes a linear relationship between transportation cost and distance. That is, it assumes that the same transportation cost per unit is incurred with each succeeding mile of distance. We have seen that this is not the case; fixed cost elements create a tapered transportation cost and rate structure per unit over distance. Our consultant at Wonka dealt with this problem by putting aside fixed "terminal" costs and considering only those that varied with distance.

Where an analysis involves large geographic areas, map distortions may result from the use of a squared as opposed to a mercator grid conforming to the global latitudes and longitudes. However, for most problems this distortion is not significant. Our consultant's grid in Fig. 9–1 is a mercator.

Only in a very few cases does the center of gravity method provide the least-cost answer. A bias in the calculation, varying with differences in weights associated with different points, prevents this. It is most extreme when one weight exceeds the sum of all other weights, as illustrated by the problem of locating a warehouse to serve only markets A and B in Fig. 13–1. **(13) What result would you get if you applied the center-of-gravity method? (14) Where would you locate the warehouse, using common sense?** Typically, a location problem capable of analysis by the center-of-gravity method will encompass many weighted points. The greater the number and the less the dominance of any one point, the less significant is the bias of the sort we have described.[3] Nevertheless, the heavy weighting for Cleveland in our previous example probably explains why the calculated center of gravity did not provide us with a lower cost estimate than for the existing plant site at Cleveland.

The center-of-gravity method does not reflect significant differences between straight-line distances and actual practical distances—for example, around bodies of water where land transportation methods are assumed. In Wonka's case, a severe distortion would have resulted in cost computations had the straight-line distance between Cleveland and Detroit over Lake Erie been used.

[3] This bias can be dealt with mathematically. The shortest distance between two points with coordinates x,y and a,b is

$$\sqrt{(x-a)^2 + (y-b)^2}$$

In Fig. 13–1, point E, with unknown coordinates x,y, from which the sum of weighted distances to the other four existing points is at a minimum, can be represented by:

$$E = 50\ \sqrt{(x-.5)^2 + (y-2.5)^2} +$$
$$150\ \sqrt{(x-2.5)^2 + (y-2.5)} +$$
$$100\ \sqrt{(x-.5)^2 + (y-.5)^2} +$$
$$100\ \sqrt{(x-2.5)^2 + (y-.5)^2}$$

This can be solved by setting w equal to 0, taking the first derivative of the cost equation, and solving alternatively for x and y.

The cost of shipping freight, per unit of distance, to and from a point is sometimes an elusive figure. Frequently, multiproduct and multiquantity shipments move at different transportation rates. This may require either detailed analysis of the costs of shipment components or accurate averaging of costs among segments of shipments which are "pooled" together for movement purposes.

Practical Use. These limitations suggest that center-of-gravity analysis is only a starting point. Additional adjustments may be required to introduce valuable flexibility into the final result. The following questions should be asked to further evaluate the results obtained from the use of this technique.

1. Is there an obvious non-linearity in transportation distance relationships? For example, does the computed result place the optimum point relatively near, say within fifty miles of, a major supplier or market? A slight adjustment of location to the nearby market or source might eliminate many local transportation costs without increasing long-distance costs.

2. Can an adjustment of the outcome be made that would place the general location in one transportation rate territory as opposed to another? Such action might provide favorable rates either into or out of the location. Yaseen cites an example:

. . . A shift of a few miles in one direction or another can secure a freight advantage over competitors to important destinations. . . .

As an example, consider a manufacturer of electrical appliances who is considering central Ohio as a location for his new plant. The majority of his distribution is in Ohio and neighboring states, but he has an important carload movement to a distributor in Los Angeles. His major competitor is located in Cleveland, Ohio.

If he selects Marysville as his location, he and his Cleveland competitor will have a rate of $5.56/cwt. to Los Angeles. Due to rate blanketing, his location 100 miles nearer the West Coast will have no effect on his competitive position. However, if he shifts only 7 miles further northwest of Marysville to Peoria, Ohio, Group C rates will replace Group B, and his rate will be $4.83. On every carload to Los Angeles he will enjoy a differential of $60 or more over his competitor.[4]

It is assumed that this adjustment in location would be considered if other rates to Eastern destinations were not affected adversely.

3. Are alternative sources of raw materials or components available that would influence logistics system adjustment?

4 Leonard C. Yaseen, *Plant Location* (New York: American Research Council, 1956), pp. 41–42.

4. Would transportation rate negotiation under the implied threat of relocation restore the attractiveness of an old location? Equalization is a term used to refer to the efforts of carriers to retain freight business even in the face of geographic handicaps by providing rates to or from a producing point that would allow them to remain competitive with others in commonly served markets. It is possible that carriers serving Cleveland might be willing to grant "rate relief" for that location to enable the continuation of the movement. Competing carriers serving other sources of supplies may be equally interested in reducing rate levels as a further incentive to the relocation of Wonka's production facilities.

5. What is the nature of freight movement into and out of the proposed location? Is it served by several modes? Is volume sufficient to generate a balanced directional movement and favorable rates? Can the firm take advantage of an existing light backhaul situation which corresponds to the direction of heavy movement of its products or the products of suppliers?

6. What is the trend of directional growth of the Company's markets? Although no specific information regarding the long-run sales potential and patterns of the firm may be available, past experience may be used to justify a location that is less than optimum under current sales conditions. For example, it appears that Wonka is looking west for its future market development, a point that might swing an otherwise borderline decision in favor of a more western location, perhaps Chicago or St. Louis in the case illustrated.

Multiple Inventory Problem

Various means of extending center-of-gravity approaches for the simultaneous location of two or more inventories, or even the location of the second inventory when one is fixed, involve a previous definition of territories to be served from each inventory location. As such, they represent simple extensions of the single inventory location application.[5] They are of limited use in any case where the definition of territories to be served from each location is not clear, and is highly interdependent with the computed locations themselves.

For estimating purposes, we probably could make use of the center-of-gravity approach in locating a second Wonka plant to supply demand encountered in the western part of the United States. (15) **Would this plant supply the Dallas as well as the Los Angeles and Tacoma distribution centers? (16) Where would it be located? (17) What additional information would you want to have, to make a final decision?**

The analysis of multiple inventory locations, whether to determine plants to be served from alternative raw material sources, distribution centers to be served from alternative plants, or customers to be served from alternative distribution centers, often requires more powerful optimizing techniques than the center of gravity approach. From those available, we have selected three of the more widely used and successful, the Bowman–Stewart model, linear programming, and the Baumol–Wolfe extension of linear programming. Finally, we will discuss a fourth, more advanced and less frequently used technique, dynamic programming. Although enough of the model and solution procedure of each is explained to allow you to evaluate their appropriate uses, please keep in mind that, unlike the center-of-gravity approach, these techniques can be solved in a practical situation only by means of a computer. Thus, there is limited value in "learning" manual solution procedures for them.

Bowman–Stewart Formulation.[6] One of the most straightforward formulations of the multiple-facility location problem utilizes a mathematical model based upon the underlying concept illustrated in Fig. 13–2. This model assumes that in the case of an increasing area of coverage from a given inventory location, if volume of business per unit of area

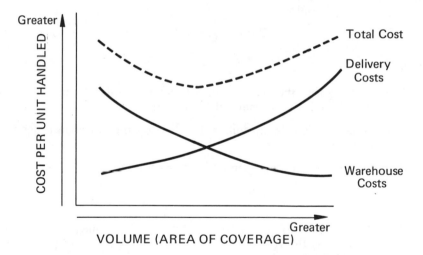

Fig. 13–2. Factors influencing the total cost to supply an area from a given location.

[5] For a description of an approach under the assumption that cross-hauling between simultaneously located plants or warehouses will be required, see William Miehle, "Link Length Minimization in Networks," *Operations Research*, 1958, pp. 232–42.

[6] Portions of this section are reprinted from Edward H. Bowman and John B. Stewart, "A Model for Scale of Operations," *Journal of Marketing*, Vol. 20, January, 1956, pp. 242–47.

(concentration of demand) is constant: (1) the warehousing cost per unit will decrease, and (2) the delivery cost per unit will increase.

Factors such as the rates of warehouse labor, insurance, and other costs at different locations were assumed to be equal. However, one important influence on costs was taken into account: whether service from a given supply point involved intrafacility transportation costs, such as from a plant warehouse to a distribution warehouse. This latter feature of the overall approach formed the second of the two major components of the model, because it allowed a determination of areas to be served directly from plant locations as well as through distribution warehouses.

It was assumed that certain costs (associated with warehousing and material handling) would vary inversely with volume, that other costs (associated with delivery) would vary directly with the square root of the area served, and that other costs would not vary with changes in either volume or area. The assumption regarding delivery costs was based on the geometric principle that radius and diameter vary with the square root of the area of a circle. This allowed the following mathematical expression of total costs to serve an area through a distribution warehouse:

$$C = a + \frac{b}{V} + c\sqrt{A},$$

where

C = cost (within the warehouse district) per dollar's worth of goods distributed, the measure of effectiveness

V = volume of goods, in dollars, handled by the warehouse per unit of time

A = area in square miles served by the warehouse

a = cost per dollar's worth of goods distributed independent of either the warehouse's volume handled or area served

b = "fixed" costs for the warehouse per unit of time, which, when divided by the volume, will yield the appropriate cost per dollar's worth distributed

c = the cost of the distribution which varies with the square root of the area; that is, costs associated with miles covered within the warehouse district such as gasoline, truck repairs, driver hours, and others

Next, actual data (representing C, V, and A above) for each existing warehouse in the system under analysis were determined. By the statistical method of least-squares multiple regression [7] it was possible to use past experience to determine mathematically the values of the coefficients or parameters (a, b, and c) which would make the model the closest predictor of the actual cost for all present warehouses using their individual volume and area figures.

Once determined, the coefficients a, b, and c were introduced into the formula. Actual values of V and A for each warehouse were substituted in the formula, a theoretical C was compared to the actual level of total costs at each location, and the correlation of the theoretical and actual costs was measured to determine the validity of the model thus developed.

In order to use the cost predictor, or model, as a tool of analysis to determine the most efficient location for units in a system, it was necessary to solve the model equation for A, the area to be served from any possible location. To do this, the density of sales per area (K) was expressed as $K = V/A$. It easily could be determined for each portion of the market area. Therefore, $V = KA$, and this quantity could then be substituted in the original model for V, giving:

$$C = a + \frac{b}{KA} + c\sqrt{A}$$

Differentiation [8] then yielded a general expression which would determine an optimum A for any b cost characteristic, c cost characteristic, or K density of sales:

$$A = \left(\frac{2b}{cK}\right)^{2/3}$$

Once A was determined, the distance from a branch warehouse to the boundary of its territory was computed by the formula for the radius of a circle, $r = \sqrt{A/\pi}$ (or 3.14).

Costs of shipping from plants to warehouses were ignored by this first

---

[7] This method minimizes the sum of the squares of the differences between the actual cost and the predicted cost. Once determined, the coefficients b and c represent the rate at which per-unit costs of type b change with volume; the rate at which per-unit costs of type a change with the square root of the area served; and the level of type a costs, which remain constant at some proportion of each dollar's worth of goods distributed. For an explanation of least-squares multiple regression analysis, see Robert Ferber, *Statistical Techniques in Market Research* (New York: McGraw-Hill Book Co., 1949), pp. 346–79.

[8] The expression for differentiation is:

$$\frac{dC}{dA} = -\frac{b}{kA^2} + \frac{c}{2\sqrt{A}} = 0.$$

The technique is explained in any standard text for the calculus.

formula, because it was assumed that as long as goods were handled through a distribution warehouse, these costs would be incurred. However, to determine areas to be served directly from plants or plant warehouses, a simple additive cost formula was devised. This formula determines the extent of the area surrounding a plant, at the boundaries of which the cost to serve customers directly from a plant warehouse equals the cost to serve them from a plant through a distribution warehouse (that is, plant to distribution warehouse, plus distribution warehouse to customer).

$$\frac{2T_oP_d + T_f + T_dH_d}{P_h(H_d - 2P_dH_m - F_t)} = \frac{2T_oD_b + T_f + T_dH_d}{P_h(H_d - 2D_bH_m - F_t)} + \frac{S_1 + B_e + 2S_oD_p + S_f + 2S_dH_mD_p + I_w}{P_s}$$

where

T_o = truck operation cost per mile
P_d = plant delivery miles
T_f = truck fixed costs per day (amortization type charges)
T_d = truck driver costs per hour
F_t = fixed driver time per day (check in, check out, coffee break, etc.)
D_b = miles from branch to delivery
S_1 = semi loading and unloading costs
B_e = branch expense per semi
S_o = semi operating costs per mile
D_p = miles from plant to the branch
S_f = semi fixed costs per day (amortization type charges)
S_d = semi driver costs per hour
I_w = inventory costs per semi per week
H_d = hours per day
H_m = hours per mile
P_h = pieces per hour
P_s = pieces per semi
2 = a multiplier reflecting cost per round trip

Most of the cost expressions in the Bowman–Stewart plant district model could be determined directly from a company's internal records. Several of the costs, such as a truck fixed cost per day or cost per mile, could be checked from outside sources. After all the specific values were inserted in the model, it could be solved for P_d, the distance from the plant to the farthest district within the plant warehouse area. Once the optimum to be served from the plant was determined, distribution centers could be spaced roughly according to relative efficiencies of scale and sales density to outlying areas.

From time to time, many of the cost relationships and the relative density of sales would change under realistic conditions. Using existing facilities as a starting point, two or more distribution centers could be relocated simultaneously to reflect changing conditions. The degree of accuracy of the coefficients a, b, and c would reflect the extent to which an optimum set of locations might be found, assuming new locations would follow the same cost patterns as old.

Further, the Bowman–Stewart formulation could be expanded to reflect emphasis on customer service, measured by the distance (in miles or time) of supply points from customers. This could be accomplished by using unrealistically high values for transportation costs (coefficient c) in areas where customer service was extremely important. It would be applicable particularly where large distances or transit times characterized relationships between existing supply points in a firm's logistics system, or where a firm's marketing territory covered a wide geographic region.

As Hoch has pointed out,[9] the application of the Bowman–Stewart and other similarly conceived models invariably produces a "tear drop" rather than a circle as the appropriate shape for a territory optimally served by a distribution center supplied from a plant inventory, particularly when the former lies within several hundred miles or less from the latter. In Fig. 13–3, Z is the point farthest from both the distribution center located at W and the plant located at P which can be served more economically from the distribution center than from the plant. In contrast, the nature of most transportation rate structures restricts the appropriate territory to point Y on a line between the distribution center and its supply plant. This is the point at which vehicle load transportation plus distribution center handling plus small-shipment transportation costs for shipments through the distribution center equal the small-shipment transportation charges directly from the plant to the customer.

Linear Programming. Linear programming is an approach to problems which assumes that the most important relationships are exactly or approximately linear in nature. For example, the most common assumption in a shipping point allocation problem is that the transportation costs are linear in relation to volume; i.e., that it costs twice as much to transport two items as to transport one. It is important to keep this assumption in mind, because although it offers opportunities for scientific

[9] L. Clinton Hoch, "Ten Most Common and Costly Mistakes in Warehouse Location," *Transportation & Distribution Management*, August, 1967, pp. 25–29.

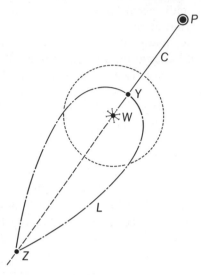

Fig. 13–3. A typical "tear-drop" (—··—··—) as opposed to circle (········) for the optimal territory served from a distribution center located in relatively close proximity to an alternative plant warehouse supply source. In this example, both Z and Y represent points which can be served with equal transportation, storage, and handling costs from both a plant at P -and a distribution center at W. *Source:* L. Clinton Hoch, "Ten Most Common and Costly Mistakes in Warehouse Location," *Transportation & Distribution Management,* August, 1967, pp. 25–29, at p. 27.

solution, it also imposes important limitations on the ultimate solution it provides.

Basic methods of linear programming are the distribution (transportation problem) and algebraic simplex methods. Each can be applied to problems of different structure and magnitude in logistics and other areas of management. We will consider the distribution method here, because it is highly appropriate for use in dealing with inventory location problems.

The Initial Allocation. The length of the calculation procedure needed to solve a linear programming problem by the distribution method can be reduced by the quality of the initial allocation of market demands to DC locations. Elaborate initial allocation methods are described elsewhere.[10] Other good ones involve the assignment of as much product

---

[10] For example, Nyles V. Reinfeld and William R. Vogel, *Mathematical Programming* (Englewood Cliffs, N. J.: Prentice-Hall, Inc., 1958) includes a detailed explanation of a "least-cost differential" method of initial assignment on pp. 27–35.

as possible to the matrix square with the lowest total cost, the next lowest total cost, on until all demand has been met and supply allocated. Another simple method of obtaining a startup point is to begin at the "northwest" (upper left-hand) corner, assigning as much as possible to matrix square M_{11} (in Fig. 13–4) and succeeding squares in the first row,

Distri-bution Center: \ Plant	Jersey City	Hershey	Richmond	Cleveland	DC (Market) Demands
Philadelphia	30[a] M_{11}[b]	M_{12}	M_{13}	M_{14}	30
Richmond	10 M_{21}	10 M_{22}	M_{23}	M_{24}	20
Cincinnati	M_{31}	20 M_{32}	M_{33}	M_{34}	20
New York	M_{41}	60 M_{42}	30 M_{43}	M_{44}	90
Dummy	M_{51}	M_{52}	M_{53}	50 M_{54}	50
Plant Capacities:	40	90	30	50	

[a] Number of units of demand at each distribution center allocated to each plant by the "northwest corner" method.
[b] Matrix cell identification number.

Fig. 13–4. The initial allocation of available supplies to demand by the "northwest corner" method.

then dropping down to the first available square in the second row to continue assignments. We will begin with the assignment of the actual allocation of product by plants to DC's at Store Display Equipment, Inc., for a recent period of time. This allocation, shown in Fig. 13–5, produced a total cost result shown in Table 13–3.

Reallocation. In order to determine whether the allocation used by Store Display Equipment was the best possible, it is necessary to perform a matrix check. We must create an artificial set of values for the purpose of checking the matrix. To do this, we can set any row (R) or column (C) matrix check value equal to any amount we wish. Generally, to simplify matters, R_1 is set equal to zero. The remaining matrix

Matrix Check Values	Column:	$C_1 = 22$ Jersey City	$C_2 = 27$ Hershey	$C_3 = 27$ Richmond	$C_4 = 27$ Cleveland	DC (Market) Demands
Row:	Plant / Distribution Center					
$R_1 = 0$	Philadelphia	23 +1[a]	27 0 30^b	29 +2	29 +2	30
$R_2 = 4$	Richmond	26 0	31 0	24 -7	31 0 20	20
$R_3 = 3$	Cincinnati	27 +2	32 +2	30 0 20	27 -3	20
$R_4 = 0$	New York	22 0 40	27 0 50	30 +3	30 +3	90
$R_5 = 13$	Dummy	40 +5	40 0 10	40 0 10	40 0 30	50
	Plant Capacities:	40	90	30	50	Total: 210

[a] Numbers in the upper right-hand corner of each matrix square denote the relationship of the square's value to the sum of matrix check values for its row and column coordinates.

[b] Underlined quantities indicate the amounts (in units) allocated to each destination from each origin.

Fig. 13–5. Initial allocation and matrix check of initial allocation, January, 19—, Store Display Equipment, Inc.

check values are set relative to it by equating each matrix square value (cost) to which items have been allocated to the sum of matrix check values for its row and column. In Fig. 13–5, this is achieved by the following process:

TABLE 13–3. Total Cost of First Allocation, January, 19___, Store Display Equipment, Inc.

Origin–Destination	Landed Cost Per Unit	Units	Total Landed Cost
Hershey–Philadelphia	$27	30	$ 810
Cleveland–Richmond	31	20	620
Richmond–Cincinnati	30	20	600
Jersey City–New York	22	40	880
Hershey–New York	27	50	1,350
Hershey–Dummy	40	10	n.s.
Richmond–Dummy	40	10	n.s.
Cleveland–Dummy	40	30	n.s.
Total			$4,260

n.s. = not shipped.

$$R_1 = 0;$$
$$R_1\,(0) + C_2\,(?) = 27, C_2 = 27;$$
$$C_2\,(27) + R_4\,(?) = 27, R_4 = 0;$$
$$R_4\,(0) + C_1\,(?) = 22, C_1 = 22;$$
$$(\text{etc.})$$

Matrix check values are obtained by using the "islands" (squares to which items were allocated) in the theoretical body of water represented by the remaining unoccupied squares in the matrix. The values are next checked against "water" squares to determine whether the first allocation is optimum (least-cost). In each case the sum of R and C matrix check values should not exceed the value of the matrix water square defined by each row and column. Saying it another way, we must ask:

$$\text{Is}\quad R_1 + C_1 > M_{11}?$$
$$0 + 22 > 23?\quad \text{No.}$$

If not, as in this case, we proceed to the next set of R and C values and their matrix square.

Whenever a matrix square is encountered that has a cost value less than the sum of its R and C matrix check values, a lower cost solution could be obtained by allocating some product to it. Even after encountering such a situation, it is best to check all of the "water" squares in the matrix first. The one whose cost value is the greatest amount less than the sum of its R and C matrix check values will offer the greatest cost reduction through the reallocation of freight to it.

Our check reveals negative water values for matrix squares M_{23} and M_{34}. In Fig. 13–5, square M_{23} yields the highest negative value of -7.

From the most negative water square, trace a path on the matrix using only island squares as points at which to make 90-degree turns. The path will resemble a series of moves that might be made by a chess rook, with the provision that the rook must come to rest only on island squares and proceed at a 90-degree angle on its next move. The object is to trace a path back to the starting water square. Island squares can be passed over by a given move. There is no specified number of moves necessary to return the path maker to his "home" water square. Because of its resemblance to the technique employed by a person cautiously crossing a shallow, rock-strewn creek, this method of reallocation is referred to as the "stepping stone" method. The path resulting from the application of this technique to the above problem is shown also in Fig. 13–5.

Because of the requirement that the path include only 90-degree turns, there will always be an even number of moves in any path. In the example, there are four. Each of these moves should next be assigned alternate plus and minus signs beginning from the first. Next, subtract the smallest quantity allocated to an island square in which a positive move is terminated from all other island squares at which positive moves are terminated. Likewise, add this same quantity to each square, be it island or water, at which a negative move is terminated. In Fig. 13–5 this results in a reallocation of ten units from squares M_{53} and M_{24} to squares M_{54} and M_{23}. In terms of dollar savings, this can be translated into $70 (ten units supplied at a cost of $24 per unit rather than $31). A second matrix check would tell us that this is not yet an optimum solution to the problem.

Two more iterations of the reallocation procedure would be required to produce the result shown in Fig. 13–6. The first of these would result in the deduction of ten units each from squares M_{24} and M_{33} and the addition of the same amounts to squares M_{23} and M_{34}. The second iteration would reallocate ten units from squares M_{54} and M_{33} to squares M_{34} and M_{53}. (You may wish to carry out these subsequent reallocations in order to check your understanding of the procedure.) Based on this example, the importance of initial care in allocating supply to demand should be clear.

Introduction of Constraints. Constraints such as, "Always work the Hershey plant to capacity, regardless of cost," "Never ship to Cincinnati from Cleveland," or "Always meet the demands of the New York warehouse" (or more typically, of a given customer), are sometimes introduced into allocation problems. They require only minor alterations in the initial formulation of data to solve a problem. Consider the second

Matrix Check Values	Column:	$C_1 = 22$	$C_2 = 27$	$C_3 = 27$	$C_4 = 27$
Row:	Plant / Distribution Center	Jersey City	Hershey	Richmond	Cleveland
$R_1 = 0$	Philadelphia	23 ___ M_{11}	27 30 M_{12}	29 ___ M_{13}	29 ___ M_{14}
$R_2 = -3$	Richmond	26 ___ M_{21}	31 ___ M_{22}	24 20 M_{23}	31 ___ M_{24}
$R_3 = 0$	Cincinnati	27 ___ M_{31}	32 ___ M_{32}	30 ___ M_{33}	27 20 M_{34}
$R_4 = 0$	New York	22 40 M_{41}	27 50 M_{42}	30 ___ M_{43}	30 ___ M_{44}
$R_5 = 13$	Dummy	40 ___ M_{51}	40 10 M_{52}	40 10 M_{53}	40 30 M_{54}

23 = cost (in dollars) of shipping one unit between a given pair of points indicated by column and row headings.

M_{11} = matrix square with coordinates of R_1 (row no. 1) and C_1 (column no. 1).

Fig. 13–6. Completed optimum allocation of demand and supply, January, 19—, Store Display Equipment, Inc.

of the constraints imposed above in the Store Display Equipment, Inc., example.

To discourage the allocation of goods to Cincinnati from Cleveland we need only to set arbitrarily the cost value of squares M_{34} in Fig. 13–6 artificially high and proceed to solve the matrix once again. Any high number might be chosen, although theoretically there is no absolute minimum quantity that will guarantee compliance with the constraint. Therefore, the safest recommendation would be to assign the largest possible value, designated by any symbol (Z will do), to M_{34} and solve as if it were a number, albeit a very large one. Other adjustments of a similar type can be made to meet any of the above limitations which might be imposed for either rational or irrational reasons.

Alternate Solutions. A given optimum solution may be undesirable for a number of reasons. But most allocation problems have several near optimum solutions offering an alternate operating plan at little cost over minimum or optimum. Whether a problem has near optimum solutions can be determined by a check of the water squares similar to that performed to determine optimality. For every water square with a cost value equivalent to the sum of its R and C matrix check values (i.e., a water square check value $= 0$), there will be an alternative optimum or basic solution.[11] By the same token, those water squares with the lowest matrix square check values will offer possibilities for alternative solutions requiring the least increment of expenditure.

Consider the optimum solution presented in Fig. 13–6. Its water square check values appear as follows:

	C_1	C_2	C_3	C_4
R_1	$23 - 22 = 1$	island	$29 - 27 = 2$	$29 - 27 = 2$
R_2	$26 - 19 = 7$	$31 - 24 = 7$	island	$31 - 24 = 7$
R_3	$27 - 22 = 5$	$32 - 27 = 5$	$30 - 27 = 3$	island
R_4	island	island	$30 - 27 = 3$	$30 - 27 = 3$
R_5	$40 - 35 = 5$	island	island	island

Because there appear to be no water squares with a check value of zero, there is no alternative basic (optimum) solution to the problem. Under these conditions, we might wish to determine the second-best alternative. Intuition would tell us that the second-best alternative would involve the allocation of product to the water square with the lowest check value in excess of zero. In the example, it is M_{11} with a check value of 1.

To derive an alternative solution from a basic solution, one need only designate the most desirable water square (M_{11} above) and proceed to use it as the starting point for a stepping-stone or island-hopping reallocation similar to that described previously. Using the matrix in Fig. 13–6, it appears that the reallocation procedure would involve matrix squares M_{11}, M_{41}, M_{42}, and M_{12}. Results of the reallocation would deduct 30 units each (the smallest quantity of product currently assigned to a square in which a stepping stone move of positive value terminates) from squares M_{41} and M_{12} and add similar amounts to M_{42} and M_{11}. In this case, the second best solution, involving no shipments from Hershey to

[11] If there are two or more of these, it can be demonstrated that there is an infinite number of quantities in which goods can be allocated to the several routes, all of which yield an optimum total result.

Philadelphia, would cost the company $30 more than the basic solution during the period under consideration. This is computed in Table 13–4.

TABLE 13–4. Cost of Comparison of Optimum vs. Next Best Solution for Store Display Equipment, Inc.

Matrix Square	Cost per Unit	Optimum Allocation (units)	Total Cost	Next Best Allocation (units)	Total Cost
M_{11}	$23	–	–	30	$ 690
M_{41}	22	40	$ 880	10	220
M_{42}	27	50	1,350	80	2,160
M_{12}	27	30	810	–	–
Total		120	$3,040	120	$3,070

Degeneracy. For any given matrix there is an exact number of island squares which allow a solution. It is one less than the sum of the number of rows and columns in the matrix, or $R + C = 1$. There is no guarantee that an initial allocation, even by a formal method, will produce the desired number of island squares. There may be either too many or too few. They should be counted after the initial allocation and before solution. If not discovered, however, an incorrect number will soon halt the solution procedure after some wasted effort on the part of the analyst.

Where an initial allocation produces too many island squares, alternatives will be introduced in the assignment of matrix check values to rows and columns, obscuring the one best method. When this is the case, island square allocations should be combined to produce the desired number before any attempt is made to check the solution for optimality.

Degeneracy results from the presence of too few island squares in a matrix, either after an initial allocation or as the result of reallocation procedures. In either case, a degenerate situation will not allow matrix check values to be assigned to all rows and columns. It can be corrected by arbitrarily allocating 0 units to any matrix square, thus creating the necessary island or islands to facilitate the establishment of matrix check values. The best of the possible squares to convert from water to an island is that which best accomplishes the objective of the solution. In the Store Display Equipment example it would be the one with the lowest cost value. Once a new island square has been created, the problem should be solved in the normal manner, regarding the matrix square with 0 units assigned to it as one would any other island square.

Occasionally, a deficiency of island squares is created during solution. This will occur when reallocation converts one more island square to water than vice versa. It requires the allocation of 0 units, as above, to one of the island squares eliminated by the allocation. The one to select for conversion from water back to an island is once again the one which best accomplishes the desired goal. Once this has been achieved, the solution can proceed as before.

The problem shown above could be converted to a series of simultaneous equations to be solved without the need of laying out a matrix of values and alternatives. This essentially is the procedure used in connection with the algebraic simplex method of linear programming in dealing with the same type of inventory location problem.[12]

Executives at the Wonka Manufacturing Company had heard a great deal about linear programming, and had suggested that its potential use for determining distribution center shipping patterns to customers be investigated. Of special interest was the Middle Atlantic region, where customers were serviced by distribution centers in Buffalo, Syracuse, Newark, Philadelphia, and Baltimore. **(18) Based upon what you know about the Wonka Company, and about linear programming, do you think this would be a good application of the technique? (19) Why?**

An Appraisal of Linear Programming. Linear programming provides as many pitfalls as opportunities. Therefore, its use should be appraised in terms of the problem to be solved.

A major advantage of the technique is that it provides the framework for the systematic appraisal of many alternatives. Even though the problem used as an example here could probably be solved by logic upon sight, it represents the most simple of a family of complex problems, most of which could not be solved in an unorganized manner. When conditions are appropriate, linear programming methods can provide rather accurate solutions in a minimum amount of time. Because they involve repetitive calculations, electronic computers readily can be put to the task of solving them.

On the other hand, solutions obtained by means of linear programming must be adjusted to take into account actual conditions and existing limitations. Reciprocal purchasing policies may require the allocation of purchases in a manner other than that indicated by formal analysis, for example.

Of course, the greatest limitation of the technique is its assumption of linearity in costs. Linear programming solutions do not take into account the size of efficient work units. Costs are rarely linear in an exact sense

[12] For an extensive discussion of the algebraic simplex, the most versatile form of linear programming, see Harold Bierman, Jr., Charles P. Bonini, and Warren H. Hausman, *Quantitative Analysis for Business Decisions*, 4th Ed. (Homewood, Ill.: Richard D. Irwin, Inc., 1973), pp. 229–59.

of the term. Quantity discounts introduce non-linearity into the average price per unit. Fixed costs of operating a vehicle create costs which are non-linear with varying distances and quantities of usage. Costs of tooling-up add fixed elements to manufacturing activities which destroy their cost linearity.

Three basic approaches have been taken to cope with this limitation of linear programming. First, cost curves have been examined to determine whether they approximate linearity over certain segments. In the diagram in Fig. 13–7, for example, per-unit costs of transportation approxi-

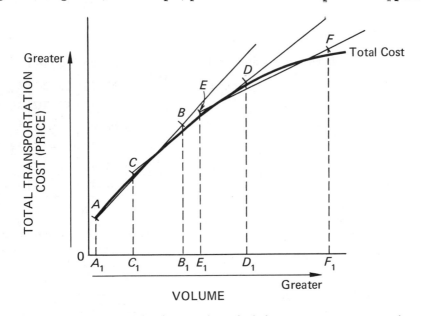

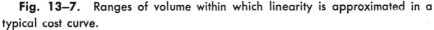

Fig. 13–7. Ranges of volume within which linearity is approximated in a typical cost curve.

mate linearity over limited segments of the cost curve, namely AB, CD, and EF, representing ranges of volume shipped, A_1B_1, C_1D_1, and E_1F_1. Techniques discussed here would be accurate in appraising only those situations in which the range of load sizes was relatively small.

Second, non-linear programming techniques have been developed which attempt to describe non-linear cost functions by specially fitted equations. Because this approach requires lengthy presentation and involves advanced mathematics, it will not be discussed here.

Third, attempts have been made to modify the effects of linear programming by combining its use with non-linear problem elements. One such example of this approach follows.

The Baumol–Wolfe Model. Baumol and Wolfe were among the first to make some allowance for non-linear cost functions while employing linear programming to allocate warehouse territories.[13] Others preceded them in dealing with different but related problems.

Baumol and Wolfe represented transportation costs from both factories (i) to all possible warehouse locations (j) and from warehouses (j) to customers (k) as two separate matrices, shown in Fig. 13–8. They then

Matrix 1

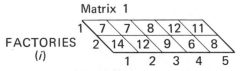

FACTORIES (i)

	1	2	3	4	5
1	7	7	8	12	11
2	14	12	9	6	8

Possible Warehouse Locations (j)

Matrix 2

CUSTOMERS (k)

	1	2	3	4	5
1	5	14	10	15	9
2	11	16	11	13	7
3	3	8	3	9	3
4	8	9	5	6	2
5	5	4	2	7	6
6	10	7	5	2	5
7	11	4	9	10	12
8	11	4	5	2	8

Possible Warehouse Locations (j)

Matrix 3

Top values: 12 21 18 27 20 / 19 26 19 21 17

Left values: 18 / 10 25 / 15 17 / 12 22 / 17 19 / 18 24 / 18 25 / i_1 25 / i_2

	j_1	j_2	j_3	j_4	j_5	
						k_1
	28	20	19	15		k_2
	20	12	15	11		k_3
	21	14	12	10		k_4
	16	11	13	14		k_5
	19	14	8	13		k_6
	16	18	16	20		k_7
	16	14	8	16		k_8

Plus additional transportation costs from plant (obscured from view in the drawing above)

j_2	j_3	j_4	j_5	
23	19	25	18	k_2
15	11	21	14	k_3
16	13	18	13	k_4
11	10	19	17	k_5
14	13	14	16	k_6
11	17	22	23	k_7
11	13	14	19	k_8

i_1

Fig. 13–8. Graphic representations of matrices for transportation costs from both plants to all possible warehouse locations to customers.

combined these linear matrices into one three-dimensional matrix in selecting least-cost routes between any given set of i, j, and k. This is shown as matrix 3 in the figure. The entire problem was subjected to the

[13] See William J. Baumol and Philip Wolfe, "A Warehouse Location Problem," *Operations Research*, March–April, 1958, pp. 252–63. The material in this section is adapted from this article.

constraints of a given amount of capacity at each of the two plant sites, i.e., $i_1 = 40$ units, $i_2 = 50$ units. Retailers' demands were given as:

$r =$	1	2	3	4	5	6	7	8
Demands in units:	10	10	10	15	5	15	10	15

Warehousing costs were assumed to be a function of the square root of the volume moving through each warehouse, so that total warehouse costs for each were:

$j =$	1	2	3	4	5
Total warehouse costs:	$75\sqrt{Z_1}$	$80\sqrt{Z_2}$	$75\sqrt{Z_3}$	$80\sqrt{Z_4}$	$70\sqrt{Z_5}$

where Z represented the volume of units assigned to move through each warehouse. Marginal warehouse costs, the cost to move an additional unit through a warehouse, were set equal to:

$j =$	1	2	3	4	5
Marginal warehouse costs:	$\dfrac{75\sqrt{Z_1}}{2Z_1}$	$\dfrac{80\sqrt{Z_2}}{2Z_2}$	$\dfrac{75\sqrt{Z_3}}{2Z_3}$	$\dfrac{80\sqrt{Z_4}}{2Z_4}$	$\dfrac{70\sqrt{Z_5}}{2Z_5}$

Only one product was assumed; however, the method could be adapted to multiproduct problems. No factor representing the value of improved transfer time from warehouse to customers was included in the method under examination.

The method used in making actual computations was that of an iterative or recursive type. That is, the same procedure was repeated over and over until no further improvement was possible in the solution. Computations for the example are as follows:

INITIAL COMPUTATION CYCLE

Minimal transportation costs, i to k:

$k =$	1	2	3	4	5	6	7	8
$i = 1$	12	18	10	13	10	13	11	11
2	17	15	11	10	11	8	16	8

Warehouses for minimal route:

$k =$	1	2	3	4	5	6	7	8
$i = 1$	1	5	1	5	3	3	2	2
2	5	5	5	5	3	4	4	4

Solution of initial transportation problem:

$i = 1$	10	0	10	0	5	0	10	5
2	0	10	0	15	0	15	0	10

Warehouse loads and costs:

$j =$	Load	Costs
1	20	336
2	15	310
3	5	168
4	25	400
5	25	350
Warehousing cost		1,564
Transportation cost		935
Total cost		2,499

SECOND COMPUTATION CYCLE (FIRST ITERATION)

Warehouse marginal costs, rounded to integers:

$$j = 1 \quad 2 \quad 3 \quad 4 \quad 5$$
$$8 \quad 10 \quad 17 \quad 8 \quad 7$$

Factory-warehouse transportation costs and marginal warehouse costs:

$j =$	1	2	3	4	5
$i = 1$	15	17	25	20	18
2	22	22	26	14	15

Minimal transportation costs, i to k:

$k =$	1	2	3	4	5	6	7	8
$i = 1$	20	25	18	20	20	22	21	21
2	24	22	18	17	21	16	24	16

Warehouses for minimal route:

$k =$	1	2	3	4	5	6	7	8
	1	5	1	5	1	4	2	2
	5	5	5	5	4	4	4	4

Solution of transportation problem:

$k =$	1	2	3	4	5	6	7	8
$i = 1$	10	0	10	5	5	0	10	0
2	0	10	0	10	0	15	0	15

Warehouse loads and costs:

	Load	Costs
$j = 1$	25	375
2	10	253
3	0	0
4	30	439
5	25	350
Warehousing cost		1,417
Transportation cost		945
		2,362

Note: Transportation costs are based on the solution of two transportation problems, one between plants (i) and warehouses (j), and the other between warehouses (j) and customers (k), as follows:

$j =$	1	2	3	4	5	
$i = 1$	25	10	0	0	5	cost 640,
2	0	0	0	30	20	

$k =$	1	2	3	4	5	6	7	8	
$j = 1$	10	0	10	0	5	0	0	0	
2	0	0	0	0	0	0	10	0	
3	0	0	0	0	0	0	0	0	cost 305,
4	0	0	0	0	0	15	0	15	
5	0	10	0	15	0	0	0	0	

yielding a total cost of transportation of 945.

THIRD COMPUTATION CYCLE (SECOND ITERATION)

Warehouse marginal costs, rounded to integers:

$$j = 1 \quad 2 \quad 3 \quad 4 \quad 5$$
$$8 \quad 13 \quad \infty \quad 7 \quad 7$$

Factory-warehouse transportation costs and marginal warehouse costs:

$j =$	1	2	3	4	5
$i = 1$	15	20	∞	19	18
2	22	25	∞	13	15

Minimal transportation costs, i to k:

$k =$	1	2	3	4	5	6	7	8
$i = 1$	20	25	18	20	20	21	24	21
2	24	22	18	17	20	15	23	15

Warehouse for minimum route:

$k =$	1	2	3	4	5	6	7	8
$i = 1$	1	5	1	5	1	4	2	4
2	5	5	5	5	4	4	4	4

Solution of transportation problem:

$k =$	1	2	3	4	5	6	7	8
$i = 1$	10	0	10	5	5	0	10	0
2	0	10	0	10	5	15	0	15

Warehouse loads:

$j =$	Load
1	25
2	10
3	0
4	30
5	25

Because the total cost for the second and third computation cycles is equal, a solution has been reached such that the total is 2,362.

The consideration of marginal warehouse costs at each stage in the computation was an attempt to introduce an element of non-linearity to what essentially is a technique based on assumptions of linearity in cost relationships.

Kuehn and Hamburger point to an inherent bias in the type of linear programming technique proposed by Baumol and Wolfe.[14] The latter is thought to indicate the use of more warehouses than is necessary, thus resulting in a cost of logistics significantly higher than optimum. They support their claim by pointing out that if Baumol and Wolfe were to have utilized only warehouse number 3, or 5, or 4, they would have accomplished their assigned task at a lower cost than by using warehouses 1, 2, 4, and 5. This is certainly true under the conditions of the problem. However, if an added weighting were to be introduced to warehouse-to-customer transportation costs in the Baumol–Wolfe formulation in order to reflect opportunity costs associated with the effect of shipping delays on customer demand, it is likely that much of the claimed bias would be eliminated. In other words, greater weight would be placed on the location of a warehouse near each major customer or customer grouping.

(20) What is the relative applicability of linear programming and the Baumol–Wolfe modification of the technique to the analysis of Wonka's distribution system? (21) Why? (22) Would your response be different if Wonka manufactured product at two or more points? (23) If it utilized public instead of private warehousing?

Dynamic Programming. Location decisions made now can influence the future logistics performance of the firm for years to come. Changing

[14] Alfred A. Kuehn and Michael J. Hamburger, "A Heuristic Program for Locating Warehouses," *Management Science*, July, 1963, pp. 643–66.

conditions warrant changing inventory location patterns. Less than optimal current locations may produce good long-term economic results. But when should locations be altered for optimum benefit? A technique for dealing with this problem of change over time is dynamic programming.[15]

The problem can be illustrated by assuming five alternative locations for serving a firm's markets, all of which might be included in a determination of optimum distribution patterns for different points in time. A year-by-year analysis of the costs of serving all markets from each inventory location requires forecasts for such items of information as transportation and warehousing costs, sales volume estimates, the relative impact on sales of the proximity of inventories to customers, and the cost of moving an inventory location. Costs or profits resulting from the use of each inventory location in each year can then be calculated.

The dynamic location plan is then found by analyzing the problem as a sequence of interdependent events, beginning with the furthest year in the future. In Ballou's example, the relative desirability of relocating an inventory is determined for the fifth year first, by subtracting the cost of moving from the profit differential from the use of alternative locations as opposed to the existing location during the fifth year from now, all on a discounted cash-flow basis with all dollar profits and costs discounted to their current value. This produces a set of calculations such as the following for location A, under the stipulation that the cost of moving an inventory in current dollars is $100,000 now or $48,225 ($100,000 discounted at an assumed 20% per year for four years) four years from now:

$$P_5(A) = \max \begin{bmatrix} \begin{array}{ccccccc} \text{Alternative} & \text{Location} & & \text{Moving} & & \text{Net} \\ (x) & \text{Profit} & & \text{Cost} & & \text{Profit} \\ A & \$1,336,000 & - & \$\quad 0 & = & \$1,336,000 \\ B & 1,398,000 & - & 48,225 & = & 1,349,975 \\ C & 1,457,600 & - & 48,225 & = & 1,409,375 \\ D & 1,486,600 & - & 48,225 & = & 1,438,375 \\ E & 1,526,000 & - & 48,225 & = & 1,477,775 \end{array} \end{bmatrix}$$

Similar calculations are made for locations B, C, D, and E, and the profit potential of optimum location decisions and the "move or stay" decision are entered into the fifth-year columns of the decision format shown in Table 13–5.

For years other than the last included in our projection, the maximum value of each location is determined by: (1) starting with the profits estimated for the location during the year in question, discounted back to the present, (2) subtracting the discounted cost of moving the inven-

[15] See Ronald H. Ballou, "Dynamic Warehouse Location Analysis," *Journal of Marketing Research*, August, 1968, pp. 271–76; published by the American Marketing Association. Portions of this section are adapted from the article with permission.

TABLE 13-5. Location–Relocation Plans for a Five-Year Planning Period
with Optimum Cumulative Discounted Profits from Location for
Year 1 to Year 5 Resulting from a Dynamic Programming
Analysis of Warehouse Locations

Year from Present Date (j)	Warehouse Location Alternative (x)				
	A	B	C^a	D	E
Year 1:					
$P_1(x)$	\$3,719,686	\$3,717,486	\$3,755,430	\$3,720,300	\$3,659,197
Policy[b]	S_A	S_B	S_C ←	S_D	S_E
Year 2:					
$P_2(x)$	\$3,525,086	\$3,540,986	\$3,583,130	\$3,553,600	\$3,499,797
Policy	S_A	S_B	S_C ←	S_D	M_C
Year 3:					
$P_3(x)$	\$3,168,986	\$3,168,986	\$3,238,430	\$3,216,000	\$3,168,986
Policy	M_C	M_C	S_C ←	S_D	M_C
Year 4:					
$P_4(x)$	\$2,402,030	\$2,402,030	\$2,402,030	\$2,459,900	\$2,418,800
Policy	M_D	M_D	M_D	→ S_D	S_E
Year 5:					
$P_5(x)$	\$1,477,775	\$1,477,775	\$1,477,775	\$1,486,600	\$1,526,000
Policy	M_E	M_E	M_E	S_D ←	S_E

[a]Arrows indicate maximum profit location plan when warehouse is initially located at C.
[b]Policy symbols refer to staying (S) in the designated location or moving (M) to a new location.

Source: Ronald H. Ballou, "Dynamic Warehouse Location Analysis," *Journal of Marketing Research*, August, 1968, pp. 271–76, at p. 275; published by the American Marketing Association.

tory location, and (3) adding the cumulative maximum profits from the optimum strategy for all subsequent years including the fifth. Twenty-five such computations produce all of the maximum values and suggested strategies for five potential locations over a five-year period, as shown in Table 13–5.

Table 13–5 contains a variety of information. For example, if our inventory currently was located at point A, an optimum location strategy for each of the next five years would be A, B, C, D, E. If point E was our starting point, the suggested strategy would be E, C, C, E, E. Thus, a move to point C at the beginning of the second year and a return to point E at the beginning of the fourth year would produce optimum results of \$3,659,197. If, for some reason, it is not possible to move from E to C until the beginning of the third year, the expected maximum profit discounted to present value for the remaining three years is shown as \$3,168,986. The strategy which produces the maximum five-year profit is C, C, C, D, C, yielding a discounted profit of \$3,755,430.

Dynamic programming has been implemented by few organizations in logistics system planning. Possible reasons for this are: (1) the lack of trust which managers are willing to place in long-range forecasts, (2) management perceptions of prohibitively high costs of relocation, precluding significant results from dynamic programming, and (3) an unwillingness to live with the assumptions that the proper set of alternative locations can be identified now for a five-year period into the future or that one set of alternatives can remain independent of other actual or potential locations for the time frame of the projection. The concept is intriguing, but apparently awaits further development before much further implementation by industry will take place.

SIMULATION TECHNIQUES

General Approach

Simulation can be viewed as the "counting up" of costs or profits resulting from a specified action. The comparison of results from successive trials leads to a selection of a good strategy in the simulation approach to a problem. The potential for the use of simulation in determining inventory locations has been enhanced in recent years by the development of distance estimating techniques, transport cost regressions related to distance, and other techniques for estimating costs from information about volumes of activity. Nevertheless, unless the brute force of the computer can be combined with the cunning of the human mind, simulation can be a time-consuming and expensive method of determining desirable location strategies. A further refinement of the general simulation approach, called heuristic programming, has raised the probability that the high promise of simulation for location analyses will be realized.

Heuristic Programming

Methods of simulation have been formulated to: (1) allow the paper operation of a logistics system utilizing many different possible warehouse combinations [16] or (2) duplicate the human mental process by programming an electronic computer in such a way that it uses, holds in reserve, or discards possible warehouse locations. The latter has been termed "heuristic" programming, in that it: (1) attempts to eliminate unnecessary or costly search and analysis, (2) reduces a problem to manageable proportions, (3) places emphasis on working toward optimum solution proce-

[16] Shycon and Maffei, *op. cit.*

dures rather than ever elusive optimum solutions themselves, and (4) closely parallels the thought process likely to be followed by the human mind in viewing the problem.[17]

In their approach to the problem of warehouse location, Kuehn and Hamburger introduced three assumptions which would reduce the size of the problem (heuristics): (1) locations with promise will be at or near concentrations of demand; (2) near-optimum warehousing systems can be developed by locating warehouses one at a time, adding at each stage of the analysis that warehouse which produces the greatest cost savings for the entire system; and (3) only a small subset of all possible warehouse locations need be evaluated in detail at each stage of the analysis to determine the next warehouse site to be added. The flow diagram explaining information inputs and analytical instructions programmed into the computer is shown in Fig. 13–9.

PRACTICAL ASPECTS OF INVENTORY LOCATION STRATEGY

Having reviewed theoretical techniques for analyzing inventory location opportunities, we turn next to several of the more practical aspects of such analyses.

Implications of Company Policy

The inventory location decision is dependent on several matters of company policy. For example, an inventory holding facility which is owned must be sold, rented, or abandoned if a new logistics system eliminates the need for that facility. It is obviously much easier to sell a facility to a prospective buyer if it is a general-purpose facility and located in an area of industrial and commercial concentration.

The possibility of leasing inventory facilities often presents itself to the company. The favorability of the leasing from the standpoint of the lessee (i.e., length of lease, release penalty, etc.), however, will often vary directly with the favorability of the location, the all-purpose nature of the construction of the facility, and other factors. In short, some firms may require facilities that cannot be leased.

A further available option is to use public warehousing facilities. They provide space that can be rented on a short-term basis under arrangements that can be terminated almost at the convenience of the using firm.

There may be instances when, for reasons of advertising value, public relations, or service to a particular customer, it is determined by manage-

[17] Kuehn and Hamburger, *op. cit.*

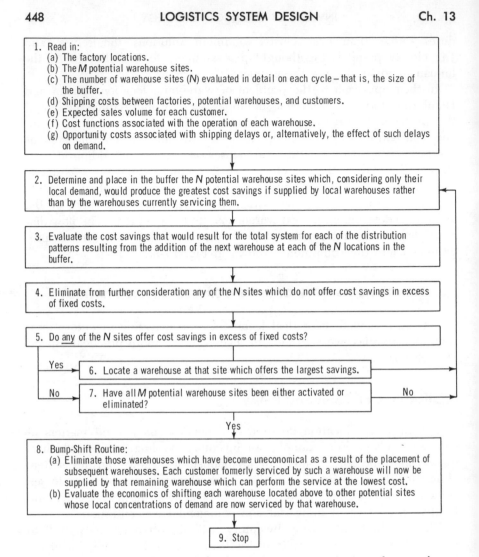

1. Read in:
   (a) The factory locations.
   (b) The M potential warehouse sites.
   (c) The number of warehouse sites (N) evaluated in detail on each cycle – that is, the size of the buffer.
   (d) Shipping costs between factories, potential warehouses, and customers.
   (e) Expected sales volume for each customer.
   (f) Cost functions associated with the operation of each warehouse.
   (g) Opportunity costs associated with shipping delays or, alternatively, the effect of such delays on demand.

2. Determine and place in the buffer the N potential warehouse sites which, considering only their local demand, would produce the greatest cost savings if supplied by local warehouses rather than by the warehouses currently servicing them.

3. Evaluate the cost savings that would result for the total system for each of the distribution patterns resulting from the addition of the next warehouse at each of the N locations in the buffer.

4. Eliminate from further consideration any of the N sites which do not offer cost savings in excess of fixed costs.

5. Do any of the N sites offer cost savings in excess of fixed costs?

   Yes ——→ 6. Locate a warehouse at that site which offers the largest savings. ——→

   No ——→ 7. Have all M potential warehouse sites been either activated or eliminated?　　　No ——

   Yes
   ↓

8. Bump-Shift Routine:
   (a) Eliminate those warehouses which have become uneconomical as a result of the placement of subsequent warehouses. Each customer formerly serviced by such a warehouse will now be supplied by that remaining warehouse which can perform the service at the lowest cost.
   (b) Evaluate the economics of shifting each warehouse located above to other potential sites whose local concentrations of demand are now serviced by that warehouse.

9. Stop

Fig. 13–9. Flow diagram of a heuristic computer program for warehouse location. *Source:* Alfred A. Kuehn and Michael J. Hamburger, "A Heuristic Program for Locating Warehouses," *Management Science*, July, 1963, pp. 643–66, at p. 647.

ment that the company will have an inventory in a particular city.

Most important of all, policies regarding customer service standards based primarily on factors other than logistics must, nevertheless, be met by a logistics system. Customer service policy serves as the greatest single determinant of the number and location of inventories.

Area of Analytic Freedom

Further constraints on the final solution of the inventory location problem are presented by four additional problems resulting from any decision to relocate an inventory.

The Effect on People.   An inventory move of any substantial distance which would require the employees of the company to move their homes or find employment elsewhere will cause certain difficulties and perhaps expense to them. Under many circumstances this may cause union–management industrial relations problems, and it will inevitably cause human relations problems. There are cases where a move may be precipitated by union problems. In one firm consolidating two inventories at a third location in the Southwest several years ago, a decision to relocate was prompted by the desire to invalidate existing seniority ratings for union warehousemen at the two old locations.

The Value of Being Known.   In addition to the more common public relations values of having a company operate a facility in a locality, there are important sales and promotion considerations. Customers may become familiar with an inventory location and may be satisfied and accustomed to doing business with the firm there. Further, transportation arrangements may have become stabilized, and carriers may have so adjusted their local operations as to give very good service to a particular existing location. A move to another location may well require repeating the process of getting one's operations smoothly integrated with the operations of servicing agencies (carriers) and customers with a certain interim loss of efficiency and service.

Moving Costs.   Whenever a move is recommended and carried out, there are, in addition to the intangible costs already mentioned, certain ascertainable costs of making the move to a new location. Probably some inventory stock will have to be transferred along with office equipment, supplies, and warehouse equipment. Employees' moving expenses may also be incurred, depending on the firm's policy in this regard.

Justification of Past Decisions.   All costs of changes in the configuration of a logistics system must be justified to other senior officers of the firm. Often some very hard questions may be asked: "Only a short while ago you decided we should relocate facilities. Now you say we should relocate them again. Why should we assume that your present decision is any better than your earlier one? Won't we just have to move again in a year or two? Aren't these moves costing us more than the 'operational' savings you claim they will give the firm?"

A location change may be in order for one or more of the company's inventory sites, but its advocate must be prepared to defend his recommendation against strong counterarguments.

Centralized vs. Decentralized Inventories

In 1948, the traffic department at General Foods Corporation was given increased responsibility for warehousing operations after it devised a plan for:

. . . elimination of district warehouses and construction of five big warehouses, to be supplied by the producing plants, each to serve a specific area with all General Foods products. The wholesaler then could order a carload of mixed products to move directly to his own siding.[18]

Twelve years later, this same company announced, in a message to its stockholders:

The half-way mark was reached in General Foods' program to establish a national network of market-centered Sales and Distribution Centers, as four more links in the coast-to-coast chain went into operation in fiscal 1960, providing faster and more dependable service to our customers in the Minneapolis–St. Paul, St. Louis, Philadelphia and Denver markets.

With similar "one-stop" service installations already operating in the Boston, Memphis, Youngstown and Atlanta markets, GF customers in eight districts now enjoy the advantages of this new sales-distribution concept.

Because the new distribution system is tailored to provide each customer with the right amount of the right products at the right time, benefits are accruing to the company as well as to our customers. Greater delivery dependability makes possible a higher return on our customers' invested capital through faster inventory turnover, and so they find it more attractive to do business with General Foods. We enjoy lower transportation costs and more efficient order processing and handling.

In the next year, GF's Market-Centered Customer Service Plan will be extended to Cincinnati, Chicago, Portland (Oregon), New York and Detroit, and subsequently to San Francisco, Los Angeles and Dallas.[19]

Recently, the number of distribution centers operated by General Foods had grown to 22. Throughout this period of change, however, the company continued to distribute its largest volume product, coffee, directly from its plants to customers located up to several hundred miles from its coffee plants.

(24) **Which of the decisions made by General Foods Corporation was right?** (25) **Are they, in fact, contrasting in policy implications?**

---

[18] "How They Got There," *Railway Freight Traffic*, August, 1947, p. 42.
[19] *Annual Report*, General Foods Corp., Fiscal 1960, p. 11.

The long-debated question of centralized or decentralized inventory locations has not stemmed the flow of executive decisions in favor of each policy. Factors tending to favor one policy or the other change from one point in time to the next, as suggested in the enumeration of benefits of each policy presented in Table 13–6.

In firms with a wide range of products of different types, both centralization and decentralization of certain inventories may be appropriate. There is a growing trend toward this type of location strategy, which can

TABLE 13–6. Benefits of Centralized and Decentralized Inventory Location Strategies, and Determinants of Their Importance

Centralized, Consolidated Location Strategy:	Varying Directly with:
Reduction of plant-to-warehouse transport costs	Proportion of former shipments of LTL size
Reduction of cross-hauling of goods between warehouses	Ineffectiveness of inventory control procedures
Reduction of safety and dead stocks per unit of throughput	Importance of safety and dead stocks for specific SKUL's
Creation of critical mass of business, attractive to first-class public warehouse operators	Volume of throughput, inventory turnover
Greater opportunity for use of private warehousing through creation of large, constant volume	Volume, regularity of throughput
More frequent inventory replenishment, further reducing safety stocks and inventory program response time	Amount of change in the volume of throughput
Opportunity for better warehouse management, control	Size of operation
Improvement of in-stock position in filling customer orders	Degree of SKUL consolidation
Improved transportation service for beyond-warehouse distribution	Importance of revenues to carrier
Elimination of duplicated effort in order picking, handling	Degree to which private warehousing is used
Decentralized, Market-Oriented Location Strategy:	Varying Directly with:
Stimulation of sales	Need of customers for proximity to stocks
Reduction of warehouse-to-customer transport costs	Cost of transportation variable with distance
Greater opportunity for use of public warehousing, creating larger proportion of costs variable with volume	Availability of, and company policies toward, public warehousing; nature of product
Improvement in order-cycle response time for customers	Degree to which overall transport service times are variable with distance
Greater sales, assuming high in-stock rates	Degree to which rapid product availability is necessary for, and substitution is practiced by, customers

be referred to as the use of a "dual" or "multiple" distribution system. (26) **Do you think Wonka's business provides us with a good opportunity for the application of this concept?** (7) **Why?** Regardless of whether it does, an exploration of the concept allows us to consider in some detail the economics of centralized inventories.

Dual or Multiple Distribution Systems

A firm may adopt two or more strategies for the distribution of various groups of items in its product line. This practice, an outgrowth of so-called ABC inventory policies or inventory echeloning, provides the ultimate extension of a concept that SKU's with varying characteristics require differentiated distribution strategies.

ABC Inventory Policies. The term "ABC inventory policy" is used generically to refer to a wide variety of practices. In all cases, such policies involve varying degrees of attention to the management of inventories for various groups of SKU's. All involve the differentiation of SKU's on the basis of such factors as: (1) rate of sale, (2) value per unit, (3) ease of storage, or (4) the strategic value of the item to a customer. Most are concerned with the provision of different levels of "coverage," through the use of safety stocks, for various categories of items.

Concentration on SKU's with High Rates of Sale. This approach employs detailed forecasts, frequent updates of inventory levels and forecast information, and the most detailed inventory management programs for the management of inventories for SKU's in the product line with the highest rates of sale. The rationale for it is that it is these SKU's which offer the greatest opportunity for savings from the application of scientific methods. SKU's with slow rates of sale typically are stocked in quantities sufficient to reduce the need for reviews of stock levels to relatively infrequent time intervals. This type of ABC program may be employed when inventory management facilities and personnel are limited and when there is little variation in other features associated with SKU's, such as unit value.

Overall customer service levels, defined in terms of the proportion of items ordered that are available in a firm's stock, can be affected most directly by the coverage provided for the SKU's with the greatest rates of sale. For example, consider Wonka's situation for levelors, outlined in Table 13–7. If the coverage level for "A" SKU's, defined as those 8 models in the line (out of 40) representing 80% of the total unit sales, increases from 90% to 97%, the in-stock order-filling rate increases from 90% to 95.6%. (28) **What effect would similar increases from 90% to 97% coverage for "B" and "C" items have?** (29) **Does this suggest the**

TABLE 13-7. The Effect on the Customer Service Level of Changes
in Inventory Coverage Levels for "A" Levelor SKU's,
Warren G. Wonka Manufacturing Company

	SKU Category			
	"A"	"B"	"C"	Total
Number of SKU's	8	8	24	40
Proportion of total SKU's	20%	20%	60%	100%
Proportion of total unit sales	81.0%	17.6%	1.4%	100%
Situation A: Non-differentiated inventory coverage[a]	90%	90%	90%	90%
Situation B: Differentiated inventory coverage[a]	97%	90%	90%	95.6%[b]

[a]Assuming each customer order is for one unit of one SKU. Where this is not the case, results will vary but this principle effect will be maintained.
[b]Calculated as (97% × 81.0%) + (90% × 17.6%) + (90% × 1.4%) = 95.6%.

possibility of further reducing the coverage for these items? (30) What additional factors would you want to take into account before taking such action?

Concentration on SKU's with High Values per Unit. Where values per unit for SKU's vary greatly, the greatest savings in inventory carrying costs may be effected either by the use of a more careful and exacting inventory program in the management of these items or by a reduction in inventory coverage levels for them. Consider the extension of our previous example, presented in Table 13-8.

The SKU's selling in the highest unit volume represent 81.0% of Wonka's total unit sales of levelors, 69.7% of the Company's unit inventory of levelors, and only 41.8% of the value of average inventories on hand. In contrast, "C" SKU's comprise 1.4% of the total unit sales, 3.6% of unit inventories, and 20.1% of the value of average inventories on hand. (31) Does this seem reasonable to you? (32) Why?

Here, a differentiated inventory coverage policy, involving the stocking of "A" and "B" SKU's to provide 97% and 80% coverage levels, respectively, and the stocking of "C" items to provide only 10% coverage, produces a $1.7 million reduction in inventory value and a significant improvement in customer service levels, as shown in Table 13-8.

Concentration on SKU's with Extensive Storage Requirements. ABC inventory policies may, where storage facilities represent a scarce resource with a high opportunity cost per unit of space, differentiate SKU's on the basis of cubic footage per unit. Extra attention may be paid

TABLE 13-8. The Effect on Customer Service Levels and Inventory Carrying Costs of Changes in Inventory Coverage Levels for Various SKU Groupings, Levelor Machines, Warren G. Wonka Manufacturing Company

	SKU Category			
	"A"	"B"	"C"	Total
Non-Differentiated Inventory Coverage:				
Proportion of total unit sales	81.0%	17.6%	1.4%	100.0%
Proportion of unit inventory	69.7%	26.7%	3.6%	100.0%
Proportion of dollar inventories	41.8%	38.1%	20.1%	100.0%
Value of dollar inventories (in millions of dollars)	$7.0	$6.4	$3.3	$16.7
Inventory coverage	90.0%	90.0%	90.0%	90.0%
Differentiated Inventory Coverage:				
Inventory coverage	97.0%	80.0%	10.0%	92.7%*
Value of dollar inventories (in millions of dollars)	$10.0	$4.0	$1.0	$15.0

*Calculated by multiplying the inventory coverage rate for each category by the proportion of total unit sales represented by each respective category, or (97% $\times$ 81.0%) + (80.0% $\times$ 17.6%) + (10.0% $\times$ 1.4%) = 92.7%.

to inventory control measures and inventory coverage reductions for SKU's requiring the greatest space per unit for storage.

Categories of product, such as frozen foods among grocery products in general, may be singled out for this type of attention because of the high cost per unit incurred in their storage.

Concentration on SKU's with High Strategic Values to Customers. Often, SKU's distributed by an organization vary in their strategic values to customers. A clutch bearing is more critical than a rear view mirror to customers of an automotive parts manufacturer, even though the latter may sell in much larger quantities. It is perhaps not surprising that such approaches have been employed from time to time by military organizations, where the penalty of unmet "customer" demand can be extremely severe, resulting in the loss of life and battle.

Extension of the ABC Rationale— Multiple Distribution Systems

Carrying ABC stocking policies a step further, organizations are beginning to implement multiple distribution systems offering differentiated location patterns and transportation methods. Features of this approach are that it allows an organization to offer somewhat uniform inventory coverage levels, a high level of dependability in order-cycle times for all SKU's, and a service response (order-cycle) time differentiated among groups of products only by the possible designation of different shipping points and transportation and handling methods for each.

Multiple distribution systems will result from the recognition of a number of "facts of logistics life." The first of these is that the relationships between sales and inventory turn rates shown in Fig. 13–10 for the Wonka Company are more or less universal among firms which do not utilize multiple distribution systems. This figure, prepared from data contained in the product profiles for machines (Table 9–4) and for parts, offers one of the most useful relationships for logistics system design purposes. Information shown in Table 13–9, collected from the files of several companies in widely varying businesses, suggests that the presence of this relationship is the rule rather than the exception. One way to deal with the problem implied by this information, where it is not

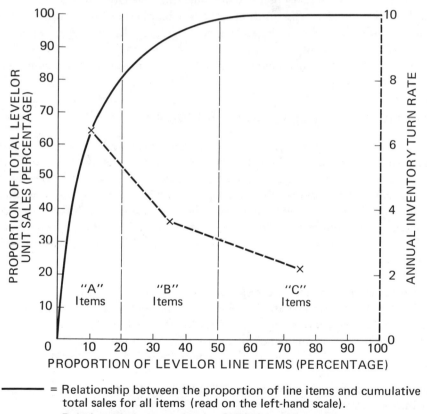

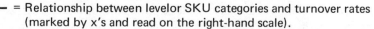

——— = Relationship between the proportion of line items and cumulative total sales for all items (read on the left-hand scale).

– – – – = Relationship between levelor SKU categories and turnover rates (marked by x's and read on the right-hand scale).

Fig. 13–10. Relationship between SKU sales and inventory turnover rates for levelor machines, Warren G. Wonka Manufacturing Company.

desirable to reduce inventory coverage for SKU groupings, is to consolidate inventories for SKU groupings with lower rates of sale, expanding sales per SKU by extending the geographic territory served by a given SKU inventory and thereby increasing the inventory turn rate.

Second, shipper surveys have indicated repeatedly a higher shipper priority on dependability of service as opposed to speed of service. Such dependability is most feasible in a system which provides uniformly high inventory coverage for all SKU's at some geographic location known to salesmen, other employees, and perhaps customers.

Third, it is a widely held (but largely undocumented) belief that customers hold lower expectations for order-cycle times for SKU's with lower rates of sale, typically the "non-standard" items, than for other SKU's. At the same time, they value dependable information about availability dates for all SKU's. Multiple distribution systems can take advantage of the former belief while meeting the latter need.

Finally, multiple distribution systems emphasize the centralization and consolidation of certain SKU groupings, not the closing or opening of warehouse or plant inventories. As such, they may represent a smaller shock to the top management psyche and a smaller commitment and risk to their proponents.

A Multiple Distribution System for Wonka?

The appraisal of advantages of a multiple distribution system for the Wonka Manufacturing Company required that our consultant: (1) establish SKU categories, (2) perform an inventory analysis, and (3) based on estimates provided by this analysis, estimate the economies of a multiple distribution system. Because the multiple distribution system concept was thought to represent greater potential for levelor parts than for machines, the analysis of the parts distribution system was carried out first.

Establishment of SKU Categories.   To simplify the analysis, our consultant, after checking with Wonka's management, decided to make the first "cut" at the problem by differentiating 20% of the SKU's representing 80% of unit sales of machines from the rest, obtained from the product-line review. He then tested the economics of distributing these "A" SKU's (with the highest rate of sale) through 16 distribution centers and consolidating the remaining "B" SKU's at the Cleveland plant distribution center.

The product-line review also yielded information which suggested that the inventory turn rate for "A" SKU's (with the highest rate of sale) was more than twice as great as that for "B" SKU's.

Because management had specified a restricted limit of seven days for

TABLE 13-9. Relationships Between Sales Volume and Inventory Turnover
Rates Experienced by a Sample of Companies in Eight Industries

Nature of Product Line Measured	Annual Inventory Turnover Rates[a]		
	Fast Moving Items[b]	Moderately Moving Items[b]	Slow Moving Items[b]
Cereal-based food products	64.8	13.5	8.8
Wire and cable, tubing	8.5	9.8	6.4
Small appliances	5.5	4.5	1.6
Small appliance parts	1.6	1.9	1.4
Grocery paper products	21.3	19.3	8.9
Writing paper products	21.9	7.0	5.4
Automotive window glass	4.7	1.7	.5
Grinding wheels	2.6	2.3	.7
Chemicals[c]	24.4	4.1	7.0

[a]Inventory turnover rates were based on an average of annual turnover (unit sales divided by average total inventory in units) rates for three selected product-line items falling into each volume sales category for each product line.

[b]Fast moving items were defined as those falling among the 20% of the items in the line selling the largest volume of units; moderately moving items were those among the next 30% in unit volume of sales; slow moving items were those in the bottom 50% of items ranked by unit sales volume.

[c]Does not include inventories held at branch (non-plant) warehouses.

Source: James L. Heskett, "The Case for Multiple Distribution Systems," to be published.

the delivery of all orders placed by dealer–customers, it was felt that the only hope for the consolidation of "B" SKU locations at one point would involve the use of air freight from Cleveland to all distribution centers more than a four-day LTL trucking haul (about 400 miles) from Cleveland. This was based on the knowledge that distribution centers were located to provide three-day LTL service to all dealer outlets. To accomplish even seven-day order-cycle times from Cleveland to all customers through distribution centers, it would be necessary to install low-cost order-transmitting units at all distribution centers and direct line connections from each to the Cleveland distribution center.

Although the possibility of distributing "B" SKU's directly from Cleveland to dealer–customers was considered, it was felt that dealers placed a sufficiently high value on receiving complete orders that Wonka's interests would be served better by holding "A" SKU's at distribution centers for delivery with "B" SKU's from Cleveland. This raised the further question of whether to "marry" shipments containing "A" and "B" items in single shipments prior to delivery. It was concluded that this would be time-consuming, expensive, and unnecessary.

Inventory Analysis. Estimates of the effect of centralized inventories on stock levels required an identification of proportions of various categories of inventories in Wonka's distribution centers. Calculations necessary for these estimates were based on the categorization of inventories into cycle, speculative, in-transit, and safety and dead stocks,[20] shown in Table 13–10. They were performed only for a small but representative sample of machine SKU's; information for two of them is shown in Table 13–10.

Cycle Stocks. Average cycle stocks in the inventory of each distribution center can be estimated as one-half of the sum of the quantities of an SKU ordered regularly by all distribution centers or one-half of the amount produced in each production run of the SKU at the plant, whichever is greater. This estimate recognizes the fact that economies of scale in production, reflected in plant EOQ's, may dictate the level of cycle stocks, regardless of the number of SKUL's in the distribution system. This proved to be the case for both Models 122L and 8M in the example shown in Table 13–10.

A word of caution is in order here. If, as in a retailing or wholesaling organization, there is no production activity, cycle stocks, measured as one-half of the buying quantities, will vary directly with the number of SKUL's or DC's, in a proportion roughly equivalent to the square root of the number of SKUL's.

Speculative Stocks. Speculative stocks at Wonka were accumulated to allow the Cleveland plant to produce at a reasonably constant rate in spite of the fact that peak machine and parts sales typically were twice those at slack selling periods. An estimate of the average quantities of speculative stock required the identification of production in advance of forecasts of distribution center needs, in the manner shown in footnoted in Table 13–10.

In-Transit Stocks. In-transit stock measurements can be based on estimates of the weighted average of transit times for shipments—in the case of Wonka, from the plant to the various distribution centers. For rail carload shipments of machines under the existing system, it was estimated to be a week, or the equivalent of one week's sales.

Safety and Dead Stocks. Dead stocks which have not produced any sales for a specified period of time often result from excessive safety stocks, accumulated in excess of need because of incorrect forecasts, concern for a high level of inventory coverage, or perhaps an incorrect positioning of stocks in the system. For purposes of multiple distribution system studies, it is sufficient to identify these stocks together as the amount that remains after the deduction of average cycle, speculative, and in-transit stocks from the total average inventory.

[20] These categories are defined in Chapter 10. It might be useful to review them, as discussed on pp. 305–6.

TABLE 13-10. Analysis of Inventories for Two Levelor SKU's, Wonka Manufacturing Company

Type of Inventory	"A" SKU Model (122L)	"B" SKU Model (8M)
Cycle Stock:		
The greater of plant production runs or the sum of distribution center order quantities[a]	3,870[a]	21.0[a]
Multiplied by .5[b]	1,935	10.5
Speculative Stock[c]	3,870	5.0
In-Transit Stock[d]	1,800	2.4
Safety and Dead Stock:		
Average inventory for the year	12,700	60.0
Sum of estimated cycle, speculative, and in-transit stocks, from above	7,805	17.9
	4,895	42.1
Percentage Analysis of Average Inventory:		
Cycle stock	15.2%	16.7%
Speculative stock	30.4	8.3
In-transit stock	14.2	4.0
Safety and dead stocks	40.2	71.0
	100.0%	100.0%

[a]Calculated for Model 122L as annual demand of 92,900 units divided by 24 production runs per year (from Table 9-4) as opposed to more than 50 distribution center ordering opportunities per year (the number of truckloads or carloads per year shipped from Cleveland to the average distribution center). Calculated for Model 8M as annual demand of 125 units divided by 6 production runs.

[b]To reflect average as opposed to maximum cycle stocks.

[c]Calculated by identifying production runs in advance of forecast need for plant production smoothing purposes, multiplying each of such run quantities by the number of months' difference between actual and necessary production, and dividing the sum of these "SKU unit months" by twelve to obtain an estimate of average speculative stocks over the year. For example, starting with the slack sales season and ending with the peak season, a simplified calculation would be as follows:

	Oct.	Nov.	Dec.	Jan.	Feb.	Mar.	Apr.	May	June	July	Aug.	Sept.	Total
Sales (units)	1	2	4	2	2	2	2	5	8	7	5	5	48
Production requirement (units)	2	4	2	2	2	2	5	8	7	5	5	4	48
Actual production (units)	4	4	4	4	4	4	4	4	4	4	4	4	48
Speculative stock balance (units)	2	2	4	6	8	10	9	5	2	1	0	0	
Cumulative speculative stocks (in unit months)	2	4	8	14	22	32	41	46	48	49	49	49	

Average speculative stocks for the year would thus be 49 unit months divided by 12, or 4.08 units.

[d]Estimated as an average of one week's sales for all distribution centers as a whole.

Note in Table 13–10 that safety and dead stocks comprise 71.0% of total inventories for our "B" SKU and only 40.2% of total inventories for the "A" SKU. This relationship occurs often, and helps explain opportunities for total cost savings in multiple distribution systems. The basic objective of the concept is to obtain significant reductions in safety and dead stocks through the consolidation of "B" items while maintaining or improving overall inventory coverage and customer service levels.

Economic Analysis of the Multiple Distribution System. Information upon which the economic analysis of a potential multiple distribution system for levelor machines was based is shown in Table 13–11. It provided a basis for a general estimate of possible cost savings from the consolidation of various SKU groupings. For purposes of rough-cut estimation, items with the highest volumes of unit sales, from Table 9–4, were called "A" SKU's and the remainder "B" SKU's. Information from the sample of items in Table 9–4 indicated that if the sample were valid, "A" SKU's represented sales of $45,750,000 and inventories of $7,000,000 at cost. "B" SKU's comprised $29,710,000 of sales and $9,710,000 of inventories at cost. Information regarding both the current use of rail carload and truckload shipments, as well as the proposed use of truck LTL and air freight for shipments from the Cleveland plant to various DC's, is shown in Table 13–11.

For purposes of establishing the profile presented in Table 13–11, it was assumed that machine order line items not shipped from distribution centers within four days of the time of their receipt constituted back-ordered items. The resulting phone calls and shipment tracing for orders comprising back-ordered line items raised the costs to process such orders from roughly $5 to about $15 per order, a considerable cost for a system processing 92,400 levelor machine orders per year.

A typical order for levelors was made up of one "A" SKU and three "B" SKU's. Because the customer service standard currently was an in-stock rate of 90% on all SKU's, this produced back-orders for "A" items on 10% of all orders and back-orders for "B" items on 25% of all orders, with the latter caused by the fact that certain orders contained two back-ordered "B" items. Because of orders containing back-ordered "A" and "B" items, the overall proportion of orders containing one or more back-ordered line items was 30%. By establishing the capability, through a Cleveland distribution center possessing 100% coverage for all "B" SKU's, of shipping all such SKU's to distribution centers for redistribution to dealer–customers within four days of the original receipt of their orders, the back-order rate could be reduced from 30% of all orders to 10%.

The inventory analysis of a sample of "A" and "B" SKU's indicated that safety and dead stocks comprised about 33% of average inventories of the former and 67% of the average inventories of the latter, as suggested

TABLE 13–11. Basic Facts and Assumptions for Analysis of Potential for a Multiple Distribution System, Warren G. Wonka Manufacturing Company

Item Category	Proportion of Product-Line Items	Proportion of Unit Sales	Annual Sales (at Cost)	Average Inventory (at Cost)	Annual Inventory Turnover Rate
"A"	20%	81%	$45,750,000 (15,890,000 lbs.)	$7,000,000	6.50
"B"	80%	19%	$29,710,000 (10,370,000 lbs.)	9,710,000	3.05
Total	100%	100%	$75,460,000	$16,710,000	4.50

Product-line value, all items = $2.87 per pound
Product-line density, all items = 8 pounds per cubic foot

Rail carload provisions: 8-day delivery, 60,000-pound minimum, $4 per cwt. rate, packing costs = .5% of product cost, 3-day variation in service time

Truckload provisions: 6-day delivery, 40,000-pound minimum, $6 per cwt. rate, packing costs = .5% of product cost, 1-day variation in service time

Truck LTL provisions: 3-day delivery (within 400 miles of Cleveland only) 1,000-pound minimum, $10 per cwt. rate, packing costs = .5% of product cost, 1-day variation in service time

Air freight provisions: 2-day delivery (anywhere in U.S.), 1,000-pound minimum, $15 per cwt. rate, packaging costs = .25% of product cost, 1-day variation in service time

Order-processing information: Annual number of orders = 92,400; current back-order rate = 30%; "A" items are back-ordered on 10% of all orders and 10% of all line items, "B" items are back-ordered on 25% of all orders and 10% of all line items; normal order-processing cost = $5; back-order processing cost = $15; extra costs for teletype and line costs under the consolidation system = $96,000; lost sales on back orders = 20% of all units back-ordered.

Other assumptions:
1. All items are currently stocked in 16 DC's.
2. By consolidating stocks in one DC, safety and dead stocks for consolidated SKU's will be reduced to 25% of their former level $\left(\frac{\sqrt{16}}{16}\right)$ and cycle stocks will remain the same.
3. Safety and dead stocks comprise 33% of the inventory for "A" SKU's and 67% of the inventory for "B" SKU's.
4. Total warehousing and inventory carrying costs = 30% of the average value (at cost) of inventory on hand.
5. The Company makes a contribution rate (excess of sales over variable costs) on sales equal to 28% of sales volume or 54% of manufacturing cost.

---

by calculations in Table 13–10. This information was particularly significant, for any increase in transportation costs for either category of SKU's (to meet service demands from a central Cleveland stock) would have to be offset in part by large reductions in safety and dead stocks under a centralized system.

Of the remaining assumptions shown in Table 13–11, two require further explanation. First, it was assumed that safety and dead stocks under the current deployment and the consolidation would vary directly in relation to the square root of the number of SKUL's, a reflection of the basic inventory management model. Thus, stocks held in 16 DC's would result in four times the safety and dead stocks for one consolidated inventory if a given level of customer service (in-stock condition) were to be maintained.

The cost of lost sales was assumed to be equivalent to the excess of sales over variable costs, an amount representing the contribution to fixed costs and profit, for items for which orders were cancelled because they were not in stock within four days after they were ordered by dealers. The rate of contribution was calculated to be 28% of sales volume or 54% of manufacturing costs for levelors.

Detailed calculations for the comparative costs of transportation, inventory carrying, packing, order processing, and contribution on lost sales under the current deployment of stocks and under a consolidated stocking policy for "A" SKU's are shown in Table 13–12.

In Table 13–12, transportation costs for rail carload, truckload, truck LTL, and air freight shipments were applied to the estimated proportions of shipments moving by each mode under each system.

In-transit inventories were estimated on the assumed average transit times for various combinations of transportation methods. Cycle and speculative stocks were assumed not to vary between systems, because such stocks were a function of production run sizes, not the number of SKUL's.

Packing costs were estimated to be about half of those for ground transportation for air shipments, based on the experiences of other firms.

Order-processing costs were calculated on the basis of the number of completely filled and partially filled orders expected under each distribution system. Costs for completely filled orders could be assigned to orders filled from the consolidated Cleveland stock as well as the stocks of the outlying DC's because they could be processed routinely according to a prearranged plan and would require no complex order preparation or duplicate communication. Annual costs for the teletype connections required by a consolidation of stocks were included in such cost estimates.

Finally, lost sales costs were estimated on the basis of the sales value of back orders on which initial orders might be cancelled under each system. This figure was then multiplied by the contribution (sales dollars in excess of variable costs) on such sales.

Estimated annual cost penalties for the proposed centralized distribution system for "A" SKU's, shown in Table 13–12, were $137,900 per year at current sales volumes. On the other hand, a similar analysis for "B"

TABLE 13-12. Economic Analysis of the Consolidation of "A" SKU's at Cleveland, Warren G. Wonka Manufacturing Company

Type of Cost	Current Deployment	Consolidation
1. Transportation:[a]		
Rail CL/truck TL	$ 799,000	$ —
Truck LTL	—	441,000
Air	—	1,720,000
Total	$ 799,000	$2,161,000
2. Inventory carrying:		
In-transit stocks[b]	$ 256,200	$ 128,100
Cycle and speculative[c]	1,405,000	1,405,000
Safety and dead stocks[d]	692,000	173,000
3. Packing[e]	228,000	146,000
4. Order processing:		
Completely filled orders[f]	323,000	347,000
Partially filled orders[g]	416,000	347,000
Extra machine and line costs[h]	—	98,000
5. Contribution on lost sales	548,000	—
Total costs	$4,667,200	$4,805,100

[a]Calculated on the assumptions that transportation rates are as shown in Table 13-11 and, based on data in Tables 9-3 and 9-4, that the following total pounds of product would be moved by each transport method:

	Current Deployment	*Consolidation*
Rail CL/truck TL	$15,890,000 (all "A" SKU's)	
Truck LTL	—	4,410,000 ("A" SKU's to DC's within 400 miles)
Air	—	11,480,000 ("A" SKU's to DC's more than 400 miles from Cleveland)

[b]Calculated for current deployment as $45,750,000 (cost of annual sales of "A" SKU's) X 20% (inventory carrying costs exclusive of warehousing costs at annual rates for goods in transit) X 1/250 (assuming 250 operating days in a year) X 7 (average days in transit by rail CL or truck TL) = $256,200. The cost under consolidation assumes an average 3 1/2-day transit time from the Cleveland plant to DC's by means of truck LTL and air transportation.

[c]Calculated on the basis of an average inventory value for "A" SKU's of $7,000,000, of which 67% are cycle and speculative stock, carried at the annual rate of 30% of the value of such stocks.

[d]Calculated on the basis of an average inventory value for "A" SKU's of $7,000,000, of which 33% are safety and dead stocks, carried at the annual rate of 30% of the value of the stocks, with such stocks under consolidation program only 25% of those currently held.

[e]Calculated as .5% of $45,750,000 in cost of product sales for current deployment and the sum of .5% of $12,700,000 for truck LTL and .25% of $33,050,000 for air shipments under the consolidation program.

[f]Calculated for current deployment program as 70% of 92,400 orders at $5 per order; calculated for consolidation program as 75% (100% – 25% back-order rate for unaffected "B" SKU's) of 92,400 orders at $5 per order.

[g]Calculated for current deployment program as 30% of 92,400 orders at $15 per order; calculated for consolidation program as 25% of 92,400 orders at $15 per order.

[h]Calculated as 20% (lost sales rate) X $\dfrac{\$45,750,000 \text{ (cost of annual sales)}}{90\% \text{ (item order fill rate)}}$ X 10% (out of stock rate for units) X 54% (contribution as a proportion of cost of sales for current deployment); lost sales costs are assumed to be eliminated under a consolidation program.

SKU's, shown in Table 13–13, suggested that the proposed system would produce annual savings of $1,083,600. (33) Why? (34) How were the results in Table 13–13 obtained?

(35) What results would be achieved by a system in which "A" and "B" SKU's would be consolidated at Cleveland and 15 distribution centers closed? This suggests that cost as well as psychological objections might be met by the implementation of a multiple distribution system for a company's product line.

Questions Raised by the Analysis. Clearly, a differentiated distribution system for various of Wonka's machine SKU's offered significant savings for the Company. At the same time, it raised questions which required further analytic effort. For example, what is the appropriate grouping of SKU's to be centralized? Is it the 80% which have the lowest sales rate? Or is it 85%, 90%, or 97%? Is unit sales rate the appropriate determinant for approaching the problem? We have explored a dual distribution system for Wonka's machine SKU's; would three or more systems produce even more favorable results? Although little theoretical work has been addressed to these questions, you can guess what form it would take by identifying the cost trade-offs involved when a portion of a company's SKUL's are centralized.

(36) Our analysis provided an estimate of possible savings to be obtained by relocating SKU's under Wonka's existing inventory manage-

TABLE 13-13. Economic Analysis of the Consolidation of "B" SKU's at Cleveland, Warren G. Wonka Manufacturing Company*

Type of Cost	Current Deployment	Consolidation
1. Transportation:		
Rail CL/truck TL	$ 518,000	$ –
Truck LTL	–	288,000
Air	–	1,122,000
Total	$ 518,000	$1,410,000
2. Inventory carrying:		
In-transit stocks	$ 166,400	$ 83,200
Cycle and speculative stocks	960,000	960,000
Safety and dead stocks	1,950,000	487,500
3. Packing	$ 148,000	$ 95,100
4. Order processing:		
Completely filled orders	$ .324,000	$ 415,000
Partially filled orders	417,000	138,000
Extra machine and line costs	–	98,000
5. Contribution on lost sales	$ 288,000	$ –
Total cost	$4,771,400	$3,687,800

*For methods and assumptions underlying calculations, see footnotes to Table 13-12.

ment program. Is this appropriate? (37) If not, would the same potential savings exist under an "improved" program? (38) What are the necessary characteristics of an "improved" program which logically would seem to offer similarly large potential savings in a multiple distribution system? (39) Why?

We have assumed that 16 SKUL's for high-volume line items and only one for SKU's with low sales rates are appropriate. Further, we have assumed that the 16 SKUL's are positioned properly. These may be heroic assumptions without a careful review, possibly by means of simulation, linear programming, or other techniques, of territories served by distribution centers, of trends in sales patterns, and of possible effects of new locations on customer service.

Finally, a comparative analysis of the effects of the current deployment and the proposed consolidation at each DC would provide a more valid estimate of comparative transportation costs. Also, a DC-by-DC calculation would reveal the relative impact on the inventories of items remaining at each DC resulting from less frequent replenishment shipments from Cleveland to the DC in question.

SUMMARY

In this chapter, a variety of techniques and concepts for determining inventory location strategy, some of them in use by management today, have been surveyed. Clearly, not all will be suited for use in the design of every logistics system. By now you should be developing a "feel" for situations in which each technique or concept might hold the greatest potential. For example, as you read about each, ask yourself whether it would be applicable to Wonka's system analysis. More important, you should be able to offer some explanation for your conclusion.

There is no proven way of selecting the best technique for each problem. In this regard, it is important to keep in mind that almost any systematic, organized concept for approaching the analysis of an inventory location problem is better than none. What we are often concerned with is the degree of improvement offered by various techniques. At this stage of development for techniques delineating good inventory location strategies, neither the butcher knife nor the scalpel is likely to kill the patient.

SUGGESTED READINGS

BROWN, ROBERT G. *Decision Rules for Inventory Management.* New York: Holt, Rinehart and Winston, 1967.
    Offers one of the few descriptions of practical techniques for developing inventory location strategies.

14

Inventory Scheduling

Inventory scheduling problems involve the timing, sequencing, and grouping of purchases, production runs, or shipments. This is an amorphous topic encompassing a wide variety of techniques and applications and denying association with any one function of an organization.

We have divided the chapter into *production* and *other* types of scheduling problems, including priority determination, system loading, route selection, and split shipment planning. This seeming hodge-podge of topics is addressed in this chapter because we believe it may be more interesting for you to survey various analytical techniques employed in dealing with scheduling problems, and to appreciate their various applications, if such material is combined and presented in one place rather than fragmented and presented in bits and pieces at many points in the book.

PRODUCTION SCHEDULING

When and in *what quantities* will goods be produced, and when must the needed raw materials be on hand? In many firms, answers to these questions have been arrived at in a haphazard manner, particularly in regard to the scheduling of production of finished goods. There has been pulling and hauling between the production department and other departments of the firm. The reason is natural enough: the production department wishes to produce "efficiently," and this has usually been interpreted to mean "produce in economic lot quantities." Unfortunately, in many firms this seldom provides a solution to the requirements of customer service as reflected in optimum finished-goods inventory levels.

Two problems exist here. First, an economic lot quantity, as viewed only from the standpoint of the operations of the production department, may not be an economic lot quantity as viewed from the standpoint of the firm as a whole. Second, even if the production "runs" are scheduled in quantities which are economic lots from the standpoint of the whole firm, there still remains the question of the "lot" of product(s) to produce today, this week, or this month vs. which to produce tomorrow, next week, or next month.

Because mathematical formulas for the determination of economic lot quantities have become sophisticated enough to include costs not directly related to the production process, such as inventory carrying costs, transportation rate discounts, and purchase discounts (for inbound materials), it is possible to determine a true economic lot size.

Assuming that economic lot sizes can be determined, the next problem concerns a determination of when which lots should be produced. It can be broken into two parts, the "gross" production planning of the items and quantities which should be produced in a given time period of a month or a week, and the "detailed" scheduling of activities within the production process, i.e., the sequence and timing of individual production operations. To a greater and greater extent, the former is being placed in the hands of those responsible for corporate logistics.

Effective coordination of inventory control and production planning imposes certain requirements on several departments in an organization. These requirements include the transmission of information (sales forecasts) and decisions (customer service standards) from the marketing department to logistics. Also, the production department must advise logistics of its production capabilities (capacity) for various products, lead times, the quantity of raw materials needed to produce a given amount of a product, and economic lot sizes (if the production department makes the latter decision). Logistics management must inform the production department of what lots of products are to be produced by what dates, and must see to it that raw materials are available as needed.

The need for and the amount of coordination necessary between logistics and production in regard to production planning depends in large measure upon the nature of the production operations of the firm. Coordination is easiest when production is "continuous to order," and probably most difficult when it is "intermittent to stock." As Timms points out, in the latter situation "materials inventories are relatively high . . . work-in-process inventory is relatively high . . . there is more choice of lot size . . . [and] . . . this complexity then extends backward to raw inventories." [1]

[1] Howard L. Timms, *The Production Function in Business* (Homewood, Ill.: Richard D. Irwin, Inc., 1962), pp. 119–20.

One-Product Situation

Inventory control principles discussed in Chapter 11 largely assumed that raw materials, component parts, or finished goods in a given order or shipment become available at one point in time, all at once. In fact, a more common situation is that in which items flow from a manufacturing or processing operation in the form of a stream. When this is the case, quantities satisfactory to meet the immediate needs of the ordering firm may accumulate soon after the first units of an order reach the end of their process or manufacture. This may allow less stringent scheduling of production processes or a shorter span between the date an order is started through the process and the date its availability is required.

Batch Flow System.   Consider a situation in which the Wonka Manufacturing Company requires from its vendor, the Eastern Pump Company, 10,000 specially designed pumping units per year for its larger levelor units. If the units are made to order, as in this case, shipment cannot be made from stock. The price per pump (V) is $100, the ordering cost ($A$) is approximately $50, and the carrying cost rate for the demand period (R) is about 25%. Wonka's operations require a constant availability of 40 pumps during each of 250 operating days during a year's time. For this reason, the Company uses a fixed order-interval policy for replenishing inventory from Eastern.

If Wonka were to receive only complete orders in a single shipment from Eastern, the frequency of orders under constant and certain demand could be computed by the formula discussed in Chapter 11, $N^* = \sqrt{Srv/2A}$, where N^* is the optimum number of orders for the period of time under consideration. Thus,

$$N^* = \sqrt{\frac{10,000 \times .25 \times 100}{2 \times 50}}$$

$$= \sqrt{2,500} = 50$$

That is, an order for pumps should be placed by Wonka 50 times per year or every 5 operating days. Its size would be:

$$Q^* = \frac{S}{N^*} = \frac{10,000}{50} = 200 \text{ pumps}$$

In this example, 50 orders or "batches" of 200 pumps each would be transported from Eastern to Wonka during a year. The inventory level at the Wonka Manufacturing Company would appear as Example A in Fig. 14–1.

If Eastern's set-up time for an order was two operating days, transit

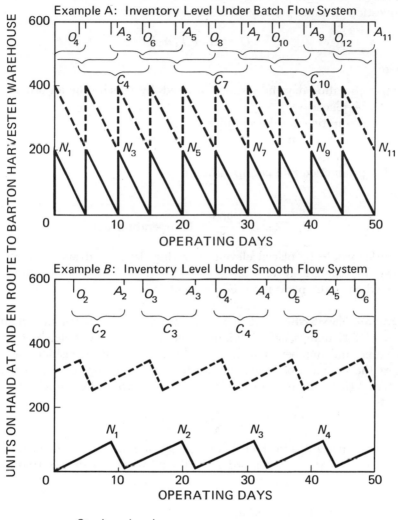

Fig. 14-1. Order cycles and inventory levels, Warren G. Wonka Manufacturing Company, under batch flow and smooth flow order scheduling (safety stocks omitted).

time to Wonka five operating days, and the rate of production of the unit in question 50 units per day, Wonka would order:

$$O_t = A_t + T_t + \frac{Q}{R}$$

where

O_t = operating days in advance of need, by which time an order must be placed
A_t = set-up time for the supplier
T_t = transit time from supplier to point of need
Q = order quantity
R = production rate per operating day

Thus,

$$O_t = 2 + 5 + \frac{200}{50} = 11 \text{ operating days}$$

An order would be placed eleven operating days in advance of need, as shown in Example A of Fig. 14–1. This period of time is sometimes referred to as the plant float requirement.

Smooth Flow System.   If there were no reason to consolidate an entire order of 200 pumps before shipment in the above example, both order lead-time and number of orders would be reduced. Consider the case where the shipment of a partial order for finished pumps is made daily by Eastern. Here, the necessary order lead time would be reduced to:

$$O_t = 2 + 5 + \frac{50}{50} = 8 \text{ operating days}$$

More important is the fact that by smoothing the flow of goods through the logistics system, larger orders could be placed with less frequency. This is based on the fact that Wonka could actually use part of its order while building its inventory to an optimum level, or order cut-off point. Assuming daily shipment of goods produced, the net daily addition of inventory to Wonka's stock would be $R - S$, or $50 - 40 = 10$ units. That is, for every 50 units shipped in, 40 would be used the same day. Whatever the cut-off point for inventory accumulation (h^*), it would be reduced at the rate of 40 units per day once shipments ceased arriving.

Production would require Q^*/R time. At the end of this time, however, the quantity on hand (h^*) would have accumulated only to $[(R - S) Q]/R$. The total cost of ordering in varying quantities could be represented as:

$$C = vS + \frac{S}{Q}A + (R - S)\frac{Q}{2R}rv$$

The quantity of Q, Q^* at which a minimum total cost is incurred for a given period of time is obtained as before, by differentiating the equation for Q.[2] The result is an equation for Q^* under a flow system of supply:

$$Q^* = \sqrt{\frac{2SA}{rv}} \times \frac{R}{(R-S)}$$

Using this formula to recompute Q under the new assumption, we would obtain the results:

$$Q^* = \sqrt{\frac{2 \times 10,000 \times 50}{.25 \times 100}} \times \frac{12,500}{(12,500 - 10,000)}$$

$$= \sqrt{200,000}$$

$$= 446$$

$$N^* = \frac{10,000}{446}$$

$$= 22.4 \text{ orders per year}$$

The new order policy would require ordering 446 pumps every 11.1 (250/22.4) operating days.

The value Q becomes the order quantity required to accommodate demand during the period in which the inventory is being built to h^* in addition to h^* itself. Thus, $Q = St + h^*$, where $t = h^*/(R-S)$; or $Q = [Sh^*/(R-S)] + h^*$. Knowing S and R, and having computed Q^*, we can compute h^* as follows:

$$446 = \frac{40h^*}{50-40} + h^*,$$

$$5h^* = 446,$$

$$h^* = 89.2 \text{ or approximately 90 units}$$

That is, nine daily shipments of 50 units each would be required to build Wonka's inventory to an optimum cut-off point.

The pattern of inventory levels for Wonka resulting from this policy is shown as Example B in Fig. 14–1. It is a pattern typical of all finished goods which become available for sale immediately upon coming from a production line.

(1) Applying concepts studied in Chapters 10 and 11, what implications would a standard purchase contract, in which a set quantity of pumps would be shipped each week during the year by Eastern Pump unless notification was received to the contrary, have for this problem? (2) What would you recommend as a policy for Wonka if, under the standard contract arrangement, the fixed cost per shipment for pickup,

$$^2 \frac{dC}{dQ} = SAQ^{-2} + \frac{R-S}{2R} rv = 0.$$

in which Wonka would be responsible for inbound transportation costs for pumps, were to be calculated as $40 and the variable cost (for handling and transportation) as $2 per pump up to 20, $1.50 per pump for each unit over 20, and $1 per pump for all units over 40?

Aggregate Analysis and Planning

Most manufacturing organizations face the need to plan the simultaneous manufacture of a number of products. Until we can develop a Utopian production facility which has unlimited capacity and no costs associated with changes in the production level, we must concern ourselves with problems such as the advance planning of production to produce relatively constant plant loads, the design of optimal changes in loading to meet seasonal needs, and the rationing of limited capacity in times of high demand levels. The nature of these tasks may differ considerably between companies manufacturing to order, of which the job shop producing custom-designed units is the extreme example, and those manufacturing to stock.

Essentially, the job shop operator may find it more difficult to move production ahead to fill in slack periods at the plant because of the unpredictable nature of future demand. Similarly, in times of insufficient production capacity to meet demand, supplies must be rationed on a much more personal basis, among customers rather than distribution center SKUL's. Because of its greater logistical implications, our primary interest here is in the operation producing to stock. The framework for the scheduling of inventories in such an operation is outlined in Fig. 14–2.

Logistics Management and the Production
Planning and Scheduling Process

Of the activities outlined in Fig. 14–2, current experience suggests that logistics management has the greatest involvement in, and often primary responsibility for, the middle range of activities encompassing what Holstein terms "master scheduling" (which we call "production planning" as opposed to the more detailed "production scheduling"), order entry, and inventory planning and control.[3]

Advance Planning–Master Scheduling. Given long-term forecasts of future demand and the results of long-term capacity planning, often the

---

[3] An interesting exception to this is the distribution division of a large manufacturer of paper products which has the responsibility not only for allocating production to various paper mills, but also that of scheduling production on individual machines within each mill.

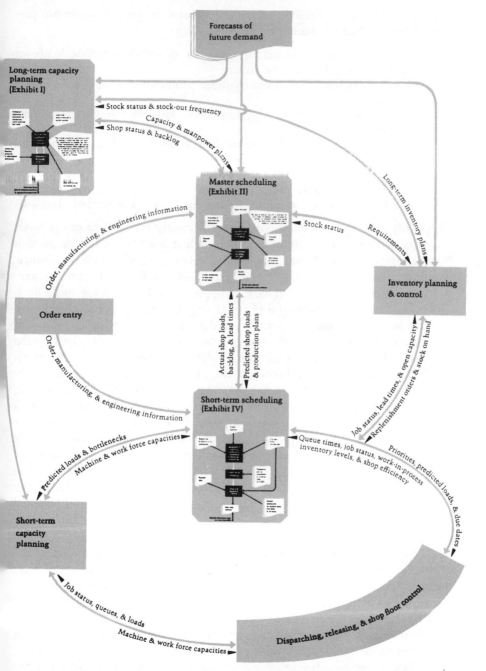

Fig. 14–2. Information flows in a production planning and control system.
Source: William K. Holstein, "Production Planning and Control Integrated,"
Harvard Business Review, May–June, 1968, pp. 121–40, at p. 139.

province of top management, intermediate-term master schedules are prepared for production, including the following:

1. The translation of general forecasts into general production loads for up to six months into the future
2. The development of item-by-item production needs for shorter periods of time
3. The reconciliation of production needs with intermediate-term production capacities
4. The development of short-term (up to 90-day) plant loadings, including the allocation of needed production among plants with overlapping production capabilities; this often is accomplished with the aid of linear programming, particularly where an attempt is made to relate the production point to the locations of expected demands

Typically, master scheduling is performed mostly for periods of up to six months into the future. Simultaneously, schedules are "locked in" so that they are relatively unchangeable for periods of up to 90 days in the future.

Basic trade-offs encountered in the master scheduling process are: (1) the desire to load to capacity as opposed to the need for some flexibility for last-minute schedule changes or additions, and (2) the desirability, particularly during periods of demand in excess of capacity, of scheduling for maximum output as opposed to more frequent production "cycles" of product groupings (involving more frequent line changes).

Many companies set aside capacity, even in the more definite short-term production schedule, to accommodate unanticipated manufacturing delays or last-minute orders from preferred customers without disrupting the production process. An example is in the manufacture of consumer paper products sold largely under private (retail chain) brands. In this business, unexpected orders, short lead-time demands from customers, and an intense level of competition for retailer orders are the rule. One manufacturer never loads its plants to more than 85% of capacity at the time schedules are "locked in." This provides the marketing and physical distribution groups in this firm with a cushion to absorb last-minute orders.

Typically, SKU's in product groupings which can be produced in the same facility and on the same equipment are cycled, or produced in turn, several times per year. Internal cycle sequence is often designed to minimize the costs of machine set-up in moving from the production of one SKU to another. This typically means that once an SKU is scratched or omitted from a given cycle, its production must await the production of all other items in the cycle. During times of heavy demand, it is often tempting to increase the lot size for individual SKU's, thus reducing the number of cycles which can be produced in a given period of time and the attendant order-cycle time for the replenishment of company stocks of individual SKU's. The desirability of such a strategy is related directly to the magnitude of set-up costs, inventory carrying costs, and the long-term profit implications from the sale of larger numbers of units in the short run as opposed to the long-term sales implications of a short-term deterioration in customer service. Problems resulting from disruptions in long-term plans for short-term profit increases usually rule out drastic adjustments in policy to take advantage of short-term opportunities.

Production Smoothing. The need for production smoothing is created by a capacity plan, typically formulated by top management, which pro vides for less capacity than that needed to meet peak annual demands. Both the formulation of the capacity plan and the master scheduling of changes in production levels within the capacity plan typically are based on intuition or simulation techniques. The nature of the problem, par-ticularly in its more complex forms, restricts the use of optimizing tech-niques in its solution.

In its most simplified form, the nature of the problem at the Wonka Manufacturing Company could be described as one in which peak sea-sonal demands were approximately twice those for slack periods, as shown in Table 14–1. Because the mix of units produced (typically six to twelve weeks in advance of shipment from distribution centers) varied little from month to month, capacity planning and production smoothing deci-sions could be made on an aggregate basis for all types of levelor SKU's. The basic economics on which such decisions were based included: (1) an investment of $500 per unit in monthly two-shift production ca-

TABLE 14–1. Sales, Production, and Inventory Projections (in Units) for the Coming Year, Warren G. Wonka Manufacturing Company

Month	Customer Orders on DC's	DC Orders on Plant	Plant Output	Planned Stocks, Beginning of Month
January	40,000	40,000	55,000	154,000
February	35,000	50,000	55,000	169,000
March	40,000	60,000	55,000	174,000
April	50,000	70,000	55,000	169,000
May	60,000	65,000	55,000	159,000
June	70,000	45,000	55,000	169,000
July	65,000	55,000	25,000	139,000
August	45,000	70,000	55,000	124,000
September	55,000	65,000	55,000	114,000
October	70,000	35,000	55,000	134,000
November	65,000	40,000	55,000	149,000
December	35,000	35,000	55,000	169,000
Total	630,000	630,000	630,000	1,823,000
				(or an average of 152,000 units on hand)

pacity (estimated to be about 75,000 units), (2) a fixed charge of $360 per year per unit of monthly two-shift production capacity for plant facilities and fixed costs of maintaining the available labor force, (3) a monthly inventory carrying cost of $1.50 per unit in stock, (4) an average contribution of $40 per unit sold, (5) a sales loss of 20% of items not produced by the plant during the month in which they were demanded by the distribution centers, and (6) a one-time production cost of $10 per unit in monthly output for increases or decreases in the monthly output.

(3) **If you were Wonka's Logistics Manager, charged with the responsibility for minimizing inventory carrying costs, what amount of plant capacity and what pattern of month-to-month production would you recommend for the Cleveland plant? (4) How would your recommendations change if you were Production Manager, responsible for minimizing unit production costs at Cleveland?**

(5) **How would your views change as President of the Company, responsible for maximizing contribution from product sales as a proportion of the total investment? (6) How would you evaluate, as our consultant to the Company, the actual policies followed by the Company of maintaining current plant capacity at 75,000 units per month and producing at the rate of 55,000 units per month during all months except July and 30,000 units during the vacation month of July, in view of the monthly sales forecasts for the coming year shown in Table 14–1?**

To evaluate these questions, you have to carry out a simplified simulation of Wonka's operation. Because the problem becomes much more complex when matters such as the timing of vacations, the scheduling of overtime or additional production shifts to increase capacity, and the possible purchase of levelors or components from subcontractors are factored in, computers have become essential for carrying out such simulations.

Allocation of Insufficient Capacity. Particularly in cyclical industries such as steel manufacture, the allocation of insufficient production capacity to SKU's or customers is a periodic task in master scheduling. At other times, accuracy in quoting delivery estimates to customers is a function of the quality of a master schedule and a company's ability to adhere to it once it is formulated.

The experience of a number of companies suggests that an organization's ability to quote accurate, realistic delivery times is a function largely of:

1. The existence of a prearranged plan for allocating and scheduling demand

2. Adherence to the prearranged plan, even during periods of stress
3. The degree to which sufficient allowance is made for slack in the loading of plant facilities
4. The quality of communications among marketing, production, and logistics regarding changes in sales demands or producing capabilities

Among prearranged plans for allocating limited supplies are allocation of capacity: (1) on a first-come, first-served basis, (2) to SKU's with the maximum production rates, (3) to SKU's found on the smallest (quickest to fill) orders, (4) to the most profitable SKU's, or to orders from the most profitable customers, or (5) to orders from the oldest, most loyal customers. Perhaps the policy most frequently followed is the latter, particularly when production is scheduled on the basis of individual customer orders rather than forecasts of distribution center replenishment orders. At Wonka, orders from distribution centers were forecast for the period of the "locked in" production schedule (90 days), production needs were estimated on a first-come, first-served basis, and production runs within each cycle were adjusted by SKU's to produce a total cycle size within 10% of that programmed for the year.

Requirements Planning. A statistical inventory control system utilizing computed economic order quantities, reorder points, and order intervals can be supplemented usefully by a replenishment program based on requirements planning. According to Thurston:

Requirements planning is the process of working backward from the scheduled completion dates of end products or major assemblies to determine the dates and quantities when the various component parts and materials are to be ordered. . . . Basically, requirements planning sets aside the "averaging process" of statistics in managing inventory and substitutes a specific enumeration of what parts to place in inventory and when.[4]

Requirements planning is useful particularly in situations in which: (1) the specific demand for a part or a completed product is known in advance, and (2) a dependable, accurate account of engineering bills of material, inventory, routing and lead-time information, sales and purchase commitments, and factory load schedules can be maintained. Typically, a raw material or parts inventory will contain some items best suited to management by statistical inventory control methods and some better suited to requirements planning.

[4] Philip H. Thurston, "Requirements Planning for Inventory Control," *Harvard Business Review*, May–June, 1972, pp. 67–71.

OTHER SCHEDULING PROBLEMS

In addition to the production-logistics coordinative scheduling techniques discussed in the first part of this chapter, there are a number of other scheduling techniques which are of importance to logistics management. Most of those discussed in the sections that follow have applications in many functions of business in addition to logistics. For purposes of emphasis, however, all examples of their application will be drawn from the area of logistics.

One further comment is in order at this point. Many of the techniques discussed here will, in actual practice, yield only "reasonable approximations" of what a decision should be. These techniques all involve the use of mathematical models which usually require that certain aspects of problems be ignored, or that several factors be lumped together for the sake of simplicity, or that mildly unrealistic assumptions about the real world be made. When the models are applied to real situations, these shortcomings become apparent. But this is no reason to abandon their use. Rather, it is wise to use the results of the calculations as a logical "point of departure" for further modification to meet the demands of an operational business situation. Whatever its limitations, and sometimes they are substantial, this process is almost certain to yield better results than random seat-of-the-pants decision making in situations where many complex variables must be balanced to achieve a particular objective. But let's not confuse the true intuitive expertise of the shipping room supervisor who has ten years of varied experience in scheduling pickup times for company shipments with random seat-of-the-pants decision making.

Priority Determination

It is not surprising that systems of priority determination largely have been developed by or for military operations. The military logistics system has several properties that exist to a degree not found in commercial systems. First, the penalty of unmet demand can be severe. Second, in less acute situations, demand is controllable. That is, it not only can be predicted, but is subject to a low rate of product substitutability in the event of unmet demand. These properties have encouraged the development of several of the MIL-Standard programs in the Department of Defense, including MILSTRIP, UMMIPS, AND MILSTEP, intended to standardize both logistics procedures and the exchange of logistics information among the many military activities, federal agencies, some friendly foreign governments, and industrial organizations.

MILSTRIP.[5] With the initiation of MILSTRIP (Military Standard Requisitioning and Issue Procedures) in 1962, the Department of Defense specified, through its Defense Supply Agency, a standardized program of uniform forms, codes, and procedures which replaced sixteen separate systems used for procuring and distributing various supply items for the separate branches of the military.

UMMIPS. A supporting program developed for use with MILSTRIP, UMMIPS (Uniform Materiel Movement and Issue Priority System), establishes a set of standards for processing, selecting, and transporting all shipments under the control of the Defense Supply Agency. Originally it specified the procedure for assigning one of twenty "priority designators" to each shipment, based on: (1) the rating, designating strategic importance, assigned to every "customer" in the Department of Defense by the Joint Chiefs of Staff, and (2) the "customer's" estimate of the urgency of need for each shipment to allow it to fulfill its mission. These designators were then grouped into four priority groups, for which maximum elapsed times from the initiation of a requisition to receipt of the material requisitioned, and even processing procedures, were prescribed. For example, for priority groups 1 and 2 shown in Table 14–2, UMMIPS specified that the Air Force would maintain the capability to process such

TABLE 14–2. Original and Current UMMIPS Response Times

Priority Designators	Maximum Elapsed Time, in Days, from Requisitioning to Receipt of Material	
	Domestic U. S.	Overseas
Original Standards[a]		
1 through 3	5 (3)[b]	7 (1)
4 through 8	8 (4)	15 (2)
9 through 15	20 (8)	45[c] (5)
16 through 20	30 (14)	60[c] (9)
Current Standards		
1 through 3	8	12–13
4 through 8	12	16–17
9 through 15[d]	31	69–84

[a]*Source:* DOD Instruction 4410.6, April 24, 1961. The parenthetical times are from Table 2–III, Army Regulation 725–50, September 22, 1961.
[b]Numbers in parentheses are days allotted for domestic U. S. transport leg.
[c]Assuming that timely surface transportation is available.
[d]Comparable to 9 through 20 in the original standards.

[5] For much of the information on which this and the following two sections are based, we are indebted to Lt. Col. Graham W. Rider, Head, Department of Management Studies at the School of Systems and Logistics, Department of the Air Force, and to a member of his faculty, Mr. A. Goldstein.

requisitions on a 24-hour basis, seven days per week, as opposed to a regular workweek schedule for shipments in priority groups 3 and 4. Elapsed time standards, priority designators, and priority groups have been revised to current levels shown in Table 14–2.

To obtain some estimate of the extent of improvement in transportation and material-handling activities which were required under these programs, the Defense Traffic Management Service (then the Military Traffic Management Agency) sampled the experience obtained from more than 21,000 shipments in 1960.[6] By relating shipment times to distances and correlating the two elements, the information on actual time-in-transit for shipments of various distances moving by various methods of transportation shown in Table 14–3 was computed.

TABLE 14–3. Time-in-Transit Study: Department of Defense Time–Distance Experience Summarized by Method of Transportation

Method of Transportation	Regression Equation	Standard Error of Estimate	Coefficient of Correlation
Carload	$T = 6.327 + 0.00270$ mile	1.25 days	+0.87
Less carload	$T = 10.917 + 0.00311$	4.48	+0.49
Truckload	$T = 3.179 + 0.00309$	1.55	+0.84
Less truckload	$T = 5.152 + 0.00335$	1.03	+0.94
Air freight	$T = 3.404 + 0.00083$	0.80	+0.64
Surface freight forwarder	$T = 7.025 + 0.00273$	1.53	+0.80

T = time in days.

Source: Keene Peterson and Herschel Cutler, "Transportation and MILSTRIP: Transport Service and Routing Decisions," in *Contributed Papers, American Transportation Research Forum, 1961*, published in multilithed form by the Forum, p. IX–11.

For the study, time-in-transit was defined as the total elapsed time between the receipt of the shipment by an originating carrier and the notification of availability of a shipment at destination. Distances were measured by means of straight lines stretched between origin and destination points. Past experience suggested that as many as 10% of the total number of shipments would probably move under priority designations 1 through 3. This provides the basis for a comparison of previous experience, shown in Table 14–3, with the expected performance of carriers (Table 14–2) under the MILSTRIP program.

The dependability in service times provided by various methods of transportation is indicated by the standard error of estimate for such

---

[6] For a more detailed report of the results of this study, see Keene Peterson and Herschel Cutler, "Transportation and MILSTRIP: Transport Service and Routing Decisions," in *Contributed Papers, American Transportation Research Forum, 1961*, published in multilithed form by the Forum, pp. IX–1 to IX–17.

times as are shown in Table 14–3. That is, 68% of all shipments moving by carload, for example, were delivered within a range of time characterized by the time indicated in the regression equation plus or minus 1.25 days. On the basis of statistical inference, 95% of all shipments would fall within two standard errors of estimate of the regression equation, or plus or minus 2.5 days. To compute the expected range and probability of times for a carload shipment moving 1,000 miles, one would make the following computations:

$$T = 6.327 + 0.00270(1,000) + 2 \text{ standard errors of estimate}$$
$$= 6.327 + 2.70 \pm 2.50$$
$$= 6.527 \text{ days to } 11.527 \text{ days}$$

That is, there is a 95% chance, based on past experience, that a carload shipment of 1,000 miles in length would have a transit time of from 6.527 days to 11.527 days. (7) **What do you find when you make the same computation for other modes of transportation shown in Table 14–3? (8) How do you explain these relationships?**

The improvement of unreliable service was thus a major objective of the MILSTRIP program. An additional finding of the study was of importance:

Consideration of the relations presented in [Table 14–3], in addition, confirms the peril of applying broad decision rules to routings, such as by specifying the use of a method of transportation for all shipments bearing a certain priority designator. To route all priority 1–3 traffic by "air," for example, will not assure "fastest" delivery. It has been demonstrated to be necessary to route traffic on an individual shipment basis to achieve reasonable economy of transport expenditures. This study suggests that it is also necessary to route traffic on an individual shipment basis to meet delivery deadlines.[7]

MILSTEP. A third program, MILSTEP (Military Supply and Transportation Evaluation Procedure), is an information system designed to determine how well the others are working. It provides a standard method for measuring supply system performance and transportation effectiveness against standards set forth by UMMIPS. By means of an In-Transit Data Card which accompanies all shipments, elapsed times are recorded and computed for the submission (order communication), requisition processing, depot processing, holding (for consolidation with other shipments), and transportation of an order. MILSTEP information: (1) indicates needed changes in the routing of shipments, (2) aids in controlling carrier service, and (3) provides the basis for changing standard UMMIPS shipment times by the various methods.

Considering the volume of government shipments moving by commercial transportation, the MIL-Standard programs described above have had a considerable impact on carriers and their performance.

(9) **Do these MIL-Standard programs have any applicability for commercial organizations?** (10) **Why?** (11) **If so, what forms might they take?**

System Loading

One of the more popular areas of operations research in recent years has been waiting-line theory. Waiting-line theory concerns itself with attempts to develop analytic descriptions of the passage of units through a given element or node on a system, usually a bottleneck requiring individual units to wait in order to be serviced. Its basic objective is to aid in the measurement of the cost of servicing units passing through the node (in terms of the service capacity required to provide varying levels of service) as opposed to the cost of unit waiting time when facilities are not capable of providing prompt service at all times.

Simulation is the process of modelling things, problems, or concepts. However, its use is not as rigidly bound by the necessity to develop simultaneous mathematical functions to describe each type of waiting-line problem as in the theoretical approach.

Together, waiting-line theory and simulation provide effective approaches to the problem of system loading and the scheduling of service capacity to meet demand.

Waiting-Line Theory. The number of waiting-line, or queuing, problems confronting logistics management is usually great. In nature they range from the processing of orders through a monitoring station to the loading and unloading of trucks at a warehouse facility. All pose the common problem of the extent to which facilities or labor should be provided at varying times to hold service and waiting costs to a minimum level. Although much of the work in waiting-line theory has been of a complex nature, it has been utilized in a number of cases instead of simulation. A simple illustration will demonstrate its rationale.

Single Line, Poisson Arrival, and Service. The most basic use of waiting-line theory is in a facility equipped to handle only one waiting line in which units arrive and are serviced over times described by normal distributions of numbers. As an example, suppose the Wonka Manufacturing Company plant warehouse had one dock and one bay for unloading trucks incoming with LTL shipments of components from a number of vendors located largely within 100 miles of the Cleveland plant. Most of the trucks were operated by common carriers. Some were owned by vendor companies. All were making deliveries on a "delivered" basis; that is, the cost of inbound transportation was borne by vendors, who controlled the deliveries.

An observation of Wonka's plant warehouse dock over a period of time yielded the information that the arrival rate of trucks during selected segments of time approximated that shown in Fig. 14–3. That is, the

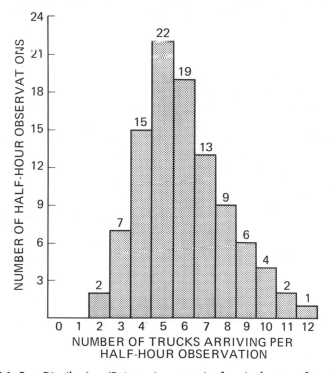

Fig. 14–3. Distribution (Poisson in nature) of arrival rates of trucks during 100 half-hour intervals, Warren G. Wonka Manufacturing Company plant warehouse.

range of arrivals per hour was from two to twelve trucks, with an average of six per hour. This distribution is called a Poisson distribution and is typical for vehicle arrivals in a variety of situations. Its mathematical properties allow it to be used in a number of theoretical formulations, including those pertaining to waiting-line theory. In the latter problem, the following relationships can be proven if arrival times are approximately Poisson and an event (in this case, arrival) can occur in any small interval of time, no matter what has happened in an adjacent time interval.

$$\bar{n} = \frac{\lambda}{\mu - \lambda}$$

$$\bar{t} = \frac{1}{\mu - \lambda}$$

$$p_n = p^n (1 - \rho)$$

where

n = number in line, including the one being serviced

$\bar{n}$ = average number in line, including the one being serviced

t = time which an arrival spends in the system

$\bar{t}$ = average time which an arrival spends in the system

λ = rate at which units arrive for service

μ = rate at which units are serviced

p = probability of an event

ρ = load factor = λ/μ

If the rate for servicing trucks were seven per hour, with a range from 4 to 10, the following results would be obtained for the case at hand:

$$\bar{n} = \frac{6}{7 - 6} = 6 \text{ trucks in line on the average}$$

$$\bar{t} = \frac{1}{7 - 6} = 1 \text{ hour waiting time per truck on the average}$$

$p_1 = 6/7\,^1\,(1 - 6/7) = 6/49 = $ probability of finding 1 truck in line

If one man could service seven trucks per hour, it might be worthwhile to investigate the total cost or economy of adding a second man, thereby reducing service time to the equivalent of eleven vehicles per hour. (12) **Why wouldn't the addition of an extra man increase the service rate to 14 vehicles per hour?** Under these conditions:

$$\bar{n} = \frac{6}{11 - 6} = 1.2 \text{ trucks in line}$$

$$\bar{t} = \frac{1}{11 - 6} = 1/5 \text{ hour or 12 minutes' waiting time per truck}$$

If the dock labor cost per man was \$4.00/hour, the maximum number that could be used in a single crew was five, and the waiting cost of vehicle and driver was \$12.00/hour, the economic analysis shown in Table 14–4 could be carried out. It indicates that a four-man crew would provide the lowest total cost for the operation. (13) **As a result of this study, would you recommend that Wonka add two men to the dock crew to increase service to incoming trucks?** (14) **Why?**

Several additional considerations would have to be made in a study of this type. Because Wonka did not suffer the costs of truck waiting time, it might not be willing to increase the cost of labor to service each

TABLE 14–4. Analysis of Service and Waiting Costs, Inbound Deliveries of
Component Parts, Warren G. Wonka Manufacturing Company
Plant Warehouse Receiving Dock

No. in Crew (L)	Service Rate, No. of Trucks per Hour (μ)	Arrival Rate, No. of Trucks per Hour (λ)	Waiting Time per Truck, in Minutes (t)	Labor Cost per Truck[a] (L_c)	Waiting Time Cost per Truck[b] (t_c)	Total Cost per Truck (C)
1	7	6	60.0	$ .571	$12.00	$12.57
2	11	6	12.0	.727	2.40	3.13
3	14	6	7.5	.858	1.50	2.36
4	16	6	6.0	1.000	1.20	2.20[c]
5	17	6	5.5	1.175	1.10	2.28

[a]At the rate of $4.00 per man-hour for dock labor.
[b]At the rate of $12.00 per truck-and-driver-hour.
[c]Optimum staffing to produce lowest total cost per truck serviced.

truck in order to help its suppliers or their hired carriers reduce their trucking costs.

Ruppenthal and Whybark investigated three similar situations in which: (1) rates of return on investment in some cases in excess of 100% per year could be provided by total cost savings from the construction of additional dock space, (2) the benefits would accrue to carriers and the investment be borne by the receiving company, and (3) there seemed to be no direct, practical means by which carrier savings could be passed on to the company owning the dock facilities.[8] As a result, investments were made in none of these cases and long lines of trucks waiting to be unloaded remained. This example illustrates the rather wide gap between recommendations suggested by operations research and engineering studies and the type of actions which are feasible for implementation by management. (15) **What means might you suggest to remedy this type of situation?**

The length of the waiting line (n) might be crucial if there was limited space for trucks to wait at Wonka's plant warehouse. In one case, Ruppenthal and Whybark found that the spur to company action was a threat from residents of the community to ask their city council to enact an ordinance restricting trucks from standing on city streets for long periods of time. In this case, the Traffic Manager responsible for the plant warehouse dock operations instituted a program similar to that employed by many companies with restricted dock facilities. He measured truck service times, obtained more complete information about

[8] Karl M. Ruppenthal and D. Clay Whybark, "Some Problems in Optimizing Shipping Facilities," *The Logistics Review,* Vol. 4, No. 20, 1968, pp. 5–32.

inbound shipments, and began scheduling vendor deliveries by quoting "appointment times." [9]

An additional alternative to be considered in Wonka's case would be the construction of a second truck bay which could be staffed by one man to achieve theoretically a service rate of 16 trucks per hour with only a two-man crew. In this case, both added labor and overheard costs would have to be balanced against reduced waiting costs.

Situations involving multiple service stations require much more complicated calculations than the simple example we have considered. Further, Poisson distributions for arrival rates on which most waiting-line theory is based may not be as common as we might assume. Rarely are arrival rates for adjacent time periods independent and random in nature. More typically, systematic dispatching customs may produce peaks and valleys in arrival rates during the day, creating actual delays and waiting-line lengths other than those suggested by waiting-line theory.

Use of Simulation.   These factors have led to the more common use of simulation to reproduce waiting-line experiences under various considerations. The vehicle of simulation, through modelling, may range in form from a model airplane to a slide rule to a set of formulas on paper. It is a concept capable of being used to emulate any real system that can be observed, measured, and described. In the case described above, it would be necessary to document arrival and service times exactly, in order to assess the impact of different procedures or facilities on vehicle flow.

Manual simulation can be carried out with the use of random selection of numbers from distributions typifying observations and measurements previously made of the system being analyzed. However, simple electronic computer routines provide random numbers and perform necessary calculations for all but the simplest of simulations much more quickly and efficiently.[10]

Route Selection

A route may be selected with the objective of minimizing distance between two points. This is particularly desirable in the operation of transportation equipment. The problem may be expanded to accommodate the additional stipulation that certain points be visited en route.

[9] *Ibid.*

[10] For an interesting non-technical discussion of the use of simulation to analyze a more complex warehouse truck servicing problem, see Donald H. Schiller and Marvin M. Lavin, "The Determination of Requirements for Warehouse Dock Facilities," *Operations Research,* April, 1956, pp. 231–43. In this case, an attempt to apply waiting-line theory was abandoned in favor of a simulation.

An additional stipulation might be that the initial origin and ultimate destination points be the same. Critical path selection in these types of problems is aimed generally at selecting the route which produces the shortest distance or time en route. Although extended mathematical formulations exist for these problems, Zionts has provided less complex interpretations of them.[11]

Routing for Shortest Distance Between Two Points. Of the many methods for finding the shortest distance between two points, two appear to be most efficient. In their non-symbolic form, they might be referred to as the matrix and listing methods. We will discuss the latter, because it provides a more graphic illustration of the technique.[12]

Basic objectives of the listing method are to: (1) find the shortest route between all points in the network and (2) indicate the path by which they are connected. The technique can be illustrated by the network shown as Exhibit 1 in Fig. 14–4. At the outset of the analysis, the lengths of the route segments to which each network node is directly connected are listed beneath the letter designation for the node. The segments in each list are ordered numerically, with the shortest (lowest value) first. This has been done in Exhibit 2 of Fig. 14–4. The iterative process then can begin.

The Method. First, to the node from which the shortest route to all other nodes is desired, give the value of 0. In Exhibit 3 of Fig. 14–4, A has been selected as this node for which information is desired. Second, delete all segments from the preceding Exhibit (2) which lead into node A (in this case, BA and CA) and transfer all remaining information to a new list (Exhibit 3). Third, select the node for which the sum of the node value and shortest segment value for a given node are lowest. At the outset, this must be the only node to which a value has been assigned (in the example, $A + AB = 0 + 3 = 3$). Fourth, place the letter designation of the selected node (A) to the right of the lists, indicating that it is the node around which the least-cost or least-distance network will be constructed. Fifth, assign the sum value from step three (3) to the node making up the other terminus of the lowest value segment used in step three (B). Sixth, again delete all segments from the preceding exhibit which lead into the node to which a value has been assigned. Seventh, repeat steps

[11] Stanley Zionts, "Methods for Selection of an Optimum Route," in *Papers—Third Annual Meeting, American Transportation Research Forum* (Oxford, Ind.: American Transportation Research Forum, 1962), pp. 25–36. Portions of the discussion in this section rely on Zionts' presentation.

[12] For an alternative explanation of this type of approach, see George B. Dantzig, "On the Shortest Route Through a Network," *Management Science,* January, 1960, pp. 187–90.

Exhibit 1

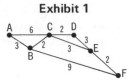

Exhibit 2

A	B	C	D	E	F
AB = 3	BC = 2	CB = 2	DC = 2	EF = 2	FE = 2
AC = 6	BA = 3	CD = 2	DE = 3	EC = 3	FB = 9
	BF = 9	CE = 3		ED = 3	
		CA = 6			

Exhibit 3

A = 0	B	C	D	E	F
AB = 3	BC = 2	CB = 2	DC = 2	EF = 2	FE = 2
AC = 6	BF = 9	CD = 2	DE = 3	EC = 3	FB = 9
		CE = 3		ED = 3	

Tree: A

Exhibit 4

A = 0	B = 0	C	D	E	F
AC = 6	BC = 2	CD = 2	DC = 2	EF = 2	FE = 2
	BF = 9	CE = 3	DE = 3	EC = 3	
				ED = 3	

Tree: A-B

Exhibit 5

A = 0	B = 3	C = 5	D	E	F
	BF = 9	CD = 2	DE = 3	EF = 2	FE = 2
		CE = 3		ED = 3	

Tree: A-B-C

Exhibit 6

A = 0	B = 3	C = 5	D = 7	E	F
	BF = 9	CE = 3	DE = 3	EF = 2	FE = 2

Tree: A-B-C-D

Exhibit 7

A = 0	B = 3	C = 5	D = 7	E = 10	F
	BF = 9			EF = 2	

Tree: A-B-C-D-E

Exhibit 8

A = 0	B = 3	C = 5	D = 7	E = 10	F = 12

Tree: A-B-C-D-E-F

Exhibit 9

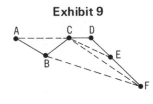

——————— Shortest route segments from all nodes to point A.

– – – – – Segments of longer routes from all nodes to point A.

Fig. 14–4. Organization of information for, and computational steps in, selection of optimum routes by the listing, or "tree-building," method of analysis.

3 through 6 until all nodes have been entered in the "tree" to the right of the lists. Further results for the example are shown in Exhibits 4 through 8 of Fig. 14–4. The translation of the "tree" in Exhibit 8 is presented in network form in Exhibit 9 of the same figure.

Appraisal. The explanation of this technique is intended to suggest the means by which more complex route-planning problems can be adapted for computer solution. Although the correct answer to the example could be obtained intuitively almost instantly without any knowledge of a systematic method, routing problems generally are of a more complex nature than that in the example.

If routing problems are committed to a computer, the matrix method requires a considerable memory capacity in the equipment used. Thus, the listing or "tree-building" method permits larger problems to be solved by computer.

Routing for Territory Coverage. Another type of routing problem arises when there is a territory to be serviced in some fashion requiring a coverage of certain points or terminals on a system. The object of the analysis generally is to determine the shortest or lowest-cost route by which designated points can be visited. The name of the problem class, "traveling salesman problems," is derived from one of its more obvious applications. It potentially has wide application in logistics for the scheduling of pickups and deliveries in a warehouse area, a local delivery or commercial zone, or a wide territory made up of points feeding materials into, or being fed by, a single location.

A systematic method proposed for approaching this routing problem relies upon mathematical formulations which have been proven to offer optimum solutions to the problem under certain limited conditions. By itself, however, the simplification of more complex approaches presented here must be considered capable of offering only good solutions, not necessarily optimum ones.

The Method. In its simplest form, the heuristic method involves computing the time or cost (or other measure of effectiveness) required to move between every point and every other point in the territory to be served. Once this is accomplished, various orders of points are tested in the following manner.

1. Select a starting point and one other point on the system. From the information in Table 14–5, these points arbitrarily might be A and B. If the vehicle and driver are expected to return to the starting point after their work, the starting point should be added to the route, producing an

TABLE 14–5. Matrix of Times Required to Traverse Distances Between
Terminal Points in the "Traveling Salesman" Routing Problem (in Minutes)

| | Network Points | | | | | | |
	A	B	C	D	E	F	G
A	0						
B	14	0					
C	17	5	0				
D	13	11	15	0			
E	10	12	6	6	0		
F	9	20	15	10	12	0	
G	13	7	16	10	10	14	0

A–B–A route. The time required to service this route would be 28
minutes, assuming that minimum time is the measure of effectiveness.

2. Selecting a third point, successively insert it between each of the
points in the route designated in step 1. Test the total time required to
serve the points in each resulting order. In the example, the time required for A–C–B–A and A–B–C–A routes would be computed as 36 and
36 minutes, respectively. Because a tie happened to occur here, one of
the shortest routes arbitrarily would be chosen as the route to which a
fourth point would be added in the same manner as before.

3. Continually check the solution to see if it violates any conditions of
the problem. Possible conditions are discussed below.

For the problem shown in Table 14–5, this simple routine would produce a routing of A–E–C–B–G–D–F–A, with a total time en route between points of 57 minutes.

Conditions. Various conditions or restrictions probably would be imposed on the solution of the problem to reflect real conditions more accurately. If time were a consideration, some estimate of the time required
to make a stop would have to be added for each stop made along the
route. In the case of the truck returning to a terminal after picking up
shipments, a provision might have to be made for the time required to
unload each shipment.

The length of a working day would impose limits on a traveler's time.
Whenever the total time required to traverse a system exceeded restriction, no more points could be added to the route without some deletion
of other points. In this case, the point to be deleted would be the one
that would produce the greatest reduction in time. In the example in
Table 14–6, if pickups required 15 minutes each, unloading after the
return to A required 60 minutes, and the length of the working day was
restricted to 190 minutes, at least one terminal would have to be deleted

TABLE 14–6. Computation of Least-Time Route to Serve Six of Seven
Terminals in Table 12–5

Route	Travel Time Required (in Minutes)	Total
A-E[a]-C-B-G-D-F-A[b]	17 + 5 + 7 + 10 + 10 + 9 =	58
A-E-C[a]-B-G-D-F-A	10 + 12 + 7 + 10 + 10 + 9 =	58
A-E-C-B[a]-G-D-F-A	10 + 6 + 16 + 10 + 10 + 9 =	61
A-E-C-B-G[a]-D-F-A	10 + 6 + 5 + 11 + 10 + 9 =	51
A-E-C-B-G-D[a]-F-A	10 + 6 + 5 + 7 + 14 + 9 =	51
A-E-C-B-G-D-F[a]-A	10 + 6 + 5 + 7 + 10 + 13 =	51

[a]Point deleted from route.
[b]Optimum route for servicing all seven points.

from the path of the vehicle servicing a given territory. It could be G, D, or F, the deletion of any one of which would reduce the required time to the maximum amount of 51 minutes, as shown in Table 14–6. This would reduce the length of the working day for the driver in question to $51 + 5(15) + 60 = 186$ minutes. Presumably, the terminal skipped could be served by a second vehicle as part of its route.

The time (or cost) required to traverse the distance between two points might depend on the direction of the path. If one path produced a favorable terrain in the form of a downhill run, for example, and the opposite an uphill run between two points, resulting times might be significantly different to traverse the route. This condition could be injected by disturbing the mirror image of the two halves of the matrix in Table 14–5 to inject a different time, say 7 minutes, to go from A to B than from B to A (14 minutes). A re-examination of the previously selected route would be required whether or not $B–A$ or $A–B$ was included as one of its segments. In this case, the re-examination would result in the selection of a new route, $A–G–B–C–E–D–F–A$.

Potential Routing Problems at Wonka. During the logistics systems appraisal process at Wonka, the Manager of the Purchasing Department, Tom Braden, suggested that the Company seriously consider establishing an in-company trucking operation, initially to pick up parts shipments from vendors located within a 100-mile radius of Cleveland. Currently, the Company was purchasing component parts for assembly and replacement stocks from approximately 300 such vendors who shipped to the Cleveland plant on the average of once a week. It was estimated that about half of these shipments moved in vendor-owned trucks and half by common carrier. The typical common carrier rate for the average 1,000-pound LTL shipment was $4.20 per cwt.; it was not known how vendors factored their trucking costs into the prices for their products.

The density of vendor locations around Cleveland produced an average distance of only about seven miles between vendor plants. Of course, the distances between vendor plants shipping on any one day was greater, estimated to be about 16 miles.

Vendor shipping operations produced peaks, valleys, and some surprises for Wonka's plant warehouse, procurement, and manufacturing groups. About 30% of incoming parts shipments were scheduled to arrive on a periodic basis, depending on Wonka's long-term inventory needs. The remainder arrived with anywhere from 24 hours to no advance notice, depending on whether documentation arrived in advance of the shipment or a phone communication preceded a given shipment. Further, approximately 30% of all weekly shipments arrived on Monday and 25% on Friday. Both peaks in activity resulted from vendor desires to clear their docks and invoice activities by the weekend. Shipments resulting from this activity arrived either on Friday or Monday, depending on whether a vendor used its own trucks or common carrier services, respectively.

(16) **Based on what you know about Wonka's parts procurement program and the proposal to implement a private trucking operation, do you feel that Wonka represents a potentially good candidate for the application of a routing technique similar to that described above?** (17) **Why?**

Other estimates of use in the private trucking appraisal were daily total "stem" time—from Wonka's plant to the first vendor plant and from the last vendor plant to Wonka's plant—of 60 to 90 minutes, depending on whether all or essentially one-fifth (a given day's shippers) of the vendor locations were included. Average pickup time for a shipment was 15 minutes, average speeds for trucks in the area were estimated to be about 20 miles per hour, and the unloading time at Wonka's plant was estimated to be about 10 minutes per shipment (a liberal estimate based on current service times experienced for vendor and other trucks). Drivers would work eight-hour days, not including lunch but including loading, driving, and unloading time.

Trucks for such an operation were estimated to cost about $14,000 each. Daily fixed costs (assuming 260 days of operation per year) of depreciation and other expenses would be about $25, variable costs other than labor about 15 cents per mile, and labor costs about $50 per day. (18) **Based on this information, what potential do you feel private trucking might have for Wonka's inbound component movements?**

Application. To date, optimizing techniques for routing problems have not been able to address a number of problem complexities, including those of interdependencies between routes and changes in operating characteristics at various times. As in other cases, we have turned to simulation as a means of obtaining good answers in a more flexible framework. However, the potential cost of the use of a simulation for daily route-planning activities can be appreciated by the fact that there are 2½ trillion ways in which a vehicle can be routed among 20 customers. The introduction of heuristics (rules of thumb) into the computer search process can reduce the problem to manageable size even for networks involving hundreds of potential vendor or customer locations.

As an example, a Dutch grocery manufacturer has implemented a vehicle-scheduling procedure that utilizes a heuristic programming package. Some 750 of its wholesale grocer customers in Holland are served each week from two distribution centers, with a total of 16 trucks. This simulation package, developed by a major computer manufacturer, involves two main programs, Network Analysis and Schedule Production.

The Network Analysis Program translates the positions of delivery points into a savings file, essentially a map of the system. The program requires the collection of data such as the following, for a reasonable representation of the company's distribution system: (1) travel time between all locations, broken down by a calculation of different average speeds for major highways, other rural roads, and urban areas, (2) limits on unloading times at various customer locations, (3) variations in the length of waiting times to unload, and (4) the suitability of an unloading area for truck–trailer combinations or straight trucks. Thus, the mere construction of the computerized "map" points up sources of existing and potential problems for the distribution system.

Locations are represented by five-digit numbers. The first digit designates a zone or traffic junction through which deliveries might be made. The next two digits designate one of 96 sections into which Holland is divided. The final two digits designate one of 99 zones within each section, thus providing for more than 9,000 location "cells" within the country.

To reduce the size of the computational task and insure an improved (not necessarily optimal) pattern of distribution, the time-honored system of delivering "on call" had to be changed. Territories served from each distribution center were divided into five segments. Deliveries for each segment were scheduled for a given day each week, with wholesalers required to place their orders by a given time each week. Sections supplied on the same working day in both distribution center territories were situated, to the extent possible, side by side along the line separating the two territories, to allow trucks from one distribution center to supply customers in the other's territory when desirable.

With this type of system organization, orders were received in time to allow the Schedule Production Program to translate a given day's orders and information from the savings file "map" into a route plan for the next day's deliveries and a loading plan (in inverse order of deliveries) for the trucks. This route plan assigns trucks on the bases of number of deliveries, sizes of loads, and restrictions on the capability to receive trucks of various sizes.

(19) **Do the major sources of economies for this company lie in the organization for, or the application of, the Vehicle Scheduling Program?** (20) **Why?** (21) **In designating customers to be included in the network, would you include those buying in truckload quantities?** (22) **Those buying in quantities of, say, less than 100 pounds per shipment?** (23) **Would this type of heuristic simulation be suitable for the problem confronted by the Wonka Manufacturing Company?**

Split Shipments

So-called "split-offs" in order shipment have become more common as the result of growing pressures to make goods available more and more rapidly for sale or further processing. Because the transportation rate per unit generally increases with a decrease in the quantity shipped, the use of split-offs incurs added transportation costs. In addition, where speed is a ruling factor, the transportation cost of a split-off is further increased by the use of faster methods than would be utilized normally. This requires that the split-off be used judiciously and with careful timing.

Routine Split-Offs. Returning to the Wonka pump supply example discussed earlier, assume that the weight per pump ordered is 150 lb. when crated for shipment. Thus a total order of 450 pumps would weigh about 67,500 lb. The minimum weight per shipment, rate per cwt., and transit times required to ship pumps from Eastern to Wonka by various methods are shown in Table 14–7.

TABLE 14–7. Transit Times, Rates, and Minimum Weights for Shipments of Pumps (Eastern Pump Company to Wonka Manufacturing Company)

Method of Shipment	Transit Time (Days)	Rate (per Cwt.)	Minimum Weight (Pounds)
Rail	8	$ 1.60	30,000
	8	1.90	20,000
Truck	5	2.00	20,000
	5	2.80	15,000
	8	3.60	10,000
	8	4.50	5,000
Air	2	8.50	5,000
	2	12.80	100

Several basic alternatives regarding the shipment of pumps would be available to Wonka, assuming that it purchased this item on an "f.o.b. origin" basis and controlled as well as paid for transportation: (1) all pumps could be shipped by air, (2) all by truck, (3) all by rail, (4) enough pumps could be shipped by air to accommodate Wonka's production until the arrival of the main portion of the shipment by truck, and (5) enough pumps could be shipped by truck to accommodate Wonka's production until the arrival of the main portion of the shipment by rail. Other alternatives, such as the use of more than two shipments (one split-off) might be considered. This is especially true for air freight, where one day's production needs (40 pumps = 6,000 lb.) would exceed the minimum weight requirement for a volume rate.

On the basis of Eastern's set-up time and production rate, the fastest that goods could be made available to Wonka would be 5 days ($O_t = 2 + 2 + \frac{50}{50} = 5$) if an air freight split-off were used. The slowest possible availability of the pumps would be 19 days ($O_t = 2 + 8 + \frac{450}{150} = 19$) if all pumps were accumulated into one rail carload shipment. In the latter case, the same transportation cost would be incurred if the shipment were split in the fifth day of production and one-half shipped at that time by carload, thus reducing the availability time to roughly 15 days.

The choice of alternatives would depend upon Wonka's estimate of the penalties of having the goods available before or after they were demanded by the production line. In cases where sales might be lost, the penalty of receiving pumps late would be limited only to the profit on the daily sales which would have been realized had the pumps been available. Where delayed arrival might mean "downtime" for the production line, the resulting costs could be tremendous. On the other hand, if Wonka's production line could not begin scheduled work on the pumps until five days after they left Eastern's plant, the early arrival of the pumps utilizing air shipment would not produce any attendant savings. On the contrary, if early arrival was accomplished, it would result in a cost penalty in the form of inventory carrying costs over a longer-than-usual period.

Consider an example in which Wonka's production of heavy-duty levelor machines using the pumps in question could begin eight days from the date of order placement. Growing costs would result if production began one or more days later. The problem basically resolves itself to a question of whether small shipments should be initiated upon completion of the daily production at Eastern's plant or whether shipments should be held until more economical shipping volumes accumulate.

Delivery dates, costs of delivery, and costs of non-availability of pumps under alternative combinations of split shipments are shown in Table 14–8.

Although less important costs of logistics and less feasible combinations of split-offs were omitted from Table 14–8 for the sake of simplicity, it appears that savings in transportation costs would more than outweigh inventory carrying cost increases and costs of idle manufacturing capacity up to an availability time of nine operating days from the time of

TABLE 14–8. Some Alternative Delivery Dates and Costs Under Methods of Splitting Pump Shipments to the Wonka Manufacturing Company

Method of Shipment	Availability Time[a]	Transportation[b]	Inventory Carrying[c]	Idle Mfg. Capacity[d]	Lost Sales[d]	Total
1. Five 50-pump shipments by truck; two 100-pump shipments by truck	8 days	$2,527.50	$256.00	–	–	$2,783.50
2. One 200-pump shipment by air; one 100-pump and one 150-pump shipment by truck	8 days	3,420.00	226.20	–	–	3,646.20
3. Three 100-pump shipments and one 150-pump shipment by truck	9 days	1,710.00	291.20	$ 100	–	2,101.20
4. Three 150-pump shipments by truck	10 days	1,350.00	321.60	600	–	2,271.60
5. One 200-pump and one 250-pump shipment by truck	11 days	1,350.00	356.80	1,600	$50	3,356.80

[a]For purposes of simplicity, computed on the assumption that shipments on the average would move by rail or truck during two plant nonoperating days (weekend). Thus, in situation 1, the set-up time would require two operating days, first day's production one operating day, and transportation five operating and two non-operating days, a total of eight operating days.

[b]Computed on the basis of rates and minimum weights shown in Table 14–7.

[c]Computed on the basis of inventory carrying costs on the average value of component pumps on hand (added at time of shipment; subtracted at time pumps enter Wonka's production line) over the shipping and storage cycle at the rate of .1% of the value of inventory on hand at the end of each operating day.

[d]Estimated.

order placement. With longer availability times, total costs would rise. The most effective split-off in this example would be to allow a 100-pump batch to accumulate before shipment by truck. This would be followed by two 100-pump shipments and one 150-pump shipment by truck.

SUMMARY

The scheduling of inventory-related activities, whether for the purpose of timing, determining priorities, or deciding upon appropriate sequences of actions, can employ a wide number of formal and informal systems and procedures. Rarely can an established technique be used without some adjustment to a specific problem, however. Correct procedures may produce ridiculous results if applied without some consideration for elements of an operation which influence, or are influenced by, a given schedule. Although made with reference to the improper use of operations research techniques, the following comment is applicable generally to much that has been said in this chapter:

Let a designated operations research group look at a traffic problem and see only the queue, to the exclusion of broader strategic possibilities, and they will be the exact counterparts of the efficiency expert who applies time study to every operation he sees. The danger lies in preoccupation with mathematical models, in forgetting that numbers often come from value judgments, in mistaking methods and techniques for substance.[13]

Many analysts have found too that the causes of so-called scheduling problems often are external to the scheduling operation itself, for example, the setting of unrealistic availability dates in the procurement of incoming supplies and materials or the sale and delivery of finished goods. This requires that an analyst explore very carefully the nature of problem constraints to assess the possibility and advisability of changing them to reduce scheduling problems. In doing so, often he finds such root causes as an ineffective method of communication which produces inaccurate or untimely information, the inability of procurement or sales personnel to divorce whimsy from reality, or their inability to exercise willpower in quoting accurate availability dates. It suggests that in dealing with such problems, a manager of logistics activities must have a basic understanding of human behavior as well as analytic techniques for inventory scheduling.

[13] Robert H. Roy, "The Development and Future of Operations Research and Systems Engineering," in Charles D. Flagle, William H. Huggins, and Robert H. Roy, *Operations Research and Systems Engineering* (Baltimore: Johns Hopkins Press, 1960), pp. 8–27, at p. 25.

SUGGESTED READINGS

BOWMAN, EDWARD H., and ROBERT B. FETTER. *Analysis for Production and Operations Management,* 3d Ed. Homewood, Ill.: Richard D. Irwin, Inc., 1967.
Offers particularly good discussions of waiting-line theory and simulation techniques applicable to scheduling problems.

BUFFA, ELWOOD S., and WILLIAM H. TAUBERT. *Production-Inventory Systems: Planning and Control,* Rev. Ed. Homewood, Ill.: Richard D. Irwin, Inc., 1972.
Organized around planning and scheduling techniques for high-volume standardized products, job shop systems, and large-scale projects. The primary emphasis for much of this material is on production processes.

EILON, SAMUEL, C. D. T. WATSON-GANDY, and NICOS CHRISTOFIDES. *Distribution Management: Mathematical Modelling and Practical Analysis.* New York: Hafner Publishing Co., 1971.
Contains extensive discussions regarding the traveling salesman problem and techniques for scheduling vehicles, loading vehicles, and determining vehicle fleet size.

MILLER, DAVID W., and MARTIN K. STARR. *Executive Decisions and Operations Research,* 2d Ed. Englewood Cliffs, N. J.: Prentice-Hall, Inc., 1969.
Contains an interesting section on the evaluation of alternative methods which can be applied to a variety of scheduling problems.

MORRIS, WILLIAM T. *Analysis for Materials Handling Management.* Homewood, Ill.: Richard D. Irwin, Inc., 1962.
An intensive analysis of quantitative techniques applied to scheduling problems in material-handling systems, including those in which conveyors are used.

NILAND, POWELL. *Production Planning, Scheduling, and Inventory Control.* New York: The Macmillan Co., 1970.
Emphasizes a number of scheduling techniques in an easy-to-follow presentation.

15

Logistics Information Flow

Information is the trigger for subsequent flows of physical material in a logistics system. The sales forecast triggers production, transportation, warehousing, and procurement activities. Customers, warehouse replenishment, and purchase orders set in motion various chains of events which culminate in physical movements of goods. The speed, accuracy, and efficiency with which information flows are effected within a system have a large bearing on the performance of the entire logistics system.

Dearden has described the typical company as operating with three major information systems, each affecting "the entire structure of an organization."[1] They are the financial, personnel, and logistics information systems, with the latter dealing with the physical flow of goods through an organization. He goes on to say:

> The assignment of the responsibility for the logistics information system is not nearly so well developed and thought out in the typical company as the other two systems are. . . . As a result, the system in many companies is relatively uncoordinated and far from optimum in development. In fact, much of the total systems activity has been started because of the problems in the logistics field. If you examine carefully the description of a typical total system, you will find that it is concerned almost exclusively with the logistics system.[2]

This, coming from one of the country's leading authorities on information systems and control, provides us with more than enough rationale for this chapter.

[1] John Dearden, "How to Organize Information Systems," *Harvard Business Review*, March–April, 1965, pp. 65–73. Other systems of lesser scope in most companies include, according to Dearden's classification, marketing, research and development, and strategic planning information systems.
[2] *Ibid.*, p. 70.

THE USES OF LOGISTICS INFORMATION

Information is used for planning, operating, and controlling the overall logistics system. These uses provide us with a convenient framework for discussing the design of information flows. As shown in Table 15–1, there are sharp contrasts in the nature of information and its use for logistics system planning, operation, and control.

TABLE 15-1. The Nature of Information, Its Uses, and Its Costs in Various Logistics Management Activities

Characteristics of Information Use in Each Management Activity	System Planning	System Operation	System Control
Degree of aggregation of information	High	Low	Moderate
Importance of information external to the current logistics system	High	Low	Moderate
Currency of information	Low	High	Moderate
Frequency of information use	Low	High	Moderate
Relative cost in each management activity of:			
Data collection	60	25	30
Data communication	5	40	15
Data processing	30	30	35
Data distribution	5	5	20
	100	100	100

Planning, as opposed to operating or control purposes, allows for greater aggregation of data. For example, in planning it may be sufficient to know the volume of material and the number of orders processed by a distribution center for a selected period of time. For operations, however, we must know the exact content of each order and its associated customer and shipping information. Effective control may require that we know the proportion of order-line items shipped late during a given period of time, perhaps by broad product categories.

Planning requires "external" information, the detailed assessment of alternative costs and technologies provided by organizations not currently parties to the logistics system being redesigned. Logistics operations require much less external information, other than environmental information regarding possible interruptions in operations, such as weather conditions or impending strikes by labor. Again, control falls between these two activities in its needs for external information, relying on the continuing monitoring of such matters as competitors' customer service levels and changes in transportation services and costs.

The basis for logistics system planning can vary from year-old data to forecasts of future needs. In contrast, certain types of operations may require instantaneous data availability and revision, while logistics control relies on weekly or monthly reports of operations, repeated only for selected activities not conforming to plan.

The emphasis of our discussion reflects the fact that formal logistics system planning of any magnitude occurs rather infrequently in most organizations. The costs associated with such efforts are concentrated in data collection and processing as opposed to data communication and distribution. Much of the data-processing activity associated with planning involves manual preparation of data, often for eventual analysis by means of computer. But contrary to popular belief, computer costs, per se, are not a major item of expense in most well-designed system-planning efforts.

In contrast, system operation is an ongoing activity involving substantial costs for the communication of transaction data. The cost breakdown in Table 15–1 assumes a centralized information-processing unit essentially trading reductions in processing costs for increases in data communication costs. Order entry, the predominant data collection activity for logistics operations, may involve varying degrees of expense for manual labor as opposed to machine processing.

System control relies on periodic knowledge of system performance. Data distribution takes on greater importance in the costs of system control activities, reflecting the reliance of effective control primarily on the communication of selected operating information upward to policy-making levels in the organization.

Over all, the development of the logistics organization and a logistics information system are mutually reinforcing actions. As Beier[3] has found:

. . . a computer-based information system does not precede the establishment of a coordinative logistics group. However, the development of such information systems contributes dramatically to the growth of logistics as a coordinating concept within the total firm.

INFORMATION FOR THE PLANNING OF PHYSICAL FLOWS

Many specific matters concerning the planning of physical flows have been raised in preceding chapters. Our purpose here is to raise questions regarding the collection and organization of data for the design of physical flows, data typically regarding what happened where, when, and in what volume. These are important questions, for the amount of existing data in an organization and the necessary efforts to organize such information may be the greatest determinants of the cost of performing a system planning effort.

[3] Frederick J. Beier, "The Impact of Information Systems in the Formation and Life Cycle of a Logistics Department: Prospects for the Future," in *Proceedings* of the National Conference of the National Council of Physical Distribution Management, Fall Meeting, October, 1971, sec. IV, page unnumbered.

Organization of Data for Current Use

Organizations typically design information systems to support operating and control activities, not planning. As a result, information for physical flow planning purposes has to be collected and organized. Basic questions here concern the degree to which analysis for planning should be adjusted to a company's current organization of data—including the level of its aggregation, its coding, and its availability for past and future periods of time—or vice versa.

Aggregation of Data. The basic objective of data aggregation is to combine as many pieces of information as possible to reduce costs of analysis without obscuring basic differences in characteristics for segments of a firm's logistics system. The nature of this activity relies heavily on the manner in which data are recorded and collected for operating purposes.

For example, information about the demand for a company's product might be identified with any or all of the following: (1) the company's 200 sales territories, (2) its 45 shipping points (plants or distribution centers), (3) its 250 products, (4) its 30 sales offices, (5) its 40,000 customers, (6) the 3,000 counties in which it sells its products, or (7) 250 major markets. The greater the detail in which information exists, the more numerous are the options for aggregation.

The extent to which existing data are aggregated will depend primarily on: (1) the use to which the analysis is to be put, (2) the savings to be obtained in processing, and (3) the degree to which a sample of "data points" accurately reflects important characteristics of a larger number of points. For example, in determining the locations for distribution centers by means of linear programming or simulation, processing costs vary to a degree with the number of combinations of potential DC locations and demand points. Thus, processing costs for a matrix of 20 potential DC locations and 250 major markets would be considerably less than for one including 100 potential DC locations and 3,000 counties. On the other hand, if the mix of products, in terms of physical characteristics, is considerably different for major markets as opposed to the multicounty territories they represent, it may be necessary to use data from 3,000 counties or attempt another means of aggregation.

Problems in aggregating data all concern compatibility of various types of information. For example, data describing the dollar amounts of various types of products sold by 200 salesmen may be collected to facilitate the payment of sales commissions. However, where salesmen are assigned by types of accounts (for example, industrial vs. commercial accounts) instead of geographical territories, this information may be of little use in pinpointing the location of demand. Further, dollar amounts must be capable of translation into physical quantities, such as pounds or cubic feet, for effective use in most logistics analysis. (1) **On what would such a valid translation depend?**

Similarly, customers often are identified in data files with the locations of their headquarters, not the plant or outlet actually receiving and using the shipment of product. Where this is the case, more detailed estimates or a different basis for aggregation must be found.

Of course, the basic information for identifying the locus of an activity associates customers, suppliers, plants, or distribution centers with locations and quantities of product. The ability to do this depends on the coding methods which the organization employs in building its data base.

Coding. The volume of data required by an effective logistics information system requires that data be coded to make them manageable, especially by computer. The degree to which information exists in coded form in a data bank, often computerized, influences its accessibility for system planning purposes. Where such data do not exist, they must be prepared from the sampling of documents such as customer orders or bills of lading, an extremely costly process.

Literally hundreds of codes, groups of letters (alpha), numbers (numeric), or other symbols can be used to describe a customer's order, its current status, and its ultimate disposition. If contents of a customer's order are coded and saved, information about the order's ultimate disposition, combined with periodic status reports prepared for control purposes, are important inputs for the planning process. Of all codes employed, those identifying the geographic location of activity are of greatest importance for logistics planning efforts. Therefore, we'll concentrate on those codes here.

Fortunately, for planning purposes, it often does not make much difference how activity locations are identified as long as orders, shipments, and receipts of goods are correctly associated with geographic locations. If necessary, codes can be devised for the most important of these activity centers after operating data are collected and aggregated. The purpose of identifying activity centers in this manner is to convert locational data into estimates of handling costs and transportation costs and times. Perhaps an example would help here.

If we wish to estimate the cost of transporting an estimated volume of product from point A to point B five years hence, we need to know the distance and an estimate of the cost–distance regression line (as in Fig. 9–6). We could obtain the shortest distance either: (1) from a map or a look-up table of origins and destinations, or (2) by computing it mathematically. For a small number of known origins and destinations, the former of these would be the most efficient. However, more typically the number of origin–destination combinations which we might wish to test would be in the tens of thousands. While we could construct a look-up table for either manual or computerized use, computational costs of manual methods would be high and the computer information storage costs could also be prohibitive. Thus, it is easier to code all possible locations by their coordinates or some other method, and use the power of the computer to calculate the distance between those origin–destination pairs in which we are interested by using the familiar old Pythagorean Theorem in the manner described in Fig. 15–1. The result can then be multiplied by factors to convert straight-line distances to rail, truck, or water miles by the shortest routes available.

One such point reference system, PICADAD, is used in the Census of Transportation in the manner described above.[4] Each point mentioned in Census data is described by a four-digit code representing the census division, the state, and the city; a second code designates special characteristics of the point, such as its inclusion in a particular Standard Metropolitan Statistical Area (SMSA), and longitudinal and latitudinal coordinates for use in calculating distance. Hence the name PICADAD, for PI (place identification), CA (characteristics of the area), and DAD (distance and direction code). By means of the latter, straight-line distance can be calculated to within 1% of the actual. This is adjusted to reflect actual route distance with a high degree of accuracy by adding 24% for motor carriers and 21% for railroads.

Grid reference systems are abstractions of point reference systems, because they identify all points in an area bounded by two latitudinal and two longitudinal lines as belonging to a grid member, the center of which is assumed to represent the locational weighting of all centers of activity in the grid member. Distances between such grid member centers are then computed in much the same fashion as described above. Extended to its most detailed level, a grid reference system becomes a point reference system.

The growing potential for the storage of coded logistics data and an increased appreciation of their value, along with the realization of the need for coordination if coded information is to be communicated between firms, have led to recent efforts to standardize basic logistics codes. As a result, the Standard Transportation Commodity Code (STCC) has been adapted from the Standard Industrial Code of basic commodities; it offers a potential for use in the classification of commodities for rate-making purposes. Currently it is used in the tabulation of shipments in the Census of Transportation. The Transportation Data Coordinating Committee (TDCC), based in Washington, D. C., has spearheaded efforts in recent years to develop and promote the use of standard codes not only for com-

---

[4] See Donald E. Church, *PICADAD: A System for Machine Processing of Geographic and Distance Factors in Transportation and Marketing Data* (Washington, D. C.: Bureau of the Census, Department of Commerce, 1965).

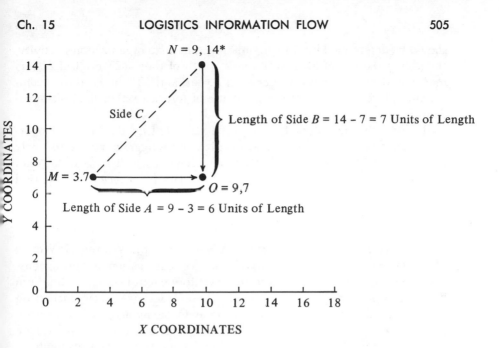

Steps in calculation:

1. Form sides A and B of a right triangle by projecting from points M and N, for which coordinates are known, to a point O at which the sides form a right ($90°$) angle.
2. Calculate units of length of sides A and B by subtracting X coordinate values for point M from those for point N for side A, and Y coordinate values for point M from those of point N for side B.
3. Calculate the units of length for side C by the Pythagorean Theorem, as follows:

$$c^2 = a^2 + b^2$$
$$c^2 = 6^2 + 7^2$$
$$c^2 = 36 + 49$$
$$c^2 = 85$$
$$c\ = 9.2 \text{ units of length}$$

To be read as $x = 9$, $y = 14$.

Fig. 15–1. Method for manual or computer calculation of straight-line distance between any two points on a two-dimensional plane using a basic principle of geometry.

modities, but also for methods of transport, for carriers, and for shipment origin, destination, and interchange points.

Time-Frame. For what period of time should data be collected for the analysis of physical flows? Theoretically, the answer to this question should be determined by: (1) seasonal factors in an organization's activity, suggesting the use of at least a year's worth of data, (2) cyclical factors requiring data for periods longer than a year, and (3) the need to accommodate future growth, suggesting the use of forecast rather than historical data.

Realistically, the alternatives may be restricted by the fact that operating data from which information for planning is aggregated are so costly to store that they get discarded quickly. This, as well as costs of data collection and processing, may require that data for a recent peak period of activity or a portion of a year be used and, by means of various estimates, extrapolated to reflect longer periods of time.

Organization of Logistics Data at Wonka. At the Warren G. Wonka Manufacturing Company, the master file of information regarding customer demand was transmitted to the inventory control system in the form of white copies of salesmen's orders. These orders were keypunched on tape and read into the computer as soon as invoicing activities were completed. The master file of information for each order-line item held on the storage tape contained the following numerically coded elements:

1. Customer number
2. Geographic codes
   a. State
   b. City
   c. County
   d. Wonka sales territory
3. Salesman's number
4. Order number
5. Salesmen's order number (if personal system was used)
6. Customer purchase order number
7. Price discount information
8. C.O.D. payment, if applicable
9. Quantity purchased
10. Price
11. Product number
    a. Basic product
    b. Package size
12. Weight of product
13. Sales category (new account, repeat sale, etc.)
14. Customer category (95 classifications, including hotel, service station, Navy, etc.)
15. Shipping date
16. Distribution center number
17. Product application number (several classifications, including floor cleaning, refinishing, etc.)

Each salesman's name was associated with the distribution center to which he was assigned unless otherwise indicated on the order.

Each day, the computer tallied information from these orders in several ways. First, the items shipped out in accordance with these orders were deducted from balance-on-hand inventories for each warehouse, product by product and item by item. Second, a running tabulation of sales was kept for 30-day periods, again for each warehouse, product, and item. Third, the most recent sales of each item at every warehouse were recorded and the inventory files updated daily as orders for those items were "closed." From this file the company could determine which products and items had experienced no sales at any warehouse location for extended time periods (normally 120 days). Such inactive items, termed "dead stock," were returned to the supplying plant as soon as possible and subsequently not stocked at that location.

Because of limited storage capacity, summary information from the data file was printed monthly, and detailed information more than six months old was "dumped" or discarded. Among the summary reports available for longer periods of time were: (1) detailed listings of warehouse shipments and inventory levels, by distribution center, and (2) sales reports by salesman by item company-wide, and by city and county. It was thought that the detailed information would have to be adjusted, or used with caution, because a salesman's order was not always filled from the distribution center to which he was assigned, a fact not always noted on the order or resulting computer entry. Further, sales territories, and even given cities, were not supplied necessarily from one distribution center if salesmen whose accounts were supplied from different DC's called on accounts in the same city, as was sometimes the case.

(2) **How would you evaluate the quantity and quality of data for planning physical flows in Wonka's logistics information system?**

Alteration of Information Systems
To Accommodate Future Planning

The infrequency of major planning efforts largely has prohibited the redesign of logistics information systems to accommodate such needs. However, data from which exception reports of "out-of-control" situations are prepared for control purposes are much the same data from which planning can draw. Thus, it is quite possible to provide, through the periodic introduction of data-saving routines, for the machine collection of information for planning. Data storage costs, however, make the indiscriminate use of such routines unwise. (3) **What can we suggest regarding alterations in information collection and retention procedures at Wonka to aid in the future planning of physical flows?**

INFORMATION FOR THE PLANNING OF
LOGISTICS INFORMATION FLOWS

The planning of logistics information flows requires a determination of: (1) what each manager needs to know to carry out his job, (2) the objectives of speed and accuracy which the system is to achieve, (3) the volume of information which the system must process, and (4) the procedures, equipment, and manpower needed to meet managerial needs and objectives within specified cost limits.

The "Need to Know" Concept

Information is valuable to a logistics manager only if he "needs to know" about a particular aspect of his organization—its customers, its suppliers, or the techniques that can be employed to improve the operations for which he is responsible. He may be curious about many phases of activity with which he is not concerned, but he is probably well advised to become involved only with the information which is required for the operation of his department, or essential to effective communication with other departments within the firm, or necessary to maintain sound relations with customers and suppliers.

This is not to suggest that a manager should bury his head in the sand of his own operational problems, but any manager who has been victimized by too much data of questionable value can testify that in many respects it is worse than not having enough data for management. This point is important, for many persons knowledgeable about the planning of information systems agree that the manager with operating responsibility is in a better position to specify his needs than is a centralized systems group.[5] Thus, a manager responsible for the logistics function may have to help his subordinates in charge of traffic, warehousing, inventory control, and order processing determine their information needs as well. Further, he will participate in the process of determining what other managers in his own and other organizations need to know from him, a process which specifies logistics information flow both external and internal to the firm.

External Flows. A variety of two-way flows of information between customers and their supplier firm are shown in Fig. 15–2. While formal, often mechanized methods provide the conduit for the flow of operating

---

[5] See for example, Philip H. Thurston, "Who Should Control Information Systems?," *Harvard Business Review*, November–December, 1962, p. 135, and Dearden, *op. cit.*, p. 68.

Upper flow (customer information):

FINANCE AND CONTROL
- Sales statistics
- Financial capacity
- Credit rating

MARKETING
- Sales statistics
- Reaction to sales promotion efforts
- Adherence to market directives
- Customers' management and manpower capacities and limitations
- Customers' financial capacity
- Competitor market activity
- Customer service requirements

LOGISTICS
- Sales statistics
- Inventory control system
- Warehouse location and capacity
- Reorder pattern and system
- Material-handling system
- Competitive and non-competitive products sold
- Receiving requirements and preferred carriers
- Specialized customer service requirements
- Recommendations for customer service improvement
- Carrier delivery performance
- Orders

C U S T O M E R

PRODUCTION
- Information on product performance
- Information on competitor product performance
- Recommendations for product or packaging improvements

PURCHASING
- Performance of component parts purchased by the firm
- Customer requirements for replacement of inadequate component parts

Lower flow (firm information):

FINANCE AND CONTROL
- Invoices
- Credit position
- Financial guidance (when requested)

MARKETING
- Customer service standards
- Market objectives
- New product introductions
- Sales promotion and advertising plans
- Prices and price discounts
- Sales budgets and goals
- Customer sales performance standards
- Competitor sales and promotion plans

LOGISTICS
- Order processing system
- Delivery (transit) time
- Material-handling system
- Carrier routing policy
- Information on status of orders
- Shipping documents
- Freight claim procedure
- Explanation of customer service failure
- Logistics guidance (when requested)

PRODUCTION
- Explanation of inadequate product performance (answering customer product complaints)
- Production guidance (when secondary production or assembly is involved)

PURCHASING
- Purchasing guidance (when requested)

Fig. 15–2. Examples of various types of external information flows between a firm and its customers.

information, in the form of customer orders or carrier "passing" (shipment progress) reports, the salesman may be a major source of logistical planning and control information. Figure 15–2 reflects the nature of information flows between a firm and its suppliers as well. Here the supplier's sales representative and the purchasing agent for the company may form the primary channel for external planning and control information.

Internal Flows. Some internal information exchanges that are of value for logistics are illustrated in Fig. 15–3. Naturally, these will be influenced by the assignment of responsibility and the nature of the organization for the management of logistics activities. Research findings substantiate the importance of internal information flows for logistics. Beier studied the impact of information systems on the development of the logistics function and its management in a number of manufacturing firms included in *Fortune's* 500 largest industrial corporations. This was one of his conclusions:

> Rather than emerging into its own little empire, a comprehensive logistics department tends to place greater emphasis on interfunctional communication. The managers of such groups often perceived their role as providing the necessary machinery to mesh the marketing and production efforts. Consequently, interfunctional group communication, i.e., horizontal communication, appeared as a mandatory prerequisite to the achievement of the firm's goals.[6]

What we have shown in Figs. 15–2 and 15–3 is a small portion of a logistics information system, the formal part. We must remember that people communicate informally, by telephone, conferences, or other means, much information that is not contained in any of the written forms and reports. While we cannot discuss the psychology of personal or informal communications, we should emphasize that *personal contact, and a proper attitude toward it, is perhaps the most important element of a sound logistics information system.*

Requirements for Speed and Accuracy

Surprisingly, the desired speed and accuracy with which various types of information should be processed is not always "as fast and accurately as possible." Delays and inaccuracies in information processing evoke penalties ranging from nothing to large amounts of expense and lost business. But the costs of elimiminating delays and inaccuracies may also range from literally nothing to substantial sums of money. Once again we find ourselves determining appropriate cost trade-offs.

For example, is a "real-time, on-line" inventory accounting and control

---

[6] Beier, *op. cit.*, page unnumbered.

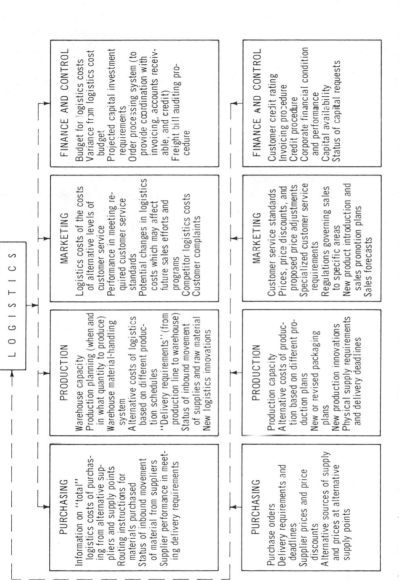

Fig. 15–3. Examples of various types of internal information flows between the logistics function and its "sister" functions in a firm.

system required, or will a nightly updating by batch processing of inventory records and replenishment order preparation be sufficient? The former, involving the use of one or more "dedicated" computers, has been more expensive. However, the relative costs of this alternative are being reduced substantially by distribution information services utilizing time sharing. (4) **What would influence your decision on this?**

Another problem in this regard is the tendency for managers to build a "safety cushion" of time into their estimates of when they will need various types of information. Do they use it or even look at it at the time they receive it? How long is it before the information is used as an input for a decision? While these questions are difficult to answer for non-routine decisions, they can be documented more accurately by interview and observation for recurring uses, such as in reporting weekly or monthly information for control purposes.

It's hard to make a case for an information system which processes information inaccurately. But some types of errors are less costly than others; some types can be detected and corrected more easily and automatically than others. This allows attention to be focused on the errors that are most costly and difficult to detect.

In order processing, for example, errors in spelling, computations of prices from an extension of the number of units ordered, and transpositions in recording item names or numbers can be detected and corrected by computer. However, a correct item name and corresponding number, incorrectly ordered by a customer, can be detected only by a knowledgeable salesman or order processor; no computer will do the job.

Volume To Be Processed

The volume of data to be processed will determine the resource mix, in terms of men and machines, that can be brought to bear on an information system. In logistics, it is the volume of routine, repetitive information processing associated with order processing and inventory control which determines the manpower and equipment requirement.

Basic questions to be raised here are the same as for the consideration of private vs. public warehousing, or private vs. common carrier transportation. They include:

1. To what extent is the need for capacity seasonal?
2. Can peak needs be met by means of a second shift or overtime operations?
3. What are the alternative costs associated with using an outside service bureau for these peaks?
4. Do we have sufficient volume to justify in-house data processing at all?

Answers to these questions may depend on the extent to which an existing in-house information-processing system uses men or machines. (5) What significance do you think this would have for such decisions?

Procedures, Equipment, and Manpower

Given a determination of necessary information and its desired speed, accuracy, and volume, the means for accomplishing the job can be analyzed. In this regard, systems analysts can use a variety of questions to shed light on existing and proposed methods by examining the extent to which information systems: (1) involve duplicated processing activities, (2) omit desirable activities, (3) move information "when ready," (4) maximize simultaneous communication and processing, and (5) suit the method to the job. We will apply these criteria to several actual company systems later in this chapter. Several brief examples may be useful here.

Duplicated processing activities may be desirable to facilitate accuracy in a system. Often, however, they have just the opposite effect. For example, the repeated manual copying of order input information, which exists even in many computer-oriented systems, creates both costs for duplicated effort and inevitable input errors.

Useful activities often omitted from information systems include: (1) the selective routing of information to points of greatest need, (2) the segregation of orders and other routine documents for differentiated handling, and (3) the verification of data accuracy at critical points in a system.

Problems of information availability, typically resulting in decision-making or information-processing emergencies, often can be traced to the fact that information is not transmitted when it is ready. This may result from such things as: (1) a lack of appreciation of the need for the data on the part of the sender, (2) a desire to "batch" data to conserve communication time and cost, or (3) an overzealous approach to data verification for accuracy. As we saw in Chapter 8, this matter is particularly critical for information transmitted between organizations, or between a firm and its suppliers or customers.

If entered and routed properly, information can be made available simultaneously to a number of processing or decision points in an organization. As a result, time lags required for inventory update, billing, and accounts receivable activities can be reduced significantly.

The matching of method and task is not a matter of mechanizing or computerizing everything possible. As McNerney has pointed out, manual methods may be most desirable for low-volume, non-routine operations. On the other hand, computers can create accurate records of a more routine nature at a high rate of speed.[7] According to McNerney:

In an attempt to justify office machinery, whether it be punched card equipment or a computer, gains or improvements which are really due to the *design* of the system are often attributed to the equipment.   In many cases, these same gains or improvements could be achieved with much less expense by modifying the existing system.   One of the real needs in evaluating data processing proposals and equipment is to ascertain whether various operations can be performed only by the use of certain equipment, and to consider alternative (and less expensive) ways of handling the same operations.[8]

Dearden offers us a final warning:

It would be unusual if the best solution were merely to automate the present manual system . . . the present system should probably be changed to take full advantage of the automation. . . . Consequently, the automation of a logistics (information) system usually requires a considerable amount of difficult systems specifications analysis.[9]

INFORMATION FOR OPERATING THE LOGISTICS SYSTEM:
ORDER PROCESSING

As we have seen, information for the operation of a logistics system passes through a series of stages which we described in Fig. 9–4 as the order, replenishment, procurement, inventory update, billing, and payment cycles—all elements concerned with or initiated by order-processing activities.   Because of its relatively routine nature and large volume in many organizations, such information lends itself to machine processing.

Order processing constitutes a significant portion of the time, and in some cases the cost, required in a logistics system.   As such, it constitutes the link between information and physical flows, and the trading of costs between them.   For example, a day saved in order-processing time may be as significant in reducing necessary inventories as a day saved in material handling or transportation.   And it may be much less costly to accomplish time savings in information as opposed to physical flows.

Equipment Trends

Equipment technology for handling information in the operation of the logistics system has developed so fast that it is risky to document the current state of the art, as we attempted to do in Chapter 3.   Nevertheless, it is useful to focus on trends of significance for logistics operations.

[7] John Peter McNerney, *Installing and Using an Automatic Data Processing System* (Boston: Division of Research, Graduate School of Business Administration, Harvard University, 1961), chaps. 4 and 5.

[8] *Ibid.*, p. 64.

[9] John Dearden, "Systems Organization and Responsibility," in John Dearden, F. Warren McFarlan, and William M. Zani, *Managing Computer-Based Information Systems* (Homewood, Ill.: Richard D. Irwin, Inc., 1971), pp. 591–609, at p. 602.

Information Input. Cathode-ray-tube (CRT) devices attached to keyboard inquiry mechanisms (envision a television set connected to a typewriter and memory device) recently have come into widespread use for order entry. Typically, they involve: (1) the receipt of a customer order by telephone or other means, (2) the entry of order information, by means of the keyboard, onto the CRT screen, (3) the verification of item name, number, and quantity with the customer by the order processor, assuming telephone communication, (4) the reservation of ordered items in inventory by pressing the "release" button on the keyboard, (5) the identification, by computer, of inaccurate order information, out-of stock items, or alternate shipping points, (6) the verification with the customer (still on the line) of corrections and other irregularities, and (7) the resulting order of such "irregular" items. The entire process, which requires a matter of seconds per order-line item, produces significantly more accurate data input, often at lower order-entry costs than manual methods.

Information Communication. In spite of dramatic increases in the capacity and capability (speed) of electronic media for handling data and the attendant reductions in costs per unit for such activities, the costs of communication for logistics information have risen proportionately to processing costs as firms have centralized information storage and processing around large-scale computer facilities. This is particularly true for systems involving real-time, on-line processing of data requiring dedicated lines for data communication as well as dedicated computing equipment.

Systems which carefully fit the communication method to the need have been most effective regarding cost. Bowersox describes, for example, a system for replenishing thousands of customers' direct orders, over 200 merchandise outlets for trading-stamp merchandise, and a small number of distribution centers from a central computer facility by means of: (1) nightly reports by air mail of store orders and directly mailed customer orders to the central computer, (2) daily teletype transmission of stock status from distribution centers to the central computer, and (3) high-speed data transmission via *Data-phone* and Wide Area Telephone Service (WATS) lines of store and customer orders and labels from the central computer facility to distribution centers.[10]

Of special interest here is the growing use of the less expensive long-line communication via space satellite, commonplace today but unheard of just a few short years ago.

[10] Donald J. Bowersox, "Total Information Systems in Logistics," *Transportation & Distribution Management,* October, 1964, pp. 23–25.

Information Storage and Access. Devices for recording and storing data on magnetic tape for subsequent recall have, during the past decade, greatly expanded capabilities for processing and storing information, particularly if such information is processed in batches. This method is particularly effective, for example, for: (1) updating inventory files periodically by sorting information about additions to, or subtractions from, inventory into an item sequence comparable to that employed for the inventory master file, (2) committing the transaction information to magnetic tape, and (3) adjusting the master file data (contained on a similar tape) by processing the transaction data against it item by item by means of machine.

More recently, the development of random-access data storage capacity and capability by means of large-scale magnetic memory cores has facilitated the development of methods for data inquiry and information input utilizing CRT or other input units, long-line communication, and real time, on-line computers.

Computation. The rapid rate of development of computing power, with an attendant high rate of equipment obsolescence, has been one of the most significant and glamorous developments in business in many years. One study estimates that in 1972 the costs of computing for comparable jobs on the largest computers were $\frac{1}{200}$ of what they were in 1959.[11]

Of lesser importance for large-scale processing but of greater interest to logistics decision makers is the development of computer time-sharing capabilities, allowing several managers simultaneous, rapid access to computers for testing the results of decisions by means of small- to medium-sized simulations as well as the use of optimizing models for decision-making purposes.

Examples

Because it is difficult to discuss order processing and logistics information operations in the abstract, several examples may help to illustrate some of the comments made thus far. We have purposely selected examples with somewhat different characteristics.

Westinghouse Electric Corporation.[12] An early, forward-looking order-processing system was implemented by Westinghouse for its Apparatus Products Group. It involved the collection of 1,500 to 1,600 orders

[11] As reported in John F. Magee, *Industrial Logistics* (New York: McGraw-Hill Book Co., 1968), p. 164.

[12] For a more complete description of this system, see "At Westinghouse," *Traffic & Distribution Management*, January, 1962, pp. 51–52.

daily by mail and telephone at more than 90 sales offices; a coding of
the order with a six-digit, self-checking address number (with which a
computer later could locate all customer information) and five-digit self-
checking product numbers; typing of the coded information (averaging
55 characters per order plus special instructions) on five-channel paper
teletypewriter tape; transmission by teletype to the company's centralized RAMAC (Random Access Method of Accounting and Control)
computer facility; conversion to punched cards for input to the computer;
computerized location of stock nearest to the customer, inventory updating, and preparation of punched cards from which invoices were prepared at headquarters, conversion of the cards to tape for teletype
transmission; and teletype receipt of information at field warehouses and
plants in the form of complete shipping orders, packing lists, labels, and
the required number of copies of bills of lading.

At the time it was implemented, this system was credited with eliminating the two to four days an order spent previously in the mail and
the two days required for its handling at the shipping point, thus reducing these portions of the order cycle by as much as six days by replacing
them with a 30-minute process under ideal conditions. As a result: (1)
inventories of one product line were reduced from $5 million to $2.7
million, (2) cash flow was improved by five days, (3) faster delivery
was accomplished for 15,000 customers, (4) several field warehouses were
closed, (5) a larger number of deliveries could be made directly from
plants, (6) inventory accounting and control was computerized, and (7)
sales, tax, and financial accounting data were produced as a byproduct
of the system.

This system made use of what, at the time, was the largest industrial
teletype network of its kind in the world, including 230 sending stations
and 243 receiving stations connected by 28,700 miles of duplex (simultaneous two-way transmission) lines feeding into two automatic switching
units in Pittsburgh. In addition, it required four additional lines for the
transmission of sales order information from the centralized order-
processing department in Pittsburgh, adding another 5,263 miles of wire
to the network.

An interesting footnote to the implementation of this (and other)
real-time information-processing systems is the fact that Westinghouse
reported that it had to synchronize working hours at its 26 field warehouses located in four time zones.

Marbon Chemical Division of Borg–Warner.[13] The diagram in Fig.
15–4 describes a system for processing customer orders implemented by
the Marbon Chemical Division of Borg–Warner, a manufacturer of syn-

[13] Based on Henry Lefer, "15-Part (Count 'Em) Form Keeps Paperwork Down
As Orders Go Up," *Handling & Shipping*, June, 1965, pp. 60–61.

thetic resins and thermoplastics for sale to manufacturers of plastics, rubber, adhesives, and paint. This method was centered around the preparation of a 15-part order form, with copies used variously for customer and salesmen communications, shipping documents, and internal notification and records.

(6) **Examine carefully the flow of documents indicated in Fig. 15–4. How many separate steps would there be in the order-processing sequence shown if each had to be accomplished sequentially?** Basically, in this system they are reduced to about eight:

1. The preparation of the 15-part form
2. The dispatch of two copies externally, two internally for action, and eleven to the Production Control Department for completion
3. The dispatch of the plant requisition, copy 2
4. If inventory is not available, the transfer of copy 3 to Production Scheduling

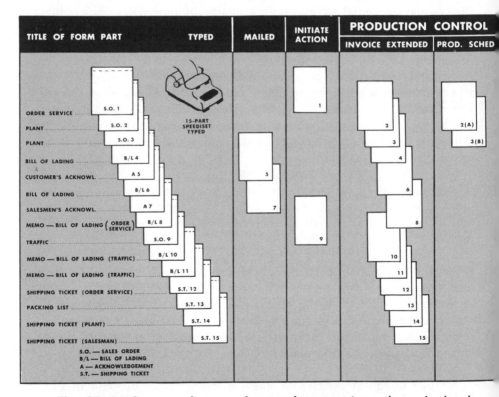

Fig. 15–4. Summary diagram of system for processing order and related *Source:* Henry Lefer, "15-Part (Count 'Em) Form Keeps Paperwork Down As Industrial Publishing Co. (div. Pittway Corp.)

5. If inventory is available, the dispatch of three copies from Production Control to Traffic
6. The subsequent dispatch of six copies to shipping from the Traffic and Production Control Departments
7. The transfer of necessary documentation to Accounting from Traffic and Shipping for carrier payment and customer billing
8. The return of copies 12 and 15 to the Order Services Department for external notice of shipment to the customer and salesman, respectively, and copies 1, 8, and 11 for matching and filing, signifying the completion of the shipment

(7) Look closely again at Fig. 15–4. Does the system shown provide for back-ordered product or for split shipments? (8) Why? (9) Assuming it might be necessary, how would you alter the procedure to accommodate this type of need?

Marbon reports that "the new system not only makes possible easier

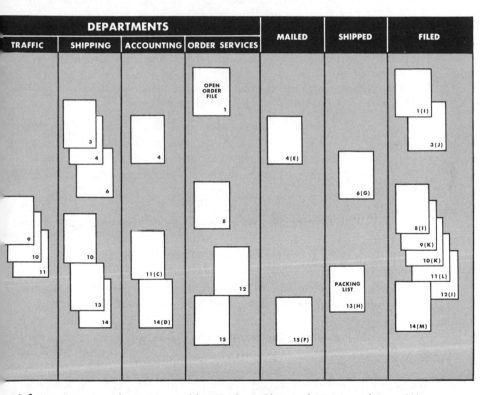

information at a plant operated by Marbon Chemical Division of Borg–Warner. Orders Go Up," *Handling & Shipping*, June, 1965, pp. 60–61; published by

and faster shipping, but by eliminating retyping also removes a major source of errors." [14]

Phillips Electric.[15] This large, European-based manufacturer of a wide range of consumer and industrial electrical products recently has developed a logistics information system called ORFO (ORdering to FOrwarding) for its Lighting Division. ORFO is implemented on a modular, step-by-step basis. Its capabilities for linking 50 National Organizations (N. O.'s, consisting of sales offices and order-receiving points in various countries) with the Company's six factories, its Eurostore facility (central distribution center), and its Eindhoven headquarters, all in The Netherlands, include the following:

1. Transfer of orders electronically from most European N. O.'s to the central computer facility at Eindhoven
2. Hourly processing of such information
3. Issuance of instructions, also according to a schedule, to the Eurostore for preparing ordered items for shipment
4. Preparation of both the invoice and the appropriate international shipping documents by computer
5. Handling of international accounting and statistics associated with the flow of material
6. Capability for guiding internal production planning, inventory control, and even Eurostore stock location selections.

Two additional features of this system are that it files orders with distant requested delivery dates until the appropriate time, and it reviews shipments from plants to the Eurostore to identify merchandise that can be shipped to customers without first being moved into the Eurostore stocks.

This system reduces order-processing times by 80%. Now that this is accomplished, "delaying factors in physical goods handling and transportation facilities will get emphasized attention." [16]

(10) **Review again the characteristics of the Westinghouse, Marbon, and Phillips methods for order processing and related activities. How do these systems measure up, to the extent you can determine, to the criteria for information system design set forth on page 513?**

Wonka Manufacturing Company. The Company received about 20,000 orders per month. The flow of documents and actions resulting from the receipt of an order is shown in Fig. 15–5.

Customer orders were received by distribution centers serving respec-

---

[14] *Ibid.*, p. 61.
[15] "Telecomputing From Ordering to Forwarding," Company document.
[16] *Ibid.*, p. 9.

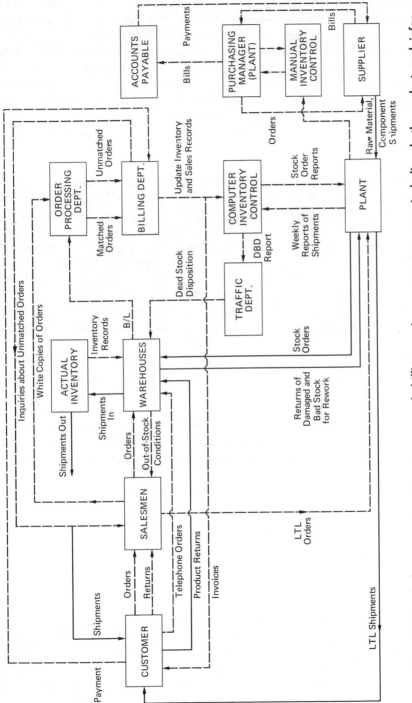

Fig. 15–5. Order processing, inventory control, billing, and payment processes, including **both product and information flows, Warren G. Wonka Manufacturing Company.**

tive customers in four ways: (1) phone call from the customer, (2) phone call from a salesman or regional sales manager, (3) the salesman's "white copy" of the order form delivered by the salesman, or (4) the salesman's white copy of the order form delivered by mail. In the first instance, a corroborating phone call from the salesman was required usually to release stocks. In all instances, the salesman was required to complete the order form, a document which then became the source of shipping, pricing, billing, and commission accounting.

Upon receipt of customer orders, DC personnel checked their daily inventory tabulations of Wonka products to determine whether they could ship all items requested on each order. For those orders on which all items were on hand, bills of lading (also known as shipping tickets) were typed up, and the items comprising those orders were selected from distribution center stocks, loaded on trucks, and delivered to the customers.

For phoned orders on which he found items requested were out of stock, several alternative courses of action were available to the salesman: (1) have the order held until a new shipment from the plant arrived at the distribution center, (2) have the order filled with items available and the balance of the order sent to the plant for direct LTL shipment to the customer, or (3) have the entire order sent to the plant for direct LTL shipment.

At times, when confronted with the knowledge that their orders would result in split-shipment (back-order) situations, salesmen would "shop" by phone to find another distribution center in the region with stock available from which to ship either the entire order or the balance unfilled by the "home" distribution center. Although company directives advised against it, "shopping" was employed, especially where several distribution centers were located relatively close together, such as in the regions served by Philadelphia, Newark, and Boston.

After making shipments, distribution center personnel deducted the amounts shipped from their own perpetual inventory records. They were requested by Wonka to mail copies of bills of lading for goods shipped daily to the Order Processing Department in Cleveland. However, bills of lading might be received in Cleveland from one to five days after a shipment actually was made.

In the Order Processing Department at Cleveland, bills of lading mailed from distribution centers were kept on file and matched with salesmen's white order copies before they were transmitted to the Billing Department. Normally, white copies of orders were received in one to five days from the time of the order. However, there were significant variations in transmittal times for the white order copy. One cause of this was the month-end "recap," or computation of the volume on which salesmen's commissions were based. Toward the end of each month, the number of orders received increased substantially, and the transmittal time declined.

Orders and bills of lading were filed as received in Cleveland, by distribution center and, within each DC file, alphabetically by account name. Twice daily, clerks attempted to match these items, and even searched through the files of geographically adjacent DC's in an attempt to detect possible errors in distribution center identification caused by a salesman's decision to order a product shipped from a DC other than the one usually used, a decision sometimes made after the order form had been filled out.

Four conditions could result at the document matching point in the Order Processing Department: (1) orders might not have matching bills of lading, (2) orders might have incomplete bills of lading, (3) bills of lading might not have matching orders, and (4) orders and bills of lading would match. In the first case, those orders in a given month were held until the beginning of the second month following the month in which the orders were written (i.e., all May orders were held until July 1). At that time, they were pulled and sent to the appropriate salesmen, who may have cancelled orders, changed shipping arrangements, written two orders, or written an order in such a way that the consignee's name on the bill of lading could not be matched. Subsequent correspondence was necessary to straighten out associated records.

In instances where incomplete bills of lading were on file (showing, for example, the shipment of three out of five line items ordered), the orders were held for five business days, and then the customer was partially billed for the goods shown to have been shipped. This often created difficulties in pricing and billing because customers sometimes did not receive the full price discount which would have been associated with a complete shipment.

The third exception condition, bills of lading without orders, was handled in a manner similar to the second. Bills of lading were held for five business days, after which the clerk wrote an order on a special form, using the information shown on the bill. This procedure often resulted in improper billing for accounts for which the appropriate pricing arrangements were normally noted by the salesmen on their orders. The manager of the Order Processing Department estimated that his clerks created 250 to 300 orders per week to cover such exceptional situations.

At the time that orders were found to match with bills of lading, the documents were sent to the Billing Department for invoicing. After an invoice was prepared and sent, the computer inventory files were updated and stock-order and dead-stock reports (of items for which no orders had been received for a year, qualifying for shipment back to the plant) were prepared for the plant Shipping Department and the Traffic Department, respectively.

As information on shipments from distribution centers to customers was recorded on five-track tape for inventory purposes at the Cleveland headquarters computer facility, weights for necessary replacement stocks for all items were accumulated by the computer. When such weights reached truckload or carload quantities, depending on the method of transportation employed for replenishing a given distribution center stock, a stock order was produced by the computer for shipment by the plant.

When a stock order was generated by the computer, it was carried through a series of steps in the Traffic Department before it reached the plant, as follows: (1) stock orders were reviewed with regional sales managers for any suggested adjustments, (2) the mode of transportation for the shipment was designated, (3) items approved for elimination from a stock order in process, by agreement between the plant manager and headquarters traffic manager, were noted on the order, and (4) stock orders for the plant were typed and hand carried to the plant.

Additions to inventory records were made as a result of documentation from: (1) stock orders received at distribution centers, (2) customer returns received at distribution centers, and (3) receipts of stocks which were inactive in other distribution centers. In each case, the processing of a variety of forms preceded the keypunching and physical entering of the information into the computer. For each stock order, for example, a document coordinator within the Traffic Department received a bill of lading and a tally sheet from the plant when the order was shipped. When the order reached the distribution center (in one to fifteen days), a receiving report was filled out, noting the number of items received in good order, product by product. Damaged goods were noted separately; they were returned to the plant and not added to inventory records in the computer. Clerical and mail delays averaged about two to three days on receiving reports, so that the total time lag between the shipment of goods from the plant to the updating of Cleveland inventory records ranged from three to eighteen days and averaged about seven.

Before proceeding, it would be useful for you to look at the basic cycles shown in theoretical form in Fig. 9–4 and compare these with the more typical "real world" of Fig. 15–5 and the discussion above.

Executives at Wonka expressed concern over time delays experienced in the information processing procedures in the Company, confirmed by information produced by the consultant in his distribution system audit, presented in Table 9–8 (page 289). Among other complaints encountered regarding communications were: (1) the failure of distribution center personnel to inform salesmen accurately about stock positions when orders were phoned in, (2) the lack of communication regarding changes in modes of transportation made by the Inventory Control and Data

Processing Departments, which were responsible for day-to-day inventory management computations, (3) the failure of those responsible for distribution center inventory control to provide advance warning regarding special orders to the Production Planning Department, even though the former could detect such needs some days in advance by analyzing computer reports of inventory balances, and (4) the communication of inaccurate estimates of shipping dates for special orders from the plant.

(11) Compare Wonka's approach to logistics information flow with the examples discussed previously. Evaluate it on the basis of the questions posed on page 513. What conclusions do you reach? (12) Specifically, what kind of changes would you recommend to the management of the Wonka Manufacturing Company, subject, of course, to cost considerations?

INFORMATION FOR CONTROLLING THE LOGISTICS SYSTEM

Logistics system control is carried out at two levels: (1) operational control concerning day-to-day matters such as inventory management and the maintenance of service levels, and (2) managerial control dealing with the monitoring of cost and other indicators leading to less frequent decisions with longer-term impact, such as the relocation of inventory.

Operational Control

Operational control provides the mechanism, whether it be a computer-oriented decision model or a person, whereby customers and various entities internal to the firm receive the level of service preprogrammed for them, defined in terms of the right goods in the requested quantities at the right time in usable condition. For this reason, information for control purposes must be total and timely—total in the sense that all items are recorded and reported, and timely in the sense that information should be up-to-date and accurate at the time actions are to be based on it.

In addition to the ongoing accounting for the inventory control necessary to provide the right items in the proper quantities, the operational control essential for the proper timing of deliveries includes monitoring the progress of orders in relation to requested delivery dates to determine the need for expediting or delaying the process. This monitoring is most effective if it takes place at a point in the process at which a decision can have significance for its further progress.

A good example of this type of operational control is that for goods in transit under a "diversion" privilege, which allows the specification of a new destination beyond the current one for a shipment, as the first destination is reached. This privilege, utilized by shippers of perishable goods to market by means of truck or railroad, allows the shipper: (1) to find the most lucrative market for his product under conditions in which demand–supply relationships in various markets change daily and (2) to pay a transportation rate computed on the basis of the distance between the origin and ultimate destination. Clearly, a frequent monitoring of shipment progress is required by the shipper and provided by the carrier under this privilege.

To an increasing extent, customers are enforcing the arrival of shipments within narrowly specified limits. Shipments that arrive early can represent cost penalties as important as those for shipments that arrive late. This has led some firms to refuse early shipments upon their arrival, emphasizing the need for operational control over order timing.

(13) **How is operational control over timing achieved in the system implemented by the Marbon Chemical Division of Borg–Warner, described earlier?**

Managerial Control

In contrast to operational control, managerial control of logistics activities deals with non-routine matters as it is necessary to do so. This requires periodic reports summarized from operating data as well as exception reports regarding performance falling outside previously designated, acceptable limits.

Although we will deal with the matter of managerial control more extensively in Chapter 21, clearly the nature of control information in terms of measures and level of detail must correspond to a manager's duties and his "need to know." LaLonde and Grashof have described control information needs at three levels of responsibility in a logistics organization, for example, involving: (1) management of activities at an individual facility, such as a warehouse, (2) responsibility for a function, such as warehousing, wherever it might take place in an organization's logistics system, and (3) responsibility for all logistics functions at the highest level in an organization.[17]

Designations of conditions under which exception reports are filed will depend upon the critical nature of the matter being reported. Stock-outs or poor service on high-volume items for which customer expectations are exacting may be of greater interest for exception reporting than a similar level of performance for low-volume, unusual items. Internal cost variances of an unfavorable nature may be allowed to accumulate longer

[17] Bernard J. LaLonde and John F. Grashof, "The Role of Information Systems in Physical Distribution Management," in Donald J. Bowersox, Bernard J. LaLonde, and Edward W. Smykay, *Readings in Physical Distribution Management* (New York: The Macmillan Co., 1969), pp. 193–205.

than unfavorable variances in customer service performance, particularly in a marketing-oriented company dealing with fickle customers. In fact, LaLonde and Grashof suggest that in many organizations complete information about each irregularity in customer service and the actions taken to correct it may well be considered appropriate for managerial control purposes at the level occupied by the manager of order processing.[18]

Wonka Manufacturing Company

Although extensive information for operational control was collected and used, particularly in the computer-oriented inventory system, information for managerial control of logistics activities was confined to reports of actual as opposed to budgeted costs for several major cost areas and an extensive program of distribution center inventory checking.

The continuing distribution center audit effort was employed to: (1) keep warehousemen "honest" in their charges to Wonka and (2) detect major discrepancies between the inventory levels reported by DC's from their inventory records and those maintained in central files at Cleveland, and the sources of the discrepancies. This required that Traffic Department personnel review, on an order-by-order basis from the monthly computer print-out containing a complete set of transactions, information regarding items for which discrepancies between DC and Wonka inventory balances were found. This activity produced several thousand dollars in savings resulting from overcharge or inventory shortage claims filed each year by Wonka against the distribution centers. But the requirements of the job were greater than the available staff, which recently had reached six full-time clerks employed in DC inventory checking. Even with six clerks, the group was now lagging about six months behind actual Company activity. The problem was further complicated by the fact that the turnover rate among members of this group was particularly high.

(14) As the manager responsible for the Traffic Department at Wonka, what action would you take regarding this situation? (15) Why? (16) Would your response be different if you were responsible for all logistics activities at Wonka?

SUMMARY

We have considered here the design of logistics information systems for planning physical flows of goods and flows of logistics information,

[18] *Ibid.*, p. 204.

operating the logistics system, and controlling such operations. Because of an organization's heavy operational reliance on order-processing information flows, we have devoted a considerable amount of attention to information systems for order processing.

The significance of this discussion lies not only in the importance of logistics information systems to the functioning of an organization. It is of basic importance to the further development of effective logistics management.

SUGGESTED READINGS

BOWERSOX, DONALD J., EDWARD W. SMYKAY, and BERNARD J. LaLONDE. *Physical Distribution Management,* Rev. Ed. New York: The Macmillan Co., 1968.
Presents diagrams of sample logistics information systems, as well as a review of the steps in planning and implementing a data communications system.
DEARDEN, JOHN, F. WARREN McFARLAN, and WILLIAM M. ZANI. *Managing Computer-Based Information Systems.* Homewood, Ill.: Richard D. Irwin, Inc., 1971.
Of particular interest in this volume are notes on "A Framework for Management Information Systems Design," and Dearden's article, "Systems Organization and Responsibility."
MAGEE, JOHN F. *Industrial Logistics.* New York: McGraw-Hill Book Co., 1968.
Focuses on the past developments and future prospects of logistics information systems.
TAFF, CHARLES A. *Management of Physical Distribution and Transportation,* 5th Ed. Homewood, Ill.: Richard D. Irwin, Inc., 1972.
Taff concentrates specifically on order processing as a physical distribution activity.

16

Comprehensive Logistics System Design

What distinguishes a comprehensive logistics system design effort from others? First, most likely it will concern itself with activities and costs of both movement and demand–supply coordination. Through total cost analysis, it emphasizes the appraisal of all costs of transportation, warehousing, packaging and material handling, order processing, inventory holding, and procurement resulting from a decision to utilize a particular method of accomplishing each activity. Further, it focuses on the analysis of the nature of change in these costs under varying conditions. Typically, such changes involve cost trade-offs.

Second, comprehensive logistics system design involves the use of people, machines, materials, and information in such a way that the parts are closely integrated to create greater productivity in the system than that suggested by the sum of its components. The concurrent design of all logistics components is rarely possible because of previous commitments and heavy and perhaps mistaken emphasis on sunk costs. However, this second identifying characteristic emphasizes, to the extent possible, the avoidance of sub-optimization of system components (the optimization of one system component to the detriment of total system cost or performance). To do this requires a systematic approach to the analysis of a logistics system. Such an approach should also be flexible enough to meet individual exigencies.

Third, a comprehensive design often views the movement of goods and the coordination of demand and supply not necessarily as activities carried on by or for one firm, but by and for firms at two or more levels in a channel of logistics. It recognizes that the price of a product to an ultimate consumer includes the costs of the sum of a number of logistics operations repeated over and over in a channel of distribution. As such, the health of all firms in a channel is interrelated, requiring an enlightened firm in the channel to analyze channel systems in terms of logistics techniques employed by its suppliers and customers as well as itself. This is a specific application of a more general philosophy advanced by some organization theorists:

> Administrative and organizational theories seem to have concentrated upon the administration of a single organization and have not specifically recognized that a system of separate organizations requires administration also.[1]

In previous chapters of this Part, we have considered attitudes, approaches, and specific techniques designed to improve various components of a logistics system. The purposes of this chapter are to discuss: (1) concepts of total cost analysis, (2) the nature of system cost trade-offs, (3) methods of implementing a total cost concept, and (4) the approach which our consultant elected in his analysis of Wonka's logistics system. The context for this chapter is provided by others in Part Four, especially Chapter 9. Before proceeding, it may be useful to review briefly the material presented there.

TOTAL COST ANALYSIS

Total cost analysis is, as its name implies, the analysis of logistics systems taking into consideration all logistics costs affected by a proposed change in the system. It was first described in detail by Lewis, Culliton, and Steele [2] although it is likely that it had been employed by a small group of firms, including at least one carrier sales organization, prior to its formal presentation in print.

Total cost analysis can take a variety of forms, ranging from a listing of cost estimates valid for any point in time to the construction of elaborate models based on observed input–output relationships. Basically, whether dealing with a simple tabulation of costs or a more complex model, we can identify cost, inventory, or other input elements as fixed or variable with changes in volume of sales, distance of movement, size of order, or some other dimension. So-called $y = a + bx$ relationships, where y represents a total cost, a the fixed portion of the cost regardless

[1] Valentine F. Ridgway, "Administration of Maunfacturer–Dealer Systems," *Administrative Science Quarterly*, March, 1957, pp. 466–67.

[2] Howard T. Lewis, James W. Culliton, and Jack D. Steele, *The Role of Air Freight in Physical Distribution* (Boston: Division of Research, Graduate School of Business Administration, Harvard University, 1956).

of changes in the variable x, and b the cost per unit of x or the variable portion of our cost structure, are convenient to construct for logistics system analyses, regardless of the complexity of the approach used. They make it possible to employ more powerful analytical techniques, such as linear programming, in the analysis by using only the variable portion of the cost estimate in the model itself and factoring into the calculation manually the fixed changes, particularly where such changes are relatively small. And they often describe quite accurately a variety of such relationships. For example, note relationships of inventory turn-over rates (and consequently, carrying costs) to various throughput volumes, as shown for the Wonka Company in Fig. 9–2. Or turn again to the presentation of the cost per unit for the shipment of levelor machines and parts over varying distances, shown in Fig. 9–6.

An Example

A classic example of early thinking regarding total cost analysis can be provided by a company which we call Brunswick Floors, Inc., a company distributing finished decorative wood products from its plant at Brunswick, New Jersey, to, among other places, the distribution center which it leases and operates at San Francisco.

Executives of the Company had gathered cost data and prepared estimates which indicated that a change from the use of rail transportation to either truck or air transportation, and a considerable reduction of the sizable quantities of inventory at both Brunswick and San Francisco could provide total cost savings. Questions were raised regarding the quantity of such savings at the current volume of business and the stages in the development of the Company's San Francisco regional market at which each combination of transportation and warehousing alternatives would be most economical.

Cost information for the Company's current volume of business is shown in Table 16–1. Once costs are stated in terms of fixed and variable components, in the form of $y = a + bx$ equations, they can be estimated for any future volume of business by graphing them, as shown in Fig. 16–1, for systems utilizing air and truck transportation.

Comparing alternative methods graphed in Fig. 16–1 or described in Table 16–1, we can set the total costs of any two (y_1 and y_2) equal to each other to find the point of volume (x), if any, at which the total cost lines described by the functions intersect. This produces the following result:

$$a_1 + b_1x = a_2 + b_2x, \text{ thus } x = \frac{a_1 - a_2}{b_2 - b_1}$$

TABLE 16-1. Annual Total Logistics Costs, Current and Proposed Systems, San Francisco Region, Brunswick Floors, Inc.*

Cost Item	Method of Transportation, Warehousing		
	Air	Highway	Railroad
Fixed costs:			
Fixed cost element, freight bill	$ 5,000	$15,000	$15,000
Warehousing, Brunswick	14,680	14,680	14,680
Warehousing, San Francisco	–	14,700	29,600
Total fixed	$34,680	$69,380	$84,280
Costs variable with volume:			
Freight cost element, variable	$70,000	$18,000	$ 7,000
Local delivery, San Francisco	10,000	10,000	10,000
Brunswick warehousing	4,100	4,100	4,100
San Francisco warehousing	–	8,200	12,300
Order preparation and placement	9,250	2,250	2,250
Capital investment in inventory	3,300	6,000	7,800
Product obsolescence and damage	2,480	5,200	2,480
Insurance	620	1,010	1,300
Taxes	420	560	650
Total variable	$100,000	$55,320	$47,880
Annual volume (pounds)	400,000	400,000	400,000
Variable cost per pound	$.250	$.138	$.119
Total cost per pound	$.337	$.312	$.330

*Each of the three systems under comparison provides the same level of service to customers: 30% of all orders delivered within 72 hours of order receipt, 80% within 96 hours; and 90% within 120 hours.

Further, we can be sure of computing least-cost line intersections if we rank the alternatives in terms of the amounts of fixed costs incurred under each, from smallest to largest. In the example, annual fixed costs for air = $34,680, truck = $69,380, and rail = $84,280. In order to find the first pertinent least-cost line intersection, we would compare air with truck. In this case, our computations would be based on the following information from Table 16-1:

$$a_1 = \$34,680, b_1 = \$.250, a_2 = \$69,380, b_2 = \$.138$$

For the example in question:

$$x = \frac{34,680 - 69,380}{.138 - .250} = \frac{-34,700}{-.112} = 309,010 \text{ lb.}$$

In other words, at an annual volume of 309,010 pounds, it would be economical in the long run to switch from air to truck. This essentially is the same result shown in Fig. 16-1, although the latter is less accurate unless graphed with extreme precision.

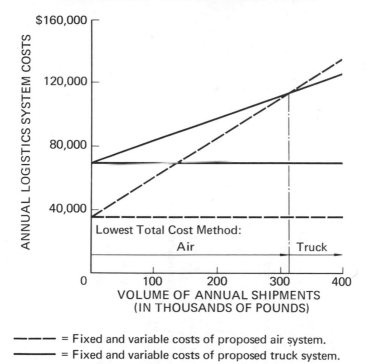

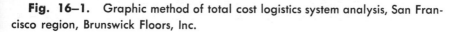

———— = Fixed and variable costs of proposed air system.
———— = Fixed and variable costs of proposed truck system.

Fig. 16–1. Graphic method of total cost logistics system analysis, San Francisco region, Brunswick Floors, Inc.

(1) Prepare similar calculations for the comparison between truck and rail alternatives. What break-even point between the two methods do you obtain? (2) At our current volume of business, assuming that Brunswick's management expects a 20% increase in volume through the San Francisco distribution center in each of the next five years, which of the alternative logistics systems would best meet the needs of the Company? (3) For what periods of time? (4) Why?

Other Cost and Activity Relationships

What we have just considered is an abstraction of a complex total cost analysis useful for illustrating the concept. In an actual situation, cost and activity relationships which must be identified and measured in a comprehensive system analysis include those shown in Fig. 16–2. Here we have set forth major logistics cost areas and have attempted to identify the major determinants (and the determinants of determinants) of each.

Cost Categories	Vary With:	Which Vary With:	Which Vary With:
Transportation costs per unit	Shipment size	Number of stock locations Frequency of shipment Total volume	
	Shipment distance	Number of stock locations Geographic market coverage	
	Costs of various modes of transportation	Value of product Density of product Geographic shipping patterns Regularity in availability of freight Shipment size	
Warehousing costs per unit	Method of warehousing	Volume of throughput Constancy of volume of activity Physical size of inventory	
	Volume of throughput	Number of stock locations Size of territory served	
	Inventory turnover rate	Inventory policy Volume of sales per SKUL	
Inventory carrying costs	Inventory control, forecasting method	Pattern of demand Predictability of demand Desirability of routinizing replenishment procedures	
	Order-cycle length	Method of transport Order-processing procedures	
	Volume of sales per SKUL	Product-line policies Engineering standardization	
	Replenishment shipment size per SKUL	Sales volume Frequency of replenishment	
Order processing costs per unit	Number of line items per order	Size of product line Nature of market	
	Average order size	Quantity discount incentives Nature of use	
	Method of order processing	Volume of orders	
	Rate of initial order fill	Accuracy of inventory data file Inventory coverage policy	
Lost sales costs	Willingness of customers to substitute	Nature of competition Type of customer need	
	Rate of contribution on sales	Ability to differentiate product, service from competition	

For example, transportation costs per unit vary inversely with shipment size, directly with shipment distance, and in relation to the costs of the various methods of transportation utilized. Shipment size, in turn, largely varies directly with the total volume of business, other things being constant. It varies inversely with the number of stock locations and the frequency of shipment, again assuming volume and other characteristics constant.

If we were to fill in the far right column of Fig. 16–2, we might conclude that the total volume of business, among other things, is influenced by the level of logistics service mentioned elsewhere in the figure. Likewise, the number of stock locations will vary with the desired customer service level, which depends on other factors. (5) As an exercise, complete the right-hand column in Fig. 16–2. As the tabulation is developed out to the right, the interrelationships in a logistics system become more and more apparent.

Clearly, even a comprehensive system analysis must limit itself to an accounting of only the major influences on cost and service. And the task of data collection and revision to fit an analytic format, even with these types of simplifications, can be tough and expensive. If carried out properly, however, it can yield relatively accurate estimates of the cost trade-offs under various alternative system designs. Before turning to methods for achieving this type of result, it is useful to consider some recurring patterns of such cost trade-offs.

LOGISTICS COST TRADE-OFFS

Throughout the text, many examples of logistics system changes have been cited. A number of these are listed in Fig. 16–3. They have been placed opposite the various kinds of costs with which they are associated in vendor, company, and customer organizations. Each example of change, based on actual industry experience, has resulted in the reduction of certain costs of logistics and an increase in others. In a sense, cost increases are traded for cost decreases presumably when a net gain results to the company instituting the change. This exchange has become more popularly known as the "trade-off" of one cost for another.

You should be thoroughly familiar with Example 1 in Fig. 16–3, after our analysis of a consolidated stocking policy for Wonka's levelor machines in Chapter 13. (6) In our analysis, did we take into account all of the trade-offs suggested in Example 1 of Fig. 16–3?

Consider Example 5, where change is represented by an increase in the use of "split shipments" to provide better supply service to the manufacturing line. It is typical of the policy pursued by several automobile manufacturers. That is, in circumstances where planned trans-

These costs often are changed	As this action is taken											
	1	2	3	4	5	6	7	8	9	10	11	12
Long-Distance Transportation From:												
Vendor to Facility[a]	−	−[c]		+[d]	+							−
Intra-Facility	+	+										+
Facility to Customer				−		+	−	−	−			
(Nature of Cost):												
For-Hire Carrier Charges	+											
Private Carriage Costs												
Local Delivery At:												
Origin(s)										−		
Destination(s)												
Material Handling:												
Vendor	−	−				−						
Company[b]		−				−				−		+
Customer												
(Nature of Cost):												
Equipment	−					+						
Labor	−					−						
Supplies	−					+						
Inventory Holding In:												
Vendors' Facilities		+	−		−			−	−			−
Company Assembly Warehouses		+	−		−			+	+			+
Company Factories												
Company Distribution Warehouses	−			+				−	+		−	+
Customers' Facilities	−			−							−	
Carriers' Equipment (En Route)	−						−					
(Nature of Cost):												
Interest on Investment							−		−			
Obsolescence									−			
Pilferage and Damage												
Inventory Taxes										−		
Insurance												
Rehandling	−[c]	+[d]	−		−							−
All of the Above												

	1	2	3	4	5	6	7	8	9	10	11	12
Warehousing:												
Vendor		+										
Company Assembly[b]		+										+
Company Distribution	−	+						+		+		−
Customer	−							−		−		
All of the Above												
(Nature of Cost):												
Fixed–Private Facilities[a]		+								−		−
Variable–Public Facilities										+		+
Packing:												
Vendor Packing		−					+					
Company Unpacking–Packing						+	+		−			
Customer Unpacking						+	+		−			
Order Processing:												
Vendor	+		+		+						+	
Company	+	−	+		+						+	
Customer											+	
Manufacturing (If Applicable):												
Fixed				+				−				
Labor Variable												
Equipment Variable												
Sales Losses Due to Logistics:												
Customer Service Deficiencies	−				−			−		−	−	
Market Territory Restrictions					−			−		−	−	−

1. Use of premium methods of transportation for outgoing finished products (accompanied by a reduction in warehouses, overhaul of communications).

2. Purchasing and shipping supplies and components by means of fewer orders of greater quantity.

3. Consolidation of shipments from supply points (allowing smaller, but requiring better timing of, purchases).

4. Increase in the number of distribution warehouses (reducing service times to customers).

5. Increase in the use of "split" shipments on supplies to meet manufacturing requirements.

6. Change from hand methods to palletization in handling of finished product (requiring customer compatibility for optimum savings).

7. Increase in the protective characteristics of packing containers (allowing shipment under different freight classification).

8. Establishment of distribution warehouses as mixing points for shipments between plants and customers (allowing volume shipments to customers).

9. Shifting packing and/or packaging operations from plant to distribution warehouse (allowing shipment in bulk).

10. Use of public vs. private warehousing facilities.

11. Use of faster communications and mechanized procedures in handling orders from customers.

12. Stabilization of labor requirements for manufacturing by establishing constant production schedule (creating inventory level fluctuations).

[a] Facility (plant or warehouse) of the company whose procedures are under study.
[b] Company taking the action.
[c] Costs which are reduced by the action.
[d] Costs which are increased by the action.

Fig. 16-3. Examples of logistics cost trade-offs reported in actual situations.

portation services do not appear likely to meet the time requirements for the provision of supplies or components to the manufacturing line, a part of the shipment is split off and shipped by faster or more dependable methods. This is likely to result in increases in: (1) transportation costs from the vendor to the company's manufacturing facility, and (2) order-processing costs of both the vendor and the company under consideration. At the same time, however, inventory holding costs of both the vendor and the company are likely to be reduced. More important, an interruption of manufacturing processes, with the attendant possibility of a customer back-order situation, will be avoided. (7) **What is the basic trade-off here?** Its identification requires knowledge of system objectives and existing costs.

System Objectives and Costs

Identification of the nature of logistics and cost trade-offs is a function of time and of the objectives of the system in which change is proposed. Time is important in establishing the relevance of change in a system. In Example 4 of Fig. 16–3, for instance, the propriety of an increase in the number of distribution warehouses would be based on the number and location of those already in operation in relation to company markets and manufacturing facilities. If a high degree of customer service were already being rendered by the system, the cost trade-off would take on primary characteristics of an increase in warehousing and inventory holding costs for a reduction in transportation cost from warehouse facilities to customers. Given a point in time at which customer service levels were relatively low, the trade-offs would include gains from an improvement in customer service.

The objectives of a given system further determine the nature of cost trade-offs in a logistics problem. For example, two basic objectives might have prompted the action in Example 5 of Fig. 16–3: (1) improvement of service to the manufacturing line and hence to customers, or (2) maintenance of the current level of service to the manufacturing line and to customers with some reduction in total logistics costs. Given the first objective, the cost trade-offs are essentially those pointed out above. The presence of the second objective, however, would simplify the nature of the trade-offs to an increase in inbound transportation costs for a reduction in inventory holding and warehousing costs.

METHODS OF IMPLEMENTING A TOTAL COST ANALYSIS

Total cost analyses of logistics systems may be accomplished by a series of intuitive probes or by more formal operations research techniques. The most successful efforts often result from a combination of the two approaches.

Intuitive Probes

Questions can be raised which help bring order out of the jumble of information collected concerning a logistics system. Further, the responses which they produce can provide direction for the selective application of more formal, often more expensive operations research techniques. The following list is not exhaustive, but should suggest other, similar questions. Many of these intuitive probes implicitly honor such time-worn shibboleths, rules of thumb, or heuristics as: (1) reduce the greatest element of cost, (2) minimize handling, or (3) maximize freight consolidation. In practice, however, it is often found that the most cost-, service-, or profit-effective systems don't minimize or maximize any single characteristic, but strike a balance between sometimes conflicting rules of thumb.

Priority Attention to the Largest or Fastest Growing Cost Items. One way of developing an analytic strategy is to identify the largest or fastest growing item of cost in the logistics system and attempt to reduce it. (8) **Referring to Table 9–10, what is this cost item resulting from the current operation of the Wonka Company?** (9) **What can we do about it?** (10) **What type of cost trade-offs might result from our cost reduction efforts?**

Measurement Against Standards. System performance can be measured against standards, reflecting both system inputs such as cost budgets, and system outputs, including customer service and other performance standards, competitors' performance, or industry averages. (11) **Which of these are of greatest value?** (12) **Why?**

Cost budgets, to the extent they reflect previous performance, good or bad, make poor standards against which to measure system performance. Only in cases of extreme deviation from budget can they provide direction for subsequent analysis. However, to the extent that they truly reflect the distinctive characteristics of a company's system, cost budgets may have a great deal of surface validity as standards.

Customer service or other performance standards, perhaps derived from observations of competitors' accomplishments, may well be useful measures. This is particularly true where little competition exists on other important dimensions, such as price. If service can differentiate one company's product from another's, the meeting of competitive standards can have an important influence on sales and profits.

Industry averages for logistics costs in relation to sales, to the extent they can be found, are difficult to apply on an absolute basis across companies in an industry. A company with a regional sales territory may have relatively low logistics costs in comparison with one with a national sales territory. Companies at different stages in their growth cycles may have significantly different relative costs, even in the same industry.

Review of the Transport-Inventory Cost Mix.

Early in our discussion, we estimated that U. S. industry in general spends about $3.00 in transportation for every $2.00 that it spends for inventory holding costs, including warehousing, material handling, insurance, taxes, obsolescence, and investment. (See Fig. 1–4). And while actual logistics cost levels in relation to sales may vary a great deal, even between companies competing in the same industry, there is an appealing rationale for the hypothesis that, whatever their actual level, logistics costs in a well-managed operation should tend toward the transport-to-inventory cost relationship described above.

Putting it another way, in industries in which the value of inventory is high and costs of transportation low in relation to sales, it may pay to spend more for transportation in order to reduce inventory costs to the point where inventory cost savings just equal added transportation expenditures. In industries where the reverse is true, it may pay to stock large amounts of inventory in many market-oriented locations to provide acceptable levels of customer service in spite of the use of low-cost, often slower and less dependable means of transportation. (13) **Can you cite examples of industries which typify each of these situations?**

The point is that in each case, adjustments are made in the design of well-managed systems to bring transport and inventory costs into a *total cost equilibrium,* one which produces roughly similar relationships for these two relatively important elements of cost for seemingly dissimilar businesses. And while it may not hold true for all companies, serious departures from the $3.00-to-$2.00 ratio may raise pertinent questions for a total cost analysis. (14) **Does this appear to be a relevant matter for our consultant reviewing Wonka's logistics system?**

Appraisal of Opportunities for Economies of Scale Through Consolidation.

Consolidation of shipments, inventories, or orders can result in significant economies of scale in a logistics system.

In this regard, for example, do customer service policies, or excessive numbers of distribution center stock points, or inventory management practices, preclude the shipment from the plant of vehicle-load shipments which usually carry dramatically lower rates per unit than smaller shipments? If so, is the rationale underlying the practice sound?

For example, in supplying the Syracuse distribution center with machines from Wonka's Cleveland plant, the inventory control model was designed to produce a replenishment order upon the accumulation of machine items for replenishment to Syracuse totalling 30,000 pounds or more, the truckload minimum quantity. If it were allowed to operate without intervention, the model would produce about 17 shipments of machines per year (510,000 pounds sales/30,000 pounds TL quantity), and perhaps only one every seven weeks during periods of slack sales. In response to pressures from the field sales force, the Traffic Department often exercised its authority to order a manual override of the model to ship smaller quantities more frequently from Cleveland to Syracuse. In fact, in the most recent year only two truckload shipments were made; the remaining machines were moved in LTL quantities at a transport premium of $13,500 over truckload transport costs (450,000 pounds × $.03 per pound excess of LTL over TL rates). It was estimated that this practice had helped increase the annual inventory turnover on machines from 3.0 to 3.8 times. **(15) Knowing this, would you recommend future adherence to inventory model rules prescribing truckload shipments for Wonka's Syracuse distribution center? (16) Would your findings lead you to look into replenishment policies for other distribution centers? (17) Using information in Table 9–3, which one would you start with? (18) Why?**

Because of its objective of shipping as many customer orders as possible within 24 hours and 90% of all customer orders within four days after their receipt at a distribution center, the Wonka Company made little attempt to consolidate shipments outbound from distribution points. In fact, however, performance measures indicated that the Company was not meeting its standards but was competitive on this aspect of its operation. Inevitably, this suggested that the Company might be able to hold orders several days longer, achieving larger shipment sizes and lower transport costs to selected centers of customer demand. An analysis of freight rates for for-hire trucking services out of Los Angeles, however, suggested that savings were not great enough to offset additional costs to finance the added working capital needed if shipments were to be delayed an average of even two (1–3) or three (1–5) days. The analysis, for which calculations are shown in Table 16–2, assumed that no sales would be lost because of delayed shipment.

As a result, it was suggested that private trucking might allow Wonka to achieve transport cost savings by shipping to customers in consolidated shipments of 15,000 to 20,000 pounds, with portions of a load destined for delivery to 15 or 20 points. By mapping demand centers and possible delivery routes, much as we did in Chapter 14, it was found that two trucks could deliver about 40% of the annual volume of machine sales

TABLE 16–2. Cost Analysis of the Consolidation of Shipments to Customers
from the Los Angeles Distribution Center,
Warren G. Wonka Manufacturing Company

Costs	Current Method	Use of Common Carrier		Use of Private/ Common Carriage	
		1-to-3-Day Consolidation	1-to-5-Day Consolidation	1-to-3-Day Consolidation	1-to-5-Day Consolidation
Transport:					
Common carrier	$291,600[a]	$262,600	$248,300	$185,500	$151,000
Private truck:					
Fixed	–	–	–	50,000[b]	50,000[b]
Variable	–	–	–	16,600[c]	16,000[c]
Added Working Capital[d]	–	63,000	94,500	63,000	94,500
Total	$291,610	$325,600	$342,800	$315,100	$312,100

[a]On transport volume of 4,820,000 pounds annually of machine having a total value of $26,510,000.

[b]Including equipment depreciation, financing, fixed maintenance, and drivers' wages.

[c]Calculated on the basis of two trips per week per vehicle, 400-mile trip lengths, and a variable operating cost of 20¢ per vehicle-mile.

[d]Calculated on the basis of $126,000 for the value of one day's sales, and an inventory carrying cost of 25% of this value per year.

(roughly 2,000,000 pounds), even taking into account the seasonal nature of machine sales, if shipments were held for consolidation for three days instead of only one. Consolidation of up to five days would allow half, or 2,400,000 pounds, of the Los Angeles outbound freight to be carried in the trucks, because of larger load weights that could be achieved per trip. (19) **The economic analysis of the proposed private trucking operation for Los Angeles is summarized in Table 16–2. What does it suggest to you? (20) How do you account for this result? (21) Are there other factors you would want to take into account in considering the adoption of private trucking and a shipment consolidation program?**

Similarly, economies in material handling might be achieved through the consolidation of warehouse stocks at fewer points. A decision to attempt to gain such economies would be based on the analysis of a number of related costs. Just as in our previous example, economies of scale from the standpoint of the user are somewhat greater when private as opposed to public warehousing is employed. This increases the risk of owning and operating a private warehouse where volumes of freight are sufficient to allow the realization of scale economies.

The variable costs of processing an order may be reduced significantly by centralizing such activities in one or two points on a logistics system. However, an attendant increase in fixed costs associated with long-line rentals for communications, as well as information sending and receiving equipment, usually accompanies such a move.

Review of System Effectiveness in Assorting and Sorting. Closely allied to questions of consolidation are those concerning product handling, typically to meet the needs of related organizational entities for different assortments of components, raw materials, and finished product. It is unrealistic to set an objective of minimizing product handling. If we were to do that, we would attempt to ship each part or machine directly and separately to customers, producing only to customer order regardless of competitive practice.

Mixing points intermediate to plants and distribution centers or customers essentially add another set of handling activities to the logistical sequence. And yet in companies in which each of several multiple plants specializes in the production of certain items in a related line of products sold to customers in common, mixing points may facilitate consolidated shipping, as shown in Figs. 16–4 and 16–5.

More often, handling which does not produce a significant change in product assortment can be questioned. Much of this takes place within the walls of a warehouse or manufacturing facility. It occurs too as a result of a lack of space or of poorly planned facilities. It may be attempted at the wrong point in the logistics system, either far in advance of need or so near the point of ultimate sale that labor and other cost penalties are incurred in the activity.

Package design and item assortments which are convenient for a plant shipping department anxious to get the product "off the dock" but which

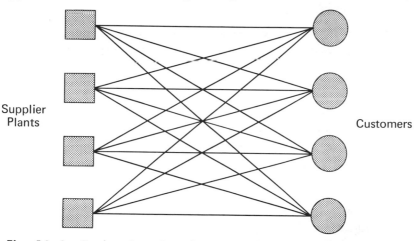

Fig. 16–4. Product flows in a logistics system employing direct plant-to-customer transportation, where company plants do not produce a full line of company products.

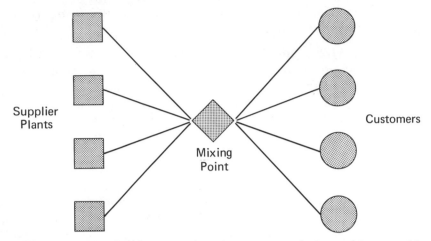

Fig. 16–5. Product flows in a logistics system employing a shipment mixing point between plants and customers.

do not conform to customer desires inevitably produce excessive handling costs for assorting and sorting. To counter this, some companies have attempted to sell standard item assortments based on an identification of repeated demand patterns. For example, sized merchandise such as wearing apparel is purchased in various sizes with predictable frequency, encouraging several manufacturers to pack standard assortments requiring no further handling of individual units after the carton leaves the plant.

Evaluation of Commitment Delay. To what extent does the system allow for the replacement of finished items in inventory with semi-assembled components, each for use in multiple finished items? To what extent does it delay shipment in relation to the receipt of an order? To what extent does it delay the commitment prior to sale of standard components to separately defined stock-keeping units, or even better, stock-keeping unit locations? Provision for commitment delay in a system will reduce costs associated with the carrying of inventory, particularly dead stocks. It must be timed to take into account geographic labor and other cost differences as well as customer buying behavior and needs. It is much more feasible in a firm which has adopted an engineering and development policy of using, when possible, standardized parts in the company's product line.

Provision for Product and Market Differentiation. In our discussion of inventory location strategy, we saw the potential cost reductions inherent in a differentiation of logistics practices for various products, portions of a product line, or markets. To what extent does a system under examination reflect these differences? As we saw, Wonka's logistics system did not, and therein existed a significant opportunity for improvement.

The Wonka situation represents a classic case. Product or market differences are often sufficiently pronounced to lead managements in the direction of differentiated logistics systems for them. But information about portions of a company's product line is often obscured in statistics for the line as a whole. Until product-line items were identified in terms of their relative rates of sale, Wonka's management treated them as part of an amorphous whole, lacking any justification for a differentiated policy.

Provision for System Balance. To what extent are system elements, indicated by their performance, compatible with one another? To illustrate this concept with some examples we have discussed previously, we might cite the use of air freight for shipments whose billing terms to customers were not changed, thereby negating the opportunity provided by air freight for reductions in accounts receivable. Or in Wonka's case, what use would a rapid communications system for customer orders serve in controlling Company inventories if the resulting update of inventory files from such information were to be delayed until after two matching documents had been received by mail from two different sources? Symptoms of system imbalance are accumulations of product, unnecessary information, unsent customer invoices, or idle equipment or personnel.

Analytic Techniques

The wide variety of analytic techniques appropriate for logistics system design can be categorized rather simply. First, all techniques serve either to optimize or simulate a given situation. Second, all of them can be categorized basically as falling into two families, according to the nature of the problem which they address: location or inventory control.

Optimizing Techniques. Typical of the optimizing techniques which we have discussed are linear programming and EOQ inventory models. These techniques provide "the one best" answer, an optimum solution of a problem for which a specific objective function has been stated, most often in terms of minimization of transportation, production, or total costs, or maximization of profit. Further, the economy of problem statement and the power of the mathematical approaches possible for optimizing techniques usually allow their use at a much lower cost for computing time than for simulation models, at least at the current state of the computing art. Problems involving up to several hundred origins and destinations can be solved, for example, by linear programming techniques in just several minutes of computer time.

As we have seen, however, optimizing approaches such as linear programming tend to oversimplify the problem statement. The range of costs and activities which can be included in such analyses is extremely limited. In addition, they require the use of restrictive assumptions. An illustration of this is the assumption of cost linearity regardless of volume in linear programming. Although there are ways of dealing with some of these restrictions, overall they constitute significant compromises for many applications.

Simulation Techniques. In contrast, simulation techniques provide relative freedom of problem expression. Whether dealing with location or inventory problems, simulation techniques emphasize a more detailed, accurate description of the way in which problem elements interact. For example, rather than emphasizing the calculation of the optimum inventory management rules, simulation techniques would attempt to describe the receipt and shipment of orders and related activities in such a way that various inventory management rules could be imposed and the resulting costs and service measures compared under various sets of rules.

Clearly, simulation techniques allow for the inclusion of more types of costs or physical activities in an analytic model. For this reason, they have broad application to a wide range of problems. Inherently, they may have a particular appeal to certain managers who like to know more about the nature of the analytic technique with which they are working. Recent research indicates that the inquisitive manager can learn a great deal about the assumptions inherent in a simulation mode by trying out different sets of policies and comparing results produced by the simulation.

To the extent that the practical application of simulation prevents the explicit description of all elements of a system, certain simplifying assumptions or calculations are included even in large-scale simulations. To the extent they are necessary, they reflect the views of the model builder, views which may or may not reflect reality. Perhaps the biggest drawback of simulation approaches, from the standpoint of some managers, is that they do not provide "the one best" answer. In fact, they neither provide any guarantee that the best answer will be found nor give any indication that the best answer has been found. In a sense, they leave more to the imagination and creativity of the user, a feature that managers may find either attractive or unattractive. A third major problem associated with many large-scale simulations is the large amount of computing time and expense they require for just one iteration of a problem. This can be particularly frustrating if the creative use of the method requires repeated "cuts and tries" at a problem. It imposes the need for the application of heuristics, or alternative-reducing rules of thumb, if simulation is to be carried out within a restrictive computing budget.

Characteristics in Common.   Formalized analytical techniques for logistics system design have certain characteristics in common. Their "results" or "answers" tend to be overrated by managers. They often raise more questions than they answer. For this reason, they both require and contribute to a high level of problem understanding on the part of management. And, in many cases, they may suggest a complete restatement of the original problem.

Any manager who places blind faith in the results produced by either an optimizing or simulation model is a fool.

Fortunately, analytic models demand a great deal of the inquisitive manager. They raise questions as well as answer them. The most significant inputs to most problem analyses are the managerial responses to questions posed by results produced by the model. For example, when our center-of-gravity model suggested to Wonka's management that the Company would not save any logistics costs if it were to move the Cleveland plant to Indianapolis (see Chapter 13), management had to ask itself a number of other questions whose implications were not factored into the model. First, of course, it had to know about the assumptions on which the center-of-gravity calculation was made. Next it was necessary to consider the impact of any potential move on labor and other costs, supplier and customer relationships, employee morale, community relations, and other matters not taken into account in the calculation. In considering such factors, management began to learn about its plant location problem, and gained a deeper understanding of why the plant had not been moved from Cleveland, and why it probably would not be moved in the near future.

Management concerns about some aspect of a company's logistics system typically give rise to a study employing analytic techniques. In the case of the Wonka Company, concerns were for rising logistics costs and declining Company profits. This led to the decision to review the Company's inventory control policy. But in the process of this analysis, the question shifted to one emphasizing inventory location strategy.

Perhaps an even better illustration is provided by the situation confronted by the Bay Area Bakery Company.[3] The question giving rise to the application of linear programming for the analysis of allocations of production from seven bakeries to some eleven major markets in the San Francisco Bay area was, "Should we build a new bakery at San Jose?" After the analysis, the original question was put aside and replaced by questions such as, "Should we reallocate our current production in a more effective pattern?" and "Should we close one or two of our less efficient or less well-located existing bakeries, regardless of whether we elect to build at San Jose?"

A Common Pitfall. A basic, sometimes critical, mistake by managements in the application of analytic techniques to logistics problems is the tendency to compare model output, particularly from optimizing models, with the results produced by the company's current methods of doing things, without regard to whether the results are the best that could be obtained under the current method. Where a significant investment in fixed facilities hangs in the balance, as in the Bay Area Bakery Company case, a decision to invest may be based on an inflated difference between optimum results from the use of an optimum method compared to mediocre results from a non-optimum method. Once the management of Bay Area Bakery, through linear programming, found how it could better use the plant facilities which it had, it realized that the proposed investment in the San Jose bakery could not be justified on a return-on-investment basis. Had it compared possible future results with current uncorrected Company performance and methods, it would have been able to justify an unnecessary investment.

We have discussed the capabilities of optimizing and simulation approaches. What, in fact, has been accomplished in the use of these techniques for logistics system design? This brings us to basic types of problems which various techniques have addressed, those associated with location and inventory.

Location Models. In addition to the location of facilities, location models are used to allocate activities, equipment, or product to various locations, all with the intent of fulfilling some stated objective such as cost minimization or profit optimization. Location models which we have considered range from center of gravity to linear programming models. Whether optimizing or simulating in character, they require certain in-

---

[3] See James L. Heskett, Lewis M. Schneider, Nicholas A. Glaskowsky, Jr., and Robert M. Ivie, *Case Problems in Business Logistics* (New York: The Ronald Press Co., 1973).

formation inputs for their execution. Included among these, you will recall, are all or most of the following:

1. Market demands, by location, stated in terms of units per period of time
2. Warehouse capacities and costs, by location, stated in terms of units of capacity per period of time and cost per unit, respectively
3. Plant capacities and costs, by location, stated in terms of units of capacity per period of time and cost per unit, respectively
4. Transport capacities and costs, by origin–destination pair, stated in terms of units per period of time and cost per unit, respectively
5. Sources of supply, capacities, and costs, by location, stated in terms of units per period of time and cost per unit, respectively
6. A statement of the objective which the model is to fulfill (explicitly stated in the case of optimizing models and implicitly stated for simulations)

Inventory Models.   Inventory models are used to deal with the questions of how much, where, and when individual SKU's should be stocked, typically on an SKUL-by-SKUL basis. In cases where demand exceeds supply, such models may have incorporated in them certain rationing or allocation rules not unlike those used in location models. We have worked with a number of inventory models, using as inputs all or most of the following types of information:

1. Demand levels, stated in terms of units per period of time
2. Order or set-up costs, stated in terms of dollars per order or machine set-up
3. Value per unit of the item for which inventory is controlled
4. Inventory carrying costs, expressed as a percentage of the value of the average inventory on hand over a given period of time
5. The cost of a stock-out, in dollars per unit out of stock
6. The length of the order cycle, stated in terms of a range of days and the probability of an order cycle of given length
7. The probability of demand of varying levels over short periods of time, often expressed in units per day

(22) **Take a moment to look over the two lists of basic inputs to location and inventory models which we have listed. Which inputs do these two families of models hold in common?** (23) **Should this raise any concerns on the part of a manager trying to decide whether to use one or the other type of model for logistics system analysis?** (24) **Do either of these types of models meet the needs of what we would call a comprehensive logistics system design effort?** (25) **Why?**

This brief exercise points up the basic problems of logistics system design efforts employing operations research techniques to date, particularly optimizing techniques for which inputs must be structured and restricted to those which we have listed. It is with such techniques that location theorists and inventory theorists have concerned themselves. Their mutual failure to take a broader view in their work, and in fact to communicate across theoretical boundaries of regional science on the one hand and inventory theory and operations research on the other, has led us to our current dilemma, one in which we have no optimizing technique capable of dealing with comprehensive logistics system design problems. If you doubt this statement, and in any case as a useful review exercise, position the various analytical approaches we have discussed in this part of the book in the matrix in Fig. 16–6. (26) **Do you find that any of the optimizing techniques we have discussed can be positioned equally well beside location and inventory models under the column headed "Optimizing Approaches"?**

Dimensions of an Integrated Optimizing Technique. Several years ago, after a rather exhaustive study of related work to that time, one of us concluded that because of their time-oriented nature, inventory models constituted the cornerstone around which an integrated optimizing technique would be designed if such a technique ever were to be developed.[4]

The use of location and inventory models reflects the two most important cost categories with which logistics is concerned: transportation and inventory. Transportation costs, in combination with volumes of goods in movement, typically have provided the heart of location models regardless of whether the model has employed linear programming, center of gravity, or some other approach. On the other hand, inventory models have been directly concerned with inventory costs.

To date, the most popular approaches to location problems have been spatially (distance) oriented. The center-of-gravity method has emphasized the minimization of ton-miles accumulated between supply and demand points on a system. Where varying rates have applied to the ton-miles involved, a weighted ton-mile measure has been used. Nevertheless, with the exception of Bowersox' use of transit time between a grocery warehouse and retail outlets in an urban setting,[5] the object of center-of-gravity models has been to minimize distance rather than time.

Linear programming models for location invariably have employed

[4] The remainder of this section is based on material in James L. Heskett, "A Missing Link in Physical Distribution System Design," *Journal of Marketing,* October, 1966, pp. 37–41.

[5] Donald J. Bowersox, "An Analytical Approach to Warehouse Location," *Handling & Shipping,* February 1962, pp. 17–20.

	Types of Techniques	
	Optimizing	Simulation
Types of Models Relevant for Logistics	Features: 1. Yield "optimum" results 2. Require many restrictive assumptions 3. Conserve computer time 4. Raise many additional questions	Features: 1. Do not yield recognizable optimum results 2. Require few restrictive assumptions 3. Require extensive computer time 4. Raise many additional questions
cation Models, typical nputs: rket demands, by location rehouse capacities and osts, by location nt capacities and costs, by location ansport capacities nd costs, by origin– estination pair urces of supply, capacities, and costs, by location tement of objective oward which solution is irected		
entory Models, typical puts: mand levels der or set-up costs lue per unit of conrolled SKUL entory carrying costs ck-out costs sts of lost sales der-cycle length and ariability mand level and variability		

Fig. 16–6. Basic categories of analytic techniques for logistics system design.

transportation costs between potential system nodes.[6] To the extent that transportation costs are assumed to be linear in relation to distance, this is a spatial measure. Finally, in the most extensively used models, based on heuristic programming, distance is the factor employed to describe nodal relationships.[7]

In contrast, inventory models have no spatial orientation in the context of the definition given earlier. The relationship of a demand point to its supply point is stated in terms of time for all models allowing uncertainty. Of course, the relevant time is not transit time between inventory locations, but rather the order-cycle time required to complete communications, order preparation, and order shipment, extending from the point of order to the supply point and back again to the point of delivery.

A major preoccupation with the time dimension is characteristic of proponents of both optimization models and simulation models for inventory management.[8]

In total, a physical distribution system can be described in terms of its inventories and their determinants. But this requires a description of inventories in transit as well as at nodal points on a network. Thus, a system of three plants, two distribution warehouses, and ten markets arranged as in Fig. 16–7 can be conceived of as having over 100 inventory "cells" of all or some goods in a product line.

The figure shows only 45 of the more important cells. Momentarily, any one cell or even most cells may be empty. Over time, however, all eventually may contain something. The elimination of a warehouse in Fig. 16–7 would eliminate not one but fifteen inventories and probably affect many of the remaining thirty.

Notice that the network in Fig. 16–7 is dimensionless. Both distance and time are unsatisfactory dimensions for the graphic description of a physical distribution system. The shortcomings of distance as a measure have been discussed. Time as a determinant of inventory levels in various cells is a promising but confusing measure, for it takes on different meanings for inventories in transit, as opposed to those at nodal points.

The level of in-transit inventories is directly influenced, among other

[6] For example, see William J. Baumol and Philip Wolfe, "A Warehouse Location Problem," *Operations Research,* March–April, 1958, pp. 252–63. For a location model employing an extension of linear programming approaches, see Robert J. Atkins and Richard H. Shriver, "New Approach to Facilities Location," *Harvard Business Review,* May–June, 1968, pp. 70–79.

[7] Alfred A. Kuehn and Michael J. Hamburger, "A Heuristic Program for Locating Warehouses," *Management Science,* July, 1963, pp. 643–66.

[8] For examples of the former, see John F. Magee, *Production Planning and Inventory Control* (New York: McGraw-Hill Book Co., 1958), and Robert B. Fetter and Winston C. Dalleck, *Decision Models for Inventory Management* (Homewood, Ill.: Richard D. Irwin, Inc., 1961). An illustration of the latter is provided by Jay W. Forrester, *Industrial Dynamics* (Cambridge and New York: The M.I.T. Press and John Wiley & Sons, Inc., 1961), especially pp. 137–86.

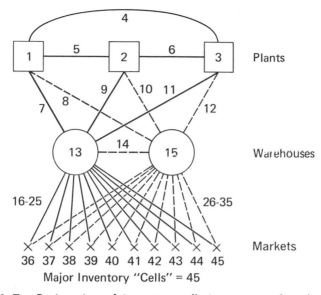

Fig. 16–7. Designation of inventory cells in a system for physically distributing goods from three plants through two distribution warehouses to ten
markets. Reprinted from James L. Heskett, "A Missing Link in Physical Distribution
System Design," *Journal of Marketing*, October, 1966, pp. 37–41, at p. 40;
published by the American Marketing Association.

things, by transit times between a given set of nodes in a system. A
different time period, that required for the completion of an order cycle,
is relevant for a determination of the inventory levels at a nodal point. [9]

The first of these statements requires a re-evaluation of the assumption
implicit in most location models—that in the location of one or more facilities on a network, a minimization of distance weighted by the freight
volume to be moved between relevant existing nodes and the proposed
nodes (least ton-mile points) will somehow lead to minimum transit
times.

As has been pointed out before, where various transport methods can
be employed to traverse a given distance, neither time nor cost necessarily
bears a close relationship to distance.

On the other hand, the relevance of order-cycle times to nodal inventories requires an examination of the implicit assumption (stretched one
step further) that distances between network nodes are somehow related
to order-cycle times for goods ordered and shipped between them. The

[9] Donald J. Bowersox implies this in his article, "Total Information Systems in
Logistics," in J. L. Heskett (ed.), *Business Logistics—Appraisal and Prospect* (Stanford: Stanford University Graduate School of Business, 1965), pp. 109–22.

rationale for the assumption logically might be the direct relationships between distance and transit time on the one hand, and transit time and order-cycle time on the other.

However, time in transit represents roughly only 40% of total order-cycle time.[10] Furthermore, in a sample of means of order-cycle times for two categories of products, carefully measured several years ago, the relationship between order-cycle times and distances for shipments moving from various manufacturers to a distribution center was so low as to be almost meaningless.[11]

One additional argument can be given for the lack of relevance of optimizing location models for the problem of logistics system design. Nearly all location models devised to date have had cost (weighted distance) minimization .as their primary objective.[12] Unless demand is assumed constant regardless of a system design, cost minimization has little to do with profit maximization in a logistics system. In addition, the costs minimized in available spatial models often are not inclusive of all those incurred in logistics activities.

In contrast, the time-oriented inventory model for conditions of uncertainty as a matter of course allows a consideration of order-cycle time and dependability as two of the determinants of demand. By facilitating the consideration of both demand (revenue) and costs, this type of model lends itself more readily than the spatially oriented model to planning with a profit-maximization objective.

These factors lead to a conclusion that concentration on spatial relationships in physical supply and distribution, although the product of nearly a hundred years of effort in the formulation of macroeconomic theory, has not yielded a valid comprehensive approach to the description and analysis of logistics systems.

Rather, such a system can be viewed most productively as a set of actual or potential inventory cells linked and partially determined by time—transit time for those inventory cells in network links, order-cycle time for those cells at network nodes.

Time rather than distance will be the unifying dimension of an inte-

[10] Evidence of this is presented in Richard A. Johnson and Donald D. Parker, "Optimizing Customer Delivery Service with Improved Distribution," *Busness Review*, October, 1961, pp. 38–46, at p. 44; and in Paul R. Stephenson, *Manufacturers' Physical Distribution Service Knowledge and Penalties: An Experimental Analysis*, unpublished Master's thesis deposited in the library of The Ohio State University, 1963.

[11] More specifically, the coefficients of determination were .11 and .16 for drug and candy products, respectively. From unpublished research by James L. Heskett in collaboration with John Rider and Paul R. Stephenson.

[12] One known exception is that reported in Frank H. Mossman and Newton Morton, *Logistics of Distribution Systems* (Boston: Allyn and Bacon, Inc., 1965), pp. 245–56, in which the effect of location on service and hence on demand is explored in the context of a conventional location model.

grated model for helping to plan and control a logistics system. This model, adapted to each company's special needs, will combine elements of a temporally oriented location model with an inventory model to produce information for planning purposes and a set of devices for the control of various elements of a company's logistics system.

STATE OF THE ART IN SYSTEM DESIGN TECHNIQUES

The preceding discussion assumes, of course, that it is desirable concurrently to consider questions regarding both location and inventory policies because of their interrelationships. What do you think about this assumption? Does a so-called optimal inventory policy produce dysfunctional results if it is not developed in the context of the locational configuration of a company's inventories? Does a company's locational arrangement influence the performance of an inventory system? Common sense would tell us that the two basic matters are closely related. But there is no evidence to indicate the seriousness of the lack of coordination in their examination. We don't know what we lose by failing to take a comprehensive approach to logistics system design.

Trend Toward Dynamic Analysis

In recent years, perhaps greater interest has been placed on the development of dynamic as opposed to static analytic techniques. These dynamic techniques measure the impact of current decisions on future results and future decisions by using outputs from one period of time as inputs for the next in an iterative computational procedure.

Dynamic Optimizing Techniques. Dynamic programming [13] has been developed as an extension of linear programming not only to optimize location and other types of decisions for various points in time, but to revise what might appear to be optimal near-term decisions to provide a more optimal long-term result. For example, a linear programming analysis might indicate the desirability of closing a plant or warehouse at the present time. Dynamic programming would assess the future need for the facility, perhaps because of increasing demand levels for future periods of time, and take into account the costs of closing and subsequently opening the facility, before presenting the cost implications *of a current decision.* Thus, dynamic programming is particularly useful in

[13] For a detailed general exploration of dynamic programming, see R. E. Bellman and S. E. Dreyfus, *Applied Dynamic Programming* (Princeton, N. J.: Princeton University Press, 1962), and Ronald A. Howard, "Dynamic Programming," *Management Science,* January, 1966, pp. 317–48.

considering the timing of decisions, invariably involving location in a logistical context, as we saw in reviewing Ballou's work.[14]

Dynamic Simulation Techniques. Dynamic simulation techniques describe rather than optimize system performance over time, incorporating decision rules determined by the user. They may range from models constructed for a special purpose to general-purpose problem-describing devices. Ballou's simulation of the interrelationships between inventory management programs at two or more levels in a channel of distribution is typical of the first of these.[15] Forrester's development of "industrial dynamics," including modelling rules, special-purpose language, and even a specially developed computer, is an example of the broader application of dynamic simulation.[16]

Perhaps the most comprehensive example of a dynamic simulation model is one designed recently by Bowersox and others, called LREPS (Long-Range Environmental Planning Simulator).[17] Among other features, this model allows a decision maker either to describe his system in the following terms or to assume changes resulting from managerial decisions along these dimensions, among others: order characteristics, product mix, new product introduction policies, the mix of customers served by the system, the location of facilities, varying echelons in a distribution channel through which various shipments may pass, inventory management policies, transportation methods, communication methods, and material-handling methods. The model measures the effectiveness of any combination of descriptors or decisions in terms of overall cost and customer service levels. In common with its sister simulation approaches, LREPS provides the richest output detail of any analytic device developed to date. Perhaps unavoidably, however, it currently shares the shortcomings outlined earlier for all simulation techniques, including cumbersome, large data input requirements and relatively high user expense in addition to the inability to pinpoint the one best answer.

Combined Approaches

Thus far we have concentrated on comprehensive approaches to logistics system design, incorporating both location and inventory models, by

[14] For a more detailed discussion of dynamic programming, see Ronald H. Ballou, *Business Logistics Management* (Englewood Cliffs, N. J.: Prentice-Hall, Inc., 1973), pp. 259–66.

[15] Ronald H. Ballou, *Multi-Echelon Inventory Control for Interrelated and Vertically Integrated Firms* (Columbus: The Ohio State University, unpublished dissertation, 1965).

[16] Forrester, *op. cit.*

[17] See Donald J. Bowersox, "Planning Physical Distribution Operations With Dynamic Simulation," *Journal of Marketing,* January, 1972, pp. 17–25.

means of either optimizing or simulation approaches. Is it possible that an approach combining optimization and simulation can provide advantages of each, especially comprehensive system design capability at a more reasonable cost? Our consultant set out to test this idea at the Wonka Company.

A SYSTEM DESIGN FOR WONKA

The overall effort of our consultant, working with Wonka personnel, involved the formulation of the study objectives, the organization of a viable working group combining talents both internal and external to the Wonka organization, the design and use of analytical devices, the reporting of findings and recommendations, and the conditioning of the environment at Wonka for the effective implementation of results.

Objectives of the Study

The first major objective of the study was to provide answers, as of one point in time, to the following questions:

1. What form of order-processing system and information-processing procedures, in terms of general characteristics described by time lags of various types, should be utilized by the company?
2. What type of inventory control policy should be used, in terms acceptable to the company's current computer programs?
3. Should the inventory control policy be applied differently to different products in the line?
4. Which products should be stocked at varying locations in the system?
5. What form of transportation, in terms of its general characteristics, should be used?
6. How many warehouses should be operated?
7. Where should they be located?
8. To what extent should each plant and warehouse be utilized, in terms of throughput?
9. What warehouses should be supplied from each plant?

Second, the study was to result in the creation of a comprehensive set of computer models which could be used by company personel in the continuing analysis of Wonka's logistics system.

Third, certain executives at Wonka were to be provided with a sufficiently good understanding of the computer models to enable them to make intelligent decisions based on their output.

The timetable established for the study is shown in Fig. 16–8. It was estimated that the study would cost Wonka $85,000 in consultants' fees

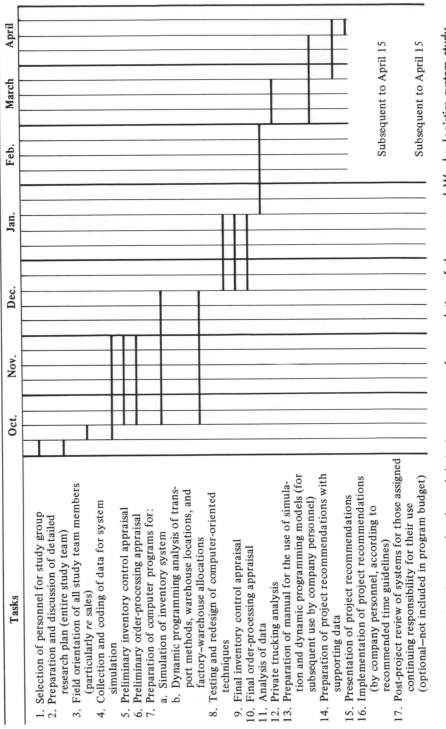

Fig. 16–8. Suggested tasks and their time sequence for completion of the proposed Wonka logistics system study.

and expenses and purchased computer time, as well as 15 man-months of executive and clerical time contributed by Wonka's personnel.

Establishment of a Working Committee

In order to facilitate coordination in the necessary tasks of collecting and analyzing information as well as implementing results, the consultant established a Working Committee for the project to include at various times himself and two other senior analysts from the consulting organization and the following personnel from the Wonka organization: Vice President, Administration; Assistant to the Vice President, Manufacturing; Manager of Field Sales Relations; Managers of Distribution, Operations Research, Order Processing, and Data Processing; and the Traffic Manager. It was agreed that the consultant would co-chair the Working Committee with the Vice President, Administration.

Design of Analytic Devices

The consultants' developmental work led to the creation of a package of computer programs called WOPACK. WOPACK was composed of two major components, WINSIM and WOLOGA.

WINSIM.   The first of these was a set of computer programs which simulated the company's current and alternative inventory control methods. Called WINSIM (short for Warehouse Inventory Simulation Model), it was designed to simulate, on a warehouse-by-warehouse basis:

1. The daily receipt, fulfillment, and diverting of customer orders
2. The preparation, transmission, production, and shipment of stock orders
3. The information flows, in terms of time lags required for each stage, required for the updating of central inventory records
4. The preparation of monthly forecasts of demand at headquarters

In all simulation work required to make an initial analysis of Wonka's inventory policies, a 180-operating day period was used. A computer system diagram for WINSIM is shown in Fig. 16–9.

By using the model and its outputs, information for management decision making could be obtained by testing the effects of changes in inventory policy and order-processing procedures on the level of inventory.

WINSIM was designed to help management answer questions such as the following:

1. What form of order-processing system and information-processing

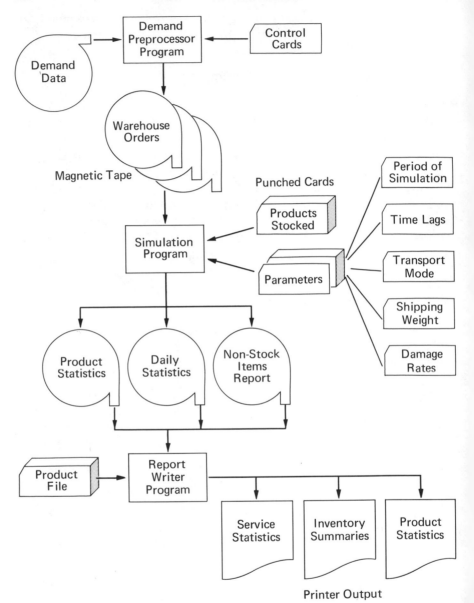

Fig. 16–9. Computer system diagram for warehouse inventory simulation (WINSIM), prepared for the Wonka logistics system study.

procedures, in terms of general characteristics described by time lags of various types, should be utilized by the Company?

2. What type of inventory control policy should be used, in terms acceptable to the Company's current computer programs?

3. Should the inventory control policy be applied differently to different products in the line?
4. Which products should be stocked at varying locations in the system?

WOLOGA. Based on the results of the analysis made possible by WINSIM, certain outputs could be used as inputs to the second of the major parts of WOPACK, called WOLOGA, a modified linear programming model.

WOLOGA, a three-stage linear programming model fashioned along lines developed for the Baumol-Wolfe model,[19] could allocate customer demand to both distribution centers and plants in either an optimizing or simulation mode. It used as inputs information regarding the effects of inventory policy on warehouse allocation (from WINSIM), the demand for Wonka's products registered by several hundred demand centers in the United States, the capacity and production cost at the plant site, the warehousing costs at each plant and public warehouse, and various types of transportation costs.

WOLOGA dealt with the following types of questions:

1. What form of transportation, in terms of its general characteristics, should be used?
2. How many warehouses should be operated?
3. Where should they be located?
4. To what extent should each warehouse be utilized, in terms of throughput?
5. Should additional plants be opened?
6. What warehouses should be supplied from each plant?
7. Should the existing plant be closed?

WINSIM and WOLOGA were designed to be used in tandem, with outputs from WINSIM used as inputs for WOLOGA and output information from WOLOGA recycled back through WINSIM to provide even better overall system design results. For example, if an effective inventory control policy identified by means of WINSIM was one which utilized truck transportation, but the subsequent use of WOLOGA indicated that at the relative cost of truck and rail alternatives, the use of rail produced lower costs, then WINSIM could again be used to develop the best possible inventory control system built around the use of rail transportation for all or some of the shipments. Thus, major elements of the WOPACK package could be used as shown in Fig. 16–10.

(27) **What are the basic advantages of combining an inventory simulator with a location optimizing device in this manner? (28) What are possible weaknesses of this device?**

19 Described on pp. 440 through 443.

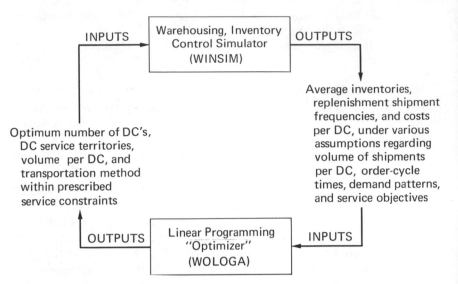

Fig. 16–10. Elements of the WOPACK simulator–optimizer package and their relationship, Wonka logistics system study.

Reporting of Findings and Recommendations

Major findings and recommendations resulting from the study included the desirability of:

1. Consolidating inventories held in distribution centers
2. Taking steps to reduce the inventory update cycle
3. Making a basic change in the forecasting model
4. Placing a moratorium on various ordering customs such as "shopping" among adjacent distribution centers by salesmen and "manual overrides" on the computer system for replenishing distribution centers from the plant
5. Creating a dual distribution system similar to that described in Chapter 13 for both machines and parts
6. Initiating private trucking operations for shipments of components inbound to the Cleveland plant
7. Staggering sales commission deadlines
8. Reorganizing for the continuing management of logistics activities

Consolidation of Inventories. The use of the WOLOGA linear programming model helped Wonka's study team identify optimum DC territories even before any other changes were made in the logistics system. The analysis was based on outputs from the WINSIM warehouse inventory simulator which provided estimates of the relationship between the volume of sales through a DC (a function of the number of DC's operated) and inventory carrying costs. It suggested that cost reductions could be achieved by closing the Pittsburgh, Buffalo, and Philadelphia

DC's and consolidating inventories formerly held in those facilities into stocks held at Cleveland, Syracuse, Baltimore, and Newark. The nature of the trade-off which produced the cost savings included major cost reductions of $205,000 in primary (plant-to-DC) transportation cost and $1,490,000 in inventory carrying (including DC warehousing) costs. Offset against this were increases of $1,075,000 in secondary (DC-to-customer) transportation costs and $185,000 in order-processing costs (including customer-to-DC telephone communications), with the latter resulting largely from a decision by the study team to recommend that increased order communications charges for certain dealer–customers under the new configuration be absorbed by Wonka. (29) **How do you explain these changes in system costs?**

No alternative locations to the 13 remaining DC's were found which produced significantly improved logistics cost performance. The net result of the proposed action was estimated to be a $435,000 reduction in system costs. Figures for inventory carrying cost savings were obtained by once again simulating costs under the new 13-DC system by means of the WINSIM model.

Reduction of Invoicing and Inventory Update Cycles. In the past, customer invoicing and the update of DC inventory records had to wait for a lengthy, undependable process (described on pages 520–25), which culminated in the matching of salesmen's order copies and warehouse shipping documents (bills of lading) at the Cleveland office. This not only produced a larger-than-necessary figure for accounts receivable, but also great inaccuracies in the DC inventory records resulting from the fact that actual shipments from DC inventories typically took place at least a week before items shipped were deducted from inventory records.

It was decided that a new procedure, which would disconnect the billing and inventory update cycles, should be tested. Basically, invoices would be prepared upon receipt of the salesmen's order copies at Cleveland. Inventories would be updated upon receipt of DC shipping documents at Cleveland. Thus, customers would be charged at the appropriate discount rate suggested by the size of the order. This procedure assumed that: (1) what was ordered would be shipped and (2) shipments would be received by the customer in roughly the same period of time required for the transmittal of salesmen's orders to Cleveland, processing, and mailing of bills to customers. By reducing accounts receivable by roughly five days under this procedure, Wonka could save $300,000 in interest expense and more than defray added costs for adjusting incorrect invoices.

Results of a test of this procedural change with the WINSIM simulator were remarkable. It was found, first of all, that a reduction in order-cycle (inventory-update) time of about five days either would allow a

30% reduction in carrying charges for safety stocks at all DC's or, more important to the functioning of the overall system with the existing forecasting and inventory control models, it would increase line-item inventory coverage on both machine and parts "A" (highest sales volume) items to nearly 100%. Similar coverage levels on machine and parts "B" items would be increased to 97% and 95%, respectively.

Revision of Forecasting Model. The forecasting model employed by Wonka, described in greater detail in Chapter 11, called for a prediction of demand based on the following formula:

$$\text{Max [Forecast demand} + (\text{Service coefficient} \times \text{MAD})]$$

where max represented the period for which demand was being forecast (in Wonka's case the period represented by both an order cycle and an order interval), the forecast demand represented the forecast for the previous period, the service coefficient (.98) indicated the level of coverage (98%) desired for items ordered from the DC inventory, and the MAD (mean absolute deviation) value represented the deviation of actual and expected demand levels for previous periods of time.

In tests with various alternatives, using the WINSIM simulator, it was found that a change in this model to:

$$\text{Max(Forecast demand}) + (\text{Service coefficient})\text{MAD}$$

produced a more predictable level of coverage and facilitated a reduction in safety stocks while maintaining the coverage level desired by Wonka. **(30) Comparing the two models, why do you think the second of the two would be more desirable?**

The effect of this change was to separate the values used for determining the inventory coverage to be provided as a buffer against deviations in the stock order cycle and interval times (max) and the inventory coverage to be provided as a buffer against deviations from the expected demand level (MAD) during these time periods. Because the current model multiplied the max figure, expressed in months, by the service coefficient and the MAD value, expressed in units, as well as the forecast demand value for any given period, it increased inventory levels far beyond those which were required to provide the level of coverage indicated by the service coefficient alone (98%).

As a result, it was estimated by means of WINSIM that savings in inventory carrying costs resulting from this adjustment would approximate another $250,000 per year.

Changes in Order Entry and Inventory Management Procedures. The uncertain availability of inventories at various DC's under the existing system had had two results: (1) salesmen "shopped" their orders until they found a DC with the desired items in stock, with a resulting inaccuracy of demand figures for DC forecasting purposes, and (2) sales managers requested that "manual overrides" be inserted into the automatic replenishment system for DC inventories, to provide extra quantities of safety stock for which chronic out-of-stock conditions existed. Both were indicative of a lack of confidence in the existing system. Assuming that the uncertainties of supply availability could largely be eliminated under the proposed methods, a moratorium was placed both on "shopping" and manual overrides, at least until the new system could be proven dependable in performance.

Creation of a Dual Distribution System. The dual distribution system described for machines (see page 456) was proposed to Wonka's management. Expected savings, based on a DC-by-DC analysis, were estimated to be $1,157,000, reduced to $987,000 by the concurrent reduction in the number of DC's from 16 to 13. This suggested that additional savings could be achieved by extending the concept to parts distribution as well. (31) **Do you think that total dollar savings from a dual distribution system for parts, for which turnover ranged from .8 times per year for "B" items to 3.5 times per year for "A" items, would exceed that for machines?** (32) **Would your reply be the same if prospective savings for parts distribution were calculated on the basis of savings per dollar of sales?** (33) **Why?**

Applying the concepts discussed in Chapter 13 to the parts distribution problem, it was found that cost trade-offs for "B" parts items produced an additional $862,000 in savings, as shown in Table 16–3. In comparison with savings for "B" machine SKU's, the dual parts distribution system produced greater savings in the costs of processing partially filled orders and smaller savings on other cost items. (34) **Why?**

Initiation of Private Trucking. The analysis of opportunities for savings which could be achieved by initiating a private trucking program for the pickup of component parts moving inbound to Cleveland, for which information is presented in Chapter 14, produced a range of possibilities. If all 15,000 shipments could be moved in a private truck fleet with pickups scheduled for various areas and totally smoothed for each day of the week, the transportation bill for incoming components could be reduced from $671,000 to only $136,350, with six trucks picking up a total of 60 shipments on each of 250 operating days of the year under a highly organized system allowing high-density pickups. (35) **How does this compare with the results of the analysis you prepared in Chapter 14?**

TABLE 16–3. Prospective Savings Under Dual Distribution System for "B" Machine and Parts SKUL's, 13-DC Configuration, Warren G. Wonka Manufacturing Company

Cost Category	Changes in Costs From Present to Proposed Program		
	Machines	Parts	Total
Transportation:			
Rail CL/truck TL	-$ 466,000	-$ 2,000	-$ 468,000
Truck LTL	+ 239,000	- 30,000	+ 209,000
Air	+ 981,000	+ 60,000	+ 1,041,000
Inventory carrying:			
In-transit stocks	- 77,000	- 6,000	- 83,000
Cycle and speculative stocks	0	0	0
Safety and dead stocks	- 1,281,000	- 385,000	- 1,666,000
Packing	- 53,000	- 6,000	- 59,000
Order processing:			
Completely filled orders	+ 77,000	+ 360,000	+ 437,000
Partially filled orders	- 250,000	- 885,000	- 1,135,000
Extra machine and line costs*	+ 42,000	+ 42,000	+ 84,000
Contribution on lost sales	- 249,000	- 10,000	- 259,000
Totals	-$1,037,000	-$862,000	-$1,899,000

*Assuming such extra costs are allocated equally to machines and parts.

This ideal situation was felt by Wonka's executives to be unrealistic because of: (1) the strong desire of some suppliers to use their own equipment, (2) the difficulty of regimenting suppliers to have their shipments ready on a given day of each week, and (3) the economic undesirability of investing in trucks to meet shipment peaks rather than some relatively constant base volume of movement. As a result, a plan was devised whereby seven trucks would be acquired to pick up a total of 45 shipments per day on a low-density basis with not all suppliers participating in the program. It was assumed that the remaining shipments, 3,750 out of the total of 15,000 would move on Monday or Friday either by for-hire transportation or private trucking methods, essentially outside the organized program for the remaining suppliers. Under this alternative, Wonka's annual private trucking costs would be $164,800 and additional transport charges $167,800, together representing an annual cost of $332,600, or some $338,400 less than current transportation costs on inbound components.

Staggering of Sales Commission Dates. At the time of the study, all sales commissions were computed on the basis of orders received from salesmen by the end of each month. As a result, 40% of all orders were received for processing during the last week of each month. To even out the order-processing burden, commission dates were staggered, with one-fourth of the sales force assigned an "end-of-month" date corresponding to each of the four Fridays during the month. Although no reductions in order-processing personnel or explicit costs could be credited to this action, it was thought that information and processing accuracy would improve significantly as a result of the corresponding reduction in peak loads and end-of-period pressures on the order-processing and accounting departments.

Reorganization. To help improve the implementation of change and the continuing successful coordination of logistics activities at Wonka, the job of Distribution Manager was shifted from the group headed by the Vice President, Marketing Services to that of the Vice President, Administration. (You may wish to refer back to the existing organization chart shown in Fig. 9–5.) In addition, planning and advisory responsibilities regarding not only distribution centers and customer service, but also traffic and transportation, inventory control, and order processing were assigned to the Distribution Manager. Because of uncertainties about future possibilities for further decentralization and increased emphasis on profit centers as opposed to cost centers in Wonka's organization, so-called "line," operating, or action responsibilities for logistics activities were not reassigned. (36) **Will this organizational arrangement accomplish its missions?** (37) **How would your recommendations regarding reorganization differ from these?** (38) **Why?**

Further Efforts. As part of its report, the study team recommended that further work be commissioned to test the effect of varying carrying cost and alpha forecast factors for different categories of products.

Finally, a "grease chart" was prepared to provide guidance for Wonka's distribution personnel in updating sales, cost, and other inputs used in the WOLOGA and WINSIM models. It indicated the frequency with which various types of data would have to be revised to keep current the data bases on which the models operated. As it was pointed out in the report, this was one of the most critical elements in the continuing use and value of the study.

SUMMARY

With the continuing development of analytic techniques, comprehensive logistics system analyses are becoming more and more feasible. These techniques can be categorized as location or inventory models, utilizing either optimization or simulation methods. To date, no truly comprehensive model spanning location and inventory problems has been developed which relies solely on optimizing techniques. The greatest progress has been made in the simulation of logistics systems of larger and larger scope.

Even with the availability of a growing portfolio of techniques, effective system analysis still relies on a combination of good common sense and the knowledge of when more formal approaches will and will not work. The comprehensive approach to Wonka's logistics system presented in this chapter has provided a good example of this combination. In total, it offered Wonka the prospect of near-term savings of $2,922,000 per year, representing a potential 15.1% reduction in logistics costs. In addition, it introduced the Company to methods for the systematic long-term planning of logistics activities and helped restructure the organization to accomplish it.

PART FIVE

SYSTEM

MANAGEMENT

If the decade of the 1960's was devoted to system design in the field of business logistics, the 1970's will see primary emphasis on the effective management of logistics systems. This is why we have attempted to extend our discussion of design and management in this Second Edition.

The total cost concept is great in theory. However, its implementation relies on people engaged in the day-to-day management of ongoing activities, on a form of organization which facilitates the achievement of the system's mission, and on a performance measurement and control program which informs managers and motivates them to manage in step with the system's mission.

In Part Five, we consider first some activity areas which require primary emphasis on day-to-day management. These are the areas of packaging and material handling, warehousing, and traffic and transportation (including in-company transportation).

Must the action as opposed to the advisory responsibilities for all logistics activities be grouped under one individual or organizational entity? Under what conditions are they most effectively centralized and decentralized? On what does the organizational form depend? These are issues to be considered in our discussion of organization.

An effective performance measurement and control program can help overcome organizational inconsistencies or difficulties, contribute to employee and managerial morale, and provide an important vehicle for meeting system goals. The implementation of such programs will receive primary attention in a growing number of organizations. It will be important to consider what will be measured, how it will be measured, and how the information will be used, in much the manner discussed in Chapter 21.

Finally, much of the real excitement in and fascination with logistics stems from its interorganizational character. The management of logistics activities is carried on to a great extent across organizational boundaries. It involves the coordination of activity among suppliers, transport carriers, customers, and other organizational entities to an extent that no other functional area of business can match. In a sense, it involves the "management" of people in other organizations. This topic, which offers perhaps the most promising opportunity for the future in logistics, occupies much of our closing chapter. The evolution of logistics management has just begun; as with all adolescents, its greatest excitement, opportunities, and rewards lie ahead.

17

Packaging and Material Handling

We have combined our discussion of packaging and material handling in part because of their close interrelationship and in part because we agree with Albl that "though the function of protection is essential, packaging to reduce distribution costs is the field which can yield the greater harvest." [1]

For example, it has been estimated that costs of packaging currently fall within the range of $21 to $24 billion annually for materials, equipment, and labor. [2] Material-handling activities by shippers, carriers, warehousemen, and receivers easily exceed $40 billion annually. In contrast, U. S. railroads and truck lines pay out in excess of $350 million annually in claims settlements. If you assume, as does one source, [3] that only 25% of all damage ever results in a claim, that only about half of all claims are paid, and that every dollar of paid claim represents $8 in hidden costs for collection (of which the carrier incurs $5 and the shipper $3), then total costs associated with package failure are as much as $4.5 billion annually. Of this amount, carriers bear $1.75 billion and shippers $2.75 billion, exclusive of sales which the latter may have lost because of loss and damage.

These subjects have another important element in common. Along

[1] Michael O. Albl, "Packaging for Total Advantages in Physical Distribution," *Handling & Shipping*, December, 1965, p. 36.

[2] For example, see *Modern Packaging* Encyclopedia Issues (December) for various years.

[3] "Management Takes a New Look at Packing, Shipping, and Loss Through Damage," in-company publication of Sealed Air Corp., 1970.

with computer technology, they represent the areas of logistics in which the greatest technological advances have been made in recent years. These advances provide a staggering array of alternatives, in terms of capabilities and costs, which we must learn to use effectively. In this sense, the engineers have developed the state of their art to a much greater degree than have managers concerned with packaging and material handling.

Our discussion is centered around packaged freight and bulk freight, and the technologies and management problems generally associated with each. This is nothing more than a convenient scheme for discussion, although an increasingly important decision in many firms concerns the appropriate point in the distribution process to convert from bulk to packaged form.

PACKAGED FREIGHT

Our discussion of packaging and material handling for packaged freight assumes a broad definition for the latter, that of all freight moving in containers which are not self-powered. In this sense, a package can range from a box for eight ounces of breakfast cereal to an 8 × 8 × 40-foot container for 60,000 pounds of otherwise unpackaged product. This relieves us of the academic exercise of having to differentiate packages, packaging materials, and shipping containers.

Packaging

There is tangible evidence that packaging technology has advanced at a rapid rate in recent years. Of particular note are the adoption of transparent materials with adhesive qualities for "skin packaging" of small, irregularly sized items; packages which can contain controlled atmosphere for preserving fresh and processed foods; designs which utilize the full structural strength of multilayered paper; and molded polyethylene forms for inner packaging. In a related area, package printing technology has advanced to the point that, if we wished, we could produce a clear advertising message or brand mark on the surface of the yolk of a soft-boiled egg. These are but a few of the many innovations described regularly in trade magazines. As a result, it is not surprising that at least one study found that packaging costs as percentages of gross sales for manufacturers of consumer goods declined from 27.9% in 1954 to 18.6% in 1967.[4]

[4] "What Does Packaging Really Cost?," *Modern Packaging*, May, 1967, pp. 90–93.

But what about the development of management for packaging, and especially for package design? Many references suggest that it has failed to keep pace in an area requiring a good understanding of a number of cost trade-offs and cross-functional relationships.

Package Design. The wide variety of considerations that must be taken into account in package design suggest the complexity of the task of managing the process. We have set forth a number of such considerations in Fig. 17–1. The importance of each of these in a given situation will vary with such matters as the characteristics of a product, the market to which it is sold, and the channels of distribution through which it is passed, as well as the cost and performance of various packaging alternatives.

Considerations for Engineering. Perhaps the most important role of package engineering is in providing an initial screen for the myriad of possible alternatives for management consideration. This essentially is embodied in considerations of strength, the amount and cost of material per unit of packaged product, the effect on production costs, and the degree to which special product needs are accommodated. At this early stage in the process, the possibility of product redesign to make more feasible certain desirable packaging alternatives should not be ruled out.

Considerations for Purchasing. Purchasing considerations will focus on costs for a given level of performance. For this reason, the purchasing function will be interested in the possibilities of standardizing package sizes around a relatively few basic dimensions, especially if the price of materials per unit is a function of the number of units of a given size purchased. In certain organizations buying products for resale without repackaging them, the merchandising (buying) group requires shipment in cartons of specified, standardized sizes for compatibility with subsequent internal storage and handling methods. The degree to which package design facilitates transportation and storage will influence transportation and warehousing costs and space needs for purchased products. For example, items which can be "nested" inside one another may well be left unpackaged until a later point in the distribution process.

The shape of a package will influence its cost. For example, the cost of a slotted, corrugated box is roughly proportional to the amount of box board which it requires. Because the amount required for a six-sided box is computed in terms of twice the length times depth plus twice the width times depth plus four times the length times width (to accommodate overlap on the top and bottom of a top-opening box), the most

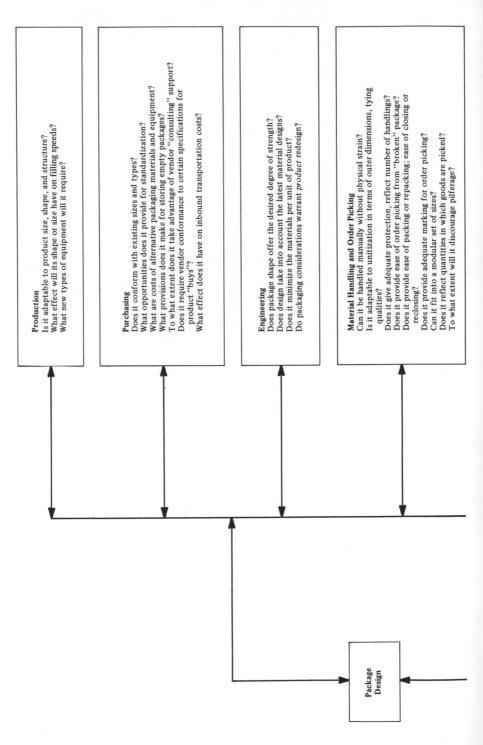

Production
Is it adaptable to product size, shape, and structure?
What effect will its shape or size have on filling speeds?
What new types of equipment will it require?

Purchasing
Does it conform with existing sizes and types?
What opportunities does it provide for standardization?
What are costs of alternative packaging materials and equipment?
What provisions does it make for storing empty packages?
To what extent does it take advantage of vendor "consulting" support?
Does it require vendor conformance to certain specifications for product "buys"?
What effect does it have on inbound transportation costs?

Engineering
Does package shape offer the desired degree of strength?
Does design take into account the latest material designs?
Does it minimize the materials per unit of product?
Do packaging considerations warrant *product* redesign?

Material Handling and Order Picking
Can it be handled manually without physical strain?
Is it adaptable to unitization in terms of outer dimensions, tying qualities?
Does it give adequate protection, reflect number of handlings?
Does it provide ease of order picking from "broken" package?
Does it provide ease of packing or repacking; ease of closing or reclosing?
Does it provide adequate marking for order picking?
Can it fit into a modular set of sizes?
Does it reflect quantities in which goods are picked?
To what extent will it discourage pilferage?

Package Design

Storage

Does it have good stacking qualities, in terms of strength, dimensions, and surface properties?
Does it conserve "cube" as much as possible?
Does it require special storage "hardware"?

Marketing—Customer

Does it conform to customer needs regarding resale, in terms of art, information, ease of display and access to contents, and size?
Does it include special use instructions?
Does it reflect customer buying habits regarding quantity and assortment?
Do its contents conform with discount price quantities?
Does it conform with customer capabilities regarding storage, handling?
Can it be disposed of easily?
Do packing considerations warrant redesign of *promotional* campaigns?

Traffic—Transportation

Does it maximize the density of the product in packaged form?
Does it protect the product from sources of damage?
Is it designed to obtain the most advantageous rate?
Does it reflect the "lowest common denominator" of carrier damage experience?
Does it suggest a change in carrier methods?
Does it reflect dimensions of carrier equipment?
Does it provide easy return of empties?
Does it provide adequate marking for shipment, handling in transit?
To what extent will it discourage pilferage?

Marketing—Ultimate Consumer

Does its size, convenience, and storability in use reflect consumer needs?
Will it "sell itself" (for self-service channels)?
Does it include sufficient instructions regarding product use?
Can it be disposed of or reused easily?
Does the package itself have utility for the ultimate consumer?
Will it be acceptable from an environmental standpoint?

Fig. 17–1. The many faces of package design: a sampling of the more important considerations in the design of product packages.

economical box, from the standpoint of materials, will have greater depth than length or width.

Manufacturers of packaging materials and equipment are sources of a great amount of free, if potentially biased, consulting advice often channelled through the purchasing engineering personnel in an organization.

Considerations for Production. The design of package size, shape, access, and closure characteristics may affect both the need for investment in new packaging equipment and the unit cost of filling packages on the production line. Automation has been introduced to such a degree in most packaging processes that considerations regarding the impact on labor morale and relations are not as important as they once were in many situations.

Considerations for Storage. The strength of a package, as well as the way in which it is stacked, will determine, for example, the height to which it can be stacked. By adopting new packages, many companies have found that they can stack to heights 50% or more higher than previously, increasing the weight and quantity of product stored per square foot of available storage space. Similarly, the shape of the package will determine cubic storage requirements; for example, a case of six rectangular cans occupies only 76% of the cube of one containing the more traditional round cans. However, in the packaging of antifreeze, one manufacturer found that some of the savings in handling and storage from the use of square cans had to be traded for a 5% package cost increase per unit of product as well as a slower filling rate for rectangular cans.[5]

If, to facilitate stacking, racks or other hardware items to share the stress of stack weight are required, this essentially represents a trade-off with package design. This is particularly true in the design of the package which is the controlling factor, the "weakest" package in a line of packages and products stored in a particular facility.

Considerations for Material Handling and Order Picking. The ease and economy with which a package allows products to be handled and picked relates to the methods used for each. By necessity or poor design, items are handled differently even within a given organization. A package handled by mechanical means at one point and manual means at another must not exceed the weight limits for the most restricted, in this

[5] D. B. Carmody, "The Impact of Packaging on Physical Distribution," in *Packaging's Role in Physical Distribution*, Management Bulletin No. 77 (New York: American Management Association, 1966), pp. 1–6.

case manual, method. Further, the protection required by the product may be a function of the number of times as well as the methods by which it is handled.

Of particular interest for material handling is the potential for unitizing the package by handling it simultaneously with a number of units of the same or other products, for example, by handling them stacked on pallets. Here, package dimensions as well as strength are important. Perfect cubes do not lend themselves to palletization without the introduction of some means of "tying" the stack of such items together. Differences in the two horizontal dimensions of a package permit an interlocking of items in a pallet load. However, unless these dimensions are correct proportionally, they may lead to an overlap of packages at the edge of the pallet, a likely source of subsequent damage, or to the need for "dead" unused space in the center of the pallet load. (1) **Turn to Fig. 17–3, on page 590. Which of the pallet patterns and package dimensions shown there meet all of these requirements?** Also, heavier and larger cartons require less overlap in unitized loading to achieve a given level of load stability.

Modular packaging has been explored by many organizations and adopted by a few for material handling and transportation. It is a concept closely related to unitization, for, as shown in Fig. 17–2, it allows the combination of packages of different modular dimensions in the same efficient handling or transportation unit, in this case a pallet quantity. It involves standardization around a few carton sizes as well. But the complexities of product-line item sizes, the need to adjust the traditional shipping quantities to the number that will fit into a modular package size, and the need to convince customers that it is feasible to sell a product in such "odd" lots has limited the implementation of modular packaging to a few products such as phonograph records. (2) **Why do phonograph records lend themselves to this concept?**

Order-picking efficiency, in terms of speed, cost, and accuracy, is a function of the adequacy and clarity of marking; the ease with which a package can be opened and selected items removed in "broken case," small, or unusual quantities; and the ease with which a package can be repacked, closed, and reused for handling or shipment.

Many organizations fail to take into account potential savings in order picking by adapting the package to quantities in which goods are ordered. For example, Friedman cites an example in which, by packaging its products in standard packs of six instead of twelve garments, one sportswear manufacturer was able to raise the proportion of items picked in standard quantities (without breaking the package) from 60% to 86%. This change, along with a change in pricing policy to encourage purchases in the new "standard" quantity, enabled the manufacturer to

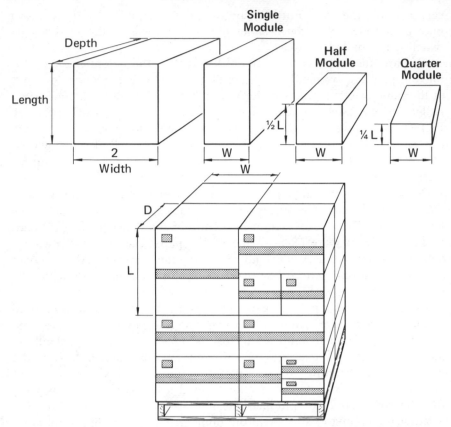

Fig. 17–2. An example of a modular system of packaging. *Source:* Walter F. Friedman, "The Role of Packaging in Physical Distribution," *Transportation & Distribution Management,* February, 1968, pp. 34–39.

implement a highly mechanized distribution center which previously was not considered feasible.[6]

Finally, in direct contrast to the desire for ease of access which a package may provide is the concern for the extent to which it may discourage "unauthorized order picking" (pilferage).

Considerations for Traffic and Transportation. Costs for transporting various products, as determined by carrier rate structures, often reflect the density (weight per cubic measure) of the packaged product, the quantity which can be carried in a vehicle load, and the degree to which the package affords protection from damage and pilferage. Additional

---

[6] Walter F. Friedman, "The Role of Packaging in Physical Distribution," *Transportation & Distribution Management,* February, 1968, pp. 34–39.

costs, not generally reflected in such rates, are those for the return of empty packages in separate shipments and carriers' costs arising out of inadequate package markings.

Carriers, particularly by air and highway, more often are constrained by cubic capacity than by weight restrictions. Their rates reflect this in lower per-unit prices for the transportation of higher-density shipments. In particular, shippers of pallet quantities have found that if the dimensions of the pallets are reduced so that two can be fitted side-by-side in a truck-trailer body with an interior width of 90 to 92 inches, the resulting load size can be nearly doubled. Interestingly, one standard pallet size of 48″ × 48″ obviously offers problems in this regard with or without package "overhang" along the edges.

A package undergoes the greatest stress in transit in many distribution systems. This particularly is true if packages or palletized unit loads are stacked to utilize the full cubic capacity of a transportation vehicle. A basic consideration in package design is the degree to which packaging costs should be traded against both basic transportation costs and those for loss, damage, and resulting claims. (3) **Notice in Table 17–1 the differences in rate classifications for different package types. What do they reflect?**

A motor carrier executive has summed up the "psychology" of assessing this trade-off:

Packaging engineers sometimes feel that the more adequately protective the packages become, the more careless the freight handlers become. We, in the carrier field, are sometimes almost persuaded that as we handle goods more safely and carefully, the shippers rely on a carrier "feather-pillow" handling approach and lighten and cheapen their packaging as a consequence.[7]

Carmody cites an example of the trade-off in describing a shipper that persuaded a railroad to purchase a new shock-control car to allow it to avoid a shift from the use of fiber drums to light-gauge steel drums costing 50% more. The shock-control car offered damage results less than 1% of those experienced with standard box cars.[8]

Clearly, there are few products of a value or character that warrants complete protection from all potential damage or theft. However, the landmark case of *Eastern Motor Express v. A. Maschmeijer, Jr.*[9] confirmed the shipper's responsibility and liability for damages caused by latent defects in the container. At the same time, the Interstate Commerce Commission has granted so-called released rates orders, under

[7] Reginald C. G. Witt, "The Purpose of Packaging," *Distribution Manager,* December, 1968, pp. 43–44, at p. 44.

[8] Carmody, *op. cit.,* p. 4.

[9] *Eastern Motor Express v. A. Maschmeijer Jr.,* 247 F.2d 826, cert. den. 78 S. Ct. 535 (1958).

TABLE 17-1. Cost Comparison for a Shipment of Calculators, Chicago to Bremen, via Great Lakes, by Container and Conventional Packing Method[a]

Item	Basis for Charge	Amount
Costs for Shipping in Six Contrans Containers		
Handling and pickup, Chicago	6 containers at $13.00 each	$ 78.00
Delivery to pier, Chicago	29,683 pounds, net	98.55
Terminal charge	41,686 pounds, gross (including containers), at $.09 per 100 pounds	37.52
Bill of lading, handling, postage, messenger		23.50
Container rental, Contrans	5 containers at $20.00 each plus 1 at $17.50	117.50
Insurance	$113,800 value at $1.735 per $100 of value	197.44
Seaway toll	41,686 pounds, gross, at $.90 per 2,000 pounds	18.76
Ocean freight	1,204 cubic feet at $1.20 per cubic foot plus 457 cubic feet at $1.375 per cubic foot, less 12½%	1,814.03
Redelivery of empty container, Bremen		36.00
Delivery charge, pier to warehouse, Bremen	Unknown	Unknown
Total		$2,421.30
Costs for Same Shipment Packed Conventionally		
Export packing		$ 409.68
Delivery to pier, Chicago	31,469 pounds, gross, at $.20 per hundred pounds	62.94
Terminal charge	31,469 pounds, gross, at $.09 per hundred pounds	28.32
Bill of lading, handling, postage, messenger		23.50
Insurance	$113,800 value at $.2075 per $100 of value	236.14
Seaway toll	31,469 pounds, gross, at $.90 per 2,000 pounds	14.16
Ocean freight	1,378 cubic feet at $1.20 per cubic foot plus 621 cubic feet at $1.375 per cubic foot	2,507.48
Delivery charge, pier to warehouse, Bremen	Unknown	Unknown[b]
		$3,282.22

[a]Adapted from "Now, Figures to Confirm Container Savings," *Handling & Shipping*, January, 1966, pp. 33–37. The costs for container shipment are actual, those for conventional packing are calculated.

[b]If these costs are different, they are probably less for the containerized alternative.

which carrier liability is limited, typically in exchange for lower transportation rates.

Of particular interest in recent years has been the cost of returning reusable pallets or containers used for unitized shipments. In some cases, it has led to the negotiation of special rates for transporting such items, entered into by carriers interested in promoting the use of the concept. In other cases, it has led to the establishment of exchange agreements whereby organizations trading with one another and using common sizes of pallets, containers, or other packages merely keep track of the balance owed one organization by the other at certain points in time.

Finally, packages well-marked for handling in transit typically will move with greater speed in less-than-vehicle quantities or in situations where carriers are responsible for assembling or distributing full loads. In one well-remembered instance, the dock personnel of a motor carrier were trying to sort for distribution a load of some two thousand cases of ten different poorly identified packages of product shipped by a well-known grocery product manufacturer. The shipper had provided only a handful of bills of lading for subsequent small-shipment deliveries, and had failed to mark the consignees' names and addresses on the cartons or otherwise organize the truckload into smaller shipments.

Considerations for Marketing to Customers. In addition to the ability of the package to deliver the product to customers in good condition, marketing managers are most concerned about the effect that the package will have on the ultimate consumer of the product, particularly if the product must "sell itself" on the shelves of a self-service retail outlet. Of nearly equal interest, however, for goods sold to customers for resale to the ultimate users are such factors as artistic design, the provision of information to aid in resale, the ease of unpacking and display, and the size of the package itself. The latter considerations are particularly important for goods to be resold through retailers. For example, supermarkets have available a fixed number of running feet of shelf and, what is more important, square feet of frontage space facing shoppers as they move through the store. Based on research indicating that supermarket sales are influenced significantly by the relative proportion of "facing" space that a product occupies, manufacturers compete vigorously by attempting to design packages to which the retailer will be willing to give additional space but which will also attract the sometimes bewildered shopper.

Of perhaps greater significance for logistics is the extent to which the shipping carton is designed to reflect customer buying habits regarding quantity and assortment. Oversized cartons with their contents half-sold consume customer space. Undersized cartons require unnecessary packaging and handling. Albl cites the following example:

For years meat packers shipped frankfurters only in cartons containing 12 one-pound packages. Most supermarkets would receive as many as 60 of those cartons for a single weekend. These small boxes were a nuisance and an expense to handle. Someone used his head and now frankfurters come in 12 to 50 pound boxes, whichever the buyer prefers. Simple? Sure, but years passed before the point came to the attention of the right person.[10]

[10] Albl, *op. cit.*, p. 38.

Of course, customer buying habits are influenced greatly by quantity discount pricing policies. Thus, it is important that packages and shipping carton overwraps conform with pricing policies.

Package and carton designs perform differently under various material-handling conditions. Variations in handling procedures and lighting conditions require not only that the package be able to withstand a variety of stresses, but that its markings be readable under all conditions it is likely to encounter.

Finally, there may be circumstances in which packaging and handling considerations warrant the redesign not only of the basic product, but of special promotions, particularly those involving special premiums sold with the basic product. As Friedman puts it:

> . . . those eye-grabbing favorites of the marketing department—the free-broom-handle type promotion—frequently bring tears to the eyes of the distribution center manager whose pounds-per-man-hour tumble as he receives, moves, picks, packs and ships the merchandise.[11]

Considerations for Marketing to the Ultimate Consumer. In addition to matters cited in the preceding section, the growing concern with environmental considerations will make it increasingly important to take matters of package disposal, reuse, or utility for other consumer uses into account in package design. The ultimate in this regard would appear to be the self-destructing beer bottle developed in Sweden recently, which disintegrates after being emptied. However, even this type of package may not be acceptable from an environmental standpoint if it represents a waste of resources. In this regard, reuse and reprocessing of packaging materials are once again on the rise, and will lead to a necessary reallocation of the costs of handling and reprocessing such materials to the consumer.

Carmody provides us with an interesting case example of packaging design:

> Union Carbide moves a considerable amount of plastic resin materials in multi-wall bags. For years, Union Carbide relied chiefly on the sewn-open-mouth and sewn-valve types of bags, and all bags were designed to carry 50 pounds of product regardless of product density. A few years ago, the company studied what the effect would be on its distribution and warehousing costs if it were to use pasted-valve instead of sewn bags.
>
> The company's distribution and handling system was based on the use of pallet loads of material: each pallet carried 40 bags or 2,000 pounds of net product. To accomplish this with the sewn bag required a bag pattern of four bags per tier, placed in pinwheel fashion on a 48-inch-square pallet, with ten tiers of bags per pallet. With bag overhang, the overall dimensions of the loaded pallet were approximately 50 inches by 50 inches. Because the pin-

11 Friedman, *op. cit.*, p. 34.

wheel arrangement left an empty space in the center of the pallet, which re-sulted in some slight instability, it was generally possible to stock these pallets only two high in a warehouse.

There were two basic problems with the old system. First, since the overall width of the pallet load in either direction was 50 inches, two pallet loads could not be loaded side by side in a truck. (Truck widths range from 88 to 92 inches.) Therefore, when truck shipments of palletized resin had to be made, the company was not able to meet the minimum payload required by the common carrier; consequently, it was forced to pay higher transportation rates per pound of product. Second, since we could store these pallet loads in the warehouse no more than two high, we could get only about 230 pounds of product per net square foot of warehouse space.

In experiments with the use of pasted-valve bags, it was found that for a slight increase in multi-wall bag cost, 50 pounds of product could be packed in a bag which would stack on a 42-inch by 48-inch pallet, five bags per tier, eight tiers high. The resulting load was quite stable, and pallets could easily be stacked three high, provided the warehouse had the necessary overhead clearance and fork lift capacity. This system provided an overall package that could be loaded into railcars, two pallets wide across the 48-inch dimension, or into trucks, two pallets wide across the 42-inch dimension. Truck freight costs were reduced substantially. Furthermore, with the ability to stack these pallet loads three high, the company was able to store approximately 380 pounds per square foot of net warehouse space. This made it possible for us to reduce warehouse space for the same quantity of product to about 60 percent of previous requirements.[12]

(4) In this example, which of the design considerations we have discussed appear to be of greatest importance? (5) In a more general sense, consider the matter of package shape. How many times has it been mentioned in our discussion? (6) In connection with which functions of the organization? (7) Are the interests of these various functions regarding package shape conflicting? (8) How? (9) Consider the same set of questions for the overall matter of package size. Your responses to these questions undoubtedly have raised additional questions about the process by which decisions are made in the design of packaging, and the organizational arrangements which facilitate the process.

Organization for Package Design

Clearly, a means must be designed to facilitate the interfunctional communication suggested by our discussion. For example, which functions in the Union Carbide organization should have been consulted in the adoption of pasted-valve bags, described earlier?

Differences of opinion arise regarding the types of organization needed to accomplish the agreed-on mission. Cornell cites evidence that:

[12] Carmody, *op. cit.*, pp. 2–3.

(1) there are few executives, but more engineers, with packaging in their job titles, and (2) packaging decisions are spread all over the typical organization. He concludes that a central focus should exist for packaging decisions, either at the divisional or headquarters level in the organization.[13] Carmody suggests that a team composed of a packaging engineer, a production man, an expert in physical distribution, a sales representative, a traffic man, and a purchasing man might be the most workable organizational arrangement.[14] (10) **How would you assess these alternative approaches?**

We have identified a number of points at which packaging and material-handling methods may conflict. To understand better the nature of these important relationships for logistics, we should explore in greater detail the technology and management of material-handling methods for packaged freight.

Material Handling

Our intent here is to provide some structure to aid thinking about material-handling systems. It is not practical to attempt a discussion of all the various types of equipment currently available to warehouse designers. Specific problems regarding material-handling systems are included in the references cited at the end of this chapter.

Equipment for Material Handling. Equipment used in material handling systems can be categorized into four major groups: individually powered vehicles, conveyors, devices for the unitization of freight, and storage aids.

In the overall design of a material-handling system, again we emphasize that efficient individual components do not necessarily guarantee an efficient system. Efficiency is not only influenced by such factors as the level and periodic fluctuations of volume handled, local wage rates for material-handling labor, and the relative cost of space. It also depends upon the manner in which the various components are fitted together to form an integrated system.

Individually Powered Vehicles. A fleet of individually powered vehicles in a material-handling system is likely to be composed of one or more of the following: fork-lift trucks, towing tractors, cranes, stacker-cranes, hand-powered equipment, and miscellaneous vehicles. Those vehicles requiring mechanical power are powered by means of electricity,

[13] Russ Cornell, "Packaging Function Moves to Top Level," *Materials Handling Engineering*, April, 1967, pp. 79–84.
[14] Carmody, *op. cit.*

diesel fuel, gasoline, or compressed gas. Except for outside or well-ventilated operations, gasoline or diesel-powered vehicles have not gained much acceptance. Rechargeable batteries provide the power source for an electrically powered fleet of vehicles. The relative costs to operate with each method of power are debatable.

Fork-Lift Trucks.   The fork-lift truck came into popular use with the advent of pallets and containers designed to accommodate fork tines (blades) which could lift them. More recently some fork-lift trucks have been designed for use without pallets or containers. The "clamp truck" is capable of picking up and moving segmentized loads which are not palletized or strapped. "Fork" trucks have many forms, depending on whether: (1) high lifting or only low lifting is required, (2) the truck will have to operate over a rough surface, in which case a high flotation truck is required (one equipped with outsized front wheels or tires), (3) large (up to 6,000 lb.) load capacity or small (commonly 2,000 lb.) load capacity is required, (4) rapid (driver–rider) or slow (walkie-type) trucks can be operated, (5) aisle width will be great (allowing the use of trucks with counter-weights under the driver's seat) or narrow (requiring the use of straddle or reach-out type trucks with running braces protruding from the front beneath the load rather than a counter-weight behind the load).

Various kinds of trucks have the capability to stack palletized goods up to heights of twenty feet or more. The actual extent to which stacking is employed will depend on other factors, including the nature of warehouse facilities and product characteristics.

Towing Tractors.   Towing tractors are used in situations where relatively long hauls of large volumes of goods are required. They pull a number of tracking trailers loaded with either palletized or non-palletized items. They can be used either in combination with fork-lift trucks or moved by hand labor.

Cranes.   Cranes for handling objects of considerable weight over a fixed path may be ceiling-mounted on fixed tracks, or they may be portable, self-powered units. The use of the latter requires relatively large, open spaces within a structure, so that they are most often used only for lifting and transporting items with handling characteristics which make the use of fork-lift trucks unsuitable or unfeasible.

Stacker-Cranes.   Increasingly popular in semi-automated material-handling systems, stacker-cranes are used in conjunction with computer memory devices to "file" pallet loads of product into banks of pallet racks and to "retrieve" them on command. Each stacker-crane operates on fixed tracks, and ranges over two facing "banks" of pallet racks, often constructed up to 100 feet high. This type of equipment is economically attractive only in situations where the costs of land are very high or additional land is simply not available, and/or when the pallet through-put volume is sufficient to realize economies of scale in the operation of these very costly installations.

Hand-powered Equipment. Even in an age of mechanization, hand-powered equipment still has a wide range of uses. It is particularly adaptable to situations in which weights are small, the available space is limited, or it is economically not feasible to install mechanically powered equipment. Hand-powered equipment includes the familiar hand-truck, a hand-crank lifting device, hand-pushed conveyor vehicles, a hand pallet-truck, and hand hooks for grabbing and lifting.

Miscellaneous Equipment. Additional equipment may be needed to complement that already described. A tiering truck, for example, can serve as a substitute for fork-lift trucks by providing a platform, capable of being transported and elevated, on which either palletized or non-palletized material may be carried. It is most often used where the material is stacked relatively high without the use of fork-lifts. One application which has popularized this type of equipment in recent years is its use in so-called retail "furniture warehouse" outlets in which large pieces of furniture are "filed" in vertical racks with seven or eight levels.

A familiar sight in storage yards and on city streets is the straddle-carry truck, capable of hauling great weights and volumes of materials such as lumber, steel, and other structural materials in a bay located under the operating cab of the vehicle and between its wheels. Special devices for some of the equipment described above may be included in this category. These include attachments for the "side-grabbing" or "side-shifting" of pallets or containers by fork-lift trucks and specialized fork attachments for handling units of unusual size or configuration.

Conveyors. Conveyors can be powered by mechanical, gravity, and hand methods. Gravity power is much less expensive than mechanical power, but it is limited by the end-height difference required by a conveyor of given slope (generally $\frac{1}{4}$ to $\frac{3}{4}$ inch per foot of running length.) Mechanically powered conveyors are referred to as belt, live-roll, chain, or trolley conveyors. Generally, the first two are associated with conveyor systems capable of being relocated. The live-roll conveyor is named after its primary feature of rollers-in-series powered from a central source. The chain conveyor, usually located in the floor of a terminal or warehouse, is the most "fixed" of all types. It cannot be shifted without considerable expense. Trolley conveyors are often mounted on the ceiling with descending hooks to which individual vehicles might be attached. As such, they are more easily altered than the chain conveyor, but are still expensive to move.

Gravity conveyors and hand-powered level conveyors are made up of the same equipment positioned in different ways. Both utilize either rollers or wheels. Wheel-type conveyors generally have fewer friction-creating surfaces. As a rule, gravity and hand-powered conveyors are highly portable. The portable feature facilitates their use in facilities with varying flows of materials.

Devices for the Unitization of Freight. In addition to the more familiar container used in long-distance transportation, this classification embodies a number of containers used primarily for storage and handling. For the purposes of this discussion, the term is limited to the types of platforms or enclosures used primarily for the accumulation of commodities into units for easy storage, order selection, and transportation. Among the more important are pallets, retail bins and drawers, and strapping or tying devices.

Pallets. Pallets are constructed of wood, steel, aluminum, corrugated cardboard, and even kraft paper, in a variety of designs to accommodate fork-lift equipment. The first of these is the most common, combining qualities of economy and reuse. Metal pallets are relatively expensive and heavy, but prove most durable in use. Cardboard and other low-cost materials provide light-weight pallets of limited durability which are particularly advantageous if the pallet is to be shipped with the product.

Pallets are expendable (constructed of medium-priced materials such as soft wood and designed for limited reuse), one-way or disposable (constructed of low-cost materials such as cardboard), or reusable. They may be constructed with sideboards to hold materials impossible to stack, or may have an overhead frame to facilitate stacking without the use of pallet racks.

A variation of the pallet for the unitized handling of freight which has gained favor in grocery product logistics in recent years is the pallet sheet or slip sheet. Used in the warehouse in conjunction with pallets and lift trucks fitted with six or more polished, long chisel forks and a pusher, side-shifter attachment, the slip sheet is simply a piece of cardboard the area of a pallet with a 5-inch flange turned up along one side. Pallet-load quantities can be picked up on slip sheets by running the tines of the fork-lift truck under the cardboard flange and the load. They are positioned, for example, in a rail car by pushing the load off the tines by means of the mechanical pusher device on the truck. Slip sheets allow for unitized freight transportation without cube-consuming pallets and the pallet return problem.

Bins and Drawers. Bins and drawers are often placed in frames to serve as ready containers of small or valuable items for order-picking purposes. Generally, this type of equipment is used for storage purposes when the item cannot be, or is not, packaged or unitized.

Tying Devices. Recently, some firms have experimented with unitization (the simultaneous handling of products of common or varying description) of freight without the use of pallets. This has been accomplished by the banding of boxes or barrels together to form a movable unit.

Products with similar cubic dimensions and physical characteristics can be unitized by gluing them to each other. Recently, a number of firms have adopted "shrink-wrap" technology in which unitized quantities of freight are encased in polyethylene or similar transparent materials and the resulting wrapping shrunk tightly around the unit by the application of heat. These innovations have proven particularly attractive, where feasible, because they often reduce the weight of equipment needed to unitize freight and eliminate the costly process of returning empty pallets to their origin.

Storage Aids. The pallet rack is the most common type of storage aid. It is, as its name implies, a rack built of pipe, structural metals, or wood to a dimension which will accommodate two or more loaded pallets in two or more tiers. Pallet racks not only facilitate the stacking of pallets by providing a stabilizing effect to the stack, but they also allow removal of a pallet on the bottom tier without disturbing the pallets above it. This is an essential feature of an operation in which pallet loads of items are picked in the selection area of a warehouse, or in which items are stored on, and picked from, pallets in the order-filling process. The pallet rack can also be used to increase the warehousing capacity of a given area by permitting the location of dissimilar products on top of each other within the pallet rack.

Various kinds of dunnage can be used in the packing of freight in warehouses or transportation vehicles. Dunnage is a term applied to objects used to brace, steady, or otherwise protect freight being stored or moved. Horizontal dunnage, for example, may consist simply of sheets of fiberboard placed between layers of a product to "tie" a load together and steady it. Vertical dunnage, on the other hand, generally is used to help support the weight of products which are piled vertically. A dunnaging technique currently being used by several shippers involves inflatable rubber "bags" which are placed between items or groups of items to cushion impact during movement.

None of the components of a material-handling subsystem can be selected without due consideration for other parts of the system. The selection of individually powered vehicles, for example, may depend upon the size of pallet needed to handle goods. But we must start somewhere, and it is perhaps most logical to proceed from the most to the least restrictive of circumstances in which such efforts take place. Assuming a fixed or given storage and material-handling structure, the material handling methods selected are probably most dependent upon the design of the unit package subsystem.

Unit Package Subsystem.   Unit or container sizes to be selected will depend upon the following factors, among others:

1. The material to be unitized
2. The type of motive equipment which can be used in a given location
3. The layout of the proposed warehouse structure, with particular regard to the spacing of supporting structural columns in the building
4. The type and dimensions of freight elevators, if any, currently installed in the warehouse
5. The possible widths of doors and aisles in the warehouse
6. The extent to which the pallet or container will be used in long-distance transportation via railroad, truck, or other modes
7. The type and size of pallets, size of motive power, and general design of the material-handling systems employed by suppliers or customers with whom unitized products might be exchanged

In the development of unit design, a wide number of alternatives present themselves. For example, a number of ways of constructing palletized units of different dimensions and characteristics from packages of the same size developed by the U. S. Navy Bureau of Supplies and Accounts are shown in Fig. 17–3. Many others have been developed by this same organization for pallets of various sizes. Ideally, unit design and modular packing box dimensions should be determined concurrently if the unit-package subsystem is to be most effectively designed.

Supporting System Components.   Concurrent with the design of a unit-package subsystem, consideration also should be given to the selection of such major supporting components as pallet racks, motorized vehicles, or conveyors.

An important consideration in the installation of pallet racks is the flexible nature of this type of equipment. It may be necessary to alter

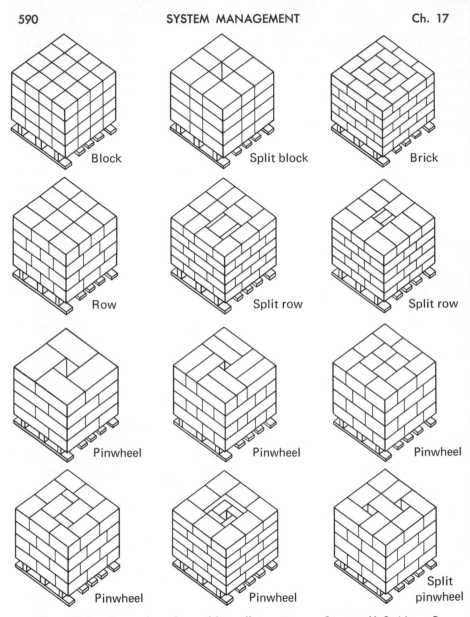

Fig. 17–3. Examples of possible pallet patterns. *Source:* U. S. Navy Bureau of Supplies and Accounts, Washington, D. C. Used with permission.

the design and layout of a material-handling operation so often that the use of detachable, knock-down, or otherwise flexible pallet and container racks may be well worth the extra expense for such equipment. A side consideration in the use of pallet racks is the rigidity which permanent pallet racks build into a material-handling system in the form of either 90° or angular pallet placement.

The most common error in the selection of motive equipment for the handling of materials is the selection of equipment with excess capacity. Extra capacity may be desirable to provide a safety factor for loads which any system is capable of handling, but if consistently unused it becomes burdensome in terms of: (1) extra initial cost of equipment, (2) generally greater floor-load requirements needed to support equipment of greater capacity, (3) extra vehicle-operating costs, and (4) extra width required in aisles down which freight must be transported, and in which it must be stacked. Except for this special consideration, much the same factors will influence the selection of motive equipment as the selection of pallet size.

The misuse of conveyors has done as much as any other action to set back warehousing practice in recent years. Part of the reason for this misuse may stem from the tendency for industrial engineers to try to extend their knowledge of material handling in manufacturing facilities into the warehouse. A production line, because of its fixed nature, is readily adaptable to the use of fixed conveyors. Generally speaking, the warehouse is not. Even though many highly efficient material-handling systems have been designed around a fixed conveyor, those firms subsequently requiring flexibility in the system have paid a penalty cost to get it.

Not only must a conveyor be selected to do a particular job in terms of carrying freight of certain dimensions and weight, but it must be selected on the basis of all the material handling it may be called upon to perform in the foreseeable future.

Compatibility with External Handling. A point that requires emphasis in the design considerations for a material-handling subsystem is that it be compatible, to the extent possible, with other material-handling activities in a channel of logistics.

In discussing unit-package design, not only should the unit package and its supporting system components be designed for easy accommodation in long-distance transportation vehicles, but they should also be designed to fit into the material-handling systems of suppliers and customers. The latter can only be achieved to a limited extent in the absence of control over the planning of suppliers and customers. However, a firm exercising some degree of economic persuasion over another may be able to influence material-handling system design to the mutual benefit of both firms. In any event, a complete disregard for the systems of larger suppliers and customers in the design of the material-handling subsystem indicates an incomplete approach to the problem.

Many material-handling subsystems, particularly in distribution centers, handle combinations of orders moving to several destinations in the same vehicle. To facilitate delivery, orders are placed in the vehicle in the reverse order in which they are to be unloaded. Many shippers have taken a cue from carriers in "building" a truckload or rail carload on the floor of the warehouse before the arrival of the vehicle. This provision in a material-handling system: (1) expedites loading, decreasing the number of truck and rail bays and detention and demurrage charges, (2) helps insure more effective and accurate carrier delivery performance, and (3) improves customer service and carrier relations. This action can be planned only in situations in which the carriers will deliver all shipments directly from the vehicle being loaded, situations usually limited to relatively short hauls and local deliveries.

Our discussion of material-handling subsystem design to this point has assumed a narrow range of latitude with many constraints for the designer. As each constraint is relaxed, allowing more subsystem components to be designed concurrently, the opportunities for improving performance increase. Consider the following example.

Swedish Cellulose Company (Svenska Cellulosa AB).[15] As part of a program to expand its exports of pulp, lumber, and newsprint to the rest of Europe, the Swedish Cellulose Company recently redesigned its entire physical distribution system, emphasizing coordinated material handling at each stage within its control to facilitate reduced inventories, faster deliveries, and reduced product damage.

The project had several major features including: (1) the reduction of origin port terminals in Sweden from twenty-five to two and destination port terminals in the remainder of Europe from one hundred to three, (2) the design of unit packages for pulp (eight steel-strapped bundles), sawed timber (four strapped bundles), and paper rolls (large units in themselves), (3) the design of truck trailers and rail cars to carry product from factories to the two export terminals, five somewhat identical terminals for material handling, and three identical self-loading ships for the transportation of mixed unit loads from Sweden to other European terminals in Rotterdam, Hamburg, and London.

With this system, Swedish Cellulose has mechanized extensively its material-handling system. Products are moved directly from the end of the production line to special trucks by five-ton fork-lifts, eighteen-ton straddle trucks, and clamp trucks with fixtures for handling units of pulp, sawed timber, and paper rolls. Similar equipment is available at all port

---

[15] This example is drawn from "Rationalized Production," a publication circulated by Svenska Cellulosa AB.

terminals. The ships are outfitted with company-designed gantry-cranes with special lifting devices, including eight electrically operated clamp-type lifting heads for units of sawed timber, and a vacuum clamp for lifting six to twelve rolls of paper at a time. The holds of the ships are carefully dimensioned and have walls of pine panelling to reduce damage. Two cranes on each ship run on rails along the deck. Only a crane operator handles the cargo units by hoisting them aboard and depositing them directly into the completely open holds, thereby eliminating the need for the horizontal movement of the units in the hold of the ship, a frequent source of damage. The loading and unloading of mixed cargo loads takes place at the rate of 8,500 tons, the capacity of each ship, in 24 hours, allowing each ship to make 33 or 34 round trips per year between Swedish and other ports.

(11) **Of the basic elements of this system, which do you think were developed first? (12) Why? (13) What are important conditions which allow the development of a system of this magnitude?**

Containerization.[16] We purposely have delayed our discussion of containers in the material-handling subsystem until this point because we feel that their significance for logistics warrants special emphasis. In a few short years, the adoption of containerization for the ocean shipping of general cargo has exceeded all estimates of growth. In 1968, 13% of "containerizable" cargo moving in the North Atlantic was shipped in containers; by 1970, the amount was 60%.[17] And yet, this recent phenomenon has produced problems for both carriers and shippers, and has received relatively little use in domestic shipping in the United States. Herein lies an interesting study in material handling and transportation economics.

History. Ironically, the idea of moving boxes without wheels is of much more recent vintage than that of putting wheels on them. Among early references to containerization are Tomkins' recollections of "furniture van bodies being transferred across the channel onto and off of English and French railroad flat cars, and off and on horse-drawn vehicles (for this was before the days of the auto truck)" around 1895.[18] In 1920, the Cincinnati Motor Terminals Company substituted motor trucks and demountable bodies for freight carts and railroad cars for the movement of less-than-carload railroad freight within the terminal and between connecting railroad terminals. This probably was the first large-

[16] As background for this section, see Chapter 4, pp. 100–101.
[17] "Many Seaports Are Finding Their Livelihood Threatened by Changes in Cargo Technology," *The Wall Street Journal*, June 28, 1971.
[18] Calvin Tompkins, "Transshipment Containers," *Shipping*, July 10, 1920, p. 27.

scale use of containerization in the United States.[19] Small containers, typically made of wood, were used for the international transportation of furniture and other items by ship in subsequent years.

Not until 1954, however, was the idea adopted in its present form as a potential means of reducing handling costs for goods bound for overseas, costs which frequently accounted for more than half of the freight bill. Malcolm McLean, then President of McLean Trucking Company, persuaded a man of comparable vision, Roy Fruehauf, then President of the Fruehauf Corporation, a truck-trailer manufacturer, to sell him $20 million of containers for what a subsequent President said was "nothing down and eight years to pay." [20] Several results can be traced in whole or in part to this transaction. Roy Fruehauf was fired by his Board of Directors three years later. The Fruehauf Corporation went on to capture more than half of what became a billion-dollar annual container market. And Malcolm McLean founded (and fifteen years later sold for approximately a half-billion dollars) Pan Atlantic Steamship Company and its successor, Sea-Land Service, for the shipment of containers initially between U. S. domestic ports from New York to Anchorage, and including Puerto Rico. When forced by an antitrust action to give up either his trucking or his shipping company, McLean bet on the more rapid growth of containerization compared to either trucking operations or the use of containers for land-bound shipments. Again, this wise choice foresaw the limited growth in the use of containers for domestic rail and water shipments. (14) **Why do you think the growth rates in container usage for shipments involving international ocean or intercoastal water movements far exceeded all others?**

Economic Advantages for Shippers. One of the early and few published documentations of shipper savings by means of containerization was that which the Victor Comptometer Corporation supplied for typical shipments of calculating machines between Chicago and Bremen, Germany, where Victor operated a distribution center serving points in Europe.[21] A portion of it is shown in Table 17–1, and indicates that the total cost of this shipment by containerization was less than 75% of that by conventional means at the time. (15) **Looking at Table 17–1, where do the major savings from the use of containerization arise? (16) Why?**

In addition to explicit dollar savings shown in Table 17–1, companies shipping containers "door-to-door" (from origin to ultimate destination) have reduced expenses for labeling (with one label per container), plant

[19] "Demountable Bodies," in Roy W. Wright (ed.), *Material Handling Cyclopedia* (New York: 1921), p. 754.

[20] "Fruehauf Corp.: Going to Sea," *Forbes,* April 1, 1968, pp. 34–40, at p. 34.

[21] "Now, Figures to Confirm Container Savings," *Handling & Shipping,* January, 1966, pp. 33–37.

space for packaging materials, pilferage, damage, inventory carrying (because of faster handling and transit time), and paperwork (with one set of papers for the entire container). In the matter of pilferage alone, it is estimated that before containerization, roughly 10% of the Scotch whisky passing through the Port of New York as regular cargo disappeared.[22]

Transit time savings have been significant with containerization. Theoretically, a container ship requires one day each for loading and discharging cargo and five days for crossing the North Atlantic between the United States and Europe, for example. In fact, container service has been provided on a weekly basis by most competing lines, allowing containerized freight to be accumulated at the port. This, in addition to a typical routing including two ports of call on each side of the Atlantic, has produced actual port-to-port transit times closer to two weeks. This is still a significant reduction from transit times via traditional methods of three weeks or more.

The Impact of Containerization on Carriers.   The irrefutable economic advantages of containerization will continue to support its rapid growth. But ironically, carrier management and labor alike have viewed this growth with great misgivings. With it, the former have seen profits decline, the latter the disappearance of jobs.

Water carriers have converted old ships and built new ones rapidly to accommodate the growth of containerization. And because of their greater cubic capacity, their greater turn-around speed, and the tendency for a cubic foot of containerized freight to contain more freight (without some of its protective packaging), even a "first generation" container ship can generate six times the capacity of a conventional freighter. This has produced an excess of capacity and a great deal of competition on the busiest routes. For example, one senior shipping executive has estimated that with a break-even load factor (ratio of space used to space available) of about 60% in the North Atlantic trade in 1971, competing carriers were realizing load factors ranging from 29% to 61%.

Break-even levels for ocean carriers have been raised by the extensive investment, originally underestimated, required for ships, containers, and shoreside facilities.

Although figures vary, it is quite possible that American flag carriers have invested nearly $2 billion in ships and containers. European and Japanese carriers probably have invested more than a billion dollars. Among recent figures for port investments for containerization were estimates that, as of 1970, New York had spent $175 million; Oakland, $35

[22] Harold B. Meyers, "The Maritime Industry's Expensive New Box," *Fortune,* November, 1967, pp. 151 ff.

million; Japanese ports of Tokyo, Kobe, Osaka, and Yokohama, $145 million, London, $40 million; and Rotterdam, $60 million.

These investments have not been matched by inland motor and rail carriers. Nor has sufficient money been spent for information systems necessary for container controls. As a result, there has been limited use of containers for "door-to-door" shipments, the type for which maximum advantages for containerization can be claimed. Also, containers have been lost, and inland turn-around time because of poor control has been much slower than expected, which has raised the investment in containers required to keep a ship moving with an economical payload.

Although container sizes have been standardized internationally, at the time when standards were established at 8-foot widths, 8-foot heights, and 10-, 20-, 30-, and 40-foot lengths, the majority of containers in use were of the non-standard dimensions of $8 \times 8.5 \times 35$ feet and $8 \times 8.5 \times 24$ feet. Further, the two American railroads that had invested most heavily in containers, the Penn Central and the Southern, had bought containers of 35-foot lengths. There is some conjecture that, as legal limitations on load dimensions and weight limits are relaxed, standards may also change.[23] In any event, there are many large vested interests that have delayed the universal use of standard equipment, further inhibiting "door-to-door" container shipments.

Finally, restrictive labor union policies have delayed the realization of the full potential economies of containerization for material handling. This potential has been demonstrated in the West Coast–Okinawa service operated for the Defense Department, in which 40,000 tons of containerized cargo can be "offloaded or onloaded" in 750 man-hours as opposed to 24,000 man-hours for break-bulk cargo in old-style ships.[24] Little wonder that labor agreements have included provisions for carrier-funded pensions for the early retirement of displaced union members on the West Coast. The East Coast settlements have reflected a different pattern, including per-ton payments to the International Longshoreman's Association and the union privilege of unloading and loading again at the port any container loaded at an inland terminal by workers outside the ILA's jurisdiction.

In spite of these temporary obstructions, containerization will continue to represent one of the most important developments in logistics. Shippers cannot ignore its savings. Regardless of whether carriers can afford to be in the business, the fact remains that they can't afford to stay out of it.

Up to now, we have assumed the use of some form of packaging for material handling. Perhaps the greatest logistical economies of all have

[23] Meyers, op. cit.
[24] Ibid.

been achieved by avoiding the use of packaging by shipping products to the greatest extent possible in bulk form.

BULK FREIGHT

The development of new methods for handling freight in bulk has both required and been made possible by the introduction of faster, more efficient methods of handling products in bulk form. Further, the range of freight which can be handled in bulk at high speeds by means of pumped air has been extended to include such commodities as barrel bungs, auto hose clamps, corn, bottle caps, toothpicks, and even money.[25]

Tankers with capacities of more than 300,000 deadweight tons and combination petroleum–ore "bulkers" of more than 200,000 tons literally have made the world's canals, which are not capable of accommodating these ships, obsolete for such large shipments. But these ships represent practical investments primarily because they can be loaded, for example, with equipment with handling capacities of 20,000 tons of ore per hour as opposed to capacities of 500 tons per hour for 1940 vintage equipment.

Bulk freight handling technology now makes it more economical to offload cargo for temporary storage and reshipment than to leave it in the transportation vehicle and handle it fewer times. This has both freed transportation equipment for more productive use and reduced the need for coordination for commodities transferred from one mode of transportation to another. For example, the handling of coal from rail cars to the pile and from the pile onto lake boats at speeds of up to 20,000 tons per hour at the Conneaut, Ohio, depot of the Bessemer & Lake Erie Railroad: (1) allowed for faster turn-around times for both rail cars and boats, (2) encouraged boat owners to order from builders boats of larger and more economic sizes, (3) encouraged shippers to store coal in piles for periods of several days to an entire winter, and (4) played a significant part in the reduction of "laid down" costs of West Virginia coal in Canada of from 15% to 20%.

In domestic transportation, the development of high-speed pneumatic conveyor mechanisms using pumps to create pressures low enough to put various commodities into "liquid" suspension, and differential pressures to induce high-speed air flows from one vehicle or container to another, has altered drastically the distribution patterns for commodities such as flour, cement, and granular plastics.

For example, bakeries converting to this system have stopped buying bagged flour. Instead, flour is being pumped directly from truck trailers into bulk storage bins, and in certain facilities from bulk storage bins

---

[25] Albl, *op. cit.*, p. 38.

directly into mixing vats. Cement producers have been able to extend the traditionally small territories served from their plants, thus increasing production economies of scale, by shipping in rail cars equipped with pneumatic conveyor mechanisms capable of transferring their contents directly to similarly equipped trucks. The rail car can serve both as a means of long-distance transportation and a temporary distribution point for subsequent truckload shipments to customers. The nature of this service has met customer requirements for product delivery in less-than-carload quantities with significant savings by eliminating traditional bagging and handling methods.

The comparative economics of two methods of handling and shipping granular plastics from the plant in Houston to customers in Ohio by this method are shown in Table 17–2.[26] Previously, these customers, all man-

TABLE 17–2. Comparative Costs of Rail–Truck, Vacuum Transfer vs. All-Truck Distribution of Granular Plastic from Houston to Points in Ohio*

Costs of Rail–Truck, Vacuum Transfer Method Per Hundredweight:	
Railroad transportation, Houston to Pataskala, Ohio, in 160,000-lb. carloads	$ .84
Vacuum transfer charge, Pataskala	.10
Weighing charge, Pataskala	.01
Billing and handling charge, Pataskala	.02
Truck transportation, Pataskala to customers, in 40,000-lb. truckloads	.42–.45
Total	$1.39–$1.42
Costs of All-Truck Method Per Hundredweight:	
Truck transportation, Houston to customers, in 40,000-lb. truckloads	$1.71–$3.01
Cost Savings for Rail–Truck, Vacuum Transfer vs. All-Truck Methods	19%–53%

*Based on information in Tom Wilcoxon, "The Bulk Rebellion Wants You!," *Handling & Shipping*, October, 1967, pp. 78–80.

ufacturers of various plastic products, received truckload shipments directly from the plant. Under the revised method, 160,000-pound rail carload shipments move from Houston to Pataskala, Ohio, where vacuum transfer equipment transfers them from the rail car to trucks according to customers' directions for subsequent shipment to customers' plants in various Ohio locations. Transfer takes place at the rate of a 40,000-pound truckload quantity in about 45 minutes. Under the shipping program, devised and operated by a leading bulk hauler by truck, Matlack, Inc., rail cars which are shipper-owned are held on a private siding leased by Matlack's subsidiary in Pataskala for periods up to 30 days at no charge. Cars not totally unloaded after 30 days are transferred to public or rail-

26 Tom Wilcoxon, "The Bulk Rebellion Wants You!," *Handling & Shipping*, October, 1967, pp. 78–89.

road-owned sidings, where they begin to collect demurrage charges. Savings under the new distribution method range from 19% to 53%.

(17) Looking again at Table 17–2, why would a leading bulk carrier by truck take the lead in organizing to facilitate this new method of transportation and material handling?

TRANSFER FROM BULK TO PACKAGED FREIGHT

Recent developments in the handling and transportation of bulk freight have led companies and entire industries to reassess points in their logistics systems at which products are converted from bulk to packaged form. These phenomena hold the promise of obsolescence for the location and continuance of certain practices, and will provide the rationale for entirely new packaging activities in new locations. (18) In general, would you expect that these developments would result in a general relocation of packaging activities nearer to, or further from, markets? (19) Why?

Bucklin provides us with a useful theoretic framework for reviewing the structure of traditional distribution channels.[27] His is a further development of the principle of postponement articulated by Alderson, which holds that an organization should:

. . . postpone changes in form and identity to the latest point in the marketing flow; postpone changes in inventory location to the latest possible points in time.[28]

Bucklin later formulated the converse of this, the principle of speculation, which suggests that:

. . . changes in form, and the movement of goods to forward inventories, should be made at the earliest possible time in the marketing flow in order to reduce the costs of the marketing system.[29]

The combined principle of postponement and speculation is stated as follows:

A speculative inventory will appear at each point in a distribution channel whenever its costs are less than the net savings to both buyer and seller from postponement.[30]

In a sense, this is the total cost concept being given interorganizational scope, a logical extension of the concept. For example, a company

---

[27] Much of this section draws upon Louis P. Bucklin, "Postponement, Speculation, and the Structure of Distribution Channels," *Journal of Marketing Research*, January, 1965, pp. 26–31.

[28] Wroe Alderson, *Marketing Behavior and Executive Action* (Homewood, Ill.: Richard D. Irwin, Inc., 1957), p. 424.

[29] Bucklin, *op. cit.*, p. 27.

[30] *Ibid.*, p. 28.

which inventories products only at its plant and produces many items to order may maximize postponement and minimize speculation. If, however, it loses sales by increasing speculation and making postponement difficult for customers, it may be advised to establish a market-oriented inventory. If the combined benefits of reduced speculation and increased postponement for the customer, and resulting increases in sales and reductions in transport costs for the supplier, are greater than increased costs of establishing the extra inventory, increasing speculation and reducing postponement for the supplier, then according to the theory a market-oriented inventory will be established.

Clearly, extending the transportation and handling of his product in bulk as opposed to packaged form allows a manufacturer to postpone his commitment of product to specific, possibly differentiated, and often more costly packages, thus reducing his speculation at very little cost to his customer.

(20) **How would you evaluate the following example, given this framework?**

. . . Individual bananas have always come in an attractive, airtight, appealing, yellow package. It is even equipped with an easy tear strip opener. However, full stalks of bananas have no regular dimension that permits efficient use of storage and transportation cube. Too, the ultimate consumer usually purchases one or two "hands," rather than a single banana or the entire stalk. Thus, we have identified two problem areas in terms of distribution costs: inefficient use of transportation and storage cube, and a shipping size which is not acceptable to the final customer.

The disposal of the stalk itself presents some interesting problems. It defies the most cunning destruction devices. It cannot economically be burned, smashed, ground, or eaten. Many city dumps refuse to accept stalks. Also, while the banana skin is easy to open, appealing, and fits the product, it offers little protection from handling damage. So, stalk disposal and product damage must be added to the list of problem areas.

Previously, bananas were moved from Central America to a produce or chain warehouse where they were ripened, cut from the stalk, weighed, packed in returnable boxes, and delivered to the stores. Each stalk was moved to the seaport, individually carried on and off the ship, in and out of the rail car, and in and out of the ripening rooms. The expense of these individual handlings materially reduced the profit from this low cost fruit.[31]

(21) **Given what you know about this situation, what kinds of alternatives might be explored for dealing with the problem?** (22) **Which do you think offers the best potential?** (23) **Why?**

The banana companies decided to do something about this. They analyzed the elements of their distribution cycle, then made a few simple, but very important changes. First, they developed a properly ventilated container into

[31] Albl, *op. cit.*, p. 38.

which the "hands" of bananas were to be packed. Then, they took the container right into the grove and cut, weighed, and packed the "hands" there. The boxes are designed to fit standard pallet quantities throughout the distribution cycle. The bananas are weighed only once, except for random checks by the purchasers.

The effect on the entire distribution system was dramatic!

1. The banana stalk had been eliminated from the picture.
2. The package now had uniform dimensions, resulting in better use of cube.
3. The shipping unit was now compatible with the consumer's buying habit.
4. Damage was drastically reduced. Packaging now protects the fruit from grove to produce counter.
5. Handling costs were greatly reduced by palletization.

Major alterations of vast systems invariably bring with them some new problems which must be overcome. For example, bananas on the stalk are easier to ripen than those packed in boxes. Each ripening room operator had to be taught how to stack the new boxes so the gas used in the ripening process would reach all of the bananas. Also, because of spoilage problems, some strains could not be boxed at all.

One of the toughest jobs was to convince the buyers (and their bosses) that a small price increase was justified to recover the cost of cutting and packing at the grove. Usually, any increase in purchase price results in a corresponding jump in selling price. The buyers had to be assured that they were actually paying less because of the elimination of labor in the ripening rooms and reduced losses from product damage. Evidence of such savings, plus the knowledge that Mrs. Housewife would be offered an unblemished product were the clinchers. All resistance has now been eliminated and boxed bananas are accepted as the standard method of distribution.[32]

(24) How would you explain what has happened here in terms of the theoretical framework of postponement and speculation developed by Alderson and Bucklin?

SUMMARY

We have considered packaged and bulk methods as the two basic modes for handling freight, concentrating particularly on non-marketing functions of packaging and newer developments in the handling of product both by means of containers and in bulk. Of final interest were determinants and trends influencing shippers in their decisions to transport and handle products either in bulk or packaged form and to establish the points in a distribution channel at which conversion from bulk to packaged form should occur.

[32] *Ibid.*, pp. 38–39.

SUGGESTED READINGS

APPLE, JAMES M. *Plant Layout and Materials Handling*, 2nd Ed. New York: The Ronald Press Company, 1963.
Although primarily oriented to the manufacturing plant, this book treats various aspects of material-handling techniques and equipment.

BOLZ, HAROLD A., and GEORGE E. HAGEMANN (eds.). *Materials Handling Handbook*. New York: The Ronald Press Company, 1958.
A compilation of exhaustive pieces on all aspects of plant and warehouse material handling. Of particular interest may be sections on industrial packaging. palletization, and warehouse and yard handling. In addition, a number of highly detailed articles deal with various material-handling methods.

BRIGGS, ANDREW J. *Warehouse Operations Planning and Management*. New York: John Wiley & Sons, Inc., 1960.

IMMER, JOHN R. *Materials Handling*. New York: McGraw-Hill Book Co., 1953.
While oriented to the handling of materials in a manufacturing operation, discusses the application of time and motion study to the problem of materials flow, the initiation and approach to material-handling studies, and cost accounting systems for effective control.

TAFF, CHARLES A. *Management of Physical Distribution and Transportation*, 5th Ed. Homewood, Ill.: Richard D. Irwin, Inc., 1972.
Presents a discussion of industrial packaging, with particular emphasis on its interrelationships with transport methods and rates, and treats the subject of material handling in general and containerization in particular.

Note: The rapidly changing technology of packaging and material handling makes it particularly appropriate to follow this subject through trade magazines on these subjects cited in footnotes appearing in our discussion and listed in Appendix C.

18

Warehousing

The operation of warehouses and carrying costs of the inventories stored in them account for an amount equivalent to more than 10% of the tangible gross national product and, in many firms, a greater proportion of the total cost of goods sold. Further, in many firms this function comprises the major portion of the operations over which logistics management has control. To the extent that inventory control is the heart of the logistics function, the warehouse is the veritable center of the logistics system for any one firm.

TYPES OF WAREHOUSING

Material-Handling (Assembly or Distribution) Warehouses

The major mission of a material-handling warehouse is to assemble, mix, and segment goods in transit. As such, it serves only as a momentary hostel for transient goods. Assembly warehouses are often used by firms purchasing large quantities of agricultural goods from a large number of sources spread over a wide region. They also may be used by industrial firms and marketing institutions which normally purchase a great quantity and wide variety of goods from suppliers in a particular region. Distribution warehouses, sometimes referred to as market warehouses, are used often for the mixing and transshipment of carload and truckload shipments moving from a large number of producing points to an even larger number of customer locations.

The most outstanding characteristic of an assembly or distribution warehouse is movement. As the diagram in Fig. 18–1 indicates, there is likely to be limited space for semipermanent storage in a material-

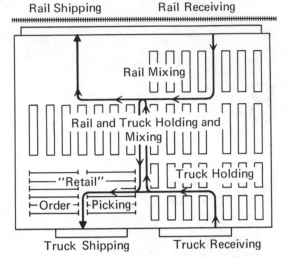

Fig. 18-1. Layout of a typical material-handling warehouse.

handling warehouse. Both carload and truckload shipments are commonly found entering and leaving the same assembly or distribution warehouse. When located between a supply area and a production point or between a production point and a market, a material-handling warehouse serves primarily as a storage-in-transit point. This type of warehouse is operated both by carriers and shippers to provide better service to industrial and trade customers or to take advantage of volume transportation rates.

As shown in Fig. 18-1, the primary activities carried on in a warehouse are receiving, holding (or storing), consolidation, selecting, and shipping. Consolidation is a term generally used to refer to the interchange of freight between carloads or truckloads in order to change the composition, but not necessarily the volume, of incoming and outgoing shipments. Selection, on the other hand, more appropriately refers to the operation where incoming loads are broken down for subsequent shipments in small quantities.

Storage Warehousing

Storage warehouses have a number of uses, all closely related to problems of demand–supply coordination. Any industry with seasonal supply or demand patterns frequently uses storage warehouses. This enables the firm to level-out production activities. Other storage warehousing is performed for the purpose of maturing, ripening, or aging products of various kinds. Still others are used for the stockpiling of strategic materials, supplies resulting from speculative purchasing decisions, and materials accumulated in anticipation of possible labor disputes, inclement weather, or cyclical production demands. The typical layout of a storage warehouse is shown in Fig. 18–2. It is identified by the relatively large proportion of space devoted to storage (long-term holding).

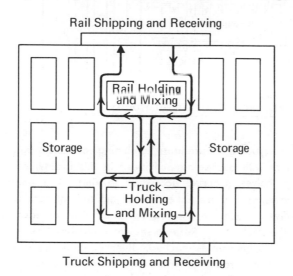

Fig. 18–2.   Layout of a typical storage warehouse.

Combination Warehousing

There are no sharp dividing lines between the storage and material-handling missions of warehouses. Most are designed to accomplish both. For example, storage and material handling are frequently combined in operations which involve conversion of bulk commodities into packaged stock. A survey conducted several years ago indicated that among companies relocating or establishing new distribution centers between 1960 and 1965, 38.3% were designed to accomplish sorting activities, 35.0% assembling, 28.0% packaging, and 7.1% fabrication. The authors concluded: "Even those of us who have followed these trends closely were surprised at the degree to which operations traditionally ascribed to the factory have been dispersed to distribution centers." [1]

An example of this type of warehouse is shown in Fig. 18–3, a diagram of the layout of a warehouse operated by a manufacturer of metal fasteners.

---

[1] Kenneth Marshall and John Miller, "Where Are the Distribution Centers Going?," *Handling & Shipping*, November, 1965, pp. 37–45.

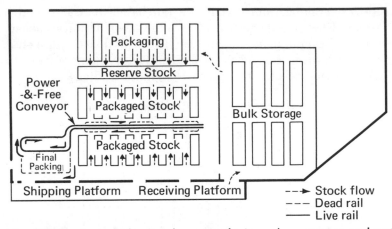

Fig. 18–3. Layout of a warehouse combining volume storage and material-handling activities with packaging activities. In this facility, packaged goods are stocked on shelves, grouped according to kind. A power-and-free conveyor moves orders, as they are picked, from stock to final packing for shipment. A powered conveyor, with unpowered switch-off rails at each stock section, loops through the stock area. Reserve shelves replenish stock shelves and are refilled when a minimum level is reached. Punched cards made from customers' orders signal for more production when bulk storage gets low. *Source:* "New Warehouse Sets Order-Filling Speed Records," *Handling & Shipping,* June–July, 1961, p. 32; published by Industrial Publishing Corp. (div. Pittway Corp.).

In speaking of warehousing, we should keep in mind that the term includes a wide range of activities and facilities. We have summarized the nature of the activities. It is important also to note that the type of facility used in warehousing may be an enclosed building, an underground cavern, a semienclosed shed, or even an open storage pile. Assembly or distribution warehousing is likely to take place primarily in the enclosed structure; storage warehousing may utilize all of the four types of facility. There are additional facility contrasts as well. Material-handling warehousing is generally typified by lateral movement, using a one-story structure and high-speed material-handling techniques, and there is likely to be less emphasis on "high-level" materials placement (the stacking of materials to heights of 20 to 24 feet). In contrast, storage warehouses may be multistory facilities, requiring less flexible and less rapid methods of handling materials.

PRIVATE OR PUBLIC WAREHOUSING?

Basically, a business firm has three alternatives in regard to warehousing. It can use public or own or lease private facilities. It is important to be able to establish criteria and evaluate each in terms of a firm's needs and financial capabilities. Except for differences in financial considerations, especially those having to do with the timing of depreciation expenses on owned facilities as opposed to lease-rental payments, leased and owned facilities have a great many characteristics in common and generally have been grouped in the category of private warehousing. The important distinction for logistics management is that between public and private warehousing.

There are advocates of both public and private warehousing, just as there are for common carrier and private transportation. Rather than engage in a pointless argument about which is best, we have elected to review the advantages and methods of engaging in both public and private warehousing. Their complementary nature is emphasized by a recent finding that of the companies using public warehousing, 75% distribute their products nationally, and presumably are among those firms for which the volume and flow of product in some areas is sufficient to support private warehousing as well.[2]

Private Warehousing

The construction, purchase, or lease of a private warehouse offers a firm advantages comparable to the operation of privately owned transportation equipment. First, it is likely to provide greater flexibility in design to meet the specific needs of the owner. This is especially important if the storage of a firm's products involves special problems such as those of temperature control, the handling of outsized objects, or other special installations not likely to be provided by the public warehouseman. Second, the operation of a private warehouse can provide the using firm greater control of the operation to insure that warehousing is conducted efficiently. A parallel to this advantage is the fact that private warehousing will, to a reasonable degree, guarantee a given service rate (cost) over a period of time. Although operating costs may rise or fall from time to time, the owning or leasing user is likely to have greater advance warning of possible changes in these costs.

In general the average cost to handle a unit through a private warehouse is less when the product moves through in a constant, high volume. It should be noted, however, that in attempting to increase volume (warehouse throughput) some firms owning or leasing warehouses have overextended market territories served by the warehouse. In these situations, they frequently incur greater transportation cost per unit than the savings in warehousing costs traded for it.

[2] McKinsey & Company, Inc. Survey of public warehousing industry conducted in 1970.

Owned or leased warehousing space may also be advantageous if it is used to house a local sales or field purchasing organization in the warehouse building itself. This action often requires the installation of special communications equipment to handle purchase or sales orders. However, the location of the sales staff at the warehouse location, in some instances, can create supervisory and organization problems which more than offset any savings that can be accomplished by the location of sales and warehousing activities in the same facility.

Finally, the use of owned or leased warehousing space may be necessitated by the desire to provide warehousing facilities near a company's manufacturing plant. Most storage space immediately adjacent to the production line is either owned or leased by the operating firm.

Public Warehousing

Public warehousing requires no investment in such facilities. Operating problems assumed by the public warehouseman also free executive talent for other activities. The public warehouseman is often well equipped to deal with problems of labor, insurance, and other matters related to warehouse design and operation.

The per-unit cost for public warehouse service is probably less than private or leased facilities when the volume of operations is low, or the level of operations fluctuates greatly from time to time. Further, the cost per unit handled is a known factor when a public warehouse is used. This facilitates future cost planning by the user.

In some localities, no personal property tax is assessed on inventory stored in public warehouses. One executive claims that:

It often develops, in fact, that a distribution system built around potential tax savings in various states—as service considerations may permit, of course—will show far greater *total* savings than one based on potential transportation and storage savings.[3]

Perhaps the greatest advantage in the use of public warehousing facilities is the great flexibility allowed in inventory location. This is particularly important when rate relationships between various modes of transportation or localities are subject to considerable change. A firm utilizing public warehousing facilities can shift the location of its inventories to reflect changes in the transportation rate structures which make existing warehouse locations comparatively uneconomical. Because it is purchased and paid for, public warehousing offers a precise documentation of warehousing costs not possible for most private warehousing operations.

[3] George R. Fraser, "Taxes Versus Transportation Costs," *Transportation & Distribution Management*, April, 1962, p. 17.

Finally, because it is available on a short-term basis, public warehousing may lend itself to test marketing activities, where the need for warehousing support is uncertain and perhaps temporary.

Criteria for Selecting Public Warehousing Services. A recent study provides information about various criteria used in the selection of public warehousing services.[4] More than a hundred users of public warehousing indicated the following ranking in importance for general factors in selection: service quality, warehousing costs, warehouse facility characteristics, warehouse services, transportation services, and clerical services. Within each of these categories, particular measures, criteria, or concerns were cited.

For example, the most important determinants of service quality were shipping and receiving accuracy, accurate record keeping, on-time shipments, and the ability to fulfill special instructions.

In warehousing cost determination, total warehousing costs were more important to shippers than individual charges for storage, handling, and clerical services. Of special importance here were transportation costs associated with a given warehouse location.

In assessing facility characteristics, users rated the cleanliness of facilities as most important, followed by the degree of security, fire, and infestation protection and the nature of handling equipment used. **(1) Does it strike you that cleanliness is an unusual measure of a facility? (2) Why?**

The primary measure in evaluating warehouse services was found to be order response time.

The assessment of transportation services in combination with warehousing was concerned primarily with motor carrier as opposed to rail or other services. This included both intercity common carrier and local cartage service. **(3) Why do you think public warehouse users responded in this fashion to the survey?**

In regard to clerical services, regular inventory reports were considered most important, followed by freight routing services. Computer facilities and freight payment services were ranked as relatively unimportant here. **(4) Can you offer some explanation for this?**

Finally, a warehouseman's reputation with the users' customers and with the warehouseman's other users was considered to be very important.

Among other findings were: "Building design and specific location are relatively unimportant, and there is a recognition that management skill is critical to a successful warehouse operation."[5]

---

[4] Kenneth B. Ackerman, R. William Gardner, and Lee P. Thomas, *Understanding Today's Distribution Center* (Washington, D. C.: Traffic Service Corp., 1972). The information in this section is based on this source.

[5] *Ibid.*, p. 163.

WAREHOUSE DESIGN

To facilitate our discussion of warehouse design, we will first assume a utopian situation in which the necessary warehousing requirements are determined, the material-handling system design selected, the facility laid out, walls and a roof built around it, and a site found to put it on. Then we will take a more realistic point of view and consider the trade-offs necessary in relating material-handling methods, layouts, buildings, and site.

Determination of Warehouse Requirements

The determination of necessary warehouse capacity requires at least two steps. The first, a determination of the supply or market area to be served by the warehouse, was discussed in Chapter 13. The second is concerned with the capacity needed in a specific facility to accommodate a given supply or market territory. It is this second step in the determination of warehouse capacity with which the following discussion is concerned.

Because of the varying nature of the building space and features required by each of the major warehousing operations, it is necessary to appraise capacity in terms of receiving and shipping, storage, and shipment processing space.

Information Required. The information necessary to determine facility capacities relates to the general level, and fluctuations in the level, of each type of warehousing activity. Different measures are necessary for each.

The sales estimate (or the purchasing schedule prepared from it) for the territory to be served by a warehouse facility is the basic document necessary to plan for the volume of movement likely to flow through a facility.

Table 18–1 presents the sales forecast for a company planning to locate a privately owned distribution warehousing facility in Cincinnati.

This type of estimate is typical of those prepared in many firms. In OKI Industries' sales organization, representatives are assigned by states, hence the state-by-state forecast. Assuming it has been determined that the optimum geographic area to be served by the Cincinnati warehouse is that bounded roughly by a circle with a radius of 100 miles and its center at Cincinnati, then sales statistics must be recast to reflect the differences in sales and logistics territories. This is shown in Table 18–2, along with a breakdown of additional information needed to complete an appraisal of capacity requirements. The additional information re-

TABLE 18–1. Sales Forecast, Ohio, Indiana, and Kentucky Territories
(OKI Industries)

State	By Month			Year's Total*
	January	February	. . . .	
Ohio	$1,600,000	$1,700,000	. . . .	$23,000,000
Kentucky	900,000	1,100,000	. . . .	16,000,000
Indiana	1,100,000	1,100,000	. . . .	17,000,000
Total	$3,600,000	$3,900,000	. . . .	$56,000,000

*If available, a longer-range forecast should be used.

quired can be provided by: (1) a sampling of bills of lading for shipments sent into the designated warehouse territory to determine the order-cycle time required for moving product from manufacturing facilities by the warehouse and the relationship of incoming to outgoing volume to be scheduled through the warehouse, and (2) longer-term estimates of trends in demands to be placed upon the warehouse operation.

Inside Requirements. Indoor space is more expensive to provide than that which is unenclosed. When considering indoor space, planners must think in terms of cubic feet as well as square feet. This trend of thought has been encouraged by the growing use of high-lift stacking equipment and higher-ceilinged, single-story structures.

Of great importance in determining the necessary height of a warehouse ceiling is the relative usage that can be obtained at each height. For example, excess ceiling height may create unused space between the top of storage stacks and the ceiling over and above the minimum amount needed for proper ventilation, a fire sprinkler system, and adequate lighting. Some of the principal determinants of efficient ceiling height are the ease with which stored goods can be stacked, the rapidity and frequency with which they must be moved through the storage area, and the size of the storage area in relation to receiving, order-picking, and shipping areas of the warehouse. In the following example, a ceiling height of 20 feet with 16-foot stacking of goods has been assumed for the warehouse under construction.

Order-Picking Space. Order picking must be carried out within physical reaching distance from the floor unless the "picking" is done with mechanical equipment. The constant movement of stock which takes place in an order-picking area precludes extensive handling of materials at great heights because of the inefficiency of repeated lifting and lowering of stock. The area must be more open in nature to accommodate unusually heavy traffic flows required for order-assembly ac-

TABLE 18–2. Information (and Its Organization) Required for Analysis of

Month	(1) Sales (millions)	(2) Sales Direct from Plant to Customer (millions)	(3) Sales Through Cincinnati Warehouse (millions)	(4) Sales Through Cincinnati Warehouse (in 000's of lb.)[a]	(5) Number of Shipments Dispatched[b]	(6) Number of Pickups[c] (all truck)
January	$ .8	$ .2	$ .6	300	6,000	120
February	1.2	.2	1.0	500	10,000	200
March	2.7	.5	2.2	1,100	22,000	220
April	3.1	.6	2.5	1,250	25,000	250
May	1.6	.3	1.3	650	13,000	260
June	1.8	.3	1.5	750	15,000	300
July	1.7	.4	1.3	650	13,000	260
August	1.5	.3	1.2	600	12,000	240
September	2.0	.4	1.6	800	16,000	320
October	3.7	.9	2.8	1,400	28,000	280
November	4.2	1.0	3.2	1,600	32,000	320
December	5.1	.9	4.2	2,100	42,000	420
Total	$29.4	$6.0	$23.4	11,700	234,000	3,190

[a]Computed on the basis of an average dollar density of $2/lb.
[b]Computed on the basis of an average order size of $100 or 50 lb.
[c]Based on an analysis of orders originating in various parts of the service territory, resulting in computation of 50 shipments per pickup in all months except March, April, October, November, and December, when greater overall volume allows consolidation of 100 shipments per pickup.
[d]Obtained by assuming a 500,000-lb. year-beginning inventory and adding Column 7 to Column 8 (for previous month), then subtracting Column 4.

tivities. It is not uncommon to find the cubic footage of stock in an order-picking area to approximate only 20% of the available cube in the area, as indicated in Table 18–2. Attempts have been made to make better use of order-picking areas by utilizing space over the areas for more permanent storage.

Generally stock is moved into an order-picking area just prior to the demand for it. Space requirements will increase just before an anticipated increase in order demand. Order demand can be estimated by first deducting from estimated sales those shipments which will travel directly to customers from plants, probably in large quantities. The remainder is that amount of sales volume which will move through the planned warehousing facilities. This can be converted to tonnage by applying a dollar-density measure for the Company's products to the sales volume expected to be delivered from the area warehouse facility.

Some amount of stock will be moved to the order-picking area in anticipation of sales over the following few days. In Table 18–2, it has

Capacity Requirements, by Month (OKI Industries' Cincinnati Warehouse)

(7)	(8)	(9)	(10)	(11)	(12)	(13)	(14)
Receipts from Factory (000's of lb.)	Month-End Inventory (000's of lb.)[d]	Month-End Inventory in Order-Picking Area (000's of lb.)[e]	Month-End Inventory in Storage and Receiving Area (000's of lb.)	Cubic Feet Needed for Order Picking, Storage, and Receiving Stocks[f]			Capacity Requirement, End-of-Month (square footage)[i]
				Order Picking[g]	Storage and Receiving[h]	Total	
700	900	100	800	100,000	320,000	420,000	21,000
700	1,100	220	880	220,000	352,000	572,000	28,600
700	700	250	450	250,000	200,000	450,000	22,500
700	150	130	20	130,000	8,000	138,000	6,900
700	200	150	50	150,000	20,000	170,000	8,500
1,200	650	130	520	130,000	208,000	338,000	16,900
1,200	1,200	120	1,080	120,000	432,000	552,000	27,600
1,200	1,800	160	1,640	160,000	656,000	816,000	40,800
1,200	2,200	280	1,920	280,000	768,000	1,048,000	52,400
1,200	2,000	320	1,680	320,000	672,000	992,000	49,600
1,200	1,600	420	1,180	420,000	472,000	892,000	44,600
700	200	60	140	60,000	56,000	116,000	5,800

[e]Assumes that a supply sufficient for four business days' (1/5 month) sales is kept on hand.
[f]Average product weight density is 5 lb./cu. ft.
[g]Cubic footage displaced by product is 1/5 of the total cubage required in the order-picking area, assuming a 20-foot-high ceiling.
[h]Cubic footage displaced by product is 1/2 of the total cubage required in the storage and receiving area, assuming a 20-foot-high ceiling and average height of 16-foot storage stacks.
[i]Assuming a uniform 20-foot-high ceiling.

been assumed that a quantity comparable to four days' sales will be kept on hand in the order-picking area. The actual quantity in any individual case can be determined by: (1) comparing the cost of restocking the order-selection area from the storage area at varying intervals with (2) the cost of space needed to maintain stocks of varying amounts in the order-selection area, plus the cost of selection (measured in distance and time required to select orders while maintaining various quantities of stock in the area). Individual quantities may be computed for each item in stock, especially if particular items move through the area in widely varying quantities.

Having determined the quantity to be maintained in the area for each stock, this quantity can be converted to cubic feet by application of the ratio of product cube to total-space cube. This is 1:5 in the example shown in Table 18–2. From the pattern of sales, it appears that these products are highly seasonal, and especially related to holidays. The seasonal demand for OKI's products requires an order-picking cube of from 60,000 cu. ft. at the end of December to 420,000 cu. ft. at the end of November.

Storage and Receiving Space. The necessary space for storage and receiving can be computed in much the same way as that for order picking. The storage of product is likely to make much better utilization of a given volume of cubic feet, primarily because it is not necessary to provide as much access to the product, requiring space-consuming aisleways and relatively low stacking.

Quantities placed in storage basically depend on: (1) the nature of the product, (2) the pattern of production in relation to sales, (3) the length of the order cycle required to replenish supplies, and (4) the desired level of customer service.

Goods for which the customer is willing to wait and for which price may be a secondary consideration, such as some industrial items and consumer specialty goods, can be produced to order. Even if produced for stock, a minimum stock is often maintained. However, most industrial products and supplies and consumer convenience and shopping goods require the maintenance of inventories and warehouses.

It is costly to regulate production levels from day to day to accommodate demand, even if sufficient capacity exists to meet peak demand periods. First, the excess capacity that must be maintained is expensive. Second, fluctuations in the size of the production labor force are costly and can cause severe industrial relations problems. Warehousing absorbs the shock caused by fluctuations in demand and supply.

The length of the order cycle required to replenish supplies becomes important in the planning of warehouse requirements only if: (1) production levels easily can be adjusted to sales levels, (2) a stock can be maintained equivalent to that required to meet demand during one order cycle, with a minimum base or safety stock for contingencies, and (3) customers cannot be persuaded to wait for a given item. In addition, the restrictions imposed by order-cycle length can be overcome to a degree by an overlapping of orders, that is, the placement of orders so that several might be in transit at once, each to arrive at a different time.

In the illustration, the manufacturing facilities appear to be run on a two-season basis, with production at a higher constant rate from June through November than from December through May. Goods placed in intermediate-term storage (30 days or more) may be organized to occupy up to 70% of the available cubic footage in a storage area, provided that the product can be stacked or otherwise stored with the aid of pallets, pallets in racks, or other devices to unitize products.

In the example, all items not in the order-picking area are assumed to be in storage. Further, goods in storage occupy only about 50% of the available cube, making allowance for receiving activities which also require space. Total storage space requirements thus range from a low of 8,000 cu. ft. at the end of April to 768,000 cu. ft. at the end of September. In all cases, cubic footage is converted to square footage by dividing by the proposed height of the building, assuming a constant ceiling height.

Interchange of Space. The value of flexibility in storage and handling equipment is illustrated by the OKI situation. If permanent facilities were to be established for each of these separate operations, it can be seen that the amount of space needed to accommodate inside activities would be 1,188,000 cu. ft., or a floor area of 59,400 sq. ft. Because the amount of space needed for one activity does not vary directly with the other, the peak order-picking period falls at a different time than the peak storage time. Therefore, the use of flexible equipment permitting the conversion of space from time to time would allow OKI to build a warehouse of 1,048,000 cu. ft. (52,400 sq. ft.) capacity to meet its needs. At an average cost of $.30/cu. ft., or $6/sq. ft. for a warehouse with a usable height of twenty feet, the saving in construction costs would amount to $42,000 with the use of movable material-handling equipment.

Only monthly sales and material-handling volume have been shown in Table 18–2. Where shipments would fluctuate extensively over short periods of time, it would be necessary to reduce sales and activity estimates to a week-by-week or even day-by-day basis.

If possible, many firms try to encourage customers to order certain products in anticipation of demand in order that other demand peaks can be met when they occur. For example, in a grocery products warehouse, less perishable items such as oranges, potatoes, and cold cuts are sent into the retail stores early in the week so that the Friday peak demand for deliveries of highly perishable fresh produce and poultry can be met. This type of planning allows more activity in less space, and saves labor costs by leveling the workload.[6]

Use of Supplementary Public Warehousing. Before reaching a decision on the amount of private warehousing space required by a given situation, it is always wise to appraise the possibility of meeting some or all of the demand through a public warehouse, assuming the alternative exists in a given community. Public warehousing charges take on an entirely variable characteristic to the user. This is contrasted by the heavy fixed charges associated with building or leasing a warehouse, combined with the much lower variable costs of operation. Thus, if public warehousing facilities can be used to meet short-run peaks in activity, the same amount of warehousing effort possibly can be provided

---

[6] For a discussion of this and other warehousing problems, see George A. Gecowets, "How To Understand Warehousing Even if You're Not a Warehouseman," *Handling & Shipping,* February, 1962, pp. 28–30.

with a smaller private facility and a lower total cost of warehousing. The type of analysis suggested is shown in Table 18–3.

The results in Table 18–3 are typical of many warehousing situations. Based on current estimates of demand, the lowest cost method for meeting the warehousing requirements for OKI at Cincinnati is to build or lease private capacity of 21,000 sq. ft. and utilize public warehousing facilities for handling over one-third of OKI's volume through Cincinnati. **(5) What other considerations would you want to take into account in appraising the extent of public warehousing use in this example? (6) How might they affect your ultimate decision regarding the size of the private warehousing facility to be built?**

Outside Requirements. Outside warehouse space requirements, unless the firm utilizes outside space for storage piles, generally will be determined by the amount of space required for the positioning of transportation equipment for loading and unloading. Both are a function of: (1) traffic fluctuations of inbound and outbound goods at the warehouse, (2) the degree of effectiveness with which equipment is scheduled, and (3) the degree to which other warehousing facilities are utilized.

Positioning of Equipment. Traffic fluctuations at the proposed warehouse can be measured roughly by the information in Table 18–2. It appears that a private warehouse of 21,000 sq. ft. would probably be required to handle a peak of about 16,000 outgoing shipments per month. Equated to pickups, this amounts to 320 truck pickups a month. Under the assumption that pickups are limited to 10 hours a day during each of the 20 working days in a month, and that a pickup of 50 shipments requires about two hours, one truck stall (spot) for shipping would accommodate 100 pickups a month. Four shipping stalls would be required to accommodate 100% of pickups at the average level of volume during peak months.

Averages cover up peaks and valleys, especially in the pickup and delivery of freight. It is possible that eight stalls might be needed to accommodate all trucks without waiting at a 21,000-sq.-ft OKI facility. The number could be reduced by: (1) the use of waiting-line theory in the planning of the facility, (2) a greater attempt to schedule pickups and to hold carriers to a prearranged schedule, (3) the off-peak scheduling of some shipments, and (4) the spotting of equipment to be loaded by second- or third-shift warehouse labor. Off-peak scheduling is a much less desirable practice with highway equipment than with rail equipment, for the truck driver often loads and unloads his own vehicle during regular pickup and delivery hours. A rail car would have to be loaded or unloaded by warehouse personnel in any event, because loading and unloading assistance is not part of the service offered by rail transportation.

TABLE 18-3. Warehousing Costs Under Varying Proportions of Use of Private and Public Warehouse Facilities of OKI Industries' Cincinnati Distribution Point

(1)		(2)	(3)	(4)	(5)	(6)	(7)
Size of Owned Facilities (sq. ft.)	Average Percentage of Private Warehouse Capacity Used	Annual Volume Moving Through Private Warehouse (cwt.)[a]	Annual Volume Moving Through Public Warehouse (cwt.)	Fixed Private Warehousing Costs[b]	Variable Private Warehousing Costs[c]	Public Warehousing Costs[d]	Total Warehousing Costs
52,400	51.7%	117,000	–	$157,200	$117,000	–	$274,200
49,600	54.2	114,620	2,380	148,800	114,620	$ 4,760	268,180
44,600	59.1	110,880[e]	6,120	133,800	110,800	12,240	256,840
40,800	61.5	110,880[e]	6,120	122,400	110,880	12,240	245,520
28,600	73.8	90,640[e]	26,360	85,800	90,640	52,720	229,160
27,600	74.7	90,640[e]	26,360	82,800	90,640	52,720	226,160
22,500	80.2	75,130[e]	41,870	67,500	75,130	83,740	226,370
21,000	81.8	75,130[e]	41,870	63,000	75,130	83,740	221,870[f]
16,900	85.5	58,630	59,070	50,700	58,630	118,140	227,470
8,500	95.7	21,560[e]	95,440	25,500	21,560	190,880	237,940
6,900	98.6	21,560[e]	95,440	20,700	21,560	190,880	233,140
5,800	100.0	21,560[e]	95,440	17,400	21,560	190,880	229,840
0	–	–	117,000	–	–	234,000	234,000

[a]Computed on the basis of an annual inventory turn of 11.0 through the private warehouse facilities.
[b]Computed on the basis of $3/sq. ft. of floor space per year.
[c]Computed on the basis of $1/cwt. moved through the warehouse.
[d]Computed on the basis of $2/cwt. moved through the warehouse.
[e]Due to the relative needs of order picking and storage and receiving space in various months of minimum usage, there is only a negligible difference in the relative use of each of these warehouse capacities; the same utilization could probably be obtained by using the smaller size of owned facilities in each case by adjusting the timing of the build-up of stocks in the order picking area.
[f]Lowest total cost alternative.

To provide sufficient space for the backing of highway vehicles for the purpose of rear-end loading, it may be recommended that a space at least 12 ft. wide and with a depth four times the length of the vehicle be allowed for each stall. Thus, a facility built to accommodate six vehicles of 50-ft. length would be 72 × 200 ft. or 14,400 sq. ft. This figure can be reduced by a third with the use of a saw-tooth dock allowing for diagonal parking of vehicles in relation to the building.

The same type of analysis could be made for inbound freight movements. It appears that these are received on a much more constant basis. A basic question that must be asked in the planning of receiving facilities is, "How does the freight arrive?" At distribution warehouses it is much more likely that rail transportation will be used for inbound freight than for outbound.

Assume that the peak volume of freight (all low in density) incoming to the proposed facility of 21,000 sq. ft. will be about 700,000 lb., roughly equivalent to thirty-five 20,000-lb. rail carloads or seventy 10,000-lb. truckloads. If approximately four hours is required to unload a truck and eight hours to unload a rail car, the capacity of one unloading spot for each would be 20 rail cars and 40 trucks per month (using a figure of 20 working days).

Influencing factors, including the use of both rail and truck transportation for incoming shipments, the spotting of equipment, and the effective scheduling of shipments, would probably require no more than one spot for a truck trailer and one for a rail car on the receiving side of the warehouse. In this case, it might be best if the incoming truck stall could be placed alongside those planned for outgoing goods in order to limit requirements for vehicle turn-around to only one side of the building.

Rail facilities needed to serve a warehouse consist of a spur line onto the property. All loading and unloading must be done while the car is situated parallel to the platform. A common distance between the middle of the car floor and the edge of the freight dock is 68 inches. Therefore, at least 12 feet of clearance between the building and the property line should be provided each spur.

Dock Requirements. In the assessment of dock requirements, provision must be made for the temporary placement of freight, the storage of dock equipment, such as dock plates (similar to the use of gangplanks on a ship), and the two-way traffic typical in most loading and unloading operations. Although it will vary from case to case, twenty-foot depths for freight docks are quite common.

The amount of running feet of dock, in the illustration, would be determined by allowing 12 feet for each of seven truck bays, or 84 feet, and at least 50 feet to accommodate the most common length of a rail car. This would amount to a requirement of 134 running feet of dock space, or 2,680 sq. ft. for outdoor shipping and receiving. If the shipping and receiving areas are to be entirely inside the building, as in many newer installations, then this figure must be included in the estimate of inside space requirements.

Based on overall appraisal of the demands to be placed on the Cincinnati warehouse of OKI, the amount of indoor and outdoor space required for the facility is shown in Table 18–4. This is roughly in accordance with a rule of thumb suggested by warehousemen, "For most warehousing operations, the building should not cover more than half of the land area."[7]

TABLE 18–4. Space Required for Warehouse (OKI Industries, Cincinnati)

		Square Feet
Indoor space:		
Building requirements (100′ × 210′)		21,000
Outdoor space:		
Truck positioning	14,400	
Rail positioning (12′ × 100′)*	1,200	
Truck and rail dock	2,680	18,280
Total		39,280

*Based on the assumption that a rail spur would be brought in flush with the short side of the building.

Material-Handling Systems and Facility Design

We have considered material-handling methods in Chapter 17. Our purpose here is to place them in the general context of facility design. Basically, the importance of the relationship varies directly with the importance of material-handling-oriented costs, such as labor and equipment, as opposed to storage-oriented costs, such as building and land, in the operation of the facility. Operations dominated by material-handling costs as opposed to storage costs, characterized by a high rate of turnover for their stocks, will require: (1) smaller length and width dimensions, (2) a single-story facility, (3) a lower ceiling, unless specialized equipment is to be used for material handling, and (4) in some cases a relatively high length-to-width ratio for a flow-through operation from one side of the building to the other.

Module Size. Clearly, the greater the number of trips required to each stock location in the warehouse per year to deposit and remove stock, the smaller is the desirable size of a warehouse module. Many public warehouse facilities designed for the rapid turnover of merchan-

[7] Ackerman, et al., op. cit., p. 77.

dise are made up, for example, of 100,000 to 120,000-sq. ft. modules. Beyond this size, economies in construction are more than outweighed by material-handling cost penalties.

Number of Storage Levels. Although subject to some debate, the matter of the number of storage levels has pretty well been resolved in favor of single-story facilities for maximum material-handling efficiency. However, a conveyor system for goods which can be handled in this fashion can make multilevel facilities more attractive, even for operations with a high material-handling requirement.

Ceiling Height. The cubic capacity of a facility is a function of height as well as length and width. The relationships among these dimensions influence at least four major categories of costs, including those for storage aids, vehicles, operations, and construction. Several years ago, for example, Walker Manufacturing Company, a manufacturer of automotive exhaust systems, mufflers, and tailpipes, followed an analytic procedure of this type in determining appropriate facility ceiling height. Results of its analysis are shown in Figs. 18–4 through 18–7.[8]

Steps used in this analysis included the establishment of a basic module of space (in this case, 100 cubic feet) and the measurement of

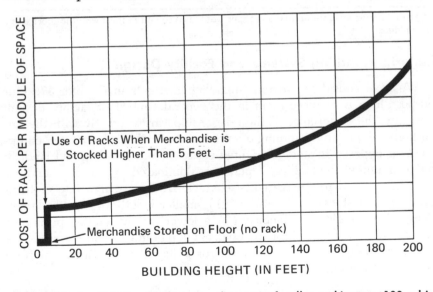

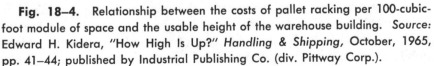

Fig. 18–4. Relationship between the costs of pallet racking per 100-cubic-foot module of space and the usable height of the warehouse building. *Source:* Edward H. Kidera, "How High Is Up?" *Handling & Shipping,* October, 1965, pp. 41–44; published by Industrial Publishing Co. (div. Pittway Corp.).

[8] The following discussion in this section is based on Edward H. Kidera, "How High Is Up?" *Handling & Shipping,* October, 1965, pp. 41–44.

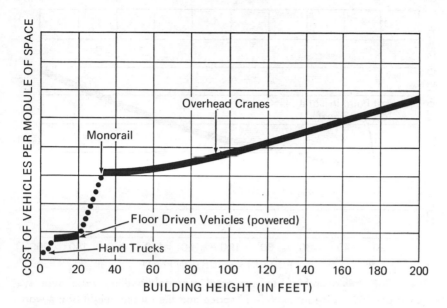

Fig. 18–5. Relationship between the costs of material-handling vehicles per 100-cubic-foot module of space and the usable height of the warehouse building. *Source:* Same as for Fig. 18–4.

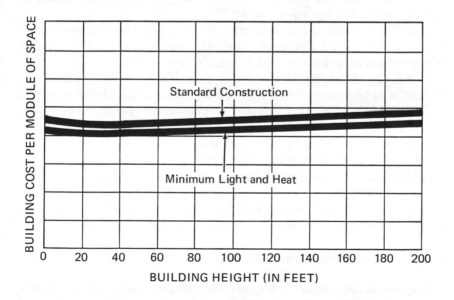

Fig. 18–6. Relationship between building costs per 100-cubic-foot module of space and the usable height of the warehouse building. *Source:* Same as for Fig. 18–4.

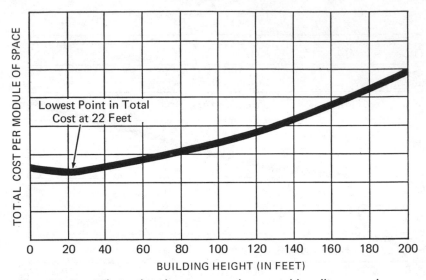

Fig. 18–7. Relationship between total material-handling–warehouse system costs per 100-cubic-foot module of space and the usable height of the warehouse building. *Source:* Same as for Fig. 18–4.

costs resulting from different combinations of material-handling methods in buildings of varying heights. (7) **How do you explain the nature of the cost curves in Figs. 18–4 and 18–5?**

In regard to building cost estimates shown in Fig. 18–6, estimates were prepared both for a building of standard construction and for one providing for minimum heating and lighting requirements.

In this case, "Changes in operating method introduced in response to changes in height produced no significant gain or loss, with the exception of automated order picking. Higher ceiling heights produced cost penalties for automated order picking." [9] Thus, operating costs were not included in the plot of total system cost shown in Fig. 18–7.

(8) **How would you appraise the evaluation illustrated in Figs. 18–4 through 18–7. (9) Do the results appear logical? (10) Are important elements omitted?**

Extremely high land values in parts of Europe have led several European manufacturers to construct vertical warehouses up to 100 feet high utilizing sophisticated stacker crane equipment operating on the principle of the automatic vertical parking lots found in some cities.

Length-to-Width Ratio. Although the distance from a point in the center of a warehouse floor to all points along its walls is minimized in

[9] *Ibid.,* p. 43.

a square building, goods rarely flow through the "center point." In fact, for operations designed for flows from one side of the building to its opposite, length-to-width ratios of up to 5-to-1 are not uncommon.

Facility Layout

Facility layout is a major determinant of the cost and service levels which can be obtained from a warehouse. Ineffective planning of warehouse layout can build a space penalty into the operation which may require years to overcome, if it is ever possible to do so.

Techniques which facilitate plant layout are transferable to the warehouse layout problem. The preparation of route sheets, operation schedules, movable templates drawn to scale to represent freight and equipment, and other devices are all effective and too numerous to discuss in detail. We will dwell briefly on some of the problems of layout which have special importance in the layout of a warehouse facility.

Limiting Factors. In layout planning, much time can be saved by first determining what alternatives cannot be considered for reasons of physical limitations of a facility. Windows, fire doors, receiving and shipping doors, elevators, and supporting columns all present problems for the layout planner. The more of these limiting factors that can be avoided by eliminating them from consideration in the planning or redesign of a warehouse, the better.

Severe restrictions imposed by supporting pillars have been avoided by the growing number of firms switching to single-story warehouse buildings. This has allowed a disregard for elevators as well. Windows have been replaced with more adequate overhead artificial lighting. The savings resulting from the more efficient use of space near curtain, or outside, warehouse walls has more than compensated for the extra cost of lighting. Receiving and shipping doors can be planned in relation to one another so that material will flow through a facility essentially in one direction. Fire door requirements may be reduced in some areas by the installation of sprinkler fire devices in the warehouse.

Materials Flow. In laying out the receiving, storage, order selection (sometimes including packaging or repackaging), and shipping areas within a warehouse, it is important to keep several points in mind.

First, to the extent possible, materials should move in one general direction through the warehouse. An effective layout discourages deviations from the flow pattern determined to be most efficient for a facility. Fixed conveyor facilities, for example, discourage a deviation from material-handling flow intended by the layout planner. (11) **To** what extent is definite directional flow present in each of the warehouse layouts shown in Figs. 18–1, 18–2, and 18–3?

Second, provision should be made, where possible or necessary, for the circumvention of one or more stages in the warehousing process. Where the turnover of stocks is of less importance, for example, layout should facilitate the movement of stock directly from incoming transportation vehicles to the order-selection area.

Third, the cross-hauling of freight within areas of the warehouse should be avoided. Layout planning must take into account the traffic volume and patterns at various levels of operation to provide adequate space for movements, especially where individually powered warehouse vehicles are used. It must also consider the efficiencies to be gained by the use of one-way corridors and other devices to route internal traffic in such a manner as to eliminate crossing traffic.

Fourth, the greatest amount of stock possible should be located closest to its point of greatest need. Further, if a one-directional flow of material is the objective, the greatest possible amount of stock should be placed at each stage of the warehousing process in such a manner that it will be easiest to locate and secure for the next stage. These sound like truisms, but the analysis needed to accomplish the goals is much more complex than the goals. The goals themselves are rarely reached.

Storage Layout. The storage area of a warehouse facility is simply laid out. It consists of storage locations and a surrounding network of aisle-ways.

Pallet Placement. There is some argument about the most efficient pattern for pallet placement. Some advocate "on the square" layout, while others prefer angular placement of varying degrees. Both types are shown in Fig. 18–8. Basically, the first of these methods requires less space for the actual placement of pallets; all of the space within the dotted line in example A of Fig. 18–8 is utilized. But square pallet placement requires more surrounding aisle space for the servicing of the actual pallet area.

Of great importance in determining the relative efficiency of pallet placement designs is the amount of access to material that is required. Lower access requirements allow a smaller proportion of pallets to be placed with aisle "facings" or exposures. Where less access is required, aisle space savings become less important and on-the-square placement may be relatively efficient. However, at the same time, space losses due to angular placement are reduced in proportion to the total space occupied by the pallet area. Also, the angular placement of pallets becomes more attractive as the length of motive pallet-handling equipment increases.

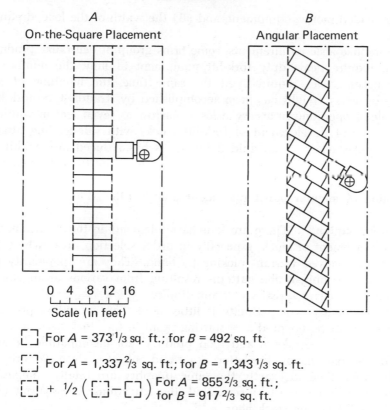

A
On-the-Square Placement

B
Angular Placement

0   4   8 12 16
Scale (in feet)

For A = 373 $1/3$ sq. ft.; for B = 492 sq. ft.

For A = 1,337 $2/3$ sq. ft.; for B = 1,343 $1/3$ sq. ft.

$\square$ + $1/2$ $\left(\square - \square \right)$ For A = 855 $2/3$ sq. ft.; for B = 917 $2/3$ sq. ft.

Fig. 18–8. On-the-square and angular pallet placement.

A strong argument for the comparative efficiency of angular placement, under conditions of long aisle length, has been advanced by Ballou.[10]

Aisle Width. Aisle width requirements vary, of course, with the size of material-handling equipment used and freight moved. If the latter is unitized, pallet or container dimensions and the size of fork-lift equipment will determine aisle dimensions.

Generally, main warehouse aisles are designed to allow two-way traffic of loaded fork-lifts. With extra allowances, this requires 10- to 12-ft.-wide corridors for material-handling systems using standard 48-inch-wide pallets.

Pallet access aisles, on the other hand, need be wide enough for only one vehicle in low traffic areas. The exact width will be determined by: (1) the length of motive equipment with pallet, (2) the turning radius

[10] Ronald H. Ballou, "Pallet Layout for Optimum Space Utilization," *Transportation & Distribution Management*, February, 1964, pp. 24–33.

of the loaded motive equipment, and (3) the width of the loaded equipment.

To reduce aisle requirements, some firms group or centralize products which require heavy-duty fork-lift equipment to limit the number of wide access aisles required. At the same time, the handling of less bulky or heavy freight has been accomplished by straddle-type fork-lifts capable of operating in access aisles as narrow as seven feet in width.

The recent development of fork-lift trucks with side-loading attachments and stacker cranes guided by tracks has reduced aisle-width requirements in some warehouses to a few inches more than the width of the widest load handled. (12) **How will this development influence the adoption of angular pallet placement plans?** (13) **Why?**

Stock Location.[11] There are four basic elements in the determination of the placement of stock, especially in order selection areas where the quantities involved warrant picking by hand. They are: popularity per item, size per unit, traffic patterns resulting from various arrangements of stock, and characteristics of compatibility.

The element of compatibility is little more than a guiding principle in that it must be honored as a starting point in the stock location problem. Generally petroleum and food products are incompatible because the former may "flavor" the latter; a nut and bolt of a given size ordered at the same time in exactly the same quantity are totally compatible items. The former must be separated; the latter must be adjacent (but not "mixed") on the stock floor.

The relative emphasis on each of the factors of stock location depends on the system of order selection under consideration. Systems can be based on principles of: (1) out-and-back selection of each item, (2) picker routing, whereby several items are picked on a single trip through the selection area, and (3) picking stations, where each station is marked and all stations are served by a fixed or portable conveyor system.

Out-and-Back Selection. This system is most often used where order items are picked in large quantities, or where the entire job is carried out with the use of fork-lifts capable of picking only one item on one pallet during one trip out and back. When this type of operation is assumed, a great deal of emphasis may be placed on the positioning of the most popular items and sets of highly compatible items near the order assembly point. However, it appears that even in this type of situation, some attempt must be made to base location on both popularity and the relative size of stock required in an order selection area. This suggests

---

[11] Material for this section is adapted from J. L. Heskett, "Cube-Per-Order Index —A Key to Warehouse Stock Location," *Transportation & Distribution Management,* April, 1963, pp. 27–31.

the use of a measure such as the cube-per-order index developed in the following example.

Six items are stocked in a warehouse. They have varying degrees of popularity. The amount of stock kept in the order selection area varies, and is determined by: (1) the cost to restock the item at varying frequencies and (2) the costs of space and order selection for the item at varying levels of stock. There are no market restrictions created by characteristics of compatibility. The number of times each item is called for, the volume required in the order selection area, and the capacity of each "zone" emanating from the order assembly point are shown in Table 18–5 and Fig. 18–9, respectively. How would total order selection costs vary under each of the predominant philosophies of stock location? If stocks with the greatest popularity, in terms of the number of times they appear on an order per day, were to be placed in zone A of the order selection area shown in Fig. 18–9, item 5 would be placed there first.

TABLE 18–5. Item Characteristics for Stock Placement Purposes

(1) Item Number	(2) Cube per Item	(3) Average Order Size (units)	(4) Number of Orders per Day	(5) Number of Days' Demand on Hand	(6) Required Cubic Footage in Order Selection Area
1	2 cu. ft.	10	100	3	6,000
2	10	6	300	2	36,000
3	16	1	900	1	14,400
4	1	4	350	3	4,200
5	16	3	1,200	1	57,600
6	4	20	300	3	72,000
			3,150		190,200

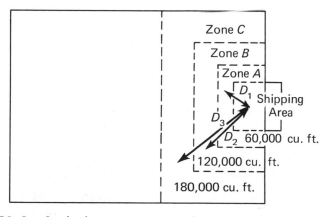

Fig. 18–9. Stock placement zones in the order selection area of a warehouse.

Because of its bulk, item 5 would take nearly all of the capacity of zone A, allowing only item 4 to be located in zone A with sufficient quantity to meet short-run demands. Items 6, 3, and 2 are the next popular and would fill zone B. Item 1 would be relegated to zone C. Order selection costs would be as shown in Table 18–6, assuming the average time and cost of selecting stock from each zone on an out-and-back basis were computed on the basis of the distances (D_1, D_2, and D_3) in Fig. 18–9. Here, the total daily cost of selecting stock would be $1,116.

Applying the size-per-unit system of stock location, locating items occupying the smallest amount of space nearest the shipping area, more stock items will be found nearer the shipping area than under any other method of space allocation. Using the method for the six items in the example, we would come up with an order selection cost (shown in Table 18–7) of $1,176 per day for the same volume of business.

TABLE 18–6. Costs of Order Selection Under Popularity Arrangement of Stock

Item Number	Number of Orders per Day	Required Cubic Footage	Zone	Order Selection Cost per Order[a]	Order Selection Cost per Day
5	1,200	57,600	A	$.20	$ 240
3	900	14,400	A–B[b]	.37[b]	433
4	350	4,200	B	.40	140
2	300	36,000	B	.40	120
6	300	72,000	B–C[b]	.41[b]	123
1	100	6,000	C	.60	60
	3,150				$1,116

[a]Based on a measurement of D_1, D_2, and D_3, in Fig. 18–9. Cost estimates assume, for the sake of the example, that all units of an item in an order can be carried in one trip out and back.

[b]Order selection cost adjusted to reflect the fact that a portion of the item stock must be located in each of two order selection zones.

TABLE 18–7. Costs of Order Selection Under Unit Size Arrangement of Stock

Item Number	Cube per Item	Total Required Cubic Footage	Zone	Order Selection Cost	Number of Orders per Day	Order Selection Cost per Day
4	1	4,200	A	$.20	350	$ 70
1	2	6,000	A	.20	100	20
6	4	72,000	A–B*	.26*	300	78
2	10	36,000	B	.40	300	120
3	16	14,400	B	.40	900	360
5	16	57,600	B–C*	.44*	1,200	528
					3,150	$1,176

*Order selection cost adjusted to reflect the fact that a portion of the item stock must be located in each of two order selection zones.

A variation of the size-per-unit system locates nearest the order assembly point entire stocks of those items which require the lowest total cubic footage in the order selection area. This system has been employed in the calculations shown in Table 18–8. It results in the lowest daily order selection cost thus far, $939.

TABLE 18–8. Costs of Order Selection Under Arrangement of Stock by Total Cubic Footage Requirements

Item Number	Total Required Cubic Footage	Zone	Order Selection Cost	Number of Orders per Day	Order Selection Cost per Day
4	4,200	A	$.20	350	$ 70
1	6,000	A	.20	100	20
3	14,400	A	.20	900	180
2	36,000	A	.20	300	60
5	57,600	B	.40	1,200	480
6	72,000	B–C*	.43*	300	129
				3,150	$939

*Order selection cost adjusted to reflect the fact that a portion of the item stock must be located in each of two order selection zones.

In general, however, none of these approaches consistently will provide the best solution to the problem. A rule can be formulated in regard to the use of these philosophies. When the sum of orders per day for a group of smaller products (items 1, 3, and 2) exceeds that for a larger product (item 5) with cubage requirements equal to the sum of the group, then grouping by size (cubic footage requirements) should be attempted. When the reverse is true, popularity provides a better basis for location.

This suggests the development of an index to weight the relative priority which each item should have in being placed near the shipping area. The index, called a cube-per-order index, provides the necessary measurement. It is defined as the required cubic footage of stock space per order filled during a given period of time.

The calculations of the cube-per-order index for each item in the example are shown in Table 18–9. They result in order selection costs $265 per day below that achieved by the item popularity criterion, $325 per day below that provided by an arrangement of items by unit size, and $88 per day below that obtainable under an item stock cube arrangement. Although the calculations in Tables 18–5 through 18–9 could be refined to reflect more accurately the continuous spectrum of distance–cost relationships, the final results would still favor an integration of size and popularity measurements in determining stock locations.

TABLE 18–9. Cube per Order Index, Location Priority, and Selection Costs for Various Items

(1) Item Number	(2) Required Cubic Footage	(3) Orders per Day	(4) Cube per Order Index (2 ÷ 3)	(5) Zone	(6) Order Selection Cost per Order	(7) Order Selection Cost per Day
4	4,200	350	12	A	$.20	$ 70
3	14,400	900	16	A	.20	180
5	57,600	1,200	48	A–B*	.26*	312
1	6,000	100	60	B	.40	40
2	36,000	300	120	B	.40	120
6	72,000	300	240	B–C*	.43*	129
		3,150				$851

*Order selection cost adjusted to reflect the fact that a portion of the item stock must be located in each of two order selection zones.

Order-Picker System. Generally order pickers are employed in the selection of small items. Manpower is used to "pick" and transport the items. Generally speaking, the cube-per-order index system of location will still offer an accurate general solution because of the desire to place orders, not items, as close as possible to one another. However, in this type of situation more than any other, the stock location planner must lay out items within a zone in a sequence that will provide a logical traffic flow through the zone. He may redesign the shape of order selection zones or create subzones to group items associated more closely with each other, not necessarily in relation to some focal point such as the order assembly point.

When the layout for an order-picker system has been determined, a dispatcher may be utilized to: (1) arrange items on an incoming order in such a fashion that they can be picked in sequence, (2) route conveyorized baskets to various picker posts placed in sequence, or (3) instruct pickers located at picking points to place onto a conveyor line specific items to be consolidated into an order.

Conveyorized System. This type of selection is adaptable to stock items of a wide range of volume and size up to the capacity of the conveyor. However, imbalance in conveyor loading produces fluctuating activity at the end of the line, causes inequities in work levels at various stations on the conveyor, and can create traffic jams on the conveyor system itself.

The cube-per-order index can be used to locate stock in conjunction with a conveyor system. Such a system guarantees that the greatest amount of cube will travel the shortest distance in order selection. This is important to efficient system operation because excess capacity, or inefficient use of capacity, is expensive. Order pickers should be stationed at irregular intervals along the line, depending on the amount of cube that must be moved from their station and the average time required to place a cubic foot of product on the conveyor.

Random Stock Location. With the advent of improved, often computerized information systems, many warehousing operations are now turning to random stock location methods, whereby incoming stock is placed in any empty, identifiable slot in the warehouse. A memory system can then provide necessary information for finding items on demand. This approach has the basic advantage of saving warehouse space and increasing capacity, because it does not allow any space to be reserved and remain unused. It can, however, result in slower order picking times if order pickers have to pick with location instructions rather than from memory or reflex.

Here again, the cube-per-order index approach could be implemented if families of product-line items with similar characteristics were treated as groupings, and random stock location were practiced within each family.

Stock Replenishment. Up to now, we have assumed that the amount of cubic footage devoted to any one stock-keeping unit (SKU) held in a picking area is fixed. However, more realistically it is a function of the frequency with which the stock is replenished either with incoming goods or product moved from storage to the picking area.

For example, assume that the stock-keeping units listed in Table 18–9 are replenished approximately every other day. Each time we replenish our stocks in the order-picking area, it costs us $300. On the other hand, if we were to replenish our stocks every day, it would reduce our required cubic footage for each stock-keeping unit by 50% in the stock selection area. If we were to replenish stocks every three days, it would increase our required cubic footage for each SKU by 50%. **(14) Should we alter our stock replenishment frequency? (15) Why?**

Based on this analysis, we are reminded again of the cost trade-offs between inventory ordering and carrying costs and those of storage, handling, and order selection.

Stock Relocation. As the cube-per-order index changes for various stock items, or as stock zone capacity changes, or other adjustments occur in the warehousing operation, stock location must be audited and, if necessary, changed. The computed daily savings for a period of time (depending on the audit cycle), when compared with the cost of relocating items, will provide information for the relocation decision.

(16) If it were estimated that the cost to reposition stock locations would be $5,000, and the estimated daily savings in order selection costs would be $50, would you recommend that the stocks be repositioned? (17) Why?

Site Selection [12]

Many general and specific factors will influence the selection of a site for the warehouse, even assuming that an analysis similar to that discussed in Chapter 13 already has been performed. Among the general factors are: (1) the quality and variety of transportation carriers serving the site, (2) the quantity and quality of labor available in the vicinity, (3) labor rates, (4) the cost and quality of industrial land, (5) taxes, (6) the nature of the community government, and (7) the cost and availability of utilities. Types of information useful for this stage of the decision process, and possible sources of information regarding each, are shown in Table 18–10.

TABLE 18–10. Types and Good Potential Sources of Information for Warehouse Site Selection

Type of Information	Good Potential Sources
General Factors:	
Quality and variety of transportation services	Common carrier executives
Quantity and quality of available labor	Personnel departments of local
Labor wage rates	companies
Cost and quality of industrial land	
Taxes	Industrial development departments
Nature of community government	of utilities
Cost and availability of utilities	
Specific Factors:	
Zoning for transportation rates	Common carrier executives
Site preparation	Consulting engineers
Flood risk	Industrial development department
Risk from adjacent hazardous industry	of utilities
Community services	Other warehouse operators in area
Local taxing practices	
Traffic congestion problems	Common carrier personnel

Source: Adapted from Kenneth B. Ackerman, R. William Gardner, and Lee P. Thomas, *Understanding Today's Distribution Center* (Washington, D. C.: Traffic Service Corporation, 1972), pp. 72–77.

At a more detailed level, the site selection process will take into account the transportation rate structure associated with a specific site,

---

[12] Much of this section is based on Ackerman, *et al., op. cit.,* pp. 72–77.

particularly in regard to the boundaries of zones which determine the jurisdiction of various transportation regulatory bodies. Significantly lower rates may be utilized for local delivery if the warehouse is located within Interstate Commerce Commission delivery limits, delivery limits set by state utilities commissions, and the so-called "exempt zone." Ackerman, Gardner, and Thomas have summarized this factor as follows:

The first zone is that established by the Interstate Commerce Commission for common motor carriers which cross state lines. The second zone is established by the State Utilities Commission for those intrastate carriers governed by its regulations. The exempt zone is that area in which unregulated or unlicensed local trucking firms may operate. A warehouse operator who plans to use private trucking may feel free to ignore these limits. However, if he can locate his warehouse within all three of these zones, he has the option of using the widest selection of common or private motor carriers without a transportation cost penalty.

Other site considerations include location risks, services, taxes, and vehicle access. Potential location risks include unsuitable soil conditions for construction and the threat of flood or nearby hazardous industry. At this point, it is appropriate to seek engineering advice regarding the costs of site preparation, which can in some cases exceed the cost of the land itself. Community services, such as fire and police protection, are important to the warehouse operator. Local taxing practices, particularly for real property, should be explored in some detail, especially if there is a chance of subjectivity in their application. Finally, traffic congestion problems which may influence carrier service to a particular site may be reviewed.

Reconciliation of Site and Design

In some cases, it may be necessary or desirable to reconcile the design to a site which is especially attractive in all aspects but its dimensions. This problem arises especially in cases of potential sites which are smaller than planned for, or which have odd dimensions. The matter must be analyzed carefully, with emphasis perhaps on the impact of a restrictive site on construction costs for storage-oriented facilities and on yearly operating costs for facilities intended for rapid turnover and extensive material-handling activities.

WAREHOUSE OPERATIONS

After the opening ceremonies, if any, are over and the top executives, consulting engineers, and visiting firemen have left, a private or perhaps a leased warehouse must be operated. Problems of warehouse operation cover the whole range of those associated with line management. The importance of this matter is suggested by the results of a recent poll in which public warehousemen cited labor relations and costs over-whelmingly as the most important problems confronting them currently.[13] It would be impossible to discuss the human elements of management here. Instead, we will concentrate on the peculiar aspects of performance measurement identified with warehousing management.

Physical Measures of Performance

Included among these measures are: (1) tons moved in and out per 24-hour period, (2) the number of orders picked in a 24-hour period, and (3) labor disputes or momentary work stoppages per period of time.

All of these measures are related to the volume of work available at any point in time. They are meaningless unless compared to some factor which will yield a ratio indicative of efficiency. In almost all cases, the required factor is manpower on hand. Thus, measures of tons moved per man, orders processed per man, and labor disputes per average labor force all provide measures of value. During periods of extremely low volume, even these measures may become distorted by the necessity of keeping a minimum work force on hand regardless of the volume.

Cost Measures of Performance

To account for the variation of costs per unit of activity at different levels of activity it is important that some attempt be made to identify separately costs which are primarily fixed or variable. Those generally falling into the former category are costs of rental or depreciation on building and equipment, utilities, insurance, fixed property taxes, maintenance, and minimum management. Costs more variable in nature are those of warehouse labor, equipment maintenance, inventory property tax, penalty charges due to delay of carrier equipment, supplies, and depreciation of containers, pallets, and other devices used in the unitization of freight.

This separate identification of fixed and variable costs will provide more accurate information regarding the effect of volume fluctuation on costs. Those units moving through the warehouse at low levels of overall volume should not be charged an excessive unit cost because of high short-run overhead burden. Nor should the warehouse management and labor be penalized with total (fixed plus variable) cost figures during periods of low volume.

[13] J. Richard Jones, "Public Warehousing: Today and Tomorrow," *Transportation & Distribution Management*, May, 1972, pp. 19–24.

Total-cost analysis is, however, essential in the overall evaluation of the efficiency of maintaining a privately operated warehouse as opposed to utilizing the service of a public warehouse. This is particularly true if long-term volume through a privately operated facility appears to be insufficient to support the physical size of the facility.

AUTOMATED WAREHOUSING

Any process as subject to repetitive activities as warehousing is a likely candidate for extensive automation. There are outstanding examples of warehouses currently in operation that are controlled almost entirely by machine. Electronic routing equipment can be used to place the incoming freight into storage, and move it from storage to order selection areas. The latter utilize a computer designed to interpret customer orders by means of punched tape or cards prepared from the order, send the necessary electrical impulses to selected areas of an automatic conveyor system which may be several miles in length, and route shipment segments to a common point of assembly by means of magnetic message media taped or painted on product cartons, photoelectric cells mounted at the side of the conveyor, or other devices. Automatic inventory management is an additional feature of this type of system. Human labor may be used only to assign stock to storage points, prepare information for computer processing, supervise the operation of the computer, and pack assembled shipments for loading. In most so-called automated installations, however, the system uses additional human labor at critical points.

Although automated warehouses are gaining a great deal of attention, their use has not been widespread as yet. And a certain amount of controversy surrounds their design and use. Among the arguments presented in favor of them are that they: (1) provide faster service to customers, (2) allow a small inventory reduction due to less order lead time, (3) allow flexibility by providing excess material-handling capacity without the need for a rapid increase in the work force, (4) remove the manager from day-to-day decision making, giving him more time for longer-range planning and decision making, and (5) relieve the warehousing operation of some labor problems through the reduced work force needed to handle goods.

There have been some notable failures among the newer automated warehousing installations. Several reasons apparently have accounted for them, including: (1) a subsequent decision to change from the centralized warehousing of large stocks to the decentralized warehousing of stocks not large enough to support automation, (2) malfunctions in the

system, causing the entire warehouse to be closed temporarily, (3) fluctuations in demand, causing machinery to lie idle a part of the time, and
(4) the realization that, rather than alleviating labor–management problems, automation may merely concentrate disputes in the hands of fewer
workers and managers with little change in the potential for work stoppages.

Automation imposes an immediate loss of flexibility in warehouse
location, because almost all automated facilities are operated on a private
basis. It may impose capacity limitations. It is expensive, although
recent installations are expected to provide annual savings of 20% to 30%
of the initial investment. Disposal of specialized automatic equipment
is difficult, especially with the rapid obsolescence of this type of equipment. In one recent failure, the automatic picking and handling machinery was so fast that it took an excessive amount of hand labor to
unload the conveyor and keep spurts of filled orders from jamming the
shipping dock.

In most cases, however, automated warehousing failures have not been
due to defective equipment but defective planning in the use of automatic equipment. Where it can be used, automation appears to offer
substantial operating economies. Whether automated or not, effective
warehousing operations appear to hinge upon the nature of the planning and management of the operation.

SUMMARY

Warehouses may be designed to perform primarily material-handling
(assembly or distribution) or storage functions. Emphasis will be placed
on material handling and other operating costs in the former; construction and other fixed costs will assume greater importance in the design
of the latter.

In organizing a warehousing program, most large firms utilize both
private and public warehousing alternatives, realizing the relative advantages of each in individual situations.

In designing a warehouse, it is useful to begin without the many
constraints which will result at a later stage in the process. This approach stresses, in this order: (1) the determination of warehouse requirements, (2) the design of the material-handling system, (3) facility
layout, and (4) site selection. At this point it may be necessary to
adjust basic plans to conform to constraints imposed by costs, available
equipment, or sites, among others.

Finally, labor costs are the most important element of warehousing
costs. Further, wages are one of the most rapidly rising cost components

in warehouse operations. This has led to a renewed interest in effective methods for managing people, and to an impetus to the introduction of increased automation into the warehouse.

SUGGESTED READINGS

ACKERMAN, KENNETH B., R. WILLIAM GARDNER, and LEE P. THOMAS. *Understanding Today's Distribution Center.* Washington, D. C.: Traffic Service Corp., 1972.
Authored by members of the management of a leading chain of distribution centers, this volume presents in concise form a guide both to the purchase of public warehousing services and to the design, construction, and implementation of privately owned or operated distribution facilities.

BRIGGS, ANDREW J. *Warehouse Operations Planning and Management.* New York: John Wiley & Sons, Inc., 1960.
Offers a good introduction to the problem of warehouse space analysis, a presentation of traditional approaches to the planning of layout and the computation of warehouse space requirements, and a discussion of the design of stock location systems.

FAMULARO, JOSEPH J. *Handbook of Modern Personnel Administration.* New York: McGraw-Hill Book Co., 1972.
Perhaps the most comprehensive of a number of textbooks and other sources of information on the subject, this compilation of writings takes up topics of special interest to us here, including job evaluation and pay plans for plant personnel, employee benefits, employee appraisal, and labor relations.

JENKINS, CREED H. *Modern Warehouse Management.* New York: McGraw-Hill Book Co., 1968.
Based on a great deal of practical experience, this book provides an up-to-date overview of warehouse management.

KAYLIN, S. O. *Understanding Today's Food Warehouse.* New York: Chain Store Age Books, 1968.
In much the fashion we have done in this chapter, Kaylin outlines the important stages in the design of a distribution center and material-handling program for a food retailing organization. Because food retailers have been leaders in warehousing practices, this discussion is of special interest.

19

Traffic

In many firms the cost of transportation is the largest component of the total cost of logistics. This certainly is true for the economy as a whole, as we saw in Chapter 1. According to one source, a manufacturing company's transportation charges amount, on the average, to 44% of all its distribution expenses after its goods leave the factories.[1]

For this reason, traffic matters may warrant a great deal of the total attention and time devoted to logistics management. However, they can be managed effectively only when they are considered as an integral part of the overall logistics system.

Our discussion will consider traffic as the management of transportation of a firm's raw materials, supplies, and finished goods, whether the transportation is purchased (from carriers) or provided by the firm itself.

For purposes of discussion, we have divided our material into two general areas of responsibility: traffic analysis and traffic control. Traffic analysis deals with the evaluation of the effect of carrier transportation service and rates on the logistics system of a firm, and a critical evaluation of carrier rates to insure that: (1) the rates charged for the movement of raw materials, supplies, and finished products are reasonable when related to the movement of related and non-related products, (2) the overall logistics system is designed to take advantage of existing carrier rate structures, and (3) adjustment of the rate structure is sought and obtained when the carrier rate structure does not meet the requirements of the logistics system. Traffic control can be defined as the monitoring of a firm's use of transportation facilities with the objective

[1] Robert P. Neuschel, "Physical Distribution—Forgotten Frontier," *Harvard Business Review*, March–April, 1967, p. 125.

of obtaining optimum use from them. It involves the selection of carriers, documentation of shipments, generation of information about carrier services and rates, measurement of carrier performance, correct payment of carrier charges, and the establishment of measures to be taken when a transportation system does not function as it is supposed to.

The management of "in-house" or private transportation is a subject of sufficient importance to warrant separate attention at the end of our discussion.

Chapter 4 provided a description and comparative analysis of transportation systems. Chapter 5 discussed the nature of transportation rates and charges. A review of those two chapters will facilitate your understanding of the discussion of the traffic function that follows. In addition, you may wish to review Chapter 6, keeping in mind these questions: **(1) What parallels do you see between the traffic and purchasing functions in an industrial firm? (2) A retailing organization? (3) Which of the considerations important in managing the purchasing process have significance for traffic as well? (4) Why?**

TRAFFIC ANALYSIS

Traffic and general management decisions regarding such matters as the selection of carriers, the negotiation of revised rates, or the implementation of private transportation first must be preceded by comprehensive analysis. This activity deals mainly with the analysis of transportation and related costs. A number of costs in addition to published rates and accessorial charges must be considered in analyzing transportation costs by any method. Although they are implicit, the following types of costs cannot be overlooked in evaluating alternative methods of transportation: (1) transit time, (2) loading and unloading, (3) packaging and dunnage, (4) non-secured in-transit loss or damage, (5) and transportation service inconsistency.

Determination of the True Cost of Transportation

Together with explicitly stated transportation rates, an evaluation of the costs enumerated above is necessary for the determination of the true cost of transportation.

Transit Time. Transportation transit time can result in two types of costs, those resulting from product deterioration or obsolescence, and in-transit inventory carrying charges. The first type is applicable to individual products and can be determined only in relation to a specific product. The second, of course, applies to all products. As transit time increases, the importance of inventory-in-transit carrying costs increases.

The burden of cost nearly always falls on the consignee. In practice, the supplier's credit period often begins with the date of shipment. Assuming a net 30-day credit period and a 15-day transit time, the consignee loses 15 days of "free credit" because of transit time. If the value of the shipment in a situation of this type approximates $50,000 and the rate of interest on goods in inventory is calculated at the annual rate of 10% of the value of such goods, the cost of the shortened credit period is $208 ($50,000 \times 10\% \times 15/365$ year).

The same principle can be used to reduce the costs of inventory and warehousing regardless of over-the-road transit time. Under conditions of relative certainty, shipments can be made to customers in advance of orders to accomplish a given level of customer service without the necessity of maintaining inventories in local markets. The use of transportation vehicles as moving warehouses in this manner can, under certain conditions, reduce inventory and warehousing costs and increase the level of customer service.[2]

Loading and Unloading. A lower quoted rate may well become a higher cost between two points when the loading and unloading costs are considered. Various modes of transportation require different types of fixed facilities for loading. For example, more extensive fixed facilities are required to accommodate a rail car as opposed to a truck trailer. The amount of manpower and equipment required for loading tends to vary, depending upon the type of vehicle that must be loaded or unloaded.

Some carriers offer more loading assistance than others. Specifically, most motor carriers make provision for loading assistance, sometimes with and sometimes without additional charge. In nearly all cases, no service of this type is included in the rates of carriers by other modes. In some areas, motor carriers assess different charges based on the type of loading procedure used. For example, on intrastate shipments within California, carriers add a charge for truckload shipments which are loaded or unloaded by "other than mechanical means." Stated conversely, a shipment loaded by mechanical means is not assessed the additional loading charge.

Demurrage and detention charges, which are penalties for failure to load or unload a rail car or truck trailer within the prescribed time limitations, may be only partially chargeable to loading or unloading procedures or failures in them. However, in selecting the mode of trans-

[2] For a case study illustration of this point, see Edward W. Smykay, "Warehouse on Wheels," *Transportation & Distribution Management*, December, 1961, pp. 13–15.

portation, it is important to consider the "free time" provided by the carrier for loading and unloading, and the contribution this free time can make to total system flexibility.

Important in a consideration of loading and unloading costs is the development of loading methods which are compatible with origin and destination warehouse material-handling systems. In this respect, some effort should be made to make a system of material handling as compatible as possible with the greatest number of suppliers and customers. Although many frustrating moments arise in the management of logistics activities, probably none is more frustrating than the sight of a warehouseman transferring units from one pallet to another because of the incompatibility of pallet sizes employed by customer and supplier.

Typically, loading and unloading costs are charged to warehousing operations. When these costs are not separated and distinguished from warehousing costs, the alternate modes of transportation are not charged with the full costs which should be assigned them. When all systems of logistics are charged the same average amount for loading and unloading, the same inadequate cost allocation results.

Packaging and Dunnage. The term "dunnage" refers to bracing and other protective devices used in the packing of products into transportation vehicles or warehouse areas. A rating classification, for purposes of pricing transportation service, is partially formulated on the basis of the amount of packaging or dunnage provided by the shipper. Typically, the more packaging provided, the lower the rating and the related rate. Several examples of rating differentials based on different amounts of packaging or dunnaging were presented in excerpts from the National Motor Freight Classification, Uniform Freight Classification, and Western Classification shown in Table 5–1 on page 141.

On items shipped in containers or packages, carriers usually prescribe minimum specifications for packaging in an attempt to limit shippers' claims for loss or damage. One of the factors in determining rate levels is the susceptibility of the product to damage. If the carrier did not specify minimum packaging standards, shippers would be inclined to ship in substandard packages and thereby place an added potential for liability on the carrier. The following is an example of the type and specificity of packaging requirements established by carriers on egg case construction.

Standard Wooden Egg Case Construction:

    (a) Ends, sides, and bottom must be of not more than 2 pieces each. Top and bottom must cover entire areas of top and bottom. Ends must have cleats at top and bottom not less than $1\frac{1}{4} \times \frac{7}{16}$ inches. Ends made of 2 pieces must have not less than 2 nails in each end of each piece, nails clinched. Sides, top and bottom must be not less than ³⁄₁₆ inch thick. Ends must be not less than ⁷⁄₁₆ inch thick. Panel ends may be used if made of ⁵⁄₁₆ inch material completely surrounded by cleats not less than 1¼ × ½ inches, securely nailed with not less than six nails in each cleat, nails clinched. Center partition must be not more than 2 pieces, not less than ⁷⁄₁₆ inch thick, and so placed when nailed that it will be squarely across the case, plumb and level with the top and bottom. Any inside dimension of each compartment must be not less than 11¾ inches. Three penny fine, cement coated, large headed nails must be used, 18 on each side, 21 on bottom and not less than 8 on top (4 in each end, except where drop-cleat cover is used 3 nails in each end will suffice). Staples may be used in lieu of nails if clinched on inside, except that coated staples when made of not less than 16 gauge steel, having prongs not less than ¾ inch in length need not be clinched when used to fasten covers. Tops may be fastened by wire spring secured to cover at each end and locked beneath upper end cleats.[3]

The so-called "damage-free" (DF) rail car provides dunnage as part of the equipment of the car. In this case, the dunnage is in the form of cross braces in the car to compartmentalize it and reduce the possibilities of damage. In the damage-free car, the dunnage is supplied by the carrier; in the more conventional car, it must be supplied by the shipper. Specialized damage-free equipment is not universally available. In fact, the supply of this type of equipment may be quite limited in certain areas or during certain seasons of the year.

In deciding whether to dunnage non-specialized cars, the shipper must relate the cost of dunnaging to the necessity of providing damage-free service to customers. The carrier generally does not vary rates depending on the type of equipment supplied. Under these circumstances, the shipper can transfer damage liability to the carrier by refusing to dunnage the car. The risk of this type of policy is the breakdown in customer service that is likely to result.

Non-Secured In-Transit Loss or Damage. The publication of released value rates allows a shipper to declare a maximum value, for purposes of loss or damage liability determination, on a given shipment. By limiting the carrier's liability, a shipper is offered a lower rate to transport a given commodity a given distance. When transporting commodities at released value rates, a shipper must either obtain additional insurance to cover losses in excess of the released value or be prepared to absorb such incremental losses.

Transportation Service Inconsistency. The failure to obtain consistently a standard transit time between two points can have at least three

---

[3] Package No. 512, Uniform Freight Classification No. 10.

adverse effects on logistics systems: (1) maintenance of excess safety stock at the delivery points, (2) lost sales, and (3) excess manpower costs. Excess costs are not always chargeable to transportation service inconsistency. Where the cause is obvious, however, it should be taken into account in a traffic analysis.

Excess Safety Stock at Delivery Points. In the discussion of inventory management, the importance of safety stocks and the determination of optimum safety stocks were discussed. It is probably safe to state that safety stocks are required as much for protection against inconsistency in the reorder cycle as they are a hedge against inconsistency in customer demand.

A major objective of traffic management is to seek consistent transit time from carriers. When transit time is regularized one of the variables of inventory planning is eliminated. The interdependency of traffic and other elements of logistics is illustrated by the fact that there is a certain and real element of risk in encouraging customers to take advantage of dependable service. The risk is that if there is inconsistency, logistics management must be ready to accept the blame for whatever the results might be.

Lost Sales. When transportation service reaches a level of inconsistency which safety stocks have not anticipated, the results at the delivery point are lost sales, back-order costs, fill-in transportation, and customer dissatisfaction. Under conditions of product substitutability, sales which are lost because of stock-outs resulting from transportation service inconsistency may never be recovered.

Excess Manpower Costs. Consignees sometimes establish standard times for delivery of shipments. For example, a wholesaler might request truckload deliveries at 6:00 A.M. in order to complete all unloading prior to 8:00 A.M., at which time the warehouse manpower is shifted to the loading of retail local delivery trucks. Assuming that three truckloads scheduled for arrival at 6:00 A.M. do not arrive until 8:00 A.M. and that a six-man crew waits for two hours with nothing to do, what is the cost to the wholesaler? Of course, he must pay the six men for the idle two hours. However, the costs of inadequate service may be greater. It may be necessary to hold the trucks until the afternoon and unload them at overtime pay rates, or try to "fit" unloading into an otherwise well-planned warehouse operating day. Finally, there are the immeasurable but nevertheless tangible costs that can result from confusion in unloading and loading operations. In situations where orders are preassembled but not shipped because of carrier inconsistency, the entire assembly process may be partially or completely "blocked."

Other Factors in Carrier Selection

In a sense, we have just enumerated a number of factors, all converted into costs, influencing the carrier selection decision. Recent research is beginning to provide insight into some subtler influences on the decision. For example, an examination of several sets of shipper data suggests that there are not necessarily any discernible relationships between transit times and shipment distances. One such set of information is presented in Fig. 19–1 for a sample of LTL shipments by a manu-

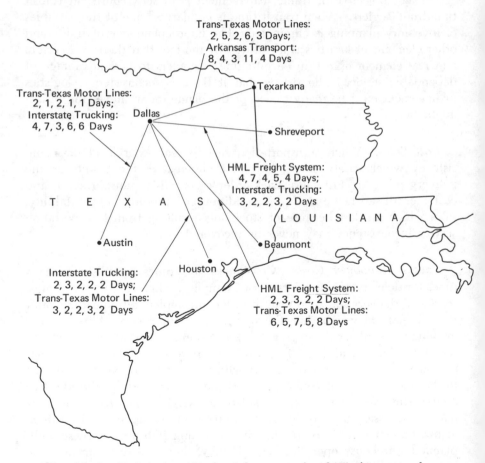

Fig. 19–1. Transit times (in days) for a sample of LTL shipments of paper products from Dallas to selected points in Texas and Louisiana by various motor carriers. (Names, locations, and data have been disguised.)

facturer of paper products from Dallas to points in the Southwest. (5) **How would you explain the relationships shown in Fig. 19–1?**

For rail carload, truck LTL, air freight, and water shipments, the greatest proportion of so-called transit time is consumed in terminal operations. There is a closer relation between total time in transit and the number of terminals or "sorting operations" through which a shipment passes than between transit time and distance.

This suggests that, in selecting motor carriers for LTL shipments or rail routings for carload shipments, significant questions should be, and will be to an increasing extent in the future, "Exactly how will this shipment move? By which route? Through how many terminals [for motor carriers] or classification yards [for railroad operations]?" The carrier offering the fewest shipment sorting points between origin and destination may well be the carrier offering the fastest and most dependable service. Although many carriers are unable, and others are unwilling, to provide such information at the present time, it may well become a competitive necessity in the future.

Upon investigation of a sample of the transit times for the last five shipments handled between selected points, requested from the carriers and shown in Fig. 19–1, the manufacturer of paper products uncovered a number of explanations for the inconsistencies in times reported.

First, Trans-Texas Motor Lines was found to serve Austin, Houston, and Texarkana directly from Dallas with no interchange. However, the volume of freight moving to Texarkana did not warrant the nightly dispatch of an over-the-road delivery to Texarkana from the Dallas terminal. Because Trans-Texas utilized terminal "hubs" through which LTL in-transit shipments to various regions might move, shipments to Beaumont from Dallas were handled in the Dallas terminal, transported to Houston, rehandled in the Houston terminal, transported to Beaumont, and resorted and handled in the Beaumont terminal for local delivery.

Second, Interstate Trucking was found to serve Houston and Shreveport directly from Dallas, but hauled the limited amount of freight it received for Austin (which it was in fact attempting to discourage) on a somewhat irregular dispatch out of Dallas and served Austin through an arrangement with a local terminal and cartage operator.

Third, HML Freight System served Beaumont directly from Dallas but routed its LTL freight for Shreveport through the Beaumont terminal also. Finally, Arkansas Transport had just extended its route by acquired rights from Texarkana to Dallas. Its ability to perform on the route apparently did not live up to the claims being made by its sales representatives.

As a result of its inquiry, the manufacturer alerted selected carriers to their poor performance, put them on notice to improve or face the loss of freight, and created a schedule for periodically surveying transit times for all of its major origin–destination pairs.

TRAFFIC CONTROL

Effective control of transportation activities requires extensive documentation and a system of information flow that produces data for decision making and specific checks to provide a comparison of actual performance. The purpose here is to emphasize the managerial aspects and implications of traffic documentation and information. More detailed descriptions of specific tasks and procedures are presented in the readings listed at the end of the chapter.

Transportation Documentation

The basic documents of transportation are the bill of lading, the freight bill, and the freight claim. Respectively, they serve the same functions as a purchase order (bill of lading), an invoice (freight bill), and a form used to settle discrepancies resulting from failure to follow instructions which govern a business transaction. In general, these documents are designed for the purpose of providing identification of shipments, the free flow of goods between carriers and shippers, the billing of freight charges, the adjustment of freight charges incorrectly billed, and the settlement between shipper and carrier of claims resulting from loss or damage to products during movement.

Bill of Lading. The bill of lading provides: (1) a contract for the movement of a shipment, (2) a receipt for goods itemized on it, and (3) in some cases, a certificate of title to the goods. There are basically two types of bills of lading, the uniform straight bill and the uniform order bill. Each may take several forms.

Uniform Straight Bill of Lading. The straight bill of lading is a non-negotiable instrument, and may serve as evidence of title to goods. Goods covered by movement under a specific bill may be delivered only to the consignee named on the straight bill of lading. An example of a uniform straight bill of lading is shown in Fig. 19–2.

Uniform Order Bill of Lading. An order bill of lading is a negotiable instrument used for the purpose of allowing a supplier to obtain payment for goods before they are delivered at destination, or providing a consignee with flexibility in the transfer of title to goods

RULES

STRAIGHT BILL OF LADING—SHORT FORM

ORIGINAL—NOT NEGOTIABLE
(To be printed on white paper)

Shipper's No. ....

Carrier's No. ....

(Name of Carrier)

RECEIVED, subject to the classifications and tariffs in effect on the date of the issue of this Bill of Lading,

At ...., 19 .....

From ....

the property described below, in apparent good order, except as noted (contents and condition of contents of packages unknown), marked, consigned, and destined as indicated below, which said carrier (the word carrier being understood throughout this contract as meaning any person or corporation in possession of the property under the contract) agrees to carry to its usual place of delivery at said destination, if on its route, otherwise to deliver to another carrier on the route to said destination. It is mutually agreed, as to each carrier of all or any of said property over all or any portion of said route to destination, and as to each party at any time interested in all or any of said property, that every service to be performed hereunder shall be subject to all the terms and conditions of the Uniform Domestic Straight Bill of Lading set forth (1) in Uniform Freight Classification in effect on the date hereof, if this is a rail or a rail-water shipment, or (2) in the applicable motor carrier classification or tariff if this is a motor carrier shipment.

Shipper hereby certifies that he is familiar with all the terms and conditions of the said bill of lading, including those on the back thereof, set forth in the classification or tariff which governs the transportation of this shipment, and the said terms and conditions are hereby agreed to by the shipper and accepted for himself and his assigns.

Consigned to ....

(Mail or street address of consignee—For purposes of notification only)

Destination .... State, ... County, ...

Delivery Address ★ ....

(★To be filled in only when shipper desires and governing tariffs provide for delivery thereat)

Route ....

Delivering Carrier .... Car or Vehicle Initials .... No. ....

No. Packages	Kind of Package, Description of Articles, Special Marks, and Exceptions	*Weight (Sub. to Correction)	Class or Rate	Check Column	Subject to Section 7 of Conditions of applicable bill of lading, if this shipment is to be delivered to the consignee without recourse on the consignor, the consignor shall sign the following statement:
....					The carrier shall not make delivery of this shipment without payment of freight and all other lawful charges.
....					
....					
....					
....					....
....					(Signature of consignor)
....					If charges are to be prepaid, write or stamp "To be Prepaid."
....					
....					
....					Received $...................
....					to apply in prepayment of the charges on the property described hereon.
....					

*If the shipment moves between two ports by a carrier by water, the law requires that the bill of lading shall state whether it is carrier's or shipper's weight.

Note—Where the rate is dependent on value, shippers are required to state specifically in writing the agreed or declared value of the property.

....
Agent or Cashier

Per ....
(The signature here acknowledges only the amount prepaid)

The agreed or declared value of the property is hereby specifically stated by the shipper to be not exceeding

.... per ....

Charges advanced:

$...........................

............................Shipper.   ....Agent.

Per ....   Per ....

Permanent postoffice address of shipper ....

Fig. 19–2. Uniform straight bill of lading.

sold while in transit. In regard to this second use, a shipment made on an order bill of lading is often consigned to the account of the shipper and later transferred to the account of the receiver, where the two are different. The negotiable feature of an order bill of lading makes it largely a document of finance.

The way in which an order bill of lading is used to obtain payment for goods before delivery is shown in Fig. 19–3. The consignor prepares

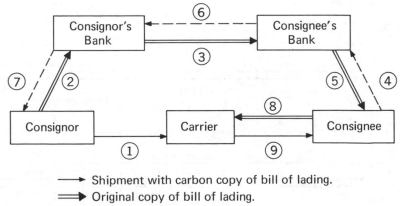

——▶ Shipment with carbon copy of bill of lading.
══▶ Original copy of bill of lading.
– –▶ Payment for goods purchased.

Fig. 19–3. The process by which the order bill of lading is used to secure payment for goods before their delivery.

the bill of lading, provides the carrier with carbon copies (step 1 in Fig. 19–3), and sends the original to his bank along with an invoice for the goods shipped (step 2). A receiver of the goods (consignee) must arrange for payment of the invoice upon its receipt by his bank (step 3). If payment is arranged (steps 4, 6, and 7), the consignee is given the original copy of the order bill of lading (step 5) to present to the carrier prior to delivery of the shipment (step 8). Delivery (step 9) will not be made unless the original bill of lading is presented to the carrier.

The bill of lading indicates where the shipment originated, where it terminated, the volume shipped, and the parties involved at the time of shipment. This document represents a valuable source of data for supply and distribution planning even though it may not contain any information about freight charges.

The responsibility for preparing bills of lading typically rests with the shipper. It is important that items being shipped be described completely on the bill. Items only partially described often carry a higher classification, and consequently a higher rate, than those more completely described. For example, note the differences in rate levels assessed on items only partially described in Table 19–1. Berman cites the example of a Wisconsin chemical company buying steel tanks for shipment under a classification, "Tanks, steel."[4] Upon checking the Consolidated Freight Classification, its personnel found that "Tanks, steel" could be further described by gauge. The lighter the gauge, the lower the shipping rate.

TABLE 19–1. Differences in Transportation Classifications and Rate Levels Assessed on Variously Described Products

Incomplete Description	Classification	Complete Description	Classification	Cost Reduction from Complete Description
Cotton shirts	100	Cotton work shirts	77½	22.5%
Chemicals	100	Crude sulfate of soda	50	50.0
Woodenware	100	Wooden forks or spoons	50	50.0
Phonographs	125	Portable phonographs	110	12.0
Toy blocks	85	Solid toy blocks	70	17.6
Hardware	70	Cotter pins—iron or steel	50	28.4

Source: Dean S. Ammer, *Materials Management*, Rev. Ed. (Homewood, Ill.: Richard D. Irwin, Inc., 1968), p. 402.

(6) How do you account for the differences shown in Table 19–1? (7) Or for the fact that invariably a more detailed description will produce a lower transportation freight classification and rate?

Freight Bill. The freight bill is the carrier's invoice for freight charges. Prepaid freight bills are presented by the delivering carrier to consignors for payment. Collect freight bills are paid by consignees. By regulation, railroad freight bills must be billed by rail carriers on the effective date of shipment and paid within 120 hours of presentation to a shipper. Bills for regulated motor carrier service must be presented within 7 days of the effective date of a shipment and paid within 7 days of presentation. On prepaid shipments, the credit period extends from the time of shipment; on collect shipments this period begins when the shipment is delivered. This may appear to be an insignificant factor for individual shipments. However, the opportunity to delay payment of freight bills until after incoming shipments have been delivered (by shipping on a collect basis) may be quite significant when related to a firm's annual freight bill.

[4] Harvey Berman, "Turn Transport Problems Into Savings," *Purchasing*, July, 1966, pp. 78–80, at p. 79.

Freight Claims.   Freight claims are documents providing information about loss or damage to products in transit, unreasonable delay in the movement of freight, and freight charges improperly assessed by a carrier. Claims are prepared by shippers for carrier consideration.

Freight Bill Auditing and Payment

It has been estimated that there are 43 billion freight rates on file with the Interstate Commerce Commission; some 36 million commodity and rating numbers in use by carriers; 288 trillion possible commodity rates; and for a shipment that passes through the hands of three carriers in its journey, more than 1 quadrillion base numbers and nearly 1.4×10^{24} factors and percentages that might apply to it.[5] In view of this, another estimate is not surprising. At present, there are more than 2,000 independent freight audit agencies in the United States which review freight bills before and after their payment for the detection of errors in the application or calculation of rates.[6] The president of one major freight auditing service claims he can save a company 5% of its freight expenses merely through auditing its bills, even after another auditor has checked them first.[7] Clearly, the effective auditing of freight bills either before or after payment requires the maintenance of timely, usable rate information by the traffic organization.

Computerized Rates.   One answer that has been advanced for the rating, auditing, and payment of freight bills is the commitment of entire tariffs to computers. The growth of this concept has been limited by the complexity of tariffs and the need for extensive memory capacity in situations where computerized tariff programs might be implemented by carriers hauling a wide range of commodities. On the other hand, most shippers have found that they can maintain "company tariffs" containing only rates applicable to methods, routes, and commodities relevant for company operations without the use of computers.

Company Tariffs.   Company tariffs or "rate ponies" can be compiled by the traffic organization or, more recently, can be purchased from companies preparing them from computerized or non-computerized files. A major advantage of most outside services is their ability, at a reason-

---

[5] Arthur W. Todd and Herbert O. Whitten, "Automation Breakthrough-Computerization of Rates and Tariffs," *Transportation Research Forum Proceedings* (Transportation Research Forum, 1965), p. 246.

[6] George L. Stern, "Traffic: Clear Signals for Higher Profits," *Harvard Business Review*, May–June, 1972, pp. 72–82, at p. 74.

[7] *Ibid.*

able cost, to update company tariffs, a task of greater magnitude and importance than the creation of the company tariff in the first place.

Post- and Prepayment Auditing.   Because the time allowed for the payment of freight bills is short, many companies audit the amounts paid after payment. The costs of recovering overpayments on freight bills are so high that other firms have turned to the prepayment auditing of bills. In some cases, this activity is performed only for bills in excess of some economic amount ranging from $10 to $100. In other cases, all bills of lading are rated by the traffic personnel when they are created so that their amounts can be compared with those on matching carrier freight bills and claims initiated quickly. This latter procedure has associated with it a high price tag for rate personnel.

Internal and External Auditing.   Questions may be raised regarding the use of freight bill auditors inside the traffic department or outside the department or the firm. Internal auditors may: (1) perform the task more quickly, assuming the availability of personnel, (2) be more familiar with the specific rates under review, and (3) be easier to control. On the other hand, external auditors: (1) typically work on an incentive basis, such as 50% of the claims recovered as the result of their work, (2) may be able to provide the peak manning levels necessary to perform the job quickly, and (3) are perhaps better able to serve in an objective manner as auditors. (8) **Why is this latter assertion logical?**

Most firms can benefit from, and many employ, an external auditor as well as at least one internal traffic department auditor.

Bank Payment Plans.   Many companies use bank payment plans, in which: (1) the carrier is instructed to submit all freight bills to the shipper's bank, (2) bills from traffic-approved carriers are paid immediately by transferring funds from the shipper's bank account to an account created for the carrier, and (3) shipper and carrier alike receive periodic reports of bills paid and the balance in their respective bank accounts. Charges assessed for these services typically are smaller than costs incurred by the shipper's accounting department in paying such bills, because the bank can consolidate separate bills from carriers and separate payments by shippers. (9) **What effect may bank payment plans have on other freight auditing and payment procedures?**

Freight Claims Processing

Freight claims result from the auditing of freight bills as well as other events. The two major types of freight claims are for loss and damage

652 SYSTEM MANAGEMENT Ch. 19

and for overcharges. In addition, in some industries claims resulting from delays in "guaranteed shipments" can be important.

Loss and Damage Claims. The carrier has liability for loss and damage that occur during the period of transportation. Common carriers are subject to bill-of-lading, common-law, and warehouseman's liabilities. Bill-of-lading liability specifies that the carrier is liable for loss or damage, without proof of carrier negligence, with the following exceptions: (1) acts of God, (2) acts of a public enemy, (3) acts of negligence of the shipper, (4) inherent nature of the goods, and (5) removal of goods from the carrier's possession by legal action against the shipper or by action of the state or federal governments exercising their police powers (for example, where the federal or state authorities might impound freight which did not comply with pure food and drug standards).

Under common law, the only exceptions to carrier liability are losses resulting from acts of God or an act of a public enemy. To enforce common-law liability on a carrier, a shipper must note on the bill of lading that it does not accept the liability limitations of the bill of lading. An additional 10% in freight charges must be paid by the shipper to extend the carrier's liability. This type of protection against loss and damage is rarely used because of the expense relative to the added protection obtained.

The carrier's bill-of-lading liability changes to that of a warehouseman after the "free time," provided in the carrier's tariff for removal of goods from a transportation vehicle, has expired. This free-time period may range from several hours to several days, depending on the mode of transportation and the tariff provisions.

As a warehouseman, the carrier is required to take the same degree of care as a prudent person would exercise in protecting his own property. The carrier is responsible for loss or damage only when the shipper can prove that the carrier was negligent by not providing ordinary care for the freight during the period of warehouseman's liability.

Loss and damage claims fall into two categories, those for damage visible at the time of delivery, and those for damage which may be concealed, either by packaging or by the nature of the products, at the time of delivery. Claims for visible damage must be filed within 9 months of the date of delivery. Claims for concealed damage must be filed within 15 days of delivery.

A claim can be filed by consignor or consignee irrespective of whether freight charges are prepaid or collect. Where customer service considerations are important, a supplier will often handle the detail connected with the filing and settlement of freight claims. This provides an opportunity to relieve some of the customer dissatisfaction which results from receiving merchandise in a damaged condition.

Overcharge Claims. An overcharge is a collection by a carrier of an amount in excess of the published rate or charge. When an overcharge is discovered before payment of a bill and within the prescribed time for the payment of bills, the shipper can return the bill to the carrier for correction before payment.

Overcharge claims result from a variety of errors, among which are: (1) use of the incorrect rate, (2) incorrect tariff interpretation, (3) arithmetic errors in extension, (4) duplicate billing by origin, destination, or intermediate carrier, (5) transposition of digits when transferring information from the bill of lading to the freight bill, and (6) incorrect preparation of the bill of lading resulting in a difference between the actual weight and the recorded weight.

Overcharge claims for interstate shipments must be presented to carriers within a 3-year period from the date of the freight bill. The regulatory agencies have jurisdiction over the settlement of overcharge claims.

A reparation claim is frequently referred to as a type of overcharge claim. It can be filed against railroads only. A rate, although legally applicable, may be unreasonable or unduly preferential. If this point is alleged and proven by a complaining shipper, the regulatory agency may determine what the reasonable rate should have been and require the rail carrier to refund the difference between a reasonable rate and the rate paid.

Claims Resulting from Delay. There are two types of service rendered by carriers—normal and guaranteed service. When the carrier (1) establishes a guaranteed schedule, usually in connection with the movement of livestock and perishables, (2) fails to meet the schedule, and (3) causes an actual loss to be incurred, the carrier may be held liable for the resulting loss. Two examples of claims arising from delay are shown in Table 19–2.

When carriers establish operating schedules which the shipper is justified in assuming to be "reasonable dispatch," claims can be filed for delay beyond the reasonable transit time if the delay was not occasioned by the occurrence of one of the bill-of-lading conditions which exempt carriers from liability, and when an actual determinable loss was incurred as a result of the delay. Claims arising from loss and damage or delay must be settled through the courts, not by regulatory bodies.

Transportation Rate Making

A published rate can be made applicable to every movement that is reasonably conceivable. The purpose of the following discussion is to describe the factors that must be considered when attempting to adjust

TABLE 19-2. Examples of Claims Arising from Carrier Delay

I. Table grapes; 30,000-lb. shipment; California to New York; guaranteed schedule, 8 days; delivery to New York in 10 days; no product deterioration:

Grape price 8th day, $.10/lb.	$3,000
Grape price 10th day, $.08/lb.	2,400
Loss due to carrier delay	$ 600

II. Table grapes; 30,000-lb. shipment; California to New York; guaranteed schedule, 8 days; delivery to New York in 14 days:

Grape price 8th day, $.10/lb.	$3,000
Grape price 14th day, $.11/lb.	
Grape price due to substandard quality $.06/lb.	1,800
Loss due to carrier delay	$1,200

an existing rate. From the standpoint of the shipper, the objective of the adjustment should be to improve the rate so that it better serves transportation and logistics objectives.

Transportation rates are determined in part by the costs of providing the service and in part by the value of the service provided to a shipper (a refined definition of "what the traffic will bear"). Every transportation rate is based on a combination of these concepts. It is difficult to handle the matter of rate making objectively because of the wide variances of opinions on the topic among transportation authorities. The primary intent here is to discuss constraints on rate making in a general manner, following it with some consideration for matters of specific rate negotiation.

Cost of Service. Although carrier cost information is available in a general sense, such information is based on industry averages and is of little value to one concerned with the question of determining whether the rates charged for the movement of specific commodities between selected points are reasonably based on costs. Cost estimation formulas developed for regulatory purposes have not been entirely successful. Based on the limitations of presently available statistical information, the shipper must resign himself to the fact that he must work with arbitrary or loosely defined carrier costs. They provide a basis for determining only whether the charges assessed for the movement of one firm's commodities are arbitrarily higher than those assessed for commodities with similar characteristics, or for commodities in general. The problem of estimating carrier cost is complex enough for the individual who is faced with the problem of transporting one commodity between two destinations. This complexity may tend toward chaos as the number of commodities, origins, and destinations increases.

Value of Service.   Value of service, the ability of a product to bear a given transportation rate burden, can place either an upper or lower limit on rate levels, depending upon the nature of the product and the service.

For example, it is assumed under this philosophy that not only are products of higher value less sensitive to transportation rate increases, but they should bear them to support lower rates for products of lower value moving comparable distances and with comparable carrier costs.

The concept can work in reverse too. It suggests that, regardless of carrier costs, certain carriers should price slower, less dependable services lower because they are worth less to shippers than faster, more dependable services provided by their competitors.

The problem is that carriers are not sufficiently sophisticated in their rate making to determine the elasticity of demand for transportation service. This results in rates based on "value of service" which do not include a valid determination of what the "value" is.

In their definitive work on competition in the transportation industries, Meyer, *et al.* have stated:

Although the proponents of such a policy [value-of-service rate-making] never put their case explicitly, it is generally argued that value-of-service rate-making is desirable for the entire economy and a necessity for the financial stability of transportation industries. The preponderance of the evidence, however, would appear to point to exactly a contrary conclusion; namely, that value-of-service rate-making as now practiced is both undesirable and unnecessary.[8]

(10) Would you agree with this statement? (11) Why?

Factors Influencing the Negotiation of Rates

Among factors influencing the negotiation of rates are the extent of intra- and intermodal competition, geography, government regulation, and competition.

Intramodal Competition.   When carrier service facilities and equipment are duplicated to provide intensive intramodal competition (competition between carriers operating within the same mode), the general result is an increase in the cost of transportation resulting from unused capacity. In addition, common carriers operating within the same mode of transportation must charge equal rates for equal service under both state and federal regulations. This effectively limits, except for short pe-

[8] John R. Meyer, Merton J. Peck, John Stenason, and Charles Zwick, *The Economics of Competition in the Transportation Industries* (Cambridge: Harvard University Press, 1959), p. 181.

riods of time, intramodal competition to variations in the quality of service provided.

Intermodal Competition. Competition between the modes of transportation furnishes significant benefits to the transportation industry and to the traffic manager. It is this type of competition that has a profound influence on the establishment of reasonable rates and services. It encourages innovation in the management of the various modes as they attempt to develop new methods of competing with each other. For example, for many years rail carriers transported automobiles in box cars for automobile transportation. Recognizing the competition of highway "truck-away" units, the rail carriers were forced to develop a tri-level "auto-car" capable of carrying as many as eighteen automobiles with little damage, and with rapid loading and unloading. More recently, they have developed a new car capable of carrying up to 30 subcompact automobiles in a vertical arrangement.

A firm must use caution in taking advantage of intermodal or intramodal competition. When a carrier offers some incentive to divert traffic to its service, it does so in contemplation of the movement of a specific volume of traffic. Although contracts which guarantee that shippers' products will move via a certain carrier or route are not allowed, a shipper should not attempt to seek advantage from a carrier unless there is a serious intent to use the service of that carrier.

Geographic Factors. Geographic factors, such as the traffic density at origin and destination and the terrain between origin and destination, are considered by carriers in determining rate levels. The volume of traffic generated by a particular area can be both an advantage and a disadvantage to a shipping firm. It can work in its favor when the area produces enough volume of freight tonnage to justify frequent and varied carrier service. The opposite may occur when the volume of freight potential in a particular area is not adequate to justify the level of service that a firm believes is necessary for the movement of its products. If a shipment moves in the "heavy-haul" direction, service is likely to be better but rates higher than for comparable movements in a "light-haul" direction.

To develop freight tonnage, carriers will sometimes establish rates which will permit commodities to compete in markets for which they are not as well located geographically as other sources of supply. Although carrier costs often do not justify this type of rate making, it exists nevertheless. Frequently carriers are forced into this practice to maintain the movement of certain commodities. This may be an advantage to products which would otherwise be eliminated from certain markets by reason of geography. On the other hand, such rate making may make it necessary for the carrier to transfer some cost burden to other commodities which are located more favorably with respect to their markets.

Government Regulation. The regulatory limitations on rate making, both in terms of the Interstate Commerce Act and the Interstate Commerce Commission's interpretation of it, are discussed in Chapter 5. It is important here to keep in mind that rates must be established within the framework of existing regulations.

Competitors. A firm at least partially must define its transportation requirements and objectives in relation to its competitors. Much of the effort expended by a firm to negotiate rates or services may be wasted if its competitors immediately receive corresponding benefits. It is important for a company to determine logistics advantages it may have over its competitors and proceed to obtain rate and service adjustments which will be unavailable to competitors by reason of volume, geographical location, fixed facility limitations, or general distribution policy.

With only a limited amount of investigation, one can determine the location and function of fixed facilities used by competitors, and the channels used by them to secure and distribute goods. Sources of information on competitors' sales in various markets, often developed by the marketing research function, provide the basis for estimates of the cost of competitors' logistics based on the relative volume moving between origins and destinations. If information concerning competitors' warehousing practices and inventory procedures is not available, a firm can develop estimates for these costs based on its own experience. To these pieces of information, a firm need only add the competitors' costs of transportation to have a relatively accurate "fix" on their logistics activity.

Figure 19–4 illustrates one type of situation where knowledge of competitors' logistics might enable a firm to improve its position relative to competitors in a particular market. Assume that firm A and competitor C have an equal monthly sales volume of 40,000 units in the same market and both serve it from a point where the transportation rates are equal. Assume that A sells through one distributor (A_1) while C ships directly to four large retail chains (C_1, C_2, C_3, and C_4). If the product weighs 50 lb. per unit, then each has 2,000,000 lb. of freight to move monthly from the supply point to the market.

(12) **Which of these firms is in a better position to take advantage of lower rates at higher minimum weights?** (13) **What are the relative transportation costs for these firms?** (14) **If you were Traffic Manager of the firm with the advantageous position, what would you suggest to further consolidate your firm's competitive advantage?**

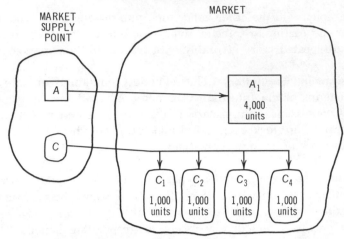

Transportation Rates from Market
Supply Point to the Market

Rate per Cwt.	Minimum (lb.)
$1.00	50,000
1.20	40,000
1.50	30,000
1.85	20,000
2.15	10,000

Fig. 19–4. An illustration of the effective use of comparative transportation advantages in plotting rate and service negotiation strategy.

In this case, for example, it might be possible and economical for A to decrease A_1's reorder cycle to two times per month and negotiate a 100,000-lb. rate to the market. This might be an attractive alternative for A that does not appear feasible for C. If a rate of $.75/cwt. at 100,000 lb. could be obtained, A's transportation advantage over C to this market (exclusive of the added inventory warehousing costs that might be incurred by both A and A_1) would be increased by $500 to $2,800.

Recognizing its competitive advantage in particular markets may enable a firm to increase its sales in that market by applying some or all of its savings from transportation to increase sales or promotional activity. This in turn could make it more difficult for competitors to build market volume to the point where they could take advantage of transportation rate discounts.

Rate Negotiation

The adjustment of rates, contrary to the belief of some, is not the answer to all problems of logistics. If rate adjustment does appear necessary and feasible, however, it should be approached with considerable caution.

Usually traffic management involves the responsibility for the movement of many commodities under many rates. In attempting to adjust and improve rates, it is often necessary to determine which of the rates, if changed, will result in a major improvement of the firm's transportation costs.

Effective carrier negotiation requires shipper control over the movements for which rate adjustment is sought. A carrier often is understandably reluctant to adjust rates for one who, in the past, had negotiated lower rates but had been unable to tender to the carrier the volume of traffic that was supposed to have moved when the requested rates became effective.

Before entering into negotiation with a carrier, it is the function of traffic management to determine the rate or rates believed to be reasonable and necessary to continue or create specific movements. The type of information required will depend on whether a shipper seeks an adjustment of a present rate or the establishment of a new rate for new market areas or products.

The bases on which an existing rate is usually adjusted are: (1) its current unreasonableness, (2) additional volume that will move after the rate adjustment, or (3) increased carrier revenue per shipment, usually as a result of increasing the minimum weight of a shipment with less than a corresponding reduction in the actual rate level. Facts must be developed which will overcome a carrier's objection to a rate adjustment that may have the effect of causing related reductions on other related or non-related commodities.

In negotiating rates for new market areas or new products, the shipper must determine as accurately as possible the ability of the product to withstand a given level of transportation charges. In addition, carrier costs for the specific movement should be estimated as closely as possible.

Timing is of particular importance in rate negotiation. Because of the time required for approval and publication of rates, a firm must plan rate negotiation as far in advance as possible. Documenting the arguments for a rate adjustment may take considerable time. This is usually followed by discussions with carriers to determine the level of rate which is agreeable to all parties. Once agreed upon, rate proposals must be circulated to all interested parties, approved by other carriers (where freight rate associations are involved), and held for a period, usually at least 30 days, before publication of an effective date for the rate. When a proposal is protested to a carrier rate bureau or regulatory body, publication of a rate may be delayed for as much as seven months, or even indefinitely. Assuming that the rate is approved after request for suspension, a complaining party still has recourse to the courts. This could further delay the time when the rate could be applied in the transportation of goods.

Control of Carrier Performance

In addition to the auditing of freight bills, traffic management can maintain controls on carrier performance by means of such devices as freight allocation, damage, and transit-time reports.

Freight Allocation Report. Freight allocation reports indicate the volume of business tendered by a shipper to various carriers. This is an important record, because a certain level of carrier performance often can be exacted on the basis of promised and tendered freight.

Damage Reports. Freight claims for loss and damage cover the actual expenses of replacing the items lost or damaged, but they do not cover the economic loss which results from lost sales because of inadequate inventory or customer dissatisfaction. On the other hand, many claims for minor damage are never filed. Nevertheless, customer dissatisfaction results from both major and minor damage.

Transit-Time Report. A shipper may be interested in the time that a carrier requires to accomplish a given delivery, but he is likely to be more concerned about the *consistency* with which the carrier can provide a standard level of service. Carriers can be requested to report on their transit-time performance. A better source of this information is a form such as that shown in Fig. 19–5. This "service report card" is sent to the customer along with other shipping documents. When the number of customers limits the feasibility of using this type of form for everyone, spot checks may be used as a substitute for total coverage.

PRIVATE TRANSPORTATION

Private carriage, along with the carriage of exempt commodities and freight moving locally or intrastate, falls outside the economic regulation of the ICC or CAB. Since most private carriage is performed by truck, we'll concentrate our discussion on this mode.

Growth

There is some controversy about the rate of growth in the use of privately owned transportation equipment by industrial and commercial

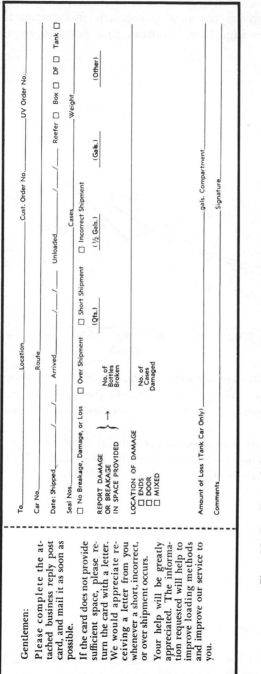

Fig. 19–5. Typical form used for measuring customer logistics service performance.

firms. The Transportation Association of America has attempted to trace the growth of private trucking, particularly in intercity traffic. Its estimates, shown in Fig. 19–6, indicates that non-ICC-regulated intercity

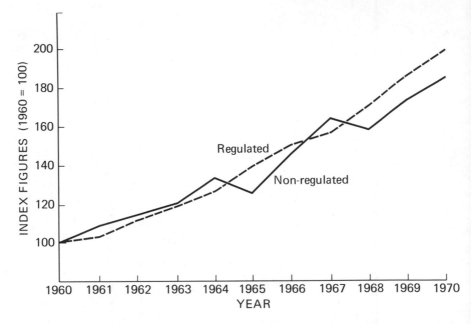

Fig. 19–6. Relative growth of dollar freight of regulated vs. non-regulated intercity truck transportation. *Source: Transportation Facts and Trends,* 9th Ed. (Washington, D. C.: Transportation Association of America, 1972).

highway transport continued to account for most of the revenue-generating activity in the trucking industry in 1970, but that its share of the total had fallen from 60% to 58% between 1960 and 1970. One estimate, which subtracts exempt commodities from the total, holds that about 40% of the total truck ton-miles moving in intercity traffic represents freight moving in shipper-operated vehicles that would not otherwise be exempt from regulation.[9]

Advantages and Disadvantages

The use of private carriage was documented several years ago in a study of 9,950 current and prospective members of the Private Carrier

[9] Allen Van Cranebrock, "Private Carriage: Facts and Fallacies," *Traffic Management,* June, 1969, pp. 44–49, at p. 45.

Conference, respresenting the 56% of the nation's major shippers who used private carriage for some or all of their transportation needs.[10] Over all, these shippers moved 61.6% of their freight by private carriage, suggesting that roughly 35% of the tonnage shipped by the largest shippers moves by private transportation. Among other things, the study indicated that the predominant reasons for using private transportation were better service (88.9% of respondents), transportation cost improvement (63.6%), freight loss and damage reduction (34.6%), the need for specialized transportation equipment (25.7%), the lack of adequate common or contract carrier service (17.6%), and the presence of specialized freight characteristics (16.3%).

Any set of factors that leads a shipper to believe he can provide his own transportation with a lower true cost than that resulting from the use of for-hire carriers favors private transportation. These factors include: (1) greater control over movements, resulting in more dependable departures and arrivals, (2) flexibility in adapting the service to a shipper's specific needs, such as loading or unloading outside regular business hours and the design of specialized equipment, (3) reduction in paperwork connected with the preparation of bills of lading, allocation records, tariff files, and claims, and (4) a more efficient use of equipment and fixed facilities than that obtained by for-hire carriers. In addition, the use of privately owned vehicles serves to create a cost yardstick against which to compare for-hire costs. It serves as a lever which might be used occasionally to obtain special for-hire carrier rate adjustments or service.

On the other hand, the use of private transportation can subject its user to: (1) increased administrative costs arising out of the replacement of for-hire carrier contacts, transactions and controls with the responsibility for the direct administration of a carrier operation, (2) greater vulnerability to fluctuations in demand for transportation service resulting in insufficient equipment some of the time and idle equipment at other times, and (3) increased labor–management problems, especially if it adds an additional union to the list of those with which the firm must negotiate. The latter problem has been alleviated to some degree by firms which are leasing both equipment and drivers from third-party organizations created to fill the need. Under these arrangements all negotiation with the drivers' union is handled by the third-party organization.

---

[10] "Private Carriage—All We Want Are the Facts," *Handling & Shipping*, October, 1967, pp. 41–45. The remainder of the data in this section, unless otherwise documentel, is drawn from this report.

Efficiency

The underestimation of administrative costs associated with private transportation is often the greatest mistake made in the appraisal of this transportation alternative. Equipment ownership or lease may involve firms in new problems related to taxes, insurance, maintenance, procurement, and personnel. This can be extremely costly. Nevertheless, there are certain circumstances in which private transportation can be less costly than for-hire transport. These arise when a shipper: (1) makes little use of terminal facilities because he ships primarily in vehicle-load lots, (2) has a balanced traffic pattern allowing a two-directional haul of goods to fill equipment moving out from and back to a certain point, or over several legs of a route, and (3) has a stable pattern and volume of shipments throughout the year to support privately owned equipment. In addition, of course, private transportation appears attractive for those products which bear unusually heavy for-hire rates, particularly cases which result from the tendency of common-carrier rates to be based on cost averages for many shippers rather than the special characteristics of one.[11]

In this regard, the study by the Private Carrier Conference, cited previously, came up with some surprising information. First, only 23.3% of the companies, a much lower rate than expected, ever hauled exempt commodities being shipped by others to help defray the costs of their trucking operations. Second, the lengths of hauls by private transportation were longer than expected, with 60% having runs over 300 miles and nearly 21% claiming hauls over 1,000 miles. (Compare this, for example, with data collected by the Census of Transportation, cited in Table 4–5 on page 123.) Third, fully 30.7% of all respondents reported they maintained a one-way operation, without the benefit of a backhaul, as shown in Table 19–3. **(15) If most interstate common carriers claim that they must pull their trailers loaded 80% of the time to break even, how would you assess the degree to which the operations described in Table 19–3 are being operated at costs lower than common-carrier rates?** Clearly, many of these shippers are motivated by something other than lower out-of-pocket costs for transportation.

TRAFFIC IN THE LOGISTICS ORGANIZATION

While the basic tasks of traffic management probably do not vary with the breadth of responsibility assigned to the function of which it is a

11 On the subject of the relative advantages and disadvantages of private transportation, see Kenneth V. Flood, "Questions in Company-Operated Transport," *Harvard Business Review,* January–February, 1961, pp. 127–35.

**TABLE 19-3. Degree of Equipment Utilization Among Firms
Operating Private Truck Fleets**

Operation Balance	Percentage of Respondents
Fully loaded all hauls	7.0%
Fully loaded one way only	30.7
Fully loaded one way—80% or more loaded return	19.2
Fully loaded one way—50% or more loaded return	16.6
Fully loaded one way—25% or more loaded return	18.5
Partial loads both ways	2.9
Triangular or multiple-leg run	1.9
Other	3.3
Total	100.0%
Base (number of responding organizations)	942

Source: "Private Carriage—All We Want Are the Facts," *Handling & Shipping*, October, 1967, pp. 41–45, at p. 43.

part, we suspect that there are subtle but important differences in the way these tasks are carried out in the traffic department of a comprehensive logistics organization.

First and perhaps most basic, there will be a tendency to assess the true as opposed to the out-of-pocket costs of various transportation rates and services.

Second, greater emphasis will be placed on coordination with carrier organizations to find lower total cost solutions to logistics problems rather than only lower rates. In this regard, a greater amount of time may be spent in understanding carrier operations and economics. Consider the following examples:

A traffic man's first visit to a truck terminal saved his company $1,000. He left his office intending to buy pallets for the shipping department, but stopped first at a motor carrier's dock to inspect a damaged shipment.

During the inspection, he noticed the carrier stacked his company's goods on pallets in a way that allowed for 25 percent more cartons, per pallet, than he did. And the pallets were the same. He eventually found that the carrier's method not only relieved his company's chronic shortage of pallets, but also better protected the goods along the route from production, through warehousing, and to the trailer and boxcar.

Another traffic manager was hard pressed to improve customer service. The shipping department told him that a shortage of trailers and boxcars made his company miss promised shipping dates.

He brought the local carriers together in his office. They told him he had the cars and trailers he needed tied up right in his own receiving area. The carriers invited him to their terminals to see how they handled equipment turnover.

He took the receiving foreman along and together they saw various methods of handling inbound and outbound shipments to get the most out of trailers and boxcars. He and the foreman mapped out an unloading schedule in receiving that eliminated trailer and boxcar shortages in the shipping area.

Within a few days, the traffic man set up a shipping department loading schedule which greatly improved customer service at and beyond his dock.[12]

Third, through its logistics organization, the traffic department communicates and coordinates its activities more thoroughly with other functions in the firm. For example, it will coordinate its appraisal of current and proposed services with sales to determine various methods of serving sales territories with varying transportation economics and service needs. It coordinates shipping schedules with purchasing and production to assure the proper arrival times for incoming raw materials. It coordinates freight bill payment with accounting to make sure that: (1) bills are paid within stringent transport regulatory limits rather than accounting timetables, and (2) transport bills payable are included in accounts payable, a matter apparently overlooked by some firms. Obviously, we could go on and on.[13]

SUMMARY

The major task of traffic management is that of compiling and using information effectively for the planning and control of carrier service and rates. In some cases, as we have shown, traffic control and planning may also include private ownership of transportation equipment. The importance of transportation costs in logistics systems has been noted, but of more significance than transportation costs is the effective use of transportation in systems which are compatible with the firm's overall logistics patterns. It is this latter characteristic which distinguishes the forward-looking traffic department from its more traditional and often-maligned counterparts in other organizations.

SUGGESTED READINGS

COLTON, RICHARD C., and EDMUND S. WARD. *Practical Handbook of Industrial Traffic Management.* Washington: The Traffic Service Corp., 1965.
This is a good source of usable information concerning traffic management. Of particular interest are the extensive sections on freight routing, freight claims, and expediting and tracing. Discussions of organizing and equipping a traffic department, and of United States Government traffic, are rather unusual features.

[12] H. G. Becker, Jr., "The Outside Half of Transportation Management," *Handling & Shipping,* August, 1966, pp. 68–69.
[13] For a more comprehensive discussion of traffic coordination and control, see Stern, *op. cit.*

FLOOD, KENNETH U. *Traffic Management*, 2d Ed. Dubuque, Iowa: William
C. Brown Co., Inc., 1965.
A comprehensive source on the subject, this book contains a particularly
useful discussion regarding company-operated transport.

MCELHINEY, PAUL T., and CHARLES L. HILTON. *Introduction to Logistics and
Traffic Management.* Dubuque, Iowa: William C. Brown Co., 1968.
Of particular interest in this treatment of the subject are chapters on a practical approach to rate finding, and the role of traffic in household goods
movements.

TAFF, CHARLES A. *Management of Physical Distribution and Transportation*,
5th Ed. Homewood, Ill.: Richard D. Irwin, Inc., 1972.
This author traces the evolution of logistics in relation to the more traditional
management function of traffic. In particular, he places the up-to-date
traffic function in the broader context of physical distribution and deals in
greater detail with various aspects of the traffic job, including routing, selection of special transportation services, and claims.

TURNER, M. S. V. *Freight Transport Planning and Control.* London: Business
Publications Limited, 1966.
Written largely from experiences in England, this volume presents an extensive review of considerations in initiating and controlling a transport
operation, including necessary controls and reporting systems, capital expenditures, and factors contributing to high vehicle utilization.

20

Organization

Management organization techniques and approaches which are rooted in and related only to the management of factory-production and mass-marketing activities are not adequate to meet the needs of firms which must deal effectively and economically with large and complex inventories of goods dispersed over wide geographic areas. Many firms with organization structures based on a historical philosophy of "produce it and sell it" find it difficult to cope with a real world in which frequently the critical problem today is to achieve efficient and economical *distribution* of their goods.

The question is how best to *accommodate change* in the management organization of some firms. Note that we say "some" firms, not all firms. It should be obvious by now that, organizationally speaking, firms having only simple and direct material flows will be relatively "untouched" by the logistics concept. Other firms will face (or have faced) a wrenching and difficult process of management organization change to make themselves effective distributors as well as effective producers and marketers of their goods.

Organization for logistics management is bound to be difficult to the extent that a company attempts simply to graft such efforts onto its current organization structures and management practices. This is characteristically a problem of implementing systems management generally. Of course, the problem is that the classic marketing–finance–production triad is itself *a system of management organization,* and to expect it to mesh easily and compatibly with a new and different management approach is expecting too much. Something has to give.

New titles abound in business: Vice President Data Processing, Vice President Distribution, Vice President Customer Services, Vice President Materials Management, Vice President Information Systems, etc. These are commingled with more traditional titles: Vice Presidents of Production, Finance, or Marketing. The result is frequently and naturally an organizational shifting and groaning like the clashing of ice masses in an Arctic ice pack.

Of course, the phenomenon of change is not new. An astute observer of his contemporary scene wrote long ago:

It must be remembered that there is nothing more difficult to plan, more doubtful of success, nor more dangerous to manage, than the creation of a new system. For the initiator has the enmity of all who would profit by the preservation of the old institutions and merely lukewarm defenders in those who would gain by the new ones.

Niccolo Machiavelli wrote this in 1513. Machiavelli knew whereof he spoke. Initiators and implementers of logistics system management concepts would do well to heed his words.

How do titles such as Traffic Manager, Purchasing Manager, Production Control Manager, or Warehouse Manager square with the title Logistics Manager? How do you pull together (*if* you should) a number of functions and activities previously and presently scattered through an organization structure? What do you do with what is left?

One corporate president became entranced with the logistics concept and set out, on paper, to transform his company's organization to accommodate all these wonderful new logistics ideas. He subsequently reported that he had approached this task with great zeal; he switched around a number of management responsibilities, modified various activities, changed many reporting relationships, centralized authority in some places while decentralizing it at other points, and, when he was finished, "I found I had made the entire company into one giant logistics department! Nobody on the chart was making or selling our products!" Somewhat chastened by this experience, he went back to the drawing board with more modest objectives in mind.

The moral of the story is that you should approach the drawing board with care and caution. Certainly one of the most useful first steps you can take is to define the issue (and its attendant problems) that you face. What are you dealing with? What are its boundaries and dimensions?

THE BASIC ORGANIZATIONAL PROBLEM

In a broad sense, logistics involves the physical flow of material which takes place in response to signals, in the form of flows of information. The process is diagrammed in simplified form in Fig. 20–1.

Information which flows from the market, in the form of orders or other indicators, provides the basis for forecasts of future demand. The

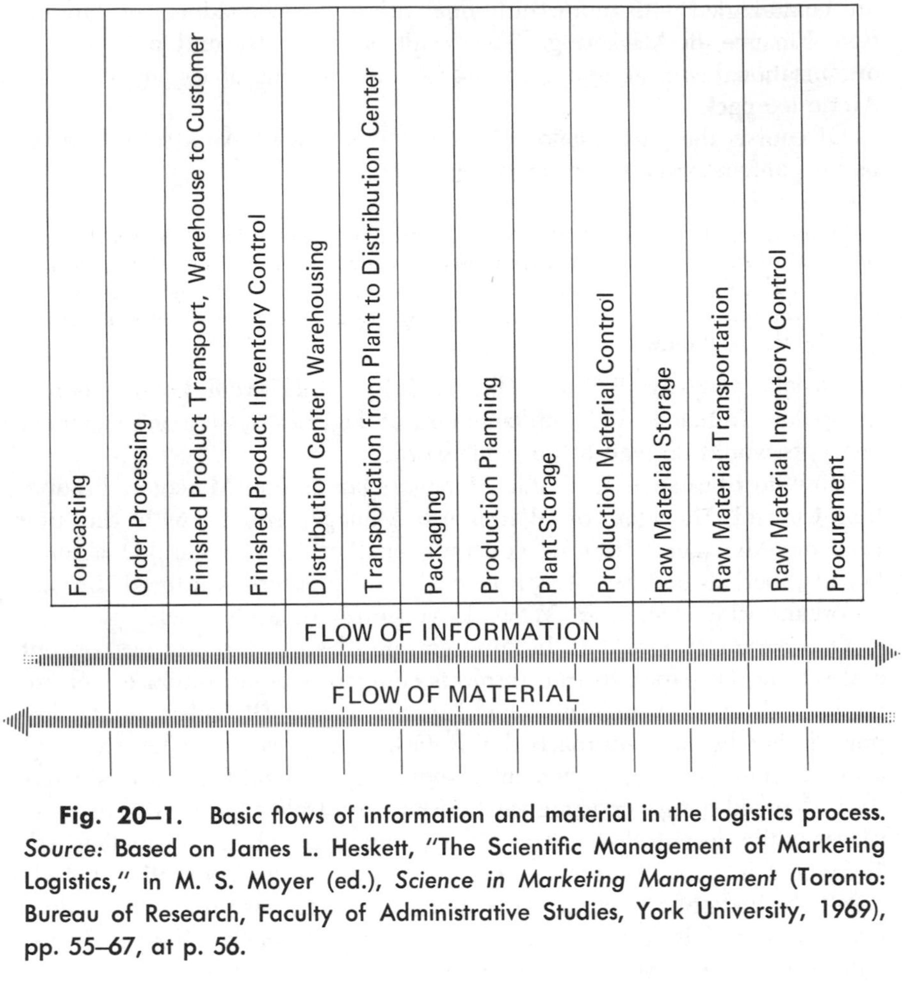

Fig. 20-1. Basic flows of information and material in the logistics process. *Source:* Based on James L. Heskett, "The Scientific Management of Marketing Logistics," in M. S. Moyer (ed.), *Science in Marketing Management* (Toronto: Bureau of Research, Faculty of Administrative Studies, York University, 1969), pp. 55–67, at p. 56.

forecasts in turn trigger replenishment orders which produce inventories at distribution centers. These orders influence production schedules which in turn help determine the timing and quantities with which raw materials are procured. At each stage in the process, this information provides the basis for purchasing for-hire or arranging in-company transportation service, buying equipment, or procuring necessary supplies for shipping purposes.

Information flows trigger material flows, beginning with the shipment of raw materials to company facilities and continuing with the transfer of raw materials to the production plant, the handling of materials through the production process, and their transportation to distribution centers for holding and subsequent shipment to markets.

In a sense, these are "horizontal" flows of information in one direction and material in the other. Organizational problems begin when we attempt to impose on this scheme the traditional "vertical" organization oriented around business functions. This type of organization, typified by the traditional pyramidal chart shown in Fig. 20–2, is based on the concept of specialization as the key to the effective management of diverse functions, especially in a large enterprise.

The specialization of management tasks leads to many perplexing questions for effective logistics management. Is the management of finished-product distribution centers the province of marketing or production? Should finished-product inventories be managed by the marketing, production, or control groups? Is the transportation of raw materials properly the responsibility of purchasing, traffic, or production? In short, such specialization can lead not only to jurisdictional disputes, but also to the duplication or neglect of certain areas of responsibility.

(1) **What are possible answers to this dilemma?** Before continuing you might stop to outline those that seem most logical to you.

So much for our introduction to some of the general questions of logistics management organization. Now we turn to those considerations, characteristics, and elements of a company's makeup that will influence the choice of the logistics management strategy a firm will choose to follow. First we will present and discuss various techniques of organizational analysis, and later we will apply these techniques to questions of logistics management organization in manufacturing firms, extractive firms, service enterprises, wholesaling institutions, and retailing institutions.

ORGANIZATIONAL ANALYSIS

The difference between simply having an organization structure which is assigned responsibility for carrying out certain activities, and actually carrying out activities in an organized manner, is the difference between form and substance. The editors of a leading business magazine devoted to the coverage of logistics topics put it bluntly:

. . . we would venture to say that many companies which are not "organized" for physical distribution management—either by chart or by use of the term—are in fact doing a first-rate physical distribution job because they understand the function, while other companies with beautifully drawn charts encompassing a physical distribution hierarchy are falling down on the job because they still haven't learned what physical distribution is all about.[1]

[1] Editorial, "Organization vs. Function in Physical Distribution Management," *Transportation & Distribution Management*, February, 1962, p. 3.

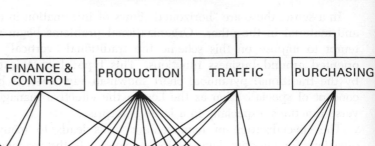
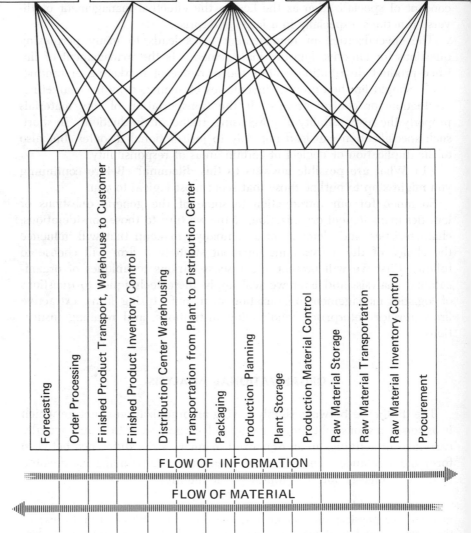

Fig. 20–2. Basic conflicts created by the imposition of a traditionally "vertical" organization structure on the logistics function involving "horizontal" flows. *Source:* Same as for Fig. 20–1, at p. 57.

As this quotation suggests, to have an organization structure without actually carrying out the function(s) of the organization is to achieve a triumph of technique over purpose.

There will be no attempt in this chapter to present something that might be termed "the ideal organization for a logistics department." No such organizational formula exists. Business is too diverse in its many forms and functions for any one type of organization to be suited to all types of business firms. As any student of management knows, or should know, organization theory does not provide an "answer" to the problem of how to organize a particular activity or function in a business firm.

Several organization charts will be presented to illustrate points discussed in the text. However, it should be clearly understood by the reader that these charts are intended only to be illustrative. They should not be construed as answers to the question, "How should logistics activities be organized?"

Our discussion is structured around a series of questions, each of which should be answered in some detail to provide an analysis of logistics activities in a given firm with a view toward organizing them. These questions include the following:

1. Are the logistics activities in the firm of sufficient importance to warrant or require their formal organization at one or more places in the company's organization structure?
2. What indications are there that the management of logistics activities need be reorganized at all?
3. What responsibilities logically might be assigned to a formally organized logistics function in this company? Which ones should be?
4. What alternative approaches can be taken to insure the communication and coordination essential for the effective management of these activities?

The answers to these four questions should provide some clear guides as to what form of organization might be appropriate for the logistics activities in a given firm.

Importance of Logistics Activities

It would not be wise for the management of a firm to ignore completely any activity carried on by the firm. The question here is not whether the activity, in this case logistics, is too small to deserve attention, but rather whether it is of sufficient importance to warrant or require that management recognize and deal with it as a significant function in the firm.

In this sense the industrial relations function is analogous to the logistics function. In a large manufacturing firm which employs thousands of production workers the industrial relations function would usually be considered so important that it would be headed by a vice president who would be consulted on any matter affecting the production work force. In contrast, another type of business firm with dollar sales as great as those of the manufacturing firm just mentioned, such as one of the famous New York art auction galleries, might have hardly more than a dozen non-managerial or non-professional employees. In such a firm it is probable that the office manager, or some person similarly titled, would handle the "personnel" function as one of a number of duties he performs.

The question immediately arises, how can one assess the importance of the logistics function in a given firm? Further, how can one express it? Can it be stated as some sort of index, or ratio, or in any quantitative manner at all? Or must it be a subjective estimate? If it is a subjective estimate, can it be made sufficiently definite to serve as a useful guide to management in deciding whether to recognize logistics as a function deserving of separate recognition in the organization structure of the firm?

Logistics Costs. As indicated previously in this text, logistics costs tend to be fragmented and included in many other cost categories because of the account classifications currently used by most firms in their accounting systems. However, it is generally a feasible task to obtain a rough, but reasonably accurate, estimate of the costs of logistics activities in a given firm, provided the person undertaking the task knows what he is about and has full access to all available financial records and data of the firm.

Two "figures" can be obtained from such an analysis. One will be a dollar amount; the other will be this amount expressed as a percentage of the company's total costs of doing business, or as a percentage of sales revenue. A further matter must then be considered before this facet of the analysis is complete.

The extent to which these costs are *controllable* must be ascertained. To illustrate this point, consider the matter of property taxes on the company's land and buildings. These may total a substantial sum, yet once the company's property is assessed for tax purposes (and all legal appeals, if any, have been exhausted) the sum of money paid annually in taxes by the firm becomes a completely non-controllable expense. Responsibility for its payment might well be delegated as a minor duty to the Treasurer of the firm no matter how large the sum. On the other hand, consider advertising expense. Whereas a business firm has no choice at all but to pay its property taxes, it may choose (wisely or unwisely) to spend nothing for advertising or to spend fully half of its gross revenues for advertising, as do some manufacturers of proprietary medicines and "health" preparations. It is probably fair to say that logistics costs ordinarily fall somewhere in between the two extreme cases just discussed; that is, a certain minimum of logistics costs will be incurred no matter what type of logistics system the firm devises. The maximum figure may be many times this amount. Additional funds may be spent to provide a very high level of customer service, to support a particular pricing policy, or to accommodate certain plant and warehouse location decisions.

The first indicator of importance is thus determined, and management now knows, for example, that logistics costs in the firm are 15% of sales. Further, it knows that the company, due to its competitive situation, chooses to sell on a delivered uniform price basis and maintains a very high level of customer service, i.e., incurs many controllable logistics costs.

What criterion can now be applied to determine whether the magnitude of logistics cost in this example is great or small? There is only one meaningful criterion: relative to other functional cost categories (e.g., production, advertising, public relations), does logistics "rate" in this firm as a function warranting separate organizational recognition from the standpoint of costs?

Size of Firm. Given firms of different size operating in the same industry, the larger firm is likely to operate more manufacturing plants, warehouses, wholesale branches, and retail outlets than the smaller. Further, because a business is typically first established as a single operating unit with relatively simple logistics patterns of geographical operations and supplier and customer relationships, logistics factors will likely receive little attention at the starting point in the firm's history. As the firm grows, and other operating units are added, the costs of logistics activities may reach very high dollar levels before the executives of the firm fully realize what has happened. Action then must be taken to provide for positive management of this once minor activity.

Customer Service Standard. This topic has previously been discussed at length and in detail, and only brief mention need be made of it here. The higher the standard of customer service the greater will be the need for recognition and careful management of logistics as a distinct function in the organization and operation of the firm.

Nature of the Product and Raw Materials. Some goods simply are easier than others to package, handle, warehouse, transport, and protect from damage. In some cases the nature of goods handled in the firm's logistics system may require considerably more care, attention, and know-how than in other cases, and thus require more careful management.

Production to Order or to Stock. If a firm manufactures (or orders from its suppliers) goods to the order of its customers, its logistics problems are simplified. In such circumstances only carelessness or a last-minute order cancellation can lead to excess inventories of either raw materials or finished goods. In contrast, a firm which produces "to stock" must accurately estimate probable demand by type and quantity of product, because the firm produces the product before it sells it. Under the latter circumstances careful forecasting and planning are essential, and even the most conscientious management can and will occasionally make mistakes, resulting at times in excess inventories or temporary failure to meet customer service requirements.

Pricing Policy. As discussed in Chapter 7, the pricing policies of the firm and its suppliers may be such that careful consideration of logistics questions is required. This is particularly the case when a firm purchases on an f.o.b. origin basis and chooses to sell on a delivered price basis. Errors in managerial judgment might lead to a situation in which the firm bought or sold much of its product in a market in which it had to absorb very heavy freight charges under its pricing policy. On the other hand, a firm might find itself selling little of its product in markets in which it had expected to earn an extra increment of profit under its delivered pricing system.

Structure of the Shipping Pattern. The "shipping pattern" of a firm, inbound, outbound, or both, may range from simple to fantastically complex. At one extreme a firm's operations might involve only one raw material which is obtained from a single source and can move by only one means of transport to the firm's only plant, production which is shipped to a single customer at one location, and only one feasible means of transport for such shipments. At the other extreme, a firm might obtain goods or materials from literally hundreds of suppliers (representing hundreds or even thousands of shipping origins) and have these goods shipped to any one of dozens of company plant warehouses at various locations. Upon completion of the production processes, finished goods might then be shipped to any one of dozens of the company's distribution warehouses and thence to hundreds or thousands of customers.

In each of these cases the logistics costs (both absolute and as a percentage of sales) may be the same, but the first situation could probably be handled by an intelligent young assistant to the office manager, while the latter case would require a sizable, well-organized, and smoothly operated logistics function managed by a very capable senior executive.

Nature of the Business. In organizations which do not manufacture products in which they deal, logistics assumes a greater relative importance in the firm's operations. Thus, in a wholesaling or retailing organization, it may be called operations and found alongside accounting and sales (or merchandising or store management), as shown in Fig. 20–3.

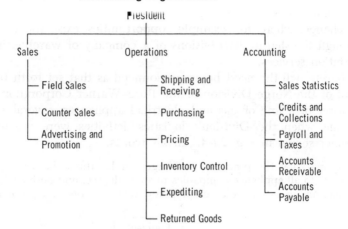

Wholesaling Organization

President

Sales	Operations	Accounting
— Field Sales	— Shipping and Receiving	— Sales Statistics
— Counter Sales	— Purchasing	— Credits and Collections
— Advertising and Promotion	— Pricing	— Payroll and Taxes
	— Inventory Control	— Accounts Receivable
	— Expediting	— Accounts Payable
	— Returned Goods	

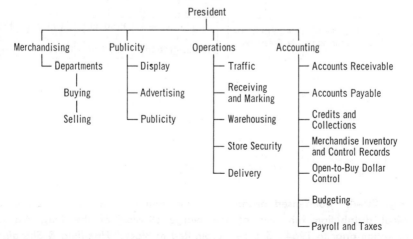

Retailing Organization

President

Merchandising	Publicity	Operations	Accounting
— Departments	— Display	— Traffic	— Accounts Receivable
Buying	— Advertising	— Receiving and Marking	— Accounts Payable
Selling	— Publicity	— Warehousing	— Credits and Collections
		— Store Security	— Merchandise Inventory and Control Records
		— Delivery	— Open-to-Buy Dollar Control
			— Budgeting
			— Payroll and Taxes

Fig. 20–3. Examples of organization for the management of larger wholesale and retail institutions.

Establishment of the Need for Reorganization

In situations in which some or all of the conditions mentioned in the preceding section are present, the question may still remain about the need for the reorganization of management for logistics. And issues regarding timing are always present. Danger signals suggesting such needs may include increasing failure to meet shipping schedules, traceable to a failure of sales and traffic to exchange information about their respective needs, forecasts, and schedules; rising inventory-to-sales ratios; increasing rates of unplanned out-of-stock conditions. Or, overlooked possibilities for coordinating efforts may provide the basis for the timing of change when, for example, opportunities exist for reducing costs through the sharing by divisions of a company of warehousing or transportation services.

Rarely will the need be as pronounced as that set forth by the President of the Norge Division of the Borg–Warner Corporation, the manufacturer of a line of gas and electrical appliances, several years ago at a time when the Division's logistics activities were organized in the manner shown in Fig. 20–4. In his words:

In analysing the problems of Norge (and I think the same problems are common to all appliance companies to some degree, and perhaps to other types of manufacturers as well) certain key facts emerge: . . . the price of our

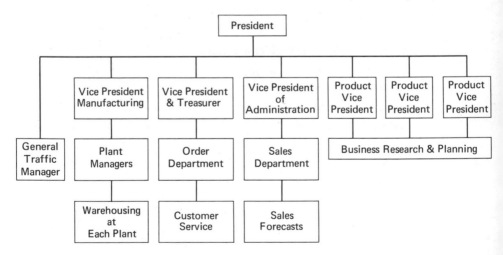

Fig. 20–4. Condensed organization diagram showing the dispersion of physical distribution functions at the Norge Division of the Borg–Warner Corporation prior to 1964. *Source:* "From Red to Black," *Handling & Shipping,* September, 1966, pp. 69–72, at p. 70; published by Industrial Publishing Co. (div. Pittway Corp.).

products virtually doubled in moving from the end of the production line to the consumer; . . . there were at least six departments within our company alone, not to mention others at our distributors and retailers, which contributed to this drastic rise . . . but which were not working under a common direction or even a common policy.

Each . . . was concerned with the costs which it incurred, but could hardly care less about whether by incurring a higher cost in their particular department they could lower *total* cost. We had a business forecasting department which forecast overall sales levels. Then, in production meetings, these forecasts were revised by the *sales* department and turned over to the *plant scheduling* department which further revised schedules to suit plant convenience. (Plant convenience, you know, means running the same model at a fixed rate forever.) The *order department* . . . was never consulted on scheduling and provided a pretty useless second guess on shipments, since by that time we either had the products or we didn't. . . . Finally, the *traffic* department shipped the "best available way" which is an optimistic way of saying shipping was purely a matter of the expedience of the moment. Somewhat independently of all this activity we had a *warehousing* department at each of the plants which came periodically to our attention as one or the other incurred expense for outside warehousing, but otherwise they were left to their own devices.

When we wound up with too much of any one product we would develop what is referred to in the industry as a "loading program." Which means we tried to push the surplus off on the distributor on the theory that if we loaded him he would in turn unload onto the dealers. At least one flaw always seemed to be present in this type of program: in order to load the distributors we had to give special terms, both price and financing, and as a result our accounts receivable relative to sales were formidable indeed, but our gross profit negligible.[2]

(2) **What are the basic needs implicit in the words of this top executive?** (3) **What alternatives suggest themselves to you for meeting these needs?** We'll see later what was done about these organizational problems.

Criteria for Responsibilities To Be Assigned to the Logistics Function

If the question regarding activities to be assigned to the logistics function could be answered adequately by a broad generalization, we could simply say that logistics includes order processing, inventory location and control, movement scheduling and allocation, production scheduling, warehousing, traffic, and whatever else comes to mind, and simply let it go at that. Unfortunately, questions of organization in business firms simply are not answered by broad generalizations.

Further, organization structure is seldom a matter of neat and abso-

[2] "From Red to Black," *Handling & Shipping*, September, 1966, pp. 69–72, at p. 70.

lute compartmentalization. There *can* be sound reasons for compromises and exceptions; their existence in the organization does not necessarily imply that it is a "sloppy" organization structure, or that the administration of the firm is poorly carried out. Of course, there *should* be sound reasons for such compromises and exceptions; they should exist as a result of deliberate decisions rather than just happening haphazardly in whatever fashion the spirit of the moment suggests.

The Use of Specialists.   Logistics activities require expertise in everything from understanding very complicated transportation rates to a detailed knowledge and understanding of the latest type of warehouse conveyor and material-handling equipment. Usually a firm cannot afford to duplicate specialists, or to establish separate organization departments for the performance of these related activities.

In some firms logistics activities are very complex and require the attention of very talented persons with specialized training, while in other firms the logistics activities may be so simple or limited that no real specialists are needed. If specialists are required, such as transportation rate specialists, or persons scheduling movements to and between plants and warehouses and on to customers by means of linear programming techniques, the fact that such specialists are "expensive" (and sometimes very hard to find) must be taken into consideration. Generally, it would be foolish to have in a purchasing department a person skilled in techniques of operations research assigned to the task of scheduling the flow of incoming materials to several plants from many materials sources if this work kept him busy only half of his time, and at the same time to have a comparably skilled person in another department who spent half of his time planning and scheduling the movement of finished goods from the company's plants to its warehouses and on to its customers. The two jobs could be combined in a single position so that the skill (and cost) of a specialist would not be wasted.

(4) Would these arguments provide support for the idea of positioning purchasing and traffic responsibilities under common management in the organization? (5) Why?

Communications.   It is essential that communication of logistics information within the firm be rapid and accurate. One way to facilitate communication is through organization. It should be emphasized, of course, that organization is no way to guarantee communication. It can increase the potential for, and ease of, fast and accurate communication, but only careful and continuous managerial attention will insure that the communication actually takes place in the manner desired.

Stolle cites the example of a machinery manufacturer selling $180 million annually with an opportunity to save $2 million and at the same time make available $3 million in capital through disposition of excess distribution facilities. According to Stolle:

This company's business is highly seasonal, and failure to maintain inventory and to make on-time delivery results directly in lost sales and profits. Distribution effectiveness "in the heat of the season" is so important that all "doing" distribution activities need to be grouped under one executive.[3]

Some firms, recognizing the importance of logistics activities in their operations, have attempted to effect necessary management coordination through communications techniques. In several of these cases, it has proven an effective substitute for functional reorganization. In others it has proven to be no more than an ineffective and costly method of avoiding organizational change.

Coordination and the Grouping of Activities. Certain titles, suggesting activity responsibility, appear often on organization charts. Examples of such logistics-oriented activities would include traffic, warehousing, order processing, and inventory control. Other logistics-related activities often do not appear in job titles. These include facility location, product-line planning, establishment of customer service standards, and packaging design. (For example, look up the incidence of these activities in the lists shown in Table 20–1.) And yet, this latter set of activities may have greater long-run significance for the organization than the first. More important, strategic decisions implied by this set of activities may require frequent coordination among individuals whose job titles do not include the names of these activities. The diagram in Fig. 20–5 suggests the nature of the coordination. Organizational groupings and responsibilities may be assembled under single individuals or in closely related departments to facilitate coordination, perhaps the most important factor in the successful application of the logistics system concept.

Logistics Activity Groupings. The survey data in Table 20–1 give some idea of the logistics activity groupings actually found in two samples of formally organized physical distribution departments in sizable manufacturing firms. Because the two studies are of comparably sized samples probably composed, in part, of the same firms, the two listings may provide us with a rough idea of trends in the development of such activity groupings. (6) **Are the statistics in Table 20–1 about what you would expect?** (7) **Why?**

[3] John F. Stolle, "How to Manage Physical Distribution," *Harvard Business Review,* July–August, 1967, pp. 93–100, at pp. 98–99.

TABLE 20-1. Responsibilities Assigned to Formally Organized Physical
Distribution Departments, 1962 and 1966[a]

Function	Percentage of Companies in Which Responsibility Is Assigned to Physical Distribution Department	
	1962 Study[b]	1966 Study[c]
Traffic and transportation	90%	89%
Warehousing and terminals (warehousing)[d]	66	70
Shipping and receiving	86	_[e]
Inventory control	72	55
Order service (processing)[d]	12	43
Distribution centers	_[e]	38
Production scheduling (planning)[d]	36	38
Customer service	–	36
Research and analysis	–	28
Forecasting and planning	–	25
Material handling	64	19
Purchasing	–	15
Export	–	15
Invoicing	–	11
Controller, finance, accounting	–	11
Packaging (protective packaging)	40	9
Methods	–	6
Personnel	–	4
Price approval	–	4
Total	100%	100%
Number of firms surveyed	50	47

[a]Responsibilities presumably include both action (line) and advisory (staff) in both surveys.

[b]*Source:* "Profile of P.D.M.," *Transportation & Distribution Management*, June, 1962, pp. 13-17.

[c]*Source:* John F. Spencer, "Physical Distribution Management Finds Its Level," *Handling & Shipping*, November, 1966, pp. 67-69.

[d]Categories in parentheses used in 1962 study only; all others used in 1966 study.

[e]Category not included in survey.

With some knowledge of the types of, and rationales for, various logistics-oriented activity groupings, it is useful to turn our attention next to the organizational alternatives for achieving the coordination implied by such groupings.

Organizational Alternatives

Among organizational alternatives for the management of logistics-oriented activities are: (1) the centralization of action responsibility for supply and/or distribution activities in single organizational entities, (2)

ORGANIZATION FUNCTIONS

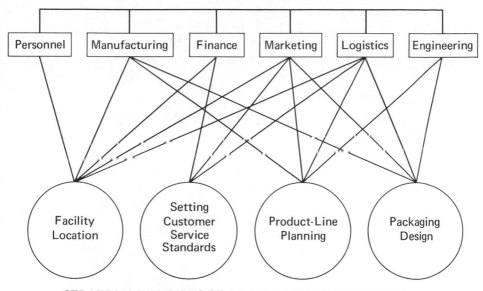

STRATEGIC DECISIONS OF A LOGISTICS-RELATED NATURE

Fig. 20–5. The importance of coordination in strategic decisions. Though these matters are critical to logistics, responsibility for them often is ill-defined.

the creation of strong central staff organizations with advisory responsibilities, and (3) the development of coordinative devices to hold together organizational elements responsible for related activities but reporting to different functional heads.

Centralization of Action Responsibility. One means of encouraging the coordination of related activities is to place them under unified authority, as shown in Fig. 20–6. In the early rush of enthusiasm for improved organizational arrangements for logistics activities, a number of authorities recommended this course of action as one means of eliminating the "gray areas" of logistics management, particularly for that element of logistics concerned with physical distribution.[4]

A centralized logistics organization, with many action (or "line") responsibilities for the planning of order processing, warehousing, transportation, purchasing, and inventory control activities, plus responsibility for their accomplishment and direct authority over the people who must

[4] See, for example, Philip F. Cannon, "Organizing for Effective Physical Distribution Management," in *Management of the Physical Distribution Function* (New York: American Management Association, 1960), AMA Management Report No. 49, p. 15.

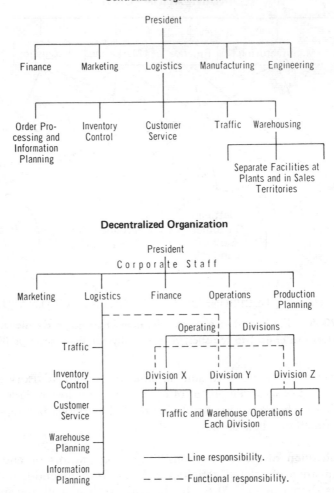

Fig. 20–6. Examples of centralized and decentralized organizations for the management of logistics activities in industrial firms. (Subfunctions under all but logistics have been omitted, for simplicity.)

carry them out, indeed has a number of advantages. It eliminates duplication and overlap in such activities, conserves manpower in the process, and facilitates the consistent administration of company policies. When action responsibilities for logistics activities are grouped under one manager, decisions affecting two or more of these activities are more likely to be made objectively, with a view toward optimizing the total effect on the firm rather than optimizing one activity at perhaps great cost to other functions and to the firm as a whole. The grouping of logistics activities under a single function provides a stronger voice in management councils, sometimes vital in tempering the plans of manufacturing or sales or both.

Creation of Strong Central Staff. Some organizations emphasize a strong central staff for planning logistics activities. This group is responsible, in effect, for designing the system and "writing the manual" by which managers with action responsibility, reporting to other functional or divisional heads, can operate it. This decentralized type of organization is shown also in Fig. 20–6.

General advantages claimed for a strong central logistics staff group in a decentralized company are that it conserves scarce planning talents, facilitates a coordinated plan, can administer performance measures and other controls for the organization, facilitates the development of talent for managing logistics activities in the various operating groups with action (line) responsibilities, and provides the incentive to such groups to perform by making them so-called profit centers.

This configuration has worked best for companies decentralized by divisions based on geographic territories, products, customer groupings, or other bases. Inevitably, the "profit" orientation of such divisions will conflict with plans deemed to be optimum for the organization as a whole by the centralized logistics staff group. Thus, its effectiveness is based on the ability of the central staff group to persuade operating managers to cooperate with an overall plan, even though by benefiting the corporation such cooperation may penalize the division. In other cases, the effective working of this arrangement depends on the ability of the central staff groups in logistics and control to devise a system of incentives, perhaps implemented by "transfer prices" between divisions, to encourage divisional cooperation with a corporate logistics plan.

(8) Having reviewed some of the arguments for both of the organizational arrangements shown in Fig. 20–6, which view appeals to you? (9) Would your answer vary by type of firm? (10) Why? (11) Would it vary by circumstances? (12) If so, what circumstances?

(13) Are the relative merits of a centralized organization greater for the purchase of transportation services from for-hire carriers (traffic) or the management of an internal, private truck fleet in a company with independent divisions, each operating its own plants but using some common sources of raw material and distributing through common distribution centers?

Rarely do all aspects of a firm's operation make it a clear-cut candidate for one of these approaches or the other. More often, a logistics organization may take on aspects of both. The logistics management for Nabisco's Special Products Division as of 1965 is shown in Fig. 20–7.

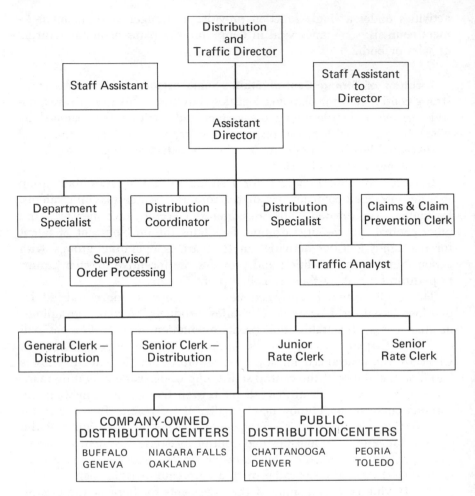

Fig. 20–7. The organization of the Distribution and Traffic Department of Nabisco's Special Products Division in 1965, suggesting the decentralization of certain activities. *Source:* Kenneth Marshall, "How Nabisco Organized a Division for Physical Distribution," *Handling & Shipping,* July, 1965, pp. 29–36, at p. 32; published by Industrial Publishing Co. (div. Pittway Corp.).

The Division was responsible for making and distributing a portion of the parent company's line of grocery products, represented by the production of eight widely scattered plants and a national market. (14) **What aspects of this organization, from Nabisco's point of view, appear to be decentralized? (15)What other aspects appear not to be decentralized?**

Nabisco's Special Products Division used several shipping arrangements, described more fully in Chapter 5, for conserving freight costs. Among these were (1) stop-offs to complete a load, in which a rail car is filled partially at one plant and then moved to a second to pick up the remainder of its load, and (2) marriage rules, under which two cars are partially loaded at different origins and move directly to the customer at a single carload rate plus a small additional cost. **(16) How would the use of these types of plans affect organizational needs?**

One survey of 46 "leading" organizations in physical distribution management found that 36% considered their responsibilities primarily line in nature, 23% regarded their responsibilities primarily as staff, and the remaining 41% cited a balance of line and staff responsibilities.[5]

Development of Coordinative Devices.   Organizational growth leads to managerial specialization and the fragmentation of responsibility, or as organization theorists term it, "differentiation." Some companies, maintaining fragmented responsibility for logistics activities, have attempted to achieve coordination of such differentiated activities through committees, individuals, or other devices.

Committees.   Some organizations have turned to committees as coordinating devices, particularly for decisions which have a long-term impact on the performance of several functions of an organization. For example, a plant location decision directly affects production and logistics costs. It has serious financial implications, and it may influence the ability of the marketing organization to meet its future commitments. **(17) Which of the strategic decisions illustrated in Fig. 20–5 might lend themselves to this approach?**

The successful application of this approach to coordination requires time, inordinate patience, and the proper attitude on the part of coordinating executives.

There is an old saying, "A camel is a horse that was put together by a committee," and there is more than a little truth in this. In practice it is simply not possible to hold a committee responsible for anything. Certainly the day-to-day operations of a logistics system are singularly unsuited to committee supervision, and the use of a committee to *manage* logistics activities is not likely to be a wise idea.

In general, the successful use of committees and other coordinative devices relies heavily on personalities and interpersonal relationships.

[5] "Profile of P.D.M.," *Transportation & Distribution Management,* June, 1962, pp. 13–17.

Given the right mix of managers, it can be highly successful. Such success, more typically, is only a sometime thing.

Integrators. Lawrence and Lorsch have identified the "integrator" as a growing force in large organizations, and through their research have attempted to identify his characteristics: [6]

1. Integrators need to be seen as contributing to important decisions on the basis of their competence and knowledge, rather than on their positional authority.
2. Integrators must have balanced orientations (as, for example, between production and sales, short-range and long-range thinking, etc.) and behavior patterns (as, for example, between people-oriented and task-oriented jobs).
3. Integrators need to feel they are being rewarded for their total product responsibility, not solely on the basis of their performance as individuals.
4. Integrators must have a capacity for resolving interdepartmental conflicts and disputes.

Among other things, Lawrence and Lorsch conclude that an integrator must be placed in a strategic location in the organization where he can obtain a wide range of information pertinent to his job. They found that this position was usually at the middle of the management hierarchy, and also concluded that "since effective integrators are predisposed to take the initiative, it is not surprising that they have high influence in their organizations." [7]

Matrix Organization. A matrix organization approach to logistics is based on the view that logistics should not be thought of as another function, but as a way of thinking about problems. DeHayes and Taylor suggest the organizational arrangement shown in Fig. 20–8 as a means of implementing the concept:

We feel that the matrix organization . . . is the epitome of the joint problem solving and shared authority that is inherent in the logistics system concept. . . . Each program manager, such as the logistics program manager, is responsible for his program within established time, cost, quantity, and quality constraints. The line organization (the vertical emphases) develops from the programs but is now a supporting relationship.[8]

Advantages cited for the matrix organization configuration for logistics are that: (1) responsibility centers, such as logistics, can be designed to accomplish planning and control in support of the overall organization's goals more effectively, (2) the nature of the matrix can be adapted

[6] Paul R. Lawrence and Jay W. Lorsch, "New Management Job: The Integrator," *Harvard Business Review,* November–December, 1967, pp. 142–51, at p. 146.
[7] *Ibid.,* p. 150.
[8] Daniel W. DeHayes, Jr., and Robert L. Taylor, "Making 'Logistics' Work in a Firm," *Business Horizons,* June, 1972, p. 43.

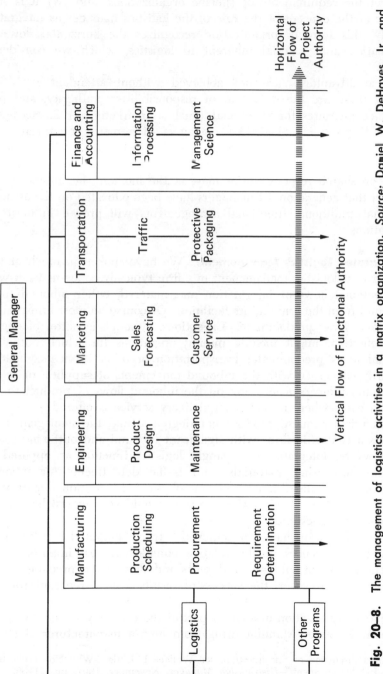

Fig. 20–8. The management of logistics activities in a matrix organization. Source: Daniel W. DeHayes, Jr., and Robert L. Taylor, "Making 'Logistics' Work in a Firm," *Business Horizons,* June, 1972, p. 44.

to meet the requirements of specific organizations, and (3) it is supportive of the concept of the role of the logistics manager as integrator. Clearly, this form of organization recognizes the horizontal flows of information and material inherent in logistics, which we considered earlier.

These advantages are not achieved without attendant problems. Among these are the definition of responsibilities, authority, and performance measures for functional (such as marketing or finance) and so-called "program" (logistics) managers in a matrix organization in such a way that conflicts can be contained or, when they arise, resolved. Further, the managerial personnel capable of operating in an organization based on shared responsibilities may, at the moment, be limited, given the fact that generations of managers have been educated on the assumption that traditional functional arrangements will prevail in most organizations.

Integrated Logistics Management.   We have spoken in much of this chapter as if logistics management in a firm typically concerns itself with unidirectional flows of information and material, either inbound to or outbound from the firm and its facilities.   Of course, in most firms, multidirectional flows predominate.   Exceptions, although a matter of degree and definition, might include mining operations for which outbound material flows predominate; transportation or other service companies primarily concerned with the inbound movements of supplies; or retailing organizations concentrating on the inbound flows of product to the store in cases where no customer delivery service is offered.

This raises a question: To what degree should the management of logistics activities in firms with significant inbound and outbound material flows be integrated in a single logistics function as opposed to separate purchasing, materials, and traffic departments for inbound flows, or traffic, distribution, or even physical distribution departments for outbound flows? [9]   (18) **What criteria would you suggest be used to deal with this question?**

In fact, few firms have yet achieved a truly integrated logistics management.   Differences in the relative complexity, cost importance, or inherent nature of inbound and outbound flows have precluded such development. However, the successful results from a reorganization to facilitate the management of one type of flow in a company can foster a similar reorganization in another part of the company. A case in point is the A. E. Staley Manufacturing Company, a manufacturer of starch

---

[9] For a discussion of this question, see Wallace I. Little, "Why Not Truly Integrated PD Management," *Distribution Manager,* November, 1967, pp. 31–36.

and other household products.[10] In this company, the results of a consolidation of responsibility for the physical distribution activities of
transportation, management of distribution facilities, inventory planning
and control, and sales–order service in a Distribution Division led to
the creation of a sister Materials Management Group responsible for
purchasing, inbound transportation, and materials control (including
order service, inbound materials control, and storage facilities).

ORGANIZATIONAL POSITIONING

In organizations in which the balance between logistics costs and
customer service is extremely important, a strong argument can be made
for a logistics organization on a level with other major functions such as
sales, manufacturing, and finance. Clearly, from this position it can be
most effective in negotiating through the maze of conflicting demands
emanating from these other major functions. A similar objectivity in
decision making may also result from a lower position in the organization
structure, if the logistics function is responsible to a somewhat "neutral"
senior executive, such as a vice president of administration. However,
its effectiveness in dealing with more senior executives in marketing,
manufacturing, and finance may be impaired.

Where the nature of a company's operation strongly favors the con-
servation of logistics costs, the function most logically will be found
reporting to finance or manufacturing. Or it may enjoy equal status
with other major functions as a materials management group responsible primarily for inbound material flows. In cases where the balance
is strongly weighted in favor of customer service, a reporting relationship to marketing may be most logical. The important point to keep in
mind is that the reporting relationship may be both indicative and supportive of an organizational bias.

A study of 47 leading physical distribution organizations in 1966, for
example, indicated that 58% were managed directly by individuals in positions two levels from the chief executive officer, with 28% managed
typically by vice presidents reporting directly to the chief executive officer, and the remainder managed from lower levels in the organization.[11]

An earlier study attempted to determine the major functions having
primary responsibility for physical distribution management in several

---

[10] See H. G. Becker, Jr., "Physical Distribution Management: A View from the
Top," *Handling & Shipping*, August, 1967, pp. 41–46.

[11] John F. Spencer, "Physical Distribution Finds Its Level," *Handling & Shipping*,
November, 1966, pp. 67–69.

hundred manufacturing, wholesaling, and retailing organizations.[12] It indicated that, however a company defines the term, physical distribution management was a responsibility of operating (manufacturing) management in 52% of the respondent organizations and a responsibility of top management in another 25%. An industry-by-industry report of results is shown in Table 20-2. (19) How would you interpret them? (20) Do you agree with the following interpretation by a management consultant?

It is interesting to note that the largest concentration (52%) of responsibility for distribution rests with the line operating management category comprised of Plant Management, General Managers, Works Managers, Superintendents, and the like. This could indicate that management is looking more to the line than the staff organization to control distribution, since distribution is viewed by many as basically operations and movement oriented, having a high labor content and thus requiring strong administrative control. It could indicate also a failure on the part of many managements to realize that, in the larger sense, the basic purpose of distribution is the strategic placement of inventory with respect to the market and that more emphasis on inventory planning and less on the actual movement of goods might produce substantial benefits.[13]

Qualifications for Logistics Management

Up to this point, we have not described directly the type of person, in terms of background and personality, most likely to meet the needs of modern logistics management.

Regardless of his responsibilities, authority, job title, or organizational position, we think that a manager of logistics activities must to some extent play the role of the integrator described earlier. What does it take to be a successful integrator?

Based on a study of a sample of so-called integrators, Lawrence and Lorsch concluded that they:

. . . pay more attention to others and to their feelings; they try harder to establish friendly relationships in their meetings; and they take on more assignments that offer opportunities for interaction . . . [they have needs to achieve which are] near the norm for managers in general, but are not especially high. . . . In fact, if integrators are too high in this motive, it may reduce their effectiveness in achieving collaboration and resolving conflict, perhaps because they will see interdepartmental conflict as a competitive rather than a collaborative challenge . . . effective integrators should try to influence others by persuasive arguments or by taking leadership roles in group activities. In

[12] "Who Are Today's Decision-Makers in Physical Distribution?," *Handling & Shipping*, September, 1964, pp. 53–57.
[13] Wendell M. Stewart, quoted *ibid.*, p. 57.

TABLE 20-2. Organizational Functions Responsible for Physical Distribution Management, by Industry

Standard Industrial Code	Industry	Functional Responsibility, by Share of Organizations in Sample					
		Corporate Management	Operating (Manufacturing) Management	Traffic	Sales (Marketing)	Purchasing	Engineering
20*	Food	29%	40%	17%	11%	0%	3%
25*	Furniture and fixtures	49	29	10	5	5	2
26*	Paper	31	30	22	4	9	4
27*	Printing, publishing	28	44	16	4	4	4
28*	Chemicals	30	30	10	13	13	3
33	Primary metals	20	53	12	7	5	3
34	Fabricated metal products	32	42	15	5	4	2
35	Machinery, except electrical	22	54	11	6	6	0
36	Electrical machinery, equipment, and supplies	23	56	12	5	4	0
37	Transportation equipment	19	55	17	4	3	2
38	Professional and scientific instruments	36	33	15	9	2	5
39	Miscellaneous manufacturing	33	47	7	8	4	0
50	Wholesale trade	47	31	12	7	3	0
52-59	Retail trade	32	44	19	3	2	0

*Indicates an industry sample size of approximately 50 companies.
Source: "Who Are Today's Decision-Makers in Physical Distribution?," Handling & Shipping, September, 1954, pp. 53-57, at p. 54.

addition, they should aspire to managerial positions that allow exercise of power, influence, and control.[14]

Finally, Lawrence and Lorsch suggest patterns of behavior they have found in effective integrators, whom they feel will be at the focal point of organizational innovation in this decade:

Effective integrators prefer to take significantly more initiative and leadership; they are aggressive, confident, persuasive, and verbally fluent. In contrast, less effective integrators are retiring, inhibited, and silent, and they avoid situations that involve tension and decisions.

Effective integrators seek status to a greater extent; they are ambitious, active, forceful, effective in communication, and have personal scope and breadth of interests. Less effective integrators are restricted in outlook and interests, and are uneasy and awkward in new or unfamiliar social situations.

Effective integrators have significantly more social poise; they are more clever, enthusiastic, imaginative, spontaneous, and talkative. Less effective integrators are more deliberate, moderate, and patient.

Effective integrators prefer more flexible ways of acting; they are adventurous, humorous, and assertive. Less effective integrators are more industrious, guarded, methodical, and rigid.[15]

In this regard, it is interesting to note that of 28 managers of physical distribution activities surveyed several years ago, many had held previous positions in two other major functions of business organizations, with 61% having had previous experience in manufacturing or operations, 43% having had such experience in traffic and transportation, 36% experience in sales, 7% in engineering, and 3% in purchasing. To underscore the rapid changes in this field, the average length of time these senior managers had held their jobs was two years, 10 months.[16]

Organizational Change

What about the problems in 1964 at the Norge Division of Borg–Warner Corporation, described earlier? A report was prepared which:

. . . defined the specific deficiencies traceable to the inadequate physical distribution system. These included habitual complaints from the parent company, objecting both to excessive investment in inventory, and receivables too high in relation to sales. From customers there were complaints about slow delivery and lack of availability. The sales department was hardly on speaking terms with the production department and with the shipping department, both of which, sales claimed, prevented attainment of sales forecasts. Traced back, these complaints were symptoms of difficulties in scheduling, forecasts of demand, storage, inventory control, shipping, customer service, and other functions.[17]

[14] Lawrence and Lorsch, *op. cit.*, p. 150.
[15] *Ibid.*
[16] "Who Are Today's Decision-Makers in Physical Distribution?," *op. cit.*, p. 57.
[17] "From Red to Black," *op. cit.*, pp. 71–72.

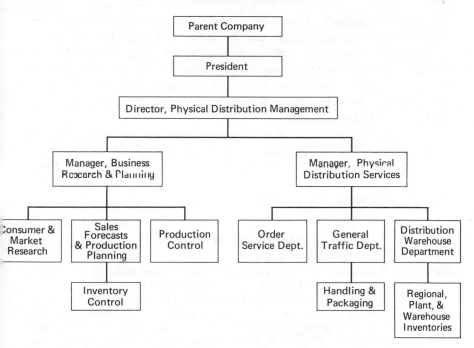

Fig. 20–9. Condensed organization diagram after the reorganization of the management of physical distribution functions at the Norge Division of the Borg–Warner Corporation in 1964. *Source:* Same as for Fig. 20–4, at p. 71.

As a result of this appraisal, the organization shown in Fig. 20–9 evolved from that shown in Fig. 20–4. (21) **What major differences do you see in these charts?**

In commenting on this reorganization, the President of Norge reflected both the pains and gains that accompany organizational reform for logistics management:

> The intervening period contains a certain amount of pain, early retirements, resignations plus reorganizations . . . there had to be a great deal of persuading and some were not really convinced until Phase One of the program was actually implemented and the results could be recognized by anyone.[18]

SUMMARY

The basic source of problems and opportunities in the organization for the management of logistics activities can be traced to the fact that logistics deals with horizontal flows of information and material which do not lend themselves to compartmentalization in the form implied by

18 *Ibid.*

the typical vertical or functional organization structure. An analysis on which organizational change can be based will take into account the importance of logistics activities in the organization, the establishment of the need for reorganization, the identification of activities for which common logistics management is most important, and consideration of alternative approaches to providing necessary communication and co-ordination of the activities.

The appropriate organizational position for logistics management will depend primarily on the relative emphasis placed on cost control or service performance as a basic objective for logistics operations. Regardless of his responsibilities, a logistics manager in most organizations, to be successful, must play the role and possess the qualities of an integrator.

SUGGESTED READINGS

BECKMAN, THEODORE N., NATHANIEL H. ENGLE, and ROBERT D. BUZZELL. *Wholesaling*, 3d Ed. New York: The Ronald Press Co., 1959.
A useful general reference for this chapter. Discusses several patterns of organization for such businesses and the factors which tend to make specific organization structures appropriate for varying types of wholesale businesses.

FREDERICK, JOHN H. *Traffic Department Organization*. Philadelphia: Chilton Co., 1956.
Presents a series of case studies built around actual traffic and distribution organizations at a time when companies were awakening to the importance of effective organization for the management of logistics activities.

HARPER, DONALD V. *Basic Planning and the Transportation Function in Small Manufacturing Firms*. Minneapolis: University of Minnesota Press, 1961.
An excellent analytical study of the organization and administration of the traffic management function in 38 small manufacturing firms in Minnesota.

MAGEE, JOHN F. *Industrial Logistics*. New York: McGraw-Hill Book Co., 1968.
Offers a discussion of the organization of the logistics function, with particular emphasis on the rationale for centralized or decentralized structures.

TAFF, CHARLES A. *Management of Physical Distribution and Transportation*, 5th Ed. Homewood, Ill.: Richard D. Irwin, Inc., 1972.
Presents a discussion of organizational issues, ranging from broad management principles to specific relationships between physical distribution and other organizational functions.

21

Performance Measurement and Control

"How can I explain logistics to my company's management?" "How can I convince my company's top management of the importance of logistics?" These questions are posed more than any others by inquiring (and aspiring) executives. The subject of performance measurement and control provides the most practical, tangible answer to both questions.

Performance measurement and control are concepts as undeniable as "safety" in the minds of most managers. But few organizations implement them with any degree of effectiveness. The individual attitude often expressed about them is, "Performance measurement and control are, of course, extremely important for the company. But, unfortunately, my job is one for which performance measures are awfully hard to establish."

Regardless of the difficulty of devising and implementing a performance measurement and control program, it is especially essential for a function such as logistics. In our discussion of organization in the preceding chapter, we concluded that it may be unrealistic to think that problems of coordination necessary for the achievement of a least total cost (or maximum profit) result can be achieved in very many cases by centralizing action responsibility for all logistics activities under one manager. If this is in fact the case, many organizations will have to resort to coordinated control and performance measurement to achieve these logistics objectives. Further, as we will see, efforts to implement an effective performance measurement and control program provide perhaps the best avenue of approach to improved planning.

RELATIONSHIP OF PERFORMANCE MEASUREMENT
AND CONTROL TO PLANNING

The relationship between planning and performance measurement and control is one of a closed loop, the nature of which is suggested by the diagram in Fig. 21–1. The plan, basically the result of the design effort

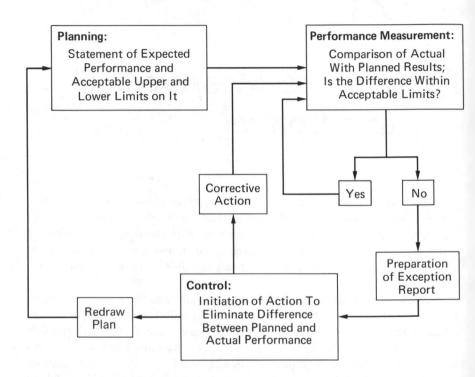

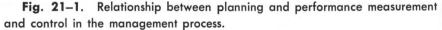

Fig. 21–1. Relationship between planning and performance measurement and control in the management process.

which we discussed at some length in Part Four, should include both a set of goals and limits around those goals which represent the bounds of acceptable performance. Periodic performance measures will determine the relationship between goals and actual performance. Where the differences between planned and actual performance levels are unacceptably large, an exception report or review audit will call the fact to the attention of management for appropriate action. The cumulative effect of such exception reports will influence future planning effort to the extent that it points out flaws in past efforts to be avoided, or provided for, in future plans.

This is the basic relationship between these important management functions. We will see next how this general statement can be applied to day-to-day management as well as to the planning and control of major projects.

FEATURES OF AN EFFECTIVE PERFORMANCE MEASUREMENT AND CONTROL PROGRAM

The subheadings in this section form a checklist which can be used to spot-check the usefulness of a logistics performance measurement and control program. It is an effort to point up in a positive manner certain shortcomings in existing programs.

Emphasis on Productivity Rather Than Production

The number of ton-miles of freight moved by a private trucking fleet during May is a measure of production. The cost per ton-mile or ratio of ton-miles to driver labor hours are measures of productivity. Production measures, signifying amounts of output, are of value for control purposes if the sole objective of such production is output. They provide a very limited frame of reference for evaluating output figures, even when there are successive output measurements over time with which to establish trends. In contrast, productivity measures relate outputs to inputs. The resulting ratios provide indicators of what must be paid for outputs, in terms of time, costs, or other inputs. As a result, they often are more useful than production measures. In the reports shown in Tables 21-1 and 21-2, you may wish to identify production as opposed to productivity measures and evaluate the relative frequency of the latter.

Proper Identification of Cost Inputs

Functional cost accounting, which identifies costs in such a way that they can be attributed to logistics, production, and marketing activities, is an art that is not only lost, but is yet to be found in many organizations. Instead, costs are collected in so-called "natural" acounts such as labor or materials, without regard to whether labor costs incurred, for example, at a manufacturing complex were incurred for activities of actual manufacture, plant material handling, or movement of product into or out of the warehouse located near the plant. Once lost, functional costs have to be reconstructed by allocating categories of costs in natural accounts

TABLE 21-1. Proposed Format for a Physical Distribution, Reporting, and Control Problem

Company: National Radiator Corp.

Period: March

System-Wide Report

	This Month	Last Month	This Month Last Year	Goal
Transportation:				
Plant to warehouses, cost per cwt.	$ .79	$ .81	$ .78	$ .78
Plant to customers, cost per cwt.	$ 1.67	$ 1.63	$ 1.60	$ 1.62
Field warehouse to customers, cost per cwt.	$ 1.43	$ 1.49	$ 1.47	$ 1.47
Between warehouses, cost per cwt., shipped from plant	$ .08	$ .04	$ .03	$ .03
Warehousing:				
Plant warehouse, cost per case handled out	$ .14	$ .14	$ .13	$ .14
Field warehouses, cost per case handled in and out	$ .53	$ .55	$ .55	$ .55
Plant, storage cost per case in average (annualized) inventory	$ .25	$ .22	$ .21	$ .21
Field warehouses, storage cost per case in average inventory	$ .30	$ .26	$ .27	$ .26
Inventory Control:				
Inventory turn, plant and field warehouses, on annualized basis	7.3	6.6	6.6	6.6
Values of total average inventory at cost (in millions)	$ 8.92	$10.02	$ 9.42	$ 9.50
Order Entry/Processing:				
Cost per order processed at plant	$ 9.90	$ 9.60	$ 9.50	$ 9.50
Cost per order processed at field warehouse	$12.30	$11.25	$11.45	$11.40
Customer Service:				
Percentage of line-item fill, field warehouse	86%	92%	89%	90%
Percentage of order fill, field warehouse	63%	75%	74%	75%
Air freight transport cost as percentage of warehouse-to-customer transport cost	3.2%	1.6%	1.5%	1.5%
Total Distribution Cost:				
Per case shipped to customers	$ 1.08	$ 1.02	$ 1.01	$ 1.00
As a percentage of sales	13.5%	12.7%	12.6%	12.5%

TABLE 21-2. Proposed Format for a Physical Distribution, Reporting, and Control Program

Company: National Radiator Corp.

Warehouse Report For: Newark, New Jersey

Period: March

	This Month	Last Month	This Month Last Year	Goal
Transportation:				
Plant to warehouse, cost per cwt,	$ .58	$ .56	$ .59	$ .60
Warehouse to customers, cost per cwt.	$ 1.36	$ 1.40	$ 1.49	$ 1.45
Warehousing:				
Cost per case handled in and out	$ .62	$ .63	$ .63	$ .63
Storage cost per case in average inventory	$ .24	$ .25	$ .31	$ .28
Inventory Control:				
Inventory turn, on annualized basis	5.7	5.9	6.1	6.0
Value of total average inventory, at cost	$673,000	$643,000	$615,000	$625,000
Cost per order processed at warehouse (include all extra charges here)	$10.95	$10.95	$11.55	$11.25
Customer Service:				
Percentage of line item fill	92%	90%	87%	90%
Percentage of order fill	77%	75%	70%	75%
Percentage of on-time shipment (within 48 hours of receipt of order)	98%	96%	97%	96%
Plant direct transportation costs to territory as percentage of warehouse-to-customer transport cost	8.3%	10.2%	16.1%	12.0%

on the basis of activity measurements, use of space, or some other assumed relationship between levels of activities and costs.

Some logistics costs are buried in other accounts. Freight on raw materials inbound to a plant or on finished products inbound to a wholesaling or retailing operation most often are charged off as "raw materials" or "cost of goods sold," respectively. Of course, companies purchasing such items only on a delivered basis may receive no record of freight as a part of the total landed cost. Warehousing costs may be charged either to production (for plant-oriented facilities) or to marketing (for distribution centers). The "loss" of inventory costs represents such a glaring example that we will consider it separately. A typical break-out of functional costs from a set of natural accounts is shown in Fig. 21–2.

Based on interviews with representatives of six major public accounting firms in 1965, Lewis reached the preliminary conclusion that "few public accounting firms are aware of any problems in the area of physical distribution." [1] Further, his survey of the literature at that time led him to the conclusion that academic accountants either were not aware of, or interested in, such problems. As a hopeful sign of progress, however, the National Council of Physical Distribution Management sponsored a study five years later designed to document the situation further. The study was supported by more than 160 well-known North American firms. [2]

Balance in Cost Inputs Reported

There is a further dichotomy in the identification of costs between explicit logistics costs, such as purchased transportation and public warehousing costs, for which documentation is readily available, and implicit logistics costs, such as inventory carrying and internal handling costs, for which documentation is not naturally accumulated.

Several years ago, one of us had the opportunity to address a national meeting of the Grocery Manufacturers of America, attended by the senior executives of companies in an industry noted for its progressive approach to logistics, especially physical distribution. During the course of the presentation, the audience was asked to respond to four questions:

1. How many of you (senior executives) know whom to hold responsible in your organization if transportation costs are too high? [In response to this question, approximately 80 chief and senior executives raised their hands.]
2. How many of you receive a periodic (monthly, quarterly, or even annual) report of transportation costs? [Again, about 80 hands went up.]
3. How many of you know whom to hold responsible for inventory levels in your organization? [This time, only about 25 hands were raised.]
4. How many of you receive a periodic report of some or all costs of holding inventory, identified as such on the report? [A number of the members of the audience glanced over their shoulders to check the responses of their colleagues. Slowly, seven hands came up.]

(1) What implications does this matter, typified by the responses described above, have for balanced total cost analysis and control in

[1] Ronald J. Lewis, "Strengthening Control of Physical Distribution Costs," *Management Services*, January–February, 1968, pp. 36–46.
[2] Michael Schiff, *Accounting and Control in Physical Distribution Management* (Chicago: The National Council of Physical Distribution Management, 1972).

Natural Accounts (Accounting)

Account	Amount ($000)	
Sales	$121,500	(A)*
Returns and Allowances	1,500	(B)
Manufacturing:		
Supervision	2,500	(C)
Labor	30,000	(D)
Materials	33,000	(E)
Supplies	5,700	(F)
Research and Development	2,500	(G)
Overhead Other Than R&D	6,300	(H)
Selling:		
Supervision	1,000	(J)
Salaries	2,800	(K)
Transportation	5,000	(L)
Overhead	3,700	(M)
Advertising and Sales Promotion	3,500	(N)
Insurance	800	(P)
General and Administrative:		
Salaries	1,000	(Q)
Office	2,700	(R)
Overhead	3,000	(S)
Interest	3,500	(T)
Taxes:		
Property	1,200	(U)
Employment	1,300	(V)
Income	2,000	(W)
Depreciation	4,000	(X)

For External Reporting:
Profit and Loss Statement

Account	Amount ($000)	
Net Sales (Y)	$120,000	(A − B)
Less: Cost of Goods Sold (Z)	80,000	(C + D + E + F + H)
Gross Profit	$ 40,000	(Y − Z)
Operating Expenses:		
General and Administrative	$ 7,500	(P + Q + R + S)
Selling	12,500	(J + K + L + M)
Advertising and Sales Promotion	3,500	(N)
Research and Development	2,500	(G)
Other Expense:		
Interest	3,500	(T)
Depreciation	4,000	(X)
Property Taxes	1,200	(U)
Employment Taxes	1,300	(V)
Net Profit Before Tax	$ 4,000	
Income Tax	2,000	(W)
Net Profit After Tax	$ 2,000	

*Capital letters identify natural accounts which are rearranged, and sometimes aggregated, in the Profit and Loss Statement as shown above.

Fig. 21–2(a). Translation of natural cost accounts into a financial statement for external reporting.

Natural Accounts (Accounting) Account	Amount ($000)		Basis for Allocation to Functional Accounts*
Sales	$121,500		
Returns & Allowances	1,500		
Manufacturing:			
Supervision	2,500	(C)	Manufacturing payroll records for supervision of handling, packaging, and packing
Labor	30,000	(D)	Plant warehouse payroll records for raw material handling, finished product handling, packaging, and packing
Materials	33,000	(E)	Freight bills for incoming raw materials (explicit) and estimated freight on goods bought delivered (implicit)
Supplies	5,700	(F)	Bills for packing, packaging supplies, pallets, fuel for material-handling equipment, other warehouse supplies
Research and Development	2,500	(G)	Labor fringe benefits according to proportion of total manufacturing payroll;
Overhead Other Than R&D	6,300	(H)	supervisory fringe benefits according to total supervision bill; heat on basis of square footage of warehouse to total; light and water estimated at 30% of the rate per sq. ft. for average of all manufacturing operations
Selling:			
Supervision	1,000	(J)	Freight bills and vouchers for private fleet services
Salaries	2,800	(K)	Payroll records for distribution center supervision, order processing, material handling, inventory control, communications on basis of supervisory estimate,
Transportation	5,000	(L)	other utilities, rent on basis of square footage in office vs. warehouse and pro-
Overhead	3,700	(M)	portion of official payroll for sales vs. distribution labor, public warehouse bills
Advertising and Sales Promotion	3,500	(N)	Insurance payments for owned warehouse facilities, transportation and material-handling equipment, and raw materials and finished product in stock
Insurance	800	(P)	
General and Administrative:			
Salaries	1,000	(Q)	Payroll records for logistics management
Office	2,700	(R)	Payroll records for headquarters personnel engaged in order processing, inventory control, forecasting, and production planning activities
Overhead	3,000	(S)	Communications and computer facility expenses on basis of executive estimate of percentage of facility use for order processing, inventory update and control, forecasting and production planning
Interest	3,500	(T)	Estimated on basis of proportion of total investment (at book value) devoted to warehouses, transportation, and handling equipment, and inventory (for explicit costs), imputed cost of capital applied to above investment (for explicit and implicit costs)
Taxes:			
Property	1,200	(U)	Estimated as proportion of book value on real property plus inventory taxes
Employment	1,300	(V)	Estimated as proportion of labor bill, executive salaries attributed to logistics
Income	2,000	(W)	
Depreciation	4,000	(X)	Book value depreciation on warehouse facilities, transportation, and material-handling equipment and inventories

*The Basis for Allocation to Functional Accounts describes for each natural account the reason for allocating a portion of that natural account to a functional account (in this case, logistics).

Fig. 21-2(b).   Descriptors of functional logistics costs as portions of natural cost accounts.

Natural Accounts (Accounting)

Account	Amount ($000)	
Sales	$121,500	(A)
Returns and Allowances	1,500	(B)
Manufacturing:		
Supervision	2,500	(C)
Labor	30,000	(D)
Materials	33,000	(E)
Supplies	5,700	(F)
Research and Development	2,500	(G)
Overhead Other Than R&D	6,300	(H)
Selling:		
Supervision	1,003	(J)
Salaries	2,803	(K)
Transportation	5,003	(L)
Overhead	3,703	(M)
Advertising and Sales Promotion	3,500	(N)
Insurance	800	(P)
General and Administrative:		
Salaries	1,000	(Q)
Office	2,700	(R)
Overhead	3,000	(S)
Interest	3,500	(T)
Taxes:		
Property	1,200	(U)
Employment	1,300	(V)
Income	2,000	(W)
Depreciation	4,000	(X)

For Internal Company Use:
Functional Accounts (Logistics in Detail)

	Amount ($000)
Manufacturing	
Accounting	
Marketing	
Finance	
Research and Development	
Labor Relations and Personnel Administration	
Other	
Logistics:	
Headquarters Management (q, r)*	$ 437
Headquarters Other (s, v)*	420
Computer	260
Communications	72
Procurement (q)	
Raw Material:	
Transport—Explicit and (Implicit) (e, t, v)	350
Handling (c, d, h)	622
Inventory:	
Interest—Explicit and (Implicit) (t)	270
Warehousing (h, x, v)	217
Tax (u)	14
Insurance (p)	17
Obsolescence	7
Production Planning	32
Packaging (f)	2,421
Finished Product Transport (t):	
Plants to Customers (l)	840
Plants to Dist. Centers (DC's) (l, x)	1,420
Plants to Plants (l)	170
DC's to DC's (l)	160
DC's to Customers (l)	2,410
Finished Product Inventory:	
Interest—Explicit and (Implicit) (t)	1,400
Warehousing (m, x, v)	1,107
Tax (u)	79
Insurance (p)	102
Obsolescence (x)	832
Order Processing (m, r, s)	237
Forecasting (r, s)	73
Total	$13,969

*Lower-case letters used to indicate that only an allocated portion of the corresponding capital letter natural account is assigned to one or more logistics functional accounts.

Fig. 21–2(c). Translation of natural cost accounts into a functional account (logistics) for internal management use.

logistics? (2) What types of bias in operating management is it likely to create?

Effective Cost Allocation

Costs must be allocated in those cases in which they are not, or cannot be, accumulated in a manner that identifies costs by causes, profit centers, or functions. Typically, they are known as indirect costs. The less definitive a cost collection and accounting system, the greater the proportion of costs that requires allocation.

There are two basic stages in the logistics cost allocation effort:

1. Allocating costs in natural accounts to functional accounts
2. Assigning logistics costs, once identified, to cost responsibility centers

The saying, "You can't satisfy all of the people all of the time," can be applied to cost allocation. Anthony puts it another way: "Whenever allocated costs are involved, the resulting . . . cost cannot be said to be accurate." [3]

The perfect procedure for allocating costs has never been found. Realization of this at the outset of the logistics cost allocation effort will encourage "satisficing" behavior and save a lot of hopeless searching for the perfect cost allocation system.

Allocating Natural Costs to Functional Accounts. Problems at this first stage typically include the following:

1. Determining plant warehousing costs (as opposed to production facility costs) for:
   a. Heat, light, and other power
   b. Interest on investment in facilities
   c. Depreciation on facilities and equipment
   d. Labor fringe benefits
2. Determining distribution center (as opposed to field sales office) costs for:
   a. Heat, light, and other power
   b. Interest on investment in shared facilities
   c. Depreciation on shared facilities
   d. Communication costs in order processing and inventory control activities
   e. Labor costs for order processing
3. Determining central computer and communication (as opposed to uses of shared facilities for other administrative activities) costs for:

[3] Robert N. Anthony, *Management Accounting, Text and Cases,* 4th Ed. (Homewood, Ill.: Richard D. Irwin, Inc., 1970), p. 381.

   a. Inventory control
   b. Order processing
   c. Forecasting
   d. Production planning
4. Determining interest expense for:
   a. Investment in facilities
   b. Investment in inventories (as opposed to accounts receivable
      and other uses of working capital)

The allocation procedure, particularly for indirect costs, requires the following:

1. Collection of the cost in a separate account
2. Identification of the functional activities to which it is to be allocated
3. Establishment of a logical basis (such as square feet of space used,
   in the case of functional activities carried out in shared facilities) on
   which to allocate costs
4. Calculation of cost per unit used for the allocation basis (in the case
   above, cost per square foot for a natural cost category like property
   tax)
5. Assignment of costs on the basis of the number of units (in this
   case, square feet) used by an activity center

Authorities on distribution cost accounting suggest guidelines for simplifying the allocation job while retaining the usefulness of results.[4] Among these are:

1. The creation of functional cost centers designed to provide management with facts required for the resolution of known policy issues
   or recurring system design needs
2. Grouping of activity centers, products, or customers to which costs
   are to be allocated in such a manner that expenses fluctuate similarly
   and in a significantly different manner than for other such groupings
3. Grouping of bases for allocation when they closely resemble one
   another
4. Elimination of the separate allocation of expenses too minor to influence results
5. Selection of bases of allocation on the criterion of the extent to
   which the basis is measurable without undue expense

Logistics costs lose their meaning if they are averaged over territories, origin–destination pairs, or distribution centers. For this reason, distribution center costing is gaining in popularity. Through the coding of expenses as they are incurred, facility-oriented costs as well as transpor-

---

[4] See J. Brooks Heckert and Robert B. Miner, *Distribution Costs* (New York: The Ronald Press Co., 1953), especially at p. 26; and Donald R. Longman and Michael Schiff, *Practical Distribution Cost Analysis* (Homewood, Ill.: Richard D. Irwin, Inc., 1955), especially at pp. 193–99 and 227.

tation to and from each distribution center can be accumulated. Transportation costs on shipments directly from plants to customers may even be coded by the distribution center territory in which such customers are located, particularly if these shipments often are occasioned by customer service deficiencies at the distribution center.

Specific bases for determining logistics cost allocations are suggested in Fig. 21–1. The identification of other costs can be accomplished by analyzing information often collected but otherwise unidentified in the accounting process, as suggested in Fig. 21–2.

Both *explicit* costs (those appearing in identifiable dollar expense accounts for financial reporting purposes), and *implicit* costs (such as inventory carrying costs assessed on the basis of a minimum acceptable rate of return to the company), are estimated in Fig. 21–2. For system analysis and design purposes, both are important. For performance measurement purposes, implicit costs are so subjective and difficult to justify to those whose performance is being measured that they are best put aside.

Assigning Functional Costs to Responsibility Centers. Problems at this stage may be less severe than those encountered at the previous one. Typically, the responsibility centers for entire categories of costs reside in functional groups at headquarters under centralized administration, or under a group of facility traffic and warehouse managers at plants and field warehouse locations under decentralized management.

Transportation and order communication costs between company facilities may have to be allocated to managers at both the destination and origin. At a more detailed level of allocation, reasons for holding inventory may be identified so that the relative amounts of inventory accumulated to accommodate logistics (transit, safety, and some speculative stock) can be related to individuals responsible for inventory control at each control point.

Separation of Controllable and Non-controllable Measures of Inputs and Outputs

Smith has pointed out:

All costs are controllable by someone. This concept refers to the level of management that is responsible for the approval of the expenditure. . . . But all costs are not controllable to the same degree.[5]

In the relative short run, over which managerial performances most often are measured and compared, many measures of logistics system

[5] George C. Smith, "Knowing Your P.D. Costs," *Distribution Age*, January, 1966, pp. 21–27.

output cannot be influenced by managers responsible for them. The basic nature of the problem is illustrated in Fig. 21–3. Here we see that those decisions which have the greatest impact on logistics performance often are made with the least participation by logistics management.

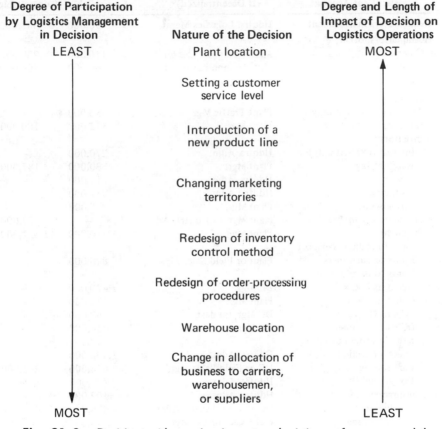

Degree of Participation by Logistics Management in Decision	Nature of the Decision	Degree and Length of Impact of Decision on Logistics Operations
LEAST	Plant location	MOST
	Setting a customer service level	
	Introduction of a new product line	
	Changing marketing territories	
	Redesign of inventory control method	
	Redesign of order-processing procedures	
	Warehouse location	
	Change in allocation of business to carriers, warehousemen, or suppliers	
MOST		LEAST

Fig. 21–3. Decisions with varying impact on logistics performance and the degree to which logistics management typically participates in them.

Because managers are most effectively judged primarily by the way in which they manage controllable elements of their business, it is important to identify the controllable elements and report them separately, or at least to establish performance measures on elements that largely are controllable. Controllable and non-controllable cost elements for one logistics organization are shown in Table 21–3.

Unless there is wide latitude in the time during which logistics activities can be scheduled and accomplished in an organization, work outputs such as cases handled in and out of a warehouse, ton-miles of private

TABLE 21-3. Controllable and Non-controllable Nature of Logistics Costs
(Over Period of Performance Measurement)

Logistics Cost Account	Basic Action Responsibility (If Decentralized)*	Amount	
		Controllable	Non-controllable
Headquarters management	Hdqtrs. Logistics Mgmt.	$ 50,000	$ 387,000
Headquarters, other:			
Computer	Mgr., Computer Center	140,000	280,000
Communications	Mgr., Computer Center	60,000	200,000
Procurement	Plant Procurement Mgr.	7,000	65,000
Raw material:			
Transport (explicit only)	Plant Traffic Mgr.	350,000	–
Handling	Plant Mgr.	522,000	100,000
Inventory:			
Interest (explicit only)	Hdqtrs. Adm.	270,000	–
Warehousing	Plant Mgr.	30,000	187,000
Tax	Hdqtrs. Adm.	14,000	–
Insurance	Hdqtrs. Adm.	17,000	–
Obsolescence	Plant Mgr.	7,000	–
Production planning	Plant Mgr. or Hdqtrs. Adm.	–	32,000
Packaging	Plant Mgr.	770,000	1,651,000
Finished product transport:			
Plants to customers	Plant or Field Sales Mgr.	840,000	–
Plants to distribution centers (DC's)	DC Mgr.	1,420,000	–
Plants to plants	Plant Mgr.	170,000	–
DC's to DC's	DC Mgr. (at dest.)	160,000	–
DC's to customers	DC Mgr.	2,410,000	–
Finished product inventory:			
Interest (explicit only)	Hdqtrs. Adm.	1,400,000	–
Warehousing	DC or Field Sales Mgr.	836,000	281,000
Tax	Hdqtrs. Adm.	79,000	–
Insurance	Hdqtrs. Adm.	102,000	–
Obsolescence	DC Mgr. or Hdqtrs. Adm.	416,000	416,000
Order processing	Field Sales or DC Mgr.	50,000	187,000
Forecasting	Field Sales or Hdqtrs. Marketing Mgmt.	–	73,000
		$10,120,000	$3,849,000

*If centralized, action responsibilities may be divided among logistics (more traditionally traffic and procurement), production, marketing, and control groups. Centralized advisory responsibility may be shared by logistics, inventory control, production planning, and forecasting groups.

transportation activity accomplished, or orders processed largely are the result of demands created by marketing and production effort. Thus, output levels rarely will be controllable over all but the shortest period of time. For this reason, the comparison of outputs to controllable inputs often will yield a measure of the manager's ability to anticipate and adjust to various demands for output activity, or putting it another way, managerial as well as labor and material inputs.

Once identified, controllable costs or other inputs can be compared with units of output on some logical basis. Naturally, every attempt should be made to relate outputs to those inputs from which they result. The relationship never will be perfect, but the goal is to achieve as much logical explanation as possible. (3) **Evaluate the degree to which relevance in output/input relationships has been achieved in Tables 21–1 and 21–2.**

For measures of the effectiveness of all inputs, including those of capital, it can be useful occasionally to compare gross overall outputs with both controllable and non-controllable inputs.

Identification of Productivity Relationships

Experience gained in the collection of cost and other information will provide the basis on which to estimate the way in which productivity measures should vary, for example, in relation to changes in the volume of an organization's activity or in relation to one another.

Performance–Volume Relationships.   Output, input, and productivity measures (relating outputs to inputs) vary with the volume of activity taking place in an organization. For example, an increasing volume of sales from a distribution center should, other things equal, produce a lower handling cost per unit of product handled for a company operating its own distribution center. This is because certain fixed work elements and a fixed labor requirement, unvarying regardless of volume, can be spread over a greater amount of volume with increased material-handling activity, at least up to a point near the theoretical capacity of a given work force.

In many situations, fixed elements of input as well as the level of output are predetermined and outside the control of an individual manager responsible for an activity. For example, the volume of shipments from a distribution center is determined by the level of sales generated in the territory served by the center as well as by the percentage of the demand the distribution center is designed to supply. Further, certain fixed elements of cost or other work inputs for material-handling activity are based on decisions outside the control of the distribution center manager responsible for the activity. In fact, only variable inputs (perhaps measured in terms of cost or man-hours) can be controlled to any degree by the manager. This requires that inputs that are fixed or variable with regard to output be identified separately for purposes of budgeting and other goal setting.

A simple approach to the identification of relationships between productivity and output involves the actual measurement of productivity at different levels of activity. In the case of material-handling activity at a distribution center, readings of tons handled in and out per man-hour of material-handling labor can be taken at different rates of throughput. A line or curve fitted to the resulting measurements, plotted in the form shown in Fig. 21–4, can provide estimates of the fixed and variable elements of the measure necessary for estimating the expected productivity results at various levels of throughput.

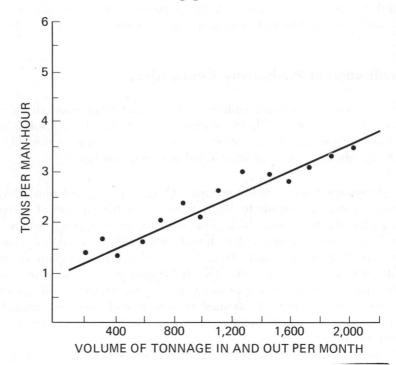

Fig. 21–4. Estimating fixed and variable elements of a productivity measure in relation to volume of activity (tons per man-hour of materials handled into and out of a distribution center, in relation to the volume of tonnage handled in and out).

Fixing Productivity Measures in Time. Many performance measures for logistics activities relate logistics costs to sales levels for a given period. This type of measure can produce puzzling results, because it relates current logistics costs to products sold during the current sales period, for which logistics costs may have been incurred largely in some preceding period. Thus, during a period of heavy sales and inventory reductions, a company might experience a ratio of transportation costs for shipments from plants to warehouses that is very low when compared with sales, especially in contrast to the high ratio incurred during a preceding period when warehouse stocks were being built in anticipation of seasonal demand.

This problem can be avoided either by eliminating performance measures relating sales outputs to logistics cost inputs or by adopting the accountant's matching concept in the collection and reporting of cost information. Under the latter alternative, attempts can be made to charge logistics costs against goods as they are sold, accruing such costs until the time of sale. Because of the complexities of assigning logistics costs under the matching concept, it is perhaps more practical to avoid the use of sales/cost ratios for all but longer periods of time (three to twelve months) over which sales and logistics activity peaks and valleys can be averaged. Such periods may be based on the length of time required for a product to pass through the entire pipeline from procurement to production line or from production line to actual sale, or the inventory cycle which a company might experience, particularly in a seasonal business.

One final note. To the extent that costs are allocated on the basis of output measures, productivity measures relating such outputs and costs will be rendered meaningless. It is hard to avoid "productivity averaging" completely, but the design of subsequent performance measures should avoid heavily averaged relationships.

Recognition of the Impact of a Control Program on Managerial Behavior

A control program influences managerial behavior. When performance measures, goals, and review and reward procedures are established in such a way that different functions of an organization work at cross purposes, they may be less desirable than none at all.

The identification of cost relationships, either within or between separate managerial groups in an organization, should lead eventually to coordinated planning and performance measurement. Coordinated planning of interfunctional strategies can in turn encourage the establishment of goals that create a minimum of conflict among production, marketing, finance, and logistics management. This is a characteristic of a well-conceived, well-implemented program of planning and control.

Although many organizations are working toward such coordinated planning, all but a handful are still establishing performance goals and measuring performance without regard for underlying implications of interfunctional strategies determined at the top management level. Consider the following situation which developed several years ago in the European subsidiary of a large multinational company.

This company, manufacturing a wide range of ceramic bathroom fixtures, among other items, found that its inventories of fixtures were badly out of balance. Stocks of colored fixtures were far too large, while white fixtures were back-ordered constantly. Although the logistics group within the organization had responsibility for establishing inventory control methods, plant managers were responsible for the items actually stored at and shipped from their respective plants. Upon investigating for possible causes of the situation, the corporate logistics staff found that plant managers were being evaluated in relation to a goal based on the dollar value of goods produced at each facility. Because colored units of a given fixture invariably carried a higher value, even though their manufacture required approximately the same labor and material input as white units, plant managers were giving priority to the manufacture of colored units in order to meet their goals.

(4) **In a situation such as this, what alternatives might you suggest for resolving the situation, if you were a member of the logistics management staff responsible for inventory control? (5) If you were a plant manager?**

Another illustrative situation is diagrammed in Fig. 21–5. Production, marketing, and finance functions, in the absence of a coordinating group such as logistics, all have a deep and somewhat conflicting interest in inventory policy. Increased cycle stocks (recalling the terms we used in Chapters 11 and 13) can allow larger, longer, less frequent, and less expensive (per unit) production costs. For seasonal items, increased speculative stocks will allow production an opportunity to maintain a constant output in spite of seasonality in sales, thus maintaining a level, less expensive work force per unit of output.

At the same time, an increase in safety stocks can produce a larger buffer against out-of-stock situations, particularly if such safety stocks are held close to markets. For this reason, a policy leading to increased safety stocks would be highly favored by marketing management.

The third party to this interrelationship, finance, often is concerned with maintaining as little inventory as possible in relation to sales, in order to conserve the working capital of the organization.

Unless the result of an inventory policy decision can be estimated, in terms of its impact on production set-up costs, per-unit production costs, inventory carrying costs, and sales, it will be impossible to select a policy that will produce the best total result for the company as a whole. The

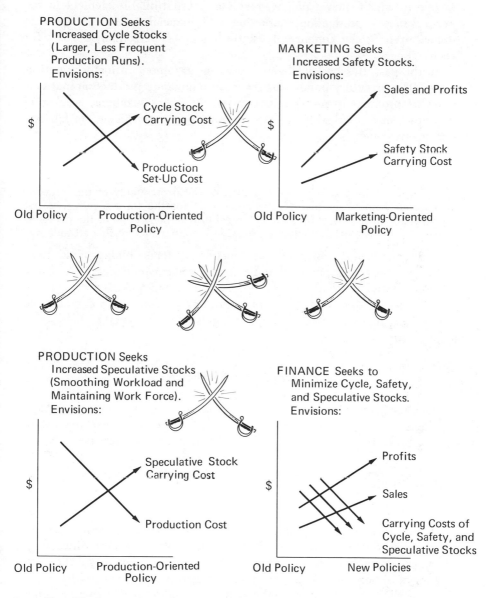

Fig. 21–5. Basic conflicts in determining the amount and type of inventory to plan for, illustrating the need for the identification of cost (and profit) relationships and coordinated planning for logistics. *Source:* Adapted from Harlan C. Meal, "Policy Conflicts and Inventory Control," *Financial Executive*, December, 1963, pp. 13–17, at p. 16.

degree to which such a policy creates an uncontrollable element in the performance of production, marketing, and financial management will go unmeasured in the concurrent establishment of performance goals for each.

In the past, this has not been a relevant argument in many organizations. The inventory policy was set to accommodate production management in production- and engineering-oriented organizations, marketing management in marketing-oriented organizations, and finance in finance- and control-oriented organizations.

The nature of a recent finding regarding the relationship between marketing and physical distribution is rather discouraging in this respect: [6]

. . . Rather than a lack of information or the poor quality of the information is the simple fact that Marketing, except for the top executive, is not concerned with the effect on P.D. (physical distribution) costs of the decisions made, and the evaluative system encourages a continuance of this attitude.

The emergence of the logistics function, systems thinking, and company-wide planning potential have forced some companies to face the problem. Models simulating the impact of various policy decisions can now be designed and used in conjunction with a company's computer to provide an important tool for developing estimates of performance inter-relationships.

PROGRAM MANAGEMENT

The management of a performance measurement and control program for logistics requires that jobs be defined, performance measures established, budgets and goals set, and performance review implemented.

Job Definition

Many organizations have established position descriptions for all executive and clerical personnel. In many, perhaps most, of these same organizations, few individuals ever refer to descriptions of jobs which they, their superiors, or their subordinates are to perform. Too often, the writing of job descriptions is a time-consuming, expensive, and useless task. Perhaps the greatest factor in the non-use of position descriptions, once they are formulated within an organization, is that they are written in such broad terms that they are impossible to interpret and administer on a day-to-day or even periodic basis.

A job definition should be short, somewhat general with respect to

[6] Schiff, op. cit., p. 1-13.

duties and responsibilities (as opposed to a statement of specific procedures to be followed on a job), and quite detailed in its specification of performance measures and review procedures. The most successful ones we have encountered contain the following elements: job title, the individual to whom the person holding the job is to report, responsibilities attendant to the job, measures by which performance in the job will be evaluated, the individual responsible for reviewing performance in the job, and the frequency and manner in which such review will be conducted.

Establishment of Performance Measures

It goes without saying that measures to be used in evaluating performance on a job should reflect the responsibilities of the position. Beyond this, however, there are additional guidelines which successful organizations have applied in establishing performance measures:

1. Be very selective in the development of quantitative measures. It is difficult for a manager to concentrate on more than a few such measures in addition to non-quantitative measures such as employee morale and the development of talent for job succession.
2. Select such quantitative measures on the basis of those that reflect:
   a. Important costs or other inputs,
   b. Scarce resources, such as facilities with limited capacities, and
   c. Measures involving inputs and outputs over which the manager being measured has the greatest control.

In establishing performance measures, it is important to obtain recommendations from the person for whom the measures are being established. The question, "How would you like to be measured on your job?" can elicit valuable information from an individual about the way he sees his job and his sense of perspective. It may also enlist his cooperation in and support of the measurement and evaluation process.

Measures which have been established successfully, with adaptations, in several logistics organizations are shown in Tables 21–1 and 21–2 (pages 700 and 701, respectively). The set of measures in Table 21–1 can be applied to a company's overall logistics activity. At a lower level of management, the measures shown in Table 21–2 can be applied to a manager of a company's distribution center. In each case, they reflect the scope and nature of logistics operations for a specific company.

(6) How would you appraise the measures used in Tables 21–1 and 21–2, using the criteria for their development suggested above? (7) How often would you suggest they be reviewed at both the system-wide and distribution-center levels? (8) In what manner? (9) What form

would your review take for the figures reported in Tables 21–1 and 21–2 for the March operating period of the National Radiator Corporation?

Budgeting and Goal Setting

Budgets not only inject discipline into the managerial process, but they provide the basis for intermediate-term financial planning, particularly the planning of cash flow. Typically, budgets are confined to the items over which a particular manager has immediate control. In a staff-oriented logistics organization with advisory responsibility, for example, such items usually include only the salaries and related administrative items for a central office staff. Clearly, in this situation, the budget has limited meaning (as opposed to broader measures of performance) for the logistics manager. He can meet his budgetary goals by hiring or firing a secretary or a rate clerk.

The budgeting of logistics costs for an entire organization may be the responsibility of the corporate staff, even though it may not be responsible for managing all logistics activities directly. Regardless of responsibility, the budgetary measures used for such activities should be flexible. That is, they should take into account the portions of a given cost which are fixed and variable in regard to the volume of logistics activity which the organization is required to carry out. If the operation of a warehouse requires a fixed charge of $100,000 per year in addition to roughly 10 cents for every case handled into and out of the facility, the budget goal should reflect the fact that on-target performance will be represented by an expenditure of $200,000 if 1,000,000 cases are handled into and out of the facility and $250,000 if the volume of such activity is 1,500,000 cases.

Budgets and performance goals should include not only a target figure for each item, but also upper and lower limits which, if violated during the course of the period for which they are established, will lead to the creation of an exception, or red-flag, report of the fact. Goals and performance measures may go "out of control," or violate limits, for a variety of reasons, all of which warrant immediate review. Causes may range from poor management to a basic change in the economics of an operation which may require an adjustment in the budget or the performance goal.

Goals for performance have broader-reaching implications than budgetary estimates. A logistics organization directly responsible for only a small administrative budget may nevertheless be measured on the basis of its ability to plan and implement a system design through others that will produce a certain result. In this case, the characteristic evaluated on the basis of such indirect measures may well be the ability of the staff advisory organization to communicate or, in the terms of Lawrence and Lorsch, to integrate.[7]

Performance Review

The failure to follow up performance measurement with a periodic review and evaluation can negate an otherwise well-devised program. The frequency of the review may depend on the importance of good performance in the job, the length of time during which the person being reviewed has held the job, or other factors. Typically, such reviews are held more often than salary and promotion reviews, perhaps every six months. In addition, impromptu reviews may take place when budgetary or performance measures go "out of control."

There are many possible approaches to performance review. All involve advance knowledge on the part of the person being reviewed of the bases on which his performance is being evaluated. One effective approach to the actual review is to have both the subordinate and his superior prepare an evaluation, based on performance figures and other information, of both qualitative and quantitative criteria. The evaluations can then be compared and discussed. Participation in the process on the part of the person being reviewed leads to greater acceptance of the actual evaluation.

PRACTICAL STEPS IN ESTABLISHING A LOGISTICS CONTROL PROGRAM

It has always seemed to us that the higher an executive rises in his organization, the more uneasy he becomes about the adequacy of measures and controls at his disposal for guiding those responsible to him. To a degree, top management is an easy mark for someone in middle management concerned about establishing visibility for himself and his management area by addressing himself to the creation of a productivity control program. Even though many members of top management don't know what logistics is, at least they'll agree that it ought to be controlled.

The possible steps in the establishment of a logistics control program sound formidable when arrayed in the manner we have discussed them above. Sometimes the gap between ideal and actual is so great that we are discouraged from taking the first steps to bridge it. And yet the payoff, in terms of increased recognition for the importance of logistics activities within an organization and the individuals responsible for them,

[7] Paul R. Lawrence and Jay W. Lorsch, "New Management Job: The Integrator," *Harvard Business Review,* November–December, 1967, pp. 142–51.

is so great that it is important to take the first steps toward the creation of such a program.

First, with a pencil and paper and the help of our preceding discussion, identify all important logistics cost categories along with other inputs of effort which the organization incurs. At this stage, the objective is to be complete. The only investment is a little of your time. There is no risk.

Second, begin collecting the cost and input data. At first, this might be done on a one-shot basis, for example, for the preceding year. Later, of course, the objective is to have such reporting carried out on a periodic, routine basis. This task may test an executive's skill in obtaining assistance from his colleagues in an organization. If top management's support must be enlisted to accomplish one of these early steps in the process, it may be necessary to proceed directly to step four, below.

It is important that the cost input collection process begin as soon as possible. Most executives we have observed have learned a great deal about the adequacy of cost information and the magnitude of the task of proper identification and collection of such information within their organizations merely by attempting to collect it. A degree of control may result just from the identification and collection process.

Third, identify and begin collecting important output measures. Production measures may be more easily obtained than those of inputs. For example, cases shipped in palletized form from a warehouse may be recorded on a shipping document. If they are not, they can be estimated from the weight shipped by a mode of transportation in which pallets are employed.

The collection of both input and output data may require a long lead time. That is why it is important to start early in the entire process. It is essential to the fourth step.

Fourth, prepare a set of desired measures by which the logistics activities within the organization might be evaluated. Such measures, rather than reflecting the nature of an individual's job, should encompass all logistics activities, regardless of the assignment of responsibility for them. They might reflect the scope of those in Table 21–1, including various measures for transportation, warehousing, inventory control, order entry and processing, customer service, and total logistics cost performance.

Fifth, these measures can then be presented to top management, along with an estimate of the importance of the logistics costs which have been collected in step two. With such justification, it takes a closed top-management mind to veto the recommended control program which can highlight such a presentation. In one presentation, which might take place months after the collection of the first information, a concerned logistics manager can:

1. Highlight the importance of logistics to his top management
2. Provide, in a practical context, an explanation of the scope of the function
3. Stress the importance of measuring logistics management performance, regardless of responsibility
4. Propose a step-by-step program for such measurement and control
5. Enlist top management support in the implementation of the program
6. Project himself as the most likely candidate for the position of manager in charge of some or all logistics activities

Sixth, assuming top management's support, a program to report regularly productivity measures such as those presented in Table 21–1 can be instituted. In all likelihood, even at this stage, sufficient information required for all of these measures will not be available on a regular basis.

Seventh, assuming support for the program is continued, organizations will develop a need for someone in the accounting or controller's function to serve as liaison between those departments and individuals responsible for logistics activities.[8] This will facilitate the regular collection and reporting of necessary information. In most cases, this effort will require that monetary and physical measures of activity be recorded and coded at the point at which they are captured for entry into the company's management information system, a basic escalation in effort requiring a policy commitment as well as the investment of funds sufficient to support the activity.

Eighth, organizations in an industry with similar interests in the measurement and control of productivity may establish cooperative efforts to exchange information, probably through a third party able to maintain confidentiality of the data. Figure 21–6 shows a page from the periodic report of a program sponsored by the National Association of Food Chains, in cooperation with the New York State College of Agriculture at Cornell University, for the control of retail distribution center productivity.

(10) The black lines in Fig. 21–6 represent the actual performance for one participating company for the quarter ending December, 1970. How would you evaluate this performance?

Such programs are most feasible when: (1) practices in different companies are somewhat homogeneous, (2) important determinants of performance can be identified to aid in the interpretation of results, and (3) measures can be devised that are sufficiently specific to be of use in the day-to-day management of operations. It goes without saying that

---

[8] It is perhaps significant that one of the major recommendations of the Schiff report, cited earlier in this chapter, was for the designation of a person with responsibilities for maintaining just such liaison.

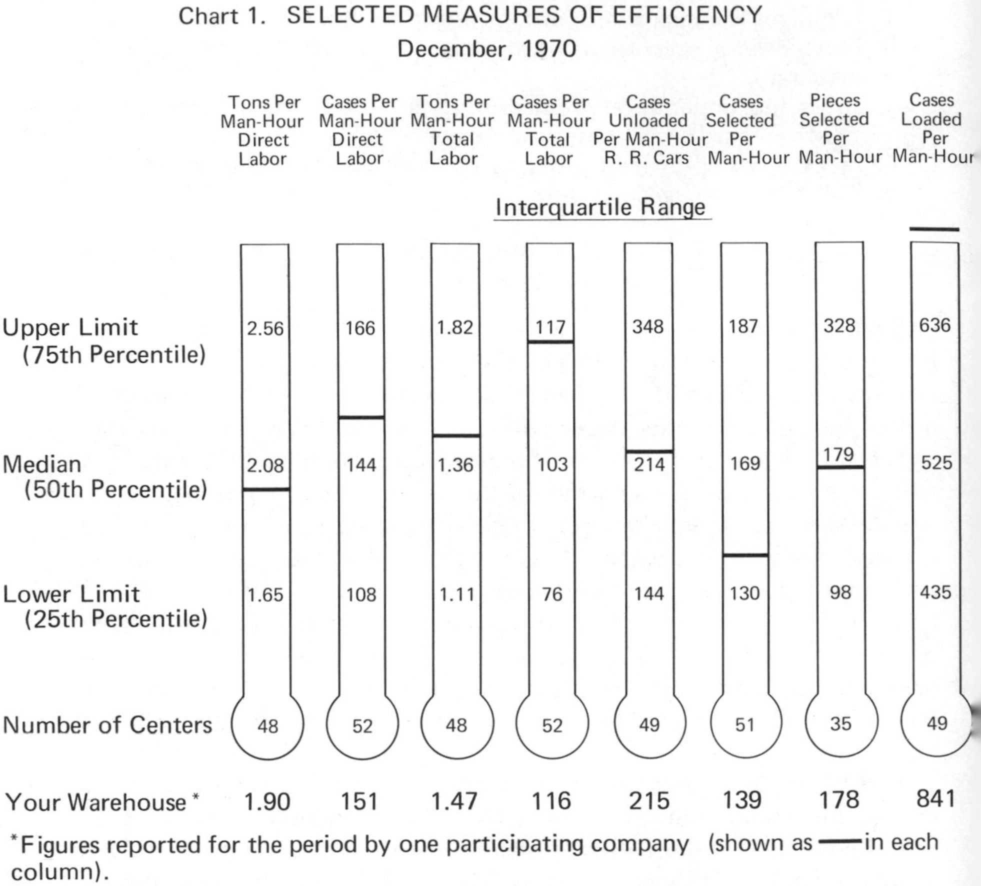

Chart 1. SELECTED MEASURES OF EFFICIENCY
December, 1970

Interquartile Range

	Tons Per Man-Hour Direct Labor	Cases Per Man-Hour Direct Labor	Tons Per Man-Hour Total Labor	Cases Per Man-Hour Total Labor	Cases Unloaded Per Man-Hour R. R. Cars	Cases Selected Per Man-Hour	Pieces Selected Per Man-Hour	Cases Loaded Per Man-Hour
Upper Limit (75th Percentile)	2.56	166	1.82	117	348	187	328	636
Median (50th Percentile)	2.08	144	1.36	103	214	169	179	525
Lower Limit (25th Percentile)	1.65	108	1.11	76	144	130	98	435
Number of Centers	48	52	48	52	49	51	35	49
Your Warehouse *	1.90	151	1.47	116	215	139	178	841

*Figures reported for the period by one participating company (shown as ▬ in each column).

Fig. 21–6. A page from the *Grocery Distribution Center Efficiency Report,* December, 1970 (published quarterly by the New York State College of Agriculture, Cornell University, as part of a project conducted in cooperation with and sponsored by the National Association of Food Chains).

accurate reporting requires honesty and good judgment on the part of participants, characteristics not always easy to maintain when a manager is under pressure for poor performance relative to his counterparts in other organizations.

Ninth, as productivity measures for budgeting and performance measurement and review purposes are collected, involved executives will begin to develop a "feel" for interrelationships among various types of outputs, inputs, and measures and goals developed for sister departments within the organization. Not until this stage of development is reached can an organization develop the type of coordinated planning that will correct the situation described in Fig. 21–5. The stage will be set for the development of interfunctional planning teams to help in the preparation of budgets and performance goals which take into account and attempt to reduce the magnitude of goal conflicts so common to production, marketing, finance, and logistics management.

Tenth, the development of a coordinated program for performance and control also will facilitate more sophisticated efforts, such as those to plan and control particular logistics projects and to measure the relative profitability of various types of business activity.

PROJECT PLANNING AND CONTROL

In contrast to the requirements for control of ongoing logistics activities are those for the selection and periodic review of efforts to implement major projects or programs, typically involving the basic redesign of all or some aspects of a logistics system. Many of the problems of project control begin in the planning process; for this reason, it is useful to consider features of an effective project control process in conjunction with planning efforts which precede it.

Standard Format for Planning and Audit Purposes

A standard format for estimating the impact of a proposed change in logistics system design can provide a checklist against which planners may compare the scope and coverage of their efforts as well as a vehicle for the systematic audit of planning and implementation efforts at a later date. One such format, which can be adjusted to meet the needs of a specific project effort, is shown in Table 21–4.

Effective Capital Budgeting Procedure

Most organizations establish cut-off points, typically expressed in terms of minimum returns on investments, below which capital investments for proposed projects will not be approved. It is useful for a project planner to have these cut-off points in mind in evaluating the usefulness of a proposed project before it is submitted to an organization's top management for consideration. It provides the basis for structuring the actual planning effort, regardless of whether there are substantial investments required for a particular project.

Capital budgeting needs require that a total cost analysis of a logistics system change be accompanied by an estimate of the required capital

TABLE 21–4. Format for Requesting Logistics Projects Authorization

Items To Be Described	Timing of Cash Inflows or Outflows			
	Year 1	Year 2	Year 3	Year 4
Summary statement of proposed project:				
Creation of an additional product distribution point by using public warehousing space at Denver, Colorado				
Required capital expenditures for:				
New facilities				
Inventory	$ 25,000	$ 5,000*	$ 5,000*	$ 5,000*
Working capital				
Cost of implementing project	4,000			
Other				
Less capital receipts from:				
Sales of equipment				
Sales of facilities				
Other				
Net capital investment required	$ 29,000	$ 5,000	$ 5,000	$ 5,000
Additional costs for, and amount:				
Order processing	$ 3,500	$ 3,500	$ 4,000	$ 4,500
Warehousing charges (in addition to current charges)	2,500	3,000	3,500	4,000
Less cost savings from, and amount:				
Warehouse-to-customer transportation	$ 13,000	$ 14,000	$ 15,000	$ 16,000
Net effect on logistics costs	–$ 7,000	–$ 7,500	–$ 7,500	–$ 7,500
Net effect on sales levels	+$100,000	+$125,000	+$125,000	+$150,000
Net effect on production costs	None			
Estimated before-tax return on investment, calculated on a discounted cash-flow basis, assuming a ten-year project life	11% (payback period is slightly less than 6 years)			

*Additional after the first year.

investment, the net impact on related major costs, and an estimate of the effect on sales.[9]

Projects involving the expenditure of money for physical facilities typically fall within the capital budgeting requirements for organized analysis and presentation set up within many organizations. However, a revision of an inventory control policy or procedure may require no new

[9] For an interesting discussion of this subject, see John R. Grabner, Jr., and James F. Robeson, "Distribution System Analysis: A Problem in Capital Budgeting," in David McConaughy and C. Joseph Clawson (eds.), *Business Logistics—Policies and Decisions* (Los Angeles: University of Southern California Research Institute for Business and Economics, 1968), pp. 143–56.

physical facilities but may have a great effect on inventories and working capital. In addition, most projects of any magnitude require capital investments, whether in the form of computer programming effort or the relocation of personnel, for their implementation. All of these considerations should be taken into account in establishing the investment required for a specific project.

While it may be impossible to provide a realistic estimate of the impact of a system change on profits, it is useful to identify effects which the change may have on major related production costs and sales levels. This will require top management personnel responsible for those activities to commit themselves to projections which can be reviewed at a later date.

Finally, all cash inflows and outflows must be positioned in time so that the estimated return on investment from the project can be calculated on a discounted cash-flow basis, taking into account the value of money today as opposed to some time in the future. The format in Table 21–4 has been designed to provide the basic inputs for the calculation of rate of return on investment on a discounted cash-flow basis.

Linkage Between Project Planning and Implementation

In most cases, the responsibilities for planning and implementing a project are divided. Central staff personnel with advisory capacity typically do the planning, handing it over to line managers with action responsibility for implementation. This, coupled with the fact that planning and implementation, especially for major projects, can be disconnected in time as well, often leads to an interruption in the vital feedback loop between control and planning shown in Fig. 21–1. When this occurs, and it occurs often: (1) planning and control of a given effort may be carried out under totally different assumptions, (2) those responsible for planning on the one hand and control on the other are given a wonderful opportunity to point their fingers at each other for sub-par performance, and (3) opportunities to improve subsequent planning efforts in the light of past successes or failures are lost.

There are several ways of creating the necessary linkage. Planning personnel may be involved in the implementation process. Those responsible for implementation and control may be engaged to help plan a project. Planning and control may be linked organizationally under one manager. Or, a project audit routine may be established for the assessment and communication of planning and control efforts associated with a given project. (11) **Under what conditions might each of these approaches be most effective?**

Regardless of the method or combination of methods used to establish a linkage between project planning and control, a systematic project audit routine can serve a useful purpose.

Project Audit Routine

Projects of minimum size, involving a minimum capital investment or minimum potential savings to warrant the cost of an audit, should be formally reviewed to determine the quality of planning and control and ways in which each could have been improved. Although such an audit should be conducted by an objective group within the organization (perhaps the finance, control, or engineering group), it should involve representatives from groups responsible for logistical planning and control.

The audit routine should be designed to determine:

1. How well the plan has been fulfilled
2. Reasons for the relative success or failure of the project
3. Whether the project should be continued in the light of the findings
4. Ways in which future planning and control efforts can be improved.

An effective audit requires that planners be able to formulate the project plan in such a way that underlying assumptions on which the plan was based can be identified, even several years after the implementation phase was initiated. It requires also that those responsible for implementation be able to verbalize the assumptions, procedures, and policies with which the plan was implemented and the operating environment in which it was done.

The timing of the audit will depend on the period of time required for the plan to register its full impact. In the case of a new warehouse facility, it might require a year's time to assess its impact on sales in the territory which it serves. A change to private from common carrier operation, and its resulting impact on customer service, might warrant a review after no more than six months.

Vehicle for Feedback

Reports tend to get filed and not read. As a part of the audit procedure, it is useful to include a post-audit debriefing for selected members of the organization responsible for logistical planning and control activities. Audit reports, along with other project documents and the minutes of the debriefing meeting, might then be placed in a reference file to be used by those involved in future projects.

PROFITABILITY CONTROL

Logistics, to a greater extent than other basic business functions, is spatially oriented. From the standpoint of profitability, it makes a lot of difference where products are sold, stored, and shipped. Lewis' summary of the view held by one of his colleagues makes the point well: [10]

. . . by allocating total costs among the various activities of marketing [including logistics] on the basis of standards or standard costs, rather than building up the individual charges at the source of their incurrence, the accountant fails to allow for the variability of . . . costs that result from locational differences.

Logistics costs, to a greater extent than costs incurred in production, marketing, and financing activities, can be associated with specific sales. This provides an unusual opportunity to relate costs to individual customers, types or groups of customers, sales territories, warehouse territories, plant territories, or specific products or product lines.

Product Profitability

The profitability of a product or product line often is influenced primarily by the margin between the allocated cost of the product sold and the sales price which a company is able to command for it in the market. Typically, the importance of logistics costs as determinants of product profitability varies inversely with the value of the product per unit of weight, notwithstanding the fact that inventory costs are related directly to product value.

One of the authors once encountered a shipping clerk for a computer manufacturer who shipped everything air express, in part because he didn't realize that at the time air express cost approximately twice what air freight did on a comparable shipment. However inadvertently he may have arrived at his policy, he was probably right. In contrast, a similar investigation of the distribution of ceramic building tile disclosed that logistics costs were not only a major factor in product profitability, but also were the most important determinants of marketing territories.

Transportation and public warehousing rates are quoted on the basis of the physical characteristics of a product, among other things. On a

[10] Ronald J. Lewis, "Strengthening Control of Physical Distribution Costs," *Management Services*, January–February, 1968, pp. 36–46, at p. 39. In this article Lewis summarizes a point of view expressed in what is perhaps the most intensive investigation of the subject: Richard Lewis, *A Logistical Information System for Marketing Analysis* (Cincinnati: South-Western Publishing Co., 1970).

company-wide basis, inventory turnover rates can be developed for each product. For these reasons, it is not difficult to associate a large portion of total logistics costs with a product, at least on an estimated basis. Those that remain, typically order entry and processing costs, can be assigned with the use of a surrogate, such as a heavier cost per unit for items found, by sample, to be out-of-stock more often than others in relation to the number of units sold.

What to do with the knowledge that certain product-line items are unprofitable, perhaps even without taking marketing costs into account, is something else. There may be many reasons for retaining an unprofitable item, among them the need to spread overhead costs over an extensive line and fulfill customers' expectations of product coverage. Nevertheless, it is useful to be able to make such decisions with the full knowledge that an item might be unprofitable.

Territory Profitability

The overall logistical profitability of a plant, warehouse, or sales territory will be influenced largely by the geographic relationship among plants, warehouses, and sales territories in question; the operational effectiveness at each facility location; and differences in customer behavior.

Costs against which to assess the relative profitability of territories can be built up starting at their origin. Beginning with a plant, warehousing and inventory costs can be determined and allocated to various categories of product. The process of cost building can then continue through the subsequent phases of the distribution process, including transportation between facilities and markets, and the storage, material-handling, inventory-carrying, and order-processing activities that take place at each facility.

In a company with excess production and marketing capacity, any operational territory that produces revenues in excess of the variable costs attributed to the revenue, termed "contribution to overhead and profit" by accountants, can be justified. However, in situations where production and marketing resources are scarce, a company may want to have knowledge of the actual and potential profitability of all feasible operational territories in order to be able to structure its effort to obtain the maximum profit from a limited production or sales volume.

Customer Profitability

Customers served through identical channels of physical product flow may have significantly different profitability for a supplier. Customer profitability varies with the size and complexity of orders placed for a given destination, the nature of the product-line items ordered, and customer demands for special logistical services.

In some cases, customer behavior may be a major determinant of the relative profitability of a sales or warehouse territory. For example, regional sales managers who do or do not encourage their salesmen to emphasize standard, high-sales-volume items as opposed to special items for which they might be substituted can have a major impact on logistics costs on a territory-wide basis. In this case, the resulting remedy may have more to do with changing sales policies than logistics procedures.

Approaches to Profitability Control

The design and implementation of a logistics profitability control system can be as complex, expensive, and debatable as a company wishes to make it. Profitability control has been made more feasible by the widespread availability and use of computers, but no one should be misled into thinking that it is now a relatively simple, straightforward matter.

Assume a company has 1,000 product-line items, 15 stock-keeping locations, a two-stage distribution system encompassing two forms of transportation at one stage and three at the other, 15,000 separate customer locations, 100,000 orders per year, and 20 identifiable logistics cost categories. If it desires to select from an information file items which would allow it to measure the profitability of each product-line item, it would have to maintain on file as many as 2,700,000,000,000,000 pieces of information, having processed each through a series of allocation programs. Further, even if such information were to be calculated each month, it would be out-of-date for certain items with distinct seasonal sales patterns, and would be criticized accordingly.

If it is to be feasible, then, a profit measurement system must be limited to the most important cost and revenue determinants and used by executives willing to recognize the assumptions and approximations inherent in such a process. For example, if the company described above were willing to categorize its 1,000 products into ten groups and build up costs for these ten groups of items from the plant warehouse through the outbound dock of its distribution warehouses, with a separate set of information for direct shipments from each of three plants to each customer destination, and a periodic sampling and assignment of costs to orders, the system might be manageable by computer.

Clearly, a more practical approach to the problem is necessary. One such approach is outlined in Table 21–5. It involves the periodic sampling of customer orders on a selective basis. Costs are applied to those

TABLE 21-5. A Program To Provide Periodic Estimates of Logistics Costs per Customer

I. From a sample of customer orders, determine:
  1. Total dollar value of orders
  2. Number of orders
  3. Number of order-line items
  4. Destination of shipment
II. By matching orders, invoices, and bills of lading, determine:
  1. Number of orders containing back-ordered items
  2. Number of line items back-ordered
  3. Number of shipments required to fill orders
  4. Size of shipments, in weight
  5. Shipment origins and destinations
  6. Proportion of weight ordered in slow-moving (80/20) items
  7. Proportion of weight ordered in fast-moving (20/80) items
III. From measurement and control system, estimate:
  1. Average cost of transportation per cwt. for:
    a. Origin–destination pairs under examination
    b. Shipments of various size categories
    c. Various methods of transportation
  2. Cost of processing an order, in terms of:
    a. Fixed cost per order containing no back-ordered items
    b. Line-item cost for orders containing no back-ordered items
    c. Fixed and variable cost per back-ordered line item
  3. Average cost of carrying inventory per cwt. for:
    a. Slow-moving items at each distribution center and plant
    b. Fast-moving items at each distribution center and plant
  4. Cost of handling product in and out per cwt. for each distribution center and plant
  5. Non-allocated logistics costs on an average-cost-per-cwt. basis
IV. When interpreted in terms of information from steps II and III, information from step I will appear as follows:

	Customer Name	
Account Activity	Arizona Tire and Rubber Company	Texas Eastern Rubber Company
Annual sales	$13,300	$8,600
Allocated logistics costs:		
Transportation:		
Plant to distribution center	370	285
Plant to customer	50	250
Distribution center to customer	475	365
Inventory holding:		
80/20 products, plant	55	30
20/80 products, plant	75	160
80/20 products, distribution center	120	75
20/80 products, distribution center	110	270
Handling:		
In and out, plant	90	65
In and out, distribution center	175	105
Order processing:		
"Routine" orders	80	40
Back-ordered goods	15	90
Total	$ 1,615	$1,735
Allocated logistics costs as a proportion of sales	12.1%	20.2%
Non-allocated logistics costs	$220	

orders based on gross allocations of major cost categories incurred at facilities, combined with the estimation of point-to-point transportation costs by means of the analysis of a minimum of information about each shipment. This relatively straightforward approach does, however, allow for an analysis of customer profitability based on order behavior. It may meet most of a company's needs for the measurement and control of profitability at a fraction of the cost of a computerized system.

(12) What would you conclude on the basis of information presented in Part IV of Table 21–5? (13) What action, if any, would you take?

SUMMARY

We have traced the subject of profit measurement and control from the features of an effective program to the more detailed application of such a program in the identification of profitability for products, operating territories, and customers. At its most sophisticated level of use, such a system can provide the means to identify cost relationships, not only over varying levels of activity but also between functions of the organization. In this way, it can provide the eventual means to assess the implications of a given policy for various functional areas, thus providing for the establishment of realistic expectations for performance in situations where compromises in performance levels between functions are necessary if the organization is to operate in the most effective manner.

Meal has summed it up nicely: [11]

One of the most important responsibilities of distribution management is to show the general management of any firm the implications of the alternative choices available to it in resolving the conflicts of interests between the various parts of an organization. It is the set of policy statements which control the routine or day-to-day decisions which will most importantly influence the face which a company presents to the outside world and which, in turn, will determine the operating results which are recorded at the end of the year. Distribution management has the responsibility for showing how the operating statement results can be influenced and will be influenced by the choice of policy statement.

In the process of accomplishing this objective, a manager can achieve important byproduct results of informing his top management in a practical sense of the scope and importance of logistics activities in general and, in particular, his own value to the organization.

[11] Harlan C. Meal, "The Formulation of Distribution Policy," *Transportation & Distribution Management*, January, 1965, pp. 21–27.

SUGGESTED READINGS

ANTHONY, ROBERT N. *Planning and Control Systems.* Boston: Division of
Research, Graduate School of Business Administration, Harvard University,
1965.
Offers a useful way of viewing the complex relationships between planning
and control in a manner that can be adapted easily to the needs of logistics
management.

BALLOU, RONALD H. *Business Logistics Management.* Englewood Cliffs, N.J.:
Prentice-Hall, Inc., 1973.
Provides an interesting review of the process of logistical control and the
information on which it is based.

HECKERT, J. BROOKS, and ROBERT B. MINER. *Distribution Costs.* New York:
The Ronald Press Co., 1953.

LONGMAN, DONALD R., and MICHAEL SCHIFF. *Practical Distribution Cost
Analysis.* Homewood, Ill.: Richard D. Irwin, Inc., 1955.
These two books, although both written some years ago, offer the most comprehensive sources of information regarding the identification, allocation,
and evaluation of marketing costs, including many which we associate with
logistics.

SCHIFF, MICHAEL. *Accounting and Control in Physical Distribution Management.* Chicago: The National Council of Physical Distribution Management,
1972.
Offers an in-depth appraisal of the state of the art in the measurement and
control of logistics costs, particularly those associated with the distribution
of goods, in fourteen companies.

22

A Look to the Future

Just two decades ago there was speculation that trailer-on-flatcar service would be reintroduced (borrowing from the rail circus troupes of the previous century) to herald a new era in coordinated, multimode transportation service.

Concern was expressed that the limits on technology imposed by strategically located waterways such as the Panama Canal and the Suez Canal not only would severely constrain the world's movements of bulk commodities, but would make control over those waterways highly desirable to any world power. The only possible relief would come from the development of large bulk ships not technologically feasible at that time.

Long-distance transportation by conveyor or vacuum tube was depicted in the Buck Rogers world of the twenty-fifth century.

Although the computer as we know it today had not yet been developed, there was speculation that the increasing use of machines for processing data on punched cards might one day afford organizations with great opportunities.

Today all of this has either happened or is possible. Trailer-on-flatcar service, after being reintroduced on a commercial scale in the early 1950's, enjoyed a rapid increase in use and is now thought to have captured much of its available market. The advent of the super-tanker, with carrying capacity of more than 20 times that thought technologically feasible at the time of World War II, has made the world's formerly important canals obsolete for large-scale bulk transportation by water. Cross-country conveyor transportation is a reality, and transport by vacuum tube is no longer a technological puzzle. The computer is commonplace, and has become an important, silent force in the operation of a business of any size today.

Closer to reality no more than a decade ago, but not yet achieved, was the introduction of scheduled container service on the world's more important trade routes, utilizing containers of standard sizes which could be interchanged between carriers of varying modes and their competitors.

Writers were speculating on the technological feasibility of real-time, on-line data processing by which a company could manage its inventories by updating inventory records instantly when orders were written, with automatic replenishment, back-ordering, and order writing by computer. Of course, only the largest firms would be able to afford such services in the foreseeable future.

Among methods of distribution which might one day be technologically feasible was that of centralized distribution, particularly of well-known products, whereby an individual consumer, through his or her phone, could call up a catalog of product information and pictures on a video screen, place an order by inputting information directly to a central warehouse, and receive products delivered directly to his home without passing through an expensive retail distribution channel.

All of these are now either in operation or technologically feasible, awaiting only the proper time and form for introduction to the public. Containerization, existent as we know it today for less than a decade, has become the predominant mode of transport for manufactured goods on more important trade routes such as the North Atlantic. Not only is real-time, on-line inventory control feasible for large firms, it is available through newly developed information and distribution utilities for smaller firms. Decentralized ordering and centralized distribution by means of video screen are feasible. A form of this system utilizing cathode-ray tubes for the recall of data regarding product names and numbers and the verification of order information is in common use in the order-processing departments of many firms today.

Clearly, the past thirty years have produced remarkable technological advances in transportation, material handling, and information processing.

Partly in response to technological change, industrial and commercial companies have reorganized to improve the management of logistics activities and make intelligent use of the newly available technology. Increased breadth, both in terms of the backgrounds of individuals attracted to the field and the scope of responsibilities which they have been given, has facilitated a trend toward the purchase of carrier services, physical facilities, and logistics system equipment as elements in a broader system of related activities. The widespread use of computer technology for operational control of logistics activities has freed time for a greater amount of appraisal of strategic alternatives on the part of logistics management. In this sense, the past decade can fairly be termed an era of organizational as well as technological change in logistics.

If we have witnessed significant technological and organizational change in the recent past, what does the foreseeable future hold? What are the implications of the fact that the U.S. population, and to some degree the size of the market that it represents, appears to be leveling out as a result of increased emphasis on birth control? Particularly, what effect will this have if the pressures for new products and product individuality continue? What types of responses will be required by the growing congestion in city centers and the continuing dispersion and rapid growth of suburban markets? Will new technology continue to provide the·primary means with which to deal with problems arising from these and other trends?

There are signs that suggest that the answer to our last question is "no." While technological and organizational change will, of course, continue, the headlines during the decade of the 1970's will be made by institutional changes—those involving the spatial reordering of functions and facilities within an organization and between cooperating organizations. This represents a logical progression in logistics from emphasis on decision making based on *internal total cost analyses* to emphasis on *internal total profit analyses and interorganizational total cost and profit analyses* of the sort suggested in Fig. 22–1.

FACTORS IN THE SHIFT OF EMPHASIS
TO INSTITUTIONAL CHANGE [1]

The focus of logistics during the current decade will turn to institutional as opposed to technological or organizational change for a variety of reasons. Included among these are the possibilities that: (1) there are physical constraints on certain methods of transportation and material handling as well as restrictive public attitudes toward the further technological development of others, (2) certain technological developments appear to be "topping out," at least for the time being, (3) existing technologies, to a growing extent, require for their success a rationalization of activity which can be brought about largely through institutional cooperation and new types of institutions, (4) there are changing attitudes toward interorganizational coordination among individuals in business as well as government, (5) continued organizational development of logistics management will yield information necessary to justify institutional change, and (6) perhaps most important, the economic

[1] This section is based on James L. Heskett, "Sweeping Changes in Distribution," *Harvard Business Review,* March–April, 1973, pp. 123–32.

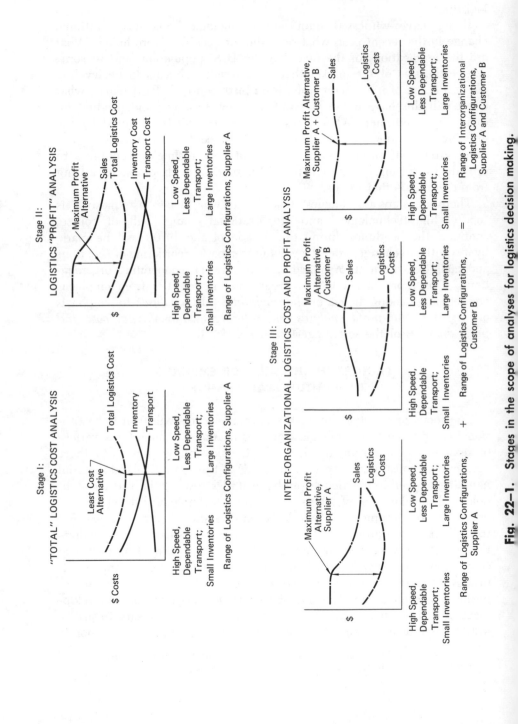

Fig. 22–1. Stages in the scope of analyses for logistics decision making.

benefits from institutional coordination and change far exceed any which foreseeable technological developments can offer.

Constraints on Technological Development

Certain transportation modes, such as rail and highway, have natural constraints imposed by the existing physical facilities. The height of a rail car can be increased only to a point; any further increase would require massive expenditures for greater clearances at bridges, tunnels, and underpass or overpass intersections that have replaced grade level railroad crossings. Truckers now speak in terms of a 6-inch increase in the width of a vehicle instead of a 10-foot increase in length, which was more feasible when highway carriers were operating with 27- and 30-foot trailers. And they will have difficulty getting even the 6 inches.

Public attitude now comprises a growing constraint on the further development of other transportation technologies. The refusal to support the development of the supersonic transport, however temporary a victory for the forces it may represent, was an important indicator. It may be significantly more difficult in the foreseeable future to obtain funds for the development of an ecologically and economically uncertain device such as the supersonic transport than for, say, an expanded system of bicycle paths for urban commuters. Throw in the current controversy and growing opposition to supertankers and the fear of the potential disasters which they could create, and the issues and arguments over possible ecological impacts of pipelines in the tundra of the Far North, and you have a clear indication that technology in the 1970's and 1980's may be in for close scrutiny.

Temporary "Topping Out" of Certain Technologies

Several years ago it was popular to look ahead to the "era of the 747," the great hope of air freight advocates. These "boxcars of the sky" were to eliminate the economic barriers to the use of air freight. Closer analysis at the time would (should) have shown that the most significant development, the introduction of the DC–8–63F airplane, already had occurred. Further, few anticipated the problems of assembling a sufficient volume of freight in one place at one time to meet the vastly greater requirements of the 747 for efficient operation. Finally, with their attention diverted to developments in the sky, most air freight advocates paid too little attention to the significant improvements which would be needed in a problem area of far greater magnitude, the handling of air freight on the ground.

The same marine architects who have produced 500,000-ton ship designs now tell us that, although designs of 1,000,000 tons are possible, the economics of building and operating such ships quite likely preclude their construction in the foreseeable future, public attitude aside. Certain diseconomies of scale begin to assert themselves.

Ingenious devices for introducing automation to the warehouse have been developed in recent years. The promise of automated warehousing, however, is yet to be realized. In fact, the requirements which it imposes on freight flow for effective utilization may in many cases be achieved only through the type of institutional cooperation discussed below.

We now have the computers and the concepts to achieve a large part of the savings possible through the effective control of inventories. More important, economical computer and communication capacity will make possible the use of models offering more individual attention to product-line items, inventory locations, and customers. But the potential gains through improved technology in this area are small compared with improvements over current operations that are possible by proper application of currently available machines and methods.

Rationalization Required by Existing Technologies

Rationalization, typified by improved allocation of effort and responsibility among cooperating and even competing institutions, has been required by the introduction of certain technologies. Conversely, technological advances have so badly outstripped institutional changes that the absence of the latter now imposes significant constraints on the former.

Perhaps the best example of this is the introduction of containerization on a wholesale basis to North Atlantic shipping several years ago.

Prospective operators planned for massive capital investment requirements for fast, expensive ships and the containers they would carry. Even the most conservative, however, did not provide for the numbers of containers which would ultimately be required for the service. They did not properly anticipate the problems of controlling container usage in the hinterlands surrounding the ports which they would serve. Ship operators paid dearly for their traditional lack of interest in, and institutional separation from, freight before it arrived and after it left their docks.

In response to this problem, operators are making extensive efforts to: (1) acquire freight forwarding, trucking, and other organizations which control freight in the hinterlands, (2) seek out arrangements under which containers can be jointly owned, and (3) collect and transmit information in such a way that more effective control can be maintained over container usage and improvements can be realized in the forecasting of volume available at various ports of call.

We have already cited the need for the assembly of large quantities of freight at a given place at one time, for shipment to a common destination, which the effective utilization of the 747 jetliner requires. It is quite possible that, until air freight volume increases significantly on a general front, self-organized groups of shippers with common origins and destinations may offer the best potential for providing this kind of volume.

Given current computers and concepts, perhaps the most acute need in inventory control activities is for more accurate data on which to base forecasts of future demand. As we have seen, the data exist. They need to be collected and transmitted in a timely way. This has led to the establishment of direct lines of communication between customers and suppliers. As Stern and Craig point out, the technology for direct computer-to-computer communication and extensive interorganizational data systems exists. The implementation of these concepts depends to a great extent on what management is willing to accept, including the possible sponsorship of interorganizational data exchange by suppliers or trade organizations.[2]

Production technologies have made possible smaller, lighter products that perform jobs better than their larger, heavier predecessors. At the same time, improvements to our intercity transportation systems have made it easier and less expensive to transport larger quantities of smaller shipments, at least to the outskirts of large metropolitan areas. What happens then? In a growing number of cities we have congestion and chaos. This is clearly a case in which technology has contributed to a problem that will be solved either by more technological development, perhaps in the form of subterranean freight access routes, or by institutional cooperation to create more efficient freight flows. (1) **Given the current financial state of most municipal governments, which type of solution do you think looks most promising to a growing number of city managers?**

Changing Attitudes Toward Interorganizational Cooperation

Many forms of interorganizational coordination not only are legal, but are becoming more and more attractive as problem-solving means to businessmen and government officials alike. The growing interest in encouraging the coordination of inbound freight movements to congested

---

[2] Louis W. Stern and C. Samuel Craig, "Interorganizational Data Systems: The Computer and Distribution," *Journal of Retailing*, Summer, 1971, pp. 73–86 ff.

city centers is just one example of a response by government and industry leaders to a difficult problem. Recently, this has led to the organization of the first symposium to explore approaches to the problem of urban freight movements.[3] Efforts in other countries are more advanced. For example, a recent study of Utrecht, Holland, disclosed that the consolidation and systematic delivery of certain types of freight moving typically in small shipments could reduce the number of delivery vehicles in the city center *from more than 600 to just six.*[4]

Feasibility studies of consolidated distribution facilities which might be operated by means of a joint venture between grocery product manufacturers and chain food store organizations utilizing the same regional distribution centers are underway. Essentially, such facilities would provide a means by which manufacturers and retailers could eliminate duplicated warehouse space and one stage in the distribution process for dry groceries.

The president of a large retail food chain recently remarked, "The idea may not be so far-fetched, and it might have advantages to both segments of the industry." Of course, the concept will have arrived when a manufacturer or his customer closes all or a part of a distribution center to take advantage of a consolidated distribution service.

Continued Organizational Development for Logistics

A number of studies have documented the organizational growth of logistics management. Clearly, the field has expanded from primary concern for fragmented activities such as transportation or inventory control to include warehousing, material handling, inventory control, order processing, and procurement activities. While organizational growth has not fulfilled the expectations of all projections which have been made for it, certain identifiable patterns of past growth which we have cited earlier should continue.

Extension of Current Growth Patterns. Organizational change, at first apparent in some larger corporations, now appears to be spreading to other companies in certain industries.

What types of industries? Several characteristics can be identified. Industries in which substantial costs of logistics, compared to sales, must be balanced against rigorous demands for customer service have provided

[3] The transcript of this symposium has been published as *Urban Commodity Flow*, Special Report 120 (Washington, D. C.: Highway Research Board, National Academy of Sciences, 1971).

[4] Described in "Nieuwe Wegen Naar Bevoorrading," published by the Transport Advies Groep Trag, Rotterdam, The Netherlands.

a spawning ground for logistics management. Included among these are grocery and chemical product manufacturing. Other industries facing severe pressures of expanded product lines have supported organizational development. These include manufacturers and distributors of products requiring extensive parts distribution activities.

Further Development: Responsibility for Coordinated Product Flow. This Second Edition has included more attention to the subjects of packaging and procurement than our earlier book. It reflects our belief that in devoting more emphasis to the matter of overall product flows within an organization, management will both increase and change the scope of responsibility for logistics activities.

Recently articulated concepts of postponement and speculation provide a means to assess future changes resulting from the analysis of overall product flows in a firm or a channel of distribution.[5] They suggest responses to various physical flow problems experienced by companies, and as such are useful for the logistics manager to keep in mind. A ready example of one such problem is that of expanded product lines.

Expanded product lines increase the cost of speculation for whoever is holding inventories. As a result, retailers and wholesalers have limited their speculative risk by reducing stocks of any one item (or investing the same amount of money in inventory for a broader product line) while at the same time expecting, and in fact depending upon, excellent response time to orders from manufacturers, to maintain a given level of customer service. This customer expectation, stated in the form of a willingness to substitute one manufacturer's product for another's in the event of the latter's inability to meet the customer's expectations, in effect raises the incentive for speculation by raising the penalties for postponement on the part of the manufacturer.

Thus caught in a squeeze between increasingly large product lines and increasing demands for service from channel institutions, a number of manufacturers have responded by holding larger quantities of stock in semifinished form closer to markets, typically in distribution centers. Here they can be cut, assembled, or packaged to order, thus postponing commitment to specific stock-keeping unit locations until the last possible moment while reducing speculation (measured in terms of the elapsed time between customer order and delivery) for the customer.

To a growing degree, logistics management will involve the operation of light manufacturing as well as distribution facilities. Perhaps the automobile assembly plant offers the most extreme example of this phenomenon. It is the closest thing to a distribution center in the channel

[5] See Chapter 17, pp. 599–601.

of distribution for automobiles produced in the United States; it also houses light manufacturing activities. Because of the complexity of the latter, however, these plants typically fall under the responsibility of production management. However, in other industries with less complex field manufacturing requirements, such as the cutting to order of plate glass, paper products, lumber, and steel, and the packaging to order of common commodities using different materials, light manufacturing in the field may be a functional responsibility of logistics management.

Principles of postponement and speculation, like total cost analysis, suggest reasons for shifting functions between facilities (in a sense, intraorganizational institutions) within the firm. They also suggest reasons for shifting such functions between firms and for creating new and eliminating old firms in a channel of distribution. Clearly, this family of concepts will have a significant impact on the future organizational growth of logistics.

Conversely, continued organizational development for logistics management will provide further support for institutional change to the extent that it will foster: (1) continued emphasis on the system (including related services provided by other companies) as the appropriate unit for analysis, redesign, and control, (2) the development of information necessary for the appraisal of new institutional arrangements, and (3) the development of a cadre of managers capable of analyzing and dealing with interorganizational problems.

Relatively Great Economic Benefits

Technological change can make more efficient the performance of a function by a company in a channel of distribution. Institutional change typically can eliminate entirely the cost of performing a function by shifting it from a company to another point in the channel, where it can be absorbed by integrating it with other activities. Only occasionally, as with momentous developments such as containerization, can technology accomplish as much. And even then, it can do this only with the institutional change necessary to implement its introduction and growth.

INSTITUTIONAL CHANGE AND INTERORGANIZATIONAL MANAGEMENT

Early in our discussion (Chapter 2) we suggested that the basic functions performed in a channel of distribution, such as selling, buying, storing, transporting, financing, providing information, and others, can only be shifted, not eliminated. They must be performed by some institutions at some point(s) in a channel. Distribution opportunities can be pinpointed by identifying which of the basic functions can be performed most effectively by each institution in the channel, and the types of institutional change needed to accommodate efficient product flow. This matter is of growing concern to companies with great dependence on, and the opportunity to assume leadership of, channels of distribution. Their concern will trigger the implementation of pricing mechanisms, implied threats, or other means to produce a coordinated channel effort that leads to the ultimate sale of more goods at a lower price and a higher per-unit profit margin for the sum of the firms cooperating in the channel.

What types of institutional change will interorganizational management call for? Early indications suggest that changes may encompass several types, arrayed in terms of their organizational impact on firms in a channel: (1) the coordination of policies and practices to facilitate the more effective performance of existing functions by cooperating channel members, (2) the shifting of functions from one institution to another in a channel of distribution, (3) the creation of joint venture or "third-party" institutions to eliminate duplicated performance of functions in such channels, and (4) the vertical integration of channel functions performed by existing organizations. Improved economics of operation will be the incentive, and anything from incentive pricing mechanisms to acquisition will be the vehicle for such change.

Coordination of Policies and Practices

It can be shown that, given a level of demand for a product in a channel of distribution, there is a quantity of goods which a customer should order, a transportation firm should carry, and a supplier should ship, to produce the lowest total cost to the sum of the channel members.[6] However, this is different from the quantity which each party to the transaction would arrive at if he were to analyze the problem taking into account only the economics of his own operation, as illustrated in Fig. 22–2. In fact, only by the greatest coincidence would all firms arrive at a decision to deal in quantities optimum to the channel without direction from one or more cooperating companies.

Further, pricing mechanisms necessary to achieve the desired interorganizational result can be calculated by those organizations supplying

[6] See James L. Heskett and Ronald H. Ballou, "Logistical Planning in Inter-Organization Systems," in Michael P. Hottenstein and R. William Millman, *Papers and Proceedings of the 26th Annual Meeting of the Academy of Management* (Academy of Management: 1966), pp. 124–36.

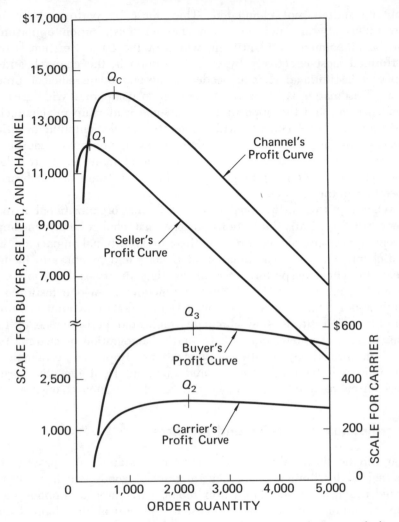

Fig. 22–2. Graph of profit curves for seller, carrier, buyer, and channel of distribution as a whole (the sum of the seller, carrier, and buyer) dealing in various order quantities, based on assumed data. *Source:* James L. Heskett and Ronald H. Ballou, "Logistical Planning in Inter-Organization Systems," in Michael P. Hottenstein and R. William Millman, *Papers and Proceedings of the 26th Annual Meeting of the Academy of Management* (Academy of Management, 1966), pp. 124–36, at p. 131.

product or services to the channel. Because these mechanisms may have the effect of redistributing profits among members of the channel, supplementary actions such as rebates may be necessary to distribute the benefits of interorganizational action to all parties to such a transaction.

Where the buyer–seller relationship is a continuing one, and the volume of product moving between them is sufficiently large, an interorganizational approach to the problem of product flow is warranted. In some cases, the introduction of technology providing distinct incentives to carry out the interorganizational transaction in a given fashion has produced the desired coordination of policies and practices.

Consider, for example, the impact of palletization on interorganizational coordination. In order to reap the maximum benefits of palletization, buyers and sellers have to coordinate their material-handling systems to make use of the same size pallet, or at least pallet sizes with modular compatibility. Thus, industry standards for pallet sizes have been established for the shipment of such things as tin cans and paper products. Where standards have not been established, wholesalers, for example, have adapted their material-handling systems to conform with those of a dominant supplier. Companies electing not to abide by such standards do so at a price, reflected in increased costs for handling goods.

What is the potential payoff from such coordination? One retailing organization selling about $200 million in goods per year, as a part of an internal cost-reduction effort, estimated that its total logistics bill came to about $6.3 million, not including the cost of inbound transportation. However, on goods purchased it was estimated that suppliers were incurring logistics costs (buried in the retailer's cost of goods sold) of nearly $15 million. This prompted a shift in emphasis from a search for opportunities largely for internal cost savings to a more balanced emphasis to include possibilities for achieving much larger savings through improved supplier–retailer coordination.

Shifting of Functions Between Organizations [7]

A large distributor of personal care and houseware products through a network of direct sales personnel desired recently to gain greater control over the delivery of product to its distributors without actually going into the trucking business. It offered truckers an interesting proposition: a guaranteed high return on their investment in return for the full authority to schedule and control their trucks, a 40% reduction in existing charges, and access to the truckers' books to verify profit levels. The 40% reduction in charges combined with the guaranteed high profit suggest the tremendous potential benefits made possible by a shift of functions and responsibilities in this case. **(2) As a trucker negotiating with this shipper, would you accept the proposition? (3) Why?**

[7] For another detailed example of this type of opportunity, see the Constellation Supers, Inc. case problem in James L. Heskett, Lewis M. Schneider, Robert M. Ivie, and Nicholas A. Glaskowsky, Jr., *Case Problems in Logistics,* (New York: The Ronald Press Co., 1973).

We have already mentioned the general shift of stock-keeping responsibility from inventory-turn-conscious retailers to wholesalers and manufacturers. This has resulted in part from the desire of retailers to reduce speculation and dead or unsalable stocks in an age of expanding product lines, as well as a realization that warehousing and material-handling costs may be significantly lower per unit for manufacturers and wholesalers than for their retailer customers. If this is the case, the shift of responsibility for the performance of these functions in the channel of distribution is a logical result of formal or informal interorganizational analysis and management.

(4) Check out the ad shown in Fig. 22–3. In what ways does it provide an illustration of shifting channel functions?

ℰUp to your neck in scrap?

Steel Service Center pre-production processing lets you climb out of it.

To generate less scrap and more profits, let your steel service center supply you with 100% usable pre-processed steel.
Blanked, sheared, slit, or flame-cut to your exact requirements. Packaged and ready for fabrication.

Result? You'll slash your scrap rate on short pieces, drops, or processing errors.

Excess scrap is just one of many hidden costs in possessing large inventories of mill-ordered steel. Find out how you can reduce even more of your *cost of possession.** Ask your local steel service center for the booklet, "When Management Takes a Closer Look at Steel Purchasing." Or write us: 1600 Terminal Tower, Cleveland, Ohio 44113.

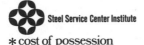 Steel Service Center Institute

* cost of possession

can run 18% to 40% of invoice price.
Factors include:
Cost of capital tied up in inventory, equipment, and storage facilities.
Operating costs for inventory handling and processing.
Other costs such as insurance, taxes, bookkeeping, scrap losses.

Fig. 22–3. An advertisement illustrating the shifting of functions in a channel of distribution for steel products. *Source: Business Week,* October 23, 1971, p. 8.

Creation of "Third-Party" Institutions [8]

Third-party organizations can provide the objectivity and "arms-length" management often needed when large, proud organizations wish

[8] For an interesting appraisal of the trend toward joint-venture or "third-party" arrangements for marketing products and services, see Lee Adler, "Symbiotic Marketing," *Harvard Business Review,* November–December, 1966, pp. 59–71.

to create a product or service requiring inputs from several cooperating companies. They are particularly attractive in a field that has been typified by fragmented, duplicated services—logistics.

Distribution Utilities. Organizational arrangements are now being used in the creation of so-called distribution utilities, companies that are capable of providing to shipper customers a complete range of warehousing, transportation, order processing, and inventory control services. A distribution utility contracts with a small-to-medium-sized manufacturer or a division of a larger firm to remove a product from the end of its production line and make it available for sale when, where, and in the quantities desired, with some pre-agreed level of customer service. This allows the manufacturer's marketing organization to concentrate on selling.

The distribution utility, to the extent that it takes possession of a product without taking title to it, is the converse of a broker, who, in common marketing parlance, buys and sells goods without ever taking possession of them.

The joint venture provides a convenient means of assembling the substantial resources that would be required if a company wished to (1) construct or acquire a network of distribution centers, (2) support the design and installation of extensive communication and information processing facilities, or (3) create an organization in which naturally skeptical manufacturer–customers can have confidence.

An example of such a joint venture is the one formed by Eastern Airlines, the Ralph M. Parsons Company, which specializes in architectural engineering and construction services, and TRW, Inc., a manufacturer of aerospace, automotive, and electronic products. Recently, these firms incorporated a new company to contract "with manufacturers and retailers to operate all or a portion of a client firm's physical distribution." [9]

Consolidated Distribution. Consolidated distribution, involving the movement of carload quantities of stocks directly from the production lines of competing manufacturers into common regional distribution centers for consolidated delivery direct to retail stores, has been discussed for some time, particularly in the grocery products industry. Until now, objections regarding loss of control over the product, possible disclosure of competitive information, and the elimination of an area of potential competitive advantage have overruled the economic advantages of averting both the manufacturer-operated and the retailer-operated distribution center, as shown in Fig. 22–4.

But consolidated distribution of this type is now a reality. The concept has been implemented recently in Canada with the creation of a

[9] From a brochure circulated by National Distribution Services, Inc., in 1973.

Product Flow Without Consolidated Distribution to a Regional Market Area

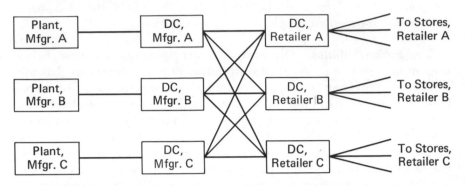

DC = distribution centers

Product Flow With Consolidated Distribution to a Regional Market Area

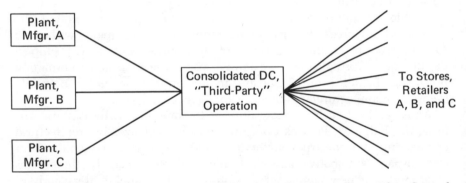

Fig. 22–4. The impact of consolidated distribution on the product flow of three competing manufacturers supplying three competing retail chain store organizations.

distribution center in Vancouver shared jointly by leading manufacturers and their chain-store customers. The success of this experiment by a task force of the Canadian Grocery Manufacturers Association, which reports that it has reduced the cost of dry grocery distribution by at least 10%, has led to its rapid expansion to two other provinces of Canada.[10]

Central Distribution Facilities. The benefits of consolidating outbound freight can usually be enjoyed by a well-managed medium-sized or large manufacturer. However, companies receiving small shipments

[10] Robert Koci, "Canada's Distribution Utilities," *Transportation & Distribution Management,* May, 1972, pp. 23–24.

from many sources have found that they must establish cooperative arrangements to enjoy similar benefits.

Thus far, such arrangements have been confined to the formation of shippers' cooperatives for the consolidation at origin of merchandise purchased by several companies for delivery to the same destination (a metropolitan area). Transportation cost savings, in the form of pro-rata rebates, from the replacement of small-package shipments by carload and truckload shipments, have been remarkable.

These same companies are beginning to explore, with the urging of city officials, the creation of consolidated storage and merchandise processing facilities, located in low cost suburban areas, as well as coordinated delivery to store sites. A private study in which one of us participated several years ago indicated that central distribution facilities could be operated at a satisfactory profit by a third party charging retailer customers only 80% of their current costs of receiving, processing, and delivering such goods themselves, typically in crowded, expensive space and traffic-clogged shipping facilities.

Vertical Integration

The possibilities we have been discussing are interorganizational alternatives to the vertical integration of logistics operations in a channel of distribution by one powerful channel member through the merger with, or acquisition of, companies with which it deals.

Vertical integration in the logistics industries flourished during the late 1960's as industrial companies began acquiring companies offering complementary logistics services such as trucking and warehousing. Interestingly, transportation companies were not leaders in this trend, possibly because of the history of stringent controls on the acquisition of companies offering competing modes of service imposed on them by the Interstate Commerce Commission. Indicators point to more active participation by transport and other companies in ventures involving the vertical integration of logistics services. The rate at which this takes place will depend, among other things, on: (1) the level of pressure on the ICC to relax its control, (2) the rate at which legal means, such as financial holding companies, are found for accomplishing vertical integration, and (3) the level of prosperity in the logistics industries themselves. In this latter regard, adversity may help rather than hinder the trend.

IMPLICATIONS FOR CARRIER MANAGEMENT

We recommend a test for a carrier manager. Ask him to answer the following five questions.

1. Do you expect your company to be offering the same services ten years hence as it does now?
2. Do you expect your company's customers to be roughly the same?
3. Do you expect their approaches to the purchase of logistics services to be the same?
4. Do you expect your company's organization to be the same?
5. Do you expect your company's ownership to be the same?

If he replies "yes" to as many as three of these questions, ask him a sixth:

6. Are you equipped to serve your organization well during an era of institutional change?

Clearly, there is no place for "status quo" thinking among carrier managements at the present time.

The impact of conscious or unconscious adherence to the logistics system concept on the part of those responsible for the management of logistics activities in industrial and commercial enterprises has been felt during the last decade by those firms providing services to such systems. Principal among these service groups is the freight carrier. Problems and opportunities created for carriers extend also to purveyors of material-handling equipment and to those dealing in packaging and packing services, equipment, and supplies. We will confine our discussion to implications for carrier management; it is easily translated and transferred to other service and supply firms.

Change in Response to Demand

In the past, industrial and commercial management has placed great emphasis on the reduction of explicit costs of transportation. Carriers have responded with intense price competition in seeking the favor of existing and potential customers.

The demand for transportation services among organizations emphasizing and coordinating the management of logistics is typified by emphasis on dependability of service and other cost-oriented rather than carrier price-oriented considerations.

New shipper policies have given rise to some shift of energies among carrier organizations from price competition alone to the design of new services which reduce the costs of logistics for customers without seriously affecting the return per unit of service to the carrier. Intense price competition among carriers probably will continue, but it will be confined more strictly to those industries which continue to emphasize transportation cost reduction to the exclusion of service improvement and whose logistics problems continue to defy more creative solution.

Selling Transportation as a System Component

Most recent attempts by carriers to establish marketing techniques in tune with increasing emphasis on the logistics system concept have included the following steps: (1) reorganization and reallocation of sales effort, (2) the development of a customer consulting program utilizing the total cost approach to physical supply and distribution systems analysis, and (3) the establishment of organizations consisting of consulting analysis and support groups commissioned to work alongside regular sales representatives to compare customer levels with carrier capability for meeting them.

Reorganization of Sales Effort. The expense involved in conducting total cost appraisals of customer logistics systems requires that carriers first reorganize their sales effort to allow less attention to some customers and more to others. This is accomplished in four steps:

1. An analysis and understanding of the capabilities of a given carrier and the types of shippers most logically attracted to its services
2. A survey of all potential shippers that might be expected reasonably to utilize services of the carrier
3. A specific identification of customers by the following types:
   a. Customers firmly committed to the use of other methods of transportation
   b. "Captive" or "automatic" customers of the carrier in question
   c. Current and potential customers with little knowledge of their total costs of logistics
   d. Current and potential customers with an interest in and a knowledge of various costs of logistics activities
4. The assignment of additional selling effort, particularly in the form of system analysis, to existing and prospective customers

Usually, it is the cost-conscious customer who is most receptive to a consulting sales approach. It is precisely this type of customer who, in the process of appraising current movement systems, is most likely to alter his utilization of different transportation services. It is he who currently should be the target of the greatest amount of creative sales effort on the part of carriers.

The shipper who is interested in the results of a carrier consulting sales study, but who cannot provide information for such a study or permission for carrier analysts to procure it, has posed many problems for advanced carrier sales effort. He has proven particularly troublesome for air freight sales effort, as indicated by Lewis, Culliton, and

Steele in their early study.[11] Where there is shipper interest, there is a prospect for carrier consulting sales efforts utilizing total cost analysis. Only limited use has been made of the total cost system analysis effort directed toward receptive clients.

Automatic customers are those bound to ship by certain methods because of location, product characteristics, or other non-personal factors. Because of the nature of automatic customers, carrier sales effort could be limited to a periodic review of their current and potential needs. Even less attention can be afforded those customers automatic to other carriers or methods of transportation. However, experience indicates that considerable time *is* devoted to automatic or captive customers because they don't present any problems for the freight sales representative.

Of those carriers currently attempting to analyze customers' logistics systems as part of their sales effort, no two have taken the same approach. For example, one railroad, recognizing that fewer than a dozen basic industries provide it with over three-quarters of its potential, has organized its market development group to pay special attention to these basic industries and then largely to key customers within these industries.

Another railroad has analyzed the needs only of those shipper firms initiating a request for such analysis. One air carrier which pioneered in the total cost analysis of shippers' logistics problems still makes some attempt to encourage its sales representatives to sell the idea of the analysis, as well as the company's service itself, to likely candidates for the use of air freight service.

Establishment of Policies. Carrier consulting sales programs, to be successful in their use of total cost analysis techniques, should be operated under the following guidelines:

1. Selective sales effort, as outlined above
2. Emphasis on the necessity for sales representatives to take action that will enhance, rather than damage, the standing of individuals representing prospective customer organizations in the eyes of their colleagues
3. Stress on the need to give the shipper–client an opportunity to voice his needs in regard to carrier equipment, freight handling, schedules, rates, and auxiliary services
4. Inclusion of transportation, storage, material handling, packing and packaging, order processing, and inventory carrying costs in an appraisal of shipper needs

[11] Howard T. Lewis, James W. Culliton, and Jack D. Steele, *The Role of Air Freight in Physical Distribution* (Boston: Division of Research, Graduate School of Business Administration, Harvard University, 1956).

5. Objective analysis of shippers' needs in regard to the transportation and material-handling components of their logistics systems,
   including recommendation of the use of competing services and
   equipment, where necessary
6. Emphasis on the importance of studying the needs of both shippers
   and receivers in a logistics system
7. Realization of the need to bring to bear on shippers' problems as
   wide a range of knowledge as a carrier marketing organization
   can provide
8. Continued reliance on the traditional carrier sales representatives
   to:
   a. Locate likely candidates for total cost analyses
   b. Provide the main contact between consulting sales talent and
      the shipper–customer

Organization of Effort.   To date, those few carriers emphasizing consulting sales techniques have tried different organizational approaches.
Most work through their regular sales representatives, to whom client
accounts are assigned, supplementing their effort with that of more
highly trained sales analysts or consultants. Some carrier sales consulting
groups, however, have the power to initiate studies and carry out all
necessary contact work.

The type of back-up support made available to regular carrier sales
representatives and their accounts varies widely. One airline emphasizing
its air freight service has reduced the size of its consulting sales staff to
two in anticipation of training all sales representatives to carry out total
cost analyses.

Another airline has developed a "dual" sales organization with one
group of sales representatives concentrating on the development of new
business through the application of total cost and other more complex
sales techniques, and one group concentrating on providing closer attention to the needs of existing air freight users. The theory behind this
approach is that the two tasks require essentially different levels of
analytical ability and different sales personalities.

Several railroads have provided their sales representatives with
engineering support to cope with problems of the design of shippers'
material-handling systems and carriers' equipment. Others have organized their analytic efforts on an industry-by-industry basis to devise
new equipment, service schedules, and rates to meet the needs of specific
industries.

Actual and Potential Results.   The development of total cost approaches to the analysis of shipper problems by both shippers and
carriers has opened up interesting opportunities for the latter. For ex-

ample, sophisticated shippers are using piggyback service, largely resulting from the bypassing of many traditional railroad classification (sorting) yards. Many shippers would continue to use it regardless of its speed of service, because they have developed the analytic and organizational mechanisms to appraise the value of dependable service.

Consider the potential of multiple distribution system development, discussed in Chapter 13, for what has been considered a growing but unprofitable business, air freight. Refer once again to Table 13–13. As you explore the sensitivity of variables included in the cost comparison shown there, you will begin to explode myths associated with air freight. For example, double the air freight rate. Or reduce the value of the freight to 75 cents per pound.

(5) Based on your comparative total cost calculations, how would you appraise a rule of thumb that has pervaded air freight marketing thinking for years: potential cargo must have a value of $2.00 per pound or more? (6) What relevant criteria should be drawn up for qualifying good prospects for a dual distribution system using air freight? (7) Compare the potential for carrying up to 20% of a shipper's volume by air with the current share of total ton-miles of manufactured goods transported by air, shown in Table 4–8, on page 127.

Adapting Prices and Services to Interorganizational Needs

Pricing. Selective rate adjustments based on the combined costs of services to shippers, carriers, and receivers have led to greater emphasis on types of rates designed to: (1) offer shippers lower cost transportation service, (2) better utilize existing carrier equipment and service schedules, and (3) produce greater overall profit for all parties to the transaction.

For example, a railroad whose customers took full advantage of a five-day free-time provision in its demurrage rules for the unloading of carloads of coal estimated that each day of delay cost it about $8 per car. Further, it concluded that its customers, through improved scheduling, could accomplish faster unloading with an increase in storage and handling cost of perhaps no more than 5¢ per ton for each day by which car turnaround time might be reduced. Based on a load of about 50 tons per car, the railroad estimated the value of a reduction in free time from five days to two to be 48¢ per ton ($8 × 3 days ÷ 50 tons). It proceeded to change its tariff to reduce free time to two days in exchange for a 30¢-per-ton reduction in rate. (8) Evaluate this action on the basis of the criteria suggested in the preceding paragraph.[12]

---

[12] For another example involving the economic analysis of the benefits of an incentive rate to a shipper, see the Roscoe Corporation case in Heskett, *et al., op. cit.*

Design of Service "Packages"

Several years ago, based on a comprehensive analysis of the economics of moving grain from producing areas in the Midwest to customers in the Southeast, the Southern Railway proposed to reduce its rates by 60% for grain consigned in quantities of no less than 450 tons (five-car quantities) for transportation in newly designed Big John hopper cars. Because of the relatively low rate for moving grain as opposed to milled products such as flour or feed, the equipment and associated rates offered the potential of restructuring the milling industry by: (1) encouraging the relocation of milling facilities from production-oriented to market-oriented sites, and (2) providing a stimulus to animal-feeding industries in the Southeast.

The study of appliance movements and shipment dimensions by another railroad resulted in the introduction of high-cube rail boxcars capable of carrying twice as many units as their predecessors. This, combined with a rate offering significant cost savings to manufacturers willing and able to load the cars to capacity, allowed manufacturers to lower their costs of appliance distribution.

Consulting Sales Approaches in Perspective

Analysis of shipper–customer movement systems has been performed by relatively few carriers. What are the reasons for this? As with other kinds of research, the benefits from a consulting sales program employing total cost analysis are not immediately apparent. The requirement of a certain amount of objectivity in analysis has made the technique vulnerable to criticism when it does not tie a customer to a given carrier or mode. Once the overall benefits of using a certain mode are understood by a customer, *there is no guarantee he will utilize the service of the firm sponsoring the analysis.* This has been a particularly acute problem in air freight services where serious sales efforts have been made by only a few airlines but the advantages of their efforts have accrued to the entire industry.

The availability of, or the necessity to train, people qualified for the demanding job of consulting sales analysis has proven a barrier to the development of more than a handful of such groups. In-company personnel often carry biases into consulting sales studies. The policies of some firms prevent the hiring of sufficient talent from outside the carrier organization to staff a new department. Organizational conflict has developed in several instances within more traditional carrier sales organizations. This conflict has revolved around the consultant–analyst's function, and the scope of his authority in customer contact. Problems have grown out of insufficient communication of ideas and coordination of effort among the carrier personnel involved.

To its credit, the consulting sales approach has spawned a number of significant changes in methods of physically distributing goods, as outlined above. In addition, it has helped individuals in shipper–customer firms build their own prestige to the point where more information for total cost system analysis has become available.

To accomplish significant results, it is essential that a carrier consulting sales program have the continuity of effort which stems from long-run organizational support. In return, there is evidence that a logistics system, once designed, is likely to tie a customer to one mode or supplier of transportation services longer than routine sales effort placing almost exclusive emphasis on rates. This is particularly true where the system is centered around specialized equipment or methods developed solely for the system. Once performed, a system analysis can be updated with a relatively small increment of effort.

CREATIVE INTERORGANIZATIONAL PROBLEM SOLVING IN LOGISTICS

Despite the constraints sometimes imposed by outdated regulatory practices and restrictive labor agreements, creative interorganizational logistics problem-solving efforts can prevail. Individuals and companies that can adopt the attitudes necessary to foster creative approaches to interorganizational problems will have an edge on their competitors. What are these attitudes and approaches? Early research in the field of inter-organization management has yielded some suggestions.[13]

Companies likely to be recognized as leaders during an era of institutional change and interorganizational problem solving will have the following characteristics.

First, they will tend to seek what bargaining theorists have termed "non-zero sum results from negotiations." Essentially, a non-zero sum result is one which reduces the total costs of the negotiating organizations, regardless of how they divide the resulting benefits. As we have seen from preceding examples, non-zero sum results can be achieved only through a basic change in procedure. Examples of this are the design of quantity price discounts to reflect efficient handling and shipping quantities, or the implementation of incentives to encourage the

[13] Much of what follows in this section is based on J. L. Heskett, Louis W. Stern, and Frederick J. Beier, "Bases and Uses of Power in Interorganization Relations," in Louis P. Bucklin (ed.), *Vertical Marketing Systems* (Glenville, Ill: Scott, Foresman and Co., 1970), pp. 75–93. For an interesting collection of papers on the subject, see Matthew Tuite, Roger Chisholm, and Michael Radnor, *Interorganizational Decision Making* (Chicago: Aldine Publishing Co., 1972).

faster unloading and turn-around of cars in our previous example. In contrast, zero sum results produce no such net benefits. Changes in prices with no accompanying changes in procedure only transfer costs and profits from one company's profit and loss statement to another's with no net economic benefit to the channel system.

Second, they will be willing to absorb risk for the mutual benefit of participants in a channel system. Recall, for example, our discussion in Chapter 14 of the work of Ruppenthal and Whybark, who used queuing theory to analyze the common problem of congestion at shippers' truck docks. They estimated that the addition of extra truck bays in several cases would reduce truck waiting time significantly, thereby producing a high return on investment.[14] Unfortunately, to implement these programs, shippers would have to make the investment to alter their facilities, the benefits of which would accrue to truckers supplying pickup and delivery services.

Presumably, such situations could be resolved if one or more truckers could reduce rates selectively to encourage the necessary investment, a practice frowned on by regulatory agencies. Or the trucker might make the investment with some assurance that he would continue to receive business from the shipper at least over a period sufficient to pay him back for his investment. Again, this practice would be looked on with disfavor by the Interstate Commerce Commission. Perhaps the only feasible course of action would be the absorption of uncertainty by the shipper by constructing the bay. In return it might obtain an informal agreement that future consideration for a rate reduction based on cost improvement would be given by the carrier. This would only work if one carrier provided all or a significant portion of the service.

Third, these companies are willing to innovate on behalf of the channel. Some companies are known as innovators in their respective business spheres, either in the testing of new technologies, organizational relationships, or contractual relationships. For example, a company which is first to establish a pool of pallets for the economic handling of goods in a channel of distribution is likely to be regarded as such an innovator, with resulting long-term rewards for successful experiments (and perhaps losses for unsuccessful ones).

Fourth, they may establish a mechanism for collecting and transmitting information and skills throughout a channel. Information that provides an early warning of inventory buildups at the retail level can be of use to all participants in a channel system. Manufacturers of such diverse products as drugs and fertilizers have provided their distributors with inventory control systems and educated them in the use of these systems. Expectations of long-term improvements in distributor prof-

[14] Karl M. Ruppenthal and D. Clay Whybark, "Some Problems in Optimizing Shipping Facilities," *The Logistics Review,* Vol. 4, No. 20, 1968, pp. 5–32.

itability and loyalty motivate such manufacturers with enlightened inter-organizational practices.

Fifth, there is an exchange of personnel with other parties to inter-organizational relationships. A factor which distinguishes management in the United States from that in most other parts of the world is executive mobility. American executives not only expect relatively frequent moves, they rarely plan to spend a lifetime working for a single firm. The migration of railroad traffic personnel into the traffic departments of major industrial firms, which seems to have occurred in recent years, can set the stage for important interorganizational achievements by executives in cooperating organizations who understand each others' problems and economic constraints.

SUMMARY AND CONCLUSION

Many technological advances which were merely speculation as recently as a decade ago are now practically taken for granted. In fact, the rate of technological change in transportation, material handling, and data handling and analysis has been so great that a period of more rapid institutional change will be required just to realize the benefits of recent technological advances.

Organizational and attitudinal changes are fostering the creation of institutional arrangements designed to capitalize on technology. Now we see growing constraints on the types of technological change which may be possible in the intermediate-term future.

These factors suggest that we may be entering a period in which institutional change will occupy a more important place alongside technological advances in the field of logistics.

Improved organization for and costing of logistics activities and their management will require appropriate responses from carriers in the development of equipment, services, and rates to meet the needs of increasingly sophisticated logistics managers in industry. It will require selective carrier marketing effort designed to allow greater attention to the needs of the "non-automatic" customer capable of taking advantage of several competing logistics system service packages.

Shippers and carriers alike, who understand the total cost and service implications of alternative logistics systems and who are prepared to negotiate rates, services, equipment designs, and facility locations that require significant economies or service improvements, will not only survive but prosper. In the process, new jobs, new types of businesses, and new institutional arrangements will be created, promising continued excitement and opportunity in the truly dynamic field we have come to call business logistics.

APPENDIXES

A

Symbols Used in the Text

D = minimum price discount required.

r = annual inventory carrying charge (as a percentage of product cost or value).

I = the average value of inventory on hand for a specified period of time.

v = average cost or value, per unit, of product.

S = demand or usage of a product for some specified period of time, in units.

C = total inventory management cost (in dollars).

Q = the quantity ordered (in units).

A = ordering or setup cost (in dollars per order or setup).

$*$ = an optimum result for any variable.

x = usage or demand during an order cycle, in units.

P = reorder point (in units of stock on hand and on order less those promised out).

N = number of orders placed per period of time.

p = probability of an occurrence.

π = cost of a stock-out situation (per unit).

$E(s)$ = expected stock-out cost per order cycle (in dollars) =

$$\pi \left[\sum_{x_P + 1}^{x_{max}} (x - P)p(x) \right].$$

W = "order up to" inventory level, or max value, in units.

σ = standard deviation.

t = length of time, in days.

σ_k = standard deviation of usage during an order interval plus an order cycle (in units).

$\bar{t}$ = average length of order interval plus order cycle (in days).

σ_{oc} = standard deviation in order interval and order cycle lengths (in days).

$\overline{x_d}$ = average usage per day (in units).

σ_{dd} = standard deviation in daily demand rates (in units).

Alpha = weighting factor for exponential smoothing.

MAD = mean absolute deviation or mean absolute error.

Q_1 = maximum quantity that can be ordered economically to qualify for a discount on unit cost (in units).

d = fraction by which the price will be reduced from the existing price if a larger quantity is ordered, in decimal fractions.

Q_o = economic order quantity based on the current price (in units).

O_t = operating days in advance of need, by which an order must be placed (in days).

A_t = set-up time for the supplier (in days).

T_t = transit time from supplier to point of need (in days).

R = production rate per operating day (in units).

h^* = optimum cut-off point for inventory accumulation (in units).

n = number in line, including the one being serviced (used in queuing theory).

λ = rate at which units arrive for service, in numbers (used in queuing theory).

μ = rate at which units are serviced, in number per period of time (used in queuing theory).

ρ = load factor = λ/μ (used in queuing theory).

L = number in labor crew.

L_c = labor cost per truck (in dollars).

B

Areas Under the Normal Curve

The table below indicates fractional parts of the total area (1.000) under the normal curve between the mean and a perpendicular erected at various numbers of standard deviations (σ) from the mean. To illustrate the use of the table, 29.103% of the total area under the curve will lie between the mean and a perpendicular erected at a distance of .81σ from the mean.

σ	.00	.01	.02	.03	.04	.05	.06	.07	.08	.09
0.0	.0000	.0040	.0080	.0120	.0160	.0199	.0239	.0279	.0319	.0359
0.1	.0398	.0438	.0478	.0517	.0557	.0596	.0636	.0675	.0714	.0753
0.2	.0793	.0832	.0871	.0910	.0948	.0987	.1026	.1064	.1103	.1141
0.3	.1179	.1217	.1255	.1293	.1331	.1368	.1406	.1443	.1480	.1517
0.4	.1554	.1591	.1628	.1664	.1700	.1736	.1772	.1808	.1844	.1879
0.5	.1915	.1950	.1985	.2019	.2054	.2088	.2123	.2157	.2190	.2224
0.6	.2257	.2291	.2324	.2357	.2389	.2422	.2454	.2486	.2518	.2549
0.7	.2580	.2612	.2642	.2673	.2704	.2734	.2764	.2794	.2823	.2852
0.8	.2881	.2910	.2939	.2967	.2995	.3023	.3051	.3078	.3106	.3133
0.9	.3159	.3186	.3212	.3238	.3264	.3289	.3315	.3340	.3365	.3389
1.0	.3413	.3438	.3461	.3485	.3508	.3531	.3554	.3577	.3599	.3621
1.1	.3643	.3665	.3686	.3708	.3729	.3749	.3770	.3790	.3810	.3830
1.2	.3849	.3869	.3888	.3907	.3925	.3944	.3962	.3980	.3997	.4015
1.3	.4032	.4049	.4066	.4082	.4099	.4115	.4131	.4147	.4162	.4177
1.4	.4192	.4207	.4222	.4236	.4251	.4265	.4279	.4292	.4306	.4319
1.5	.4332	.4345	.4357	.4370	.4382	.4394	.4406	.4418	.4429	.4441
1.6	.4452	.4463	.4474	.4484	.4495	.4505	.4515	.4525	.4535	.4545
1.7	.4554	.4564	.4573	.4582	.4591	.4599	.4608	.4616	.4625	.4633
1.8	.4641	.4649	.4656	.4664	.4671	.4678	.4686	.4693	.4699	.4706
1.9	.4713	.4719	.4726	.4732	.4738	.4744	.4750	.4756	.4761	.4767
2.0	.4772	.4778	.4783	.4788	.4793	.4798	.4803	.4808	.4812	.4817
2.1	.4821	.4826	.4830	.4834	.4838	.4842	.4846	.4850	.4854	.4857
2.2	.4861	.4864	.4868	.4871	.4875	.4878	.4881	.4884	.4887	.4890
2.3	.4893	.4896	.4898	.4901	.4904	.4906	.4909	.4911	.4913	.4916
2.4	.4918	.4920	.4922	.4925	.4927	.4929	.4931	.4932	.4934	.4936
2.5	.4938	.4940	.4941	.4943	.4945	.4946	.4948	.4949	.4951	.4952
2.6	.4953	.4955	.4956	.4957	.4959	.4960	.4961	.4962	.4963	.4964
2.7	.4965	.4966	.4967	.4968	.4969	.4970	.4971	.4972	.4973	.4974
2.8	.4974	.4975	.4976	.4977	.4977	.4978	.4979	.4979	.4980	.4981
2.9	.4981	.4982	.4982	.4983	.4984	.4984	.4985	.4985	.4986	.4986
3.0	.49865	.4987	.4987	.4988	.4988	.4989	.4989	.4989	.4990	.4990
4.0	.4999683									

C

Information Sources

This compilation of current sources of information is intended to supplement the suggested readings at the end of the text chapters, and will be a useful reference listing for the management of logistics activities.

The sources have been grouped into five categories: professional journals and commercial periodicals; general business periodicals; professional, industry, and trade associations; government publications; and miscellaneous references.

Professional Journals and Commercial Periodicals

The entries below represent the more important journals and periodicals related to business logistics. For a comprehensive index of publications in the field of logistics, see *Business Periodical Index*, published monthly by H. W. Wilson Co., Bronx, N. Y. 10452.

Air Cargo. Monthly. Ziff–Davis Publishing Co., New York, N. Y. 10016.

Airline Management and Marketing (including *American Aviation*). Monthly. Ziff–Davis Publishing Co., New York, N. Y. 10016.

Bell Journal of Economics and Management Science, The. Semiannually. American Telephone and Telegraph Co., New York, N. Y. 10007.

Commercial Car Journal. Monthly. Chilton Co., Inc., Philadelphia, Pa. 19139.

Distribution/Warehouse Cost Digest. Monthly. Marketing Publications, Inc., Washington, D. C. 20004.

Distribution World-Wide. Monthly. Chilton Co., Inc., Philadelphia, Pa. 19139.

Economic Geography. Quarterly. Worcester, Mass. 01610.

Fleet Owner. Monthly. McGraw–Hill, Inc., New York, N. Y. 10036.

Handling & Shipping. Monthly. Industrial Publishing Co., Cleveland, Ohio 44113.

Industrial Development and Manufacturers Record. Bimonthly. Conway Publications, Atlanta, Ga. 30319.

The International Journal of Physical Distribution. Three times per year. IPC Transport Press, Ltd., London SE1, England.

Jet Cargo News. Monthly. Houston, Tex. 77018.

Journal of Air Law and Commerce. Quarterly. School of Law, Southern Methodist University, Dallas, Tex.

Journal of Marketing Research. Quarterly. American Marketing Association, Chicago, Ill. 60601.

Land Economics. Quarterly. University of Wisconsin, Madison, Wis. 53706.

Logistics and Transportation Review, The. Faculty of Commerce and Business Administration, University of British Columbia, Vancouver 8, Canada.

Logistics Spectrum. Quarterly. Society of Logistics Engineers, Los Angeles, Calif. 90015.

Management Science. Monthly. The Institute of Management Sciences, Providence, R. I. 02903.

Material Handling Engineering. Monthly. Industrial Publishing Co., Cleveland, Ohio 44113.

Modern Materials Handling. Monthly. Boston, Mass. 02116.

Modern Packaging. Monthly. McGraw–Hill, Inc., New York, N. Y. 10019.

Modern Railroads. Monthly. Cahners Publishing Co., Chicago, Ill. 60603.

National Defense Transportation Journal. Semimonthly. National Defense Transportation Assoc., Washington, D. C. 20006.

Oil and Gas Journal. Weekly. The Petroleum Publishing Co., Tulsa, Okla.

Operations Research: Journal of the Operations Research Society of America. Bimonthly. Operations Research Society of America, Baltimore, Md. 21202.

Pacific Air & Truck Traffic. Monthly. Pacific Shipper, San Francisco, Calif. 94111.

Pacific Traffic. Monthly. Corte Madera, Calif. 94925.

Packaging and Shipping. Monthly except June, August, and December. Bonnell Publications, Inc., Plainfield, N. J. 07060.

Pipe Line Industry. Monthly. The Gulf Publishing Co., Houston, Tex. 77001.

Production and Inventory Management Journal. Quarterly. American Production and Inventory Control Society, Washington, D. C. 20037.

Purchasing Magazine. Biweekly. Conover–Mast Publications, Inc., New York, N. Y. 10017.

Purchasing Week. Weekly. McGraw–Hill, Inc., New York, N. Y. 10036.

Railway Age. Weekly. Simmons–Boardman Publishing Corp., New York, N. Y. 10013.

Traffic Bulletin. Weekly. Traffic Service Corp., Washington, D. C. 20005.

Traffic Management. Monthly. Cahners Publishing Co., New York, N. Y. 10017.

Traffic World. Weekly. Traffic Service Corp., Washington, D. C. 20005.

Transport Topics. Weekly. American Trucking Associations, Inc., Washington, D. C. 20036.

Transportation and Distribution Management. Monthly. Traffic Service Corp., Washington, D. C. 20005.

Transportation Journal. Quarterly. American Society of Traffic and Transportation, Inc., Chicago, Ill. 60606.

Waterways Journal. Weekly. The Waterways Journal, Inc., St. Louis, Mo. 63101.

General Business Periodicals

Occasionally, general journals and periodicals publish articles that become important references on the economics and management of business logistics. Those listed below are especially significant for the frequency with which such articles appear. A topical index of many of those periodicals can be found in the *Business Periodical Index,* published monthly by H. W. Wilson Co., Bronx, N. Y. 10452.

Business Horizons. Quarterly. Graduate School of Business, Indiana University, Bloomington, Ind. 47401.

Business Topics. Quarterly. Graduate School of Business Administration, Michigan State University, East Lansing, Mich. 48823.

Business Week. Weekly. McGraw–Hill, Inc., New York, N. Y. 10036.

California Management Review. Bimonthly. Graduate School of Business Administration, University of California, Berkeley, Calif. 94720.

Dun's Review and Modern Industry. Monthly. Dun and Bradstreet Publications Corp., New York, N. Y. 10017.

Fortune. Monthly. Time, Inc., New York, N. Y. 10020.

Harvard Business Review. Bimonthly. Graduate School of Business Administration, Harvard University, Boston, Mass. 02163.

Journal of Business. Quarterly. University of Chicago Press, Chicago, Ill. 60637.

Wall Street Journal. Daily. Dow Jones & Co., New York, N. Y. 10004.

Professional, Industry, and Trade Associations

The associations listed here provide forums for airing research and policy issues of importance to the field of logistics. The listing does not include the many manufacturing-oriented industry associations which have special committees to handle specific logistics problems within the given industry.

The associations described below sponsor the exchange of research data or, because of the research they conduct in support of policy-making activities, circulate significant amounts of information.

Names are alphabetized according to the key word in the association's name, rather than the first word in its formal title. The nature of its membership and its basic objective are described, and there is a listing of the main publications each organization sponsors.

Much of the information in this section was adapted from Margaret Fisk (ed.), *National Organizations of the U. S.,* 7th Ed. (Detroit: Gale Research Co., 1972), vol. 1.

ADMINISTRATIVE MANAGEMENT SOCIETY (AMS). Willow Grove, Pa. 19090. Members: Office administrators, supervisors, personnel men, educators, and equipment manufacturers. Promotes the application of scientific methods to commerce and industry for the purpose of increasing productivity (particularly in the office), lowering costs, and improving the quality of output. Publications include *Administrative Management Magazine,* monthly.

AIR TRANSPORT ASSOCIATION OF AMERICA (ATA). Washington, D. C. 20036. Members: Domestic U. S. trunk, domestic local service, international, territorial, and intra-Hawaii and intra-Alaska airlines engaged in transporting goods and mail by aircraft between fixed terminals on regular schedules. Promotes legislation of interest to its members. Publications: *Quarterly Review of Airline Traffic and Financial Data,* and *Facts and Figures About Air Transportation,* annually.

AUTOMOBILE MANUFACTURERS ASSOCIATION (AMA). Detroit, Mich. 48202. Members: Manufacturers of passenger and commercial cars, trucks and buses for highway transportation. Publications: *Motor Truck Facts,* annually.

THE CONFERENCE BOARD (CB). New York, N. Y. 10022. Members: Business organizations, trade associations, government bureaus, libraries, labor unions, colleges and universities, and individuals. A fact-finding institution which conducts research and publishes studies on business economics and management experiences. Publications include reports of continuing research in business and industry.

DELTA NU ALPHA. Cleveland, Ohio 44107. Members: Transportation, traffic, and physical distribution management educators and managers. Concerned with advancing the profession of management in these areas. Publication: *Delta Nu Alphian,* 11 times per year.

AMERICAN ECONOMIC ASSOCIATION (AEA). Northwestern University, Evanston, Ill. 60201. Members: Educators, business executives, government administrators, journalists, lawyers, and others interested in economics and its application to present-day problems. Encourages historical and statistical research into actual conditions of industrial life and provides a non-partisan forum for economic discussion. Publications include: *American Economic Review,* quarterly, *Journal of Economic Literature,* quarterly, and *Papers and Proceedings,* annually.

AMERICAN INSTITUTE OF INDUSTRIAL ENGINEERS (AIIE). New York, N. Y. 10017. Members: Industrial engineers and industrial engineering students. Concerned with the design, improvement, and installation of integrated systems of men, materials, and equipment. Publication: *Journal of Industrial Engineering,* monthly.

ASSOCIATION OF INTERSTATE COMMERCE COMMISSION PRACTITIONERS (AICCP). Washington, D. C. 20423. Members: Lawyers and transportation and traffic specialists admitted to practice before the Interstate Commerce Commission. Among its objectives are: To promote the proper administration of the Interstate Commerce Act and related Acts, and to uphold the honor of practice before the ICC. Among its publications are the *ICC Practitioners Journal,* six times per year.

SOCIETY OF LOGISTICS ENGINEERS (SOLE). Los Angeles, Calif. 90015. Members: Individual management and technical practitioners in the field of logistics; includes scientists, engineers, educators, managers, and other specialists in commerce, aerospace, and other industries, government, and the military. Covers every logistics specialty, including maintainability, systems and equipment maintenance, maintenance support equipment, human factors, training and training equipment, spare parts, overhaul and repair, handbooks, field site activation and operation, field engineering, facilities, packaging, material handling, and transportation. Publication: *Soletter*, bimonthly,

AMERICAN MANAGEMENT ASSOCIATION (AMA). New York, N. Y. 10020. Members: Executives in industry, commerce, government, charitable and non-charitable, and non-commercial organizations; university teachers of management. Concerned with providing the training, research, publications, and information services required by managers to do a better job, and organizing and encouraging an exchange of management thinking and experience within the profession. Publications include many research studies on matters pertaining to logistics in its several series of publications on General Management and Packaging, including *Special Reports, Management Reports,* and *Management Bulletins.*

THE INSTITUTE OF MANAGEMENT SCIENCES (TIMS). Providence, R. I. 02903. Members: Scientists and managers in business, labor, government, teaching, and research. Concerned with the advancement of scientific knowledge and the improvement of management practices, with concentration on management technology, electronics, applied mathematics, psychology, economics, and other sciences. Publications include *Management Science*, monthly (alternating Theory and Application series).

AMERICAN MARKETING ASSOCIATION. Chicago, Ill. 60601. Members: Marketing and marketing research executives, sales and promotion managers, advertising specialists, teachers, and others interested in marketing. Fosters research and sponsors seminars, conferences, and student marketing clubs. Publications include: *Journal of Marketing,* quarterly, *Journal of Marketing Research,* quarterly, *Proceedings,* annually, and bibliographies, books, monographs, and pamphlets on marketing.

INTERNATIONAL MATERIAL MANAGEMENT SOCIETY (IMMS). Ann Arbor, Mich. 48105. Members: Engineers, educators, and executives. Concerned with the advancement of the theory and practice of materials management and packaging in manufacturing, distribution, warehousing, transportation, and military operations. Publications include the *IMMS Journal,* monthly (as part of *Modern Materials Handling Magazine*) and the *IMMS Review,* quarterly.

ASSOCIATION OF OIL PIPE LINES (AOPL). Washington, D. C. 20006. Members: Oil pipe line companies, most of which are regulated by common carriers. Assembles factual and statistical data and information relating to the pipe line industry for presentation to Congress, governmental departments, agencies and commissions, trade associations, and to the public generally.

OPERATIONS RESEARCH SOCIETY OF AMERICA (ORSA). Baltimore, Md. 21202. Members: Persons engaged or interested in operations research in industry, government, and military services. Publications: *Operations Research,* bimonthly, *Bulletin of the ORSA,* semiannually, and *Transportation Science,* quarterly.

SOCIETY OF PACKAGING AND HANDLING ENGINEERS (SPHE). Chicago, Ill. 60604. Members: Practicing engineers in the fields of packaging or material handling. Sponsors special university courses and conducts seminars on these topics.

PACKAGING INSTITUTE (PI). New York, N. Y. 10017. Members: Users and manufacturers of packaging materials, machinery, and services. Sponsors discussions, seminars, and research to help producers of packaged materials solve technical, engineering, and economic problems. Publication: *Proceedings,* annually.

PARCEL POST ASSOCIATION (PPA). Washington, D. C. 20036. Members: Wholesalers, retailers, mail-order houses, and other firms using parcel post service for distribution of products. Concerned with the promotion of the efficient and economical distribution of small-package shipments by whatever means.

NATIONAL COUNCIL OF PHYSICAL DISTRIBUTION MANAGEMENT (NCPDM). Chicago, Ill. 60606. Members: Business executives with a professional interest in the field of physical distribution management. Includes members from industrial concerns, as well as consultants and educators. Concerned with advancing and promoting the management science of integrating transportation, warehousing, material handling, protective packaging, inventory size and location, and customer service.

AMERICAN ASSOCIATION OF PORT AUTHORITIES (AAPA). Washington, D. C. 20006. Members: Port administrative organizations of the United States, Canada, and Latin America. Sets standards in such phases of port activity as modern terminal design, operations and cargo handling, fire prevention, maintenance, and administration. Publication: *World Ports,* eight times per year.

AMERICAN PRODUCTION AND INVENTORY CONTROL SOCIETY (APICS). Washington, D. C. 20037. Members: Production and inventory control managers and teachers. Concerns itself with curricula and certification, educational doctrines, language, and techniques for production and inventory control. Publications: *APICS News,* monthly, *Production and Inventory Management,* quarterly, *APICS Bibliography, APICS Production and Inventory Control Training Manual,* and *APICS Dictionary.*

ASSOCIATION OF AMERICAN RAILROADS (AAR). Washington, D. C. 20036. Members: American railroad companies and their representative executives. This is the central coordinating and research agency of the American railway industry. Publishes documents regarding policy issues involving rail transportation.

RAILWAY SYSTEMS AND MANAGEMENT ASSOCIATION (RSMA). Chicago, Ill. 60611. Members: Representatives of accounting, traffic, engineering, mechanical, transportation, communications, purchasing, stores, executive, personnel, and freight claim departments in the railroad industry, and its suppliers. Promotes methods that improve control, provide essential information faster, and reduce overall costs in the railroad industry; encourages research into railroad problems. Publication: *Proceedings,* six to eight times per year.

REGIONAL SCIENCE ASSOCIATION (RSA). Wharton School, University of Pennsylvania, Philadelphia, Pa. 19104. Members: Academic and professional individuals Concerned with the practice and advancement of analysis of geographic regions, and with related spatial and areal studies. Publications include *Journal of Regional Science.*

NATIONAL ACADEMY OF SCIENCES–NATIONAL RESEARCH COUNCIL (NAS–NRC). Washington, D. C. 20418. Members: Private organization of scientists and engineers dedicated to the furtherance of science and its use for the general welfare. Publications include an annual numbered series of books, monographs, and reports covering subjects including transportation and urban development.

NATIONAL ASSOCIATION OF SHIPPERS ADVISORY BOARDS (NASAB). American Association of Railroads, Washington, D. C. 20036. Members: Shippers and receivers of rail freight. Concerned with fostering the cooperation of shippers and railroads in the development of transportation. Publication: *Proceedings,* annually.

ASSOCIATION FOR SYSTEMS MANAGEMENT (ASM). Cleveland, Ohio 44138. Members: Executives and specialists in systems work serving business, commerce, education, government, and the military. Concerned with communications, electronics, equipment, forms control, human relations, organization, procedure writing, and systems application. Publications include *Journal of Systems Management,* monthly.

ASSOCIATED TRAFFIC CLUBS (ATC). Washington, D. C. 20034. Members: Men and women in the traffic and transportation fields; including railroads, bus lines, trucking firms, and traffic managers of industrial firms. Among other objectives and activities, these organizations award scholarships and fellowships for study and research in transportation. Publications include the *ATC News Bulletin,* bimonthly.

AMERICAN SOCIETY OF TRAFFIC AND TRANSPORTATION (AST&T). Chicago, Ill. 60606. Members: Persons engaged in transportation or traffic administration. The purpose of the organization is "to establish standards of knowledge, technical training, experience, conduct and ethics, and to encourage the attainment of high standards of education and technical training requisite to the proper performance of the various functions of traffic, transportation, and physical distribution management." Publications include the *Transportation Journal,* quarterly.

NATIONAL INDUSTRIAL TRAFFIC LEAGUE (NITL). Washington, D. C. 20004. Members: Industrial traffic managers. Concerned with the formulation of policy on a wide range of matters of interest to industrial traffic managers. Publications include *The Legislator,* weekly.

NATIONAL DEFENSE TRANSPORTATION ASSOCIATION (NDTA). Washington, D. C. 20006. Members: Men and women of the armed forces, federal government, and private industry in the fields of transportation. Purpose: "To assist in the development of a sound national transportation system that will be responsive to the nation's military and industrial needs in peace and war." Publications include: *National Defense Transportation Journal,* bimonthly.

TRANSPORTATION ASSOCIATION OF AMERICA (TAA). Washington, D. C. 20036. Members: Representatives of all sections of the transportation industry; users, investors, airlines, freight forwarders, highway carriers, pipelines, railroads, and water carriers. Its major objective is: "To resist all trends which may lead to government ownership or operation of any form of transportation." Publications include: *What's Happening in Transportation,* biweekly, and *Transportation Facts and Trends,* annually (with quarterly supplements).

TRANSPORTATION RESEARCH FORUM (TRF). Members: Managers and researchers in the field of transportation. Provides a forum for the exchange of research information regarding transportation. Publication: *Proceedings,* annually.

AMERICAN TRUCKING ASSOCIATIONS (ATA). Washington, D. C. 20036. Members: Individual state trucking associations, comprising motor carrier company managers. Defines policy, promotes legislation, conducts research, and provides specific services (such as accounting service) for the trucking industry. Publications include: *Transport Topics,* weekly, *Quarterly Digest, Proceedings of Trucking Industrial Forum,* annually, *Bibliography of Motor Freight Transportation Trends,* annually; safety manuals, handbooks, driver-training manuals, booklets on the trucking industry, and freight claims forms and booklets.

AMERICAN WAREHOUSEMEN'S ASSOCIATION (AWA). Chicago, Ill. 60606. Members are operators of public warehousing facilities. Serves as a forum for the exchange of information regarding warehousing practices.

WATER TRANSPORT ASSOCIATION (WTA). New York, N. Y. 10036. Members: Common carriers serving the Great Lakes, inland waterways, coastal and intercoastal trades. Operates information service in support of legislative and other matters of interest to its membership. Publications include speech reprints and research reports, distributed occasionally.

THE AMERICAN WATERWAYS OPERATORS, INC. (AWO). Washington, D. C., 20036. Members: Carriers engaged in the transportation of commodities by water, shipbuilders, operators of terminal facilities, naval architects, and companies providing midstream fuel and supply services. Promotes the interests of the barge and towing industry as a whole. Publications include

The Barge and Towing Industry Catalog of Publications, Films, and Information Resources.

WESTERN HIGHWAY INSTITUTE (WHI). San Francisco, Calif. 94104. Members: Motor carriers, suppliers, and others interested in highway transportation research. Serves as a research and engineering agency for the organized motor carrier industry in the western United States and Canada. Publications include a *Newsletter,* bimonthly.

Government Publications

The best sources of macroeconomic statistics are the publications of the federal government. Listed below are publications of the Government Printing Office pertaining to logistics. The GPO catalog number for each item is included.

For a continuing bibliography of these publications, see the *Monthly Catalog of United States Government Publications,* published by the Superintendent of Documents, Government Printing Office, Washington, D. C. 20402.

U. S. Census of Transportation, prepared every four years by the Bureau of the Census, Department of Commerce, including Volume 1, National Travel Survey; Volume 2, Truck Inventory and Use Study; Volume 3, Commodity Transportation Survey: Part 1, Shipper Groups, Part 2, Production Areas and Selected States, Part 3, Commodity Groups. C 3.6/2: C 33/2/970 (for 1967 Census, published in 1970).

Civil Aeronautics Board Reports to Congress, prepared annually by the Civil Aeronautics Board. C 31.201:970 (for 1970).

Freight Commodity Statistics, prepared annually by the Interstate Commerce Commission, including: Class I Railroads, IC 1 ste. 29:969 (for 1969); Motor Carriers of Property, IC 1 mot. 22:968 (for 1968).

Annual Report of Interstate Commerce Commission, prepared by the Interstate Commerce Commission. IC 1.1:970 (for 1970).

Annual Report of Maritime Administration, prepared by the Maritime Administration, Commerce Department. C 39.201:970 (for 1970).

Transportation Revenue and Traffic of Large Oil Pipe Line Companies, prepared quarterly by the Bureau of Accounts, Interstate Commerce Commission. IC 1.

Translog, journal of military transportation management prepared monthly by the Military Traffic Management and Terminal Service, Department of the Army, Department of Defense. D. 101.66/2 (volume numbers and numbers).

Annual Report, Transportation Department, prepared by the Transportation Department. TD 1.1:970 (for 1970).

Transport Economics, a commentary prepared monthly by the Bureau of Economics, Interstate Commerce Commission. IC 1.17.

National Transportation Statistics, Summary Report, prepared annually by the Office of Systems Analysis and Information, the Department of Transportation.

Transport Statistics in the United States, prepared annually by the Bureau of Accounts, Interstate Commerce Commission, including: Part 1, Railroads,

Railway Express Agency, Inc., and Electric Railways; Part 5, Carriers by Water; Part 6, Oil Pipe Lines; Part 7, Motor Carriers; and Part 8, Freight Forwarders. IC 1.25:969 (for 1969)/part number.

Miscellaneous References

Included in this listing are publications offering useful reference tools, statistics, and planning devices. Alphabetization of titles is according to the main topic, not necessarily the first word in the title.

Much of the information included here was obtained from *Guide to American Directories*, 8th Ed., Bernard Klein (ed.), published by B. Klein Publications, Inc., Rye, N. Y. 10580.

Bullinger's Postal and Shippers' Guide for the U. S. and Canada. Published annually by Bullinger's Guides, Inc., Westwood, N. J. 07675.

Dun & Bradstreet Reference Book of Transportation. Published in May and November by Dun & Bradstreet, Inc., New York, N. Y. 10007. Alphabetical and geographical listing of Class I, II, and III motor carriers, air carriers, freight forwarders, pipelines, railroads, and water carriers.

Interstate Port Handbook. Published annually by the Rockwell F. Clancy Co., Chicago, Ill. 60601. Provides information on the location of ports, harbors, docks, and terminals used on the inland waterways and Great Lakes.

Janes Freight Containers. McGraw–Hill Inc., New York, N. Y. 10036. Provides data on port facilities, inland services, and port traffic of the world.

Leonard's Guide. Published in local editions and a national edition annually, with quarterly supplements, by G. R. Leonard & Co., Chicago, Ill. A guide to carrier rates.

Lloyd's Register of Ships. Published annually by Lloyd's Register of Shipping, New York, N. Y. 10004. Contains names, owners, and other data about all merchant ships over 100 tons gross, throughout the world.

The Marketing Information Guide. Published monthly by Trade Marketing Information Guide, Inc., Washington, D. C. 20036. An annotated bibliography.

Modern Materials Handling Directory Issue. Published annually by Cahners Books, Boston, Mass. 02110. Includes equipment trade names and manufacturers.

Moody's Transportation. Published annually by Moody's Investors Service, New York, N. Y. 10007. Financial information regarding various transportation forms.

National Distribution Directory. Published annually by Guide Services, Inc., Atlanta, Ga. 30324. Directory of approximately 4,000 local cartage, warehousing, and distribution services.

National Highway and Airway Carriers and Routes. Published semiannually by the National Highway Carriers Directory, Chicago, Ill. 60607. Contains information for 2,000 highway and air cargo carriers regarding operating data, executive personnel, number of units operated, location of terminals, and other items.

National Zip Code Directory. Published by National Zip Code Directories, Washington, D. C. 20005.

Official Guide of the Railways. Published monthly by National Railway Publication Co., New York, N. Y. 10001. Lists leading American railroads, including executives and timetables.

Official Motor Freight Guide. Published semiannually by Official Motor Freight Guide, Inc., Chicago, Ill. 60607. Contains individual guides for 31 major cities, containing the towns and cities served by motor carriers and cargo airlines operating in each city.

Packaging Information Sources. Published by Gale Research Co., Detroit, Mich. 48226. An annotated bibliography covering the literature that deals with various aspects of the packaging industry.

Packing & Shipping Directory. Published annually by Bonnell's Publications, Inc., Plainfield, N. J. 07060. Contains information about firms supplying materials and services for handling and physical distribution of industrial goods by land, sea, and air.

Bibliography on Physical Distribution Management. Published and updated periodically by the National Council of Physical Distribution Management, Chicago, Ill. 60606. An annotated bibliography.

Directory of Key Plants. Published biennially by Market Statistics, Inc., New York, N. Y. 10017. A listing of approximately 42,000 key industrial plants with SIC classifications and employment figures.

Plant Location. Published annually by Simmons–Boardman Publishing Corp., New York, N. Y. 10013. Provides industrial site selection agencies and data, listed geographically by states and provinces in the United States and Canada.

Site Selection Handbook. Published annually by Conway Research, Inc., Atlanta, Ga. 30319.

Official Directory of Industrial & Commercial Traffic Executives. Published annually by the Traffic Service Corp., Washington, D. C. 20005. Includes names and addresses of over 14,400 traffic, transportation, and distribution executives.

Transportation Information Sources. Published by Gale Research Co., Detroit, Mich. 48226. An annotated guide to libraries, government and statistical sources, periodicals, research and university programs, professional organizations, and trade associations having information about transportation.

Current Literature in Traffic and Transportation. Published monthly by The Transportation Center at Northwestern University, Evanston, Ill. 60204. An annotated bibliography.

Trinc's Blue Book of the Trucking Industry. Published annually by Trinc Transportation Consultants, Division of Dun & Bradstreet, Inc., Washington, D. C. 20005. Presents information about the ownership, addresses, officers, directors, control, and operating performance of 3,500 Class I and II motor carriers.

Membership Directory—American Warehousemen's Association. American Warehousemen's Association, Chicago, Ill. 60606.

Index